The Sporting News

This DAY *in* SPORTS

The Sporting News

This DAY *in* SPORTS

A DAY-BY-DAY RECORD OF
AMERICA'S SPORTING YEAR

RON SMITH

MACMILLAN PUBLISHING COMPANY
NEW YORK

This is a Carlton Book

First published in the United States by
Macmillan Publishing Company

Macmillan Publishing Company
Simon & Schuster Macmillan
866 Third Avenue
New York, NY 10022

Printed in Great Britain

Printing number
1 2 3 4 5 6 7 8 9 10

Library of Congress Card Catalog Number: 94-20098

Library of Congress Cataloging-in-Publication Data

The sporting news' this day in sports / Carlton Books.
p. cm.
Includes index.
ISBN 0-02-897264-3
1. Sports — United States — History — Miscellanea. 2. Sports —
United States — Calendars. I. Carlton Books. II. Sporting news.
GV583.S6845 1994
796'.0973 —dc20

94-20098
CIP

Design: Suzy Hooper
Project art editor: Robert Fairclough
Project editors: Martin Corteel & Tim Smith
Production: Sarah Schuman

54.00

A foreword by JOHN RAWLINGS, the editor of

The Sporting News

WELCOME TO THE REAL WORLD: November 22, 1963. June 6, 1944. December 7, 1941. July 4, 1776. Those dates stand alone in history, instantly recognizable and able to provoke feelings, memories and even passions for generations of Americans. They are imbedded in time, etched into the fiber of the period and event that they represent.

Now welcome to the world of sports. This world has nothing to rival the John F. Kennedy assassination, Pearl Harbor or D-Day, but it is not lacking for color, excitement and amazing athletic achievements that will withstand the test of time and memory.

And it has its own special dates, the threads that intertwine sports with American culture while providing a point of reference and perspective – and a special history of its own.

OCTOBER 3, 1951 – *Bobbie Thomson's "Shot Heard Around the World."*

OCTOBER 13, 1960 – *Bill Mazeroski's Game 7 home run beats the Yankees in the World Series.*

DECEMBER 23, 1973 – *Franco Harris' Immaculate Reception gives the Steelers a shocking NFL playoff victory.*

FEBRUARY 24, 1980 – *The U.S. Olympic hockey team completes its Miracle on Ice.*

Time, indeed, is relative and the date each breaking story assigns itself becomes the identification tag for posterity. That's what this book is all about. It's sports from a different angle, a *This Day in Sports* glimpse of how the memorable professional, amateur and collegiate events unfolded in relation to the calendar.

The chronicling of sports is nothing new; there are thousands of published books and magazines that address its history in various specialized and chronological manners. *The Sporting News* has been reporting, researching and analyzing sports news for more than 108 years.

But this book takes a different approach, treating each page as a calendar date with the major sports stories that made that date memorable. It celebrates the birthdays of the major sports stars and it mourns their deaths. It's not an all-inclusive encyclopedia. But it is fun, it is easy to read and it is nostalgia at its best.

And it's quick proof that, true to an adage, there is a time and a place for everything.

MILESTONES · IN SPORTS ·

1935

Bucknell 26, Miami 0 in the first Orange Bowl game at Miami.

1935

Tulane 20, Temple 14 in the first Sugar Bowl game at New Orleans.

1937

Texas Christian 16, Marquette 6 in the first Cotton Bowl game at Dallas.

1942

Oregon State upset previously unbeaten and untied Duke, 20–16, in the only Rose Bowl game not played in Pasadena, Calif. The game was moved to Durham, N.C., because of war-time restrictions.

1961

George Blanda's 88-yard pass to Billy Cannon broke open a tight contest and propelled the Houston Oilers to a 24–16 victory over the Los Angeles Chargers in the American Football League's first championship game.

1963

Down 42–14 with 12 minutes remaining in the Rose Bowl, No. 2-ranked Wisconsin used the passing of quarterback Ron Vander Kelen to stage a furious rally that fell just short in a 42–37 loss to No. 1 Southern California.

1982

Pittsburgh's John Brown caught a 33-yard pass from Dan Marino with 35 seconds remaining to give the Panthers a 24–20 Sugar Bowl victory over Georgia.

1989

Top-ranked Notre Dame defeated No. 3 West Virginia, 34–21, in a Fiesta Bowl battle of unbeatens, clinching the Fighting Irish's first national championship since the year 1977.

1954 WHO WAS THAT GUY?

Running back Dicky Moegle shredded Alabama's defense for 265 yards and three touchdown runs in Rice's 28–6 Cotton Bowl victory over the Crimson Tide. But the story of this game was the touchdown Moegle did not score – at least not physically.

As Rice halfback **Dicky Moegle** *heads down the sideline, Alabama's* **Tommy Lewis** *gets ready to make his infamous tackle.*

Rice was leading, 7–6, midway through the second quarter when Moegle, who had already run 79 yards for one touchdown, set off on what appeared would be a 95-yard TD jaunt.

However, as he streaked down the right sideline, clear of traffic and well ahead of his nearest pursuer, a figure suddenly jumped off the Alabama bench and slammed Moegle to the ground.

The tackle had been made by Crimson Tide fullback Tommy Lewis, who wasn't even in the game and explained his action later by saying, "I guess I'm too full of Alabama."

The referee awarded Moegle his touchdown and the talented back later ran 34 yards for another in one of the greatest performances in major bowl history. But his effort was overshadowed by the one impulsive play of Lewis, who, ironically, had scored Alabama's only touchdown on a one-yard first-quarter run.

JANUARY 1

A STAR IS BORN

1911: Hank Greenberg, a Hall of Fame first baseman-outfielder who batted .313 over a 13-year career and once hit 58 home runs in a season.

★ ★ ★

1925: George Connor, a football Hall of Fame tackle-linebacker for the Chicago Bears from 1948–55.

★ ★ ★

1927: Doak Walker, a former SMU Heisman Trophy-winning running back and a football Hall of Famer.

★ ★ ★

1945: Jackie Ickx, a Belgian race car driver and six-time winner of the 24 Hours of LeMans.

★ ★ ★

1967: Derrick Thomas, a current National Football League linebacker

★ ★ ★

DEATH OF A LEGEND

1923: Willie Keeler (baseball).

★ ★ ★

1902 MICHIGAN COMES UP ROSES

The powerful Michigan Wolverines, living up to their "point-a-minute" reputation, parlayed five Neil Snow touchdown runs and a smothering defense into a 49–0 victory over West Coast representative Stanford in the inaugural Rose Bowl game. The contest, played before 7,000 fans at Tournament Park in Pasadena, Calif., was a mirror image of Michigan's regular season.

Coach Fielding Yost's Wolverines won all 11 of their games, outscored opponents 550–0, did not allow an opponent to penetrate their 35-yard line and kept four teams from crossing midfield.

The decisive thrashing stunned Rose Bowl officials,who had hoped to make this New Year's Day game an annual event.

The 1902 **Stanford Cardinals,** *losers in the first Rose Bowl.*

1970 TEXAS CATCHES A BREAK

Cotton Speyrer's diving catch at the 2-yard line kept a desperation Texas drive alive and Billy Dale put the clincher on a Longhorn national championship with 1:08 to play when he ran one yard for a touchdown that secured a 21–17 Cotton Bowl victory over Notre Dame.

The Longhorns, their 10–0 record and No. 1 ranking on the line, faced a 17–14 deficit and a fourth-and-two situation at the Irish 10 with time running out on their championship hopes. James Street, who had driven Texas 66 yards, badly underthrew Speyrer, who dove for the ball and made an outstanding grass-level catch. Dale won the game moments later.

Notre Dame, which had taken the lead earlier in the final period on a Joe Theismann-to-Jim Yoder 24-yard TD pass, tried to put together a desperation drive of its own. But Texas' Tom Campbell sealed the verdict by intercepting a Theismann pass at the Longhorn 14.

The Fighting Irish, making their first bowl appearance in 45 years, stunned the Longhorns by taking a 10–0 second-quarter lead, thanks primarily to a 54-yard Theismann TD bomb to Tom Gatewood. Texas came back on a one-yard touchdown run by Tom Bertelsen and a three-yarder by Ted Koy.

JANUARY

2

1987 LIONS ROAR AGAIN

Penn State's relentless defense picked off five Vinny Testaverde passes and recovered a pair of Miami fumbles, allowing the Nittany Lions to prevail, 14–10, in a national championship-deciding battle of unbeatens in the Fiesta Bowl.

It wasn't pretty. The Lions were outgained, 445 yards to 162, and outpassed, 285–53, but the opportunistic defense consistently found ways to keep the high-powered Hurricanes out of the end zone.

The winning touchdown was set up, fittingly, by linebacker Shane Conlan's second interception of the game midway through the final period. D.J. Dozier ran six yards for the go-ahead score, but the game was far from over.

The Hurricanes came roaring back. Testaverde, the Heisman Trophy winner who completed 26 of 50 pass attempts, hit a clutch fourth -down pass for 32 yards and connected on five more throws that took Miami to the Nittany Lion 6-yard line. But that's where Testaverde ran out of magic.

His fourth-down pass was picked off by linebacker Pete Giftopoulos with nine seconds remaining on the watch.

The favored Hurricanes compounded their turnover problems with nine costly penalties. The national championship was Penn State's second in five years.

1984 MIAMI HOLDS OFF NEBRASKA'S CHARGE

Defensive back Ken Calhoun knocked away Turner Gill's two-point conversion pass with 48 seconds remaining in the Orange Bowl and preserved Miami's 31–30 upset victory over No. 1-ranked Nebraska, clinching the Hurricanes' first-ever national championship.

Miami, a one-time loser ranked No. 4 and 5 by the two major polls, held a 31–17 lead with 4:44 remaining and appeared to be on its way to victory. But the powerful Cornhuskers, riding a 22-game winning streak and a prohibitive 11-point favorite, mounted a desperate rally that almost produced a victory.

First Jeff Smith, a replacement for injured star running back Mike Rozier, ran one yard to cap a 76-yard drive. Then Smith bolted 24 yards on a fourth-and-eight play in the final minute. Probably needing only a tie to secure a national championship, Nebraska Coach Tom Osborne decided to gamble. He lost.

Miami had squandered an early 17–0 lead built on a pair of Bernie Kosar touchdown passes.

California's **Roy Riegels** *heads toward the wrong end zone with a Georgia Tech fumble in a New Year's Day Rose Bowl classic.*

A STAR IS BORN

1927: Gino Marchetti, a football Hall of Fame defensive end for the Dallas Texans and Baltimore Colts from 1952–66.

★ ★ ★

1963: David Cone, a current major league pitcher.

★ ★ ★

1965: Greg Swindell, a current major league pitcher.

DEATH OF A LEGEND

1986: Bill Veeck (baseball).

1929 RIEGELS TAKES WRONG TURN

A funny thing happened to California defender Roy Riegels on his way to a touchdown against Georgia Tech in the Rose Bowl. He took a wrong turn and ended up on the wrong path to immortality. Riegels was in the right place at the right time when a fumble by Georgia Tech's Stumpy Thomason bounced into his arms at the Yellowjacket 35-yard line midway through the second quarter of a scoreless game. He took off for the end zone.

"I was running toward the sidelines when I picked up the ball," Riegels explained later. "I started to turn toward my left, toward Tech's goal. Somebody shoved me and I bounded right off into a tackler. In pivoting to get away from him, I completely lost my bearings."

And California lost a football game. Riegels ran toward his own goal, with teammate Benny Lom in hot pursuit. Riegels was caught and turned around at the goal line, but Tech players slammed him to the turf at the 3. When Cal tried to punt out of trouble, Vance Maree blocked the kick through the end zone for a safety. After the Yellowjackets extended their lead on Thomason's 15-yard, third-quarter touchdown run, Cal fought back on a 10-yard TD pass from Lom to Irv Phillips – but too late.

Final score: Georgia Tech 8, California 7.

MILESTONES • IN SPORTS •

1939

Forty-one seconds away from a perfect, unscored-upon season, Duke surrendered a 19-yard touchdown pass (Doyle Nave to Al Krueger) to Southern California and dropped a heart-breaking 7–3 decision in the Rose Bowl.

1939

Blue 7, Gray 0 in the first Blue-Gray post season all-star game at Montgomery, Ala.

1965

The AFL's New York Jets pulled off a major coup when they signed Alabama quarterback Joe Namath to a three-year contract, the day after he guided the Crimson Tide in a 21–17 Orange Bowl loss to Texas.

1966

Playing in the melting snow on Green Bay's Lambeau Field, the Packers sloshed to their third NFL championship in five years with a 23–12 victory over the Dallas Cowboys.

1966

Philadelphia 76ers center Wilt Chamberlain joined former St. Louis great Bob Pettit as pro basketball's only career 20,000-point scorers.

1982

In the highest-scoring playoff game ever contested, Rolf Benirschke's 29-yard field goal at 13:52 of overtime gave the San Diego Chargers a 41–38 victory over Miami.

1985

UNLV scored an NCAA-record 93 second-half points and combined with Utah State for an NCAA total-points record in a 142–140 triple-overtime victory – Jerry Tarkanian's 600th as a college basketball coach.

1986

New York Islanders right winger Mike Bossy joined hockey's exclusive 500-goal club.

1920 Yankees Buy A Legend

The New York Yankees, still looking for their first American League pennant and World Series championship, paid Boston Red Sox Owner Harry Frazee an incredible $125,000 for the contract of 26-year-old pitcher-outfielder Babe Ruth.

The lefthanded-hitting Ruth, who set a major league record with 29 home runs in 1919, spent most of his five full Boston campaigns as a pitcher, compiling an 89–46 regular-season record and a 3–0 World Series mark.

But as the young slugger began displaying his awesome hitting prowess, his time on the mound began to diminish.

Yankee co-Owner Jacob Ruppert immediately named Ruth as his everyday right fielder.

Harry Frazee *(left) with* **Jacob Ruppert** *(pointing),* **Tillinghast Huston** *(right) and baseball Commissioner* **Kenesaw Mountain Landis.**

Frazee reportedly parted with his young star because of his own financial difficulties.

1993 Buffalo Shocks Houston

Down 28–3 at halftime and 35–3 early in the third quarter, the Buffalo Bills pulled off the biggest comeback in professional football history and walked away with a wild 41–38 overtime victory over the stunned Houston Oilers in an AFC wild-card playoff game at Orchard Park, N.Y.

Kicker Steve Christie capped the crazy afternoon with a 32-yard field goal at 3:06 of the extra period. The game-winner was set up by Nate Odomes' interception of a Warren Moon pass and a 15-yard penalty.

Moon built Houston's first-half lead with touchdown passes of 3 and 27 yards to Haywood Jeffires, 7 yards to Webster Slaughter and 26 to Curtis Duncan. When safety Bubba McDowell picked off a Frank Reich pass and ran it back 58 yards for a third-quarter score, Buffalo's task looked nothing short of impossible.

But the turnaround came fast and furious. Reich, starting in place of injured Jim Kelly, fired four TD passes of his own in the second half and a four-touchdown Buffalo blitz in the third quarter cut the Bills' deficit to 35–31. When Reich fired 26 yards to Andre Reed in the fourth period, Buffalo suddenly led, 38–35.

The Oilers did drive 63 yards to a game-tying Al Del Greco field goal with 12 seconds remaining, but they were just delaying the inevitable.

A STAR IS BORN

1939: Bobby Hull, a hockey Hall of Fame left winger and the NHL's second 50-goal man. He scored 913 goals in the NHL and WHA combined.

★ ★ ★

1962: Jim Everett, a current National Football League quarterback.

★ ★ ★

1964: Cheryl Miller, a three-time women's college basketball player of the year.

★ ★ ★

DEATH OF A LEGEND

1991: Luke Appling (baseball).

1987 Browns Get Kick Out of Overtime

Mark Moseley, getting a reprieve after missing an easy 23-yard field goal in the first overtime, connected on a 27-yarder at 2:02 of the second extra session and gave the Cleveland Browns a 23–20 divisional playoff victory over the New York Jets.

Moseley's kick brought an end to the third-longest game in National Football League history. He had kicked a 22-yard field goal with seven seconds left in regulation to force overtime.

The Browns had appeared hopelessly out of the game when Jets back Freeman McNeil scored on a 25-yard run with 4:14 remaining in the fourth quarter. But Cleveland quarterback Bernie Kosar, aided by several New York penalties and mistakes, rallied the Browns on two long drives that produced a one-yard Kevin Mack TD run and Moseley's game-tying field goal. The Browns' final drive started on their own 33 yard line with 51 seconds remaining and no timeouts.

Kosar tied a playoff record with 33 completions and set marks with 64 attempts and 489 passing yards. The victory gave the Central Division champs their first berth in an AFC title game.

Record-setting Cleveland quarterback **Bernie Kosar.**

January 3

Milestones in Sports

1931

High-scoring Montreal Maroons star Nels Stewart set a record for efficiency when he scored two goals 4 seconds apart in the third period of a 5–3 victory over the Boston Bruins.

1972

Southern University's Rod Milburn, the outdoor world record-holder in the 120-yard hurdles, set an indoor mark of 13.4 seconds when he ran first in the U.S. Track and Field Federation indoor championships at Houston.

1973

A 12-member group headed by shipbuilding tycoon George Steinbrenner bought the New York Yankees from CBS for $10 million.

1981

Johan Kriek became the first South African to win a grand slam tournament when he defeated American Steve Denton, 6–2, 7–6, 6–7, 6–4, in the Australian Open final.

1982

Johnny Miller sank a par putt to defeat Spaniard Seve Ballesteros on the ninth hole of a sudden-death playoff in Sun City, Bophuthatswana, earning the richest prize ever offered in golf – $500,000.

1983

Dallas running back Tony Dorsett broke through the Minnesota defense and ran 99 yards for a touchdown in a 31–27 loss to the Vikings. It was the longest run from scrimmage in NFL history.

JANUARY

4

MILESTONES · IN SPORTS ·

1970

The 9-year-old Minnesota Vikings became the first expansion team to win an National Football League championship when they blew away the Cleveland Browns, 27–7, in 8-degree temperature at Bloomington, Minn.

1976

The Dallas Cowboys ran roughshod over the Los Angeles Rams, 37–7, in the NFC championship game and became the first wild-card team to qualify for a Super Bowl berth.

1986

Navy center David Robinson set an NCAA record for blocked shots when he swatted away 14 during the Midshipmen's 76–61 victory over North Carolina-Wilmington.

1992

New York star Mike Gartner joined the National Hockey League's exclusive 1,000-point club when he scored a goal in the Rangers' 6–4 loss at New Jersey.

A STAR IS BORN

1930: Don Shula, won 300+ NFL games as coach for the Baltimore Colts and Miami Dolphins.

★ ★ ★

1935: Floyd Patterson, twice former heavyweight boxing champion of the world.

★ ★ ★

DEATH OF A LEGEND

1931: Roger Connor (baseball).

★ ★ ★

1986 Dickerson Runs Wild

Eric Dickerson, who set the National Football League's one-season rushing record with 2,105 yards in 1984, put on a dazzling one-man show as the Los Angeles Rams recorded a 20–0 divisional playoff victory over Dallas that earned them a berth against Chicago in the NFC championship game.

The Rams held a precarious 3–0 lead when Dickerson took his first handoff of the second half and bolted 55 yards for a touchdown. After the Rams had stretched their advantage to 13–0, Dickerson took a fourth-quarter handoff and broke free for a 40-yard TD that virtually sealed the verdict.

The former Southern Methodist star finished the game with a playoff-record 248 yards on 34 carries, the most yards ever gained by a Rams back and the most ever allowed by a Dallas defense. The former professional playoff record of 206 yards had been set by San Diego's Keith Lincoln in a 1963 American Football League game.

Joining Dickerson in the spotlight was a Los Angeles defense that forced six turnovers and sacked Dallas quarterback Danny White five times.

Eric Dickerson, *the Rams' 248-yard playoff weapon.*

1970 'Super' Chiefs Scalp Raiders

Chiefs' back **Robert Holmes** *gets the call against the Raiders.*

Wendell Hayes and Robert Holmes scored touchdowns and the Kansas City Chiefs earned a berth in Super Bowl IV while dropping the curtain on the American Football League with a 17–7 title game upset of regular-season champion Oakland.

With the AFL-NFL merger set for next season, it was fitting that the Chiefs and Raiders, hated rivals, should battle for the league's final championship. The Raiders had beaten the Chiefs twice during the regular campaign and finished with the AFL's best record. Kansas City, a second-place finisher in the West, upset the East champion New York Jets in a playoff semifinal.

The Raiders struck first when Charlie Smith ran three yards for an opening-period touchdown. But it was all Chiefs after that. With Len Dawson calling the signals, Kansas City drove to a tying second-quarter TD that Hayes scored with a one-yard run. Then they took the lead in the third period on Holmes' five-yard romp. A 22-yard Jan Stenerud field goal closed out the scoring.

Raiders quarterback Daryle Lamonica threw four interceptions.

1984 Gretzky Posts Another Record

Edmonton's Wayne Gretzky, adding another offensive distinction to his already amazing ledger, scored four goals and handed out four assists in a 12–8 victory over Minnesota.

This feat made him the first player to score eight or more points in a game twice in his career.

Gretzky had joined an elite group of eight-point scorers in a contest last November against New Jersey. Former Toronto star Darryl Sittler heads that list by virtue of a 10-point performance in 1976 and six other players had scored eight in a contest.

But the Oilers' Great One was not the only offensive star in the high-scoring matchup at Northlands Coliseum. Mark Messier had six assists, including a record-tying four in the second period, and Jari Kurri notched three goals. Gretzky also extended his consecutive-games scoring record to 41.

1963

Unpatriotic Lincoln Propels Chargers

It was a day to remember for the San Diego Chargers and Keith Lincoln, one to forget for the defenseless Boston Patriots. With Lincoln putting on the greatest one-man playoff show ever witnessed, the Chargers cruised to a 51–10 American Football League championship game victory at San Diego's Balboa Stadium.

Lincoln carried 13 times for a professional playoff-record 206 yards and caught seven passes for 123 more. He scored on a 67-yard first-quarter run and caught a 25-yard fourth-quarter touchdown pass from John Hadl. Lincoln capped his big day by completing a halfback pass for 20 yards.

Lincoln, however, was just one of San Diego's many weapons on a day full of big plays. Running back Paul Lowe ran 58 yards for a touchdown, wide receiver Lance Alworth made a 48-yard TD catch, starting quarterback Tobin Rote fired two touchdown passes and Hadl came in to throw for one TD and score another himself.

The championship game victory was the Chargers' first after two previous losses.

JANUARY

5

MILESTONES
• IN SPORTS •

1910

The newly-formed Canadiens played their first game at Montreal's Jubilee Rink, thrilling 3,000 fans with a 7–6 victory over Cobalt, Ontario.

1957

Rather than accept a trade to the New York Giants, Brooklyn Dodgers' second baseman Jackie Robinson announced his retirement from baseball.

1975

Houston pitcher Don Wilson, who fired two no-hitters in a nine-year career with the Astros, committed suicide by carbon monoxide poisoning when he ran his car engine inside the closed garage at his Houston home.

1983

Edmonton's Wayne Gretzky recorded his 100th point of the season (an assist) in his 42nd game – an 8–3 Oilers' victory over Winnipeg.

A STAR IS BORN

1864: Ban Johnson, the Hall of Famer who founded and served as long-time president of the American League.

★ ★ ★

1898: Riggs Stephenson, a 14-year major league outfielder and career .336 hitter.

★ ★ ★

1932: Chuck Noll, the man who coached Pittsburgh to four Super Bowl championships in the 1970s.

★ ★ ★

1938: Jim Otto, a football Hall of Fame center for the Oakland Raiders from 1960–74.

★ ★ ★

1954: Alex English, a career 25,613-point scorer in 15 National Basketball Association seasons.

★ ★ ★

DEATH OF A LEGEND

1954: Rabbit Maranville (baseball).

★ ★ ★

1963: Rogers Hornsby (baseball).

★ ★ ★

1982: Wally Post (baseball).

★ ★ ★

1987: Dale Mitchell (baseball).

★ ★ ★

1988: Pete Maravich (basketball).

★ ★ ★

1991

72-Point Effort Wasted

U.S. International senior Kevin Bradshaw scored 72 points, but not even that record-setting performance could save the 1–16 Gulls from defeat. They dropped a 186–140 decision to Loyola Marymount in another record-setting confrontation at Gersten Pavilion in Los Angeles.

Any time the Gulls and Lions get together, you can expect records to fly. And this was more of the same. The 186 points scored by Loyola Marymount was the most ever in an NCAA contest and Bradshaw's explosion broke the 21-year-old mark of 69 points that Louisiana State's Pete Maravich scored against Alabama in 1970. The record is for points against a Division I opponent.

The 26-year-old Bradshaw connected on 23 of 59 shots from the floor and seven of 22 three-pointers. He also gathered in 10 rebounds. Bradshaw, who said he realized he was on a record pace with about 10 minutes remaining, tied Maravich's mark with a free throw with 1:27 to play and dropped a second charity toss to break the record.

The Lions broke their own one-game scoring mark (181 in 1989 against U.S. International) when Rahim Harris stole a pass, drove swiftly to the basket, and dunked the ball with about only a minute of play remaining.

U.S. International hotshot **Kevin Bradshaw.**

1986

Roof Leak Keys NBA Rainout

In what probably ranks as a National Basketball Association first, a game between the Seattle SuperSonics and Phoenix was called because of rain with the Suns leading, 35–24, during second-quarter play at the Seattle Coliseum.

Actually, the contest was called because of a leaky roof that was dropping water on the playing surface, making footing treacherous and conditions uncomfortable for players.

The leak had been detected in the morning and tarps had been placed on the roof to prevent any further seepage. But gusty winds blew the tarps away and a water spot was detected on the floor at game time. When the leak intensified, play was held up. After an hour delay, officials, with no real solution in sight, decided to call it a night. And the NBA experienced its first ever rainout.

JANUARY

6

A STAR IS BORN

1920: Early Wynn, a baseball Hall of Fame pitcher and 300-game winner.

★ ★ ★

1957: Nancy Lopez, a member of the LPGA Hall of Fame and wife of former baseball star Ray Knight.

★ ★ ★

MILESTONES IN SPORTS

1973

John McKenzie, Larry Pleau and Jim Dorey scored second-period goals to lead the East to a 6–2 victory over the West in the WHA's first All-Star Game at Quebec.

1973

Ben Hogan, Bobby Jones, Walter Hagen, Arnold Palmer and Jack Nicklaus were voted the five greatest golfers of all time in a Golf Writers Association of America poll.

1980

The Los Angeles Rams earned their first Super Bowl berth when three Frank Corral field goals provided all the scoring in a 9–0 NFC championship game victory over Tampa Bay.

1980

The Philadelphia Flyers extended their NHL-record unbeaten streak to 35 games with a 4–2 victory over Buffalo.

1981

John Tonelli exploded for five goals to lead the NHL's New York Islanders to a 6–3 victory over Toronto.

1985 MARINO, DOLPHINS BOMB PITTSBURGH

Miami quarterback Dan Marino, terrorizing the team he grew up idolizing, passed for an AFC championship game-record 421 yards and four touchdowns to lead the Dolphins to a 45–28 victory over the Pittsburgh Steelers and their record-tying fifth Super Bowl berth.

Miami's **Dan Marino** *bombed Pittsburgh in the AFC title game.*

Marino, who was born and raised in Pittsburgh and played quarterback for the University of Pittsburgh, showed no mercy during the one-sided contest at Miami's Orange Bowl. He connected with Mark Clayton on a 40-yard touchdown strike in the opening quarter, Mark Duper on a 41-yarder in a 17-point Miami second period, Duper again on a 36-yard TD pass in the third quarter and Nat Moore on a seven-yarder in the final stanza.

Miami's offensive machine rolled up 569 total yards against the out-manned Steelers, who never could get back into the game after trailing, 24–14, at halftime. Marino's performance fell just short of San Diego quarterback Dan Fouts' playoff-record 433 yards, set during a double-overtime game against the Dolphins in 1982.

1951 NBA'S LONGEST GAME

Ralph Beard hit a short shot with one second left in the sixth overtime, giving the Indianapolis Olympians a 75–73 victory over Rochester in the longest National Basketball Association game ever played.

The game at Rochester's Edgerton Sports Arena was decided when Beard dropped his shot after taking a full-court pass from Paul Walther, who had grabbed the rebound of a missed Arnie Risen shot. Walther spotted Beard racing toward the other goal and hit him with a perfect pass that led to the only basket of the sixth overtime.

That was pretty much the story of all the extra sessions. After ending regulation in a 65–65 tie, both teams played conservatively. In two of the overtimes, neither team scored. In two others, each team scored two points. In the scoreless fourth extra session, neither team even got off a shot.

The Olympians' victory snapped Rochester's winning streak at seven games. Risen led all scorers with 26 points while Alex Groza and Beard scored 17 apiece for Indianapolis.

1980 SUPER STEELERS DEFEAT OILERS

Pittsburgh quarterback Terry Bradshaw fired a pair of second-quarter touchdown passes to overcome an early Houston lead and the Steelers went on to grind out a 27–13 victory over the Oilers and earn a trip to their record fourth Super Bowl.

The Steelers and a capacity crowd of 50,475 at Three Rivers Stadium were stunned when Houston safety Vernon Perry stepped in front of a Bradshaw pass with 2:30 gone in the opening period and ran it back 75 yards for a touchdown. Toni Fritsch's 21-yard field goal early in the second quarter made it 10–3, but Bradshaw and company quickly showed the poise and determination that have produced three Pittsburgh Super Bowl championships in the 1970s.

The strong-armed quarterback hit tight end Bennie Cunningham on a 16-yard touchdown pass in the second quarter and gave the Steelers their first lead with a 20-yarder to John Stallworth. The Steelers added 10 fourth-quarter points and Franco Harris ran down the clock as the Steelers finished off the Oilers for the second straight year in the AFC title game.

Indianapolis Olympians scoring ace **Alex Groza.**

MILESTONES IN SPORTS

1920

Joe Malone scored twice to lead Quebec to a 4–3 victory over the Toronto Arenas and become the NHL's all-time leading goal-scorer with 59.

1925

Montreal's Harry Broadbent scored five goals and led the Maroons to a 6–2 NHL victory over Hamilton.

1927

The Harlem Globetrotters, formed and organized by Abe Saperstein, played their first game in Hinckley, Ill.

1950

The Senior Bowl, the annual postseason all-star game in which college seniors are introduced to play-for-pay football, made its debut in Jacksonville, Fla.

1972

The Los Angeles Lakers stretched their incredible winning streak to 33 games with a 134–90 victory over Atlanta. The streak was the longest ever compiled by a professional sports team.

1981

Los Angeles star Marcel Dionne notched his 1,000th career NHL point with a goal in the Kings' 5–3 victory over the Hartford Whalers.

1980 LONG FLYERS' STREAK ENDS

Rookie Mike Eaves scored one goal and assisted on two others and the Minnesota North Stars brought an unceremonious end to Philadelphia's record 35-game unbeaten streak with a 7–1 victory in a National Hockey League showdown before the largest crowd (15,962) ever to witness an NHL game at the Metropolitan Sports Center.

The North Stars, who entered the contest with the NHL's third-best record, spotted the Flyers a goal before roaring back. After Philadelphia's Bill Barber scored at 3:49 of the opening period, Eaves tied the game, Greg Smith gave the North Stars the lead and Steve Payne made it 3–1. Goaltender Gilles Meloche shut the door on the Flyers and the game gradually got out of hand.

Thus ended one of the great streaks in modern North American sports. The Flyers had not lost since October 13, their second game of the season, and had compiled a 25–0–10 mark in the three months since. The previous longest streak, 28 games, belongs to the 1976–77 Montreal Canadiens.

The Flyers now sport a 26–2–10 record. The North Stars are 20–9–8.

Niagara's long-range sharpshooter **Gary Bossert.**

1987 BOSSERT BOMBS SIENA

Niagara senior guard Gary Bossert put on the greatest long-range bombing show in college basketball history when he scorched Siena for an NCAA-record 12 three-pointers and 37 points in a 97–88 victory at Loudonville, N.Y.

Bossert knocked home 12 of 14 shots from beyond three-point range and set four national records. In addition to his record for 12 treys in one game, Bossert set a mark for one-game three-point field goal percentage (85.7) and consecutive three-pointers made (11) in both a game and a season.

Amazingly, he did not even shoot a two-pointer.

A STAR IS BORN

1913: Johnny Mize, a baseball Hall of Fame first baseman-outfielder who batted .312 over his 15-year major league career.

★ ★ ★

1922: Alvin Dark, a career .289 hitter over 14 seasons and later a major league manager.

★ ★ ★

1945: Tony Conigliaro, a former Boston Red Sox slugger whose career ended prematurely because of a beanball accident.

★ ★ ★

DEATH OF A LEGEND

1990: Bronko Nagurski (football).

★ ★ ★

1990: Joe Robbie (football).

★ ★ ★

1990: Horace Stoneham (baseball).

★ ★ ★

JANUARY 7

1991 ROSE LEAVES PRISON

Pete Rose, baseball's all-time hit king, who was convicted on federal tax evasion charges last July, completed his initial five-month sentence at a Marion, Illinois, work camp and then began Phase II of his rehabilitation process.

The 49-year-old Rose who was banned from baseball in 1989 for his alleged gambling activities and then convicted last year on charges of failing to report more than $350,000 of baseball-related income, will check immediately into a Cincinnati halfway house.

His three-month stint there will include various work activities and 1,000 hours of community service, a sentence that will carry over after his release.

Rose, who was driven away from the Marion facility by his wife Carol, has spent the last five months working eight-hour days in the prison welding shop. He made 11 cents an hour at that job.

After his community service is complete, Rose will remain on probation for another nine months.

The income tax evasion charges stemmed from money Rose received for autograph signings and baseball memorabilia sales.

The lifetime ban that remains in force for an indefinite period was handed down by then-baseball Commissioner A. Bartlett Giamatti, who investigated reports that Rose bet on baseball games.

JANUARY

8

MILESTONES IN SPORTS

1947

An NHL rookie record: Toronto's Howie Meeker scored five goals in a 10–4 victory over Chicago.

1984

Washington's Bengt Gustafsson scored five goals to lead the Capitals to a 7–1 NHL victory over the Philadelphia Flyers.

1984

The Los Angeles Raiders, two-time losers to Seattle during the regular season, beat the Seahawks, 30–14, in the AFC championship game and dashed their hopes of appearing in a first Super Bowl.

1986

Former Giants star Willie McCovey, a career 500-home run hitter, became the 16th first-ballot electee to baseball's Hall of Fame.

1992

The NCAA toughened its requirements for controversial Proposition 48 by raising the number of college preparatory courses and the minimum grade-point average incoming freshmen need to qualify for participation in the various sports.

1972 Freshmen Get Okay For Varsity Sports

The National Collegiate Athletic Association ended its annual convention at Hollywood, Fla., with the surprising announcement that freshmen will be eligible to play varsity football and basketball at major colleges and universities beginning in the fall.

The decision, which is sure to create a lot of controversy, brings those two major sports in line with all other sports, which have not been bound by freshman restrictions for the last two years. The new rule is not mandatory, but victory-hungry coaches are sure to embrace their new-found freedom.

While the question of freshman eligibility in basketball was passed by a strong voice vote, a count had to be taken for football. It passed, 94–67.

A STAR IS BORN

1953: Bruce Sutter, a long-time National League star relief pitcher and a former Cy Young Award winner.

★ ★ ★

1957: Dwight Clark, a former wide receiver for the San Francisco 49ers.

★ ★ ★

1957: Calvin Natt, a former National Basketball Association forward who scored 10,293 points in his 12-season career (1979-91).

★ ★ ★

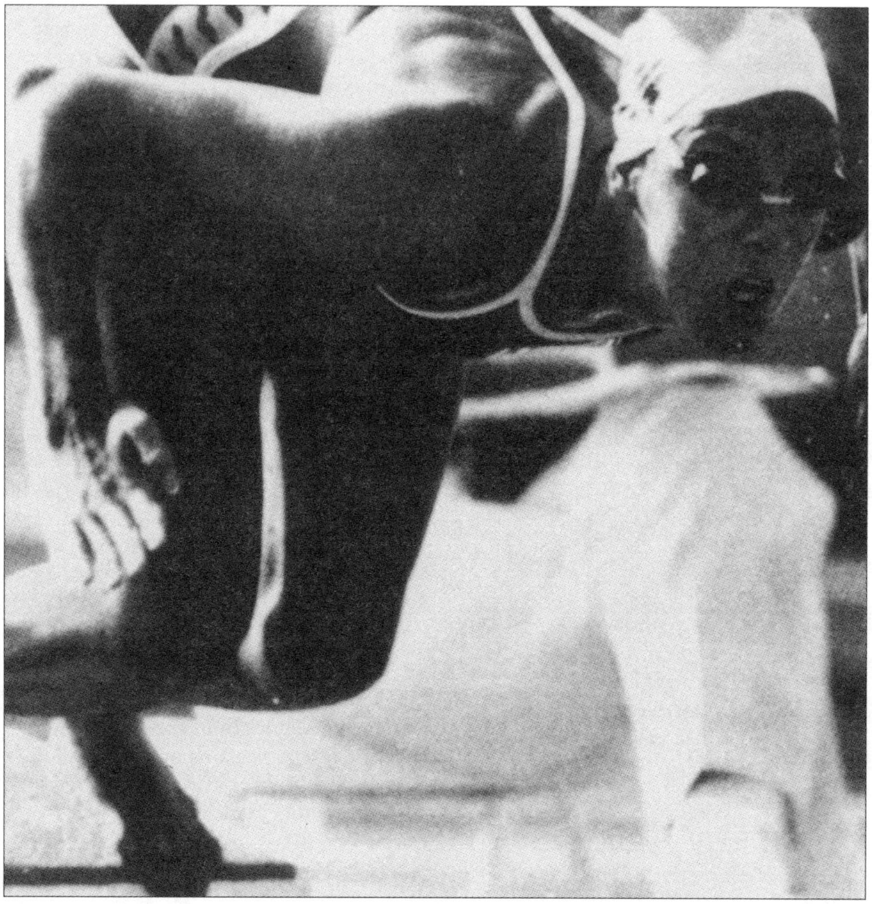

American 14-year-old swimming sensation **Tracy Caulkins.**

1978 Caulkins Smashes Records

Tracy Caulkins, a 14-year-old Nashville girl, broke three American records and assisted on another in the two-day United States women's international swimming competition at Brown University.

Caulkins finished her record run by covering the 400-yard individual medley course in 4:16.75, topping the previous mark of 4:19.04. Then she competed as part of the 400-yard medley relay team that set an American record of 3:43.72.

The youngster had set American marks the previous day in the 200-yard breast stroke and the 200-yard individual medley. Her one loss in the event was to 13-year-old Russian Julia Bogdanova in the 100-yard breast stroke.

The meet pitted 105 young swimmers from the United States, Belgium, Canada, Great Britain, Italy, Norway, Sweden, West Germany and the Soviet Union in 13 events. The powerful East Germans were supposed to attend, but backed out at the last minute.

1984 NCAA Tournament Expands Its Basketball Field to 64

The executive committee of the National Collegiate Athletic Association, acting on the first day of the NCAA's annual convention, voted to expand the field of its championship basketball tournament to 64 teams.

David Gavitt, chairman of the Basketball Tournament Committee, said he hoped this expansion would be the last. The tournament, which started as a six-team event in 1939, will field 53 this year after playing last year with 52 and two years ago with 48 teams.

With 275 Division I basketball programs vying for berths, about 23 percent of their hopes will be fulfilled. The new size was recommended by both the tournament committee and the National Association of Basketball Coaches.

1972 Bucks Stop Long Laker Win Streak

Milwaukee center **Kareem Abdul-Jabbar** *helped bring down the curtain on the Lakers' 33-game winning streak.*

Kareem Abdul-Jabbar scored 39 points and grabbed 20 rebounds, leading the fired-up Milwaukee Bucks to a 120–104 victory over Los Angeles that ended the Lakers' incredible 33-game National Basketball Association winning streak.

The Lakers, in compiling the longest run of success ever enjoyed by a professional sports team, had not lost since October 31 and entered the game against Milwaukee with a 39–3 record. But the defending NBA-champion Bucks were primed for the showdown and they gave a capacity crowd of 10,746 at Milwaukee Arena plenty to cheer about.

Especially Jabbar, who outplayed Lakers counterpart Wilt Chamberlain in every sense of the word. Jabbar provided the fourth-quarter spark, hitting the first two baskets of an 18–2 fourth-quarter run that broke open a two-point game and lifted the Bucks to their 36th victory in 44 games.

The Lakers' record run was 13 victories higher than the previous best NBA streak. That, ironically, was set by last season's Bucks, who won 20 in a row en route to their championship.

1977 Super Raiders Sack Vikings

Dave Casper caught a one-yard touchdown pass from Ken Stabler, Pete Banaszak ran one yard for another touchdown and Errol Mann kicked a 24-yard field goal in a decisive second quarter that helped the Oakland Raiders sack the Minnesota Vikings, 32–14, in Super Bowl XI.

The second-quarter explosion before 103,438 fans at the Rose Bowl in Pasadena, Calif., broke open a tight contest and sent the frustrated Vikings on their way to a record fourth Super Bowl loss in as many tries. Three of those losses were to first-time Super Bowl winners, including the Raiders.

The key play occurred early, when the Vikings appeared ready to score at Oakland's 3-yard line. But running back Brent McClanahan fumbled, linebacker Willie Hall recovered and the Raiders were on their way. Stabler directed a consistent offense that featured the receiving of Fred Biletnikoff and the running of Clarence Davis and Mark van Eeghen.

1963 An Era Ends In Cleveland

Former Cleveland Browns coach **Paul Brown.**

In a bizarre and shocking conclusion to one of the greatest success stories in professional sports history, Cleveland Browns Owner Art Modell fired Coach and General Manager Paul Brown, the man who molded his team into a four-time All-America Football Conference and three-time National Football League champion.

With Brown calling all the shots, Cleveland won all four of the now-defunct AAFC's championship games and then shocked the NFL community by winning a title in 1950, its first year in the league. The Browns either won or tied for the NFL's Eastern Conference crown in eight of their first nine seasons and went all the way three times. Brown's NFL coaching record was 111-44-5, his AAFC mark 47-4-3.

The parting of Brown and Modell is the result of a long-term deterioration of a once-strong relationship. Modell had privately expressed a desire to reorganize for some time. Before his dismissal, Brown was the only coach in the 17-year history of the franchise.

Brown could have served out the six years of his contract as a vice president but declined.

January 9

Milestones in Sports

1942

Heavyweight boxing champion Joe Louis made short work of Buddy Baer, knocking out the challenger with 4 seconds remaining in the first round of a title bout at New York's Madison Square Garden.

1977

Roscoe Tanner used a booming serve and powerful placements to blow away Guillermo Vilas in the men's final of the Australian Open, 6–3, 6–3, 6–3.

1978

Ingemar Stenmark of Sweden continued his pace in World Cup competition when he won his sixth straight slalom of the season – the day after he had won his sixth giant slalom.

1988

Minnesota's Anthony Carter caught 10 passes for an NFL playoff-record 227 yards as the Vikings advanced to the NFL championship game with a 36–24 victory over San Francisco.

A Star Is Born

1934: Bart Starr, a football Hall of Fame quarterback and leader of the Green Bay Packer winning machines of the 1960s.

★ ★ ★

Death of a Legend

1971: Elmer Flick (baseball)

★ ★ ★

1989: Bill Terry (baseball)

★ ★ ★

1994: Harvey Haddix (baseball)

★ ★ ★

JANUARY

10

A STAR IS BORN

1835: Harry Wright, a baseball Hall of Famer best remembered as the game's first professional manager.

★ ★ ★

1938: Frank Mahovlich, a hockey Hall of Fame left winger and a member of the NHL's 500-goal club.

★ ★ ★

1938: Willie McCovey, a baseball Hall of Fame first baseman who blasted 521 career home runs.

★ ★ ★

1939: Bill Toomey, an American decathlon champion in the 1968 Summer Olympic Games at Mexico City.

★ ★ ★

DEATH OF A LEGEND

1973: Turk Edwards (football).

★ ★ ★

1982 CLARK SAVES 49ERS WITH LEAPING CATCH

Dwight Clark made a leaping fingertip catch of a Joe Montana pass in the end zone to tie the game and Ray Wersching kicked the extra point with 51 seconds remaining to give the San Francisco 49ers a dramatic 28–27 victory over Dallas and a berth in Super Bowl XVI.

Clark's second TD catch of the game at Candlestick Park capped an 89-yard drive that consumed 4 minutes, 3 seconds with the 49ers backed squarely against the wall. Montana faced a third-and-three situation at the Cowboys 6-yard line when he rolled right to avoid the Dallas rush and made a desperation heave that appeared to be hopelessly overthrown. But Clark, at 6-foot-4, went high to pull in the pass that gave the 49ers the 1981 NFC Championship Game victory.

The catch was the eighth of the game for Clark, who totaled 120 yards. Montana threw for three touchdowns and 286 yards overall. Dallas quarterback Danny White threw for two touchdowns and Tony Dorsett ran for another in a losing effort.

San Francisco wide receiver **Dwight Clark.**

MILESTONES IN SPORTS

1920

A six-goal explosion by Newsy Lalonde set an NHL one-game record and led Montreal to a 14–7 victory over Toronto.

1975

Johnny Miller fired a stunning 10-under-par 61 and bolted to a commanding six-stroke lead in the second round of the Phoenix Open.

1980

In an intense, dramatic fight to the finish, Bjorn Borg defeated Jimmy Connors in a tiebreaker, 3–6, 6–3, 7–6, during play in the Colgate Grand Prix Masters tournament at New York's Madison Square Garden.

1984

Former baseball greats Luis Aparicio, Harmon Killebrew and Don Drysdale were elected to the Hall of Fame, the largest group of players picked in 12 years.

1967 O'GRADY GETS HIS REVENGE

Journeyman golfer Mac O'Grady, three months removed from a six-week PGA Tour suspension, overcame some shaky putting and captured the MONY Tournament of Champions by a single stroke over Rick Fehr.

O'Grady fired a final-round 71 over the 7,022-yard La Costa Country Club course to earn the $90,000 first prize. That more than made up for the $5,000 fine he paid when he was suspended by Commissioner Deane Beman for constant criticism of him and other PGA Tour officials.

The 35-year-old O'Grady had struggled throughout his career and needed 17 tries at the qualifying school before getting his PGA Tour card. The victory, obviously, was sweet vindication in a lot of ways.

It didn't come easy. O'Grady three-putted three greens and barely held off Fehr, who also shot a final-round 71. On the final hole, O'Grady lagged a 60-foot putt to within four feet and then tapped in for his victory-securing par.

O'Grady's four-round total was 10-under-par 278.

1992 VIKINGS HIRE BLACK COACH

Minnesota, which didn't hire its first black assistant until 1988, became the second modern-era National Football League team to hire a black head coach when it tabbed Stanford University boss Dennis Green to replace the retired Jerry Burns.

Green joins the Los Angeles Raiders' Art Shell as the only black head coaches in a league that is more than 60 percent black. NFL Commissioner Paul Tagliabue, who has been encouraging all 28 teams to increase their minority hiring, hailed the Vikings' choice and praised Green as a man with all of the right qualifications.

The 42-year-old Green, who compiled a 10–45 record during five seasons at Northwestern, led Stanford to an 8–4 mark last year. The Cardinal had not enjoyed a winning campaign since 1980.

Green's NFL experience came in two stints under San Francisco Coach Bill Walsh. Green served as an offensive assistant in 1979 and again from1986–88.

Minnesota's **Dennis Green,** *the NFL's second modern-era black coach.*

The hiring of Green overshadowed Tampa Bay's appointment of former Cincinnati Coach Sam Wyche the same day.

A STAR IS BORN

1890: Max Carey, a baseball Hall of Fame outfielder who once held numerous major league basestealing records.

★★★

1896: Paddy Driscoll, a pro football Hall of Fame player and coach in a long career that ranged from 1919–68.

★★★

1952: Ben Crenshaw, a former Masters golf champion.

★★★

1963: Tracy Caulkins, an outstanding swimmer and winner of three gold medals at the 1984 Los Angeles Olympic Games.

★★★

1970 CHIEFS GIVE AFL ANOTHER SUPER WIN

The Kansas City Chiefs, led by the passing of beleaguered quarterback Len Dawson, delivered another big blow to the notion of NFL superiority with a 23–7 victory over prohibitive favorite Minnesota in Super Bowl IV.

Dawson, whose name had surfaced in a Detroit gambling investigation during Super Bowl week, completed 12 of 17 passes and fired a 46-yard third-quarter touchdown strike to Otis Taylor in giving the American Football League its second major Super Bowl upset in as many years. Joe Namath and the New York Jets had upset Baltimore in Super Bowl III after Green Bay captured the first two post-merger agreement championship games in lopsided fashion.

A national television audience and 80,562 fans at Tulane Stadium in New Orleans were stunned by the decisiveness of the Chiefs' victory. They dominated the powerful Vikings defensively and confounded a Minnesota defense that had allowed less than 10 points per game in a 12–2 regular season.

Mike Garrett scored Kansas City's other touchdown on a five-yard run and Jan Stenerud kicked three field goals.

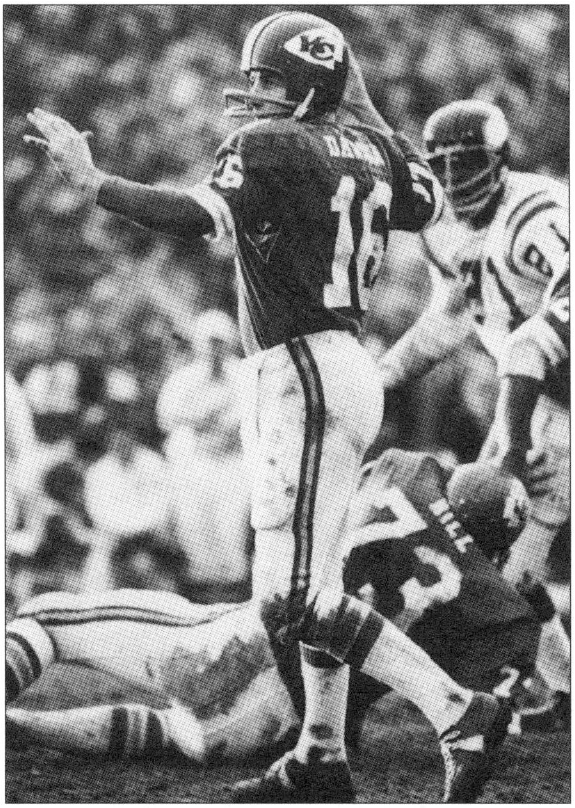

Chiefs quarterback **Len Dawson** *picked apart the Vikings.*

1973 A.L. ADOPTS DH RULE

American League owners, claiming a designated hitter rule would add more scoring and excitement to the game, adopted the controversial DH as a three-year experiment at a meeting in Chicago. It was the first major rule change in 80 years and triggered one of the biggest controversies in baseball history.

The rule, simply stated, allows each A.L. team to replace weak-hitting pitchers in the lineup with players who will bat, but not play defensively. Proponents hailed the idea as a needed boost to the offensive side of the game. Purists maintained the rule would usher in an era of platoon baseball, eventually leading to 18 men on each side – nine hitters and nine defensive specialists.

The A.L. passed the rule with a shaky 8–4 vote. The National League vetoed the idea but gave its permission for the A.L. to use it on an experimental basis, beginning in the 1973 season.

1976 FLYERS BEAT UP RUSSIANS

The Philadelphia Flyers, showing little regard for detente or their Russian guests, bullied their way to a 4–1 exhibition hockey victory over the Soviet Central Army team in a controversial international matchup at the Philadelphia Spectrum.

The Flyers, two-time defending Stanley Cup champions known for their brawling style, unleashed their intimidating tactics on the stylish Soviets early and never let up. As the Russians became visibly agitated, the Broad Street Bullies became even more aggressive.

The situation turned ugly midway through the opening period when Philadelphia defenseman Ed Van Impe viciously drilled high-scoring Valery Kharlamov from behind. When no penalty was called, Soviet Coach Konstantin Loktev ordered his goalie off the ice. The referee responded by handing the Russians a delay of game penalty and Loktev answered by sending his team to the locker room.

After a conference between NHL officials and members of the Soviet delegation, Loktev was ordered to recall his team and play resumed – 16 minutes after the incident. To add insult to injury, Reggie Leach scored 17 seconds into the power play and the Flyers went on to an easy victory.

Loktev later called the game an exhibition of "animal hockey."

JANUARY 11

MILESTONES IN SPORTS

1946

Pittsburgh Steelers co-Owner Bert Bell was named NFL commissioner when the contract of Elmer Layden was not renewed.

1948

Montreal's famed Punch Line of Toe Blake, Maurice (Rocket) Richard and Elmer Lach was broken up when Blake suffered a career-ending double fracture of his ankle in a game against the New York Rangers.

1974

Boston Celtics sixth man John Havlicek became the NBA's eighth career 20,000-point scorer.

1981

Jim Plunkett's 14-of-18, 261-yard performance carried Oakland to a 34–27 AFC championship game victory over San Diego and allowed the Raiders to become the conference's first wild-card team to advance to a Super Bowl.

1984

The Denver Nuggets defeated the San Antonio Spurs, 163–155, in the highest-scoring regulation game in NBA history.

1987

John Elway's five-yard touchdown pass to Mark Jackson with 37 seconds remaining in regulation tied the game and Rich Karlis' 33-yard overtime field goal gave the Broncos a 23–20 AFC championship game victory over Cleveland.

JANUARY 12

A STAR IS BORN

1944: Joe Frazier, a former heavyweight boxing champion and adversary of Muhammad Ali in the 1960s and early '70s.

★★★

1951: Bill Madlock, a major league infielder and four-time N.L. batting champion who averaged 305 over 15 seasons.

★★★

1960: Dominique Wilkins, a current National Basketball Association forward.

★★★

1906 Football Comes To Pass

A rules committee commissioned by the newly formed National Intercollegiate Football Conference, reacting to public outrage and a call for drastic reform from President Theodore Roosevelt, redefined college football with changes designed to eliminate brutality from the game.

The most far-reaching new rules, designed to open up play and get rid of the mass-formation style that had caused numerous deaths and injuries, were the legalization of the forward pass and creation of a neutral zone between the offensive and defensive lines. Other changes included reducing game time from 70 to 60 minutes, increasing first-down distance from five to 10 yards on three plays and another umpire besides the referee and linesman.

Teams attempting to pass would lose possession of the ball if unsuccessful.

1969 Namath Fulfills Prophecy

Quarterback Joe Namath, who had boldly guaranteed a victory for the American Football League over powerful Baltimore in Super Bowl III, directed the prohibitive underdog New York Jets to a 16–7 victory over the Colts in one of the biggest upsets in American sports history.

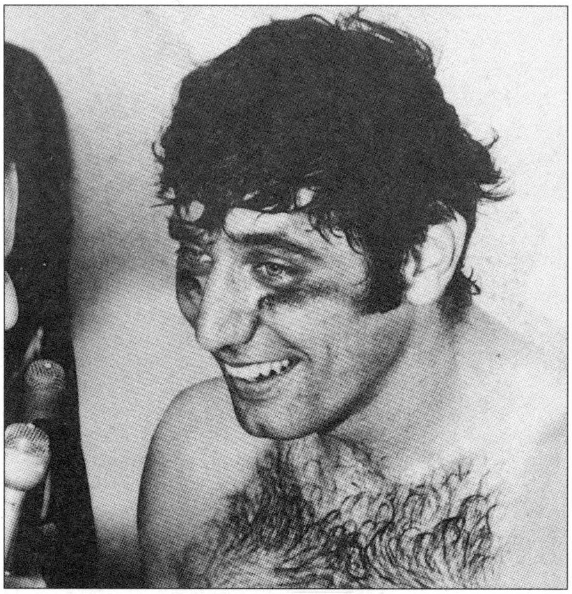

Jets quarterback **Joe Namath** *after Super Bowl III.*

The brash Namath, who had made his prediction three days earlier, performed flawlessly in the game at Miami's Orange Bowl, confounding an excellent Colts defense with a mixture of pinpoint passes and Matt Snell runs. The Jets defense took care of the rest, dominating the line of scrimmage and harassing Baltimore quarterbacks Earl Morrall and Johnny Unitas into four interceptions and numerous other bad passes.

The game's turning point came in the first quarter when the Colts missed two scoring opportunities – one on a wide field goal attempt and another on an end zone interception that followed a Baltimore fumble recovery at the Jets' 12-yard line. The New Yorkers took control after that and gave the AFL a much-needed dose of respect. Dismayed after blowout victories by the National Football League's Green Bay Packers over Kansas City and Oakland in the first two Super Bowls, the AFL suddenly had reason to smile.

Snell scored the Jets' only touchdown midway through the second quarter on a four-yard run and Jim Turner added three field goals. Baltimore's only score came late on Jerry Hill's one-yard run.

MILESTONES IN SPORTS

1958

The NCAA rules committee, making the first change in football scoring rules since 1912, added the two-point conversion option after touchdowns.

1960

Syracuse forward Dolph Schayes, already the NBA's career scoring leader, became the league's first 15,000-point man.

1975

Blazing Johnny Miller, an eight-time winner on the PGA Tour last year, shot a 24-under-par 260 for a record-setting 14-stroke victory in the Phoenix Open. The 260 was the second lowest four-round total ever posted.

1986

Chicago Blackhawks star Denis Savard tied an NHL record for quick goals when he scored 4 seconds into the final period of a 4–2 victory over Hartford.

1992

Troy State pounded defenseless DeVry Institute, 258–141, in a Division II college basketball battle that set eight NCAA scoring records

Pittsburgh's hard-charging running back **Franco Harris.**

1975 Steelers Earn 1st NFL Title

Franco Harris rumbled for 158 yards and a third-quarter touchdown and Pittsburgh's vaunted defense smothered Minnesota as the Steelers earned their first ever National Football League championship with a 16–6 victory over the Vikings in Super Bowl IX at Tulane Stadium in New Orleans.

The victory ended 42 years of frustration for Pittsburgh Owner Art Rooney.

It was made possible by an opportunistic defense that limited the powerful Vikings to 119 yards and also forced quarterback Fran Tarkenton into three interceptions.

Steelers quarterback Terry Bradshaw, after seeing his team take an unlikely 2–0 lead into halftime, got his ground game rolling in the second half and capped the scoring with a four-yard TD pass to tight end Larry Brown after Harris' nine-yard TD run had given the Steelers a 9–0 lead.

Sandwiched between the two scores was Minnesota's touchdown – a blocked punt recovered by Terry Brown in the Steelers' end zone.

The loss was the Vikings' third in the last six Super Bowls.

1974 Miami Pulls Off Double

Larry Csonka bulled his way for two touchdowns and Miami quarterback Bob Griese picked apart Minnesota's "Purple People Eaters" defense as the Dolphins cruised to a 24–7 victory in Super Bowl VIII and became only the second back-to-back winner of football's showcase event.

Miami running back **Larry Csonka** *was a human battering ram in Super Bowl VIII.*

Unlike the 1972 Dolphins, the 1973 edition was not perfect. But Miami finished its second straight impressive season with a 15–2 record and carried an armor of invincibility into its matchup with the Vikings. The Dolphins proceeded to dominate, both offensively and defensively, and joined the Green Bay Packers as two-time Super Bowl winners. The Vikings became the first team to lose two Super Bowls.

Mixing runs by Csonka, Jim Kiick and Mercury Morris with conservative passes to Jim Mandich and Marlin Briscoe, Griese controlled the clock masterfully. Csonka's five-yard run in the opening quarter gave Miami a 7–0 lead and Kiick's one-yard run, also in the first period, stretched the advantage to 14–0. The lead would grow to 24–0 before the Vikings finally scored on a four-yard scramble by quarterback Fran Tarkenton.

Csonka finished off his big afternoon with a Super Bowl-record 145 rushing yards.

1986 NCAA Adopts Prop 48 Rule

The Division I universities of the National Collegiate Athletic Association, ignoring the strong objections of predominantly black institutions, approved a controversial system for determining whether incoming freshmen will be eligible to compete in sports.

Under the new Proposition 48, scores from the Scholastic Aptitude Test or American College Test will play a major role in determining a freshman's athletic fate. For the next two years, a freshman who maintains a 2.2 grade-point average in high school must achieve at least a 660 (out of 1,600) on the S.A.T. or a 13 (out of 37) on the A.C.T. to be eligible. If the student has a 2.1, the score requirements increase to 680 and 14. If he has a 2.0, it's 700 and 15. Beginning in 1988, the rule will be standardized so the student must maintain at least a 2.0 grade point plus get a minimum of either 700 or 15.

Calling the use of standardized entrance examinations discriminatory, the 17 predominantly black schools in the NCAA combined their efforts to try and defeat the proposal. The rule passed by a vote of 206–94.

A freshman athlete who fails to meet the minimum requirements under the new guidelines must sit out a year and concentrate on his studies.

Milestones in Sports

1962

Third-year Philadelphia center Wilt Chamberlain set an NBA scoring record for a regulation game when he posted 73 points in the Warriors' 135–117 romp past the Chicago Bulls.

1973

The NCAA raised its controversial 1.6 high school grade-point average requirement for incoming freshman athletes to 2.0. Youngsters without the 2.0 cannot compete in intercollegiate athletics or be awarded a scholarship.

1982

Hank Aaron, baseball's all-time home run king, and Frank Robinson, the only man to win MVP awards in both leagues, were voted into the Hall of Fame in their first year of eligibility.

1991

Two-sport star Bo Jackson suffered a career-threatening hip injury when he was tackled during the Los Angeles Raiders' 20–10 AFC divisional playoff victory over Cincinnati.

1991

Edmonton's Mark Messier scored his 1,000th career point (an assist) in a 5–3 victory over Philadelphia.

January 13

A Star Is Born

1886: Art Ross, a hockey Hall of Fame coach, innovator and namesake for the trophy that goes annually to the NHL scoring champion .

★ ★ ★

1962: Kevin Mitchell, a current major league outfielder.

★ ★ ★

Death of a Legend

1978: Joe McCarthy (baseball).

★ ★ ★

1965 Warriors Trade Wilt

The Philadelphia 76ers, looking for an inside force to help them scale the championship ladder, pulled off a shocking trade when they acquired 7-foot-1 center Wilt Chamberlain from San Francisco for three players and an estimated $300,000 in cash.

The stunning announcement came moments after the annual All-Star Game at St. Louis. Chamberlain, a five-time NBA scoring champ who averaged an incredible 50.4 points in 1961–62, will go to the 76ers with Connie Dierking, Paul Neumann and the rights to Lee Shaffer going to San Francisco.

Chamberlain has dominated offensively since his NBA arrival in 1960–61, but has yet to lead a team to championship heights. The former Kansas star currently is averaging 38.9 points per game.

JANUARY

14

MILESTONES IN SPORTS

1943

An inspiring debut: Montreal's Alex Smart scored a hat trick and added an assist in his first NHL game, a 5–1 Canadiens victory over Chicago.

1954

A match made in heaven: Former New York Yankee center fielder Joe DiMaggio married movie actress Marilyn Monroe.

1962

Margaret Smith, playing on her home turf, defeated Jan Lehane, 6–0, 6–2, and captured her third straight Australian singles championship.

1976

Millionaire yachtsman and media magnate Ted Turner completed his purchase of the Atlanta Braves baseball franchise.

1981

Frank Robinson, who broke a color barrier in 1975 when he made his debut as baseball's first black manager at Cleveland, was named new manager of the San Francisco Giants.

1973 MIAMI FINDS PERFECTION

Bob Griese passed for one touchdown and Jim Kiick ran one yard for another as the Miami Dolphins staked a perfectly legitimate claim to the title of greatest National Football League team ever assembled with a 14–7 victory over Washington in Super Bowl VII at the Los Angeles Coliseum.

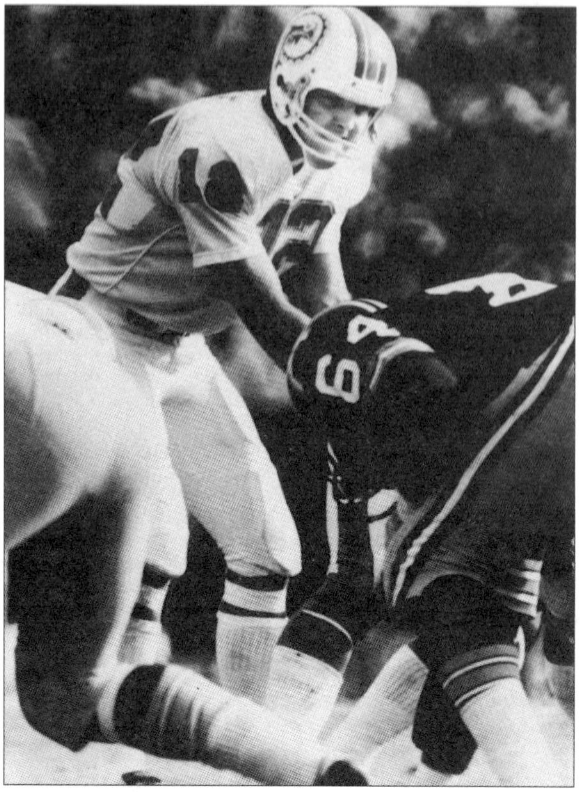

Bob Griese, *Miami's near-perfect quarterback.*

Perfectly legitimate as in 17–0, the Dolphins' final record. With the victory, Miami completed its 1972 season as the only undefeated, untied team in the 53-year history of the NFL. And the Dolphins closed out their showcase campaign in impressive style.

Primarily, it was a show choreographed and orchestrated by Miami's "No-Name Defense," which badgered and smothered the Redskins. The Dolphins, paced by Griese's 28-yard TD throw to Howard Twilley, Kiick's run and Larry Csonka's 112 rushing yards, were leading 14–0 and had things well under control in the fourth quarter when a bizarre play involving kicker Garo Yepremian made things a little tighter than they should have been.

Yepremian was attempting a 42-yard field goal when the kick was blocked by lineman Bill Brundige. The ball bounced back to Yepremian, who fielded it and frantically tried to pass. The ball slipped out of his hand and the wobbly throw went right to Washington's Mike Bass, who ran 49 yards for a touchdown.

The Redskins did get the ball back with 1:14 remaining, but the Dolphins stopped them cold and put the cap on the greatest season in football history.

1968 PACKERS CLAIM ANOTHER TITLE

The Green Bay Packers put another dent in the American Football League's claim of parity when they overpowered the AFL-champion Oakland Raiders, 33–14, in professional football's second Super Bowl at Miami's Orange Bowl.

As in their lopsided victory over Kansas City in the 1967 Super Bowl inaugural, the Packers simply had too much of everything – poise, discipline and talent. After building a 16–7 halftime lead on three Don Chandler field goals and Bart Starr's 62-yard touchdown pass to Boyd Dowler, the Packers really took control in the second half. They increased their lead to 33–7 before finally surrendering a consolation TD on Daryle Lamonica's 23-yard strike to Bill Miller.

The Packers were only 9–4–1 during the NFL's regular season. Oakland won the AFL championship with a 14–1 mark.

Green Bay's **Boyd Dowler** *crosses the goal line after catching a 62-yard TD pass from quarterback* **Bart Starr.**

1940 HISTORIC RULING FREES 91 TIGERS

In a historic ruling that could set back the Detroit organization for years, baseball Commissioner Kenesaw Mountain Landis freed 91 Tigers because the parent club had covered up movement of its players.

Landis' decision marked the most far-reaching free agency ruling ever handed down and freed talent the Tigers valued in excess of $500,000. Eighty-seven of the new free agents are minor leaguers and four were cut loose from the Tigers' parent roster.

The major leaguers are second baseman Benny McCoy, outfielder Roy Cullenbine and pitchers Lloyd Dietz and Steve Rachunok. Wally Moses, recently acquired from the Philadelphia Athletics for McCoy, will have to be returned.

The hiding of players within the farm system has been a source of irritation to Landis. In 1938, he freed 74 members of the St. Louis Cardinals organization, but most of those were lower-classification minor leaguers. The Tigers also must pay $50,000 in compensation to 14 players.

A STAR IS BORN

1932: Don Garlits, a drag racing champion who has won 35 National Hot Rod Association top-fuel events.

★ ★ ★

DEATH OF A LEGEND

1947: Bill Hewitt (football).

★ ★ ★

MILESTONES
• IN SPORTS •

1939

The NFL-champion New York Giants defeated a team of league all-stars, 13–10, in the first Pro Bowl game at Wrigley Field.

1972

Heavyweight champion Joe Frazier recorded a fourth-round technical knockout of Terry Daniels in a title bout at New Orleans.

1977

Boy Wonder jockey Steve Cauthen, the 16-year-old from Walton, Ky., scored with five winners during a meet at Aqueduct and brought his six-day total to 23, a New York state record.

1979

Tim Young's five-goal explosion lifted the Minnesota North Stars to an 8–1 NHL victory over the New York Rangers.

1981

Former St. Louis Cardinals righthander Bob Gibson became the 11th player to be elected to baseball's Hall of Fame in his first year of eligibility.

A STAR IS BORN

1891: Ray Chapman, the Cleveland shortstop who died in 1920 when he was struck by a pitch from New York's Carl Mays.

★ ★ ★

1901: Luke Sewell, a 20-year major league catcher in the 1920s and '30s.

★ ★ ★

1920: Bob Davies, a basketball Hall of Fame guard for 10 seasons in the NBA's formative years.

★ ★ ★

DEATH OF A LEGEND

1993: Henry Iba (basketball).

★ ★ ★

1967 Green Bay Wins First Super Bowl

The Green Bay Packers, defending the honor of the National Football League and justifying their status as prohibitive favorites, recorded an emphatic 35–10 victory over Kansas City in the first championship game contested between the NFL and rival American Football League.

The historic "Super Bowl," the result of a merger agreement between the two leagues last June, was played in the Los Angeles Coliseum before 61,946 fans and an estimated 60 million television viewers. The NFL-champion Packers were heavily favored. The AFL-champion Chiefs were upstarts trying to gain respect.

They did so in the first half. Bart Starr connected with Max McGee on a 37-yard touchdown pass and Jim Taylor ran 14 yards for another Green Bay TD. But the Chiefs answered with a seven-yard pass from Len Dawson to Curtis McClinton and a 31-yard Mike Mercer field goal. The 14–10 halftime score left observers scratching their heads.

But it was all Packers after intermission. McGee caught a 13-yard TD pass and Mike Pitts ran for a pair of scores while the Green Bay defense held the Chiefs to one penetration into Packer territory.

1968 Hockey Player Masterton Dies

Minnesota North Stars center Bill Masterton, who had returned to hockey in 1967 after a four-year retirement, died of a massive internal brain injury he suffered 30 hours earlier when he hit his head on the ice in a game against Oakland

Masterton, a 29-year-old Winnipeg native, is the first player in the 51-year history of the National Hockey League to die as the result of a game-related injury. The helmetless Masterton was hit in front of the Oakland goal, fell backward and hit his head on the ice. He was immediately rushed to a Bloomington, Minn., hospital where he remained until his death.

Masterton's return to hockey was the result of recent expansion and the resulting creation of more jobs. He had scored four goals and seven assists this season.

The accident sparked outcries throughout the league for legislation to make helmets a mandatory piece of equipment for all players.

1978 Dallas Charge Tames Broncos

The Dallas Cowboys, ruthlessly humiliating former teammate Craig Morton with a first-half defensive charge that produced four interceptions and seven turnovers, powered their way to an impressive 27–10 victory over the Broncos in Super Bowl XII at the New Orleans Superdome.

Morton, the former Dallas quarterback, never had a chance. Chased and harassed all afternoon by defenders Harvey Martin and Randy White, he succumbed to the pressure and the Cowboys took control. One interception led to a Tony Dorsett touchdown run and Efren Herrera kicked two first-half field goals while missing three others.

Denver, held to 72 first-half yards and trailing 13–0 at intermission, finally scored early in the third quarter on a 47-yard Jim Turner field goal. But the Broncos' comeback attempt was quickly short-circuited.

Dallas quarterback Roger Staubach stretched the Cowboys' lead with a 45-yard touchdown pass to Butch Johnson and the capper came on a halfback option TD pass from Robert Newhouse to Golden Richards.

In the end, the Broncos' only consolation was a turnover-free second half.

The victory was the second for Dallas in Super Bowl play. The Cowboys defeated Miami in Super Bowl VI.

JANUARY **15**

Dallas Cowboys sack master **Randy White.**

JANUARY

16

1972 COWBOYS LASSO DOLPHINS

The Dallas Cowboys, always the bridesmaid in their postseason adventures, finally moved into the football spotlight when they crushed the up-and-coming Miami Dolphins, 24–3, in Super Bowl VI at Tulane Stadium in New Orleans.

The Cowboys, who finished second to Green Bay in the 1966 and '67 National Football League title games and to Baltimore in last year's Super Bowl, choreographed their first NFL championship around the passing of Roger Staubach and the running of Duane Thomas.

Staubach, who completed 12 of 19 passes, fired a pair of seven-yard touchdown strikes, to Lance Alworth and tight end Mike Ditka. Thomas gained 95 yards rushing and ran three yards for a third-quarter touchdown that increased Dallas' lead to 17–3. Ten of the Cowboys' points came as a result of two Miami turnovers.

The young Dolphins, playing in their first-ever championship game, managed only 185 yards of total offense.

Dallas Cowboys running back **Duane Thomas.**

1970 CURT FLOOD FILES SUIT, TESTS RESERVE CLAUSE

In a case that could destroy the reserve system under which major league baseball has operated for decades, a suit was filed in Federal Court on behalf of former St. Louis Cardinals outfielder Curt Flood charging that the sport is in violation of the nation's antitrust laws.

Flood, with support from the Major League Players Association, named the commissioner of baseball, the presidents of the National and American leagues and the 24 clubs in his $3 million action. A hearing was set to consider Flood's immediate release from the "reserve clause" restrictions that tie a player contractually to one team indefinitely.

The action was taken in response to last October's trade that sent Flood from St. Louis to Philadelphia. The long-time center fielder said he would suffer "irreparable damage" if he is not allowed to play for the team of his choice in 1970. If Flood wins his case, which could go all the way to the U.S. Supreme Court, he could cause irreparable damage to baseball and other professional sports.

Baseball was ruled a business and, therefore, not subject to the nation's antitrust laws in a 1922 Supreme Court ruling. Subsequent Supreme Court decisions in 1953, 1955 and 1957 upheld the earlier decision.

Curt Flood: *One man against the establishment.*

1942 BASEBALL HAS GREEN LIGHT

U.S. President Franklin D. Roosevelt, responding to a letter from Commissioner Kenesaw Mountain Landis, gave baseball the green light to continue play as American troops fight overseas in World War II.

Landis had written the President, asking whether baseball should continue or cease operation in deference to the more serious matters being decided in Europe and other parts of the world. President Roosevelt delivered an emphatic "Play Ball" message in his "Green Light" letter and suggested that baseball schedule more night games for hard-working Americans.

"I honestly feel that it would be best for the country to keep baseball going," the President wrote. He added that the 6,000 play ers employed by the 300 or so major and minor league teams could provide valuable entertainment and a nice diversion for at least 20 million people.

Roosevelt left the final decision up to owners and emphasized drafted players should not be deferred.

A STAR IS BORN

1873: Jimmy Collins, a baseball Hall of Fame third baseman who played at the turn of the century.

★ ★ ★

1911: Dizzy Dean, a baseball Hall of Fame pitcher and the last National Leaguer to win 30 games in a season.

★ ★ ★

1935: A.J. Foyt, four-time winner of the Indianapolis 500 and all-time leader in Indy car victories.

★ ★ ★

1966: Jack McDowell, a current major league pitcher.

★ ★ ★

MILESTONES • IN SPORTS •

1972

Jack Nicklaus rammed home an 18-foot birdie putt on the first hole of a sudden-death playoff to defeat Johnny Miller and claim first prize in the Bing Crosby tournament at Pebble Beach, Calif.

1974

Former New York Yankee teammates Mickey Mantle and Whitey Ford were elected to the baseball Hall of Fame on the same ballot. Mantle was the seventh player to earn first-ballot election.

1977

Bruce Lietzke, a PGA rookie looking for his first professional victory, sank a 70-foot birdie putt on the fourth hole of a sudden death playoff and defeated veteran Gene Littler in the Tucson Open.

1985

The major basketball colleges voted approval for a 16-team preseason National Invitation Tournament featuring many of the country's top-ranked teams.

1988

CBS-TV fired Jimmy (The Greek) Snyder, a tout on its NFL Today show for 12 years, because of derogatory comments he made about blacks during a Washington, D.C., TV interview.

JANUARY 17

Baltimore's **Jim O'Brien** *(80) celebrates his winning kick in Super Bowl V.*

1971 O'Brien, Colts Kick Cowboys

A 32-yard field goal by Jim O'Brien with five seconds remaining gave the Baltimore Colts a 16–13 victory over Dallas in Super Bowl V and the National Football League's first championship after the AFL-NFL merger.

The Colts, one of the three NFL teams that had joined the newly formed American Football Conference, posted their victory before 79,205 fans at Miami's Orange Bowl. The game's classic ending saved the day for what otherwise was a comedy of errors.

The Colts committed six turnovers (three fumbles, three interceptions) and the Cowboys chipped in with four (one fumble, three interceptions). Both teams missed excellent scoring opportunities, the Colts failing to convert a first-and-two situation at the Dallas 2-yard line and Cowboys running back Duane Thomas losing a fumble at the Baltimore 2.

The Cowboys scored on a pair of Mike Clark field goals and a seven-yard touchdown pass from Craig Morton to Thomas. The Colts answered on a 75-yard Johnny Unitas-to-John Mackey TD pass and a two-yard Tom Nowatzke run. The winning field goal was set up when linebacker Mike Curtis picked off a Morton pass with less than two minutes remaining.

1975 Smith's Record Vault

Steve Smith got the International Track Association professional season off to a flying start when he raised his own world indoor record in the pole vault to 18–2$\frac{1}{2}$ during competition at the Montreal Forum.

Smith, using a fiberglass pole, thrilled the crowd of 8,753 by clearing 17–10 on his second-to-last jump, and the record-breaking height on his final vault. The 23-year-old Californian shattered his own indoor mark of 18–1$\frac{3}{4}$.

Smith was inspired by the presence of outdoor world record-holder Bob Seagren who could do no better than 17–4. Seagren, who had cleared 18–5$\frac{3}{4}$ on his outdoor record-setter, missed three times at 17–10. Smith had to retire after his record vault because of leg cramps.

A STAR IS BORN

1929: Jacques Plante, a hockey Hall of Fame goaltender who is credited with being the first to wear a mask.

★ ★ ★

1940: Kip Keino, an outstanding Kenyan distance runner and gold medalist in the 1,500-meter race at the 1968 Mexico City Olympic Games.

★ ★ ★

1942: Muhammad Ali, a three-time heavyweight boxing champion and generally considered one of the greatest fighters of all time.

★ ★ ★

1970: Jeremy Roenick, a current National Hockey League center.

★ ★ ★

1988 Byner Fumble Costs Browns

John Elway's 20-yard touchdown pass to Sammy Winder with 4:01 left snapped a 31–31 tie and the Denver Broncos survived a harrowing final two minutes to record a 38–33 AFC championship game victory over the Cleveland Browns.

The Broncos, in qualifying for their second straight Super Bowl, needed a stout defensive stand and a little luck to hold off the Browns. After Elway's strike to Winder, Cleveland quarterback Bernie Kosar drove the Browns to the Denver 8-yard line with 1:12 remaining. Earnest Byner, who had enjoyed a big day both as a rusher and receiver, took a handoff and found a clear path to the end zone. But as he crossed the 5, defender Jeremiah Castille poked the ball from Byner's grasp and the Broncos recovered at the 3. Denver took a late safety while closing out its victory.

The Broncos appeared to be cruising when they took a 21–3 first-half lead and answered an early second-half Cleveland touchdown with an 80-yard Elway-to-Mark Jackson strike. But Kosar rallied the Browns and finally forced the tie with a four-yard pass to Webster Slaughter with 10:48 remaining. That's when Elway took over.

MILESTONES IN SPORTS

1974

Playing without injured center Bill Walton, UCLA stretched its NCAA-record basketball winning streak to 88 with a 68–44 victory over Iowa.

1980

The NBA's Utah Jazz placed former All-Star guard Pete Maravich on waivers and agreed to buy out the remaining 2$\frac{1}{2}$ years of his five-year contract.

1981

Marvelous Marvin Hagler, making his first defense of the middleweight championship, scored an eighth-round technical knockout of Venezuelan Fulgencio Obelmejias in a bout at Boston.

1984

Ingemar Stenmark of Sweden turned in a strong second run and came back from third place to capture the slalom – his 76th World Cup ski victory – in a meet at Parpan, Switzerland.

1986

Tim Witherspoon earned a 15-round majority decision over Tony Tubbs in a WBA heavyweight title fight at Atlanta.

JANUARY

18

MILESTONES · IN SPORTS ·

1938

Only one player earned election in baseball's third Hall of Fame class – former pitching great Grover Cleveland Alexander.

1972

In an exciting conclusion to the NBA's showcase event, Jerry West of the Los Angeles Lakers hit a 21-foot jump shot to give the West a 112–110 victory over the East in the All-Star Game at Inglewood, Calif.

1975

Alvaro Pineda, one of America's top jockeys, was killed at Santa Anita race track when his mount, Austin Mittler, reared and threw him against the top of the starting gate.

1980

Harlan Hoosier, a 13-year-old amateur boxer from Beauty, Ky., died from brain contusions he suffered during a tournament at Lenore, W. Va.

1981

Bruce Lietzke, setting a 90-hole tournament record of 335 with a final-round 69, captured the Bob Hope Desert Classic by two strokes over Jerry Pate.

1976 PITTSBURGH EARNS SECOND SUPER TITLE

The Pittsburgh Steelers, seeking to become football's third two-time Super Bowl winner, scored 14 fourth-quarter points and held off a late Dallas rally to defeat the Cowboys, 21–17, in Super Bowl X at Miami's Orange Bowl.

Terry Bradshaw's 64-yard touchdown bomb to Lynn Swann, a safety and Roy Gerela's two field goals produced Pittsburgh's fourth-quarter points and helped the Steelers overcome a 10–7 Dallas lead. The Cowboys responded with a 34-yard Roger Staubach touchdown pass to Percy Howard with just under two minutes remaining and then tested the "Steel Curtain" defense in the final minute with one last shot at victory.

But Staubach, who had beaten Minnesota with a 50-yard "Hail Mary" pass in a divisional playoff game, was intercepted by safety Glen Edwards. The victory allowed Pittsburgh to join Green Bay and Miami as a two-time Super Bowl victor.

Pittsburgh Steelers' wide receiver **Lynn Swann.**

A STAR IS BORN

1938: Curt Flood, a former major league center fielder and the man who challenged baseball's reserve clause in the courtroom.

★ ★ ★

1954: Scott McGregor, a major league lefthander who won 138 games in 13 seasons with the Baltimore Orioles.

★ ★ ★

1961: Mark Messier, a current National Hockey League center.

Cleveland fireballer **Bob Feller** *took a voluntary pay cut.*

1950 FELLER TAKES PAY CUT

Bob Feller, Cleveland's fading but still explosive 192-game winner, signed his 1950 contract for an estimated $45,000 – taking a $20,000 pay cut at his own suggestion.

The fireballing righthander, unhappy with his 19–15 and 15–14 performances of the last two years, said he did not deserve to be making the $65,000 guaranteed salary he pocketed last year when he appeared in 36 games and pitched 211 innings.

"You can call this a very drastic pay cut," said Indians General Manager Hank Greenberg. "Feller thinks it's drastic, too. But he himself made the suggestion. In fact, he offered to take more than the 25 percent maximum pay cut allowed."

Feller, who pitched his first major league game with the Indians in 1936 as a raw 17-year-old out of Van Meter, Iowa, has enjoyed five 20-victory seasons in an outstanding career that was interrupted for four years when he served in the Navy during World War II. He will be pitching in his 12th big-league season.

1985 DECKER SHINES IN COMEBACK

Mary Decker, competing for the first time since her controversial collision with Zola Budd in last August's Los Angeles Olympic Games, flashed quickly into the lead and never let up en route to a world record in the 2,000-meter run at the Sunkist Invitational indoor track and field championship.

Decker was uncatchable as she ran a 5:34.52 at the Los Angeles Memorial Sports Arena, breaking the 5:43.30 record held by Russian Yekaterina Podkopayeva. Decker's main competition, Ruth Wysocki, finished 30 yards back in 5:45.93. Wysocki had defeated Decker in the 1,500-meter event at last year's Olympic trials.

Decker looked surprisingly strong in her first race in four months. When last seen, she was lying on the infield, grimacing in pain after falling during the 3,000-meter Olympic final at Los Angeles. The fall came when she made contact with Budd, the young distance runner from South Africa.

Decker was critical of her opponent after the incident and said Budd had cost her a chance to win a gold medal. Many observers felt the criticism was unwarranted.

1974 NOTRE DAME ENDS UCLA WIN STREAK

In a wild and crazy ending to college basketball's greatest victory run, the UCLA Bruins missed five shots in the final 21 seconds of an intersectional battle at Notre Dame and saw their amazing 88-game, three-year winning streak come to an unfortunate end in the most unlikely of fashions.

Unlikely because top-ranked UCLA appeared to be in control of its destiny after a first half in which the Bruins shot 70 percent from the field and built a 17-point lead against the second-ranked Fighting Irish. Unlikely because the Bruins owned a seemingly safe 70–59 lead with 3:32 left to play.

But the team that had won seven straight NCAA Tournament championships suddenly wilted in the face of a tough Irish press. On its first five possessions under pressure, UCLA misfired and the Irish converted each turnover into points. The comeback was completed when Notre Dame's Dwight Clay hit a jumper from the corner, giving the Irish a 71–70 lead.

After a timeout with 21 seconds remaining, the Bruins inbounded and Tommy Curtis missed a 25-foot jumper. Dave Meyers' tip attempt also missed and an Irish player knocked the ball out of bounds. With six seconds to play, big Bill Walton misfired on a 12-footer and two more Bruins missed follows.

Ironically, the Bruins' last loss had come three years earlier on the same court. The defeat was the first in the careers of Bruin stars Walton, Greg Lee and Keith Wilkes.

Johnny Miller *was hotter than the desert sun when he completed his Arizona sweep.*

1975 MILLER CONTINUES TORRID STREAK

Johnny Miller, in the midst of one of the greatest hot streaks ever witnessed on the PGA Tour, blazed around the Tucson National Golf Club course in a record 61 strokes and completed his Arizona sweep with a tournament-record four-round total of 263, nine strokes ahead of second-place John Mahaffey.

Miller, who recorded a PGA-record 14-stroke victory over Jerry Heard in last weekend's Phoenix Open while compiling the second-best four-round total (260) in history, was at it again in the final round at Tucson. Miller birdied five of his first seven holes and recorded an eagle on 11. He finished with sub-par scores on 10 of the 18 holes and missed birdie putts on the other eight.

Miller, who shaved 49 strokes off par in the two Arizona events combined, won eight times last year. He completed play at Tucson with rounds of 66, 69, 67 and 61.

JANUARY 19

MILESTONES · IN SPORTS ·

1932

Charlie Conacher scored five goals and Toronto roared past the New York Americans, 11–3, in an NHL game at Toronto.

1937

Former greats Napoleon Lajoie, Tris Speaker and Cy Young were selected as baseball's second class of Hall of Fame inductees.

1972

Former Los Angeles Dodgers pitching great Sandy Koufax became the youngest Hall of Fame electee at age 36. He was selected along with Yogi Berra and Early Wynn.

1975

When former UCLA greats Kareem Abdul-Jabbar and Bill Walton faced off for the first time as professionals, Milwaukee's Abdul-Jabbar had 50 points, 15 rebounds and 11 assists. Portland's Walton had seven points.

1979

Renaldo Nehemiah and Greg Foster both were credited with an indoor world-record time of 6.95 seconds when they finished in a dead heat in the 60-yard high hurdles at the Philadelphia Track Classic.

A STAR IS BORN

1932: Joe Schmidt, a football Hall of Fame linebacker and coach for the Detroit Lions (1953–65).

★ ★ ★

1957: Ottis Anderson, a National Football League running back.

★ ★ ★

1966: Stefan Edberg, a Swedish tennis star and winner of five grand slam championships.

★ ★ ★

1969: Junior Seau, a current National Football League linebacker.

★ ★ ★

DEATH OF A LEGEND

1979: Tuffy Leemans (football).

1952 PGA BREAKS COLOR BARRIER

The Professional Golfers Association took its first big step toward integration when its Tournament Committee approved the participation of blacks in PGA co-sponsored events.

PGA President Horton Smith made the historic announcement and said that he hoped blacks might compete in the upcoming Phoenix Open. That, however, might be over-optimistic. There still are several obstacles to overcome.

Blacks will face the same rules that apply to all golfers who are not regular tour players. That means they would have to be invited among the 10 players exempted from qualifying or they would have to be included among the 10 invited to attempt to qualify. Only a special law could allow them to bypass the normal procedure.

JANUARY

20

MILESTONES
IN SPORTS

1966

Former Boston great Ted Williams received 93.3 percent of the possible votes in becoming the third first-ballot electee into baseball's Hall of Fame.

1974

Johnny Miller completed an unprecedented sweep of the first three events on the PGA Tour when he shot a final-round 68 in the Tucson Open and defeated Ben Crenshaw by three strokes.

1979

Affirmed, horse racing's Triple Crown winner in 1978, suffered his fifth consecutive loss when he finished second to Radar Ahead in the San Fernando Stakes for 4-year-olds at Santa Anita race track in California.

1980

Four-year veteran Jeff Mitchell shot a final-round 67 and recorded a four-stroke victory in the Phoenix Open – his first ever victory on the PGA Tour.

1982

Wayne Gretzky scored three goals and assisted on two others as the Edmonton Oilers defeated St. Louis, 8–6 – a few hours after it had been announced the Great One had signed a whopping 21-year contract.

1983

An NHL milestone: A goal by Darryl Sittler, his 1,000th career point, helped the Philadelphia Flyers beat Calgary, 5–2.

Elvin Hayes *(left) battles UCLA's* Lew Alcindor.

1968 UCLA Meets Its Match

Houston's Elvin Hayes, a clear-cut winner in his personal battle with UCLA big man Lew Alcindor, connected on two free throws with 28 seconds remaining to give the Cougars a 71–69 victory over the Bruins in a classic battle of unbeatens at the Houston Astrodome.

The much-publicized meeting between college basketball's two elite teams lived up to advance billing. A full house at the Astrodome and a national television audience watched as the second-ranked Cougars ended UCLA's 47-game winning streak, the second longest in history, and extended their own to 18. Houston has won 49 straight games at the Astrodome.

The 6-foot-8 Hayes was spectacular, scoring 39 points, grabbing 15 rebounds and blocking four shots. Alcindor was average, probably the result of an eye injury that had forced him to miss UCLA's last two games. Alcindor scored only 15 points and was obviously playing at less than his top form.

Houston led most of the game, with UCLA managing to force ties on three occasions. Bruins guard Lucius Allen, who scored a team-high 25 points, connected on a pair of free throws with only 44 seconds remaining to set up Hayes' late heroics.

1980 Steelers Show Record Form

Terry Bradshaw's 73-yard fourth-quarter scoring strike to John Stallworth gave Pittsburgh the lead and Franco Harris' one-yard touchdown run with 1:49 remaining provided insurance for the Steelers' hard-fought 31–19 Super Bowl XIV victory over the Los Angeles Rams.

The game, played in the Rams' backyard at the Rose Bowl, was a seesaw affair for three quarters. The Steelers scored first on Matt Bahr's 41-yard field goal, the Rams answered with a one-yard touchdown run by Cullen Bryant. Harris scored on a one-yard run for Pittsburgh, the Rams answered with a pair of Frank Corral field goals.

After Bradshaw had fired a 47-yard scoring strike to Lynn Swann and Vince Ferragamo had connected on a 24-yard TD pass to Ron Smith in the third quarter, the Rams held a precarious 19–17 advantage. That's when the Steelers' championship game experience took over.

The victory was the record fourth for Pittsburgh in six years. Los Angeles was making its first appearance in pro football's showcase event.

A STAR IS BORN

1931: Glenn (Fireball) Roberts, a race car driver who won 34 NASCAR events before he died in a fiery accident during the 1964 World 600.

★★★

1937: Bailey Howell, an 18.7-point career scorer during 12 National Basketball Association seasons in the 1960s.

★★★

1940: Carol Heiss, an American figure skating champion at the 1960 Rome Olympic Games and silver medalist at the 1956 Games.

★★★

DEATH OF A LEGEND

1947: Josh Gibson (baseball).

★★★

1985 Montana Leads 49er Blitz

San Francisco quarterback **Joe Montana** *shredded Miami for 331 yards and three touchdowns in Super Bowl XIX.*

Joe Montana, staging one of the most dazzling one-man shows ever witnessed in a championship game, threw for a Super Bowl-record 331 yards and three touchdowns, ran for another score and flawlessly directed the San Francisco 49ers to a 38–16 Super Bowl XIX victory over Miami at Stanford Stadium in Palo Alto, Calif.

Montana, who capped his do-everything day by scrambling for 59 yards, connected for TD strikes of 33 yards to Carl Monroe and 8 and 16 yards to Roger Craig. Montana completed 24 of 35 passes to win his personal duel with record-setting Miami quarterback Dan Marino and scored himself on a six-yard second-quarter scramble.

Marino completed 29 of 50 passes for 318 yards, but he was the Dolphins' only weapon against a swarming defense that pressured him into several bad throws. The Super Bowl victory was the second in four years for the 49ers.

MILESTONES
• IN SPORTS •

1921

Federal Court Judge Kenesaw Mountain Landis, selected last November as baseball's first commissioner, officially began his new job.

1945

Bill Thoms and Ken Smith scored once and Frank Mario twice in a 1:20 span of the second period to lead Boston to a 14–3 rout of the New York Rangers.

1969

Stan Musial became the fourth first-ballot electee into baseball's Hall of Fame and Roy Campanella became the Hall's second black selection.

1990

Always controversial John McEnroe was disqualified from the Australian Open tennis tournament for cursing the supervisor of referees during a fourth-round match against Mikael Pernfors.

1990

Pittsburgh Penguins star Mario Lemieux put on a show for his home fans with a four-goal explosion that led the Wales Conference to a 12–7 victory over the Campbell in the NHL All-Star Game.

1979

Steelers Win Record 3rd Super Bowl

Pittsburgh Steelers wide receiver **John Stallworth** *burned Dallas twice in Super Bowl XIII.*

Terry Bradshaw triggered Pittsburgh's powerful offensive machine with four touchdown passes and the Steelers became football's first three-time Super Bowl winner with a 35–31 victory over Dallas in Super Bowl XIII at Miami's Orange Bowl stadium.

Bradshaw played longball against the Cowboys' defense, connecting with wide receiver John Stallworth on 28 and 75-yard touchdown throws and with running back Rocky Bleier on a seven-yard strike before half-time. But the Steelers could not shake the Cowboys, who scored on a 39-yard pass from Roger Staubach to Tony Hill and linebacker Mike Hegman's 37-yard touch-down return of a Pittsburgh fumble.

After Dallas pulled to within 21–17 in the third quarter on a Rafael Septien field goal, the Steelers pulled away in the fourth period on a 22-yard Franco Harris TD run and an 18-yard Bradshaw-to-Lynn Swann touch down pass.

The ever-resourceful Staubach rallied Dallas with late TD passes to Billy Joe DuPree (seven yards) and Butch Johnson (four yards), but it was too little too late.

JANUARY

21

A STAR IS BORN

1940: Jack Nicklaus, the all-time leader in major championships (20) and generally acclaimed as the greatest golfer who ever lived.

★ ★ ★

1963: Hakeem Olajuwon, a current National Basketball Association center.

★ ★ ★

DEATH OF A LEGEND

1984: Johnny Weissmuller (swimming).

★ ★ ★

1989: Carl Furillo (baseball).

★ ★ ★

1993: Charley Gehringer (baseball).

1980

Bomb Drops On Seminoles

Virginia Tech's Les Henson redefined the word "dramatic" when he sank a shot at the buzzer to give the Hokies a 79–77 Metro Conference victory over Florida State in a college basketball game at Tallahassee, Fla.

The Hokies and Seminoles were tied in the waning moments of an evenly-matched battle of 10-game winners and Florida State was playing for the last shot. With five seconds remaining, Pernell Tookes fired up a jumper near the free-throw line, the ball bounced off the rim and was grabbed by Henson, who was standing right on the baseline with his back toward the Virginia Tech goal.

Henson wheeled and heaved the ball down-court as players from both teams began retreat-ing toward their respec-tive benches. Swish! The ball sailed cleanly through the net. Florida State fans sat in stunned silence as the Virginia Tech bench, momentarily unwilling to believe what it had just witnessed, began to celebrate an unlikely victory.

"Just incredible," said Tech Coach Charlie Moir of the 93-foot bomb. "I'll probably never see a shot like that again."

1978

Duran Stops DeJesus

Roberto Duran, the light-ning-quick Panamanian with fists of steel, stunned Esteban DeJesus in the 12th round and claimed the undisputed lightweight championship in a bout at Las Vegas.

Duran, who had split two earlier fights with DeJesus and entered the ring as the recognized World Boxing Association champion, caught his Puerto Rican opponent with a right cross early in the round and sent him sprawling. DeJesus, the recognized World Boxing Council champ, jumped to his feet but appeared groggy as Duran backed him into a corner. As Duran delivered a flurry of lefts and rights, DeJesus sagged into the ropes and the fight was stopped.

Duran, who led on all three officials' cards, had dominated since the fifth round. The victory was Duran's 61st and his 51st by knockout.

JANUARY

22

1973 FOREMAN SHOCKS FRAZIER

George Foreman, a former Olympic boxing gold medalist and the winner of 37 straight professional fights, sent unbeaten heavyweight champion Joe Frazier reeling to the canvas six times and recorded a stunning second-round technical knockout in a title fight at Kingston, Jamaica.

Foreman, the Super Heavyweight Olympic winner in the 1968 Summer Games at Mexico City, used his long reach to keep the champion away from him in the early going and then rocked Frazier with a powerful left hook to the body. Sensing that he had him on the ropes, Foreman moved in with left-right combinations and sent the champion down with a right uppercut.

Frazier took the mandatory eight count and then resumed his attack on the challenger. It was bad strategy. Foreman sent him down with another uppercut and then did it again with a straight right just before the bell.

It was more of the same in the second round. Frazier went down three more times and referee Arthur Mercante finally halted the bout. Frazier, who had won a piece of the heavyweight title in 1968 with a victory over Buster Mathis, was making his 10th title defense overall and third since outpointing Muhammad Ali in a classic match two years earlier.

MILESTONES • IN SPORTS •

1973

An era came to an end in Baltimore when quarterback Johnny Unitas, the holder of virtually every NFL passing record, was traded to San Diego for future considerations.

1982

Edmonton scoring machine Wayne Gretzky set an NHL record by notching his 61st goal of the season in the Oilers' 50th game.

1988

Mike Tyson strengthened his hold on the world heavyweight boxing championship when he recorded a fourth-round technical knockout of former champion Larry Holmes at Atlantic City.

1988

Seven major league players, including stars Kirk Gibson and Carlton Fisk, were declared no-risk free agents as a result of arbitrator Thomas Roberts' collusion ruling in favor of the Major League Players Association.

1989 MONTANA RALLIES 49ERS TO VICTORY

Joe Montana, enhancing his status as one of professional football's greatest all-time pressure quarterbacks, threw a 10-yard touchdown pass to John Taylor with 34 seconds remaining in Super Bowl XXIII, giving the San Francisco 49ers a 20–16 victory over Cincinnati at Miami's Joe Robbie Stadium.

Montana's TD winner capped a 92-yard drive that he engineered masterfully over the final 3:10 of play. Mixing passes and runs, Montana drove the 49ers methodically downfield after the Bengals had taken the lead on Jim Breech's 40-yard fourth-quarter field goal.

The 49ers had tied the game earlier in the period on Montana's 14-yard touchdown pass to Jerry Rice.

Montana finished with a Super Bowl-record 357 passing yards and he needed every one of them to overcome the big-play Bengals. Cincinnati's Stanford Jennings turned in the most dazzling play of the game when he ran a third-quarter kickoff back 93 yards for a touchdown.

San Francisco quarterback **Joe Montana** *burned the Bengals in the final minute of Super Bowl XXIII.*

The Super Bowl victory was San Francisco's NFL-best third of the 1980s under Coach Bill Walsh.

Washington defenders miss connections with Raiders back **Marcus Allen** *on his 74-yard Super Bowl touchdown run.*

1984 ALLEN'S RUSHING RECORD

Marcus Allen provided the offense with a record-setting 191 yards and two touchdowns and the Los Angeles defense took care of the rest as the Raiders recorded an easy 38–9 Super Bowl XVIII victory over the defending-champion Washington Redskins at Tampa Stadium.

Allen scored on second-half runs of five and 74 yards, but it was the Raider defense that did the most serious damage. Los Angeles scored one touchdown when Derrick Jensen blocked a Jeff Hayes punt and fell on it in the end zone and added another on Jack Squirek's five-yard interception return of a Joe Theismann pass. Sandwiched between was quarterback Jim Plunkett's 12-yard scoring toss to speedy Cliff Branch.

The Raiders set Super Bowl records for points by one team (38) and margin of victory (29).

A STAR IS BORN

1948: George Foreman, the still-active former heavyweight boxing champion.

★ ★ ★

1957: Mike Bossy, a hockey Hall of Fame right winger and the second NHL player to score 50 goals in 50 games.

MILESTONES · IN SPORTS ·

1950

An Associated Press poll selected the 1914 Miracle Braves' incredible dash to a World Series championship as the biggest upset of the half century.

1953

A Baltimore group headed by Carroll Rosenbloom was awarded a National Football League franchise – the holdings of the recently-defunct Dallas Texans.

1975

Former Pittsburgh slugger Ralph Kiner, facing his 15th and final chance to win election into baseball's Hall of Fame, received the required votes in his last year of eligibility.

1979

Willie Mays, former star center fielder for the New York and San Francisco Giants, gained election to baseball's Hall of Fame on the first ballot, earning 409 of a possible 432 votes.

1988

Talented West German Steffi Graf, a driving force in the new guard of women's tennis, earned her first Australian Open championship with a 6–1, 7–6 victory over veteran Chris Evert.

1929 YANKEE INNOVATION: UNIFORM NUMBERS

Yankee co-Owner **Jacob Ruppert**, *pictured with Manager* **Miller Huggins**, *added permanent numbers to the New York uniforms in 1929.*

New York co-Owner Jacob Ruppert, in an innovative move that will be watched closely by other major league teams, announced that the Yankees will wear permanent numbers on the backs of their uniforms in the 1929 season to help fans make quick player identifications.

Ruppert said the move is being made because many fans do not attend games on a regular basis and cannot easily pick out the players they have come to see. He also said identification was difficult for even the regular fan during pregame batting practice and when rookies make their first few appearances.

The numbers will be large, like those currently being used by football teams. Baseball teams have experimented with numbers before, but never as a permanent fixture to the uniform.

1944 15–0: RED WINGS CLUB NEW YORK IN MISMATCH

The Detroit Red Wings, putting on an impressive display of power hockey for their home fans, clubbed the outmanned New York Rangers, 15–0, in the most lopsided National Hockey League shutout ever recorded.

The Red Wings swarmed all over the ice and made life miserable for Rangers goalie Ken McAuley, who literally feared for his well-being. The New York netminder recorded 43 saves but still could not stop the onslaught.

By contrast, Detroit rookie goaltender Connie Dion faced only nine shots while recording his first career shutout.

Ten different players contributed points for the Red Wings with only defenseman Cully Simon and Dion not figuring in the scoring. The primary weapon was Syd Howe, who connected three times and set an all-time Detroit career record with 149 goals. Murray Armstrong, Carl Liscombe and Don Grosso scored two goals apiece.

The Red Wings got progressively stronger as the game proceeded. They scored two goals in the first period, five in the second and eight more in the third.

JANUARY 23

A STAR IS BORN

1936: Jerry Kramer, an outstanding offensive guard for the Green Bay Packer championship teams of the 1960s.

★ ★ ★

1969: Brendan Shanahan, a current National Hockey League winger.

DEATH OF A LEGEND

1956: Billy Evans (baseball).

1987 MARTINA UPSET IN FINAL

Hana Mandlikova, showing a poise and determination that had been missing in past matches against Martina Navratilova, pulled off a stunning straight-set victory over the defending champion in the final of the Australian Open.

Mandlikova took advantage of numerous Navratilova mistakes and her own inspired play to record her 7–5, 7–6 victory.

The 30-year-old Martina enjoyed a 5–4 lead and was serving for the first set when the 24-year-old second seed came to life.

Mandlikova won the next six games, closing out the first set and rushing to a 3–0 lead in the second. Martina fought back, but Mandlikova won the second-set tiebreaker, 7–1, and earned her second Australian title.

Navratilova, who had her 58-match victory streak snapped, had not dropped a set going into the final. She was seeking her fourth Australian title.

JANUARY

24

1978 NAMATH RETIRES

Broadway Joe Namath, the flamboyant, rifle-armed quarterback who led the New York Jets to the biggest upset in Super Bowl history, ended his 13-year career with the simple announcement, "I'm not going to play next year."

Namath, speaking from his Fort Lauderdale, Fla., home, said he made his decision last year as he was playing out his final campaign as a 35-year-old backup for the San Francisco 49ers. The other 12 years of his outstanding career had been spent with the Jets, who signed him out of the University of Alabama in 1965.

The talented and controversial Namath had to fight through an injury-plagued career. He underwent four knee operations, battled a difficult torn hamstring muscle and missed time because of a broken wrist and separated shoulder. But still he thrived.

His biggest season was 1967, when he became the first 4,000-yard passer in National Football League history. In 1968, Namath led the Jets into the Super Bowl and then boldly predicted a New York victory over the heavily favored Baltimore Colts. He delivered, 16–7, and gave the fledgling American Football League a needed dose of respect. Namath finished the Jets portion of his career with 27,057 passing yards and a 50.2 completion percentage.

1981 50-50: BOSSY JOINS EXCLUSIVE NHL CLUB

New York's Mike Bossy rifled a shot past Quebec goaltender Ron Grahame with 1:29 left to play in a game at the Nassau Coliseum and joined former Montreal great Maurice (Rocket) Richard as the only players in National Hockey League history to score 50 goals in their first 50 games of a season.

Islander **Mike Bossy**, *hockey's newest 50–50 man.*

With 4:10 remaining in the final period, the Islanders right winger still was two goals short in his historic quest. Tied up all night by the double and triple-teaming tactics of the Nordiques, Bossy finally managed his first shot on an Islander power play and managed to flip a backhander past Grahame for his 49th goal.

That gave New York a 5–4 lead. After the Islanders had increased their margin to 6–4, Bossy sent the New York crowd and his teammates into delirium with his record-tying shot.

Richard's record had stood since the 1944–45 season.

A STAR IS BORN

1957: Mark Eaton, a current National Basketball Association center.

★ ★ ★

1968: Mary Lou Retton, who became the first American gymnast to win an individual all-around gold medal at the 1984 Los Angeles Olympic Games

★ ★ ★

1964: Rob Dibble, a current major league pitcher.

★ ★ ★

MILESTONES • IN SPORTS •

1939

Three baseball Hall of Fame additions: George Sisler, Eddie Collins and Wee Willie Keeler.

1972

Ownership groups in Atlanta and Long Island, N.Y., were awarded franchises, increasing the National Hockey League's membership total to 15 teams.

1973

Former Milwaukee lefthander Warren Spahn, a 363-game winner during his outstanding career, became the sixth player to be elected to the Hall of Fame in his first year of eligibility.

1986

Winger Mike Bossy joined the National Hockey League's 1,000-point club when he assisted on a goal in the New York Islanders' 7–5 victory over Toronto.

1990

Winston-Salem State's Clarence (Big House) Gaines, in his 44th year of coaching college basketball, joined former Kentucky coaching great Adolph Rupp as the only members of the 800-victory club. Winston-Salem State defeated Salisbury (N.C.), 79–69, for the milestone victory.

1982 WERSCHING GETS KICKS IN WIN OVER BENGALS

Joe Montana threw for one touchdown and ran for another and Ray Wersching kicked four field goals to lift the San Francisco 49ers to a 26–21 victory over the Cincinnati Bengals in Super Bowl XVI at the Pontiac Silverdome.

The battle of Super Bowl first-timers actually was decided in the first half by a series of Cincinnati turnovers. Dwight Hicks intercepted a Ken Anderson pass to spark a drive that Montana capped with a one-yard dive into the end zone and a fumble recovery by Lynn Thomas led to Montana's 11-yard TD pass to Earl Cooper.

Wersching's first field goal, a 22-yarder, came with 18 seconds remaining in the half and gave the 49ers a commanding 17–0 lead. The Bengals added insult to their own injury when they failed to cover the ensuing kickoff and Wersching added a 26-yarder just before half.

Cincinnati did rally in the second half for three touchdowns, but Wersching kicked two more field goals that provided the margin.

The victory punctuated a dramatic San Francisco turnaround from a 6–10 record in 1980 to a 13–3 1981 mark that really set the stage for its Super Bowl victory.

JANUARY

25

1981 EAGLES GO KER-PLUNK

Oakland's 'Super' quarterback **Jim Plunkett.**

Jim Plunkett punctuated his resurrection from the lower depths of Oakland's roster with a three-touchdown performance in Super Bowl XV as the Raiders rolled to a 27–10 rout of the Philadelphia Eagles at the New Orleans Superdome.

The Raiders, who finished the regular season at 11–5, became the first wild-card playoff entry to win an NFL championship. Plunkett, who had served with the Raiders since 1978 as a forgotten back-up, was a big reason for that drive after taking over for the injured Dan Pastorini in the fifth game of the 1980 regular season.

Plunkett was outstanding in the Super Bowl. The former Heisman Trophy winner threw a two-yard first-quarter touchdown to Cliff Branch and then hooked up with Kenny King a few minutes later on the longest pass play in Super Bowl history – an 80-yarder that made the score 14–0. Plunkett later threw a 29-yard scoring pass to Branch.

The Eagles, hounded by a furious Oakland pass rush, never could get back in the game after the first quarter. Three of quarterback Ron Jaworski's passes were intercepted by linebacker Rod Martin and he completed only 18 of 38 throws, one an eight-yard fourth-quarter touchdown strike to Keith Krepfle.

1960 ROOKIE WILT GETS 58

Wilt Chamberlain, the most explosive rookie ever to play in the National Basketball Association, scored 58 points and grabbed 42 rebounds to lead the Philadelphia Warriors to a 127–117 victory over Detroit at Memorial Gymnasium in Bethlehem, Pa.

Wilt Chamberlain *already stood head and shoulders above NBA opponents as a Philadelphia rookie.*

The towering 7-footer, who is threatening to rewrite the NBA record books, connected on 24 field-goal attempts and 10 of 13 free throws in the second-highest single-game scoring performance ever staged. Minneapolis Lakers forward Elgin Baylor had set the record earlier in the season when he exploded for 64 points.

Chamberlain, the league's leading scorer, topped his previous high of 55. Twenty-three of his points came in a 35-point final period that put the game out of reach.

A STAR IS BORN

1924: Lou Groza, a professional football Hall of Fame tackle-placekicker for the Cleveland Browns from 1946-67.

★ ★ ★

1926: Dick McGuire, a long-time National Basketball Association player and coach.

★ ★ ★

1937: Don Maynard, a football Hall of Fame wide receiver and the long-time favorite target of New York Jets quarterback Joe Namath.

★ ★ ★

1959: Mark Duper, a current National Football League wide receiver.

★ ★ ★

1962: Chris Chelios, a current National Hockey League defenseman.

★ ★ ★

1965: Esa Tikkanen, a current National Hockey League left winger.

★ ★ ★

DEATH OF A LEGEND

1991: Hoot Evers (baseball).

★ ★ ★

MILESTONES IN SPORTS

1924

Opening ceremonies were held for the first Winter Olympic Games at Chamonix, France.

1939

Joe Louis recorded a first-round knockout of John Henry Lewis at New York's Madison Square Garden, retaining his heavyweight boxing crown.

1988

Utah guard Rickey Green was credited with scoring the NBA's 5 millionth point during a game against Cleveland at Salt Lake City.

1991

St. Louis Blues winger Brett Hull became the fifth player in NHL history to score 50 goals in 50 games.

1992

Jim Courier upset top-seeded Stefan Edberg, 6–3, 3–6, 6–4, 6–2, and became the first American male in 15 years to win the Australian Open.

1987 A GIANT STEP FORWARD

Phil Simms fired three touchdown passes and outdueled his more-heralded counterpart, John Elway, as the New York Giants overpowered the Denver Broncos in a 39–20 Super Bowl XXI rout at the Rose Bowl in Pasadena, Calif.

Simms was outstanding as he completed 22 of 25 passes for 268 yards. One, a six-yarder, went to Zeke Mowatt for a first-quarter touchdown, another, a 13-yarder, went to Mark Bavaro for a third-quarter score and a third, a six-yarder, went to Phil McConkey for a fourth-quarter TD.

Elway wasn't too shabby either, but most of the damage he inflicted came in a first half that frustrated Denver fans. The Broncos scored on a 48-yard Rich Karlis field goal and Elway's four-yard run, but they also squandered several excellent scoring opportunities that could have increased their 10-9 halftime advantage.

Elway finished 22 of 37 for 304 yards and threw a late 47-yard TD pass to Vance Johnson, but the Giants already had taken control with a 17-point third-quarter explosion.

That explosion carried them to victory in their first-ever Super Bowl appearance, and sent the Broncos down to their second defeat in as many tries. Denver had dropped a 27–10 decision to Dallas in its first Super Bowl in 1978.

JANUARY

26

MILESTONES
• IN SPORTS •

1921

Toronto's Corb Denneny became the third National Hockey League player to score six goals in one game and the St. Patricks recorded a 10–3 victory over Hamilton.

1950

An Associated Press poll named Jesse Owens, the American hero of the 1936 Summer Olympic Games, the "greatest star" of the half century.

1960

Burnsville (W. Va.) High School star Danny Heater scored 135 points in a 32-minute basketball game as his team defeated Widen High, 173–43.

1970

Arthur Ashe became the first black man to win an Australian Open championship when he defeated Dick Crealy, 6–4, 9–7, 6–2.

1985

Edmonton center Wayne Gretzky scored his 50th goal of the season in the Oilers' 49th game – a 6–3 victory over the Pittsburgh Penguins.

1992

Washington quarterback Mark Rypien passed for two touchdowns and Gerald Riggs ran for two more as the Redskins defeated Buffalo, 37–24, in Super Bowl XXVI at the Metrodome in Minneapolis.

1986

Bears Crush New England

Quarterback Jim McMahon directed a flawless offensive plan and end Richard Dent led a ruthless defensive charge as the Chicago Bears crushed the New England Patriots, 46–10, in Super Bowl XX at the New Orleans Superdome.

The victory was icing on an 18–1 season that gave the Chicagoans a look of invincibility. Mike Ditka's Bears had been just as dominating during the regular campaign, surrendering a National Football League-low 198 points while rolling up 456 of their own.

McMahon was the trigger man for an offense that produced 408 yards against the Patriots and he capped his performance with two short touchdown runs. Dent, who harassed New England quarterback Steve Grogan the entire game, led a defense that limited the Patriots to seven rushing yards and 184 overall. The defense also produced nine points.

Reggie Phillips scored a touchdown when he returned a third-quarter Grogan interception 28 yards and the Bears concluded their scoring with a fourth-quarter safety, tackling Grogan in the end zone. Kevin Butler contributed three field goals.

Mary Decker, *the 21-year-old record-setting miler.*

1960

Owners Select Rozelle

Frustrated National Football League owners, bringing an end to seven days of bitter haggling, compromised on their choice of commissioner candidates and elected 33-year-old Los Angeles Rams General Manager Pete Rozelle.

Rozelle, who becomes the NFL's sixth commissioner dating back to 1920, was not even on the candidate list when the meeting opened at Miami Beach. San Francisco lawyer Marshall G. Leahy and former FBI man Austin H. Gunsel were the leading vote-getters through the first 22 ballots, but the 12 owners were hopelessly deadlocked. Seven supported Leahy, five wanted Gunsel – and neither side would budge.

That's when Los Angeles Owner Carroll Rosenbloom suggested Rozelle as an alternative candidate. The owners, needing a three-fourths majority to elect a commissioner, gave Rozelle eight votes with three abstaining and one sticking with Leahy. Rozelle was given a three-year term at $50,000.

He will replace Bert Bell, who suffered a heart attack and died during a Philadelphia game last October. The issues facing Rozelle are expansion and the looming battle against the new American Football League.

New National Football League Commissioner **Pete Rozelle.**

1980

Decker Sets Mile Record

Mary Decker, the 21-year-old speed demon from Eugene, Ore., overpowered the field in an international track and field meet at Auckland, New Zealand, and lowered the world record in the women's mile to 4:21.7.

Decker, the 1,500-meter gold medalist in last summer's Pan American Games, made her move on the final lap of the race at Mount Smart Stadium and was 100 meters ahead of her nearest competitor with 100 meters to go. Linden Wilde of New Zealand finished a distant second in 4:36.6, nearly 15 seconds behind Decker.

Decker, who broke the year-old record of 4:22 set by Natalia Maracescu of Rumania, took advantage of a fast Tartan track and sunny weather. She ran the first quarter in 1:02.5, the half mile in 2:08 and the three-quarters in 3:16.5.

A STAR IS BORN

1950: Jack Youngblood, an outstanding defensive end for the NFL's Los Angeles Rams from 1971–84.

★ ★ ★

1961: Wayne Gretzky, the holder of virtually every National Hockey League offensive record and generally recognized as the greatest player in the league's long history.

★ ★ ★

DEATH OF A LEGEND

1893: Abner Doubleday (baseball).

★ ★ ★

1932: William Wrigley (baseball).

★ ★ ★

1980: Lynn Patrick (hockey).

★ ★ ★

1983: Paul (Bear) Bryant (football).

1991 GIANTS PAY THE BILLS

The New York Giants, using a stiff defense and ball-control tactics designed to keep Buffalo's high-powered offense off the field, recorded an exciting 20–19 victory over the Bills in Super Bowl XXV when Scott Norwood's 47-yard field goal attempt sailed wide with eight seconds remaining.

It was an exciting finish to an otherwise nondescript Super Bowl. The Giants ground out 386 total yards and consumed huge chunks of the clock. Ottis Anderson rushed for 102 yards and a touchdown and was a big factor in New York's ability to control the ball for a Super Bowl-record 40:33.

Buffalo built a 12–3 lead on Norwood's 23-yard field goal, a one-yard touchdown run by Don Smith and a second-quarter safety. The Giants fought back just before halftime on Jeff Hostetler's 14-yard TD pass to Stephen Baker and took a 17–12 lead in the third quarter on Anderson's one-yard run. The Bills regained the advantage on Thurman Thomas' 31-yard run in the final period, but Matt Bahr's 21-yard field goal after another time-consuming drive proved to be the clincher for the Giants' second Super Bowl win.

1982 TECHSTERS WIN 54TH IN ROW

Pam Kelly scored 18 points and Louisiana Tech won its women's NCAA-record 54th straight basketball game with an 83–60 victory over the University of Georgia at Marietta, Ga.

Tech, which raised its record to 20–0, led 35–24 at the half and put the contest out of reach behind Angela Turner's second-half scoring. Turner fired in 12 of her 14 points in the first 11 minutes after intermission and Tech gradually extended its lead to 23.

Louisiana Tech began its record journey on December 1, 1980, after dropping a 77-69 decision to South Carolina.

After the Georgia victory, Tech's record streak was snapped two days later in a 61–58 loss at Old Dominion.

A STAR IS BORN

1901: Art Rooney Sr., the founder and long-time owner of the National Football League's Pittsburgh Steelers.

★ ★ ★

1927: Joe Perry, a football Hall of Fame fullback for the San Francisco 49ers and Baltimore Colts from 1948–63.

★ ★ ★

1967: Dave Manson, a current National Hockey League defenseman.

★ ★ ★

DEATH OF A LEGEND

1991: Dale Long (baseball).

1973 UCLA STREAK REACHES 61

Bill Walton *and two members of UCLA's record-setting Walton Gang,* Keith Wilkes *(52) and* Pete Trgovich *(25).*

The Walton Gang stepped on the court at Notre Dame's Athletic and Convocation Center before 12,000 revved-up fans, methodically shot down the Fighting Irish for its record-setting 61st straight victory and then rode off into the sunset.

The Walton Gang, alias the UCLA Bruins, is nothing short of the best college basketball team ever assembled. The Bruins, winners of six consecutive national championships and eight overall, proved that once again against the Fighting Irish with a resounding 82–63 victory.

The top gun, as usual, was center Bill Walton, who scored 16 points, grabbed 15 rebounds, handed out four assists and blocked 10 Notre Dame shots. Slick forward Keith Wilkes scored 20 points in a game that the Bruins had in hand after only the first seven minutes.

The victory allowed UCLA to top the record winning streak of the San Francisco Dons, who won 60 straight games while recording back-to-back NCAA Tournament victories in the mid-1950s. A UCLA team led by Lew Alcindor won 47 games before losing to Houston in 1968.

Ironically, UCLA's last loss (January 23, 1971) had come against Notre Dame on the same court the record was set.

MILESTONES IN SPORTS

1980

Jimmy Connors captured his third straight U.S. Pro Indoor tennis championship when he dispatched John McEnroe, 6–3, 2–6, 6–3, 3–6, 6–4 in a 3-hour, 16-minute maration at Philadelphia.

1982

Cleveland's Geoff Houston scored 24 points and handed out a near-record 27 assists as the Cavaliers posted a 110–106 NBA victory over the Golden State Warriors.

1984

Wayne Gretzky scored a first-period goal to extend his NHL-record point-scoring streak to 51, but the Edmonton Oilers had to settle for a 3–3 tie with New Jersey.

1984

Carl Lewis set an indoor world record in the long jump when he soared 28–10¼ in his final leap during the Wanamaker Millrose Games at New York's Madison Square Garden.

JANUARY

28

MILESTONES
IN SPORTS

1943

Chicago's Max Bentley scored four goals and assisted on three others as the Blackhawks posted a 10–1 NHL victory over the New York Rangers. Bentley had all four goals and an assist in the third period.

1960

The making of a dynasty: A new NFL franchise, awarded to Dallas interests, was named the Cowboys.

1959

The NFL's Green Bay Packers named a new coach – Vince Lombardi.

1972

Oral Roberts star Eddie Woods grabbed 30 rebounds in a 109–104 victory over Louisiana Tech – the second consecutive game he had reached that lofty plateau.

1982

Edmonton center Wayne Gretzky's NHL-record 51-game scoring streak ended when he failed to get a point in a game against Los Angeles and goaltender Markus Mattsson.

1958 Campanella Paralyzed

Roy Campanella, the three-time National League Most Valuable Player who helped lead the Brooklyn Dodgers to five N.L. pennants and one World Series championship in his 10 big-league seasons, saw his career come to an abrupt end when a car he was driving overturned on a slippery road in Glen Cove, N.Y., leaving him paralyzed from the shoulders down.

The accident occurred at 3:34 a.m. about a mile from Campanella's Glen Cove home. The burly catcher was driving a rental car that skidded on wet pavement and crashed into a telephone pole. Campy was pinned for about a half hour as rescuers pried open the doors.

Campanella, who compiled a .276 career average and hit 242 home runs, was rushed to the hospital where he underwent a four-hour operation to repair fractured vertebrae in his neck. But doctors warned that he may never recover movement in the lower part of his body.

Campanella was scheduled to move with the team to Los Angeles for the 1959 campaign.

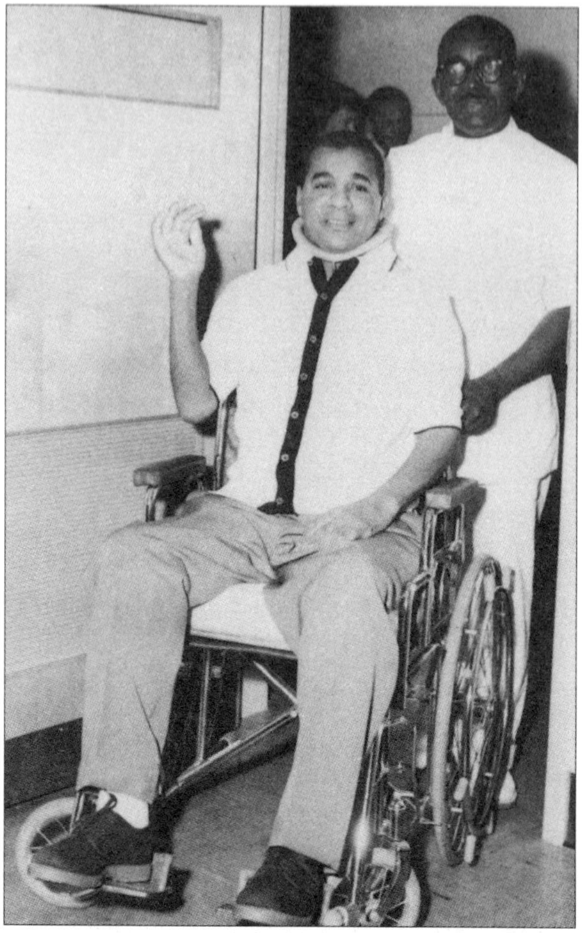

Dodger catcher **Roy Campanella** *after his automobile accident.*

1961 Two Jumpers Beat Record

American John Thomas and Russian Valeri Brumel, two high jumpers competing thousands of miles apart on the same day, both soared over the indoor world-record height of 7–foot–2½, a mark set by Thomas last March.

Brumel, an 18-year-old newcomer to the 7-foot level, soared over the bar at 7–4½ during an indoor meet in Leningrad to establish a new world record, either indoor or outdoor. News of the Russian's feat reached Thomas as he was preparing to compete in the Boston Athletic Association Games.

Thomas, who had cleared the 7-foot barrier 53 times entering the competition, proceeded to go 7–1 on his first jump, 7–2 on his second and 7–3 on his third after two misses. But with everybody watching intently to see if Thomas could reclaim his lost record, the 19-year-old Boston University student took the advice of his coach and called it a night.

The day ended with both jumpers having cleared heights never before attained.

A STAR IS BORN

1847: George Wright, a baseball Hall of Fame infielder who played in the formative years of the 19th-century National League.

★★★

1932: Parry O'Brien, a pioneer shot putter who revolutionized the event's technique with his innovative "glide."

★★★

DEATH OF A LEGEND

1991: Red Grange (football).

★★★

1990 Montana Fires 5 TD Passes

Joe Montana, the acknowledged master of late-game heroics, took a different tack in Super Bowl XXIV when he blistered the Denver Broncos with five touchdown passes and led the San Francisco 49ers to a 55-10 victory and their second straight National Football League championship, their record-tying fourth overall.

Jerry Rice caught three of Montana's record-setting TD throws, John Taylor caught one and Brent Jones one. Four of the five were 20 yards or longer and Montana's 297 passing yards concluded an impressive postseason in which he managed to complete 65 of 83 pass attempts for 800 yards and 11 touchdowns.

The Broncos never really had a chance against the explosive 49ers. Rice caught a 20-yard first-quarter TD pass and Jones caught his from seven yards out. After Tom Rathman had run one yard for another TD, Rice caught a 38-yard scoring toss that gave San Francisco a 27–3 halftime advantage.

It was more of the same in the second half as the 49ers set Super Bowl records for points and margin of victory. They also matched Pittsburgh's record of four Super Bowl championships.

1958 MUSIAL BECOMES SIX-FIGURE PIONEER

St. Louis slugger **Stan Musial,** *the N.L.'s first $100,000 man.*

Seven-time batting champion Stan Musial, the heart and soul of the St. Louis Cardinals for 16 big-league seasons, became the first six-figure star in National League history when he signed a contract for $100,000.

With cameras whirling and flashbulbs popping in a Hollywood-like setting, Cardinals President August A. Busch Jr. presided over the ceremony at the Anheuser-Busch Brewery offices. The unpretentious Musial, known affectionately to St. Louis fans as Stan The Man, said he would have been happy to settle for an eighth straight $80,000 contract.

But Busch decided otherwise and Musial joined a six-figure club that was founded in 1949 by former New York Yankee Joe DiMaggio. He replaces Pittsburgh's Ralph Kiner as the N.L.'s highest paid player.

Busch predicted that his 37-year-old star, the N.L.'s defending batting champ, would lead the Cardinals through another great battle during the 1958 campaign.

1988 JOHNSON BREAKS RECORD

Ben Johnson streaked to a record-shattering victory in the men's 50-yard dash and fellow Toronto sprinter Angelia Issajenko matched the women's 50-yard record in the Toronto Sun Challenge track and field meet.

Johnson, the world record holder in the 100-meter dash (9.83) and the indoor 50 and 60-meter events, was greeted warmly by his home crowd and responded by bursting out of the blocks to a 5.22 clocking in his first heat. But that was just the preliminary.

The muscular Canadian turned on the jets in the final and broke his own 50-yard record (5.20, set two weeks earlier) with a blazing 5.15. Two other Canadians, Desai Williams and Mark McKoy, finished second and third.

Issajenko, the world record holder for the 50 meters, followed Johnson's lead and equaled the 5.74 posted by American Evelyn Ashford in 1983.

A STAR IS BORN

1960: Greg Louganis, an outstanding American diver who won two gold medals in consecutive Olympic Games (1988 and '92).

★ ★ ★

1960: Steve Sax, a current major league infielder.

★ ★ ★

1964: Andre Reed, a current National Football League wide receiver.

MILESTONES IN SPORTS

1950

An Associated Press poll selected Jack Dempsey over Joe Louis as the greatest boxer of the half century.

1959

The Kentucky Wildcats handed 29-year Coach Adolph Rupp his 600th college basketball victory when they defeated Georgia, 108–55, in a game at Lexington, Ky.

1964

Boone Trail High School of Mamers, N.C., defeated Angier High, 56–54, in 13 overtimes – a record for longest scholastic game ever played.

1968

Billie Jean King captured her first Australian championship with a 6–1, 6–2 victory over seven-time winner Margaret Smith.

1971

Milestone: Philadelphia 76ers guard Hal Greer became the sixth player in NBA history to score 20,000 career points.

1973

The National Hockey League added franchises in Kansas City and Washington, bringing its membership to 17.

1985

New York Islanders veteran Bryan Trottier joined the NHL's exclusive 1,000-point club when he scored a goal in a 4–4 tie with Minnesota.

1963 FOOTBALL HONORS FIRST HALL OF FAME CLASS

Eleven of professional football's brightest stars from yesteryear and six of the men who founded and built the National Football League were named as charter members of the NFL's new Hall of Fame.

The shrine is being constructed in Canton, O., the city where the NFL was founded in 1920. Former players who will be among its first inductees are Jim Thorpe, Red Grange, Bronko Nagurski, Sammy Baugh, Dutch Clark, Don Hutson, Mel Hein, Ernie Nevers, Cal Hubbard, Fats Henry and Johnny (Blood) McNally. Former founding fathers and officials are George Halas, Curly Lambeau, Tim Mara, Bert Bell , Joe Carr and George Preston Marshall.

Bell and Carr were former NFL commissioners. Halas founded the Chicago Bears, Mara the New York Giants, Lambeau the Green Bay Packers and Marshall the Washington Redskins.

"These are the milestone men of pro football," said Dick McGann, director of the new Hall. "Their deeds and dogged faith wrote the history of this great game." All 17 were voted in unanimously by a board of selectors. There were no special formulas or requirements necessary for election.

The Pro Football Hall of Fame at **Canton, Ohio.**

JANUARY

30

1994 DALLAS SUPER AGAIN

Emmitt Smith rushed for a pair of second-half touchdowns and safety James Washington scored on a 46-yard return of a Thurman Thomas fumble as the Dallas Cowboys became the third NFL team to win four Super Bowls with a 30–13 victory over Buffalo.

The victory, the Cowboys' second in a row and the NFC's 10th straight over the AFC, came after a sluggish first half in which the Bills built a 13–6 advantage. But the second half was all Cowboys after Washington tied the game by scooping up one of two critical Thomas fumbles and scoring.

Smith took over on Dallas' next possession, running for 61 of his game-high 132 yards and scoring from 15 yards out to give the Cowboys a 20–13 advantage. Washington's fourth-quarter interception set up Smith's second TD.

The loss was Buffalo's fourth straight, tying Denver and Minnesota for Super Bowl futility. The Cowboys were the first to win a Super Bowl after opening the season 0–2.

A STAR IS BORN

1943: Dave Johnson, a former major league infielder and current major league manager.

★ ★ ★

1955: Curtis Strange, an outstanding American golfer who won consecutive U.S. Open titles.

★ ★ ★

1983 RIGGINS RUNS WILD AS REDSKINS TRIUMPH

A fourth-quarter 43-yard touchdown burst by 230-pound John Riggins wiped out a 17–13 Miami lead and sent the Washington Redskins on their way to a 27–17 Super Bowl XVII victory over the Dolphins at the Rose Bowl in Pasadena, Calif.

Bulldozing Washington running back **John Riggins.**

Riggins, who ran for a Super Bowl-record 166 yards, broke through the Dolphin defensive line on a third-and-one play and raced untouched into the end zone. The Redskins, suddenly in possession of their first lead, used Riggins to ground out the clock and iced their victory with a six-yard scoring pass from Joe Theismann to Charlie Brown.

In avenging a 14–7 loss to the Dolphins in Super Bowl VII, the Redskins rolled up 400 total yards compared to 176 for Miami. Riggins, who also caught a pass for 15 yards, outgained the entire Miami offense. The Dolphins managed only nine first downs, two in the second half.

But still they owned a 17–10 halftime lead, thanks to David Woodley's 76-yard TD pass to Jimmy Cefalo, Fulton Walker's 98-yard kickoff return and Uwe von Schamann's 20-yard field goal. And despite their second-half ineptitude, they carried their advantage into the final period.

But that's when Riggins took over and literally carried the Redskins to their 15th victory in 16 games dating back to 1981.

MILESTONES • IN SPORTS •

1967

Roy Emerson made short work of American Arthur Ashe and cruised to the Australian singles championship with a 6–4, 6–1, 6–4 victory at Adelaide, Australia.

1972

Wilt Chamberlain became the NBA's all-time leading rebounder when he grabbed No. 21,722 against Portland and passed former Boston rival Bill Russell.

1980

Chris Evert-Lloyd, saying "I'm burned out," won a first-round match in a Seattle tournament and then announced she would drop off the tour for the remainder of the year.

1982

Super welterweight champion Wilfred Benitez used his superior quickness to keep Roberto Duran off balance and scored a unanimous 15-round decision over the former champion in a WBC bout at Las Vegas.

1982

Scott Hamilton defended his national figure skating championship with a dynamic performance before 15,100 fans at New York' s Market Square Arena.

Margaret Smith, *seven-time Australian singles champion.*

1966 MARGARET SMITH EARNS 7TH AUSTRALIAN TITLE

Margaret Smith, the talented Australian who last year became the second woman to record a tennis grand slam, opened up her 1971 campaign with another victory – and she did it the easy way.

Smith captured her seventh straight Australian singles championship when American Nancy Richey, suffering from a knee injury, forfeited the prestigious title. Richey had reached the final earlier in the day when she defeated 18-year-old Australian Kerry Melville, 6–2, 8–6, in a semifinal battle.

But the knee began acting up and doctors advised that the Texan could do serious damage if she played the final. Smith, who defeated American Carole Graebner, 6–2, 6–4, in her semifinal, also won by default last year when Brazilian Maria Bueno withdrew from the final because of a cramp.

Richey needed only 18 minutes to beat Melville in the opening set, but fell behind, 5–3, in the second before rallying for the victory. Smith beat Graebner in 65 minutes.

1970 Maravich Sets Mark For Points

LSU scoring machine **Pistol Pete Maravich.**

Pistol Pete Maravich, Louisiana State's slender, mop-headed scoring machine, passed former Cincinnati star Oscar Robertson as the top collegiate point producer of all-time when he connected on a 15-foot jump shot during the Tigers' 109–86 victory over Mississippi.

Maravich, who finished with 53 points for a career total of 2,987, hit his record-setter late in the game, nearly six minutes after tying Robertson's career mark of 2,973 points. The overflow crowd at LSU Coliseum gave their star a long standing ovation that carried over into a postgame celebration.

Maravich, the two-time All-America and national scoring champion, began his senior season 687 points behind Robertson and ranked 14th on the scoring charts. He broke the record with 13 games remaining in his final campaign.

Maravich had 25 points in the first half to pull within 15 of Robertson's record.

1988 Hot Williams Burns Broncos

Washington's Doug Williams, seeking to become the first black quarterback to lead his team to a National Football League championship, fired four touchdown passes and combined with rookie running back Tim Smith to lead the Redskins to a 42–10 Super Bowl XXII victory over Denver.

Williams was masterful as he completed 18 of 29 passes for a Super Bowl-record 340 yards in the game at San Diego's Jack Murphy Stadium. He was especially masterful in a record-breaking 35-point second-quarter explosion that helped to wipe out a 10–0 deficit and turned the game into a rout.

Williams fired touchdown passes of 80 and 50 yards to Ricky Sanders, 27 yards to Gary Clark and eight to Clint Didier in the amazing period. Smith added a 58-yard touchdown run to the second-quarter fireworks en route to a Super Bowl-record 204-yard rushing effort.

The game started out well for three-time Super Bowl loser Denver and quarterback John Elway, who connected with Ricky Nattiel on a 56-yard TD pass on the first play of the game. But after Rich Karlis added a 24-yard field goal for a 10–0 advantage, everything started going rapidly downhill.

Elway completed only 14 of 38 passes in the game and threw away three interceptions.

A STAR IS BORN

1913: Don Hutson, a football Hall of Fame end for the Green Bay Packers (1935–45) and the long-time NFL record-holder for career touchdowns (99).

★ ★ ★

1913: Wayne Millner, a pro football Hall of Fame end for the Boston and Washington Redskins from 1936–45.

★ ★ ★

1919: Jackie Robinson, a Hall of Fame infielder and the man who broke baseball's color barrier for the Brooklyn Dodgers in 1947.

★ ★ ★

1931: Ernie Banks, a baseball Hall of Fame shortstop and a 512-home run hitter in 19 seasons with the Chicago Cubs.

★ ★ ★

1947: Nolan Ryan, a major league pitcher who retired after the 1993 season with 324 victories and career records for no-hitters (seven) and strikeouts (5,714).

★ ★ ★

DEATH OF A LEGEND

1992: Mel Hein (football).

January 31

Milestones in Sports

1920

Quebec's Joe Malone set a still-standing NHL record when he scored seven goals in a 10–6 victory over Toronto.

1941

Joe Louis retained his heavyweight boxing championship when he knocked out Red Burman in the fifth round of a title bout at New York's Madison Square Garden.

1950

An Associated Press poll named former Minneapolis Lakers great George Mikan as the greatest basketball player of the half century.

1989

Pittsburgh's Mario Lemieux scored his 54th goal in the Penguins' 50th game, the third-best 50-game total in NHL history.

1993

The Dallas Cowboys turned a record nine turnovers and two defensive touchdowns into a 52–17 victory over the Buffalo Bills in Super Bowl XXVII at Pasadena, Calif.

1989 Bombs Away: 331 Points Set Record

Hank Gathers scored 41 points and an incredible 11 other players joined him in double figures as Loyola Marymount and U.S. International played the highest-scoring game in college basketball history – a 181–150 contest won by the Lions at their Gersten Pavilion home in Los Angeles.

The combined 331 points broke the previous record of 306 – set by the same two teams three weeks earlier. Loyola Marymount also won that contest, 162–144, at San Diego. The Lions' 181 points broke the NCAA record of 164 they shared with the University of Nevada Las Vegas and the Gulls' 150 were the most ever scored by a loser, breaking their own record.

Loyola Marymount, which also got 34 points from Jeff Fryer, led 94–76 at halftime.

FEBRUARY

1

MILESTONES
· IN SPORTS ·

1956

Hayes Alan Jenkins of Colorado Springs gave the U.S. its third straight men's figure skating gold medal when he led an unprecedented 1–2–3 American sweep in the Winter Olympic Games at Cortina d'Ampezzo, Italy.

1964

Yale senior Wendell Mottley set a world indoor 440-yard dash record with a 48-second clocking during the Boston Athletic Association Games at Boston Garden.

1964

Montreal's Bobby Rousseau broke loose for five goals and the Canadiens skated past the Detroit Red Wings, 9–3.

1988

New Jersey's John Bagley, a 6-foot-1 guard, became the shortest player in NBA history to perform a triple-double. Bagley recorded 19 points, 10 assists and 10 rebounds in the Nets' 108–103 victory over Dallas.

1993

Gary Bettman officially opened his first term as National Hockey League commissioner.

1987

Warriors Survive 4-Overtime Battle

Joe Barry Carroll recorded season highs of 43 points and 24 rebounds and the Golden State Warriors survived a wild and intense battle with the New Jersey Nets to post a four-overtime, 150–147 victory at Oakland.

The seventh quadruple overtime game in NBA history–and the first in three years – was decided when Carroll scored six points in the final session and helped the Warriors open a 149–144 lead with nine seconds remaining.

But Leon Wood made things tight with a three-point basket and, after Chris Mullin had hit one of two free throws, Wood's halfcourt shot at the buzzer bounced off the rim.

The marathon contest, which falls two short of the NBA record for overtimes, featured 26 lead changes and 21 ties. Four of those ties came at the end of regulation (108–108), the first overtime (118–118), the second extra session (127–127) and the third (138–138).

The loss was the fifth straight for the Nets, who now are 11–33.

Golden State guard Sleepy Floyd, who set an NBA record by playing 64 minutes, supported Carroll with 29 points while Mullin added 25. Dwayne Washington had a career-high 29 for New Jersey while Mike Gminski added 25 and Orlando Woolridge 24.

A STAR IS BORN

1904: Carl Reynolds, a 13-year major league outfielder who posted a .302 career average during the Depression era.

★★★

1940: Herve Filion, harness racing's all-time leading winner with more than 13,000 career victories.

★★★

1944: Paul Blair, an outstanding defensive center fielder for 17 major league seasons.

★★★

1968: Mark Recchi, a current National Hockey League right winger.

★★★

DEATH OF A LEGEND

1928: Hugh Jennings (baseball).

★★★

Rangers goalie **Terry Sawchuk,** *the all-time shutout king.*

1970

Sawchuk Gets 103rd Shutout

Goaltender Terry Sawchuk, the New York Rangers' 40-year-old insurance policy, extended his own National Hockey League record when he posted career shutout No. 103 with a 6–0 victory over Pittsburgh at Madison Square Garden.

The venerable Sawchuk, acquired by the Rangers to give Ed Giacomin a rest as the season winds down, skated off the ice to a standing ovation after stopping 29 Penguin shots and earning his first whitewash since his 1967–68 campaign with the Los Angeles Kings.

Sawchuk had to share the spotlight with Dave Balon, who enjoyed the first hat trick of his career, and Jean Ratelle, who scored twice. But the man with more than 400 career victories was clearly the center of attention in the Rangers' locker room.

"I'm old and I'm tired," he told reporters, "but I try my best."

1984

Stern Takes NBA's Reins

David Stern, Larry O'Brien's right-hand man for the last five years, officially took over as the National Basketball Association' s fourth commissioner with a mandate to bring pro basketball to areas where there are no teams. The 41-year-old Stern, who has served as the league's executive vice-president in charge of business and legal affairs since 1980, replaces O'Brien, who will continue as a consultant and advisor to the league. Not well-known outside of NBA circles, Stern is highly respected for the results he has achieved for the league in labor negotiations and legal matters and his supervision of the circuit's intensified marketing efforts and television expansion.

The former Columbia Law School graduate is particularly knowledgeable in the area of cable television and has supervised the NBA' s broadcasting operations. Highly recommended by O'Brien, Stern was selected by a unanimous vote of the NBA Board of Governors in November.

New NBA Commissioner **David Stern.**

1949 HOGAN HURT IN CRASH

Ben Hogan, considered by many the top player on the professional golf tour, suffered a variety of career-threatening injuries when the car he was driving collided with a Greyhound bus near the small town of Van Horn, Tex.

Hogan had opened the season with victories in the Crosby and Long Beach Open tournaments and then lost a playoff to Jimmy Demaret in the Phoenix Open. However, as he was driving with wife Valerie back to their home in Fort Worth, Tex., their Cadillac collided with a bus trying to pass a truck.

Hogan suffered a fractured pelvis, a broken collar bone, a broken rib, a broken ankle and damage to his left knee. When blood clots began to form, his condition became serious and an abdominal operation was performed.

Sweet-swinging **Ben Hogan's** *outstanding career was threatened by a serious automobile accident.*

It actually could have been worse. Hogan saw the accident coming and threw his body over his wife, trying to shield her from the impact. This heroic action saved his own life. The force of the blow drove the steering column through the driver's seat.

MILESTONES IN SPORTS

1936

Ty Cobb, Babe Ruth, Honus Wagner, Christy Mathewson and Walter Johnson were voted charter members of baseball's new Hall of Fame.

1954

Rio Grande College's Bevo Francis, who had set a single-game small-college scoring record of 84 points two weeks earlier, shattered that mark with 113 in a 134–91 victory over Hillsdale.

1956

A new queen of the world figure skating scene: Tenley Albright became the first American woman ever to capture an Olympic gold medal in the Winter Games at Cortina d'Ampezzo, Italy.

1962

Marine John Uelses, using a new fiberglass pole, became the world's first 16-foot pole vaulter when he scaled 16–0$\frac{1}{4}$ during competition in the Millrose Games.

1977

Toronto's Ian Turnbull set an NHL record for defensemen when he scored five goals in a 9–1 victory over Detroit.

1980

The Dallas Mavericks paid an admission price of $12 million and were accepted as the NBA's 23rd franchise.

1989 WHITE NAMED N.L. PRESIDENT

Bill White, a .286 career hitter in 13 seasons with three major league teams, was selected as baseball's 13th National League president after receiving quick approval from the 12 N.L. club owners. White became the highest ranking black executive in a professional sports league.

White, who has broadcast New York Yankee games for the last 18 years, was tabbed by a five-man search committee headed by Los Angeles Dodgers Owner Peter O'Malley. The decision to accept the job was difficult because White will take a considerable pay cut, but he chose to accept the challenge of replacing A. Bartlett Giamatti, baseball's new commissioner.

White, who spent seven seasons as a first baseman with the St. Louis Cardinals and also played with the Philadelphia Phillies and New York and San Francisco Giants, was a six-time All-Star.

The search committee focused most of its efforts on finding a black. Other candidates included Simon Gourdine, the former deputy commissioner of the National Basketball Association, and also the former major league star Joe Morgan.

1967 NBA HAS A RIVAL

The American Basketball Association formally set up shop as a second major league and unveiled the tallest commissioner in the history of sports – 6-foot-10 former National Basketball Association great George Mikan.

Mikan had been the centerpiece of the five-time NBA-champion Minneapolis Lakers in the late 1940s and early 1950s. In his first official action as NBA commissioner, he declared a "no-war" policy in regard to player procurement and offered an olive branch to his former employers.

"We do not intend to raid the NBA for players," Mikan said. "I haven't read the current NBA contract and I don't know what it says, but we feel we must honor contractual obligations."

That, however, doesn't mean the ABA will ignore overtures from star players whose contracts have run out or refrain from spending freely for talent from the college ranks.

The league, which hopes to open with a 70-game schedule, will begin play in the fall with 10 teams.

Franchises already have been placed in an Eastern Division (New York, Pittsburgh, Indianapolis, Minneapolis and New Orleans) and a Western Division (Dallas, Houston, Kansas City, Oakland and Anaheim).

FEBRUARY 2

A STAR IS BORN

1895: George Halas, the famed "Papa Bear" who founded, coached and served as inspiration for the Chicago Bears NFL franchise for more than a half century. He was a charter member of the pro football Hall of Fame.

★ ★ ★

1923: Red Schoendienst, a baseball Hall of Fame infielder for 19 seasons and later manager of the St. Louis Cardinals.

★ ★ ★

1926: Bob Richards, the only pole vaulter to win the event in consecutive Olympic Games (1952 and '56).

★ ★ ★

DEATH OF A LEGEND

1918: John L. Sullivan (boxing).

★ ★ ★

FEBRUARY

3

MILESTONES
• IN SPORTS •

1962

New Zealander Peter Snell became the first runner to cover 800 meters in less than 1:45 when he was clocked in 1:44.3 during a track and field meet in Christchurch, New Zealand.

1964

Kentucky handed its legendary coach, Adolph Rupp, his 700th career victory with a 103–83 decision over Georgia. The victory lifted Rupp's 33-year record to 700–135.

1980

Spectacular Bid, with Bill Shoemaker in saddle, set an American record for 1¼ miles when he won the Strub Stakes in 1:57.8 at Santa Anita Race Track in Arcadia, Calif.

1980

New York Ranger veteran Phil Esposito scored his milestone 699th and 700th career goals in a 6–3 victory over the Washington Capitals.

1980

Larry Holmes defended his WBC heavyweight boxing championship with a sixth-round technical knockout of Lorenzo Zanon in a title bout at Las Vegas.

1982

Chicago's Grant Mulvey scored five goals, four of which came in the opening period, and added two assists in the Blackhawks' 9–5 victory over the St. Louis Blues.

1990 SHOEMAKER FINISHES FOURTH IN FINAL RIDE

Bill Shoemaker, horse racing's most successful and beloved jockey, slipped off into the sunset after riding Patchy Groundfog to a fourth-place finish in his much-publicized final mount at the Santa Anita track in Arcadia, Calif.

Bill Shoemaker *(right) brings down the curtain on his fabulous horse racing career aboard Patchy Groundfog at Santa Anita.*

Shoemaker, the 58-year-old Hall of Famer who finished his record-setting career with 8,833 winners in 40,350 mounts, made the Legend's Last Ride Handicap at Santa Anita his final stop on a worldwide farewell tour that began last June.

Shoemaker had his 3–5 favorite in the lead on the homestretch, but Patchy Groundfog wilted as 63,200 fans watched in disappointment.

Shoemaker, who visited 20 countries and most of the major tracks across the United States on his farewell tour, also recorded 6,136 career second places and 4,987 thirds. His winnings totaled more than $123 million and he rode four Kentucky Derby winners, five Belmont Stakes winners and two Preakness Stakes champions.

1944 HOWE SCORES 6 GOALS

Detroit center Syd Howe exploded for six goals in a 12–2 victory over the New York Rangers, the greatest one-game performance since the infancy of the National Hockey League in 1920 and 1921.

The 32-year-old veteran performed his rare double hat trick in two-goal bursts. He scored twice in an 18-second span of the opening period, twice in a 62-second span of the second stanza and twice in a 57-second span of the third. The Red Wings scored three goals in each of the first two periods and exploded for six in the finale.

Quebec's Joe Malone set the all-time single-game record in 1920 when he scored seven times and four players, Montreal's Newsy Lalonde, Malone, Toronto's Corb Denneny and Ottawa's Cy Denneny, notched six in the 1920 and 1921 campaigns. But nobody had managed to accomplish the feat since.

Teammate Don Grosso scored a goal and then tied two NHL records with six assists and seven points.

1962 UELSES SOARS 16 FEET

John Uelses, a 24-year-old U.S. Marine corporal using a new fiberglass pole, soared over the 16-foot pole vault barrier for the second time in two days and removed any doubt about his current superiority in the event.

Uelses had cleared 16–0¼ the previous night during competition in the Millrose Games at New York's Madison Square Garden. But in the celebration that followed the record performance, well-wishers inadvertently dislodged the crossbar from its perch, preventing a remeasurement as required by rules that govern track and field records. As a result, there was some doubt that the world's first ever 16-foot vault would be recognized.

No problem. Competing in the indoor games of the Boston Athletic Association at Boston Garden, Uelses duplicated his performance – and added a half inch to boot. His vault of 16-1 was re-measured at 16–0¾, a mark that likely will be accepted as a world indoor record. George Davies, at 15–10¼, still will be listed as the outdoor record-holder.

It took Uelses three tries to get over 15–4 and he then vaulted 15–8½ before making his record jump.

A STAR IS BORN

1890: Larry MacPhail, a Hall of Fame executive who, as Cincinnati general manager, introduced night baseball in 1935.

★ ★ ★

1938: Emile Griffith, an outstanding boxer who held both the world welterweight and middleweight championships.

★ ★ ★

1940: Fran Tarkenton, a football Hall of Fame quarterback for the Minnesota Vikings and New York Giants from 1961–78.

American **Terry McDermott** *pushes around the final turn during his dramatic Olympic speed-skating victory.*

1964

McDermott Wins Gold

Terry McDermott, a 23-year-old barber from Essexville, Mich., roared to a shocking victory in the 500-meter speed skating final and gave the United States its first gold medal of the Winter Olympic Games at Innsbruck, Austria.

McDermott did not figure to pose a threat to Russian Yevgeny Grishin, the world record-holder in the event. But Grishin, racing in the second heat, slipped slightly on the first turn, putting his gold medal hopes in jeopardy. Still, he was tied for the lead with Russian Vladimir Orlov and Norway's Alv Gjestvang when McDermott took the ice.

The sun had just popped out, the wind had stopped and conditions were ideal for a fast run. McDermott, using skates he had borrowed from his coach, hit the 100-meter mark in 10 seconds, a tenth behind Grishin's time. But then he turned on the jets.

As he hit the final turn with the lead, the crowd went wild. He hit the finish line at 40.1 seconds, an Olympic record.

February 4

Milestones in Sports

1964

Lew Alcindor, a 7-foot-1 phenom, scored 28 points and grabbed 19 rebounds in less than three quarters as Power Memorial Academy defeated Xavier High School, 94–59, for its New York State-record 49th straight victory.

1969

John Madden, a 33-year-old Oakland assistant, became the youngest head coach in the NFL when he was named to succeed John Rauch as Raiders boss.

1976

U.S. District Court Judge John W. Oliver upheld the ruling of arbitrator Peter Seitz, who had declared pitchers Andy Messersmith and Dave McNally as free agents.

1988

Four new basketball Hall of Famers: Wes Unseld, Clyde Lovellette, Ralph Miller and Bobby McDermott.

1991

A special baseball committee ruled that permanently ineligible players be left off the Hall of Fame ballot, thus disqualifying Pete Rose from immediate consideration.

A Star Is Born

1929: Neil Johnston, a basketball Hall of Fame center and three-time National Basketball Association scoring champion.

★ ★ ★

1959: Lawrence Taylor, a current National Football League linebacker.

★ ★ ★

1961: Denis Savard, a high-scoring NHL center.

★ ★ ★

Death of a Legend

1909: John Clarkson (baseball).

★ ★ ★

1943: Frank Calder (hockey).

★ ★ ★

1969

Owners Elect Kuhn

Major league baseball owners, stalemated in their efforts to elect a new commissioner, settled on compromise candidate Bowie Kuhn and elected the 42-year-old Maryland-born attorney to a one-year term.

Kuhn, who will carry the title Commissioner Pro-Tem, replaces William D. Eckert, who was forced to resign after fulfilling three years of his seven-year term. While not well known to the public, Kuhn is a familiar face to baseball insiders and is well-schooled in the business end of the sport.

That comes from his long association with the National League through the corporate law firm of Willkie, Farr and Gallagher. Kuhn has been involved with baseball since 1950 and most recently served as legal counsel for the player relations committee.

Kuhn's surprise election came as the result of a stalemate between National and American League owners at a meeting in Miami Beach. The A.L. faction wanted New York Yankee President Michael Burke, the N.L. favored San Francisco Giants vice president Chub Feeney.

When neither side would budge, Kuhn was accepted by both parties as an interim choice.

Bowie Kuhn *(left), baseball's compromise commissioner.*

1987

Conner Gets His Revenge

Dennis Conner, the only American ever to lose an America's Cup title to a foreign competitor, gained both revenge and vindication when he sailed Stars & Stripes to a 1-minute, 59-second victory–and a four-race sweep of Australia's Kookaburra III.

Conner, the skipper three years ago when the Australians won their first America's Cup in the 132-year history of the event, had spent the last three years preparing to get it back. He also had spent the last three months with his crew winning 47 match races in the grueling America's Cup regatta. And when Stars & Stripes matched up against Kookaburra III, it was really no contest.

With more than 100,000 spectators watching from various vantage points of the Fremantle, Australia, waterfront, Stars & Stripes jumped to a quick 5-second lead. But the final race over the 24.3-nautical mile course was really decided when Conner, on his second attempt, crossed in front of the Australian yacht by almost two boat lengths. Conner and crew lengthened the lead the rest of the way and cruised to victory.

FEBRUARY

5

A STAR IS BORN

1934: Hank Aaron, a Hall of Fame outfielder who collected 3,771 hits and finished his 23-year career as baseball's all-time home run king with 755.

★★★

1942: Roger Staubach, a football Hall of Fame quarterback for the Dallas Cowboys and a former Heisman Trophy winner from Navy.

★★★

1949: Darrell Waltrip, a three-time NASCAR national champion and a one-time winner of the Daytona 500.

★★★

1968: Roberto Alomar, a current major league second baseman.

★★★

DEATH OF A LEGEND

1970: Rudy York (baseball).

★★★

1943

LaMotta Outlasts Sugar Ray

Unsung Jake LaMotta, a determined and relentless brawler, punched a gaping hole in Sugar Ray Robinson's armor of invincibility when he scored a unanimous 10-round decision over the previously undefeated welterweight champion before 18,930 fight fans at Detroit's Olympia Stadium.

LaMotta, who had lost to Robinson four months earlier, patiently ignored the champion's dancing and jabbing tactics in the early rounds and relentlessly worked the body. Robinson appeared to be in control until late in the eighth round, when LaMotta suddenly rocked him with a right to the body and left to the head that sent him sprawling through the ropes.

Robinson was saved by the bell, but LaMotta's attack picked up steam in the ninth and 10th rounds when he stunningly secured his 41st career victory against five losses.

That pales in comparison to Robinson's amazing ledger. The loss was his first in 130 career bouts. He had won 89 as an amateur and 40 more since turning professional in 1940. He has recorded 32 pro knockouts.

Brawling **Jake LaMotta** *(left) en route to his stunning victory over* **Sugar Ray Robinson.**

1948

Two Americans Strike Gold

On an historic day for American sports, Washington housewife Gretchen Fraser sped to victory in the women's slalom and Dick Button captured gold at the Olympic Ice Stadium, giving the United States its first-ever Winter Games medals in Alpine skiing and figure skating.

Fraser's victory caught everybody by surprise. Going off first on the opening slalom runs, she zigzagged down Mount Piz Nair in 59.7 seconds, a mark that only Austria's Erika Mahringer could top (59.6). But Fraser was even more impressive on her second run, finishing at 57.5 for a combined total of 1:57.2 that blew away her competition.

Button, recognized as the best figure skater in the world, was expected to win – and he didn't disappoint. The Harvard freshman enjoyed a big lead after the compulsory school figures and attacked his free-style with fervor and grace. Gliding confidently around the ice, the youngster skated with poise and performed five jumps in a flawless routine that earned him the highest score ever handed out by Olympic judges. Included in his innovative program was a daring double axel never before performed in a major competition. Button's victory was sealed when Hans Gerschwiler of Switzerland, the second-place skater, fell early in his routine.

Olympic ice skating champion **Dick Button.**

1960

Russell Pounds Boards

Boston center Bill Russell, cleaning the boards with his usual ferocity, grabbed a National Basketball Association-record 51 rebounds and led the Celtics to a 124–100 victory over Syracuse at Boston Garden.

Russell broke his own National Basketball Association mark of 49 rebounds, set in November 1957. The 6-foot-10 former University of San Francisco star also contributed 23 points, two less than teammate Frank Ramsey.

Russell was steady as she goes, pulling down 24 caroms in the first half and 27 in the second.

The Celtics' 15th straight home-court victory was secured with a 43-point second quarter.

George Yardley and Dick Barnett led Syracuse with 19 points apiece.

MILESTONES IN SPORTS

1980

Montreal's Guy Lafleur set an NHL career All-Star Game scoring record when he notched his 19th point (an assist) in a 6–3 Wales Conference victory over the Campbell Conference.

1983

Carl Lewis, representing the Santa Monica Track Club, set an indoor world record in the 60-yard dash when he was clocked in 6.02 seconds during competition in the Dallas Times Herald invitational meet.

1987

Five new basketball Hall of Famers: Walt Frazier, Pete Maravich, Rick Barry, Bob Houbregs and Bobby Wanzer.

1991

Los Angeles sniper Dave Taylor earned his 1,000th career NHL point with an assist in the Kings' 3–2 victory at Philadelphia.

1960 Robertson's Scoring Record

Oscar Robertson, the talented Cincinnati senior guard who has carried the Bearcats to a 17–1 record, became college basketball's all-time scoring leader during a 67–55 victory over Houston when he hit a second-half layup that gave him 2,589 career points.

A STAR IS BORN

1895: Babe Ruth, the New York Yankees Hall of Fame outfielder who ushered in the long-ball era and blasted 714 career home runs.

★ ★ ★

1927: Smoky Burgess, a major league catcher who built a reputation as one of baseball's all-time great pinch-hitters from 1949–67 .

DEATH OF A LEGEND

1993: Arthur Ashe (tennis).

The Big O, who scored 16 points in the first half, hit his record-setter in the opening minute after intermission and moved past former Wake Forest star Dickie Hemric on the scoring charts. Hemric finished his four-year, 104-game career with 2,587 points. Robertson passed him in his 76th career game during his third season.

Robertson finished the afternoon with 29 points and a career total of 2,600. The Bearcats ensured their victory in the final three minutes of the game at Cincinnati.

Robertson, who is averaging more than 33 points per game, is gunning for his third consecutive national scoring title. He averaged 35.1 points per game in 1957–58 and 32.6 last season.

Cincinnati star **Oscar Robertson** *(12) earned acclaim as college basketball's all-time leading scorer.*

February 6

Milestones in Sports

1967

Muhammad Ali recorded a unanimous 15-round decision over Ernie Terrell and retained his heavyweight championship in a bout at the Houston Astrodome.

1969

Five new additions to the Pro Football Hall of Fame: Allie Sherman, Greasy Neale, Turk Edwards, Leo Nomellini and Ernie Stautner.

1969

Unhappy with his front-office role for the Green Bay Packers, Vince Lombardi accepted an offer from the Washington Redskins to become part owner, executive vice-president and head coach.

1986

Five goals by Buffalo's Dave Andreychuk keyed the Sabres' 8–6 victory over the Bruins at Boston.

1990

St. Louis' Brett Hull joined his father Bobby in the NHL's 50-goal club when he scored in a game against Toronto.

1970 NBA Votes to Add 4 Teams

The National Basketball Association voted to add four teams and expand its membership to 18 for next season. The expansion was announced after an NBA Board of Governors meeting with new franchises to be located in Portland, Houston, Cleveland and Buffalo. Each of the new ownerships will pay $3.7 million.

The vote was 11–3 in favor of expansion and the board decided to let the new teams participate in this year's college draft. The expansion teams will be allowed to pick seventh, eighth, ninth and 10th and other players will be supplied off the rosters of existing teams through an expansion draft.

The newcomers also will be allowed to share in television revenue when the new contract is negotiated, a privilege which is not often given to expansion teams.

1993 Arthur Ashe Dies of AIDS

Arthur Ashe, a pioneer who paved the way for black men in amateur and professional tennis, died in New York City of pneumonia, a typical complication of AIDS, at age 49.

Ashe announced in April that he had AIDS after learning the news was about to be published. He said he probably contacted the disease from an unscreened blood tranfusion during his second open-heart surgery in 1983. After the announcement, Ashe founded the Arthur Ashe Foundation for the Defeat of AIDS and joined other institutions dedicated to fighting the dreaded disease.

Ashe's list of tennis firsts is long and impressive. He was the first black man to win a grand slam tennis event and the first to win the Wimbledon (1975), U.S. Open (1968) and Australian Open (1970) championships. He was the first black member of the U.S. Davis Cup team and the only black amateur to capture a U.S. Open. He was ranked No. 1 in the world in 1968 and 1975 and he led the U.S. to a pair of Davis Cup titles.

Off the court, the former UCLA graduate actively fought anti-apartheid policies in South Africa and helped found the Association of Tennis Professionals.

FEBRUARY

7

MILESTONES
IN SPORTS

1949

New York Yankee center fielder Joe DiMaggio became major league baseball's first six-figure superstar when he signed a contract for $100,000.

1950

Boston slugger Ted Williams, baseball's second six-figure star, became the game's highest-paid player when he signed with the Red Sox for $125,000.

1980

Rick Vaive scored two goals and Vancouver snapped Philadelphia's 26-game home-ice unbeaten streak, 4–1.

1988

Chicago's Michael Jordan captured MVP honors with a 40-point performance in the NBA All-Star Game, a 138–133 victory for his East team over the West.

1976 Toronto's Sittler Has 10-Point Game

Toronto center Darryl Sittler scored six goals and added four assists in the greatest one-man National Hockey League show ever staged and the Maple Leafs did a little staging of their own with an 11–4 victory over Boston.

Darryl Sittler *exploded for a single-game-record 10 points against the Boston Bruins.*

The 25-year-old Sittler opened with a pair of first-period assists, he scored three goals and handed out two assists in Toronto's six-goal second period and he scored all three of the Leafs' third-period goals to wrap up his incredible offensive barrage.

His fifth goal against Boston rookie goalie Dave Reece came mid-way through the final stanza and wiped out the old NHL mark of eight points in a game shared by former Montreal stars Maurice (Rocket) Richard (1944) and Bert Olmstead (1954). Former Quebec star Joe Malone set the NHL record for most goals in a game with seven in 1920 and six players had notched six goals, but only two since 1921.

Sittler's outburst came against a Boston team that had won seven straight games.

A STAR IS BORN

1889: Earl Whitehill, a 218-game winner during his 17 major league seasons in the 1920s and '30s.

★ ★ ★

1953: Dan Quisenberry, a submarine-throwing righthander who briefly held the major league record for saves (45) in one season.

★ ★ ★

1957: Carney Lansford, a major league third baseman and former American League batting champion.

★ ★ ★

DEATH OF A LEGEND

1952: Wilbur Henry (football).

★ ★ ★

1959: Napoleon Lajoie (baseball).

★ ★ ★

1979: Warren Giles (baseball).

★ ★ ★

1969 Diane Crump Becomes First Female Jockey

Diane Crump, a 20-year-old jockey with nerves of steel, became the first female to ride at a United States parimutuel track when she guided longshot Bridle'n Bit to a 10th-place finish at Hialeah in Miami.

Six jockeys, including veteran Ron Turcotte, cancelled their mounts for the seventh race, refusing to ride against a woman. But four others decided to take part in the historic event and replacements quickly were found for the dropouts.

The race went off smoothly and Crump handled herself well. Riding a 48–1 longshot, she broke Bridle'n Bit on top, faded to last place on the backstretch and recovered to pass two horses in the 12-horse field. After covering the mile and an eighth over a wet track, the mud-splattered Crump was mobbed by fellow jockeys, well-wishers, reporters and photographers.

Asked about her plans for the future, Crump said she would ride again on February 18 and expressed hope that she would begin getting mounts on the daily card.

1970 Pistol Pete Fires In 69

Louisiana State's Pete Maravich, the greatest career scorer in the history of college basketball, fired in a record 69 points in a 106–104 loss to Alabama and then fired a few rights and lefts in a postgame brawl with Crimson Tide fans.

Maravich's point barrage was the largest ever against a Divison I opponent. Niagara's Calvin Murphy had set the previous one-game best of 68 against Syracuse in 1968. Maravich, whose 3,157 career points are 83 more than former Cincinnati star Oscar Robertson scored in his brilliant career, had set a previous personal one-game high of 66 last year against Tulane.

Maravich connected on 26 field goals and 17 of 21 free throws in a game that the 6–12 Crimson Tide broke open with a flurry midway through the second half. After the Tigers' sixth loss in 18 games, Maravich went after a spectator and other LSU players became involved in a brawl that was broken up before anybody actually got hurt.

1964 KIDD, HEUGA WIN MEDALS

Billy Kidd and Jim Heuga, a pair of 20-year-old Americans with big hearts and dogged determination, zoomed to surprising second and third-place finishes in the slalom and captured the first-ever men's Alpine skiing Winter Olympic medals for the United States.

Kidd, who clocked a competitive 70.96 seconds on a morning run down the Innsbruck, Austria, course in blizzard-like conditions, streaked through the gates in a 60.31-second afternoon run. That put the pressure on first-round leader Josef (Pepi) Stiegler, but the stocky blond Austrian was up to the challenge. He posted a 62.10, only seventh best in the afternoon, but good enought to hold off Kidd.

Heuga's performance was amazing under difficult circumstances. The Californian got a bad draw and started 24th and 22nd on his runs, when the track was rutted and the icy slopes laid bare.

He finished his morning run in 70.16 and his afternoon drive in 61.36 to earn a well-deserved bronze medal.

Skier **Billy Kidd** *performed an American Alpine first in the Winter Olympic Games at Innsbruck, Austria.*

FEBRUARY 8

MILESTONES IN SPORTS

1936

The Philadelphia Eagles, selecting first in the National Football League's inaugural college draft, picked University of Chicago halfback and Heisman Trophy winner Jay Berwanger.

1950

An Associated Press poll voted once-beaten thoroughbred Man o'War the greatest horse of the half century.

1962

Philadelphia center Wilt Chamberlain scored 59 points in a 136–120 victory over the New York Knicks, topping the magic 3,000-point barrier and raising his own one-season record total to 3,039.

1963

The Dallas Texans, having obtained permission from other American Football League owners, transferred their franchise to Kansas City and subsequently became the Chiefs.

1983

Edmonton's Wayne Gretzky set an NHL All-Star Game record with four goals – all in the third period – as the Campbell Conference defeated the Wales, 9–3, at New York's Nassau Coliseum.

1986

Billy Olson, bettering the indoor world record set earlier in the day by Russian Sergei Bubka, pole vaulted 19–5¾ during competition in the U.S. Olympic invitational indoor track meet.

1987 MANTLE CUT OFF

Former New York Yankee great Mickey Mantle signed a $100,000-per-year contract to work for an Atlantic City gambling casino and was told by baseball Commissioner Bowie Kuhn to sever all ties to the game.

The 51-year-old Hall of Fame center fielder, who blasted 536 home runs in 18 big-league seasons with the Yankees, was introduced as the new director of sports promotions for the Claridge Hotel and Casino, but his primary job will be to play golf with clients. The salary matches the largest Mantle ever made as a player. "It's nothing I'm ashamed of," said the three-time American League MVP. "It's not like I'm standing outside the hotel and trying to get people to come in and lose their money." Mantle's fate is the same suffered by former Giants great Willie Mays three years ago. Mays joined Bally International as a public greeter and golfer and was ordered by Kuhn to relinquish his baseball ties.

A STAR IS BORN

1921: Hoot Evers, a 12-year major league outfielder with a .278 career average in the 1940s and '50s.

★ ★ ★

1937: Billy Cannon, a former Heisman Trophy-winning running back from Louisiana State.

★ ★ ★

1960: Dino Ciccarelli, a current National Hockey League right winger.

★ ★ ★

1970: Alonzo Mourning, a current National Basketball Association center.

DEATH OF A LEGEND

1956: Connie Mack (baseball).

1987 LOPEZ WINS BIG ONE

Nancy Lopez shot a 2-over-par 74 to win the $30,000 first prize in the Sarasota Classic. But, more importantly, the victory was the 35th of her outstanding career and automatically qualified her for induction into the Ladies Professional Golf Association's Hall of Fame.

Lopez's three-stroke victory over Kathy Baker and Anne Marie Palli came on the same Bent Tree Country Club course where she won her first professional tournament in 1978.

The 30-year-old Lopez finished with a 7-under total of 281 and increased her career earnings to $1,743,244, the fourth-best total on the tour.

The victory was the first for Lopez since her return late last year after giving birth. Her last victory had come in the 1985 Portland Championship. Lopez becomes the 11th player to qualify for the Hall of Fame and the first since JoAnne Carner in 1982.

She will become eligible for induction in July, when she completes her 10 years of membership in the LPGA.

New LPGA Hall of Famer **Nancy Lopez.**

FEBRUARY

9

1992 MAGIC STEALS SHOW

Former Los Angeles Lakers star Magic Johnson, who announced his shocking retirement last November after testing positive for the HIV virus, made a dazzling one-game return to the National Basketball Association hardcourts with an All-Star Game performance that will not soon be forgotten.

Johnson, voted into the starting lineup by National Basketball Association fans despite not playing at any point during the regular season, was the brightest star on display in the Western Conference's 153–113 victory over the Eastern Conference at Orlando.

Despite his three-month layoff, Magic stepped into the spotlight with 25 points, nine assists and five rebounds in 29 minutes. He was 9 of 12 from the floor, 3 of 3 from three-point range and 4 of 4 from the free throw line.

Magic's big afternoon got off to a rousing start and ended in a blaze of glory. He was introduced as the last of 25 All-Stars, received a tremendous ovation from fans and players and responded by scoring eight points in the first five minutes of the game. He closed the classic by hitting all three of his long-range bombs in the final 2:42.

There was no argument when Johnson was awarded his second All-Star Game Most Valuable Player award.

1966 NHL DOUBLES SIZE IN U.S. EXPANSION

The 49-year-old National Hockey League, trying to compete with more affluent professional circuits for dollars and exposure, doubled its pleasure with the addition of six teams in the United States and the decision to take its product coast to coast.

The new franchises, which will begin play in the 1967–68 season, will be located in Los Angeles, the San Francisco Bay Area, Minneapolis-St. Paul, St. Louis, Pittsburgh and Philadelphia. The new ownerships must pay $2 million and provide a satisfactory playing arena seating at least 12,500.

Those teams will join New York, Boston, Chicago, Detroit, Montreal and Toronto in a 12-team league that will be divided into two divisions. The $12 million will be divided among the six existing teams and the new clubs will be stocked through a yet-to-be-determined drafting procedure.

The NHL opened operation in 1917 as a four-team, all-Canadian circuit. Boston was organized as its first American team in 1924.

WBC junior middleweight champion **Terry Norris** *made short work of the comeback-minded* **Sugar Ray Leonard.**

A STAR IS BORN

1914: Bill Veeck, the former owner of the Cleveland Indians, St. Louis Browns and Chicago White Sox and baseball's master showman.

★★★

1925: Vic Wertz, a hard-hitting outfielder who is remembered as the victim of Willie Mays' outstanding catch in Game 1 of the 1954 World Series.

★★★

1958: Sandy Lyle, a British golfer who has won British Open and Masters championships.

★★★

1961: John Kruk, a current major league first baseman.

★★★

DEATH OF A LEGEND

1994: Bud Wilkinson (college football coach).

MILESTONES IN SPORTS

1920

Baseball's Joint Rules Committee banned the spitball, telling teams they can designate hurlers who will be allowed to throw the pitch for one more season.

1940

Heavyweight champion Joe Louis struggled to a 15-round split decision over Arturo Godoy in a fight at New York's Madison Square Garden.

1971

Former pitching great Satchel Paige became the first Negro League star to be elected to a special baseball Hall of Fame section created for those players who were banned from major league play before 1947.

1988

Pittsburgh's Mario Lemieux put on a show for St. Louis hockey fans, scoring three goals and three assists in the Wales Conference's 6–5 All-Star Game victory over the Campbell Conference.

Hall of Famer **Satchel Paige.**

1991 NORRIS BATTERS SHOCKED LEONARD

In a stunning and sudden reversal of fortunes, Sugar Ray Leonard's outstanding boxing career came to a remorseful end when the 34-year-old five-time champion was battered, bruised and cut by a relentless Terry Norris in a fight at New York's Madison Square Garden.

The 23-year-old WBC junior middleweight champion worked Leonard over with a variety of punches that produced a lopsided 12-round decision. The beating was so thorough that Leonard, his lips cut and his left eye swollen shut, announced his retirement shortly after the decision had been announced.

Leonard, who held the welterweight, junior middleweight and middleweight titles at various points of his career, was fighting for the first time in more than a year – and it wasn't pretty. Norris (27–3) sent the former Olympic champion crashing to the canvas in the second and seventh rounds and controlled the fight from start to finish.

Leonard finished with a 36–2–1 record.

1968 FLEMING HAS GOLD CHARM

Peggy Fleming, the 19-year-old darling of the American sports world, glided and whirled her way into the hearts of the Olympic judges with a stunning free-style performance and captured the first United States gold medal at the Winter Olympic Games held in Grenoble, France.

Fleming entered the final day of competition with a prohibitive 77.2-point lead over her nearest competitor and performed her final routine with the same artistry and perfection she had displayed in her compulsory school figures.

Dressed in a chartreuse dress with rhinestones glittering under the arc lights of the Stade de Glace, Fleming stepped on the ice midway through the three-hour spectacle and roared into a fast-paced routine that included numerous jumps, spins and axels performed with flawless execution and breathless panache.

She closed with a double-toe loop and a leap into a flying sit spin, a maneuver that brought a roar from the crowd. The Olympic gold was the icing on the cake for a career that includes two world championships and five American titles.

American darling **Peggy Fleming** *captures the hearts of Olympic judges with her gold medal-winning performance in the Winter Games at Grenoble, France.*

FEBRUARY 10

MILESTONES IN SPORTS

1908

Tommy Burns, making his sixth defense of the heavyweight boxing championship, recorded a fourth-round knockout of Jack Palmer in London.

1969

Louisiana State scoring machine Pete Maravich exploded for 66 points, but the Tigers dropped a 110-94 college basketball decision to Tulane.

1974

Hubert Green carded a final-round 65 and recovered from a three-stroke deficit to beat Bert Yancey by two shots and claim the Bob Hope Desert Classic tournament title at Palm Springs, Calif.

1992

American Bonnie Blair blazed to a world-record time of 39.10 seconds in the 500-meter speed skating final, winning her first Olympic gold medal in the Winter Games at Albertville, France.

1962 BEATTY BREAKS MILE BARRIER

Little Californian Jim Beatty became the first runner in history to break the 4-minute mile barrier indoors when he ran a 3:58.9 at the Los Angeles Times indoor track and field meet.

Beatty ran the first quarter in 59.1 seconds, hit the half-mile clock at 1:59.6 and the three-quarters at 3:01.2. He trailed Jim Grelle at the half mile, passed him on the eighth of 11 laps and opened a wide lead for the victory. Grelle, who ran a 4:07.1, finished second and Dave Martin finished third at 4:15.1. All three runners represent the Los Angeles Track Club.

Beatty broke the previous indoor mark of 4:01.4 set in 1959 by Ron Delany of Ireland. But he wasn't the only record-setter at the Los Angeles Sports Arena on this day.

New Zealand's Peter Snell broke his fourth world record in the previous three weekends when he captured the 1,000-yard run in 2:06. The 23-year-old Snell had broken indoor records for the 800-meter and 880-yard runs and the outdoor mile record (3:50.4) in his recent hot streak.

Canadian Bill Crothers finished second to Snell in 2:07.4, a time that also managed to smash the previous indoor 1,000-yard record.

A STAR IS BORN

1893: Bill Tilden, a winner of six straight U.S. singles championships and the dominant tennis player in the world during the 1920s.

★ ★ ★

1894: Herb Pennock, a Hall of Fame lefthanded pitcher who compiled a 5-0 record in World Series play for the New York Giants from 1912–34.

★ ★ ★

1950: Mark Spitz, the American swimmer who won an Olympic-record seven gold medals at the 1972 Munich Games.

★ ★ ★

1955: Greg Norman, an Australian golfer and one of the top names on the PGA Tour.

★ ★ ★

DEATH OF A LEGEND

1989: Glenna Collett-Vare (golf).

★ ★ ★

1992 TYSON FOUND GUILTY

Mike Tyson, who pounded challengers into submission through most of a boxing career that lifted him to great heights as the heavyweight champion of the world, was knocked to the canvas when an Indianapolis jury found him guilty of raping an 18-year-old girl last July.

Tyson, known during his fighting days as Iron Mike, watched stoically as the eight-man, four-woman jury pronounced him guilty on one count of rape and two counts of criminal deviate conduct after 10 hours of deliberation. The 25-year-old Tyson had been accused of attacking an 18-year-old Rhode Island girl who was in Indianapolis as a contestant in the Miss Black America pageant.

The incident took place in the hotel suite of the former champ, who was an invited guest of the Indiana Black Expo festival. The woman claimed she had been forcibly raped. Tyson claimed the 18-year-old had been a willing sexual partner.

As a result of the verdict in the 13-day trial, Tyson could face from six to 20 years in prison.

FEBRUARY

11

MILESTONES IN SPORTS

1949

Willie Pep recorded a unanimous 15-round decision over Sandy Saddler at New York's Madison Square Garden, becoming the first boxer ever to win the world featherweight championship a second time.

1957

Detroit's Ted Lindsay was elected president of the newly formed National Hockey League Players Association.

1971

Jean Beliveau scored his 500th career goal in Montreal's 6–2 victory over the Minnesota North Stars.

1972

Propelled by a big first run, American Barbara Cochran held off France's Danielle Debernard and captured the women's slalom gold medal by two-hundredths of a second in the Winter Olympic Games at Sapporo, Japan.

1973

Ending an 18-month dry spell, Arnold Palmer charged home with a final-round 69 and won the Bob Hope Desert Classic by two strokes over long-time rivals Jack Nicklaus and Johnny Miller.

1973

The Philadelphia 76ers set a one-season National Basketball Association record for futility when they dropped a 108-90 decision to the Lakers at Los Angeles – their 20th consecutive loss.

1990 Tyson Loses Heavyweight Stunner

James (Buster) Douglas *appears ready to pounce after sending heavyweight champion* **Mike Tyson** *to the canvas during the 10th round of a shocking title bout at Tokyo.*

James (Buster) Douglas, who figured to be the 38th victim on undefeated Mike Tyson's death march, pounded the heavyweight champion to the canvas in the 10th round of a fight at Tokyo and then watched the referee count down one of the greatest upsets in boxing history.

It was a shocking and controversial conclusion to what was supposed to be a quick-and-easy defense for the supposedly invincible champion. Douglas was such an underdog that Las Vegas oddsmakers had refused to even post a betting line. But the fight was much livelier than expected and the real fun began when Tyson sent Douglas sprawling in the eighth round.

Tyson supporters complained after the fight that Douglas (29–4–1) had been inadvertently given a long count by the referee and said the fight should have ended then and there with a Tyson victory. Television replays appeared to support the claim, but the bout continued and Douglas remained on his feet.

Then, suddenly, the challenger connected in the 10th with three straight left jabs and followed with five big punches that sent Tyson down. He was counted out 1:23 into the round and the stunning upset was complete.

Tyson, known in boxing circles as Iron Mike, had recorded 33 knockouts in his previous 37 bouts.

1974 Players Win First Hearing

Pitcher Dick Woodson, a 10–8 performer for the Minnesota Twins last season, was declared a winner by Detroit lawyer Harry H. Platt in the first major league baseball salary dispute decided by binding arbitration.

The historic ruling was handed down after Platt had listened to arguments for more than four hours. Woodson, who owned a 32–29 record over four big-league seasons, had demanded a $29,000 salary and the Twins had countered with a $23,000 offer. Under terms of the new Basic Agreement negotiated last year, the arbitrator had to choose one of the figures without compromise.

Woodson was one of 48 major leaguers who filed for the arbitration process, which gives them an alternative to costly holdouts. All cases were to be decided by February 22, although negotiations between the players and teams could continue up to the time of the hearing.

Pitcher **Dick Woodson** *defeated the Twins in baseball's first arbitration case.*

1979 Soviets Dazzle NHL

The Soviet national hockey team punctured the American and Canadian notion of National Hockey League superiority when it dazzled and finessed its way to a 6–0 victory over an NHL All-Star team in the decisive third game of the first Challenge Cup series at New York's Madison Square Garden.

Simply put, the NHL style of hard checks and grind-it-out hockey was no match for the speed and finesse of the Russian team. Getting excellent goaltending from Vladimir Myshkin and efficient passing and scoring from four different lines, the Soviets took command early and the confused NHL stars could not turn the momentum.

When the NHL team began delivering some hard, intimidating checks, the Russians simply turned on the afterburners. They exploded for four goals in a 6-minute span of the final period to seal the verdict.

The NHL players had been cocky after beating the Soviets, 4–2, in the opener of the three-game series. But the Soviets rallied for a 5–4 Game 2 victory after trailing early, 4–2.

A STAR IS BORN

1863: Jimmy Ryan, a baseball star of the pre-1900 National League.

★ ★ ★

1909: Max Baer, a boxer who briefly held the heavyweight championship in 1934.

★ ★ ★

DEATH OF A LEGEND

1950: Kiki Cuyler (baseball).

1981 CONTRACT ERROR SETS FISK FREE

In one of their biggest blunders since 1920 when they sold Babe Ruth's contract to the New York Yankees, the Boston Red Sox were forced to give six-time All-Star catcher Carlton Fisk his freedom because they mailed him a new contract two days beyond the specified deadline.

Arbitrator Raymond Goetz officially set Fisk free, ruling the Red Sox had inadvertently violated the Basic Agreement between players and owners with their negligence. Fisk, a .285 career hitter, can sell his services to any team and likely will draw a lot of attention.

The Red Sox also could have lost star center fielder Fred Lynn. But, realizing that Fisk and Lynn both could be set free, Boston officials quickly worked out a trade with the California Angels. The Angels met Lynn's salary demands and consummated the deal that sent pitchers Frank Tanana and Jim Dorsey and outfielder Joe Rudi to Boston with righthanded pitcher Steve Renko joining Lynn on the West Coast.

Fisk and Lynn had claimed negligence and took the Red Sox to arbitration over the winter, asking to be freed from their contracts. The 33-year-old Fisk saw his case through and was rewarded for his effort.

1972 U.S. EARNS HOCKEY SILVER

The powerful Soviet Union ice hockey team defeated Czechoslovakia, 5–2, to capture the Olympic gold medal and give the Cinderella United States team an unexpected silver.

The loss left the Czechs with a 3–2 record and six points, the same as the United States. Because the Americans had defeated the Czechs earlier in the tournament, they were awarded the silver medal. The U.S. also was helped when Finland upset Sweden, 4–3, leaving the Swedes with five points.

The U.S. finished its play with a 6–1 victory over Poland. The team that wasn't expected to qualify for medal-round play coasted past the Poles, thanks to a pair of goals by Craig Sarner, three assists by Kevin Ahearn and the inspired goaltending of Michael Curran, who lost his shutout on a 30-foot final-period slap shot.

The hockey medal was the Americans' first since the incredible gold-medal upset of 1960.

Southern University's **Rod Milburn,** *the world record-holder in the 120-yard hurdles.*

MILESTONES IN SPORTS

1958

Boston center Bill Russell scored 18 points and grabbed 41 rebounds in the Celtics' 119–101 victory over the Syracuse Nationals.

1968

Frenchman Jean-Claude Killy captured the men's giant slalom at the Winter Olympic Games in Grenoble, France, moving within one victory of an Alpine triple crown.

1972

Southern University's Rod Milburn, the outdoor world record-holder in the 120-yard hurdles, set an indoor mark of 13.4 seconds when he ran first in the U.S. Track and Field Federation indoor championships at Houston.

1982

Mary Decker-Tabb pulled away quickly and ran a women's indoor mile world record 4:21.47 in the Millrose Games at New York's Madison Square Garden.

1983

Marvelous Marvin Hagler raised his career record to 56–2–2 with a sixth-round knockout of Tony Sibson in a welterweight championship fight at Worcester, Mass.

A STAR IS BORN

1870: Jesse Burkett, a baseball Hall of Fame outfielder who compiled a .339 career average over 16 seasons from 1890–1905 and won three N.L. batting titles.

★ ★ ★

1904: Chick Hafey, a Hall of Fame outfielder and career .317 hitter in the 1920s and '30s.

★ ★ ★

1926: Joe Garagiola, a light-hitting major league catcher who went on to greater fame as an announcer, broadcaster and television personality.

★ ★ ★

1934: Bill Russell, a basketball Hall of Famer and five-time MVP who led the Boston Celtics to 11 National Basketball Association championships. He later became the league's first black coach.

★ ★ ★

1958: Bobby Smith, a current National Hockey League star and a career 1,000-point scorer.

★ ★ ★

DEATH OF A LEGEND

1985: Van Lingo Mungo (baseball).

★ ★ ★

1994: Ray Dandridge (baseball).

★ ★ ★

1993 SHARKS LOSE 17TH STRAIGHT

Six different Edmonton players scored and Bill Ranford made 28 saves in his first shutout of the season as the Oilers recorded a 6–0 victory and handed the San Jose Sharks their National Hockey League record-tying 17th consecutive loss.

It was another ugly performance for the team that now ranks with the 1974–75 Washington Capitals on the NHL's all-inept list. The second-year Sharks have won just six times in 56 games.

San Jose has been outscored 88–31 during its losing streak and 19–1 over its last three games. Most embarrassing was loss No. 16, a 13–1 blasting in Calgary. Even Flames goaltender Jeff Reese got into the act in that one, receiving credit for three assists.

FEBRUARY 13

MILESTONES IN SPORTS

1920

The Negro National League was organized during a meeting at a YMCA in Kansas City.

1960

Five drivers were hospitalized and three others slightly injured in a spectacular 37-car crash at the Daytona International Speedway during a 250-mile race for sportsman-modified cars.

1964

Slick-fielding Chicago Cubs second baseman Ken Hubbs was killed when the plane he was flying crashed on a frozen lake near Provo, Utah.

1973

Montreal star Frank Mahovlich assisted on a goal during a 7–6 loss to Philadelphia, earning his 1,000th career point.

1977

Philadelphia's Julius Erving scored 30 points and grabbed 12 rebounds in a dazzling All-Star Game display, but his Eastern Conference team lost a 125–124 thriller to the West.

1990

Bryan Trottier of the New York Islanders became the NHL's 15th 500-goal scorer when he connected in a 4–2 loss to Calgary.

1991

Leroy Burrell made two world-record runs in the 60-yard dash during an indoor meet at Madrid. Burrell ran a 6.48 and 6.40.

1954 Selvy Scores 100 Points

Furman star Frank Selvy, in an unprecedented scoring burst that is unlikely ever to be challenged, exploded for 100 points in a 149–95 victory over little Newberry College of South Carolina.

The high-scoring Selvy was phenomenal as he connected on 41 of 66 field-goal attempts and 18 free throws. His effort shattered the previous record of 73 points in one game, set by Temple's Bill Mlkvy in 1951. Selvy's outburst was tempered, however, by the fact that it came against a school with a male enrollment of 269. Selvy went on to finish his season with an NCAA-record 41.7-point average and a second straight national scoring title. He topped the 50-point plateau eight times.

1984 Armstrong Pulls Shocker

Gold medalist **Debbie Armstrong** *gets a warm welcome from hometown Seattle fans after returning from Yugoslavia.*

Debbie Armstrong, a 20-year-old non-winner on the World Cup circuit, swept to victory over fellow American Christin Cooper and captured an unexpected gold medal in the women's giant slalom at the Winter Olympic Games.

Armstrong's victory and Cooper's silver medal marked the first 1–2 sweep recorded by Americans in an Olympic Alpine event. Cooper had been mentioned as a medal contender, but Armstrong was a long shot.

Cooper took the lead on her first run, snaking down the 1,332-meter Mount Jahorina course in 1:08.87, one-tenth of a second faster than Armstrong. But on the second run, Cooper slipped, giving Armstrong the opening she needed. She streaked down the slope in 1:12.01, beating her teammate by half a second. Armstrong's total was 2:20.98, Cooper's 2:21.38.

1976 Hamill Shows Golden Touch

American sweetheart **Dorothy Hamill** *shows off her Olympic figure skating gold medal during the awards ceremony at Innsbruck, Austria.*

American sweetheart Dorothy Hamill, following in the tradition of Tenley Albright, Carol Heiss and Peggy Fleming, put on a breathless exhibition of figure skating artistry and easily captured Olympic gold in the Winter Games at Innsbruck, Austria.

Hamill, eye-catching in her low-cut red dress, totally mesmerized the audience at the Olympic Ice Hall with a four-minute performance full of jumps, spins and showmanship.

She skated to Russian music and executed every maneuver flawlessly before closing with her standard signature – the Hamill camel (a camel into a sit spin with a spin coming out).

When the routine ended, bouquets and spring flowers rained down from the stands on the smiling Hamill. The judges rained down a few flowers of their own, giving the Riverside, Conn., girl eight 5.8s and a 5.9 in technical merit and a solid line of 5.9s for artistic interpretation.

No other skater came close. Dianne de Leeuw of the Netherlands finished second without one 5.9 on her scorecard.

A STAR IS BORN

1918: Patty Berg, one of the greats of women's golf and winner of 16 major championships.

★ ★ ★

1919: Eddie Robinson, the college football coach at Grambling State University since 1941 and the all-time leader in career coaching victories.

★ ★ ★

DEATH OF A LEGEND

1964: Ken Hubbs (baseball).

★ ★ ★

1975 LARRIEU CLAIMS RECORD

American distance queen Francie Larrieu, who does her training with the UCLA men's track team, added the 1,500-meter run to her long list of indoor world records during competition in the Maple Leaf Indoor Games at Toronto.

Larrieu, the only female member of the Pacific Coast Club in Long Beach, Calif., covered the metric mile in 4:10.4, the equivalent of a 4:30 mile. She lowered the previous record by six-tenths of a second and finished well ahead of Canadian Glenda Reiser.

The 22-year-old Larrieu adds the 1,500 meters to an impressive resume that includes indoor world records for the mile, the two-mile, the 1,000-meter and the 3,000-meter. She was timed in 64.9 at the quarter and at 2:11.7 at the half mile.

A STAR IS BORN

1907: Johnny Longden, one of the all-time great jockeys who rode 6,032 career winners and guided Count Fleet to a 1943 Triple Crown.

★ ★ ★

1912: Byron Nelson, an outstanding golfer in the 1940s who included two Masters, two PGA Championships and one U.S. Open among his victories.

★ ★ ★

1913: Woody Hayes, the long-time Ohio State football coach who posted a career record of 238–72–10.

★ ★ ★

1935: Mickey Wright, one of the all-time greats of women's golf. She posted 82 career victories and won 13 major championships.

★ ★ ★

1960: Jim Kelly, a current National Football League quarterback.

★ ★ ★

DEATH OF A LEGEND

1948: Mordecai (Three Finger) Brown (baseball).

★ ★ ★

1992 BLAIR MAKES GOLD RUSH

Speed skater **Bonnie Blair**, *the first American woman to win three gold medals in Winter Olympics competition.*

Bonnie Blair, an unpretentious 27-year-old battler from Champaign, Ill., became the first American woman to win three gold medals in Winter Olympics competition when she posted a victory in the 1,000-meter speed skating final at Albertville, France.

Blair, who had won gold medals in the 500 meters at Calgary four years ago and the same event four days earlier at Albertville, had just enough left to win the 1,000 sprint. Having lost in the 1,500-meter two days before, Blair ground out a 1:21.90 clocking and then waited and watched as her chief rival, China's Ye Qiaobo, went for the gold.

Everybody knew it was close as Qiaobo hit the finish line and the wait was unnerving. Finally the board flashed the final result – Blair had won by an incredible 2 hundredths of a second.

Blair also had beaten Qiaobo in the 500-meter race – by 18 hundredths of a second. The skaters were hindered all week by ice that turned mushy because of unseasonably warm weather.

1988 ALLISONS ENJOY DAYTONA SWEEP

Bobby Allison charged into the lead with 18 laps remaining and then held off a late challenge by his son Davey to post a 2½-car length victory in the Daytona 500 – stock car racing's top event.

Allison, driving a Buick Regal, became the first 50-year-old driver to win a 500-mile race and extended his record as the oldest man ever to win a NASCAR event. His 84th NASCAR victory also was the first stock car race in which a father and son had finished 1–2.

The race was one of the closest ever run at Daytona with a record 17 drivers on the winning lap. The lead changed hands 26 times among 12 drivers. Allison's average speed – 137.531 miles per hour – was the third slowest ever. Part of the reason was seven caution flags that covered 42 laps.

One of the slowdowns was because of a wreck involving seven-time Daytona winner Richard Petty on the 106th lap. Petty's car skidded sideways coming off a turn and was hit by Phil Barkdoll's car. It rose into the air and did seven barrel rolls before coming to a rest and being hit again.

Petty was taken to the hospital for observation, but was released later.

FEBRUARY 14

MILESTONES IN SPORTS

1951

Sugar Ray Robinson, avenging an earlier upset loss, scored a 13th-round technical knockout over Jake LaMotta in a middleweight title bout at Chicago.

1953

William & Mary star Bill Chambers grabbed an NCAA-record 51 rebounds in a 105–84 victory over Virginia.

1971

Chicago's Bobby Hull moved into second place on the all-time goal-scoring charts with No. 546.

1975

Julius Erving scored 63 points, but his New York Nets dropped a 176–166 decision to San Diego in the highest-scoring professional game ever played.

1986

Edmonton's Wayne Gretzky enjoyed the third seven-assist game of his career – an 8–2 Oilers victory over Quebec.

1988

American speed skater Dan Jansen, who had learned earlier in the day that his sister had died of leukemia, fell on the first turn of the 500-meter final at Calgary, ending his bid for Olympic gold.

1990

Pittsburgh's Mario Lemieux saw his point-scoring streak end at 46 games – five short of Wayne Gretzky's National Hockey League record.

FEBRUARY

15

A STAR IS BORN

1929: Graham Hill, a British race car driver who captured the Formula 1 world championship two times and won the Indianapolis 500 in 1966.

★ ★ ★

1940: John Hadl, one of the outstanding passers among all-time National Football League quarterbacks.

★ ★ ★

1948: Ron Cey, a 17-year major league third baseman who hit 316 career home runs.

★ ★ ★

1968: Tim Cheveldae, a current National Hockey League goaltender.

★ ★ ★

1978

Leon Spinks Stuns Ali

Leon Spinks, a toothless brawler from the streets of East St. Louis, pulled off one of the bigger upsets in boxing history when he gained a 15-round split decision over Muhammad Ali and walked away with the sport's biggest prize – the heavyweight championship.

New heavyweight champion **Leon Spinks** *celebrates his unexpected victory over* **Muhammad Ali.**

The 24-year-old Spinks was a crazed aggressor from the opening bell and Ali, seemingly amused by his young opponent at the beginning, danced, taunted and employed both his peek-a-boo and rope-a-dope defenses. But nothing seemed to bother Spinks and the 36-year-old Ali, taking a lot of punishment, finally decided to get serious.

Realizing he was in danger of losing the Las Vegas fight, Ali went after Spinks in the 10th and 11th rounds, jolting the former Marine corporal with a couple of good rights. The 15th round turned into a wild-swinging donnybrook as both fighters, hoping to avoid turning matters over to the judges, pulled out all stops and went for a knockout.

As it turned out, Ali needed one. When the decision was announced, his second reign as heavyweight boxing champion came to an unexpected end.

MILESTONES
• IN SPORTS •

1974

Boston's Phil Esposito joined the NHL's 1,000-point club, assisting on a goal in the Bruins' 4–2 victory at Vancouver.

1975

Montreal's Yvan Cournoyer exploded for five goals and seven points in a 12–3 rout of the Chicago Blackhawks.

1975

American distance queen Francie Larrieu set a world indoor record in the mile when she was clocked at 4:29 during competition in the San Diego indoor games.

1980

Edmonton rookie Wayne Gretzky tied an NHL record with seven assists and set an NHL mark for points by a rookie (96) in the Oilers' 8–2 victory over Washington.

1981

Richard Petty averaged 169.651 miles per hour in his Buick and won his record seventh Daytona 500 stock car race.

1992

Paul Wylie earned a surprising Olympic silver medal in the figure skating competition during the Winter Games at Albertville, France.

1976

Pearson Wins In Wild Finish

David Pearson, driving his battered Mercury across the finish line at 20 miles per hour, captured stock car racing's biggest prize – the Daytona 500 – as Richard Petty sat helplessly in his Dodge less than 50 yards away from his sixth victory.

In a wild conclusion to an exciting race, Petty and Pearson, the two most successful drivers on the Grand National circuit, entered the final lap in a virtual deadlock. Petty held a slight advantage as their cars entered the final turn side by side, about a quarter of a mile from the finish line.

Suddenly Petty's Dodge slid into the Mercury and sent it spinning into a concrete wall at 180 mph. The Mercury bounced off the Daytona International Speedway barrier and hit the Dodge, which went into a spin along the wall. When all was said and done, the two cars sat stalled on the infield, not far from each other and only about 50 yards from the finish line.

Both drivers frantically tried to get their cars started, Pearson finally succeeding. As Petty watched in horror, Pearson chugged his Mercury onto the track and completed his first Daytona 500 victory – slowly but surely.

1936

Henie Meets A Challenge

The great Sonja Henie, forced to give her best career performance to hold off the unexpected challenge of England's Cecilia Colledge, did just that in an inspiring free-style routine that earned her a third consecutive Olympic figure skating gold medal at Garmisch-Partenkirchen, Germany.

World champion figure skater **Sonja Henie.**

Henie, the blonde Norwegian who has dominated women's figure skating for 10 years, carried a three-point margin over Colledge into the free-style program, but Colledge skated first and thrilled the 11,000 spectators with a conservative, but error-free program that earned her an average 5.7 mark from the judges. That put the pressure on Henie. Needing a mistake-free program of her own, the world champion swung into her repertoire of difficult figures that included a double axel Paulsen jump and a series of difficult turns, spins and twirls. The routine ended with a graceful split, and the judges rewarded her with a 5.8 and 424.5 total points, six more than Colledge.

Henie claimed her crown in a hard-fought competition that featured 22 skaters representing 12 nations. The top American was Maribel Vinson (5th).

A STAR IS BORN

1866: Billy Hamilton, a Hall of Fame outfielder and holder of many pre-1900 stolen base records.

★ ★ ★

1953: Lanny McDonald, a hockey Hall of Fame right winger and a career 500-goal scorer.

★ ★ ★

DEATH OF A LEGEND

1961: Dazzy Vance (baseball).

★ ★ ★

1972 Wilt Reaches 30,000 Plateau

Los Angeles Lakers center Wilt Chamberlain stepped into uncharted territory when he scored his 30,000th career point in a game against the Phoenix Suns, but his joy was tempered somewhat by the unusual ending of the contest. The Suns scored the winning basket of a 110–109 victory at Phoenix with three seconds remaining when Chamberlain was called for goaltending.

Ironically, Chamberlain's milestone points also came on a goaltend – when Neal Walk tried to block his shot with 2:09 left in the third period. With that basket, the National Basketball Association's all-time leading scorer broke new ground.

Chamberlain finished the game with 19 points (six field goals, seven of 12 free throws), but his attempted block of a Connie Hawkins shot resulted in the Suns' late victory. The loss was only the Lakers' ninth in 60 games.

In addition to his 30,000 career regular-season points, Chamberlain also has scored 3,210 in playoff competition.

1984 Johnson Fulfills Olympic Boast

Bill Johnson, a 23-year-old Californian who had boasted that everyone else would be fighting for second place, backed up his words with a scintillating burst down Mount Bjelasnica that earned him the first Olympic men's downhill gold medal in American history.

The cocky Johnson, known as a "glider" who performs well on straight courses without turns, told reporters before the race at Sarajevo, Yugoslavia, "I don't even know why everyone else is here. They should hand it (the gold medal) to me."

After heavy snow and powerful winds had postponed the downhill three times, Johnson finally got his chance to back up those words.

Needing to catch Switzerland's Peter Mueller for the gold, Johnson streaked down the mountainside and clinched the win with a sizzling closing burst that gave him a final clocking of 1:45.59, 27 hundredths of a second faster than Mueller and 34 hundredths faster than Austria's Anton Steiner.

American skier **Bill Johnson** *tells the world he's No. 1 after his gold-medal victory in the Olympic downhill.*

1926 Lenglen Posts Dramatic Win

In a fascinating tennis match that virtually made the world stand still, French champion Suzanne Lenglen posted a grueling 6–3, 8–6 victory over young American Helen Wills, reestablishing her unofficial title as queen of women's tennis.

The buildup to the match in Cannes, France, was enormous and the interest in the result phenomenal. It easily ranked as the greatest women's sporting event ever staged and was close to holding that distinction among men's events.

The more experienced Lenglen, who had lost only one time in her storied career, was expected by many to make short work of her 20-year-old opponent. But that didn't happen. In a baseline battle that tested the resolve and physical condition of both women, the California girl fought through the first set and then was serving for set point at 6–5 in the second when a bad line call broke her concentration.

A Lenglen return that clearly was out was given to the French woman and she quickly posted two more points for the game. Wills, the three-time U.S. champion, took the next two games to deuce, but Lenglen won both and closed out the match.

World newspapers called it the most dramatic match in tennis history.

February 16

MILESTONES IN SPORTS

1921

Montreal's Newsy Lalonde exploded for five goals and the Canadiens overpowered Hamilton, 10–5.

1968-1969

Two milestones: Montreal's Jean Beliveau and Detroit's Alex Delvecchio became the second and third members of the National Hockey League's 1,000-point club.

1970

Heavyweight champion Joe Frazier pounded Jimmy Ellis and recorded a fifth-round technical knockout during a bout at New York's Madison Square Garden.

1975

Jimmy Connors defeated Vitas Gerulaitis and became the first modern player to win three straight U.S. National Indoor tennis championships.

1980

Mary Decker became the first woman to break the 4:20 barrier in the mile when she was clocked at 4:17.55 during a track and field meet in Houston.

1992

Martina Navratilova became the winningest singles player in tennis history when she captured her 158th title (the Virginia Slims of Chicago) and moved past long-time rival Chris Evert.

1992

Chicago's Michel Goulet scored his 500th career goal in a 5–5 tie against the Calgary Flames.

FEBRUARY

17

MILESTONES
IN SPORTS

1923

Ottawa's Cy Denneny became the NHL's all-time leading scorer for a second time when he notched his 143rd career goal in a 2–0 victory over Montreal.

1941

Joe Louis made his 14th successful heavyweight title defense and knocked out Gus Dorazio in the second round of a bout at Philadelphia.

1980

Buddy Baker, driving his Oldsmobile at a stock car-record 177.606 mph, captured his first Daytona 500 on his 18th attempt.

Daytona 500 winner **Buddy Baker.**

1985

Laffit Pincay Jr. rode four winners at Santa Anita Race Track and joined Bill Shoemaker and Johnny Longden as the only jockeys to win 6,000 thoroughbred races.

1985

Bill Elliott held off a late challenge from Neil Bonnett and drove his Ford to victory in the prestigious Daytona 500.

1968 KILLY EARNS ALPINE TRIPLE

Jean-Claude Killy, the cover-boy idol of French ski fans, captured a tense and controversy-filled slalom and became only the second Alpine skiing triple crown winner in the history of the Winter Olympic Games.

Frenchman **Jean-Claude Killy,** *skiing's second Olympic triple crown winner.*

Killy, who already had won the downhill and giant slalom before his excited countrymen in Grenoble, France, was the first man down the slope in the second heat of the final event. He maneuvered through the 1,040-meter course and its 131 gates in a dense fog, posting a two-heat time of 99.75 seconds. All he could do now was wait and watch.

One by one his competition fell by the wayside. Then Austrian Karl Schranz started his run, only to pull up when a spectator interfered. Given a second chance, Schranz bolted to apparent victory with a time of 99.22.

Killy got a reprieve, however, when reports circulated that Schranz had missed a gate before the spectator interference. If so, he would be disqualified. That's what happened – two hours after the race – and Killy had his third victory.

Before Killy, only Austrian skier Toni Sailer in 1956 had managed to capture an Alpine triple crown.

A STAR IS BORN

1936: Jim Brown, a football Hall of Fame running back and the all-time career touchdown (126) leader. He ranks third in career rushing (12,312 yards).

★ ★ ★

1959: Neil Lomax, a former quarterback in the National Football League.

★ ★ ★

1963: Michael Jordan, the former NBA guard and five-time scoring champion who led the Chicago Bulls to three consecutive championships. He was generally considered one of the greatest players in league history.

★ ★ ★

1966: Luc Robitaille, a current National Hockey League left winger.

★ ★ ★

DEATH OF A LEGEND

1959: Tim Mara (football).

★ ★ ★

1986: Red Ruffing (baseball).

★ ★ ★

1989: Lefty Gomez (baseball).

★ ★ ★

1974 AMERICANS SET INDOOR RECORDS

American distance runners Tony Waldrop, Mary Decker and Francie Larrieu went on a record-setting binge during the San Diego indoor games, knocking off four world marks and reestablishing themselves at the forefront of the world track scene.

Waldrop, who rose from obscurity to join the world's elite milers over the winter, continued his impressive rise by setting the indoor mile record with a 3:55 clocking. Tom O'Hara had set the previous record (3:56.4) in 1964 and Jim Ryun matched it in 1970 – at San Diego.

Decker, the 93-pound 15-year-old from Oregon, knocked more than four seconds off her pending world indoor mark for the 880-yard run. She was timed in 2:02.4, breaking her week-old mark of 2:06.7.

Larrieu remained the queen of American distance running with a world-record performance in the 2-mile run. Larrieu, who already held world marks in the 1,500-meter and mile, ran the 2-mile in 9:39.4 to become the first woman to break the 10-minute barrier in the event indoors.

1985 BRAMBLE ROCKS MANCINI AGAIN

Livingstone Bramble, fighting the hostile crowd as well as Ray (Boom Boom) Mancini, recorded a 15-round unanimous decision over the popular former champion and retained his World Boxing Association lightweight crown in a battle at Reno, Nev.

Mancini simply was no match for Bramble, although the final judges' cards were surprisingly close. Bramble controlled every round except the sixth, but won by only a single point on each card.

Buoyed by the lusty cheering of the 11,758 fans who packed into the Lawlor Events Arena, Mancini kept plugging away against the man who had taken away his title with a 14th-round knockout last June. It became extra tough for Mancini when Bramble opened a big gash over his right eye – a cut that would require 27 stitches.

With blood streaming into his eyes almost every round, Mancini fought on and even rallied a little in the late going. Still, he could not present a serious threat to the champion and nobody was surprised by the decision.

FEBRUARY 18

1962 FIREBALL FINALLY FINISHES

Glenn (Fireball) Roberts, ending a run of bad luck that had cost him victories in the first three Daytona 500s, wheeled his black and gold Pontiac to a world speed record and captured racing's most prestigious stock car event.

Roberts averaged 152.529 miles per hour to surpass the speed record for a continuous 500-mile race set in last year's Daytona by Marvin Panch. He negotiated the 200 laps around the Daytona International Speedway's 2 1/2-mile track in 3:10.41, 10 minutes faster than Panch's 1961 winning time.

Victory was sweet for the Daytona Beach driver, who had led each of the three previous Daytona races but had never finished. Once he was victimized by blown tires, twice by engine trouble.

Not this time. Roberts led for 144 laps and outdueled young Richard Petty, who finished 27 seconds back in a Plymouth. Roberts held off Petty despite having to make an extra pit stop.

A STAR IS BORN

1895: George Gipp, a Notre Dame fullback who died in 1920 and later served as the inspiration for Coach Knute Rockne's "Win one for the Gipper" speech.

★ ★ ★

1915: Joe Gordon, an outstanding second baseman in the 1930s and '40s, an American League MVP and later a major league manager.

★ ★ ★

1926: Len Ford, a football Hall of Fame end in the late 1940s and '50s for the Los Angeles Dons and Cleveland Browns.

★ ★ ★

1938: Manny Mota, a 20-year major league infielder-outfielder and one of the game's all-time great pinch-hitters.

★ ★ ★

1949: John Mayberry, a 15-year major league first baseman who hit 255 home runs and enjoyed three 100-RBI seasons from 1968-82.

★ ★ ★

1969: Alexander Mogilny, a current National Hockey League right winger.

★ ★ ★

DEATH OF A LEGEND

1933: Gentleman Jim Corbett (boxing).

★ ★ ★

1951 3 CCNY STARS ARE ARRESTED

Ed Roman, Ed Warner and Al Roth, three stars from last year's City College of New York basketball team that recorded an unprecedented double by sweeping the National Invitation Tournament and the NCAA Tournament, were arrested and charged with "fixing" games at Madison Square Garden.

District Attorney Frank Hogan, who is heading up the investigation, said all three players admitted receiving sums up to $1,500 each for making sure the margin of victory in three 1951 contests stayed below the point spread that CCNY was favored by. The Beavers lost all three of the games in question.

The arrests were made as the team and Coach Nat Holman were returning from Philadelphia, where they had just beaten Temple. They were questioned all night and, confronted by incriminating evidence, admitted receiving payoffs.

Also arrested were Salvatore Tarto Sollazzo, a known gambler, Eddie Gard, a Long Island University senior and Sollazzo's apparent intermediary, and Connie Schaff, a basketball player at New York University. Schaff had attempted to line up an NYU teammate for a gambler, but his overtures were rejected.

MILESTONES IN SPORTS

1919

Ottawa star Cy Denneny notched his 52nd career goal in a 4–3 victory over Toronto, becoming the NHL's all-time top scorer.

1928

Sonja Henie, a 15-year-old figure skating phenom from Oslo, Norway, dazzled the judges at the St. Moritz, Switzerland, Winter Games and walked away with her first Olympic gold medal.

1981

Wayne Gretzky's five goals and two assists were too much for the St. Louis Blues in a 9–2 Edmonton victory.

1990

Derrike Cope drove his Chevrolet to victory in the Daytona 500 when leader Dale Earnhardt blew a tire on the last lap.

1979 KING RICHARD RULES DAYTONA

Stock car king Richard Petty, content to fight it out for third place with Darrell Waltrip and A.J. Foyt a half mile behind the leaders, captured his record sixth Daytona 500 when leaders Donnie Allison and Cale Yarborough crashed on the final lap.

Not only did Allison and Yarborough lock bumpers, they also traded hot words on the infield. Yarborough also traded punches with Allison's brother, Bobby, as Petty celebrated his unlikely victory a few yards away.

The 41-year-old Petty, driving an Oldsmobile, finished a car length ahead of Waltrip in earning the $73,500 first prize and lifting his career earnings to more than $3 million. Foyt finished third with Allison and Yarborough claiming the fourth and fifth spots.

Yarborough was incensed after the race, claiming Bobby Allison, out of contention, had dropped back to run interference for his brother. The accident occurred when Yarborough tried to pass Donnie Allison on the inside.

After the crash, Yarborough jumped from his Oldsmobile and headed for Donnie Allison, sitting in his Oldsmobile. Bobby jumped in front of Yarborough and threw a punch. Yarborough retaliated by hitting Bobby on the head with his helmet. The fight was broken up quickly and cooler heads prevailed.

Cale Yarborough *(left), having knocked* **Bobby Allison** *to the ground, looks toward a rushing* **Donnie Allison** *(right) during an infield scuffle near the end of the Daytona 500.*

FEBRUARY 19

MILESTONES IN SPORTS

1955
Montreal star Bernie Geoffrion accounted for half of the Canadiens' goals in a 10–2 victory over the Rangers.

1977
The New York Rangers' Rod Gilbert became the NHL's 11th 1,000-point man when he scored a goal during a 5–2 loss to the New York Islanders.

1984
Cale Yarborough became the second driver to win consecutive Daytona 500s when he swept to victory in his Chevrolet Monte Carlo.

1989
Ignoring orders from his crew to stop and refuel, a gambling Darrell Waltrip drove his Chevrolet on fumes across the finish line and claimed his first Daytona 500 victory.

1984 MAHRE TWINS PULL 1–2 SLALOM SWEEP

Phil and Steve Mahre, the world-class ski-racing twins from Yakima, Wash., wrapped up the Alpine segment of the Winter Olympic Games in a blaze of glory when they finished 1–2 in the men's slalom.

The Mahre twins, *Phil (left) and Steve, gave the U.S. a 1–2 Olympic slalom sweep.*

Phil captured the gold medal on the final day of competition at Sarajevo, Yugoslavia, with a two-run time of 1:39.41. Steve, the leader after a strong first run, won silver with a combined time of 1:39.62. The Mahre sweep gave the United States eight medals in the Games, including an unprecedented five (three golds) in Alpine skiing.

The Mount Bjelasnica course was steep and icy and 25 skiers missed gates or fell. But not the Mahres. Steve turned in a 50.85 first run, seven-tenths of a second faster than fourth-place Phil. But Phil blazed through a 47.86 second run that moved him into first. Steve could not catch his brother.

The medal was Phil's second in Olympic competition – he had won silver in the Lake Placid slalom in 1980. Steve's medal was his first.

1970 KUHN SUSPENDS McLAIN

Denny McLain, the Detroit righthander who was on top of the baseball world just two seasons ago when he won 31 games, was suspended indefinitely by Commissioner Bowie Kuhn because of "1967 bookmaking activities and his associations at that time."

McLain, who voluntarily appeared before a Federal grand jury in Detroit the previous day, was handed his sentence after a 5½-hour meeting with Kuhn. The commissioner said the action was taken because of "certain admissions made candidly to me by Mr. McLain and not on allegations contained in a recent magazine article."

Kuhn was referring to a recent Sports Illustrated story that alleged McLain had run a bookmaking operation in 1967, had failed to pay a large debt and had had his foot stomped by a hoodlum, forcing him to miss several weeks of the pennant race. The story also said the man he allegedly owed money later died mysteriously in an automobile accident.

The 25-year-old McLain, who won 24 games and shared Cy Young honors with Baltimore's Mike Cuellar last year, will not be allowed to play or practice with the Tigers. He is the first baseball player suspended for gambling since two New York Giants were banned from baseball in 1924.

The most notorious gambling suspensions came in 1921, when eight members of the Chicago White Sox were banned for life for their involvement in fixing the 1919 World Series.

A STAR IS BORN

1916: Eddie Arcaro, a jockey has won two Triple Crowns. He rode Whirlaway in 1941 and Citation in 1948.

★ ★ ★

1957: Dave Stewart, a current major league pitcher.

★ ★ ★

1962: Hana Mandlikova, a tennis star who has won two Australian Opens, one French Open and one U.S. Open.

★ ★ ★

DEATH OF A LEGEND

1985: George Uhle (baseball).

★ ★ ★

1953 WILLIAMS CRASH LANDS

Ted Williams, Boston's Splendid Splinter and four-time American League batting champion who is fighting a different kind of a war these days, survived a major scare when he crash landed his F-9 Panther jet after flying a bombing mission in Korea.

U.S. Marine flying ace **Ted Williams.**

Williams, who is wearing the colors of the U.S. Marine Corps instead of the Red Sox, was on a routine bombing mission when his plane was hit by small-arms fire. Rather than bail out over enemy lines, Williams flew the burning plane back to an allied airfield and crash landed – just in time.

Shortly after the 35-year-old Marine captain escaped from the cockpit, the plane exploded.

MILESTONES · IN SPORTS ·

1952

Andrea Mead Lawrence won the women's slalom and became the first American to win two ski gold medals in Winter Olympic competition. She earlier had won the giant slalom in the Games at Oslo, Norway.

1954

Furman gunner Frank Selvy became the first major college basketball player to top the career 1,000-point barrier.

1971

Ireland's Eamonn Coghlan set a world indoor mile record when he was clocked at 3:50.6 during the Jack-in-the-Box invitational meet at San Diego.

1971

Boston's Phil Esposito, en route to his record 76-goal season, became the first player in NHL history to score his 50th goal in the month of February during a game against Los Angeles.

1976

Dwight Stones broke his own indoor world high jump record when he went over the bar at 7–6 1/4 in the U.S. Olympic invitational meet at New York.

FEBRUARY 20

1988

Boitano Holds Off Orser's Challenge

Brian Boitano, the four-time American national champion and 1986 world champion, added an Olympic gold medal to his long list of accomplishments when he skated an inspired free-style performance that gave him a hair-thin advantage over Canadian Brian Orser.

The competition before Orser's countrymen and a large U.S. contingent at the Calgary Saddledome was both tense and spectacular. Holding a slight lead over Orser heading into the long program, Boitano put on the performance of his life.

His execution was flawless and his jumps and spins energized. He performed eight triples without a miss and he finished his 4-minute, 40-second program to a long standing ovation. He received five 5.9s and four 5.8s for technical merit and his artistic scores ranged from one 5.7 to three 5.9s.

The pressure was squarely on Orser's shoulders and the 1984 Olympic runnerup (to American Scott Hamilton) and reigning world champion responded big. His outstanding performance was marred by one near fall on a triple jump – and that probably cost him a gold medal .

Orser received eight 5.8s and one 5.9 for technical merit and three 5.8s, five 5.9s and one perfect 6.0 for artistic impression. Five of the nine international judges favored Boitano and two others had the skaters tied on points. The American captured the tie-breakers based on his superior technical merit.

American **Brian Boitano** *(above) defeated Canadian* **Brian Orser** *in a tense Olympic figure skating duel.*

A STAR IS BORN

1890: Sam Rice, a Hall of Fame outfielder and a .322 career hitter over his 20-year major league career (1915–34).

★ ★ ★

1934: Bobby Unser, a race car driver with 35 career CART victories and three visits to the Indianapolis 500 winner's circle.

★ ★ ★

1942: Phil Esposito, a hockey Hall of Fame center who won five NHL scoring titles and finished with 717 career goals.

★ ★ ★

1963: Charles Barkley, a current National Basketball Association forward

1981

Lewis Leaps Into Spotlight

Carl Lewis, the University of Houston's multi-talented 19-year-old long jumper and sprinter, captured the spotlight at the Southwest Conference indoor track and field championships when he posted one world record and just missed getting another.

Lewis, the defending NCAA long jump champion, soared 27–10 1/4 during the Fort Worth, Tex., competition to break the world record of 27–6, set last year by Mississippi College's Larry Myricks. Lewis' previous long jump best was 27–4.

After that victory, the tall, muscular sophomore captured first place in the 60-yard dash with the third-fastest indoor time ever recorded. His 6.06 seconds was just off Stanley Floyd's 6.04 mark, set two weeks ago in the Dallas Times-Herald competition.

1976

Coopman Is Easy For Ali

Muhammad Ali toyed with challenger Jean-Pierre Coopman for four rounds and then knocked out the Belgian with a big right uppercut in the fifth as he successfully defended his heavyweight crown in a title fight at the Roberto Clemente Coliseum in San Juan, Puerto Rico.

The 34-year-old Ali's fifth title defense in his second reign as champion was easy and effortless. Coopman plodded around the ring throwing plenty of punches, but few connected and those that did had little effect.

Ali, meanwhile, stood flat-footed for most of the first four rounds, peppering Coopman with a flurry of punches whenever the urge struck him. In the fifth round, Ali began to dance, circling left and right and bothering the challenger with quick jabs. Suddenly, Ali came in with a big uppercut that knocked Coopman to the canvas. After the referee counted him out, Ali helped drag the fallen challenger to his corner.

The victory lifted Ali's career record to 50–2.

FEBRUARY

21

A STAR IS BORN

1903: Tom Yawkey, a baseball Hall of Fame official who owned the Boston Red Sox for 43 years.

★ ★ ★

1925: Jack Ramsay, a former college basketball coach who went on to the NBA and compiled 864 career victories.

★ ★ ★

1937: Ron Clarke, an outstanding Australian runner in the 1960s who set 17 world records in distances ranging from 2 miles to 20, 000 meters.

★ ★ ★

1952

Button Is Golden Boy

Harvard senior Dick Button, reaffirming his superiority in the world figure skating community, performed a never-before-seen triple loop that amazed the judges and helped earn a second Olympic gold medal during competition at St. Moritz, Switzerland.

Button probably did not need the daring new maneuver to win his second straight Winter Games championship. But, like in 1948 when he unveiled a daring double axel in his free-style winning performance, Button awed the crowd with his confidence – and audacity.

He was flawless from beginning to end, but the highlight of his breathtaking routine came when he executed three complete revolutions and landed cleanly to routinely finish the rest of his program.

It came as no surprise when all nine judges awarded Button first place.

1992

America Gets 2 Medals

Kristi Yamaguchi, displaying an elegance and artistry befitting a world champion, glided and swirled her way to Olympic gold with an inspirational final routine at Albertville, France.

Yamaguchi, the first American female Olympic champion since Dorothy Hamill in 1976, was not perfect. She fell while performing a triple loop and she cut a triple salchow to a double. But all of the other top five competitors fell and the defending American and world champion won because her footwork, spins, arm movement and presence were near perfect.

Japan's Midori Ito, who fell on a triple axel early in her routine, skated brilliantly the rest of the way and rose from fourth to a second-place finish. The Japanese and Czechoslovakian judges gave Ito first-place marks, but the rest supported Yamaguchi.

American Nancy Kerrigan, another proponent of style and grace, won the bronze medal. It marked the first time since Carol Heiss won gold and Barbara Roles bronze in 1960 that the U.S. had won two medals in women's figure skating.

MILESTONES IN SPORTS

1960

Philedelphia center Wilt Chamberlain scored 58 points in a victory over the New York Knicks–the record fourth time this season he had topped the 50-point barrier.

1968

Major league players and owners ratified baseball's first Basic Agreement.

1970

Chicago's Bobby Hull became the NHL's third 500-goal scorer when he connected twice during a 4–2 victory over the New York Rangers.

1970

LSU's Pete Maravich scored 64 points, but the Kentucky Wildcats got 51 from Dan Issel and claimed a 121–105 victory.

1982

Tom Watson sank a dramatic 43-foot putt on the third hole of sudden-death overtime to defeat Johnny Miller in the Los Angeles Open.

1982

Penguins End Record Streak

Two third-period goals by Pittsburgh's **Mike Bullard** *helped end the Islanders' record 15-game winning streak.*

The lowly Pittsburgh Penguins, who had snapped their nine-game winless streak the night before against powerful Philadelphia, stunned the New York Islanders, 4–3, at the Pittsburgh Civic Arena and ended the Islanders' NHL-record 15-game winning streak.

Two third-period Mike Bullard goals and the clutch goaltending of Michel Dion gave the Penguins all the amunition they needed to end professional hockey's longest run of perfection. Dion faced 16 final-period New York shots and Bullard drove the game-winner past Roland Melanson with 4:29 left to play.

"We bombarded the guy," said frustrated Islander Bobby Nystrom after the game. "Well, it's the sign of a good team to be frustrated after losing."

The two-time defending Stanley Cup champions traded early goals with the Penguins before Bob Bourne gave them a 3–2 second-period advantage. The Islanders peppered Dion with shots in the final stanza, but it was Bullard who found the net for Pittsburgh. He tied the game at 4:20 and then scored the winner 11 minutes later.

New York had victimized Pittsburgh four times during its streak, which started on January 21.

"I knew somewhere along the line it would come to an end," said Islanders Coach Al Arbour. "It's a disappointment, but I'm very proud of our players."

FEBRUARY

22

1980 U.S. Shocks Russians

Mark Johnson drove home a rebound to tie the game and Mike Eruzione scored on a 30-foot slap shot, giving the United States Olympic hockey team a 4–3 victory over the powerful Soviet Union in one of the most startling upsets in sports history.

Americans **Mark Johnson** *(10) and* **Robert McClanahan** *(24) jump for joy after Johnson's third-period goal tied the game and set the stage for a startling Olympic upset of the Soviet Union.*

The semifinal shocker at Lake Placid, N.Y., kept the U.S. unbeaten through seven games and put the Americans in position to win their second-ever gold in Winter Games play. The 1960 team performed that feat first when it shocked the Russians in a semifinal match and beat Czechoslovakia in the final.

The Americans, a rag-tag group of minor league journeymen and collegians, can clinch gold in two days with a victory over Finland. But they will be hard-pressed to match either the dramatics or the emotional fervor created during and after their upset of the Soviets.

As the U.S. team and goalie Jim Craig held off rush after rush from the swarming and fast-skating Soviets, the large American crowd began to grasp the significance of what they were witnessing. Patriotic songs, foot stomping and flag-waving hysteria accompanied the ecstatic countdown as the desperate Russians threw everything they had at Craig. To no avail. When the final horn sounded victory, parents and fans dashed onto the ice for an emotional hugfest as thousands more remained in the stands chanting, "U.S.A, U.S.A." Across the nation, fireworks, car horns and other noise signaled unrestrained joy.

The Americans had their upset. Phase I of the Miracle on Ice was now complete.

A STAR IS BORN

1874: Bill Klem, who generally is considered the greatest umpire of all time. He was the first arbiter elected to the baseball Hall of Fame.

★★★

1934: Sparky Anderson, a long-time major league manager whose teams have compiled more than 1,900 victories.

★★★

1940: Chet Walker, an 11-year NBA forward who scored 18,831 career points in the 1960s and '70s.

★★★

1950: Julius Erving, an outstanding ABA and NBA forward who scored 30,026 points in his professional career – third on the all-time list.

★★★

1965: Pat LaFontaine, a current National Hockey League center.

1955 Maureen Connolly Retires

Maureen Connolly, the only female ever to capture all four major tennis tournaments in one year, shocked her fans and the sport's establishment when she announced her retirement at the still-tender age of 20.

Connolly, the ranking queen of the courts and one of the greatest players in the history of tennis, made her stunning announcement in the wake of a horse riding accident that severely injured her leg. She said the slow rehabilitation was one factor in her decision and her plan to marry Norman Brinker, a former member of the United States equestrian team, was another. Little Mo injured her leg last July when her horse, frightened by a passing truck, pinned her against the vehicle. Connolly, a three-time Wimbledon and U.S. singles champion, was a winner in all nine major championships she entered. In 1953, she became the first woman to complete a grand slam, winning the Wimbledon, U.S., French and Australian championships.

1959 Petty Wins In Mad Dash

Johnny Beauchamp *(with trophy) was accorded royal treatment after apparently winning the inaugural Daytona 500, but the victory later was awarded to* **Lee Petty.**

Lee Petty won an intense dash to the finish line in the inaugural Daytona 500, but he didn't know that until three days later. That's when the race result was finally decided by pictures from a classic photo finish.

The 500-mile stock car extravaganza, run on the 2½-mile oval track of the new Daytona International Speedway, was a tight duel from start to finish. But the intensity really picked up with 15 laps remaining when Petty's Oldsmobile and Johnny Beauchamp's Thunderbird began dueling bumper-to-bumper, neither yielding an inch.

It became even more tense when the cars pulled side by side with three laps to go and ran that way the rest of the race. As they hit the finish line, it was too close to call, but NASCAR head Bill France tried anyway, declaring Beauchamp the winner. Officials viewed pictures and movies over the next two days and finally reversed France's call.

The 44-year-old Petty was credited with an average speed of 135.42 miles per hour–the fastest ever achieved by an American-built stock car.

MILESTONES · IN SPORTS ·

1969

Barbara Jo Rubin became the first woman jockey to win a race at an American track when she rode Cohesian to victory in the ninth race at Charles Town, W. Va.

1981

Quebec brothers Peter and Anton Stastny both scored a rookie-record eight points – in the same game. Peter scored four goals and four assists and Anton had three goals and five assists in the Nordiques' 11–7 victory over Washington.

1988

High-scoring Bradley star Hersey Hawkins poured in 63 points in the Braves' 122–107 college basketball victory over the University of Detroit.

1988

American Bonnie Blair zipped to a speed skating gold medal and a world record (39.10) in the 500-meter sprint at the Winter Olympic Games in Calgary.

1990

La Salle All-America Lionel Simmons posted 27 points against Manhattan and became college basketball's fifth career 3,000-point scorer.

FEBRUARY

23

MILESTONES IN SPORTS

1906

Heavyweight champion Tommy Burns held off the challenge of Marvin Hart in a 20-round fight at Los Angeles.

1938

Joe Louis' second heavyweight title defense was an easy one – a third-round knockout of Nathan Mann in New York.

1960

Carol Heiss, following in the footsteps of Tenley Albright, gave the United States its second straight women's Olympic figure skating gold medal when she won the competition at Squaw Valley, N.Y.

1983

Mark Pavelich exploded for five goals and the New York Rangers cruised to an easy 11–3 NHL victory over Hartford.

1985

Stormy Indiana Coach Bob Knight made headlines when he threw a chair across the floor in a fit of rage over officiating during a game against Purdue at Bloomington, Ind.

1987

Seattle's Nate McMillan tied Ernie DiGregorio's NBA rookie assist record when he handed out 25 during a victory over the Los Angeles Clippers.

1991

Chicago's Michel Goulet notched his 1,000th career point during a 3–3 tie with Minnesota.

1980 HEIDEN'S GOLD RUSH

Eric Heiden, the world's fastest skater and America's newest golden boy, completed his nine-day blitz of the world and Olympic record books when he knocked more than six seconds off the world mark for the rugged 10,000-meter race and captured his fifth gold medal.

American golden boy **Eric Heiden,** *who won a record five Olympic speed skating gold medals.*

Heiden dominated the speed skating segment of the Lake Placid Winter Games like nobody before him. He already had posted victories in the 500, 1,000, 1,500 and 5,000-meter events when he lined up for the grueling 6.2-mile finale and a shot at history.

The 21-year-old Wisconsin native did not miss his mark. Going off in the second pair, he pushed, pounded and drove himself to his third world record of the Games, posting an amazing 14:28.13 time that easily shattered the world record.

That gave Heiden an unprecedented five individual golds and every one was a record. He set world marks in the 1,000, 1,500 and 10,000 and Olympic marks in the 500 and 5,000.

1960 GOODBYE EBBETS FIELD

As former Dodger officials, players and fans watched sadly from the Ebbets Field rotunda, a white wrecking ball with stitches painted onto its sides delivered the first crushing blows to a baseball monument.

So began the 10-week destruction of one of the most adored ballparks ever built. Once a cathedral in the Borough of Churches, Ebbets Field was abandoned in 1958 by the once-proud franchise that had graced its flagpole with nine pennants and one passionately-earned World Series championship.

Built in 1913 by Charles Ebbets, the stadium was unique in design and an inviting playground for some of the zaniest fans and players baseball has ever known. Super fan Hilda Chester, with her clanging cowbell, was a fixture, as was the infamous Sym-Phony band. Such players as Duke, Pee Wee, Newk, Jackie, Campy and Skoonj formed the heart and soul of Dem Bums. Uncle Robbie managed Brooklyn's Daffiness Boys for 18 glorious years.

A brief pre-demolition ceremony was conducted at home plate as Lucy Monroe sang the national anthem and former Dodger broadcaster Al Helfer introduced such long-time Dodgers as Carl Erskine, Ralph Branca and Roy Campanella.

Pieces of **Ebbets Field** *are carted away by former fans.*

1983 GENERALS PULL SIGNING COUP

The new United States Football League, looking for "instant credibility" in its coming battle with the established National Football League, pulled off what it considered a major coup when its New Jersey Generals signed University of Georgia junior running back Herschel Walker.

Walker's three-year contract makes him professional football's highest-paid player.

Walker, the reigning Heisman Trophy winner, will receive a reported $1.5 million per season, more than double what Chicago running back Walter Payton makes as the NFL's highest-paid player. The 20-year-old tailback set 10 NCAA rushing records, gained 5,259 yards and led the Bulldogs to a national championship in three memorable seasons at Georgia.

The signing ended a week-long controversy. Despite Walker's denials, the NCAA had announced two days earlier that he had signed with the Generals and thus forfeited his final season of eligibility. The signing also broke a stated USFL policy against signing underage players, an unwritten rule long adhered to by the NFL.

A STAR IS BORN

1923: Dante Lavelli, a pro football Hall of Fame end who played on the great Cleveland Browns teams from 1946–56.

★ ★ ★

1940: Jackie Smith, one of pro football's outstanding tight ends during a long National Football League career.

★ ★ ★

1943: Fred Biletnikoff, a pro football Hall of Fame wide receiver for the Oakland Raiders from 1965–78.

★ ★ ★

1963: Bobby Bonilla, a current major league outfielder.

★ ★ ★

1980 U.S. Makes A Miracle

The United States Olympic hockey team, completing its Miracle on Ice journey into the history books, defeated Finland, 4–2, captured the gold medal at the Lake Placid, N.Y., Winter Games and touched off a second round of patriotic fervor that engulfed a proud nation.

Following on the heels of the Americans' semifinal victory over the powerful Soviet Union, one of the most startling and dramatic sports upsets of all time, the U.S. team appeared tired and emotionally drained as it took the ice to complete its gold-medal run against the Finns.

This was a ragtag team of college stars and itinerant minor leaguers who had banded together under the direction of Coach Herb Brooks with little hope of even making the medal round, much less contending for a gold medal. But, playing against more experienced and talented opponents, the Americans somehow won four times and tied once in the preliminary round and then pulled its semifinal shocker against the Russians. The game against Finland was almost an afterthought in the wake of the emotional triumph of two days earlier.

And it showed. The Finns scored first on a goal by Jukka Porvari and the Americans tied on a shot by Steve Christoff. Finland regained the lead on Mikko Leinonen's goal and held its 2–1 advantage through two periods. The Americans, who had trailed at some point in six of their first seven games, would have to come from behind again.

The Americans' hard-checking style began to take its toll in the final period. First Phil Verchota scored to tie the game and then Rob McClanahan gave the U.S. its first lead. Brilliant U.S. goalie Jim Craig held off the Finns through three desperate power plays, the Americans added an insurance goal and the wild, ecstatic countdown began.

When it reached zero, flags waved, fans sang patriotic songs and many of the 10,000 inside the Olympic Field House stormed onto the ice to celebrate and congratulate their conquering heroes. Chants of "U.S.A." and "We're No. 1" filled the Olympic Village and Americans everywhere, most of whom had watched the final minutes on television, blared car horns, shot off fireworks and creatively joined in the nationwide outpouring of emotion.

Telegrams began pouring in and even President Jimmy Carter called Brooks to offer congratulations for the second U.S. hockey gold medal in Winter Games history.

The first, ironically, came 20 years earlier when the U.S. defeated the Soviet Union in a semifinal contest and beat Czechoslovakia in the Olympic final.

1982 Gretzky Passes Phil Esposito

Young Edmonton center **Wayne Gretzky.**

February 24

Edmonton center Wayne Gretzky became the greatest one-season goal-scorer in National Hockey League history when he tallied three times in a 6–3 victory over Buffalo, breaking former Boston star Phil Esposito's record of 76.

The Great One's first goal came with 6:36 left in the game and broke the mark Esposito had owned since the 1970–71 campaign. He scored again with 1:44 to play and brought his season total to 79 with a 45-foot shot that beat Buffalo goalie Don Edwards with 17 seconds remaining.

The record-setter was vintage Gretzky, who has scored an NHL-record 176 points in 64 games. He froze defenseman Richie Dunn in his tracks, shot around him and fired the puck past the helpless Edwards. The 21-year-old Gretzky also had a pair of first-period assists.

Milestones in Sports

1974

Leonard Thompson captured his first PGA Tour victory when he beat Hale Irwin by one stroke in the Jackie Gleason Inverrary Classic at Fort Lauderdale, Fla.

1978

New Jersey guard Kevin Porter handed out an NBA-record 29 assists during a 126–112 victory over the Houston Rockets.

1988

Finland's Matti Nykanen became the first Winter Olympics triple gold winner in the Nordic ski events when he won the 90 and 70-meter individual jumping medals and helped produce a 90-meter team victory at Calgary.

1993

Detroit's Steve Yzerman became the NHL's 37th 1,000-point man when he assisted on a goal in a 10–7 loss at Buffalo.

A Star Is Born

1874: Honus Wagner, a baseball Hall of Fame shortstop who batted .329 over his 21-year major league career in the early 1900s.

★ ★ ★

1956: Eddie Murray, a current major league first baseman.

★ ★ ★

1965: Paul Gruber, a current National Football League offensive tackle.

★ ★ ★

Death of a Legend

1926: Eddie Plank (baseball).

★ ★ ★

1990: Tony Conigliaro (baseball).

★ ★ ★

FEBRUARY
25

A STAR IS BORN

1895: Bert Bell, a football Hall of Famer, one-time owner of the Philadelphia Eagles and former commissioner of the National Football League.

★ ★ ★

1918: Bobby Riggs, a former tennis star of the 1930s and '40s who later lost to Billie Jean King in the much-publicized "Battle of the Sexes" match.

★ ★ ★

1919: Monte Irvin, a Hall of Fame infielder-outfielder who played in both the old Negro League and the major leagues.

★ ★ ★

1938: Herb Elliott, an Australian distance runner in the late 1950s and '60s who ran 17 sub-4-minute miles and set three world records.

★ ★ ★

1947: Lee Evans, an American quarter-miler whose 400-meter world record at the 1968 Olympic Games stood for 20 years.

★ ★ ★

DEATH OF A LEGEND

1934: John McGraw (baseball).

★ ★ ★

1966: James D. Norris (hockey).

1964

CLAY STUNS LISTON IN BOXING SHOCKER

In one of the most stunning upsets in boxing history, young Cassius Clay backed up his boasts, humbled his critics and knocked down the notion of Sonny Liston's invincibility with a seventh-round technical knockout over the heavyweight champion in a title bout at Miami Beach.

The brash 22-year-old, who had spent his pre-fight days predicting victory and spouting homemade poetry, was everything he had claimed to be ("I am the greatest") – and more.

Holding his hands low and seemingly offering his face up for sacrifice, Clay danced, feinted and avoided Liston's powerful left hooks with grace and dexterity as he jabbed and fired shots at the champion's face with lightning quickness and precision.

Liston, who never even hurt the former light heavyweight Olympic champion, took plenty of punishment in return. Clay opened a gash under Liston's left eye, cut his cheek and had him tired, bleeding and confused by the end of the sixth round. When Liston failed to answer the bell for the seventh because of a shoulder injury, Clay became heavyweight champion of the world.

True to form, the youngster, who had indeed "floated like a butterfly, and stung like a bee," danced a victory jig and offered a challenge for disbelieving reporters: "Eat your words," he yelled, and most of them did exactly that the next day in print.

Young **Cassius Clay** *(left) toys with heavyweight champion* **Sonny Liston** *en route to his shocking upset.*

1987

SMUs GIVEN DEATH PENALTY

In the harshest punishment ever handed down to a football program, the National Collegiate Athletic Association barred Southern Methodist University from fielding a team next fall, limited its 1988 schedule and put the Mustangs in a ground-level situation with a series of other penalties.

The punishment was meted out as a result of numerous rule violations, ranging from illegal recruiting to under-the-table payments to players. The former Southwestern Conference power had been placed on probation six previous times and the NCAA decided to scrap the school's program and make it rebuild from scratch.

Among the penalties handed down were a reduction of scholarships, a coaching staff cutback and four years of probation. SMU players were given permission to transfer to other schools without losing the usual year of eligibility. The NCAA's seven-page report stated that the harsh punishment was intended to "eliminate a program that was built on a legacy of wrongdoing, deceit and rules violations."

MILESTONES IN SPORTS

1924

Maryland prep star Marie Boyd established a high school girls record when she scored 156 points in a single game.

1959

Lee Petty, who finished in a February 22 photo finish with Johnny Beauchamp in the first Daytona 500, was officially declared the winner, reversing the original decision.

1962

Wilt Chamberlain scored 67 points, but that wasn't enough as the New York Knicks rode Richie Guerin's 50 points to a 149–135 victory over the Philadelphia Warriors.

1977

New Orleans' Pete Maravich scored 68 points, an NBA record for a guard, during a victory over the New York Knicks.

1989

Heavyweight champion Mike Tyson scored a fifth-round technical knockout of Frank Bruno during a bout at Las Vegas.

1973

BASEBALL GETS HISTORIC PACT

Opening the door for spring training to begin and a new season to get underway, major league owners and players agreed on provisions for an historic new Basic Agreement that sets up a binding arbitration process for salary disputes and gives 10-year players the right of trade refusal.

While a number of advancements were made in benefits, the highlight of the agreement for the players clearly was the arbitration concession. Whereas players previously had little recourse in salary disputes, the new process allows them to submit demands to an arbitrator, who will compare them to the owners' offers and make an either/or decision.

The other major concession was the "10 and 5" rule, which allows a player with 10 or more years of major league service, the last five of which have been spent with one team, to reject a trade. This represents an important modification of baseball's ever-controversial reserve system.

1961 Panch Sets Speed Mark

Marvin Panch, a hometown Florida boy driving a 1960 Pontiac, took advantage of the furious pace set by pole-sitter Glenn (Fireball) Roberts and blazed to a world speed record en route to an emotional victory in the third annual Daytona 500 stock car spectacular.

After Roberts dropped out of the race with engine trouble on the 188th lap, Panch took over and steamed home with an average speed of 149.601 miles per hour, the highest ever recorded for a continuous 500-mile auto race. The previous best mark of 138.767 had been set last year by Jim Rathmann in the Indianapolis 500.

With 65,000 fans watching the proceedings on a sunny day at the Daytona International Speedway, Roberts stormed into the lead and held it most of the way until bad luck struck with only 13 laps remaining in the 200-lap event. His starter motor broke loose, swung down and punched a hole in the oil pan. Roberts pulled into the pits engulfed by a cloud of smoke.

Panch, a 35-year-old Daytona Beach driver, crossed the finish line less than 15 seconds ahead of a 1961 Pontiac driven by Joe Weatherly and captured the $23,000 first prize.

1960 Jenkins Wins Olympic Gold

David Jenkins gave the performance of his life just when he needed it most and the result was a well-earned figure skating gold medal in the Winter Olympic Games at Squaw Valley, N.Y.

Jenkins, following in the footsteps of his brother, Hayes Alan Jenkins, the 1956 Olympic gold medalist, brought the near-capacity crowd at Blyth Arena to its feet with a rousing free-style performance.

Trailing Czechoslovakia's Karol Divin after the compulsory figures, Jenkins jumped into his routine with a single axel and then reeled off numerous jumps and spins that left everybody gasping. His near-flawless performance earned him first-place votes from all nine judges and one perfect 6 – a rare occurrence in world-class figure skating.

Jenkins received one 5.8, seven 5.9s and his 6 for technical merit and three 5.9s and six 5.8s for artistic impression. His total score of 1,440.2 placed him well out of reach of Divin, the skater in second-place .

Jenkins adds the Olympic gold medal to his three straight world championship titles.

The Jenkins brothers: *Hayes (left) and David (center) with fellow skater* **Ronnie Robertson.**

1935 Yankees Release Ruth

A glorious era ended for New York baseball when Babe Ruth, baseball's longtime Sultan of Swat, was given his unconditional release by the Yankees so that he could sign a career-concluding contract with the National League's Boston Braves.

The Babe thus returns to the city where he began his major league career in 1914 as a lefthanded pitcher and occasional outfielder for the American League's Red Sox. Ruth, whose contract was sold to the Yankees in 1920, ends his A. L. career with 708 home runs, 659 of them coming in the Yankee pinstripes. He combined with slugging first baseman Lou Gehrig to lead the Yankees to seven A.L. pennants and four World Series championships in 15 seasons.

Ruth requested the release so he could join the Braves as an executive, assistant manager and active player. He signed a three-year contract and said he intends to continue being involved as an active player for as long as his body will permit.

Yankee great **Babe Ruth** *(third from left) decided to end his career with the Boston Braves.*

Milestones in Sports

1965

Fresno State senior Darel Newman tied the indoor record for the 60-yard dash when he ran 5.9 seconds in the Golden Gate invitational.

1973

Triple Crown winner Secretariat was syndicated for a record $6.8 million with the agreement he would race the rest of the year before retiring to stud.

1981

Boston battled Minnesota – literally – in a 5–1 Bruins victory. The game was marred by 84 penalties totaling 406 minutes and 12 players were ejected.

1987

Michael Jordan scored a Chicago-record 58 points and led the Bulls to a 128–113 victory over the New Jersey Nets.

A Star Is Born

1887: Grover Cleveland Alexander, a baseball Hall of Fame pitcher from 1911–30 who won 373 games, tying Christy Mathewson for the all-time National League lead.

★ ★ ★

1959: John McEnroe, a current tennis star with four U.S. Open titles and three Wimbledon championships.

★ ★ ★

1957: Joe Mullen, a current National Hockey League right winger.

★ ★ ★

Death of a Legend

1992: Jean Yawkey (baseball).

FEBRUARY

27

A STAR IS BORN

1902: Gene Sarazen, a dominant golf winner in the 1920s and '30s. He won all four major titles at least once.

★ ★ ★

1933: Raymond Berry, a football Hall of Fame receiver in the 1950s and '60s.

★ ★ ★

1961: James Worthy, a current National Basketball Association forward.

1960 AMERICANS ICE POWERFUL SOVIETS

A ragtag group of American hockey players, not even expected to make the medal round of the Olympic competition at Squaw Valley, Calif., pulled off an incredible 3–2 upset of the heavily favored Soviet Union team and put itself in position to win a first-ever U.S. gold medal.

The victory touched off wild celebrations on the ice, throughout the Olympic Village and around the country as a wave of patriotism gripped the American continent.

Never before had a U.S. hockey team defeated the powerful Soviets and never before had such lofty heights been attained in such dramatic fashion.

It was obvious from the beginning that the Cinderella Americans were overmatched in both speed and skill level. But not in heart. Bill Cleary scored first for the U.S., but Russian Venjamin Aleksandrov tied the game 59 seconds later. The Soviets continued to swarm on Jack McCartan, but the American goaltender held them off – until Mikhail Bychkov broke through late in the first period.

McCartan continued to play inspired hockey in the second session and Bill Christian finally broke through at 11:01 for the tying goal. Somehow the Americans held off the Russians through the remainder of the period and the first half of the third before lightning struck.

That came on a shot by Bill Christian off a pass from brother Roger. Suddenly, with 5:01 left to play, the U.S. had a shocking 3–2 lead.

McCartan, who made 27 saves, spent much of the closing minutes on his stomach and back, holding off repeated Russian sorties. When the final horn sounded, sticks went flying into the air, well-wishers dashed onto the ice and the celebration began.

Never mind that the U.S. would have to play Czechoslovakia the next day for a gold medal. Ultimate victory already had been achieved.

1959 BOSTON WINS SLUGFEST

In an unprecedented offensive explosion enjoyed thoroughly by 12,315 fans at Boston Garden, the Celtics powered their way to a 173–139 victory over the Minneapolis Lakers.

The game produced seven NBA records, including most combined points (312) and most points by a losing team. The previous record for combined points was 282, set in a 146–136 St. Louis victory over Syracuse.

The other five records were set by the Celtics: most points by one team, most points in a half (90), most points in one quarter (52) and most field goals in a game (72). Bob Cousy set an individual record for assists with 28. The Celtics, who ran up an 83–64 halftime advantage, stretched it to 121–95 after three quarters. Boston was led by Tom Heinsohn, who scored 43 points, Cousy (31) and Bill Sharman (29).

Bob Cousy, ***Boston's record-setting assist man, handed out 28 in the Celtics' 173–139 victory over the Minneapolis Lakers.***

MILESTONES IN SPORTS

1966

Peggy Fleming, a 17-year-old high school girl from Colorado Springs, captured the world figure skating championship with a near-flawless routine that earned her first-place votes from all nine of the judges at Davos, Switzerland.

1977

Chicago's Stan Mikita became the National Hockey League's eighth 500-goal scorer when he connected during a 4–3 Blackhawks loss to Vancouver.

1980

The Hartford Whalers, who already had hockey great Gordie Howe on their roster, picked up Golden Jet Bobby Hull from the Winnipeg Jets for future considerations.

1983

Ireland's Eamonn Coghlan became the first miler to break 3:50 indoors when he was clocked in 3:49.78.

MILESTONES · IN SPORTS ·

1940

An historic doubleheader at Madison Square Garden: Pittsburgh beat Fordham and New York University beat Georgetown in the first televised college basketball games.

1970

Cincinnati's Pete Rose, living up to his earlier prediction, became the first baseball singles hitter to sign a six-figure contract.

1971

Jack Nicklaus became the first golfer to win all four majors two times when he recorded a two-stroke victory over Billy Casper in the PGA Championship.

1990

The Edmonton Oilers and Los Angeles Kings did more than play hockey when they combined for an NHL-record 85 penalties in a game at Los Angeles.

1960 CINDERELLA STRIKES GOLD

The Cinderella United States ice hockey team, in danger of missing its chance to win a first-ever Olympic gold medal, exploded for six third-period goals and crushed Czechoslovakia, 9–4, in an historic victory at Squaw Valley, Calif.

The Americans, obviously tired and emotionally drained after their stunning 3–2 victory over the Soviet Union the previous night, skated to a 3–3 first-period tie with the Czechs and fell behind, 4–3, after the second period of the medal-deciding contest. The Americans needed a lift.

They got it from an unexpected source – Soviet captain Nikolai Sologubov. The Russian made a surprise visit to the U.S. locker room between periods, suggesting that the sagging Americans bolster themselves with oxygen to counteract the mile-high thin air. The Americans took his advice and stormed out for the final 20 minutes.

Roger Christian, who scored four goals, tied the game at 5:59 on a 20-foot shot. Bob Cleary gave the U.S. a 5–4 lead at 7:40 off a rebound. At 11:01, a Czech player was sent to the penalty box and Bob Cleary, Christian and Bill Cleary scored in a 67-second span.

The underdog Americans added one more goal and the gold was secure – the first in Winter Games history for a U.S. team.

A team of American upstarts shocked the world with their hockey gold medal in the 1960 Winter Olympic Games.

FEBRUARY 28

A STAR IS BORN

1890: Joe Malone, a hockey Hall of Famer from the league's formative years and holder of the one-game NHL record of seven goals.

★ ★ ★

1940: Mario Andretti, a race car driver who has crossed over to win a Daytona 500, an Indianapolis 500 and a Formula 1 world championship.

★ ★ ★

1956: Adrian Dantley, a 15-year NBA star who scored 23,177 career points.

★ ★ ★

1973: Eric Lindros, a current National Hockey League center.

★ ★ ★

DEATH OF A LEGEND

1988: Harvey Kuenn (baseball).

1981 MURPHY STREAK HITS 78

Calvin Murphy, a pint-sized guard for the NBA's Houston Rockets, raised his record string of consecutive free throws to 78 during his team's 104–103 loss to San Diego.

Murphy, who had not missed from the foul line since December 27, was 5 for 5 in his 27-point effort against the Clippers at Houston. Each one added to the record he set February 19 when he passed former star Rick Barry's previous NBA mark of 60.

Murphy, in fact, surpassed the best efforts at both the professional and collegiate levels. Bob Lloyd of Rutgers set the NCAA Division I record in 1967 with 60 straight free throws and Monmouth's John Barone set the Division II mark of 65 in 1970. Murphy's streak ended the next day at San Antonio.

Diminutive Houston guard **Calvin Murphy.**

1986 DRUG BATTLE INTENSIFIES

Commissioner Peter Ueberroth stepped up his crusade against baseball's growing drug problem when he handed seven major league stars one-year suspensions without pay.

Ueberroth, saying the seven had either used drugs themselves or helped in the spread of the drug problem, suspended New York Mets first baseman Keith Hernandez, New York Yankee infielder Dale Berra, Oakland pitcher Joaquin Andujar, Cincinnati outfielder Dave Parker, San Francisco outfielder Jeffrey Leonard, Kansas City outfielder Lonnie Smith and Los Angeles infielder Enos Cabell. Six of the seven described their association with drugs during testimony in last year's Pittsburgh trials of seven men charged with cocaine distribution. Andujar was implicated during their testimony.

Ueberroth, however, did offer the players a chance to avoid the suspension – if they would adhere to some strict guidelines. To regain active status, the players must donate 10 percent of this year's salary to drug-prevention programs, submit to voluntary drug tests for the rest of their careers and perform 200-plus hours of community service.

FEBRUARY

29

MILESTONES
· IN SPORTS ·

1932

Former heavyweight champion Jack Dempsey knocked out two opponents in less than three minutes of an exhibition in Dayton, O . Dempsey beat Jack Phillips in 1:22 and Pat Sullivan in 1:10.

1940

Jimmy Demaret fired a pair of 71s and captured the 54-hole St. Petersburgh Open by one stroke over Byron Nelson – his fifth victory on the PGA winter tour.

1964

Bill McClellon, a New York high school sophomore, set a national scholastic indoor high jump record for the second time in two weeks, leaping 6–8 in a local championship meet.

1972

Atlanta slugger Hank Aaron became the highest paid player in baseball history when he signed a three-year contract for a reported $600,000.

1992

Ray Bourque's 1,000th career point came on an assist during Boston's 5–5 tie against Washington.

1980 HOWE GETS GOAL 800

Venerable Gordie Howe, hockey's 51-year-old marathon man, stepped into uncharted territory when he extended his own goal-scoring record to a new level, notching No. 800 in a game at Hartford.

The Whalers right winger reached his latest National Hockey League milestone at 1:27 of the third period in a game against St. Louis. He whistled a 10-foot wrist shot between the pads of Blues goalie Mike Liut and the Whalers went on to record a 3–0 victory.

The goal was Howe's 1,069th in the professional ranks, including playoffs and a six-year stint in the World Hockey Association. He began his career with Detroit in 1946, retired from the Red Wings in 1971 and sat out two seasons before signing to play with sons Marty and Mark for the WHA's Houston Aeros. He later joined the Whalers and returned to the NHL this season when the team was one of four WHA clubs admitted to the league as part of a merger agreement.

Howe, who helped the Red Wings to four Stanley Cup championships in his early years, is a six-time NHL scoring champion and six-time league Most Valuable Player.

Gordie Howe, *the NHL's first 800-goal scorer.*

Five-time ice skating world champion **Dick Button.**

1952 BUTTON AGAIN

Dick Button, performing the free-style portion of his program with a panache and precision that nobody in the world can duplicate , capped off his second straight Olympic gold medal with an unprecedented fifth consecutive world figure skating championship at Paris.

Button, the Harvard senior who had captured his gold medal eight days earlier in the Winter Games at Oslo, held a commanding 35-point lead after the compulsory figures and added to his advantage during the free-skating portion of the program. His well-designed routine, full of difficult jumps and intricate maneuvers, earned first-place votes from all seven of the judges and 1,352.4 total points.

That was well ahead of two Olympic teammates, who completed an American sweep. Jimmy Grogan compiled 1,271 points for second place and Hayes Jenkins 1,262.2 for third.

A STAR IS BORN

1904: Pepper Martin, a former major league outfielder and career .298 hitter over 13 seasons with the St. Louis Cardinals' Gas House Gang.

★ ★ ★

1924: Al Rosen, a two-time American League home run champion in the 1940s and '50s.

★ ★ ★

1936: Henri Richard, a hockey Hall of Famer and 1,000-point scorer who played on 11 Stanley Cup champions with Montreal.

1924 RUTH ILLNESS SCARES YANKS

The New York Yankees received a major scare when defending American League home run champion Babe Ruth collapsed in a Hot Springs, Ark., hotel lobby and was confined to bed with a mild attack of influenza.

Ruth went down in the lobby of the Hotel Majestic and had to be assisted to his room where he was treated by a doctor. The diagnosis was clean – a case of the flu – but the physician warned it could develop complications, such as pneumonia, if not handled with care.

Ruth is coming off an outstanding season in which he hit .394, belted 41 homers and drove in 131 runs. He is the most dynamic and popular player in the game and news of his health problem was greeted with great concern, both by the Yankees and his legions of fans.

But the attending doctor said his progress is being monitored closely and he should be fine with complete rest and a few precautionary steps to see that symptoms of the illness do not reoccur.

MILESTONES · IN SPORTS ·

1934

Heavyweight champion Primo Carnera defended his crown with a unanimous 15-round decision over challenger Tommy Loughran at Miami, Fla.

1941

Elmer Layden, one of Notre Dame's legendary Four Horsemen, was named first commissioner of the National Football League.

1969

New York Yankee center fielder Mickey Mantle ended his outstanding 18-year baseball career with a .298 batting average and 536 home runs at age 37.

1983

Tamara McKinney became the first American woman and the second American overall to win a World Cup overall Alpine skiing championship.

1990

The NFL, as a result of a $950 million deal with ABC-TV, expanded its playoff field to 12 teams with the addition of two wild-card games.

MARCH 1

1949 Joe Louis Finishes Championship Reign

Joe Louis *ended his heavyweight-championship reign just short of 12 years.*

Joe Louis, who held the world heavyweight championship longer than any man in history and successfully defended it an amazing 25 times, relinquished the crown with the announcement of his retirement in a letter to National Boxing Association Commissioner Abe J. Greene.

Louis, the first heavyweight champion to retire undefeated since Gene Tunney in 1928, held the crown for 11 years, 8 months and 1 week after knocking out James J. Braddock in the eighth round of a fight on June 22, 1937, at Chicago. His latest title defense, last June at New York's Yankee Stadium, produced an 11th-round knockout of Jersey Joe Walcott.

In between, the Brown Bomber fought all comers and never gave an inch. His only professional loss was to former champion Max Schmeling, a slight he later avenged with a first-round knockout.

Louis also announced his plans to go into the promotional side of boxing. In a second note to Greene, Louis requested permission to stage a heavyweight bout next June at Chicago Stadium between top contenders Ezzard Charles and Walcott for the vacated title. Greene gave Louis the go-ahead.

1973 Robyn Smith Rides High

Robyn Smith, looking to become the first female jockey to ride a winner in stakes competition at a major United States track, guided North Sea to a four-length victory in the $27,450 Paumonok on the opening day of racing at New York's Aqueduct Park. Smith guided her 4-year-old colt over the six-furlong Aqueduct course in 1:09 3/5, overcoming second-place Onion and pre-race favorite Nose for Money. Alfred Gwynne Vanderbilt's North Sea, like his 117-pound jockey, went off as a long shot.

Smith expressed thanks to Vanderbilt "for giving me the chance to ride. He told me that he was scared that I'd win my first stakes riding for somebody else, and I'm glad that I was able to do it for him."

Smith shared hugs in the winner's circle with Vanderbilt and North Sea trainer Bobby Lake.

A STAR IS BORN

1926: Pete Rozelle, a football Hall of Fame executive who guided the NFL to great heights as commissioner from 1960 to 1989 – a period that included expansion from 12 to 28 teams, a merger with the AFL and creation of the Super Bowl.

★ ★ ★

1961: Mike Rozier, a 1983 Heisman Trophy-winning running back for Nebraska and former professional football star.

★ ★ ★

DEATH OF A LEGEND

1963: Irish Meusel (baseball).

★ ★ ★

1988 Gretzky Sets Assist Record

Wayne Gretzky's feed to teammate Jari Kurri produced a first-period goal that vaulted him past former great Gordie Howe on the all-time assist list and sparked the Edmonton Oilers to a 5–3 National Hockey League victory over the Los Angeles Kings at Edmonton.

Gretzky's record-setting assist, No. 1,050, came in the 681st game of his amazing nine-year career. The great Howe needed 26 seasons and 1,767 games to amass 1,049. Gretzky is just 27 years old.

Gretzky, who already owns most of the NHL's offensive records and will produce many more before he is finished, passed from the side of the net to Kurri at 12:44 of the first period. The winger flipped the puck past Kings goalie Roland Melanson. Teammate Esa Tikkanen went on to claim honors with a three-assist game.

MARCH

2

MILESTONES

IN SPORTS

1966

Left wing Bobby Hull became the NHL's first two-time 50-goal scorer when he reached the plateau in the third period of a 5–4 Blackhawks victory over Detroit at Chicago Stadium.

1970

LSU's Pistol Pete Maravich broke former Houston star Elvin Hayes' one-season scoring record when he fired in 55 points in a 97–87 victory over Mississippi State and brought his season point total to 1,263.

1980

Spectacular Bid became horse racing's second $2 million winner when Bill Shoemaker rode him to victory in the $350,000 Santa Anita Handicap.

1980

American Olympic sensation Eric Heiden failed in his bid to win a fourth straight world speed skating championship when he finished second to Dutch skater Hilbert van der Duim at Heerenveen, The Netherlands.

1989

Detroit Red Wings forward Bob Probert was arrested by customs officials on the American side of the Windsor-Detroit Tunnel when he allegedly tried to smuggle cocaine across the Canadian-U.S. border.

1993

Winnipeg's sensational Teemu Selanne broke Mike Bossy's rookie goal-scoring record when he brought his season total to 54 with a hat trick in the Jets' 7–4 loss to Quebec.

1962

WILT POSTS 100 POINTS

Philadelphia scoring machine Wilt Chamberlain, in a one-for-the-books performance that could stand forever, connected on 36 field goals and 28 free throws for 100 points in the Warriors' 169–147 victory over the New York Knickerbockers before 4,124 fans at Hershey, Pa.

Not only did the 7-foot-1 giant shatter his own National Basketball Association one-game scoring record, he did it by an incredible 22 points. Using his patented fall-away jumper and dominating in close, Chamberlain made 36 of 63 field-goal attempts and complemented that effort with an uncharacteristic 28-of-32 performance from the line.

Chamberlain, who also grabbed 25 rebounds, topped his own single-game record of 78 points – a mark set earlier this season. He matched the 100-point college scoring record of Furman's Frank Selvy against Newberry in 1954. With the hot Chamberlain scoring at will, the Warriors jumped to a 19–3 lead and never looked back. Richie Guerin (39 points), Cleveland Buckner (33) and Willie Naulls (31) had big games for New York, but their efforts were lost in Wilt's large shadow. Al Attles was Philadelphia's second-high scorer with 17.

A STAR IS BORN

1896: Clair Bee, a former college and professional basketball coach who is credited with inventing the 1–3–1 zone defense and proposing two important innovations: the 3-second rule and the 24-second clock.

★ ★ ★

1909: Mel Ott, a baseball Hall of Fame outfielder who batted .304 and hit 511 home runs over his outstanding 22-year career with the New York Giants.

★ ★ ★

1965: Ron Gant, a current major league outfielder.

★ ★ ★

DEATH OF A LEGEND

1962: Walt Kiesling (football).

1951

NBA'S STARS SHINE BRIGHT

Boston's **Ed Macauley** *dazzled the hometown fans in the inaugural NBA All-Star Game.*

Boston's Ed Macauley scored a game-high 20 points and held big George Mikan to 4-of-17 shooting from the field as the East team scored an easy 111–94 victory over the West in the National Basketball Association's inaugural All-Star Game at Boston Garden.

Macauley hit 7 of 12 field-goal attempts and 6 of 7 free throws, but his biggest contribution might have been limiting the 6-foot-11 Mikan, Minneapolis' star center, to 12 points. With Macauley and Philadelphia's Joe Fulks (19 points) leading the charge, the East broke to a 31–22 first-quarter lead, extended it to 53–42 by halftime and coasted the rest of the way.

The All-Star contest, a brainstorm of NBA publicist Haskell Cohen and Boston Celtics founder Walter Brown, drew 10,094 enthusiastic fans. It will become an annual affair, in the tradition of baseball's All-Star Game.

Joe Lapchick (New York) coached the East and John Kundla (Minneapolis) the West while Indianapolis' Alex Groza led the losers with 17 points.

1969

ESPOSITO REACHES PLATEAU

Boston's **Phil Esposito,** *hockey's first 100-point man.*

Boston center Phil Esposito scored a pair of third-period goals in the Bruins' 4–0 victory over Pittsburgh and became the first National Hockey League player to reach the 100-point plateau in a single season.

Esposito, who had set the NHL's one-season scoring record the night before when he registered his 98th and 99th points, sent a capacity Boston Garden crowd of 14,659 into delirium when he beat Penguins' goaltender Joe Daley 17 seconds into the final period, extending Boston's advantage to 2–0.

The game was interrupted for 15 minutes as the fans showered the ice with hats and other debris. When Esposito scored again at 6:41, the arena shook and play was delayed for another five minutes.

The goals were the 39th and 40th of the season for the talented center, who scored 35 goals and 84 points last year. Chicago star Bobby Hull held the previous one-season record of 97 points, set in 1965–66.

1977 FRATIANNE SURVIVES

Linda Fratianne, a 16-year-old Californian with a bulldog mentality, got up after a fall in her free-style program and dazzled the judges with her grace and technical execution en route to the women's world figure skating championship at Tokyo.

Fratianne went down while attempting a triple salchow jump midway through her final-day program. But she quickly got to her feet and went right into a triple toe loop that dazzled the crowd. She was in top form the rest of the way.

Eight of the nine judges gave Fratianne first-place votes as she received 10 ordinals for 189.26 points. East Germany's Anett Poetzsch finished second with 185.18 points and West Germany's Dagmar Lurz took third at 182.48.

Fratianne's victory follows on the heels of Dorothy Hamill's triumph in 1976. The last American winner before Hamill was Peggy Fleming in 1968.

American **Linda Fratianne,** *the world figure skating champion.*

MARCH

3

A STAR IS BORN

1912: Joe Stydahar, a Hall of Fame two-way tackle who helped the Chicago Bears win three NFL championships from 1936 to '46.

★ ★ ★

1920: Julius Boros, an outstanding professional golfer who won two U.S. Open titles and one PGA Championship in the 1950s and '60s.

★ ★ ★

1962: Jackie Joyner-Kersee, one of the greatest women athletes of all time. Joyner-Kersee, a world-class long jumper, won Olympic heptathlon gold medals in 1988 and '92 and a silver in 1984.

★ ★ ★

1962: Herschel Walker, a current National Football League running back.

★ ★ ★

MILESTONES • IN SPORTS •

1920

In the biggest one-team goal-scoring explosion in NHL history, the Montreal Canadiens skated to a 16–3 victory over the Quebec Bulldogs.

1951

Temple's Bill Mlkvy fired in 73 points, the third-highest one-game total in NCAA basketball history, as the Owls pounded Wilkes College, 99–69.

1968

Jean Beliveau became the NHL's second 1,000-point man when he scored a goal in Montreal's 5–2 loss at Detroit.

1977

An American first: Phil Mahre recorded his second consecutive victory in a World Cup giant slalom competition at Stratton, Vt.

1985

Bill Shoemaker became the first jockey to reach $100 million in career purses when he rode Lord at War to victory in the Santa Anita Handicap at Arcadia, Calif.

1975 LARRIEU WORKS DOUBLE TIME

Francie Larrieu, the 22-year-old distance queen from California, broke women's world records for the mile and 1,500 meters in the same race as she sparked the United States to a lopsided victory in the annual U.S. – Soviet Union indoor track and field meet at Richmond, Va. Larrieu, who was turned down in her request to also qualify for the 2-mile event, broke her own indoor mile mark when she ran a 4:28.5, setting a 1,500-meter mark of 4:09.8 in the process.

The UCLA junior ran her first quarter in 65 seconds, the half-mile in 2:12.9 and three-quarters in 3:20. When she crossed the finish line well ahead of the pack, she was greeted by a standing ovation.

Larrieu's effort helped the American women pull away for a 73–44 victory over their Russian counterparts. The U.S. men won, 98–62, giving the Americans a 171–106 overall victory. But the final results were tarnished by the knowledge that many of the top Soviet competitors had remained home to prepare for the upcoming European indoor championships. American men finished 1–2 in 13 events.

Larrieu had originally broken the record a month earlier in San Diego.

1984 OWNERS SELECT UEBERROTH

Major league baseball's 26 owners, ending a 16-month search for a more business-minded successor to Bowie Kuhn, elected Peter V. Ueberroth as the game's sixth commissioner, subject to completion of his work as president of the Los Angeles Olympic Organizing Committee.

Kuhn, who has held the job for 15 years, will continue in his lame-duck role until October 1 when Ueberroth becomes free of his Olympics commitment and begins his five-year term. Kuhn was blocked from re-election by five National League owners in November 1982 and has delayed his departure three times since his term officially ended last August.

Ueberroth is a 46-year-old Californian with a business background. Much of the dissatisfaction with Kuhn stemmed from his lack of business expertise in a period of financial transition. Ueberroth is well known for turning a small travel agency into a $300 million business.

Ueberroth had insisted he would not take the job unless changes, including the controversial re-election procedure that deposed Kuhn, were made in the bylaws. Now a simple majority in each league is needed rather than a three-fourths majority.

MARCH

4

A STAR IS BORN

1888: Knute Rockne, the outstanding college football coach who guided Notre Dame to consensus national championships in 1924, '29 and '30 and 105 victories in 13 seasons.

★ ★ ★

1891: Dazzy Vance, a Hall of Fame righthander who compiled a 197–140 record in a 16-year career that ended in 1935.

★ ★ ★

1966: Kevin Johnson, a current National Basketball Association guard.

★ ★ ★

DEATH OF A LEGEND

1860: John Montgomery Ward (baseball).

★ ★ ★

1990: Hank Gathers (basketball).

1990 College Star Gathers Dies

Loyola Marymount star Hank Gathers, who pulled a rare college basketball double last season when he led the nation in both scoring and rebounding, collapsed during a West Coast Conference tournament game against Portland and died nearly two hours later at a Los Angeles hospital.

The 23-year-old Gathers, a 6-foot-7, 210-pound center with a 28.8-point average this season, scored on a dunk midway through the opening half against Portland, ran toward midcourt and suddenly collapsed. Gathers appeared to suffer convulsions as a hushed crowd at Gersten Pavilion looked on.

He was rushed to the hospital and died an hour and 41 minutes later of unknown causes. But doctors suggested his death could have been related to a heart arrythmia condition that was being treated with medication.

Gathers, who recorded nation-leading averages of 32.7 points and 13.7 rebounds last year as a junior, had collapsed in the second half of a December game against California-Santa Barbara. He underwent several days of tests and was diagnosed as having an irregular heartbeat. Gathers, a Philadelphia native, began taking medication and was cleared to play basketball.

Loyola Marymount basketball star **Hank Gathers.**

1968 Frazier Stops Buster Mathis

Smokin' Joe Frazier, staking a strong claim to Muhammad Ali's vacated heavyweight crown, battered and bruised big Buster Mathis for 10 rounds before finally knocking him out in a bloody battle at New York's Madison Square Garden.

Most of the blood belonged to Mathis, who took a savage right to the chin and left hook to the temple that knocked him through the ropes and onto the ring apron at 2:33 of the 11th round. Mathis, bleeding profusely from his nose, struggled valiantly to get to his feet but was mercifully counted out.

Frazier, unbeaten in 20 professional fights with 18 knockouts, was aggressive from the opening bell, battering the 243-pounder who had scored two victories over him as an amateur. By the end, Mathis' white nylon trunks were splattered with blood and he was serving as nothing more than a human punching bag.

The victory put Frazier in position to claim the crown that was stripped from Ali because of his conviction for draft evasion. Frazier is the recognized undisputed champion in New York, Massachusetts and Illinois.

1962 Chamberlain Does It Again

What can you do for an encore after wiping away virtually every National Basketball Association single-game scoring record with a 100-point salvo that was borderline unbelievable? Plenty, if you're Wilt Chamberlain.

The 7-foot-1 Philadelphia center tailed off to 58 points in his return engagement against the New York Knicks, but in topping the 50-point plateau for a fifth consecutive game he stretched his season total to 3,921 – an NBA record. With three games remaining, Chamberlain would need to average just over 26 points to become the NBA's first 4,000-point man.

Chamberlain, who carries a 50-point average, connected on 24 field goals and 10 free throws in the Warriors' 129–128 victory at Madison Square Garden. Ironically, the game was decided by a Chamberlain pass that resulted in Paul Arizin's field goal with 30 seconds remaining.

Chamberlain, who had hit the century mark two days earlier against the Knicks in a game at Hershey, Pa., single-handedly offset the offensive heroics of New Yorkers Willie Naulls (39 points) and Richie Guerin (31).

MILESTONES IN SPORTS

1970

Ismael Laguna of Panama regained the world lightweight boxing title when he scored a ninth-round technical knockout of Mando Ramos at LA.

1972

Argentina's Carlos Monzon defended his world middleweight boxing title with a fifth-round technical knockout of American Denny Moyer in Rome.

1973

Chris Evert recorded her first victory as a professional, defeating England's Virginia Wade in the S & H Green Stamps event at her home town of Fort Lauderdale, Fla.

1981 HAMILTON ARRIVES

Scott Hamilton, a diminutive American with a flair for theatrics, electrified 14,600 fans at the Hartford Civic Arena with a pulsating free-skate performance that vaulted him from third place after the original program to the world figure skating championship.

The 5-foot-3 Hamilton, the next-to-last skater on the card, captured the

World champion **Scott Hamilton.**

hearts of the judges and crowd with five minutes of feverish twists and jumps that moved him past fellow American David Santee in the gold-medal chase. Santee, who had to follow Hamilton on the ice, settled for second place, giving the U.S. a rare 1–2 finish.

The 22-year-old Hamilton, the second American man to win a championship since 1970, was nearly perfect in his execution. The judges ignored one minor slip and awarded him a series of 5.8s and 5.9s, a level above the marks received by Santee. Hamilton's performance was so inspiring that the crowd rewarded him with an emotional standing ovation – even before he had completed his routine.

1971 BUCKS SET WIN RECORD

Lew Alcindor scored 34 points and Oscar Robertson directed Milwaukee's offense with flawless efficiency as the Bucks set a National Basketball Association record with their 19th consecutive victory – a 108–95 triumph over the Pistons at Detroit's Cobo Arena.

The Bucks were all business as they stepped onto the floor and raced to a 23–6 lead. They held a 31–18 advantage after a quarter and led 55–42 at halftime before the Pistons fought their way back into the game.

With Dave Bing scoring 14 of his 39 points in the third quarter, Detroit pulled to within 77–74. But Alcindor resumed his domination inside, John McGlocklin fired away from the outside and the veteran Robertson controlled the game's tempo.

Milwaukee pulled away to its 64th season victory – the second most in NBA history.

The Bucks, who had put together an earlier 16-game winning streak, topped the consecutive-win mark set last season by the New York Knicks. McGlocklin supported Alcindor with 26 points while Robertson scored 18 and handed out 16 assists.

A STAR IS BORN

1921: Elmer Valo, a 20-year major league outfielder who batted .282 from 1940–61.

★ ★ ★

1947: Kent Tekulve, an outstanding major league relief pitcher who appeared in a National League-record 1,050 games and recorded 184 saves over a 16-year career that ended in 1989.

★ ★ ★

1966: Michael Irvin, a current National Football League wide receiver.

1922 BABE RUTH CALLS 'TAILS', WINS CONTRACT SQUABBLE

Babe Ruth, *the New York Yankees 'coin-flip' contract winner.*

Babe Ruth correctly called "tails" and New York Yankee Owners Jacob Ruppert and Colonel Tillinghast Huston paid the price – a three-year contract that easily made the Sultan of Swat baseball's highest-paid player.

Ruth and Huston had reached an impasse during their marathon negotiating session at Hot Springs, Ark., so the game's premier slugger offered a solution – a coin flip to decide between the Yankees' best offer and Ruth's demand. Huston liked the idea, contacted Ruppert in New York for approval and met with his star outfielder for the final resolution.

Huston flipped a half dollar and Ruth made the winning call. Ruth, who will sit out the first six weeks of the 1922 season under a suspension from Commissioner Kenesaw Mountain Landis for participating in an unauthorized barnstorming tour, will receive more than $50,000 per season – about $10,000 more than he made last year when he blasted 59 home runs. He also reportedly will earn $500 for every home run he hits, which could produce a significant total.

MARCH 5

MILESTONES • IN SPORTS •

1965

Ernie Terrell defended his WBA heavyweight championship with a unanimous 15-round decision over Eddie Machen at Chicago.

1966

Marvin Miller, a 48-year-old attorney, was elected as the first full-time executive director of baseball's Major League Players Association.

1975

Steve Shutt's two goals paced Montreal to a 4–3 victory over Atlanta – the Canadiens' NHL-record 21st consecutive victory on the road.

1976

Ron Turcotte became the sixth jockey in New York horse racing history to ride six winners in one day, accomplishing his feat at Aqueduct.

1977

The Mahre twins, Phil and Steve, both took home medals for their slalom performances in World Cup competition at Sun Valley, Idaho. Phil finished first, Steve third.

MARCH

6

1966 SEAGREN SOARS 17 FEET

Bob Seagren, a 19-year-old California college student, became the first athlete to pole vault 17 feet indoors when he cleared 17–0 1/4 in the National Amateur Athletic Union track and field championships at Albuquerque, N.M.

Seagren cleared the record-setting height on his second try and then missed three times at 17–4 1/2. He broke the indoor mark of 16–10 held by John Pennel, the first pole vaulter to clear the magical 17-foot barrier outdoors.

Ironically, Seagren and Pennel are close friends who share an apartment in Glendale, Calif. Both had cleared 16–6 in the AAU meet and were tied with Jeff Chase. Seagren cleared his 17-foot height while both Pennel and Chase faltered.

"I hurried all of my jumps – it was just so anticlimactic," Seagren said after his three misses at 17–4 1/2.

Bob Seagren, *the world's first 17-foot indoor pole vaulter.*

A STAR IS BORN

1898: Jimmy Conzelman, a Hall of Fame player and coach from the formative years of the National Football League.

★★★

1900: Lefty Grove, a Hall of Fame lefthander who won 300 games in a 17-year career from 1925–41 with the Philadelphia Athletics and Boston Red Sox.

★★★

1941: Willie Stargell, Pittsburgh's Hall of Fame outfielder who hit 475 home runs over a 21-year career that ended in 1982.

★★★

1947: Dick Fosbury, an Olympic gold medal-winning high jumper (1968) who introduced the back-first "Fosbury Flop" jumping technique.

★★★

1972: Shaquille O'Neal, a current National Basketball Association center.

★★★

DEATH OF A LEGEND

1943: Jimmy Collins (baseball).

★★★

1990: Joe Sewell (baseball).

1982 SPURS NEED 3 OVERTIMES, GERVIN'S 50

George Gervin scored 50 points, including eight straight in the third overtime, as the San Antonio Spurs held off Milwaukee, 171–166, in the highest-scoring game in National Basketball Association history.

The 337 points were an NBA record, far outdistancing the previous mark of 316 accomplished twice – both in regulation games. Amazingly, neither team led by more than six points at any time during the contest at San Antonio.

Brian Winters, who led the Bucks with 42 points, almost single-handedly wiped out San Antonio's late 124–118 advantage by scoring Milwaukee's last 13 points of regulation. His three-point play at the buzzer tied the game at 131–131.

The Bucks jumped to leads in the first two overtimes but the Spurs rallied to tie at 145 and 157. With Gervin taking charge in the finale, San Antonio pulled ahead, 165–161, and the Bucks were unable to close the gap.

Gervin got plenty of scoring support from Mike Mitchell, who added 45. Winters hit 13 straight field goals during one stretch of the game.

San Antonio sharpshooter **George Gervin.**

1976 HAMILL EARNS WORLD TITLE

Dorothy Hamill, the American darling of the recent Winter Olympic Games at Innsbruck, Austria, added a world figure skating championship to her growing list of accomplishments in the final act of her competitive career.

Hamill, the women's Olympic gold medalist, was close to perfection as she outdueled East Germany's Christine Errath in the world competition at Goteborg, Sweden. Hamill won both the short and long programs and brought the crowd to its feet with a rousing performance in the free-skate segment.

After flawlessly executing a program that included numerous double jumps, spins and her famous "Hamill Camel," the 19-year-old was rewarded with three near-perfect 5.9 scores for technical merit and a full string of 5.9s for artistic impression. Errath, performing a more difficult program, had 5.9s for her technical execution, 5.8s for artistic impression.

Hamill, who had announced that the world competition would be her last, is the first American to win the prestigious title in eight years.

MILESTONES IN SPORTS

1920

Mickey Roach of the Toronto St. Patricks became the seventh NHL player to score five goals in a game during an 11–2 victory over Quebec.

1983

The 12-team United States Football League kicked off its first professional season with games in five U.S. cities.

1984

Winnipeg's Dale Hawerchuk made NHL history when he earned five assists in the second period of the Jets' 7–3 victory over Los Angeles.

1988

Julie Krone earned her female-record 1,205th career victory aboard Squawter in the ninth race at Aqueduct.

1990

Jennifer Capriati, a 13-year-old tennis phenom playing in her first professional match, defeated 28-year-old Mary Lou Daniels, 7–6, 6–1, at Boca Raton, Fla.

A STAR IS BORN

1950: Franco Harris, an eight-time 1,000-yard rusher who finished his 13-year NFL career with 12,120. Harris helped the Pittsburgh Steelers win four Super Bowl titles in the 1970s.

★ ★ ★

1960: Ivan Lendl, a professional tennis star who finished 1992 with eight major championships and 91 overall titles to his credit .

★ ★ ★

1960: Joe Carter, a current major league outfielder.

★ ★ ★

1970: Teemu Selanne, a current National Hockey League right winger.

★ ★ ★

DEATH OF A LEGEND

1902: Pud Galvin (baseball)

MILESTONES • IN SPORTS •

1921

Ottawa's Cy Denneny became the fifth NHL player to score six goals in a game when he blistered Hamilton during a 12–5 Senators victory.

1924

Cincinnati Manager Pat Moran, with the Reds in Orlando, Fla., for spring training, died in a local hospital of Bright's disease at age 48.

1951

Ezzard Charles, defending his heavyweight championship for the seventh time, scored a unanimous decision over Jersey Joe Walcott at Detroit.

1974

A nine-member New Orleans group agreed to pay $6.5 million for the right to form the NBA's 18th franchise.

1989

Calgary's Lanny McDonald became the NHL's newest 1,000-point man when he scored a goal in the Flames' 9–5 victory over Winnipeg.

MARCH 7

1970 NOTRE DAME CRUISES AS CARR SCORES 61

Notre Dame Coach Johnny Dee and NCAA Tournament record-setter **Austin Carr.**

Notre Dame sharpshooter Austin Carr shattered the NCAA Tournament single-game scoring record when he poured in 61 points and led the Fighting Irish to a 112–82 first-round Mideast Regional basketball victory over Ohio University at Dayton, O.

Carr befuddled four different Ohio defenders as he connected on a record 25 of 44 shots from the field and 11 of 14 from the free throw line. He hit from 35 feet and he scored in close as he brought his season point total to 1,009 and led the Irish to their 21st victory in 27 games.

The Bobcats, who finished at 20–5, stayed close through most of the first half, but Notre Dame pulled away with a 14–2 burst in a four-minute stretch just before intermission. Carr, who got a 24-point assist from teammate Collis Jones, scored 35 of Notre Dame's 54 first-half points.

The 6-foot-3 junior broke the NCAA scoring record held by Princeton's Bill Bradley since 1965. Bradley poured in 58 points in a contest against Wichita State.

1983 MAHRE TRIPLES HIS PLEASURE

Phil Mahre, the only American ever to win an Alpine skiing World Cup overall championship, clinched his third straight title with a victory over Sweden's Ingemar Stenmark in the giant slalom at Aspen, Colo.

Mahre gained 25 World Cup points and brought his season total to 250, 47 more than the second-place Stenmark. With Stenmark refusing to compete in next week's downhill competition at Lake Louise in Canada, nobody can catch Mahre.

The American champion raced through the 52-gate course in 1:15.89 on his second run, giving him a sparkling two-run total of 2:31.49. Stenmark, badly needing a victory, could do no better than 2:32.09, good for third place behind Luxembourg's Marc Girardelli (2:31.65). Mahre led Stenmark by 13-hundredths of a second after the first run.

"That's it. I won it," Mahre exalted after the competition. "Everything just came together today. The first run wasn't quite as good as the second. But I concentrated very well and put everything together all the way down the mountain."

1987 TYSON, HEARNS WIN

Mike Tyson brought the WBC and WBA heavyweight titles under one umbrella with a unanimous 12-round decision over James (Bonecrusher) Smith and Thomas Hearns captured his third world title with a 10th-round knockout of light heavyweight Dennis Andries in championship bouts at Las Vegas and Detroit.

Tyson, already the WBC champion, took away Smith's WBA title with a convincing victory that raised his professional record to 29-0. The 20-year-old slugger, looking for his 26th knockout, was thwarted by the 33-year-old Smith's rush-and-grab tactics that kept him on his feet but never really allowed him to be a factor in the fight.

Andries was not so fortunate. Hearns knocked down the champion six times before ending the fight at 1:26 of the 10th round. Andries went down four times in the sixth and once in the ninth.

The 28-year-old Hearns, a former welterweight and super-welterweight champion, is the 12th boxer to win titles in three classes. Wilfredo Gomez was the last to do it in 1985. Hearns is 44–2 with 37 knockouts.

Andries, a 31-year-old Guyana native, was making his second defense of the title he won in April 1986.

MARCH

8

1937

Hockey Great Morenz Dies

Howie Morenz, a Canadian folk hero generally accepted as the greatest player in National Hockey League history, collapsed and died in a Montreal hospital where he was recovering from a leg injury he had suffered six weeks earlier during a game. He was 34.

The colorful and talented Morenz was the biggest gate attraction during the formative years of a league that was badly in need of stars.

A speedy center who began his career in 1923–24 with Montreal, Morenz was known for his lightning rushes and a hard shot that made him one of the top scorers in the NHL.

For 14 seasons, all but two with the Canadiens, he terrorized goaltenders, scoring 270 goals and 467 points while leading the Canadiens to three Stanley Cup championships. Little No. 7 was a two-time league scoring champion and three-time winner of the Hart Trophy.

Morenz's career came to a sudden end on January 28 when he was checked into the boards during a game against the Chicago Blackhawks, fracturing his left leg and ankle. He still was recovering from those injuries at the hospital when he suffered a heart attack and died.

1971

Frazier Shocks Ali In 15-Round Classic

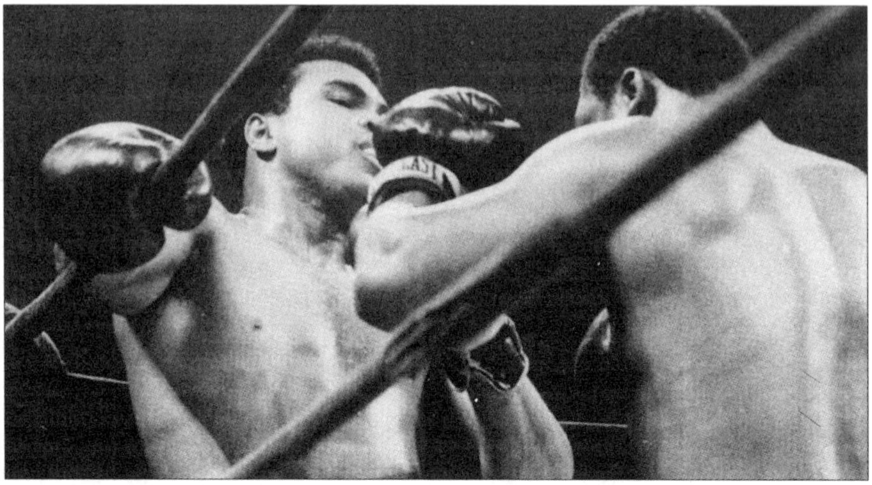

Joe Frazier *delivers a hard left to the head of Muhammad Ali on his way to a unanimous 15-round decision and the heavyweight championship.*

In a classic battle at Madison Square Garden, Joe Frazier retained his heavyweight crown with a unanimous 15-round decision over undefeated Muhammad Ali, the man who had preceded him on the championship throne.

The 27-year-old Frazier, who had earned the title with a series of victories after it had been stripped from Ali in 1967, settled the heavyweight controversy by unleashing a savage attack to the body from the opening bell and flooring his 29-year-old opponent with a wild left hook in the 15th round – the third knockdown of the former champ's career.

The buildup for this fight was enormous and the television audience, estimated at 300 million, was not disappointed. Ali clowned and taunted periodically in the early rounds, Frazier mocked Ali in the middle of the fight after he had taken control.

By the end, the relentless Frazier was the stronger, more dangerous fighter and Ali's butterfly wings had been clipped. After the decision had been announced, Ali was taken to the hospital for X-rays of his swollen jaw.

The loss was Ali's first in 31 professional fights. Frazier is 27–0 with 23 knockouts.

A STAR IS BORN

1938: Pete Dawkins, a former Army running back who won the 1958 Heisman Trophy.

★ ★ ★

1942: Dick Allen, a sometimes-controversial major leaguer who belted 351 home runs over a 15-year career that ended in 1977.

★ ★ ★

1953: Jim Rice, a former Boston outfielder who batted .298, hit 382 homers and drove in 1,451 runs over a 16-year career that ended in 1989.

DEATH OF A LEGEND

1937: Howie Morenz (hockey).

★ ★ ★

1991: James (Cool Papa) Bell (baseball).

MILESTONES IN SPORTS

1930

Money, money, money: New York Yankee star Babe Ruth signed his contract for an incredible two-year figure of $160,000.

1975

Martina Navratilova, an 18-year-old defector from Czechoslovakia, defeated Australian Evonne Goolagong for the first time in seven matches, 6–2, 4–6, 6–3, and captured the national indoor tennis championship at Boston.

1981

Tom Kite birdied two of the last three holes and claimed an exciting one-stroke victory over Jack Nicklaus in the Inverrary Classic at Lauderhill, Fla.

1982

Tom Kite sank a 20-foot birdie chip shot on the first hole of a sudden-death playoff and handed Jack Nicklaus and Denis Watson a stunning defeat in the Bay Hill Classic at Orlando, Fla.

1991

Dale Hawerchuk scored a goal in Buffalo's 5–3 loss to Chicago, becoming the 31st NHL player to reach 1,000 points.

1958

Silky Sullivan Rallies Again

Silky Sullivan, displaying the same burst of speed that had gained him national attention in his earlier prep races, came from 20 lengths back and scored a three-length victory over Harcall in the $130,500 Santa Anita Derby in Arcadia, Calif.

Silky Sullivan, with Bill Shoemaker in saddle, turned on the jets as he rounded the final turn and literally blew past the other nine 3-year-olds as a record crowd of 63,000 roared its approval. He finished with a brilliant final-quarter time of 24 2/5 seconds en route to a 1:49 2/5 clocking.

Silky Sullivan had displayed the same closing burst in earlier races, almost winning one in which he fell behind by 35 lengths. Shoemaker, riding Silky Sullivan for the first time, kept him closer than that in this race and the colt responded.

As the pack hit the homestretch, Silky Sullivan passed quickly and set his sights on Aliwar, the late leader. He pulled even on the outside and drew away without too much effort.

1971 THE BUCKS STOP HERE

Bob Weiss scored six points in overtime and the Chicago Bulls brought down the curtain on Milwaukee's National Basketball Association-record 20-game winning streak with a 110–103 victory at Chicago Stadium.

Proving once and for all that the Bucks really are human, the Bulls played them to a 99–99 standstill through regulation and then outscored them, 11–4, in the extra session.

Weiss scored the first four points of the overtime period and Chet Walker added a basket before the Bucks could score. Another two-pointer by Weiss and an aggressive Chicago defense sealed the verdict.

The Bucks, who started their streak February 6, lost for the first time in more than a month despite the 39-point effort of center Lew Alcindor. Bob Love led Chicago with 23 points while Jerry Sloan and Tom Boerwinkle chipped in with 21 apiece.

The previous longest NBA winning streak, 18 games, was put together by the New York Knicks in the 1969–70 season.

The Bulls and guard **Bob Weiss** *brought an end to Milwaukee's NBA-record 20-game winning streak.*

1935 BUCKEYES' OWENS STREAKS TO RECORD

Ohio State record-setter and Olympic sprinter **Jesse Owens.**

Ohio State sprinter Jesse Owens, fighting off strong challenges from two Michigan runners, won the 60-yard dash in a world-record 6.1 seconds in the 25th annual Western Conference track and field meet at Chicago.

Owens, known as the Buckeyes' Black Comet, shot out of the starting blocks like a flash but could not shake Wolverines Sam Stoller and Willis Ward, the event's defending champion. His spectacular closing burst gave him a final one-yard advantage over Stoller, who barely edged his teammate for second.

Owens, who doubles as a world-class long jumper, smashed the 12-year-old record of Loren Murchison by a tenth of a second. Murchison's mark had been tied six times.

Despite Owens' heroics, the Buckeyes could do no better than finish a distant second to Michigan. The Wolverines retained their team title with a meet-record 49 1/2 points, 27 better than Ohio State.

1974 WALDROP EXTENDS AMAZING STREAK

North Carolina senior Tony Waldrop ran his amazing streak of sub-four-minute indoor mile victories to seven with a 3:59.5 clocking in the National Collegiate championships at Detroit.

The 22-year-old Waldrop, who has finished under four minutes in every indoor race he has run since January 19, outsprinted Illinois star Mike Durkin over the final two laps and barely finished the 11-lap race under the once-sacred barrier. A slow pace kept Waldrop from seriously challenging his indoor world-record time of 3:55.

Waldrop, who needed a 55-second final quarter to keep his streak intact, easily pulled away from Durkin, who finished second with a time of 4:01.2. Brigham Young's Paul Cummings was third at 4:02.5.

To show how dominant Waldrop has been, the previous best string of sub-four-minute indoor performances, turned in by Tom O'Hara in 1964, was three. Jim Ryun did it in consecutive races in 1967.

MARCH 9

MILESTONES IN SPORTS

1948

NHL President Clarence Campbell, making his stance on gambling perfectly clear, issued lifetime suspensions to the New York Rangers' Billy Taylor and Boston's Don Gallinger for betting on games.

1958

Detroit forward George Yardley became the first NBA player to score 2,000 points in one season, finishing with a 27.8 average.

1977

Oral Roberts dropped a 90–89 decision to Oregon in the opening round of the NIT, but Anthony Roberts finished with a tournament-record 65 points.

1984

Tim Witherspoon captured the WBC heavyweight championship with a 12-round majority decision over Greg Page at Las Vegas.

1986

Gilbert Perreault highlighted Buffalo's 4–3 victory over New Jersey with milestone goal No. 500.

A STAR IS BORN

1912: Arky Vaughan, a Hall of Fame shortstop who compiled a .318 average over a 14-year career that ended in 1949.

★ ★ ★

1964: Phil Housley, a current National Hockey League defenseman.

★ ★ ★

1965: Benito Santiago, a current major league catcher.

MARCH 10

A STAR IS BORN

1938: Ron Mix, a Hall of Fame offensive tackle from 1960–71 for teams in the AFL and NFL.

★ ★ ★

1946: Curley Culp, an outstanding defensive tackle over a 14-year NFL career that ended in 1981.

★ ★ ★

DEATH OF A LEGEND

1985: Bob Nieman (baseball)

1962 BUDD EQUALS RECORD TWICE

Villanova senior Frank Budd matched the 60-yard dash world-record time of 6 seconds in the IC 4-A indoor track and field championships at New York's Madison Square Garden – and he did it twice.

Budd, a chunky 22-year-old New Jersey native, rocketed to his record-tying victory in an afternoon quarterfinal heat, matching the mark set by Herb Carper in 1960 and equaled three times by Roscoe Cook. Two timers caught him at 0:06 and a third at 0:06.1. In cases where the official times vary, majority rules.

Four hours later and with 11,972 fans now watching his effort, Budd streaked to a victory in the 60-yard dash final and again matched the record. This time two of the official stopwatches clocked him at 0.06 and a third recorded him at 0.05.9.

1974 BOBBY WINS UNSER DUEL

Bobby Unser zoomed across the finish line 58-hundredths of a second ahead of brother Al and captured the California 500 in the closest 500-mile race in the history of the United States Auto Club.

Bobby *(above) nipped brother* **Al** *in an all-Unser conclusion to the California 500 stock car classic.*

Bobby averaged 157.017 mph in winning the battle of Eagles and earning his second career 500-mile victory. Bobby had won the Indianapolis 500 in 1968 while Al, the younger and more successful of the brothers, had won at Indy in both 1970 and '71.

After pre-race favorite A.J. Foyt was sidelined by car trouble on the 23rd lap, the race belonged to the Unsers. Either Bobby or Al, part of a racing family that included their father, two uncles and another brother, led every lap after the 89th. Thirty-nine laps were run under a yellow caution flag.

Al enjoyed a 7.1-second lead after 162 of the 200 laps, but Bobby chipped away and finally passed him on the backstretch of lap 171. Bobby stretched his lead to 1.8 seconds with two remaining, but Al's final-lap burst threw a scare into his brother and set the stage for a record-setting finish.

MILESTONES IN SPORTS

1909

Recently crowned heavyweight boxing champion Jack Johnson fought to a six-round no-decision against unheralded Victor McLaglen at Vancouver.

1913

The Quebec Bulldogs completed their quick-and-easy two-game sweep of the Sydney Millionaries in a battle for hockey's coveted Stanley Cup.

1970

The Detroit Pistons posted a 115–112 victory over Boston, eliminating the defending NBA-champion Celtics from playoff contention for the first time in 20 years.

1971

Boston's Phil Esposito tied Bobby Hull's one-season goal-scoring record when he notched No. 58 in the Bruins' 8–1 victory over California at Oakland.

1980

Sweden's Ingemar Stenmark captured the special-slalom event at Cortina D'Ampezzo, Italy – his eighth World Cup victory of the season and 48th overall.

1985

Dick Motta became the fourth NBA coach to record 700 career victories when his Dallas Mavericks defeated the New Jersey Nets, 126–113.

1993

It's official: Minnesota North Stars Owner Norman Green received NHL permission to move his team to Dallas for the 1993–94 season.

1967 DAVE PATRICK UPSETS RYUN

In a surprising conclusion to the indoor track and field season, Villanova's Dave Patrick outdueled distance king Jim Ryun and set a world indoor half-mile record of 1:48.9 in the National Collegiate championships at Detroit.

Patrick finished 12 yards ahead of his 19-year-old opponent, who holds world records at five distances. Knowing Ryun's reputation as a late-race sprinter, Patrick pulled off his upset by setting a torrid pace and pulling far enough ahead that Ryun couldn't catch him.

The strategy worked. Patrick led the six-man field by 10 yards after the second of $5^1/2$ laps as Ryun stayed back in the pack. He ran the quarter mile in 52.4 seconds and was 20 yards ahead with two laps to go. Ryun made his move with $1^1/2$ laps remaining, moving from fifth to third and then to second, giving everything he had. But all he could manage was a 1:50.7 finish, good for second place.

Patrick beat the 1:49 indoor mark posted by Tom Von Ruden three weeks earlier.

1971 Records Fall In Boston

Phil Esposito shattered three National Hockey League records and teammate Bobby Orr claimed two more as the high-scoring Boston Bruins rolled to a 7–2 victory over the Los Angeles Kings at Inglewood, Calif.

Esposito scored a pair of goals, bringing his record season total to 60 and his record point total to 128. He broke Bobby Hull's mark of 58 goals and his own mark of 126 points, both set two seasons ago. He also broke the record for most goals in a season including playoffs (59), set by Montreal's Jean Beliveau in 1955–56.

But the talented Boston center was not alone on the record chase. Orr recorded three assists to raise his record one-season total to 88, one more than he managed last year, and his four points gave him 122, surpassing by two his 1969-70 record for a defenseman. Orr's 35th goal extended his own defenseman record to 35.

Esposito's record-breaker came at 7:03 of the opening period, after the Kings had taken a 1–0 lead, and his second came at 15:40 of the second period. Orr's record-breaking assist came at 6:11 of the final stanza.

A Star Is Born

1923: Louise Brough, an outstanding women's tennis player who won four Wimbledon singles titles and one United States singles championship in the1940s and '50s.

★ ★ ★

1959: Phil Bradley, a former outstanding college football quarterback at Missouri who went on to a major league baseball career in the 1980s.

★ ★ ★

Death Of A Legend

1972: Zach Wheat (baseball).

★ ★ ★

March 11

Milestones in Sports

1978

UCLA senior Mike Tully set a world amateur record of 18–5¼ during pole vault competition at the collegiate indoor track and field championships at Detroit's Cobo Arena.

1979

Upset specials in the second round of the NCAA Tournament's East Regional: St. John's 80, No. 2-seed Duke 78 and Pennsylvania 72, No. 1-seed North Carolina 71.

1983

American Rosalynn Sumners earned eight of nine first-place votes in the freestyle program and captured her first world figure skating championship at Helsinki, Finland.

1989

Switzerland's Vreni Schneider ended his World Cup season with a record 14 victories, two more than Sweden's Ingemar Stenmark managed in 1978.

1990

Scrappy center Denis Savard assisted on a goal for career point No. 1,000, but his Chicago Blackhawks dropped a 6–4 decision to the St. Louis Blues.

1993

Canadian Kurt Browning claimed his fourth men's figure skating title in five years at the world championship competition at Prague, Czechoslovakia.

1974 Kuhn Orders Aaron to Play

Commissioner Bowie Kuhn ordered Atlanta officials to revise their plan of having slugger Hank Aaron sit out the team's season-opening series at Cincinnati so he can resume his chase of Babe Ruth's career home run record at Fulton County Stadium in front of Braves fans.

Hank Aaron's *pursuit of Babe Ruth's all-time home run record came with many accessories, such as this special recording with words written by Detroit broadcaster Ernie Harwell (left).*

Kuhn, in his never-ending search for the "best interests of baseball," issued a statement virtually ordering the Braves to use Aaron in two games of the Cincinnati series, pointing out that the veteran outfielder had played in approximately two of every three games in 1973.

The controversy arose when the Braves announced they were thinking of using Aaron, who finished the 1973 season with 713 home runs, only as a pinch-hitter in Cincinnati. That would allow him, they reasoned, to go after record-tying homer No. 714 and record-breaker 715 in the upcoming homestand at Atlanta.

But Kuhn took issue with Atlanta chairman Bill Bartholomay, saying, "He has not been able to persuade me that the procedure he wishes to follow is good for baseball. As a result, I have advised him that I am disapproving the announcement and that, barring disability, I will expect to see the Braves use Henry Aaron in the opening series in Cincinnati. . . ."

1982 Hamilton Again

Scott Hamilton, executing seven triple jumps in a freeskate program that dazzled the judges, became the first American to win back-to-back world championships in 12 years when he scored a narrow victory at Copenhagen.

The championship came down to Hamilton's near-perfect technique versus the flamboyancy of European champion Norbert Schramm of West Germany. The 23-year-old Hamilton earned five 5.9s for technical merit but only two for artistic impression. The 21-year-old Schramm had five 5.9s for artistic merit but nothing above a 5.8 for his technical work.

That translated into victory for the 5-foot-3 Hamilton, whose jumping ability and technique first caught the international eye last year at Hartford, Conn.

Hamilton is only the second American to win a world championship since Tim Wood won back-to-back titles in 1969 and '70. And he is just the third since 1959 when David Jenkins won his third straight title.

MARCH

12

1961 Canada Slugs Soviets

The "Smoke-Eaters" from Trail, British Columbia, scratched, clawed and fought their way to a 5–1 victory over the Soviet Union and returned the ice hockey world championship to Canada after a one-year absence.

The Canadians, claiming their third title in four years, were faced with a must-win situation at Geneva, Switzerland. Czechoslovakia already had won, raising its final record to 6–0 and increasing the pressure. A victory would give the Canadians the championship based on tournament goal differential; a loss would drop them into a second-place tie with the Soviets.

As expected, the game opened with the heavyweights trading checks and trying to establish momentum. Canada finally broke through on a Henry Smith goal, but the deciding blows were not delivered until the second period.

That's when Canada's Dave Rusnell suddenly exploded and punched Vladimir Jursinov in the face. The Russian fought back and soon both teams were involved in a 30-second melee that seemed to take the heart out of the Soviets.

Goals by Canadians Jack McLeod and Hal Jones broke open the tight game and the suddenly-meek Russians played on without inspiration as Canada cruised to its championship.

1966 Hull Scores Record 51st

Bobby Hull, Chicago's Golden Jet, shattered the one-season goal-scoring record that had stood for 21 years when he blasted a slap shot past New York Rangers goalie Cesare Maniago in the third period of the Blackhawks' 4–2 victory at Chicago Stadium.

Hull's 51st goal came on a Blackhawks power play and tied the score at 2–2. Hull connected on a 40-foot drive from in front of the net at 5:34 of the final period, $2^{1}/_{2}$ minutes after teammate Chico Maki had put Chicago on the board with the first of his two goals.

The talented left winger broke the record of 50 goals set in 1944–45 by Montreal's Maurice (Rocket) Richard and matched twice – in 1960–61 by Montreal's Bernie Geoffrion and last year by Hull. Richard scored his 50 in a 50-game schedule, Geoffrion in 70 games. Hull reached 51 in Chicago's 61st game of the season.

Hull later assisted on Maki's game-winner and Doug Mohns added an insurance goal for Chicago at 18:41.

Record-setter **Bobby Hull**, *Chicago's Golden Jet.*

A STAR IS BORN

1938: Johnny Rutherford, an outstanding race car driver who won the Indianapolis 500 three times and won a CART national points championship in 1980.

★ ★ ★

1942: Jimmy Wynn, a powerfully-built outfielder who blasted 291 home runs over a 15-year major league career that ended in 1977.

★ ★ ★

1951: Alberto Juantorena, an outstanding Cuban track star who earned gold medals in both the 400 and 800-meter races at the 1976 Montreal Olympic Games.

★ ★ ★

1956: Dale Murphy, a two-time National League Most Valuable Player who retired in 1993 with 398 career home runs.

★ ★ ★

1962: Darryl Strawberry, a current major league outfielder.

★ ★ ★

DEATH OF A LEGEND

1973: Frank Frisch (baseball).

★ ★ ★

1987: Woody Hayes (football).

★ ★ ★

MILESTONES IN SPORTS

1973

The New York Raiders defeated the Chicago Cougars, 8–7, in a World Hockey Association game that was notable because no penalties were called.

1983

New York Islanders star Mike Bossy scored a pair of goals in a 6–2 victory over Washington, becoming the first player to reach the 50 plateau in each of his first six NHL seasons.

1984

The flamboyant British ice dancing team of Jayne Torvill and Christopher Dean became the first to record nine perfect scores of 6.0 during competition in the world figure skating championships.

1985

Boston's Larry Bird set a franchise record when he blistered Atlanta for 60 points in the Celtics' 126–115 victory over the Hawks at New Orleans.

1987

Canada's Brian Orser outdueled defending champion and chief rival Brian Boitano to capture the men's world figure skating championship at Cincinnati.

1966 Johnny Longden Wins Last Ride

Johnny Longden, the Grand Old Man of the track, rode off into the horse racing sunset after guiding underdog George Royal to a nose victory in the San Juan Capistrano Invitation Handicap – the final race and winner in a record-setting 40-year career.

The 59-year-old Longden went out in style as 60,792 fans at Arcadia, Calif., cheered him to career victory No. 6,032. And he did it with a dramatic stretch run that brought George Royal from fifth place with about a quarter mile to go in the $1^{3}/_{4}$-mile test for 5-year-olds. George Royal edged past front-runner Plaque at the wire.

The victory, Longden's second of the day, brought his career purse winnings to $24,665,800 and left him almost 700 wins ahead of second-place Bill Shoemaker on the all-time list. Longden also rode 4,914 second-place finishers and 4,273 thirds in a career that started in 1926.

Among the highlights of that career was Longden's 1943 Triple Crown victory aboard Count Fleet.

A STAR IS BORN

1872: Willie Keeler, a Hall of Fame outfielder who batted .345 in a turn-of-the-century career that ended in 1910.

★ ★ ★

1886: Frank (Home Run) Baker, a Hall of Fame third baseman (1908–22) who batted .307 over a 13-year career that produced only 96 homers, belying his nickname.

★ ★ ★

1918: George McAfee, a speedy Hall of Fame halfback who spent eight seasons with the Chicago Bears in a career interrupted by World War II.

★ ★ ★

1922: Frank Gatski, a Hall of Fame center and linebacker who appeared in 11 National Football League championship games, eight on the winning side, from 1946–57.

★ ★ ★

1938: Joe Bellino, a former Navy collegiate halfback who captured the 1960 Heisman Trophy.

★ ★ ★

1964: Will Clark, a current major league first baseman.

★ ★ ★

1961 PATTERSON KOs SWEDE

Floyd Patterson survived two first-round knockdowns and roared back to knock out Swedish rival Ingemar Johansson in the sixth round of a world heavyweight championship fight at Miami Beach.

Patterson, beating Johansson for the second time in three tries, retained his title after tumbling to the canvas twice in the opening minutes, courtesy of Johansson's powerful right hand.

Both times the champion jumped up at the count of two, took the mandatory eight count and continued the fight. Before the round had ended, Patterson dropped Johansson with a solid left hook.

The next five rounds were fierce and furious. Both fighters pummeled away, looking for the quick knockout, and neither appeared interested in going the scheduled 15 rounds. Patterson enjoyed the upper hand, but the champion continued to take punishment from well-aimed Johansson rights.

The end came at 2:45 of the sixth when the 26-year-old Patterson connected with a left to the body, another left to the nose and two clubbing rights that sent the 28-year-old Swede sprawling. Johansson managed to regain his feet at the count of seven, dropped back down and arose again, just after the 10 count had been completed.

MILESTONES • IN SPORTS •

1960

National Football League owners voted to allow the Cardinals ownership to move its home base from Chicago to St. Louis.

1960

Arnold Palmer one-putted nine of the last 10 greens, birdied the last two holes and defeated Doug Sanders by one stroke in the Pensacola Open – his third consecutive PGA Tour victory.

1963

Undefeated Cassius Clay, priming for his upcoming fight with heavyweight champion Sonny Liston, scored an unimpressive 10-round decision over Doug Jones at New York.

1981

SMU's Keith Connor set a triple jump world record of 56–9½ during competition in the National Collegiate indoor track and field championships at Detroit.

1982 ZAYAK SKATES TO TITLE

World figure skating champion **Elaine Zayak.**

Elaine Zayak, a 16-year-old American buried in seventh place because of a fall in the short program, rebounded with a dazzling series of triple jumps in the free-style segment and claimed the women's world figure skating championship at Copenhagen.

Zayak had finished second in the United States national competition because of three falls in her free-style program. When she fell in the short program on the first day of the world competition, nobody gave her a chance.

But Zayak dazzled the judges with seven well-executed triples and an otherwise flawless routine that vaulted her past East Germany's Katarina Witt and Austria's Claudia Kristofics-Binder, the two favorites.

Zayak, who received first-place votes from six judges after her free-style performance, became the sixth American to win the women's title since World War II.

1975 HOT CORDERO RIDES TO GLORY AT AQUEDUCT

Jockey Angel Cordero capped his amazing hot streak with a ho-hum two-victory card at Aqueduct, one day after he had ridden a New York record-tying six winners in one program.

Cordero, riding with a damaged tendon in his left knee, brought his 16-day Aqueduct record to 48 winners in 112 races, a 43 percent success rate. That string included three days of four winners, three of five and the six-bagger in which he won the day's first five races. Only four other jockeys had won six races in one program at New York tracks, but two did it with weight allowances afforded apprentice riders.

Cordero, a 32-year-old Puerto Rican, followed his biggest career outing with just two winners, but he kept his bettors happy by finishing in the money on all seven of his mounts. Cordero has not been blanked since the Aqueduct session opened February 24.

Jockey **Angel Cordero** *en route to another victory at Aqueduct.*

MARCH

14

1963 ASSIST RECORD TIED

San Francisco guard Guy Rodgers tied a National Basketball Association record with 28 assists, but the St. Louis Hawks upstaged his brilliant effort with a 114–109 victory over the Warriors at the Cow Palace in San Francisco.

Rodgers was outstanding in scoring 14 points and matching the one-game assist record set by Boston's Bob Cousy in 1959 against Minneapolis. He set up many of Wilt Chamberlain's 15 dunk shots en route to a game-high 39 points, but he also fed Al Attles (15), Tom Meschery (15) and Wayne Hightower (12) for easy baskets.

It wasn't enough. The Hawks used the shooting of Bob Pettit and Cliff Hagan to rally from a 12-point halftime deficit and finally pulled ahead near the end of the third quarter. They never trailed again, even though Pettit sat out much of the final period with foul trouble.

Pettit led the Hawks with 35 points.

1976 SHOEMAKER RIDES 7,000TH WINNER

The incomparable Bill Shoemaker reached another unprecedented horse racing milestone when he rode his 7,000th career winner in the fifth race at Santa Anita. And he did it aboard Royal Derby II, a horse that had not seen the winner's circle in almost three years.

Bill Shoemaker, *horse racing's all-time winningest jockey.*

The 44-year-old Shoemaker, horse racing's all-time winningest jockey, was making his 12th attempt at the elusive milestone. But he did not figure to be a factor in the 1 1/8-mile test. And true to form, Royal Derby II broke poorly out of the starting gate and was buried in sixth place, 10 lengths behind the leader, midway through the final turn.

But Shoemaker, finding working room on the outside, somehow coaxed his 7-year-old 3–1 longshot to momentary glory. A spirited homestretch burst caught the leaders and Royal Derby II zipped passed them to a 3 1/4-length victory that brought an excited cheer from 41,000 appreciative racing fans.

"I knew it was bound to happen sooner or later," said a smiling Shoemaker, who had broken former great Johnny Longden's career record of 6,032 victories in 1970.

1981 REED DROPS BOMB

Arkansas guard U.S. Reed fired up a 49-foot "prayer" that was answered with a swish at the final buzzer and the Razorbacks claimed a 74–73 victory over defending-champion Louisville in the second round of the NCAA Tournament's Midwest Regional at Austin, Tex.

Reed's miracle was needed after Louisville, the defending NCAA champion, had taken a 73–72 lead with five seconds remaining on Derek Smith's fall-away jump shot. Arkansas inbounded the ball to Reed whose progress was stopped by two Cardinals a step short of the halfcourt line. He let go his bomb and players from both teams watched in amazement as the ball sailed through.

"It was a prayer shot," said Louisville Coach Denny Crum, who had watched his high-scoring Cardinals struggle the entire game against Arkansas' tough zone defense. Smith was held to 10 points while Rodney and Scooter McCray led the team with 11 apiece.

Reed finished with 19 points, second to teammate Darrell Walker's 23. Louisville, coming off its 1980 NCAA Tournament title, closed with a 21–9 record.

MILESTONES IN SPORTS

1962

Detroit star Gordie Howe joined Maurice (Rocket) Richard as the NHL's only 500-goal scorers when he connected in the Red Wings' 3–2 loss to the Rangers at New York.

1972

The NBA's Cincinnati Royals announced plans to transfer the franchise to Kansas City.

1972

The Los Angeles Lakers continued on their record-setting way when they defeated Detroit, 129–116, for their 29th victory on the road.

1986

Edmonton's Paul Coffey tied a 9-year-old NHL record for defensemen when he scored eight points (2 goals, 6 assists) in the Oilers' 12–3 victory over Detroit.

1991

An NCAA Tournament first: A No. 2 seed, Syracuse, was knocked off in the first round by 15th-seeded Richmond, 73–69, in an East Regional game.

A STAR IS BORN

1946: Wes Unseld, an outstanding National Basketball Association center from 1968–81 and a former NBA coach.

★ ★ ★

1961: Kirby Puckett, a current major league outfielder.

★ ★ ★

1969: Larry Johnson, a current National Basketball Association forward.

★ ★ ★

DEATH OF A LEGEND

1925: Walter Camp (football).

★ ★ ★

1972: Len Ford (football).

★ ★ ★

1969 RUSSIANS POUND U.S.

The powerful and relentless Soviet Union ice hockey team, beginning its quest for a seventh consecutive world championship, scored 11 second-period goals against a helpless team from the United States and coasted to a 17–2 victory at Stockholm, Sweden.

It was a men-against-boys mismatch as the Russians came out firing against a ragtag group of American amateurs who had played just two games together. Goalie Mike Curran was heroic in a first-period effort that produced 19 saves, many in one-on-one confrontations, while allowing just three goals.

But the second period was a different story. With Vlacheslav Starchinov leading the assault, the Russians peppered Curran with shot after shot and the goalie broke down, allowing 11 goals. He was replaced at the start of the third period by John Lothrop with the Russians leading 14–0 and obviously intent on running out the clock. American goalies faced 66 shots, the Soviet goaltenders just 13. Starchinov scored four goals and two other Russians earned hat tricks. It was the most lop-sided defeat ever endured by an American team in the world championships.

MILESTONES IN SPORTS

1979

American Leon Coleman tied the world record in the 50-meter hurdles twice during a U.S.-Soviet Union track and field meet at Lenin Stadium. Coleman ran 6.4 seconds in both the semifinal and final rounds.

1985

Larry Holmes successfully defended his heavyweight championship with a 10th-round technical knockout of David Bey at Las Vegas.

1988

On the move: Cardinals owner Bill Bidwill received NFL permission to move his franchise from St. Louis to Phoenix.

1991 BUBKA CLEARS 20 FEET

Sergei Bubka, the high-flying Russian with a knack for reaching great heights, became the first pole vaulter to clear the 20-foot barrier during competition in an international indoor track and field meet at San Sebastian, Spain.

Bubka, who has unofficially broken the indoor world record 13 times since 1984, soared 20–0¼ on his first attempt without even touching the bar. Bubka had missed three times at that height a week earlier in a meet at Seville.

The 27-year-old champion has broken the outdoor record nine times, but not since 1988, when he cleared 19–10½. Bubka's barrier-breaker came 10 years after Thierry Vigneron of France cleared 18 feet and a little more than 20 years after the 18-foot barrier fell. It took 13 years to go from the 14 to 15-foot height, 22 years to get from 15 to 16, 18 months to reach 17 and seven years to get to 18.

Russian **Sergei Bubka**, *pole vaulting's first 20-foot man.*

MARCH 15

A STAR IS BORN

1918: Punch Imlach, a former NHL coach who guided Toronto to four Stanley Cup titles in the 1960s.

★ ★ ★

1926: Norm Van Brocklin, a Hall of Fame quarterback who led two NFL teams to championship game victories (1951, '60) and later coached in the league.

★ ★ ★

1946: Bobby Bonds, a 14-year major league star (1968–81) who batted .268 and hit 332 home runs.

★ ★ ★

1961: Terry Cummings, a current National Basketball Association forward.

DEATH OF A LEGEND

1990: Tom Harmon (football).

1989 FRIEDER RESIGNS MICHIGAN JOB

Bill Frieder, admitting his timing could have been better, resigned as Michigan basketball coach to take the head job at Arizona State, two days before the Wolverines were scheduled to open play in the NCAA Tournament.

The 47-year-old Frieder had hoped to coach his team through the postseason, but Michigan Athletic Director Bo Schembechler turned controls over to assistant Steve Fisher. "I don't want someone from Arizona State coaching the Michigan team," Schembechler said.

Frieder, who compiled a 191–87 record in nine seasons as coach after serving seven years as an assistant to former Michigan boss Johnny Orr, said he was forced to make a quick decision by Arizona State and couldn't pass up the opportunity.

"I do regret the timing," said Frieder, who directed Michigan to six straight NCAA Tournament invitations. Make no mistake about it, I love Michigan. This is a career move for me."

The young and talented Wolverines, featuring a freshman-dominated line-up, finished the regular season 24–7 and have the weapons to advance far in the NCAA Tournament. Frieder will be taking over a sagging Arizona State program and a team that finished 12–16 last season.

Former Michigan coach **Bill Frieder** *before his career move.*

MARCH

16

MILESTONES IN SPORTS

1935

American Glenn Cunningham performed an unprecedented track double when he won the 1,000-meter race in world-record time and came back later to win the Colombian mile.

1947

Detroit's Billy Taylor set an NHL record with seven assists as the Red Wings posted a 10–6 victory over the Blackhawks at Chicago.

1970

With the addition of teams in Cleveland, Buffalo, Houston and Portland, the NBA realigned its 18 teams into four divisions – Atlantic, Central, Southern and Pacific.

1991

Americans Kristi Yamaguchi, Tonya Harding and Nancy Kerrigan made figure-skating history when they finished 1–2–3 in the World Championships at Munich, Germany. It was the first one-country sweep in the 73-year history of the event.

Glenn Cunningham, *the American distance king.*

1994 HARDING ENDS CAREER

Tonya Harding, the U.S. national figure skating champion who was implicated in a vicious assault on fellow figure skater Nancy Kerrigan, ended her competitive career when she pleaded guilty to a felony charge that she tried to cover up the attack.

The 23-year-old Harding, who continued to deny any part in planning the January 6 assault with ex-husband Jeff Gillooly and bodyguard Shawn Eckardt, took the plea-bargain in Multnomah County, Ore., with the guarantee she would no longer be subject to prosecution in any jurisdiction.

In accepting the plea, Harding agreed to resign from the U.S. Figure Skating Association, pay a $100,000 fine, accept three years of supervised probation, donate $50,000 to the Special Olympics, pay $10,000 in court cases and perform 500 hours of community service. Harding also agreed to undergo a psychiatric examination.

The much publicized assault occurred January 6 in Detroit after Nancy Kerrigan had completed a practice session for the U.S. Figure Skating Championships.

As Kerrigan left the rink, a man charged at her, clubbed her on the knee with a heavy object and fled. Kerrigan was rushed to a hospital and was forced to withdraw from the competition, which Harding won.

In the days that followed, Gillooly and Eckardt were implicated as the masterminds of the assault, allegedly to help Harding's chances of winning the national title, and they claimed Harding took part in the planning. Shane Stant, an Eckardt acquaintance, later was arrested as the hit man and Stant's uncle, Derrick Smith, was charged as the getaway driver.

Harding's national championship gave her an automatic berth on the U.S. Winter Olympics team and Kerrigan was given a spot by a special vote of the U.S. Olympic Committee. But when the USOC scheduled a special hearing with hopes of removing Harding from the team, the skater responded by suing the organization for $20 million. The USOC backed down.

The Harding-Kerrigan rivalry, a soap opera that was played out daily by the world press leading up to the Games, finally took to the ice at Lillehammer, Norway, but failed to fulfill expectations. Kerrigan skated well and earned a silver medal, barely losing to young Oksana Baiul of Ukraine.

Harding struggled throughout the competition and finished in eighth place.

A STAR IS BORN

1906: Lloyd Waner, a Hall of Fame outfielder who batted .316 over an 18-year career that ended in 1945.

★★★

1956: Ozzie Newsome, an outstanding tight end who caught 662 passes for 7,980 yards over a 13-year career (1978–90) with Cleveland.

★★★

1966: Rodney Peete, a current National Football League quarterback.

★★★

DEATH OF A LEGEND

1972: Pie Traynor (baseball).

★★★

1985: Eddie Shore (hockey).

★★★

1938 TEMPLE WINS NIT DEBUT

The 1938 **Temple Owls** *made short work of Colorado in the inaugural NIT final.*

Don Shields scored 16 points and the 6-foot-6 tandem of Mike Bloom and Don Henderson batted away numerous Colorado shots as the tall and talented Temple Owls defeated the Buffaloes, 60–36, in the final of the inaugural National Invitation Tournament.

The 14,497 fans who watched the one-sided contest at New York's Madison Square Garden were treated to a basketball clinic by the hot-shooting Owls. They raced to a 10–1 lead and extended their advantage to 33–18 by halftime. They shot, passed and defended better than the Buffaloes and the result was never in doubt.

The Eastern Conference champions, who finished their season 23–2, were so dominant that Coach Jimmy Usilton removed his starters after six minutes of the second half. Everybody got in on the scoring, although Howie Black and Ed Boyle claimed honors behind Shields with 14 points apiece. Jack Harvey led Colorado with 11.

1973 76ERS LOSE RECORD 68TH

Elvin Hayes scored a career-high 43 points and the Baltimore Bullets handed the lowly 76ers their National Basketball Association season-record 68th loss with a 120–115 decision at Philadelphia.

The 76ers reached their record-setting low with five games remaining in the regular season and a chance to extend their futility even farther. The loss was their eighth straight and dropped their season mark to 9–68.

Most of the damage was done by Hayes, who connected on 19 field goals and five free throws while blocking six Philadelphia shots. Two of those blocks came in the final two minutes, when Baltimore was breaking a 115–115 deadlock and taking control of the game.

The loss broke the record shared by the 1967–68 San Diego Rockets and the 1970–71 Cleveland Cavaliers. Fred Carter paced Philadelphia with 39 points, one under his career high. The 76ers actually led through most of the first half.

Baltimore's **Elvin Hayes** *scored 43 points and the 76ers lost for an NBA season-record 68th time.*

MARCH 17

MILESTONES • IN SPORTS •

1897

Bob Fitzsimmons knocked out Gentleman Jim Corbett in the 14th round of a fight at Carson City, Nev., and claimed the world heavyweight championship.

1908

Heavyweight champion Tommy Burns scored a first-round knockout of Jem Roche in a bout at Dublin, Ireland.

1977

Jimmy Young recorded a unanimous 12-round decision over former champion George Foreman in a heavyweight shocker at San Juan , P.R.

1989

Georgetown, the No. 1 seed in the East Regional, survived a major upset bid by Princeton and held on for a 50–49 victory in an NCAA Tournament opening-round game at Providence, R.I.

1990

Julio Cesar Chavez stopped Meldrick Taylor with two seconds remaining in the 12th round in a junior welterweight championship fight at Las Vegas.

A STAR IS BORN

1899: Charley Root, a 201-game winner who is best remembered as the pitcher who gave up Babe Ruth's "called shot" homer in the 1932 World Series.

★ ★ ★

1902: Bobby Jones, the outstanding golfer who made history in 1930 when he performed the sport's first and last one-season grand slam.

★ ★ ★

1914: Sammy Baugh, a Hall of Fame quarterback who led the NFL in passing six times over a 16-year career that ended in 1952.

★ ★ ★

1919: Hank Sauer, a former major league outfielder who batted .267 in 15 seasons from 1941–59.

★ ★ ★

DEATH OF A LEGEND

1965: Amos Alonzo Stagg (football).

★ ★ ★

1981: Paul Dean (baseball).

★ ★ ★

1937 CENTER JUMP IS ELIMINATED

Basketball's National Rules Committee, trying to take away the advantage of teams with extra-tall players, approved the far-reaching recommendation of the National Coaches Association that eliminates the center jump after baskets.

The center jump, a basketball tradition, will be used only at the beginning of games and the start of overtimes in the coming season. When one team scores a basket, the other will get the ball out of bounds. After the season, results will be reviewed and the rule will either be changed or made permanent.

The change has been used on an experimental basis by the Southern Division of the Pacific Coast Conference for the last three years. The Big Ten Conference already had voted to experiment with the new rule for the coming season. The coaches association had voted 60–9 to recommend adoption.

The rules committee also took into consideration a questionnaire it had prepared and sent to college and prep basketball coaches all over the country. Those coaches favored elimination of the center jump by a lopsided 891–658 margin.

1906 SILVER SEVEN UPSET

The three-year Stanley Cup reign of Ottawa's Silver Seven came to an end when they recorded a 9–3 victory over the Montreal Wanderers but dropped the two-game total-goals tie-breaker, 12–10.

The Silver Seven, who had won eight consecutive series and outscored opponents 151–74 over that span, put themselves into a deep hole when they dropped the opener to Montreal, 9–1. With the Eastern Canadian Hockey Association championship and Stanley Cup on the line, only an extremely lopsided second-game victory could avert the Wanderers' upset bid.

Amazingly, the Silver Seven almost pulled it off. With Harry Smith scoring six goals, the Silver Seven stretched a 3–1 halftime lead to 9–1 and suddenly the goal count was tied, 10–10. Now the Wanderers, playing before a loud Ottawa crowd, had their backs against the wall and they responded well.

With time running down, Montreal's Lester Patrick broke the tie and then added another goal for good measure. A 9–3 loser, Montreal nevertheless completed what no other team had been able to do for three years.

MARCH

18

Maurice (Rocket) Richard, *the Canadiens' controversial superstar.*

1955 FANS RIOT IN MONTREAL

A major riot that started at a hockey game and carried over to the streets of Montreal waged on for more than seven hours and resulted in thousands of dollars in losses for area merchants.

The riot was a heated response to a decision by National Hockey League President Clarence Campbell to suspend Montreal Canadiens star Maurice (Rocket) Richard for the remainder of the regular season and the Stanley Cup playoffs. Richard's suspension followed a game in Boston in which the volatile right winger violently attacked another player with his stick and struck a linesman two times.

Campbell's decision sent shockwaves through the hockey-crazed city. And anger turned to violence when 14,000 fans jammed the Montreal Forum for a first-place battle with the Detroit Red Wings and thousands more were turned away, providing a tense undertone outside the arena as well as in.

The emotional trigger was pulled by Campbell himself, who showed up for the game midway through the first period and took his seat. As the Red Wings were taking a 4–1 lead over the Canadiens, the fans were taking out their wrath on the league president, throwing programs, overshoes, eggs, tomatoes, peanuts, pennies and any other debris they could find in his direction.

The situation had grown dangerous by the end of the opening period and fire safety officials halted the contest, resulting in a forfeit victory for Detroit. But the fans did not care about that. They took their anger to the streets.

Over the next seven hours, a normally tranquil 15-block area of Montreal was gripped in terror. Streetcars caught in traffic jams were targets of flying bottles, corner newsstands were pushed over and set afire, automobiles were overturned and stores were looted and burned. More than 100 persons were arrested and not even the televised pleas of Richard could calm the storm.

The turmoil was called the worst in Montreal since the anti-conscription riots of World War II.

MILESTONES IN SPORTS

1953

Branch McCracken's Indiana Hoosiers won their second NCAA Tournament championship with a 69–68 squeaker over Kansas.

1955

New Yorker Louis Jones lowered the 400-meter world record four-tenths of a second to 45.4 during competition in the Pan American Games at Mexico City.

1972

Carolina's Larry Miller set an ABA single-game scoring record when he fired in 67 points and led the Cougars to a 139–125 victory over Memphis.

1983

WBA champion Michael Spinks outpointed WBC champion Dwight Braxton and claimed a unified light heavyweight championship in a 15-round title bout at Atlantic City.

1990

The second-longest shutdown in baseball history came to a merciful end when owners and players agreed to a four-year contract after a 32-day lockout of spring training camps.

1992

National Football League owners, meeting in Phoenix, fell four votes short of the necessary three-quarters majority and dropped the controversial instant-replay review rule.

A STAR IS BORN

1956: Ingemar Stenmark, the Swedish ski champion who captured two gold medals at the 1980 Lake Placid Winter Olympic Games and three World Cup overall titles.

★ ★ ★

1961: Curt Warner, a four-time 1,000-yard rusher in his seven National Football League seasons (1983–89) with the Seattle Seahawks.

★ ★ ★

1964: Bonnie Blair, the American speed skater who earned one gold medal at the 1988 Winter Olympic Games, two at the Winter Games of 1992, and a record two more at the Lillehammer Games of 1994.

★ ★ ★

DEATH OF A LEGEND

1984: Charley Lau (baseball).

★ ★ ★

1953 BRAVES GOING TO MILWAUKEE

Baseball's geographical map was changed for the first time in more than half a century when National League owners voted unanimously to allow Boston Braves Owner Lou Perini to shift his team to Milwaukee for the 1953 season.

Workers load baseball equipment into a moving van for the long haul from Boston to Milwaukee.

Perini, who also agreed to pay the American Association's Milwaukee Brewers $50,000 and secured approval for the team to move to Toledo, O., sought the move because "since the advent of television, Boston has become a one-team city." The Braves had shared the city with the Red Sox since 1901, the year the American League was formed.

It didn't help, either, that the Braves finished in seventh place last season and attracted only 281,000 fans – costing Perini a reported $700,000 in losses. The Braves will play their 1953 games in Milwaukee's County Stadium, a new facility that seats 35,911.

The move breaks up a baseball structure that has existed without change since 1903, when the Baltimore Orioles became the New York Highlanders, a predecesor of the current Yankees.

The Braves were charter members of the National League and trace their Boston roots back to 1876.

1960 OHIO STATE CAGES BEARS

Ohio State hit a blistering 16 of 19 first-half shots and rode that momentum to an easy 75–55 victory over favored California in the NCAA Tournament championship game at San Francisco.

The game had been billed as offense versus defense and the Buckeyes, the highest-scoring team in the nation, clearly won the battle against the team that held opponents to a national-best 49.5-point scoring average. All five Ohio State starters scored in double figures and the normally offensive-minded Buckeyes buckled down and held the Golden Bears to 34 percent shooting from the floor.

The issue was decided early. Stars Jerry Lucas and John Havlicek connected on seven of 10 first-half shots and the other three Buckeye starters, Larry Siegfried, Mel Nowell and Joe Roberts, were a combined 9 for 9. With that kind of shooting, Ohio State raced to a 37–19 lead and never looked back.

Lucas scored 16 points, Nowell 15, Siegfried 13, Havlicek 12 and Roberts 10 for the 25–3 Buckeyes while the outmanned Golden Bears (28–2) had only two double-digit scorers, Dick Doughty (11) and Bill McClintock (10).

Mel Nowell *and his Ohio State teammates made short work of California in the 1960 NCAA Tournament championship game.*

MARCH

19

MILESTONES IN SPORTS

1961

Veteran golfer Bob Goalby fired a PGA-record eight consecutive birdies en route to a final-round 65 and a three-stroke victory over Ted Kroll in the St. Petersburg (Fla.) Open.

1967

Bobby Hull, one of two NHL players to score 50 goals in a season, reached the lofty plateau for a third time in Chicago's 4–4 tie with Montreal.

1981

The Buffalo Sabres exploded for an NHL-record nine goals in the second period of a 14–4 victory over Toronto.

1981

Another 1,000-point man: Philadelphia's Bobby Clarke reached the career milestone with a goal in the Flyers' 5–3 victory over Boston.

1984

Denny McLain, the former Detroit pitcher who won 31 games in 1968, was named on a five-count federal indictment with charges ranging from possession and distribution of cocaine to bookmaking and extortion.

1988

St. Louis playmaker Bernie Federko joined the 1,000-point fraternity when he assisted on a goal in a 5–3 Blues loss to Hartford.

1966 TEXAS WESTERN UPSETS KENTUCKY

Guard Bobby Joe Hill scored 20 points and the unheralded Miners of Texas Western used a quick, aggressive defense to throttle powerful Kentucky and pull off a stunning 72–65 upset in the NCAA Tournament championship game at College Park, Md.

The Miners, the first all-black national champion in college basketball history, used their quickness and discipline to wear down the No. 1-ranked and all-white Wildcats of Adolph Rupp. That Texas Western, the nation's third-ranked team despite a soft schedule, had even advanced to the Final Four was something of a basketball shocker.

But the Miners quickly showed why and they did it with a surprising three-guard offense and a pair of hard-working big men, 6-foot-7 David (Big Daddy) Lattin and 6-5 Harry Flournoy.

Coach Don Haskins' strategy worked to perfection. The Miners controlled the tempo with quickness, Hill creating havoc for Kentucky's guards and Texas Western's big men dominating inside. The Miners raced to a 34–31 halftime lead, stretched the margin to 68–57 in the second half and forced Kentucky to foul.

The Miners made 28 of 34 free throw attempts while Kentucky shot just 13. Lattin added 16 points for Texas Western while Louie Dampier and Pat Riley scored 19 apiece for Kentucky.

1955 DONS EARN FIRST NCAA TITLE WIN

High-flying Bill Russell dominated inside and guard K.C. Jones did a masterful defensive job on high-scoring La Salle center Tom Gola as San Francisco completed its storybook season with a 77–63 victory over the Explorers in the NCAA Tournament championship game at Kansas City.

With the 6-foot-1 Jones using his superior quickness to control the 6–6 Gola and free Russell to perform his defensive magic inside, No. 1-ranked San Francisco dominated the No. 3-rated Explorers. Russell swatted away numerous shots and scored 18 first-half points as the Dons rolled to a 35–24 advantage and never were threatened after intermission. Russell finished with 23 points and 25 rebounds but had to share honors with Jones, who added an uncharacteristic 24 points to his superb defensive effort. The Dons closed with a 28–1 record while La Salle dropped to 26–5.

A STAR IS BORN

1871: Joe McGinnity, a Hall of Fame righthander who won 247 games in an iron man 10-year career that ended in 1908.

★ ★ ★

1914: Jay Berwanger, a former University of Chicago halfback and the first winner of the Heisman Trophy (1935).

★ ★ ★

1927: Richie Ashburn, a major league outfielder who batted .308 over a 15-year career that ended in 1962.

DEATH OF A LEGEND

1981: Frank Lane (baseball).

MARCH

20

MILESTONES
• IN SPORTS •

1972

Immaculatta 52, West Chester State 48 in the inaugural national championship game of the Association for Intercollegiate Athletics for Women.

1973

Former Pittsburgh star Roberto Clemente, who died in a plane crash 11 weeks earlier, was ushered into baseball's Hall of Fame in an unprecedented special election. Clemente became the shrine's first Latin American electee.

1988

Mike Tyson, defending his WBC heavyweight championship, scored a second-round knockout of Tony Tubbs at Tokyo.

1992

Iran Barkley scored a surprising 12-round split decision over Thomas Hearns and claimed the WBA light heavyweight championship in a bout at Las Vegas.

Tom Gola, *La Salle's top offensive weapon*

1965

Bill Bradley Scores 58

Princeton star Bill Bradley, playing his final college game before beginning his studies as a Rhodes scholar, set a Final Four record by blistering Wichita State for 58 points in the Tigers' 118–82 victory in the NCAA Tournament consolation game.

Bradley was sensational as he connected on 22 of 29 field-goal attempts and 14 of 15 from the free throw line while rounding out his performance with 17 rebounds and four assists. Many observers thought his point total could have been much higher, but the sharpshooter passed up a number of 20-foot jumpers to set up teammates.

Princeton, a 93–76 loser to Michigan in a semifinal contest, earned its third-place trophy by jumping to a 53–39 halftime lead and then dominating a one-sided second half.

Bradley also set a record for most points ever in a Final Four with 177 over five games.

Princeton's **Bill Bradley** *scored 58 points in his college finale – a victory over Wichita State in the NCAA Tournament consolation game.*

1965

Hot Goodrich Sparks UCLA

Gail Goodrich, UCLA's little big man, destroyed Michigan with a dazzling 42-point effort that lifted the Bruins to a 91–80 victory and their second consecutive NCAA Tournament championship.

The 6-foot-1 lefthander was everywhere as he blazed around the taller Wolverines and connected on 12 of 22 shots and 18 of 20 free throws en route to a title-game record point total. The No. 2-ranked Bruins, giving away size to top-rated Michigan, devastated the Wolverines with their vaunted press that sparked a 12–1 run near the end of the half.

UCLA entered halftime with a 47–34 advantage and stretched the lead to as much as 20 after intermission before Coach John Wooden began substituting freely. Much of the second half was spent at the free throw line, where the opportunistic Bruins hit 25 of 33 attempts.

The Bruins (28–2), the fifth team to win back-to-back NCAA championships, got a big lift from sixth man Kenny Washington, who hit 7 of 9 shots from the floor and scored 17 points. Washington had scored 26 a year earlier in UCLA's title-game victory over Duke.

Michigan (24–4) got a 28-point effort from star forward Cazzie Russell, who hit 10 of 16 shots from the field.

A STAR IS BORN

1945: Pat Riley, a former National Basketball Association forward and a current coach in the NBA.

★ ★ ★

1948: Bobby Orr, a hockey Hall of Famer generally considered the greatest defenseman in the history of the NHL. He won two scoring titles in a 12-year career (1966–79).

★ ★ ★

DEATH OF A LEGEND

1937: Harry Vardon (golf).

★ ★ ★

1984: Stan Coveleski (baseball).

★ ★ ★

1954

La Salle Earns NCAA Respect

Tom Gola, La Salle's little big man, doubled his pleasure with 19 points and 19 rebounds as the Explorers rolled to a 92–76 victory over outmanned Bradley in the NCAA Tournament championship game at Kansas City.

La Salle teammates Charlie Singley and Frank Blatcher scored 23 points apiece, but it was the 6-foot-6 Gola who controlled the game with his passing, defense and inside play after Bradley had forged a 43–42 halftime lead.

Gola, playing his double role as playmaker and inside force to perfection despite four fouls, sparked a 30–14 second-half run that lifted the Explorers to their 26th victory in 30 games and gave them the last laugh on writers and coaches who had ranked them No. 11 in the regular season-ending polls.

Even with its victory, however, La Salle fell short on the respect barometer. Most pollsters favored No. 1-ranked and undefeated Kentucky, which sat out postseason play in protest of three top players being ruled ineligible.

MARCH

21

MILESTONES IN SPORTS

1941

Joe Louis' 15th defense of his heavyweight championship produced a 13th-round technical knockout of Abe Simon at Detroit.

1973

Montreal's Frank Mahovlich became the NHL's fifth 500-goal scorer and helped the Canadiens to a 3–2 victory over Vancouver.

1975

Georgia Tech set NCAA baseball records for most lopsided shutout and biggest winning margin when the Yellowjackets defeated Earlham (O.), 41–0.

1986

American Debi Thomas edged East German Katarina Witt and became the first black to win a world figure skating championship.

1989

Lanny McDonald, who scored his 1,000th career point exactly two weeks earlier, notched goal No. 500 in Calgary's 4–1 victory over the New York Islanders.

A STAR IS BORN

1939: Tommy Davis, a former major league outfielder who batted .294 over an 18-year career that ended in 1976.

★ ★ ★

1956: Ingrid Kristiansen, a Norwegian distance runner who won two Boston Marathons and one New York City Marathon.

★ ★ ★

DEATH OF A LEGEND

1975: Joe Medwick (baseball).

★ ★ ★

1976: Joe Fulks (basketball).

★ ★ ★

1988: Edd Roush (baseball).

★ ★ ★

1964

UCLA GETS FIRST TITLE

UCLA's devastating full-court press forced the bigger, slower Duke Blue Devils into 29 turnovers and the Bruins raced to a 98–83 NCAA Tournament championship game victory in an impressive end to their undefeated season at Kansas City's Municipal Auditorium.

The Bruins' first national championship, like so many of their regular-season victories, was secured in one frantic series during which the UCLA press proved decisive. With Duke holding a 30–27 advantage with 7:14 remaining in the half, UCLA suddenly ran off 16 unanswered points in a blazing $2^1/2$-minute stretch that decided the game.

Key figures in that blitz were guard Gail Goodrich, who finished with a game-high 27 points, and sixth man Kenny Washington, who hit 11 of 16 field-goal attempts, scored 26 points and grabbed a game-high 12 rebounds.

Surprisingly, the bigger Blue Devils were outrebounded, 43–35. The 30–0 Bruins finished as college basketball's third undefeated national champions.

1959

GOLDEN BEARS HOLD OFF STUBBORN WEST VIRGINIA

Cal Coach **Pete Newell** *shares the NCAA Tournament championship trophy with players (left to right) Bob Dalton, Al Bunch and Bernie Simpson.*

Darrall Imhoff tipped in his own missed shot with 15 seconds remaining and California withstood a furious late run by West Virginia to record a 71–70 victory in the NCAA Tournament championship game at Louisville, Ky.

Cal's first national title was not secured until Imhoff connected to give the Golden Bears a three-point lead after the pressing Mountaineers had whittled their 13-point deficit to one. Willie Akers scored an uncontested layup with eight seconds left, but Cal inbounded and ran out the clock.

The patient, defensive-minded Golden Bears seemed to have things well in hand when they stretched their 39–33 halftime margin to 57–44 midway through the second half. But West Virginia went into a full-court press and California uncharacteristically fell apart.

With star forward Jerry West doing most of the damage, the Mountaineers cut into the lead and almost pulled it out. But the 6-foot-10 Imhoff, four inches bigger than West Virginia's tallest player, saved the day.

Denny Fitzpatrick led all Cal scorers with 20 points, but West took game scoring honors with 28.

1953

CELTS' COUSY GOES WILD

Boston guard Bob Cousy, connecting on 30 of 32 free throw attempts in a chippy game at Boston Garden, scored a National Basketball Association playoff-record 50 points as the Celtics posted a 111–105 four-overtime victory over Syracuse Nationals.

The Celtics, who advanced past the opening round of the playoffs for the first time in history, needed everything their little playmaking guard could muster.

The former Holy Cross star made a long set shot that tied the game with five seconds left in the third overtime and then scored nine points in the final extra session to insure the Celtics' two-game series sweep.

The game was both evenly matched and ugly. Even because both teams scored 27 field goals and attempted 65 free throws.

It was ugly because the teams combined for 107 fouls and much of the contest was played at the free throw line.

Cousy made 10 field goals but no other player managed more than five in 68 minutes of action.

Cousy's record topped the 47-point performance of Minneapolis center George Mikan in a 1952 playoff game.

MARCH 22

A STAR IS BORN

1926: Billy Goodman, a former major league infielder who batted .300 over a 16-year career that ended in 1962.

★ ★ ★

1928: Ed Macauley, a basketball Hall of Famer who scored 11,234 points over a 10-year NBA career that ended in 1958–59.

★ ★ ★

1972: Shawn Bradley, a current National Basketball Association center.

1969 ALCINDOR ERA ENDS WITH ANOTHER TITLE

The Lew Alcindor college basketball era came to a spectacular close when the 7-foot-1 UCLA center scored 37 points, grabbed 20 rebounds and led the Bruins to a 92–72 victory over Purdue and their record third consecutive NCAA Tournament championship.

The outmanned Boilermakers were matched against a man on a mission and Alcindor dominated both offensively and defensively. He connected on 15 of 20 field-goal attempts and 7 of 9 free throws in 36 minutes while throwing a defensive blanket over the Purdue big men.

The victory was never in doubt. UCLA led 50–41 at halftime and built on that margin in the second half. A key to the Bruins' dominance was the defensive job Kenny Heitz did on high-scoring Boilermaker guard Rick Mount, the nation's leading scorer with a 33.5 average. With the bespectacled Heitz dogging his every move, Mount made only 12 of 36 shots and scored most of his 28 points after the game had been decided.

UCLA (29–1) became the first team to win three consecutive NCAA championships and Alcindor closed his three-year varsity career with an incredible 88–2 record.

MILESTONES IN SPORTS

1958

Kentucky 84, Seattle 72: Adolph Rupp's Fiddlin' Five earned a fourth NCAA Tournament championship for Kentucky.

1967

Muhammad Ali defended his heavyweight championship with a seventh-round knockout of Zora Folley at New York's Madison Square Garden.

1968

UCLA, avenging an early-season showdown loss at the Astrodome, pounded the Houston Cougars, 101–69, in a Final Four semifinal game at Los Angeles.

1974

Peter Revson, an American auto racer practicing for the South African Grand Prix at Johannesburg, died in a fiery crash when he lost control of his Ford UOP Shadow.

1975

Delta State's women ended Immaculatta's four-year AIAW Tournament winning streak with a 90–81 championship game victory at Harrisonburg, Va.

1986

Trevor Berbick claimed Pinklon Thomas' WBC heavyweight crown with a 15-round unanimous decision over the champion in a match at Las Vegas.

1970 UCLA WINS FOURTH CONSECUTIVE CHAMPIONSHIP

Still champions: UCLA Coach **John Wooden** *with star players* **Sidney Wicks** *(center) and* **Curtis Rowe.**

The UCLA Bruins, out to prove they could win an NCAA championship without Lew Alcindor, raised more than a few eyebrows when they overpowered Jacksonville, 80–69, and completed their unprecedented fourth straight title run with an emphatic victory at College Park, Md.

Despite giving away a lot of size, UCLA dominated inside with 6-foot-8 Sidney Wicks, 6-9 Steve Patterson and 6-6 Curtis Rowe. That trio, faced with the prospect of defending against Jacksonville's 7-2 Artis Gilmore and 6-10 Rod McIntyre, was more than up to the task.

Gilmore scored 19 points, but Wicks slapped five shots back in his face and made life difficult for the talented big man. Frustrated by the defense of Wicks, Gilmore went through a $16\frac{1}{2}$-minute stretch without scoring.

With Gilmore under control, the rest was easy. UCLA (28–2) forged a five-point halftime lead and then methodically stretched it out in the second half. Rowe led balanced UCLA with 19 points, with Wicks and Patterson adding 17 apiece and John Vallely putting on 15.

1989 ROZELLE RETIRES, FOR PETE'S SAKE

Pete Rozelle, the former "boy commissioner" who guided the National Football League through almost three decades of prosperity, stunned team owners and fans when he announced his retirement at the NFL meetings in Palm Desert, Calif.

The 63-year-old Rozelle, a compromise choice to succeed Bert Bell as commissioner in 1960, said he simply wanted to get out and enjoy life while still able.

"I didn't want to die in office like Bert Bell before me," a tearful Rozelle commented, adding that he wanted to get out "while I can still enjoy some years without stress."

Among Rozelle's accomplishments were a successful revenue-sharing plan, a merger with the American Football League, the rise of the Super Bowl into a major sporting event and the blossoming of the NFL as a prime-time television attraction.

But Rozelle had spent recent years handling an endless stream of court cases over drug controversies, ownership problems and labor-management disputes. He said he would remain in office until a new commissioner is appointed.

1957 Tar Heels Edge Kansas

Joe Quigg sank two free throws with six seconds remaining in the third overtime and then batted away a desperation pass intended for Kansas big man Wilt Chamberlain, giving North Carolina a 54–53 victory in the NCAA Tournament championship game and completing the Tar Heels' undefeated season.

Kansas star **Wilt Chamberlain** *(right) watches as a North Carolina player launches a shot during action in a triple-overtime NCAA Tournament championship game.*

Despite their 31–0 record, the Tar Heels were underdogs to the 24–2 Jayhawks – primarily because of the 7-foot Chamberlain, the most devastating big man college basketball had ever produced.

But North Carolina stayed away from Chamberlain and hit a torrid 64.7 percent of its shots while building a 29–22 halftime lead. When the Tar Heels cooled off after intermission, Kansas battled back and carried a three-point advantage into the final two minutes. A Quigg field goal and a Tommy Kearns free throw tied the score at 46–46 and forced overtime.

North Carolina, with high-scoring Lennie Rosenbluth on the bench with five fouls, held the ball for much of the first two extra sessions. Kansas finally broke a 52–52 deadlock in the third overtime on a Gene Elstun free throw, setting up Quigg's late heroics.

1974 Hungry Wolfpack Ends UCLA Run

In a heavyweight battle that brought down the curtain on UCLA's seven-year NCAA Tournament championship streak, North Carolina State posted an 80–77 double-overtime victory over the Bruins in a Final Four semifinal matchup at Greensboro, N.C.

Playing close to home and still reeling from a lopsided early-season loss to UCLA, N.C.-State (30–1) traded punches with the Bruins through a first half in which the lead was never more than five points for either team. UCLA pulled ahead by 11 points twice in the second half, but David Thompson and 7-foot-4 Tom Burleson brought the Wolfpack back on both occasions.

The score was tied 65–65 at the end of regulation, 67–67 after a cautious first overtime. UCLA jumped to a seven-point lead in the second extra session and appeared headed for victory.

But the vaunted UCLA mystique suddenly fell apart amid a series of turnovers and missed shots. N.C.-State fought back and a Thompson basket produced a 76–75 lead. Two Thompson free throws and two more by Monte Towe clinched the Wolfpack upset.

Thompson finished with 28 points, one less than Bill Walton, who played the final game of his outstanding UCLA career.

North Carolina State's **David Thompson** *(44) battles UCLA's Bill Walton.*

1963 Loyola Wins Late

Vic Rouse's put-back of a missed shot with one second remaining in overtime capped a frantic Loyola of Chicago comeback and gave the Ramblers a 60–58 victory over Cincinnati in an NCAA Tournament championship game at Louisville, Ky.

With 12 minutes left in regulation, the misfiring Ramblers trailed, 45–30, and turned to a full-court press. This paid dividends and Cincinnati turnovers began turning into Loyola points, triggering the biggest title-game comeback in tournament history.

A basket by Les Hunter finally cut the deficit to one and the Ramblers fouled with 12 seconds remaining to stop the clock. Larry Shingleton made one free throw, but Loyola rebounded the miss and Jerry Harkness hit a last-second jump shot that forced overtime at 54–54.

Each team scored a pair of baskets in the extra session and Loyola got its chance to win in the final seconds. The Bearcats concentrated on the high-scoring Harkness, who whipped a pass to Hunter for a jump shot. The ball rolled off the rim to Rouse, who put in the winner.

A Star Is Born

1923: Arnie Weinmeister, a Hall of Fame defensive tackle who played just six seasons in the All-America Football Conference and the NFL from 1948–53.

★ ★ ★

1929: Roger Bannister, a British distance runner who cracked the four-minute mile barrier with a time of 3:59.4 on May 6, 1954.

★ ★ ★

1943: Lee May, a slugging first baseman who belted 354 home runs in an 18-year career that ended in 1982.

★ ★ ★

1955: Moses Malone, a current National Basketball Association center.

Death of a Legend

1977: Joe Stydahar (football).

March 23

Milestones in Sports

1948

Kentucky 58, Baylor 42: Adolph Rupp's Wildcats won their first NCAA Tournament championship.

1952

Chicago's Bill Mosienko set an NHL record by scoring three full-strength goals in a 21-second span of the third period in a 7–6 victory over the New York Rangers.

1968

UCLA 78, North Carolina 55: The Bruins earned their second straight NCAA Tournament championship and fourth in five years.

1974

The women of Immaculatta captured their third straight AIAW championship with a 68–53 victory over Mississippi College.

1979

Larry Holmes defended his WBC heavyweight championship with a seventh-round technical knockout of Osvaldo Ocasio at Las Vegas.

1991

In the opening game of the new World League of American Football, the London Monarchs posted a 24–11 victory over Frankfurt Galaxy.

1994

Los Angeles center Wayne Gretzky became the most prolific scorer in NHL history when he notched career goal No. 802 in the second period of a 6–3 loss to Vancouver and moved past Gordie Howe on the all-time list.

MARCH

24

1936 HOCKEY'S LONGEST GAME

Modere Bruneteau, a rookie who had scored only two goals during the regular season, beat Montreal goalie Lorne Chabot on a two-man break and gave Detroit a 1–0 victory in the longest National Hockey League game ever played.

Bruneteau's goal at 16:30 of the sixth overtime, off a pass from Hector Kilrea, brought a merciful end to a series-opening playoff game between the Red Wings and Maroons.

The contest totaled 176½ minutes – 11 minutes and 44 seconds longer than a 1933 playoff game between Toronto and Boston.

The marathon game, viewed by 9,500 fans at the Montreal Forum, was a tight-checking affair that dragged on until 2:20 a.m. Both teams had plenty of scoring chances, but both goalies, Chabot and Norman Smith, were spectacular.

Smith, playing in his first playoff game, frustrated Montreal with an incredible 90 saves.

After both teams had nearly ended the game late in the fifth overtime period, Detroit finally broke through in the sixth. Kilrea and Bruneteau broke in alone on Chabot and the goaltender was helpless. Kilrea slid a nice pass to the rookie who faked Chabot off his feet and then calmly fired the loose puck into the vacated net.

1962 CINCINNATI WINS AGAIN

The Bearcats of Cincinnati, desperately wanting to prove that their 1961 national championship-deciding upset of Ohio State was no fluke, repeated that feat in impressive fashion, thrashing the No. 1-ranked Buckeyes, 71–59, in the NCAA Tournament final at Louisville, Ky.

The battle for Ohio bragging rights might have been decided one day earlier, however, when high-scoring Buckeyes center Jerry Lucas sprained his knee in a semifinal victory over Wake Forest. Heavily taped and obviously struggling, Lucas scored 11 points, far below his season average.

But even a healthy Lucas might not have been enough to derail Cincinnati's championship plans. With center Paul Hogue controlling Lucas and putting on his own offensive show, the Bearcats pulled to a 37–29 halftime lead. The advantage ballooned to as much as 18 points in one-sided second half.

An inspired Hogue finished with 22 points and 19 rebounds while Tom Thacker chipped in 21 points for the 29–2 Bearcats. Reserve center Gary Bradds led Ohio State (26–2) with 15.

San Francisco basketball Coach **Phil Woolpert.**

1956 DONS CRUISE TO 2ND TITLE IN ROW

Bill Russell scored 26 points, grabbed 27 rebounds and intimidated high-scoring Iowa center Bill Logan into a 12-point performance as San Francisco rolled to an 83–71 NCAA Tournament championship game victory over the Hawkeyes and staked its claim as the best college basketball team in history.

Not only did the Dons become the third back-to-back winner of the prestigious event, they became the first to do it with a perfect record (29–0). They also did it without playmaking guard and defensive whiz K.C. Jones, who was ineligible for postseason play.

Iowa actually provided a challenge for the powerful Dons – in the first half. The Hawkeyes raced to a 15–4 lead and forced San Francisco to play catchup for one of the few times this season. But the Dons were up to the task, finally taking a 24–23 lead and stretching the margin to 38–33 by halftime.

They made the rest look easy. With the ever-scowling Russell scoring from in close and forcing Logan away from the basket with his intimidating defensive play, San Francisco steadily pulled away to achieve its NCAA-record 55th consecutive victory.

Jubilant Cincinnati players give Coach **Ed Jucker** *a victory ride after their second straight NCAA Tournament championship game upset of Ohio State.*

MILESTONES IN SPORTS

1947
Utah pulled off a stunning upset of powerful Kentucky in the NIT championship game, posting a 49–45 victory at Madison Square Garden.

1961
A horse racing record: Jockey Johnny Longden recorded career victory No. 5,500 aboard Spring Victory at Golden Gate Fields in California.

1975
Muhammad Ali, making his first heavyweight title defense, scored a 15th-round technical knockout of Chuck Wepner at Cleveland.

1978
The Buffalo Bills granted the request of star running back O.J. Simpson and traded the most prolific one-season rusher in NFL history to the San Francisco 49ers.

1980
Louisville 59, UCLA 54: Darrell Griffith scored 23 points and led the Cardinals to their first NCAA Tournament championship .

A STAR IS BORN

1893: George Sisler, a Hall of Fame first baseman who batted a lofty .340 over a 15-year career that ended in 1930.

★★★

1938: Larry Wilson, a Hall of Fame safety during a 13-year career with the St. Louis Cardinals from 1960–72.

★★★

1951: Pat Bradley, a current LPGA professional who has won all four majors at least once.

★★★

1958: Bruce Hurst, a current major league pitcher.

★★★

DEATH OF A LEGEND

1926: George Vezina (hockey).

MILESTONES
· IN SPORTS ·

1916

Big Jess Willard, making his first heavyweight title defense after beating Jack Johnson, fought to a 10-round no decision against Frank Moran at New York's Madison Square Garden.

1947

Holy Cross 58, Oklahoma 47: The Crusaders win their first NCAA Tournament championship at New York's Madison Square Garden.

1958

37-year-old Sugar Ray Robinson made boxing history when he scored a 15-round split decision over Carmen Basilio and won the world middleweight title for an unprecedented fifth time.

1962

Bobby Hull's 50th goal, tying the one-season record of Maurice (Rocket) Richard and Bernie Geoffrion, propelled the Chicago Blackhawks to a 4–1 victory over the New York Rangers.

1967

UCLA 79, Dayton 64: The first year of the Bruins' Lew Alcindor era ended with a 30–0 record and an NCAA Tournament championship game victory.

1972

Goal No. 600: Bobby Hull reached another milestone when he scored with 2:26 remaining and gave Chicago a 5–5 tie with the Boston Bruins.

1972

UCLA 81, Florida State 76: The first year of the Bruins' Bill Walton era ended with a 30–0 record and sixth straight NCAA tournament victory.

1974

North Carolina State 76, Marquette 64: UCLA's seven-year reign officially ended with the Wolfpack's first NCAA Tournament championship.

1982 Gretzky's Milestone

Wayne Gretzky, Edmonton's 21-year-old point-producing machine, scored two goals and assisted on two more in the Oilers' 7–2 victory over Calgary, becoming the first player to cross the National Hockey League's magical 200-point barrier.

The amazing Gretzky scored his 200th point of the season at 9:16 of the opening period when he fed Pat Hughes in front of the Calgary net for a 20-foot slapshot that beat Flames goalie Rejean Lemelin. His 201st point came two minutes later when he fed teammate Dave Semenko at the side of the net with the Oilers holding a two-man advantage.

Gretzky punctuated his 200-point feat with two second-period goals – both in shorthanded situations. Through Edmonton's 76 games, the record-setting third-year center has 90 goals and 113 assists. He has been held scoreless just eight times.

1961 Bearcats Surprise No. 1 Ohio State

Cincinnati's **Paul Hogue** *(22) has rebounding position on Ohio State's Jerry Lucas during the 1961 NCAA title game.*

Cincinnati, slowing Ohio State's high-powered scoring machine to 26 points in the final 25 minutes, posted a shocking 70–65 overtime victory over the No. 1-ranked Buckeyes and claimed the NCAA Tournament championship at Kansas City.

The Bearcats used a hard-nosed defense and balanced scoring to win the battle of Ohio and hand the Buckeyes their first loss after 27 victories. Coach Ed Jucker's team slowed the pace, frustrated Ohio State's fast-break offense and turned in one of the biggest upsets in postseason history.

But it was not easy. Playing a little faster pace than Jucker would have liked, Cincinnati trailed at halftime, 39–38. But defense was the name of the game in the second half and the teams fought nose to nose, Cincinnati pulling ahead by six, falling behind by five and finally pulling even at the end of regulation, 61–61, on Bob Knight's layup with 1:41 remaining.

The Bearcats scored the first points of overtime on two Paul Hogue free throws and steadily pulled away to their first championship.

Bob Wiesenhahn led Cincinnati (27–3) with 17 points while Carl Bouldin added 16, Tom Thacker 15 and Tony Yates 13. Ohio State's top gun Jerry Lucas scored 27 points, but high-scoring forward John Havlicek was held to four by the stingy Bearcats.

1934 Smith Masters Augusta

Horton Smith, a Chicago club pro who had never won a major championship, fired a final-round 72 and recorded a one-stroke victory over Craig Wood in the inaugural Masters golf tournament at Augusta, Ga.

Smith, a tall Missourian using a borrowed driver, took the lead with a 10-foot birdie putt on 17 and earned the first-place check of $1,500 when he rammed home a four-footer on 18, giving him a four-round total of 284. Wood had finished earlier in the day with a 71–285, one stroke better than Paul Runyan and Billy Burke.

Smith appeared to be faltering when he bogeyed 14 and 15, missing four-foot putts on both holes. But he came back to par 16, got his dramatic birdie on 17 and sank his title-clincher on 18 with Wood watching him from the clubhouse.

Despite the exciting finish, much of the attention was diverted to Bobby Jones, the proud Georgian who came out of retirement to compete on his home course. Jones, the former golf grand-slammer who attracted huge galleries and was constantly distracted by friends and well-wishers, finished 13th with a 294 total.

MARCH
25

A STAR IS BORN

1910: Dutch Leonard, a righthanded pitcher who won 191 games over a 20-year career that ended in 1953.

★ ★ ★

1920: Howard Cosell, the former Monday Night Football and Wide World of Sports broadcaster known for his "tell it like it is" style.

★ ★ ★

1966: Tom Glavine, a current major league pitcher.

★ ★ ★

1969: Travis Fryman, a current major league infielder.

MARCH

26

MILESTONES
• IN SPORTS •

1944

St. John's, playing before a partisan crowd at New York's Madison Square Garden, became the first back-to-back winner in the history of the NIT with a 47–39 victory over DePaul.

1949

Kentucky 46, Oklahoma A&M 36: The Wildcats became only the second team to claim back-to-back NCAA Tournament titles.

1952

Kansas 80, St. John's 63: Clyde Lovellette sparked the Jayhawks' first NCAA title victory with a championship game-record 33 points.

1970

Pistol Pete Maravich, the most prolific scorer in the history of college basketball, signed a rich five-year contract with the NBA's Atlanta Hawks.

1974

George Foreman scored a surprisingly easy second-round technical knockout of challenger Ken Norton in a heavyweight championship fight at Caracas, Venezuela.

1977

Delta State knocked off LSU, 68–55, and captured its third straight women's basketball championship.

1992

Former heavyweight champion Mike Tyson, convicted on rape charges in federal court, was sentenced to six years in prison and fined $30,000.

1979

Spartans Do A Magic Act

Earvin (Magic) Johnson outdueled Larry Bird in a high-profile college basketball matchup and Michigan State withstood a late Indiana State rally to record a 75–64 victory in the NCAA Tournament championship game at Salt Lake City, Utah.

Johnson, a 6-foot-8 point guard, scored a game-high 24 points and riddled the previously undefeated Sycamores with pinpoint passes that set up easy baskets. Magic got plenty of support from Greg Kelser and Terry Donnelly, who combined for 34 points, and a defense that swarmed on Bird. The talented senior connected on just 4 of 11 first-half shots and 7 of 21 in a 19-point effort.

With Bird out of the flow, Michigan State raced to a 37–28 halftime lead and stretched the advantage to 50–34 early in the second half. But Bird refused to let the Sycamores die easily. Playing on guile and determination, he combined with guard Carl Nicks to bring Indiana State back within six.

With 10:10 remaining, it was time for Michigan State's Magic act. Johnson scored seven points in the next five minutes and the Spartans, back in control, went to a delay game that sealed their victory.

A STAR IS BORN

1960: Marcus Allen, a current National Football League running back.

★ ★ ★

1962: John Stockton, a current National Basketball Association guard.

★ ★ ★

DEATH OF A LEGEND

1973: George Sisler (baseball).

Oklahoma A&M big man **Bob Kurland,** *one of college basketball's original 7-footers.*

1946

Aggies Double The Pleasure

Oklahoma A&M center Bob Kurland, towering over the college basketball world like a giant sequoia, scored 23 points and led the Aggies to a 43–40 victory over North Carolina and their second straight NCAA Tournament championship.

Kurland, one of the game's first 7-footers, was too much for the Tar Heels, whose biggest man was 6-6 Horace (Bones) McKinney. Kurland held McKinney to five points and the North Carolina center fouled out midway through the second half trying to keep Kurland away from the basket.

Even without McKinney, the Tar Heels put up a fight, cutting a 13-point second-half deficit to three on the shooting of John Dillon. But Kurland scored the next seven points and A&M was never seriously threatened again.

The victory gave Coach Henry Iba's 31–2 Aggies the distinction of becoming college basketball's first two-time champions.

1973

Walton Gang Rides High

UCLA center Bill Walton, putting on a basketball clinic for 19,301 Final Four fans in St. Louis and a national television audience, scored 44 points and led the Bruins to their seventh consecutive NCAA Tournament championship with an 87–66 demolition of Memphis State.

Walton, to put it simply, was unstoppable. The 6-foot-11 giant put on the greatest show in title-game history by hitting 21 of 22 field-goal attempts and 2 of 3 free throws while grabbing 13 rebounds. His 44 points were a championship-game record.

Despite Walton's dominance, Memphis State fought to a 39–39 halftime tie behind the play of guard Larry Finch and center Larry Kenon. Thirty of the Tigers' 39 points were scored by that duo, who took advantage as Walton spent the last five minutes of the half on the bench with three fouls.

But Walton returned with a vengeance in the second half and Memphis State faded. Even the big man's fourth foul and a sprained ankle in the final minutes couldn't prevent the inevitable – UCLA's record 75th straight victory.

Finch scored 29 points and Kenon added 20 in a losing cause.

UCLA's **Walton Gang** *rode into St. Louis and captured the Bruins' seventh straight NCAA Tournament championship.*

1978 Givens Bombs Duke In 41-Point Classic

Hot-shooting lefthander Jack Givens connected on 18 of 27 field-goal attempts and scored 41 points, lifting his Kentucky Wildcats to a 94–88 victory over Duke in the NCAA Tournament championship game at the Checkerdome in St. Louis.

Givens' big game was the result of a 2–3 Duke zone defense that stretched out from the baseline and concentrated on stopping 6-foot-10 center Rick Robey and guards Kyle Macy and Truman Claytor. That strategy left the middle open just beyond the free throw line and it didn't take long for Givens to find his spot.

With the 6-4 forward hitting nine of his 12 first-half shots and scoring 23 points, Kentucky bolted to a 45–38 advantage. Refusing to give up the defensive strategy after intermission, Duke continued conceding Givens his shots and he responded with a 9-of-15 second half. The Wildcats gradually pulled away.

The final score was close only because Duke front-liners Gene Banks (22 points), Jim Spanarkel (21) and Mike Gminski (20) fought back hard against Kentucky substitutes. Robey added 20 points for 30–2 Kentucky, which captured its fifth NCAA title.

MARCH

27

A STAR IS BORN

1880: Miller Huggins, the diminutive Hall of Fame manager who guided the New York Yankees to their first three World Series championships in the 1920s.

★ ★ ★

1903: Walt Kiesling, a football Hall of Fame player and coach who was most prominent in the formative years of the National Football League.

★ ★ ★

1940: Cale Yarborough, a championship auto racer who has won four Daytona 500 stock car races and three NASCAR titles.

★ ★ ★

1953: Annemarie Moser-Proll, an outstanding Austrian skier who won six World Cup overall titles and a 1980 Olympic gold medal.

★ ★ ★

1963: Randall Cunningham, a current National Football League quarterback.

★ ★ ★

MILESTONES IN SPORTS

1942

Champion Joe Louis continued his unflinching assault on heavyweight title contenders with a sixth-round knockout of Abe Simon at New York's Madison Square Garden.

1945

Oklahoma A&M 49, New York University 45: The Aggies and 7-foot center Bob Kurland captured their first NCAA Tournament championship.

1971

UCLA 68, Villanova 62: The Bruins earned their record fifth straight NCAA Tournament championship.

1983

Heavyweight champion Larry Holmes scored a unanimous 12-round decision over Lucien Rodriguez at Scranton, Pa.

1990

After a 48-year NHL title drought, the New York Rangers claimed the Patrick Division regular-season championship with a 7–4 victory over the Quebec Nordiques.

1939 Oregon Wins First NCAA

John Dick scored 15 points and Oregon, utilizing an up-tempo offense and a variety of defenses, raced to a 46–33 victory over Ohio State in the inaugural NCAA Tournament championship game at Northwestern University in Evanston, Ill.

The NCAA-sponsored event, the National Association of Basketball Coaches' answer to the 1-year-old National Invitation Tournament, was a showcase for Oregon's futuristic style. Running an effective fast break and mystifying the Buckeyes with a mixture of man-to-man and zone defenses, the Ducks raced to a 21–16 halftime lead and stretched out their advantage after the intermission.

Ohio State's faulty strategy contributed to its demise. The Buckeyes chose to double-team Oregon star Laddie Gale and Ducks Coach Howard Hobson simply used him as a decoy. With Gale drawing all the attention, Dick and guard Bobby Anet found themselves open for easy baskets.

The tournament opened with eight teams playing at regional sites around the country. Six of the nation's top teams spurned the event to play in the NIT at New York's Madison Square Garden.

1951 Spivey Leads Kentucky To Third Championship

Center Bill Spivey, shaking off an uninspired first half, scored 22 points and grabbed 21 rebounds as Kentucky became the first three-time NCAA Tournament winner with a 68–58 championship game victory over Kansas State at Minneapolis.

Spivey, a talented 7-footer, was outhustled in the early going by 6-8 Kansas State center Lew Hitch, who outscored him 10–4 and led K-State to a 19–13 lead. Only the inspiring effort of Cliff Hagan, who was fighting a cold and high temperature, kept Kentucky close and gave Coach Adolph Rupp a chance to deliver his own brand of inspiration to his big center at halftime.

Spivey was a different player after intermission. Taking charge of the game at both ends of the court, he dominated Hitch and Kentucky began pulling away from the Big Seven Conference champions. When the game ended, Spivey had nine more points and 12 more rebounds than Hitch and Kentucky had an easy victory. Hagan fought through his sickness to hit 5 of 6 field-goal attempts. But it wasn't enough. Rupp's Wildcats had previously won NCAA titles in 1948 and '49.

Kentucky big man **Bill Spivey.**

MARCH

28

MILESTONES
IN SPORTS

1942

Stanford 53, Dartmouth 38: The Indians captured college basketball's fourth NCAA Tournament title.

1944

Utah 42, Dartmouth 40: The Utes needed overtime to win their first NCAA Tournament championship.

1982

Louisiana Tech 76, Cheyney State 62: The Lady Techsters captured the first NCAA Tournament championship for women.

1984

In a sneaky move that stunned the NFL, Colts Owner Robert Irsay hired a fleet of moving vans, cleaned out his Baltimore offices and took his team to a new home in Indianapolis.

A STAR IS BORN

1940: Kevin Loughery, a current National Basketball Association coach.

★ ★ ★

1944: Rick Barry, a basketball Hall of Fame forward who scored 25,279 points in his combined ABA-NBA careers from 1967–80.

★ ★ ★

DEATH OF A LEGEND

1931: Ban Johnson (baseball).

★ ★ ★

1953: Jim Thorpe (football, baseball, track).

★ ★ ★

1958: Chuck Klein (baseball).

★ ★ ★

1977 Marquette Wins One for Coach Al

Guard Butch Lee scored 19 points and an inspired Marquette team, trying to win one for retiring Coach Al McGuire, connected on its final 12 free throw attempts and 23 of 25 in the game while posting an emotional 67–59 victory over North Carolina in the NCAA Tournament championship game at Atlanta.

With Lee firing away, the Warriors played an inspired first half and raced to a 39–27 lead over the favored Tar Heels. But North Carolina came out firing after intermission, posting 16 of the first 18 points and taking a 43–41 advantage. When forward Bernard Toone tied the game at 45 with 12:45 remaining, the Tar Heels went into their famous four-corner offense, holding the ball and looking for the easy basket.

The strategy backfired. After three minutes of passing and dribbling, North Carolina missed an easy shot and Marquette scored on the other end. With momentum lost, the Tar Heels faltered and the Warriors stretched their lead, turning to a delay game of their own that resulted in a string of game-clinching free throws.

The final seconds of the Marquette victory ticked away with McGuire sitting on the sideline, sobbing emotionally into his hands.

1972 Rupp Era Ends At Kentucky

Coaching legend Adolph Rupp, who guided the Kentucky basketball program to 875 victories and four NCAA Tournament championships over 42 seasons, announced his retirement after guiding his final team to a 21–7 record.

Rupp actually was forced out by a Kentucky law that requires mandatory retirement at age 70. Rupp, a former University of Kansas player under another legendary coach, Phog Allen, turned 70 last September and was allowed to guide the Wildcats for a final season.

True to form, the 1971–72 Wildcats shared the Southeastern Conference championship and reached the final of the NCAA Tournament's Mideast Regional before losing to Florida State. Under Rupp, Kentucky has won or shared 27 Southeastern Conference titles, four NCAA titles and one NIT championship.

Rupp, who coached his first game at Kentucky in 1930, overtook Allen for the top spot on the all-time coaching victory list in 1967 when the Wildcats defeated Notre Dame for No. 722. He finished his career with a final mark of 875–190.

Kentucky Coach **Adolph Rupp** *in the late 1940s with Wildcat star* **Alex Groza.**

1990 Jordan Soars For 69

Michael Jordan took his above-the-rim aerial act to new heights in Richfield, O., when he scored a career-high 69 points and led the Chicago Bulls to a 117–113 overtime victory over Cleveland.

Jordan connected on 23 of 37 field-goal attempts and 21 of 23 free throws in topping the 60-point barrier for the fourth time in his National Basketball Association career. His previous high was 63 points against Boston in the 1986 playoffs and he twice scored 61 in 1987.

Only three NBA players have scored more points in a game. Wilt Chamberlain did it six times (100, 78, 73, 73, 72, 70), David Thompson once (73) and Elgin Baylor once (71). Jordan scored 16 in the first quarter, 15 in the second, 20 in the third, 10 in the fourth and 8 in overtime. He is averaging more than 33 points per game.

The high-flying Chicago star also grabbed a career-high 18 rebounds while recording six assists and four steals.

A STAR IS BORN

1867: Cy Young, a 19th century Hall of Fame pitcher with the record for career victories (511).

★ ★ ★

1925: Emlen Tunnell, a football Hall of Fame safety from 1948–61 with the NFL's New York Giants and Green Bay Packers.

★ ★ ★

1944: Denny McLain, the last major league pitcher to win 30 games in a season (1968).

★ ★ ★

1945: Walt Frazier, a basketball Hall of Fame guard with 15,581 points over a 13-year NBA career that ended in 1979–80.

★ ★ ★

1955: Earl Campbell, a three-time NFL rushing champion and 1977 winner of the Heisman Trophy.

A STAR IS BORN

1988: Ted Kluszewski (baseball).

1976 INDIANA COMPLETES A PERFECT SEASON

Scott May and Kent Benson combined for 51 points as Indiana overcame a six-point halftime deficit to defeat Big Ten Conference-rival Michigan, 86–68, in the NCAA Tournament championship game and become the seventh team to claim the title with a perfect record.

The powerful Hoosiers, unable to contain swift Michigan guard Rickey Green in a 35–29 first half, took control of their 32nd consecutive victory with a second-half blitz that staggered the Wolverines. Scoring on virtually every possession, Indiana went from its six-point deficit to a 73–59 lead as 17,540 fans at Philadelphia watched in disbelief.

The rest was easy and Michigan's last hopes were dashed when center Phil Hubbard fouled out with 7:27 left to play. May, the 6-foot-11 Benson and guard Quinn Buckner combined for 36 of Indiana's first 38 second-half points and 67 in the game.

Kent Benson *tells the world what it already knows – the Hoosiers are No. 1.*

1950 CCNY PULLS OFF SHOCKING SWEEP

CCNY players **Al Roth** *(25) and* **Floyd Layne** *in action against North Carolina State.*

City College of New York, completing its shocking and unprecedented sweep of college basketball's two postseason classics, defeated No. 1-ranked Bradley, 71–68, and claimed the championship of the NCAA Tournament at New York's Madison Square Garden.

CCNY, a team that had struggled badly through the second half of the season and barely qualified for the NIT, swept through that event in surprising fashion, upsetting Bradley, 69–61, in the final. As NIT champion, the Beavers qualified for the NCAA field and put together another shocking string of victories, setting up a rematch with Bradley in the title game.

By now, the Cinderella Beavers were poised and confident. They shredded the Braves' zone defense en route to a 39–32 halftime lead and stretched their advantage to 58–47 midway through the second half. In desperation, Bradley switched to a man-to-man defense and began chipping away.

The lead was 69–63 with a minute remaining when Bradley's Joe Stowell hit a free throw and Gene Melchiorre made two layups off steals. The pesky Melchiorre stole the ball again with time running out and drove for a go-ahead basket, but Irwin Dambrot took the ball out of his hands and fired the length of the court to Norm Mager, who made the clinching basket.

The victory completed a 24–5 season for the opportunistic Beavers of Nat Holman.

1982 JORDAN SINKS HOYAS

North Carolina freshman Michael Jordan hit a 16-foot jump shot with 15 seconds remaining and the Tar Heels held on to record a hard-fought 63–62 victory over Georgetown in the NCAA Tournament title game at New Orleans.

The Tar Heels' second national championship did not come easy. The powerful Hoyas displayed a potent inside-outside combination with 7-foot freshman Patrick Ewing and guard Eric (Sleepy) Floyd. No. 1-ranked North Carolina countered with slashing James Worthy, 6-9 Sam Perkins and Jordan.

Ewing showed a surprising scoring touch as Georgetown claimed a 32–21 halftime advantage. The second half was a basketball clinic in which the lead see-sawed back and forth, neither team able to pull ahead by more than four points. After Floyd's short jumper gave Georgetown its final lead with 57 seconds remaining, North Carolina called a timeout and set up the play to Jordan. When his jumper fell, the Hoyas still had time to win. But guard Fred Brown, thinking he saw teammate Eric Smith with his peripheral vision, instead fired a pass to Worthy, securing North Carolina's victory.

Worthy finished with 28 points while Ewing led Georgetown with 23.

MILESTONES IN SPORTS

1929
The 5-year-old Boston Bruins swept to the Stanley Cup with a two games to none victory over the New York Rangers.

1940
Joe Louis made quick work of Johnny Paychek with a second-round knockout in a heavyweight title bout at New York's Madison Square Garden.

1941
Wisconsin 39, Washington State 34: An NCAA Tournament championship for the Badgers and a major victory for the Big Ten Conference.

1966
It took Muhammad Ali 15 rounds to record a unanimous decision over George Chuvalo in a heavyweight championship bout at Toronto.

1970
Chicago goaltender Tony Esposito made Toronto his 15th shutout victim of the season in a 4–0 Blackhawks victory at Chicago Stadium.

1977
The National Football League adopted a 16-game regular-season schedule and four-game preseason slate to begin in 1978.

1990
Houston center Akeem Olajuwon became the third player in NBA history to get a quadruple-double when he recorded 18 points, 16 rebounds, 11 blocked shots and 10 assists in the Rockets' 120–94 victory over Milwaukee.

MARCH

30

A STAR IS BORN

1940: Jerry Lucas, a basketball Hall of Famer who scored 14,053 points over an 11-year NBA career that ended in 1973–74.

★ ★ ★

DEATH OF A LEGEND

1952: Deacon Phillippe (baseball).

★ ★ ★

MILESTONES IN SPORTS

1916

The pre-NHL Montreal Canadiens captured their first Stanley Cup, beating the Portland Rosebuds of the PCHA in a five-game final series.

1919

The Stanley Cup final was cancelled with Montreal (NHL) and Seattle (PCHA) tied at 2–2–1 because of a life-threatening influenza epidemic.

1940

Indiana 60, Kansas 42: The Hurryin' Hoosiers win their first NCAA Tournament championship.

1943

Wyoming 46, Georgetown 34: The NCAA Tournament championship trophy headed west for the third time in five years.

1966

Star Los Angeles Dodger pitchers Don Drysdale and Sandy Koufax ended their 32-day double holdout by signing a combined package worth more than $210,000.

1968

TENNIS 'OPENS UP' IN HISTORIC VOTE

Members of the International Lawn Tennis Federation, following the lead of Wimbledon officials who already had opened their championships to professionals, voted unanimously to endorse worldwide open tennis in an historic meeting at Paris.

The meeting, attended by 66 representatives of 47 countries, provided a shocking turnaround for a long-debated issue that had been voted down on numerous occasions. The British, expecting a severe reprimand for their decision to allow both professionals and amateurs to compete in their prestigious Wimbledon tournament, instead received praise for their pioneering role. There were no dissenting voices.

The ILTF decision is not binding. The various national organizations will be able to plot their own course and thus shape the future of tennis. The United States Lawn Tennis Federation immediately scheduled a meeting for Dallas.

1987

HOOSIERS GRAB SMART VICTORY

Keith Smart, *Indiana's sharpshooting guard*

Keith Smart, who scored 12 of Indiana's final 15 points, nailed a 16-foot jump shot with five seconds remaining and lifted the Hoosiers to a 74–73 victory over Syracuse in the NCAA Tournament championship game at New Orleans.

Smart took over after the Orangemen went to a box-and-one defense to contain long-range bomber Steve Alford, who had hit four of five three-point attempts that sparked Bobby Knight's Hoosiers to a 34–33 half-time lead.

Alford, who finished with 23 points, scored his final basket with 4:01 remaining, tying the game at 65–65.

Even with Smart firing on all cylinders down the stretch, the Hoosiers trailed, 73–70, with 38 seconds remaining. But Syracuse's Howard Triche missed the back end of a one-and-one free throw and freshman Derrick Coleman missed the front end of another, giving Indiana life. Smart's short jumper cut the lead to one and his game-winner over Triche sealed Indiana's fifth NCAA title.

1981

THOMAS' INDIANA KICK UP HEELS

Sophomore guard Isiah Thomas scored 19 of his game-high 23 points in a dazzling second-half display to spark Indiana to a 63–50 victory over North Carolina in the NCAA Tournament championship game at Philadelphia.

Indiana's fourth national title was a tribute to Thomas' quickness and court savvy. In the opening minutes of the second half, Thomas made two steals and layups, three jump shots and several point-producing passes that stretched a 27–26 Hoosier halftime lead to 43–34. In the closing minutes of the game, he was a ball-handling wizard.

Thomas' heroics followed a first half in which North Carolina had threatened to blow the Hoosiers out of the box. The Tar Heels scored eight of the first 10 points, enjoyed another 8–0 run and led, 20–14, when Randy Wittman began shooting holes in the North Carolina zone. Wittman's 18-foot corner jumper with one second on the clock gave Indiana its first lead and set the stage for the Hoosiers' second-half blitz.

The game was played despite protests after President Ronald Reagan sustained gunshot wounds in an afternoon assassination attempt.

Neither the players nor the fans who had planned to watch the game onTV knew whether it would be played until shortly before game time.

The NCAA Tournament committee made the announcement after learning that the President was out of danger after surgery.

1974
The new World Football League earned instant credibility when Toronto owner John Bassett Jr. raided the Miami Dolphins' championship roster and signed receiver Paul Warfield and running backs Larry Csonka and Jim Kiick.

1980
Mike Weaver claimed John Tate's WBA heavyweight championship with a 15th-round knockout at Knoxville, Tenn.

1986
Louisville 72, Duke 69: Pervis Ellison, a 6-foot-9 freshman center, was too much for the Blue Devils in the NCAA Tournament championship game.

1991
The women of Tennessee captured their third NCAA Tournament championship in five years with a 70–67 overtime victory over Virginia.

A STAR IS BORN

1878: Jack Johnson, boxing's first black heavyweight champion (1908–15) who compiled a professional record of 78–8–12.

★★★

1928: Gordie Howe, a hockey Hall of Fame right winger who played 32 seasons in the WHA and NHL and ranks second in all-time goals and points.

★★★

1971: Pavel Bure, a current National Hockey League right winger.

★★★

DEATH OF A LEGEND

1931: Knute Rockne (football).

★★★

1980: Jesse Owens (track and field).

★★★

1931 ROCKNE DIES IN CRASH

Notre Dame's Knute Rockne, regarded by many as the greatest coach in college football history, died when the plane that was carrying him from Kansas City to Los Angeles crashed into a pasture near Bazaar, Kan.

The 43-year-old Rockne, who compiled a 105–12–5 record and produced two undefeated teams in 13 glorious seasons as coach of the Fighting Irish, was on his way to Los Angeles to tend to personal business and to make a football film. He was one of eight passengers who died when the Trans-Continental and Western Airways aircraft lost its engines and went down.

Among the football innovations credited to Rockne were the backfield shift and improvements in offensive line play. The former Notre Dame end (1910–14) also formulated revolutionary forward passing strategies.

Rockne will be remembered for his "Four Horseman" team of 1924 and his "win one for the Gipper" speech that inspired Notre Dame to a big victory over Army in 1928. His 1929 and '30 teams both enjoyed undefeated seasons.

Former Notre Dame football coach **Knute Rockne.**

1991 DUKE SHOCKS UNLV

Duke forward Christian Laettner dropped a pair of free throws with 12 seconds remaining and the Blue Devils dropped the curtain on the University of Nevada-Las Vegas' 45-game winning streak with a shocking 79–77 victory over the Runnin' Rebels in a Final Four semifinal game at Indianapolis.

UNLV, heavily favored to win its second consecutive NCAA championship, entered the game with the fourth longest winning streak of all time. The Rebels had embarrassed opponents all season, outscoring them by an average of 27.6 points per game.

But it quickly became clear Duke would not die easily and that seemed to unnerve the Rebels. Seeking revenge for a 30-point loss to UNLV in last year's NCAA title game, the Blue Devils stayed within striking distance and faced only a five-point deficit with 2½ minutes remaining.

Guard Bobby Hurley cut UNLV's lead to two with a three-point bomb, Brian Davis converted a three-point play and suddenly Duke had a lead. The Rebels tied the game on Larry Johnson's free throw, but Laettner's 27th and 28th points gave Duke its final lead.

Hard-working Duke forward **Christian Laettner.**

MARCH 31

1975 WIZARD BOWS OUT

Richard Washington and Dave Meyers combined for 52 points and UCLA gave retiring Coach John Wooden his record 10th NCAA Tournament title with an inspired 92–85 championship game victory over Kentucky at San Diego.

Wooden, who had announced his plan to retire after UCLA's semifinal victory over Louisville, watched as the Bruins fought to a 43–40 halftime lead and stretched their advantage to 10 points with 12 minutes remaining. But the burly Wildcats refused to die.

With Kevin Grevey leading the charge, Kentucky pulled to within one, 76–75, and set the stage for the game's key play. Meyers, trying to get off a shot, collided with Grevey and was charged with his fifth foul. When he screamed and pounded the floor in disgust, he also drew a technical.

The Wildcats, suddenly in position to take charge, bungled the opportunity. Grevey missed both the front end of his one-and-one and the technical and Kentucky committed a turnover. Having regained lost momentum, the Bruins pulled away from the discouraged Wildcats.

Washington scored 28 points and Meyers 24 for the 28–3 Bruins. Grevey paced 26–5 Kentucky with 34 points .

APRIL 1

1991 DUKE BREAKS THROUGH

Christian Laettner scored 18 points and grabbed 10 rebounds to spark the Duke Blue Devils to a 72–65 victory over Kansas and their first NCAA Tournament championship in an emotional game at the Indianapolis Hoosier Dome.

The victory was especially sweet for Coach Mike Krzyzewski, who was making his fifth appearance in the Final Four since 1986. Duke had pulled off a shocking semifinal victory over defending champion Nevada-Las Vegas and many questioned whether the Blue Devils would be emotionally drained.

No problem. With point guard Bobby Hurley directing traffic and controlling the first-half tempo, Duke jumped to a 42–34 lead and never faltered. Laettner and Bill McCaffrey provided the firepower and the Blue Devils methodically stretched their advantage to 14 points with just 6:10 remaining.

The Jayhawks, with 18-point scorer Mark Randall doing most of the damage, made a final run and pulled within 70–65 with 32 seconds remaining, but Brian Davis' emphatic dunk closed the door on Kansas' comeback hopes.

Duke shot 56 percent from the floor but won the game from the foul line with a 20-of-28 performance. Kansas was 4 of 8 from the line.

MILESTONES • IN SPORTS •

1938

Quick and easy: Joe Louis defended his heavyweight crown with a first-round knockout of Harry Thomas at Chicago.

1981

Edmonton's 20-year-old Wayne Gretzky broke Bobby Orr's one-season record for assists when he notched No. 103 by setting up Jari Kurri for a first-period goal in a 4–4 tie with Colorado.

1982

The New York Knicks, trailing Cleveland by 26 points with 4 minutes remaining in the third quarter, fought back for a stunning 111–110 NBA victory at Madison Square Garden.

1990

Jack Nicklaus, making his debut on the PGA Seniors Tour, rolled to a four-stroke victory in the Tradition at Scottsdale, Ariz.

1992

Voting 560–4, players staged the first in-season strike in NHL history, walking out with five days remaining on the regular-season schedule.

A STAR IS BORN

1939: Phil Niekro, a 318-game winner in a distinguished pitching career that ended in 1987.

★ ★ ★

1944: Rusty Staub, a talented outfielder who collected 2,716 hits and batted .279 in a 23-year baseball career that ended in 1985.

★ ★ ★

1965: Mark Jackson, a current National Basketball Association guard.

★ ★ ★

DEATH OF A LEGEND

1914: Rube Waddell (baseball).

★ ★ ★

1985 VILLANOVA SLAYS GIANT

Villanova, heavy underdog to a Georgetown team generally considered one of the best of all time, methodically executed the big bad Hoyas with a near-perfect performance that produced a 66–64 championship game victory and one of the monumental upsets in NCAA Tournament history.

Coach **Rollie Massimino** *(above) pulled the strings and guard* **Gary McLain** *(below) handled Georgetown's suffocating pressure defense in Villanova's stunning upset of the Hoyas.*

Villanova, a two-time regular–season loser to Big East-rival Georgetown and a 10-time loser overall, was not considered a major threat to the defending NCAA champions. But with point guard Gary McLain handling the ball superbly against Georgetown's relentless full-court pressure, the Wildcats connected on 13 of 18 first-half shots and a late Harold Pressley basket gave them a 29–28 lead. When the crowd at the Lexington, Ky., arena saluted the Villanova players with a half-ending ovation, nobody realized the best was yet to come.

The Wildcats were as close to perfection over the final 20 minutes as a team can get. With 6-foot-9 Ed Pinckney shackling Georgetown 7-footer Patrick Ewing and Villanova's defense forcing David Wingate and Reggie Williams to take tough shots, the Wildcats picked right up where they had left off.

McLain continued to handle the pressure, Villanova continued its torrid shooting and the Wildcats stayed in the game. Georgetown claimed four one-point leads, but couldn't stretch its advantage. When Villanova took a 55–54 lead with 2:36 remaining on Harold Jensen's jump shot, the stage was set for Villanova's upset. McLain directed an effective delay game, the frustrated Hoyas fouled and the Wildcats hit their shots. In record fashion.

A 9-of-10 second-half blitz gave Villanova a tournament-record .786 field-goal percentage and the perfect antidote for an opponent with superior manpower. The Wildcats also hit 11 of 14 shots from the foul line. Dwayne McClain scored 17 points and Pinckney added 16, but the real hero was McLain, who hit all three shots he took and committed just two turnovers.

MILESTONES
IN SPORTS

1969

Lew Alcindor, the 7-foot-1 center who led UCLA to three straight NCAA Tournament championships, spurned a lucrative offer from the ABA's New York Nets and signed a five-year NBA contract with the Milwaukee Bucks.

1983

Luther Bradley of the USFL's Chicago Blitz picked off a professional football-record six passes in a 42–3 victory over the Tampa Bay Bandits at Tampa Stadium.

1985

In an attempt to increase action and stop stalling tactics, the NCAA adopted a 45-second clock for use in all 1985–86 college basketball games.

1986

Edmonton's Paul Coffey scored his 46th and 47th goals, breaking former Boston star Bobby Orr's one-season record for a defenseman and leading the Oilers to an 8–4 victory over Vancouver.

1990 Rebels With Cause Sweep Away Duke

The Runnin' Rebels of the University of Nevada-Las Vegas, the glowering and much-maligned bad boys of college basketball, used a relentless pressing defense to force 23 Duke turnovers and handed the Blue Devils a 103–73 thrashing in the championship game of the NCAA Tournament at Denver.

Coach Jerry Tarkanian's Rebels were their usual trash-talking selves as they shackled Duke stars Christian Laettner and Bobby Hurley, forced a tournament-record 16 turnovers and buried the Blue Devils with the inside-outside combination of guard Anderson Hunt and big man Larry Johnson.

Hunt connected on 12 of 16 shots and scored 29 points while Johnson hit 8 of 12 and finished with 22. The Rebels owned a 57–47 halftime lead and really turned up the pressure after intermission with an 18-point run.

It was sweet revenge for Tarkanian, the oft-investigated NCAA whipping boy who watched his team shoot 61 percent from the floor and hit 18 of 29 three-point attempts en route to its 35th victory in 40 games.

It was like a casual stroll down victory lane as Tark the Shark watched the proceedings like any other spectator, lounging in his chair with his hands folded behind his head, admiring the performance of his fine-tuned machine.

The 30-point victory margin was the largest in championship game history and the title was UNLV's first.

UNLV Coach **Jerry Tarkanian's** *Rebels battled their way to the school's first NCAA title.*

1986 NCAA Adopts 3-Point Shot

In a move that could change the course of college basketball, the National Collegiate Athletic Association adopted the three-point field goal for men's play in the 1986–87 season.

The controversial decision came after five years of experimentation with the three-pointer among 20 conferences. Different leagues tried the rule from different distances and the 12-member NCAA rules committee finally settled on 19 feet, 9 inches as the one most desirable to college coaches.

The National Basketball Association awards three points for shots outside an arc 23 feet, 9 inches from the basket. College coaches thought that distance was too far.

Dr. Edward S. Steitz, athletic director at Springfield College and secretary-editor of the rules committee, praised the innovation, saying it will force teams to play more defense away from the basket while expanding the role of the little man and the pure shooter in the game.

1984 Hoya Paranoia Rocks Houston

Scowling Michael Graham and sweet-shooting Reggie Williams, a pair of Georgetown freshmen, took center stage in what had been billed as a battle of big men and led the Hoyas to an 84–75 victory over Houston and their first NCAA Tournament championship.

The Battle of Seattle was supposed to be decided by the inside play of 7-footers Akeem Olajuwon of Houston and Patrick Ewing of Georgetown. But when the two stars got into early foul trouble, the game took on a different tone.

Using its patented pressure defense to wear down Houston's guards and force turnovers, the Hoyas broke a 14–14 tie with eight consecutive points and methodically built a 40–30 halftime lead while Ewing sat on the bench with two fouls. Olajuwon picked up his third foul with 42 seconds left in the half and his fourth 23 seconds after intermission.

Only the torrid shooting of guard Alvin Franklin kept the Cougars in contention. Franklin hit 14 of Houston's next 20 points after Olajuwon's exit, cutting Georgetown's lead to three. But that was as good as it got. With Graham scoring 14 points and dominating inside and Williams scoring 19, the Hoyas pulled away to their 34th victory in 37 games.

The loss was the fifth in 37 decisions for Guy Lewis' Cougars.

APRIL 2

A STAR IS BORN

1870: Hughie Jennings, a Hall of Fame infielder who batted .312 over a 17-year career at the turn of the century.

★ ★ ★

1907: Luke Appling, a Hall of Fame shortstop who batted .310 over a 20-year career (1930–50) with the Chicago White Sox.

★ ★ ★

1910: Arnie Herber, a football Hall of Fame quarterback who built his reputation with the Green Bay Packers in the 1930s.

★ ★ ★

1915: Al Barlick, a Hall of Fame umpire in a 30-year career that ended in 1971.

★ ★ ★

1927: Billy Pierce, a smooth lefthanded pitcher who won 211 games in an 18-year major league career that ended in 1964.

★ ★ ★

1945: Don Sutton, a consistent if unspectacular 324-game winner over a 23-year pitching career that ended in 1988.

★ ★ ★

1945: Reggie Smith, a .287 batter and 314-home run hitter in 17 productive major league seasons (1966–82).

★ ★ ★

DEATH OF A LEGEND

1972: Gil Hodges (baseball).

APRIL

3

1933 HOCKEY'S LONGEST GAME

Ken Doraty, the smallest player on the ice, fired a shot past Boston goalie Tiny Thompson in the sixth overtime period and brought an end to the longest game in National Hockey League history – a 1–0 Toronto victory at Maple Leaf Gardens. The pulsating triumph came in the decisive fifth game of a semifinal playoff series and earned Toronto the right to meet the New York Rangers in the Stanley Cup finals. The game was viewed by 14,500 fans, the largest crowd ever to attend a hockey game in Canada, and most of them stayed to the end.

That end came after three 20-minute periods and five 20-minute overtimes. The total game time was 164 minutes and 46 seconds, far outdistancing the previous mark of 128:52 by the Rangers and Montreal in 1930.

Springfield and Boston of the Canadian-American League played 100 overtime minutes last season before settling for a 2-2 tie.

The Maple Leafs carried the play throughout, but Thompson's sensational goaltending kept Boston alive. Both teams had goals overruled – one on an offsides and the other because of a pre-shot whistle.

Doraty scored his game-winner off a pass from Andy Blair, giving Toronto goalie Lorne Chabot a hard-earned shutout.

MILESTONES • IN SPORTS •

1977

Boston's Jean Ratelle picked up his 1,000th career point in his 1,007th game when he assisted on a goal in the Bruins' 7–4 victory over the Toronto Maple Leafs at Boston Garden.

1982

Another milestone: Gilbert Perreault's 1,000th National Hockey League career point came on an assist in Buffalo's 5–4 victory at Montreal.

1985

The NBA placed another franchise on the West Coast by giving the Kings permission to move operations from Kansas City to Sacramento.

1985

Owners and players agreed to expand Major League Baseball's championship series from a best-of-five to a best-of-seven game format.

1991

Bo Jackson, released by Major League Baseball's Kansas City Royals after suffering a serious hip injury while playing for the National Football League's Los Angeles Raiders, signed a share-the-risk contract with the Chicago White Sox.

1989 MICHIGAN FINISHES ITS LONG JOURNEY

Michigan guard Rumeal Robinson hit a pair of free throws with three seconds remaining in overtime and the Wolverines claimed their first NCAA Tournament championship with an 80–79 victory over Seton Hall at Seattle.

The exciting victory climaxed a traumatic postseason run that was choreographed by interim coach Steve Fisher, who had taken control of the team just before the tournament when Coach Bill Frieder announced he had taken the coaching job at Arizona State. Under Fisher, the Wolverines posted five consecutive victories and carried a 29–7 record into the title game.

Glen Rice, *Michigan's long-range bomber.*

With Glen Rice bombing from the outside and Robinson directing traffic, Michigan rolled to a 51–39 second-half advantage and appeared headed to easy victory. But John Morton, who scored a game-high 35 points, brought the Pirates back and his three-point shot with 25 seconds remaining forced overtime.

The extra session came down to the final seconds and Seton Hall, holding a one-point advantage, missed a short jumper. When Robinson darted downcourt for the potential go-ahead basket, he was fouled, setting the stage for his winning free throws.

Rice led Michigan with 31 points.

1962 PARET'S DEATH SPARKS PROBE

Benny (Kid) Paret, pummelled into unconsciousness March 24 by welterweight champion Emile Griffith in a title fight at Madison Square Garden, died at a New York hospital, sparking a loud public outcry against the "vicious sport of boxing."

Griffith had dominated the 25-year-old Paret through the early rounds and went for a knockout early in the 12th.

The champion worked his 25-year-old Cuban opponent into the corner and assaulted him with about twenty-five blows as he stood defenseless against the ropes.

With Paret helpless and possibly out on his feet, referee Ruby Goldstein inexplicably allowed the carnage to continue. Paret finally fell to the canvas, bleeding and unconscious.

An ambulance rushed him to the hospital, where he underwent an emergency operation to relieve pressure on his brain. But he remained comatose until his death.

A legislative committee was set up to determine the course of boxing in New York.

It heard testimony from many of those present at the controversial fight and ordered both Griffith and Goldstein to testify.

A STAR IS BORN

1934: Jim Parker, the first offensive lineman elected to the football Hall of Fame exclusively as an offensive performer. He played from 1957–67 for the Baltimore Colts.

★ ★ ★

1945: Bernie Parent, a hockey Hall of Fame goaltender who posted 55 shutouts and a 2.55 goals-against average and led Philadelphia to consecutive Stanley Cup titles in 1974 and '75.

★ ★ ★

1964: Shane Conlan, a current NFL linebacker.

A STAR IS BORN

1888: Tris Speaker, a Hall of Fame outfielder who batted .345 and collected 3,515 hits over a 22-year American League career that ended in 1928.

★ ★ ★

1924: Gil Hodges, a slugging first baseman who hit 370 career home runs, most of them with the Brooklyn and Los Angeles Dodgers from 1943–61.

★ ★ ★

1939: Bill Bridges, an outstanding basketball forward who scored 13,558 points and grabbed 4,871 rebounds during 15 combined ABA and NBA seasons.

★ ★ ★

1939: JoAnne Carner, an outstanding woman golfer who won five U.S. Amateur championships and two U.S. Opens in the 1950s, '60s and '70s.

★ ★ ★

1963: Dale Hawerchuk, a current National Hockey League center.

★ ★ ★

DEATH OF A LEGEND

1967: Guy Chamberlin (football).

★ ★ ★

1971: Carl Mays (baseball).

★ ★ ★

1983

N.C. State Ices Cinderella Season

North Carolina State's Lorenzo Charles caught teammate Dereck Whittenburg's desperation shot in mid-air and slammed it home with one second remaining, completing the Wolfpack's 54–52 upset of Houston and its shocking run to an NCAA Tournament championship.

N.C. State entered the game as a heavy underdog to Houston's high-scoring "Phi Slama Jama" dunking fraternity. The Wolfpack, 25–10, had reached the final by virtue of several comeback victories that were nothing short of amazing.

N.C. State continued its magic against a talented Houston team that featured 7-foot Akeem Olajuwon, Clyde Drexler, Michael Young and Larry Micheaux. The key was a compact zone that forced Houston's inside power out of the lane.

With 6–11 Thurl Bailey scoring 15 points, the Wolfpack raced to a shocking 33–25 halftime lead. But sanity prevailed after intermission when the Cougars put together a 17–2 run that produced a 42–35 lead. When Houston Coach Guy Lewis went to his spread offense, however, the pace slowed and N.C. State clawed its way back, finally tying at 52 on two jumpers by Whittenburg.

When Houston freshman Alvin Franklin missed a pair of free throws with less than a minute to play, the Wolfpack worked for a last shot. But a pass to Whittenburg was deflected and the senior grabbed the loose ball, firing a desperation shot that fell into the waiting hands of Charles.

Die-hard North Carolina State Coach **Jim Valvano.**

APRIL

4

MILESTONES • IN SPORTS •

1968

Louisiana State sharpshooter Pete Maravich set an NCAA single-season record when he finished his sophomore campaign with a 43.8-point scoring average.

1985

Three Tulane basketball players and five other persons were indicted in a point-shaving scandal and university President Eamon M. Kelly announced that the school will drop its program.

1986

Edmonton's Wayne Gretzky surpassed his own NHL single-season points record when he raised his total to 214 with three assists in a 9–3 loss to Calgary.

1974

Aaron Catches Babe at 714

Atlanta slugger Hank Aaron, wasting little time in his quest to unseat Babe Ruth as baseball's all-time home run king, belted record-tying homer No. 714 on his first swing of the new season, six minutes after the Braves–Reds opener had started at Cincinnati's Riverfront Stadium.

The 40-year-old Aaron, who entered the new campaign one home run short of Ruth's career record, connected with a Jack Billingham pitch and drove it 400 feet over the left-field wall for a three-run homer. With the number "714" flashing on the huge scoreboard above the upper deck in center field, Aaron trotted around the bases and into the record books. He was met at home plate by enthusiastic teammates and the game was held up while tributes were passed his way.

The home run, which came on a 3–1 pitch in Aaron's 11,289th career at-bat, sailed to the left of the 375-foot sign. The shot gave Atlanta a quick 3–0 lead, but the Reds came back to post a 7–6 victory in 11 innings.

1988

Manning Seals Kansas' Win

Danny Manning scored four of his 31 points from the free throw line in the final 10 seconds to propel Kansas to a shocking 83–79 victory over Big Eight Conference-rival Oklahoma and the Jayhawks' first NCAA Tournament championship in 36 years.

In an entertaining game at Kansas City, both teams displayed a relentless pressure defense and pushed the ball downcourt in a 50–50 first-half battle during which Oklahoma hit 7 of 11 three-point shots and Kansas connected on 4 of 5 while shooting 71 percent from the floor.

With Stacey King dominating inside and Dave Sieger bombing from the outside, the 35–3 Sooners built a 65–60 second-half lead and did everything they could to shake the 27–11 Jayhawks. But Manning would not let that happen.

The All-America forward added a jumper to a six-point Kansas burst that broke a 71–71 deadlock and, when Oklahoma cut the margin to one minutes later, he secured the game from the free throw line.

Danny Manning, *the top gun in Kansas' imposing arsenal.*

APRIL

5

A STAR IS BORN

1871: Glenn (Pop) Warner, a football innovator and college coach who produced a 313–106–32 record and three national champions from 1896–1938.

★ ★ ★

1951: Rennie Stennett, a former major league second baseman best remembered for his record seven-hit effort in a 1975 game for Pittsburgh.

★ ★ ★

1984 JABBAR SETS NBA SCORING RECORD

Kareem Abdul-Jabbar completed his 15-year chase of the National Basketball Association's most coveted record when he connected on a 12-foot baseline sky hook during a game against Utah and became the game's all-time leading scorer.

Abdul-Jabbar made history in the fourth quarter of the Los Angeles Lakers' 129–115 victory over the Jazz at the Thomas and Mack Arena in Las Vegas. Having tied Wilt Chamberlain's 11-year-old mark of 31,419 points a few minutes earlier on a dunk, the 7-foot-2 Abdul-Jabbar let fly with his patented sky hook over Jazz defenders Mark Eaton and Rickey Green.

When the ball floated through, the game was stopped and ceremonies were conducted at mid-court. Abdul-Jabbar took the microphone and said, "It's hard to say anything after all is said and done."

The 36-year-old Abdul-Jabbar was removed from the game with 31,421 points. He made 10 of 14 shots and both free-throw attempts for 22 points. He set the record in 1,166 games, 121 more than Chamberlain, who retired after the 1972–73 season.

1967 WILT KEYS 76ER WIN

Wilt Chamberlain scored 20 points and grabbed a National Basketball Association playoff-record 41 rebounds as the Philadelphia 76ers rolled to a 115-104 victory over Boston and nudged the eight-year defending-champion Celtics to the brink of elimination from the post-season tournament.

Chamberlain's record-setting domination of the boards and a 30-point effort by Hal Greer gave the 76ers a three games to none lead in the Eastern Conference Finals and put the Celtics into a near-hopeless situation. No team has been able to recover from a 3–0 playoff deficit since the NBA began play in the 1946-47 season.

The Celtics fell behind in the third quarter, but fought back to within a point, 102–101, with three minutes remaining. But Wally Jones hit three consecutive long jump shots, Chet Walker made a layup and Greer hit five free throws as the 76ers regained control.

The game ended with ecstatic Philadelphia fans filling Convention Hall with chants of "Boston is dead! Boston is dead!"

The Celtics' incredible run of success had started 10 years earlier when they won their first NBA championship with a seven-game victory over St. Louis. After losing the next year to the Hawks, Boston reeled off eight consecutive title runs – an unprecedented feat in any of the four major sports. The previous best streak had been five in a row by baseball's New York Yankees and Hockey's Montreal Canadiens.

MILESTONES · IN SPORTS ·

1971

Former Notre Dame quarterback Joe Theismann spurned the NFL's Miami Dolphins and signed a two-year contract with the Toronto Argonauts of the Canadian Football League.

1972

Del Insko became the fourth driver in harness racing history to record 3,000 career victories when he guided Actor Melody to the finish line in the fourth race at Yonkers Raceway.

1976

Nine years after banning the dunk shot from college and high school basketball, the National Basketball Rules Committee brought it back, legalizing it for the 1976–77 season.

1987

Betsy King parred the second hole of a sudden-death playoff and earned her first major title by beating Patty Sheehan in the Dinah Shore classic at Rancho Mirage, Calif.

1915 WILLARD SHOCKS JOHNSON

Jess Willard, a 6-foot-6, 250-pound Kansas farm-boy, connected with a wild right to the jaw of Jack Johnson in the 26th round of a heavyweight title bout at Havana, Cuba, bringing an end to the $6^1/2$-year reign of boxing's first black champion.

Johnson, who had powered his way past every "Great White Hope" sent to dethrone him since winning the championship from Tommy Burns in 1908, was clearly the superior boxer in his match against the giant Willard. But Willard's strategy was simple: Survive the early rounds and let the intense heat of Havana take its toll on the 37-year-old champion.

The strategy worked. Johnson pummeled Willard for 20 rounds, bouncing him around the ring like a giant pinball, but he couldn't put him down. Then, suddenly, Johnson ran out of gas and the fight turned.

Jack Johnson's *stranglehold on white America ended in the ring against big* **Jess Willard.**

It was just a matter of time. Unable to move with his early quickness and no longer able to muster punching power, Johnson took a left jab to the heart and the windmill right to the jaw that sent him sprawling. Just like that, it was over. Johnson announced his retirement after the fight.

1992 DUKE WINS 2ND IN ROW

Duke point guard and quarterback **Bobby Hurley.**

The Duke Blue Devils, seeking to become the first team to win back-to-back national championships in 19 years, dashed Michigan's title hopes with a late 23–6 run that produced a 71–51 victory in the NCAA Tournament final at the Minneapolis Metrodome.

Duke, which held the freshman-laden Wolverines to eight points and three field goals over the final 9:57, led 48–45 when the run began at 6:51 on Christian Laettner's reverse layup. The Blue Devils made eight of their final 10 shots and scored on their final 12 possessions to wrap up their 34th victory in 36 games.

Laettner recovered from a horrible start to finish with a game-high 19 points, one more than Grant Hill. Bobby Hurley called an outstanding game from the point, scored nine points and handed out seven assists.

Michigan, which started five freshmen, held a 31–30 halftime lead, but missed all nine three-pointers it attempted after intermission. Chris Webber led the Wolverines with 14 points.

The victory allowed Duke to become the first top-ranked team to win a championship since North Carolina in 1982.

1987 LEONARD SHOCKS HAGLER

Sugar Ray Leonard, fighting for just the second time in five years, scored a shocking 12-round split decision over Marvelous Marvin Hagler and claimed the World Boxing Council's middleweight championship in a showy spectacle at Caesar's Palace outdoor arena.

It was a popular decision for the 15,336 fans who chanted, "Sugar Ray, Sugar Ray." It was not so popular for Hagler, who lost for the first time since 1976 and third time in a career that has produced 63 victories.

Hagler was on a seek-and-destroy mission from the opening bell. But every time he caught up to the elusive Leonard, he would be greeted by seven or eight swift blows. That pattern continued through the early rounds before a tiring Leonard began to feel the power in Hagler's accurate counter-punches.

But neither man could take control and the bout ended with the fighters standing toe to toe and slugging it out. The verdict was turned over to the judges, who narrowly awarded Leonard his 34th victory in 35 fights.

Leonard was coming back from an eye injury.

Sugar Ray Leonard *(right) delivers a blow to Marvin Hagler's head during their middleweight battle at Caesar's Palace.*

1958 PALMER CLAIMS MASTERS

Arnold Palmer shot a final-round 73 over a soggy and slow Augusta National course and then watched for two hours from the clubhouse before claiming the Masters championship and his first major title.

The 28-year-old former U.S. Amateur champion did not exactly burn up the course en route to his 73 and four-round total of 284. But neither did anybody else because of an overnight thunderstorm that threatened postponement of the final round.

Palmer took control at the par-5 13th hole, where he clubbed a 3-wood to the green and dropped a 20-foot putt for an eagle 3. After losing a stroke when he three-putted the 18th, the youngster watched from the clubhouse as Doug Ford and Fred Hawkins missed 18th-hole birdie putts that would have forced a playoff.

Ford recorded a final-round 70, the best of the day, and Hawkins a 71. They tied for second at 285.

APRIL 6

MILESTONES IN SPORTS

1900

James J. Jeffries defended his heavyweight championship with a first-round knockout of Jack Finnegan at Detroit .

1973

The A.L. launched its designated-hitter experiment on Opening Day at Boston's Fenway Park when New York Yankee Ron Blomberg drew a first-inning bases-loaded walk in an eventual 15–5 Red Sox victory.

1977

The California Angels ruined the Mariners' debut at Seattle's Kingdome with a 7–0 victory.

1992

Rick Sutcliffe fired a five-hit shutout as Baltimore christened Oriole Park at Camden Yards with a 2–0 Opening Day victory over the Cleveland Indians.

A STAR IS BORN

1903: Mickey Cochrane, a Hall of Fame catcher and manager with the Philadelphia Athletics and Detroit Tigers from 1925–37.

★ ★ ★

1908: Ernie Lombardi, a Hall of Fame catcher who batted .306 over a 17-year career that produced two N.L. batting titles in the 1930s and '40s.

★ ★ ★

1951: Bert Blyleven, a 22-year righthanded pitcher who won 287 games before ending his career in 1992.

★ ★ ★

APRIL

7

A STAR IS BORN

1859: Walter Camp, a college football pioneer credited with such innovations as downs, the line of scrimmage, the center snap, 11 players per side and All-America teams.

★ ★ ★

1873: John McGraw, the Hall of Fame manager who guided the New York Giants to 10 pennants and three World Series championships from 1902–32.

★ ★ ★

1918: Bobby Doerr, Boston's Hall of Fame second baseman who batted .288 and collected 2,042 hits over 14 major league seasons from 1937–51.

★ ★ ★

1954: Tony Dorsett, a former Heisman Trophy winner from Pittsburgh who ranks as the all-time collegiate career rusher (6,082 yards) and No. 2 all-time in the NFL (12,739).

★ ★ ★

1975 LEE ELDER BREAKS MASTERS BARRIER

Lee Elder, obviously unhappy about the horde of reporters that greeted his historic arrival at Augusta National Golf Club, fought his way to the clubhouse and registered as the first black to compete in a Masters tournament.

Lee Elder, *the first black to compete in a Masters tournament.*

The 40-year-old Elder and his wife Rose drove up the driveway fronting the white clubhouse in a red limousine at 2:05 p.m. Large crowds of reporters and well-wishers had gathered before noon – his expected arrival time.

When the couple emerged from the car, they were engulfed by photographers and reporters who began firing questions. "I'm not talking," said Elder, who made his way into the clubhouse, registered and then went to the locker room.

Elder, who qualified for the Masters by winning the Monsanto Open in Pensacola, Fla., last year, played rounds at Augusta National in October and March at the invitation of Cliff Roberts, co-founder of the tournament. But he limited action after his arrival to hitting a few practice shots – and avoiding the media.

1928 'OLD' LESTER RESCUES RANGERS

Desperate New York Coach Lester Patrick, a 44-year-old former defenseman, put on the goalie pads of injured Lorne Chabot midway through Game 2 of a Stanley Cup final series against the Montreal Maroons and led the Rangers to an inspiring and memorable 2-1 victory before a shocked crowd at the Montreal Forum.

The game was scoreless early in the second period when Chabot took a Nels Stewart shot just above the eye and was rushed to a hospital. With no other goaltenders on his roster, Patrick faced a decision. Already trailing in the series one game to none, he could substitute a player without goaltending experience. . . or step in himself, an illogical alternative that Patrick chose.

Wearing Chabot's bloody, sweat-soaked gear, Patrick flopped around the net like a wounded duck. But with the determined Rangers stepping up their checking and limiting Montreal shots, the New Yorkers made it through the second period scoreless and played the Maroons to a 1–1 standstill in the third period.

When Frank Boucher threaded his way through the Maroon defense and beat Montreal goalie Clinton Benedict at 7:05 of overtime for the winning goal, the Rangers carried Patrick off the ice on their shoulders. Their white-haired boss had made 18 saves – and earned himself a great deal of respect.

The inspired Rangers went on to win the next three games and earn their first Stanley Cup.

MILESTONES IN SPORTS

1970

Milwaukee fans, who had lost their N.L. Braves four years earlier, got their first look at A.L. baseball when the newly-arrived Brewers dropped a 12–0 Opening Day decision to California at County Stadium.

1977

Steve Cauthen, a 16-year-old apprentice, became the first jockey in New York racing history to twice win six races on a single card, performing the feat for a second time at Aqueduct.

1979

Houston righthander Ken Forsch held the Atlanta Braves hitless in a 6–0 victory at the Astrodome—the earliest (by date) no-hitter in baseball history.

1985

Herschel Walker romped for a USFL-record 233 yards and led the New Jersey Generals to a 31–25 victory over the Houston Gamblers.

1977 CANADIAN JAYS ENJOY TAKEOFF

The expansion Blue Jays captured the heart of Toronto fans when they introduced American League baseball to Canada with a resounding 9–5 victory over Chicago in a baseball season opener at Exhibition Stadium.

The Blue Jays followed the lead of the National League's Montreal Expos, an expansion franchise that fielded the first team on foreign soil in 1969. The Toronto opener was played on a cold afternoon before 44,649 fans who cheered heartily as their new team wiped out an early 4–1 deficit with an impressive 16-hit barrage.

The biggest offensive weapon was wielded by Toronto first baseman Doug Ault, who drove in four runs with a solo first-inning home run, a two-run third-inning blast and an eighth-inning single. Al Woods joined the fun, becoming the 10th man in history to homer on his first major league at-bat.

Jerry Johnson, working in relief of starter Bill Singer, pitched $2^2/3$ innings to claim the historic victory.

A STAR IS BORN

1910: George Musso, a football Hall of Fame lineman who played from 1933–44 with the NFL's Chicago Bears.

★ ★ ★

1912: Sonja Henie, a Norwegian figure skater who won 10 world championships and three consecutive Olympic gold medals (1928, '32, '36).

★ ★ ★

1940: John Havlicek, the Boston Celtics Hall of Fame forward who scored 26,395 career points and played on eight NBA championship teams in the 1960s and '70s.

★ ★ ★

1946: Jim (Catfish) Hunter, a five-time 20-game winner who posted 224 career victories and played on five World Series champions from 1965–79.

★ ★ ★

1954: Gary Carter, a 19-year major league catcher who retired in 1992 with 324 career home runs.

DEATH OF A LEGEND

1978: Ford Frick (baseball).

1974 715: AARON PASSES RUTH

Atlanta slugger Hank Aaron claimed Babe Ruth's career home run crown when he belted his record-setting 715th round-tripper off Los Angeles lefthander Al Downing in the Braves' season opener at Atlanta Stadium.

The record-breaking home run swing of Atlanta's **Hank Aaron.**

Aaron, who had finished the 1973 season one homer short of Ruth's 714 career mark and then tied the Bambino with his first swing of the season in Cincinnati, drove a 1–0 Downing pitch into the Braves' left-center-field bullpen for a two-run shot that tied the game at 3–3.

The historic home run was greeted by skyrockets and other fireworks that lit up the sky as Aaron circled the bases. He was met at home plate by a gigantic hug from his mother and a mob of happy teammates. Ceremonies honoring his feat lasted another 10 minutes as 53,775 fans saluted their 40-year-old star.

The home run was captured by national television cameras, which had followed Aaron through spring training in an unprecedented media blitz. Aaron, playing in his 20th campaign, had walked in his first at-bat of the night. The Braves went on to defeat the Dodgers, 7–4.

APRIL 8

1975 ROBBY BREAKS COLOR BARRIER

Frank Robinson, officially taking up the mantle as baseball's first black manager, directed the Cleveland Indians to a 5–3 season-opening victory over the New York Yankees and punctuated his big day by hitting a home run.

Robinson, making his historical debut before 56,204 fans and hundreds of cameras on a frigid afternoon at Cleveland's Municipal Stadium, got the game off to a dramatic start when he connected with a first-inning Doc Medich pitch for his 575th career home run. The homer stirred up the crowd and seemed to inspire the young Indians.

After the home run, the rest was easy as Robinson flawlessly pulled the managerial strings while handling his part-time role as designated hitter. Robinson, baseball's first player-manager since 1959, ranks fourth on the game's all-time home run chart.

Rachel Robinson, the widow of Jackie Robinson, threw out the ceremonial first pitch, 27 years after her husband had broken the color barrier as a player for the Brooklyn Dodgers.

Frank Robinson officially broke the managerial color barrier six months earlier when General Manager Phil Seghi introduced him as the Indians' new field boss.

1987 DODGER OFFICIAL RESIGNS

Al Campanis, the Los Angeles Dodgers official who suggested on network television that blacks may lack the qualities to become baseball managers or front-office executives, resigned under a blitz of media and personal pressure.

The 70-year-old Campanis, a Dodger vice president and a member of the organization since 1943, created an uproar when he appeared on ABC's Nightline with Ted Koppel as part of a show dealing with the 40th anniversary of Jackie Robinson breaking baseball's color barrier.

When Koppel asked why baseball had no black managers, general managers or owners, Campanis replied, "I truly believe that they may not have some of the necessities to be, let's say, a field manager or perhaps a general manager."

Koppel then asked him if he really believed that and Campanis responded, "Well, I don't say that all of them, but they certainly are short. How many quarterbacks do you have, how many pitchers do you have, that are black?"

Former Dodger vice president **Al Campanis.**

MILESTONES IN SPORTS

1989

With 46,847 California fans watching at Anaheim Stadium, one-handed Angels pitcher Jim Abbott lost his major league debut, 7–0, to Seattle.

1990

Nick Faldo parred the second hole of a sudden-death playoff against Raymond Floyd and earned his second consecutive Masters golf championship.

1991

Bill Shoemaker, who retired in 1990 as the winningest jockey in horse racing history, suffered partial paralysis when the car he was driving crashed at Corvina, Calif.

1992

Tennis great Arthur Ashe, saying he was victimized by a blood transfusion during open-heart surgery in 1983, revealed he had been battling the AIDS virus since 1988.

1993

Miami guard Brian Shaw set a National Basketball Association 3-point field goal record when he connected for 10 in a 117–92 Heat victory at Milwaukee.

APRIL

9

A STAR IS BORN

1898: Curly Lambeau, an NFL charter member and Hall of Famer as a player, coach and owner of the Green Bay Packers. He led Green Bay to six NFL championships and 230 victories.

★★★

1928: Paul Arizin, a basketball Hall of Fame forward who scored 16,266 points in a 12-year career with the NBA's Philadelphia Warriors from 1950–62.

★★★

DEATH OF A LEGEND

1971: Will Harridge (baseball).

★★★

MILESTONES • IN SPORTS •

1913

Brooklyn dedicated new Ebbets Field, but Philadelphia spoiled the occasion with a 1–0 victory over the Dodgers.

1947

Commissioner A.B. (Happy) Chandler suspended Brooklyn Manager Leo Durocher for the 1947 season, citing a series of unpleasant incidents "detrimental to baseball."

1965

Houston's new Astrodome, a.k.a. the Eighth Wonder of the World, opened its gates to rave reviews as the Astros recorded a 2–1, 12-inning exhibition victory over the New York Yankees.

1973

Tommy Aaron posted a final-round 68 and held off Jack Nicklaus and J.C. Snead for a one-stroke victory in the Masters at Augusta.

1978 PLAYER IS THE MASTER

South African **Gary Player**, *a three-time Masters champion.*

South African Gary Player, the only foreigner to win a Masters golf tournament, donned the coveted Green Jacket for a third time when he blistered the Augusta National course for a final-round 64 and recorded an exciting one-stroke victory over three challengers.

Player, who started the round seven strokes behind third-round leader Hubert Green, recorded seven birdies on his last 10 holes and then watched from the side of the 18th green as Green, Rod Funseth and Tom Watson all missed putts that would have forced a sudden-death playoff.

Green, who shot a final-round 72, missed from 2 1/2 feet. Watson and Funseth, who finished with 69s, missed from 12 and 24 feet, tying Green for second place with 72-hole totals of 278.

The 42-year-old Player, who previously had won at Augusta in 1961 and '74, became the oldest golfer to win a Masters. The victory was his 19th on the PGA Tour and 112th worldwide.

1978 WILD SHOOTOUT DECIDES TITLE

San Antonio's George Gervin, needing 59 points to win a National Basketball Association scoring title, fired in 63 in a night game at New Orleans after Denver's David Thompson had scored 73 in an afternoon game at Detroit to apparently claim the honor.

The final-day shootout was possible because all four teams had nothing at stake in the season-closing games. Both the Nuggets and the Spurs concentrated on getting the ball to their stars and both teams lost, Thompson's Nuggets to the Pistons, 139–137, and Gervin's Spurs to the Jazz, 153–132.

Thompson was phenomenal in scoring the third-highest single-game total in NBA history. He connected on 28 of 38 shots from the floor and 17 of 20 from the free throw line. He scored 53 of his points in the first half.

Gervin made 23 of 49 field-goal attempts and 17 of 20 from the foul line. He, too, enjoyed a 53-point first half and completed his day with a 27.22 average. Thompson finished at 27.15.

Thompson's big game ranked behind only the 100 and 78-point efforts of former great Wilt Chamberlain, who also scored 73 twice.

Despite his 73-points, Denver's **David Thompson** *had to settle for second place in the NBA scoring race.*

1989 FALDO SINKS PUTT, HOCH

With darkness, rain and fog engulfing Augusta National Golf Club, Nick Faldo rolled in a 25-foot birdie putt on the second hole of a sudden-death playoff with Scott Hoch and claimed the 53rd Masters championship.

The dramatic putt completed an amazing final day for the Englishman. He had started the final round well back in the pack but fired a 65 that included birdies on four of the final six holes.

One by one his challengers faltered until only Hoch had a chance to win in regulation. But Hoch, playing in a driving rain, missed a four-foot par putt at 17 and finished with a 69, forcing the playoff.

Hoch missed a golden opportunity on the first extra hole—the 10th. Faldo hit into a bunker and missed a 15-foot par putt. But Hoch reached the green in regulation, rolled a putt to two feet and lipped his potential winner.

Visibility was little more than the length of Faldo's winning putt when the match ended dramatically.

MILESTONES
• IN SPORTS •

1949

Sam Snead fired his second consecutive 67 and earned his first Masters championship with a four-stroke victory over Johnny Palmer.

1961

South African Gary Player shot a final-round 74 and became the first foreigner to win the Masters with a one-stroke victory over Arnold Palmer and Charles Coe.

1962

The expansion Colt .45s pounded out an 11–2 victory over Chicago in their franchise debut at Houston's Colt Stadium and Cincinnati spoiled the opening of new Dodger Stadium with a 6–3 victory at Los Angeles.

1971

Jim Bunning pitched the Phillies to a 4–1 victory over Montreal in the first game at Philadelphia's new Veterans Stadium.

1973

Kansas City unveiled new Royals Stadium, complete with a 40-story-high, crown-shaped scoreboard and a huge fountain display. The Royals christened the park with a 12-1 victory over the Texas Rangers.

1976

Pitcher Andy Messersmith, a free agent by virtue of arbitrator Peter Seitz's landmark ruling four months earlier, was signed by Atlanta to what Braves Owner Ted Turner termed "a lifetime contract."

1993

Laurie Boschman scored two late goals and the Ottawa Senators ended their National Hockey League-record 38-game road losing streak with a 5–3 victory over the New York Islanders.

1960 Palmer's Late Charge

Arnold Palmer, making one of his patented late charges, closed his final round with a pair of birdies and claimed his second Masters championship with a one-stroke victory over Ken Venturi.

Palmer, the leader after each of the first three rounds, fell behind Venturi on Augusta National's back nine and faced a one-stroke deficit with six holes to play after Venturi had posted his 70. But the hard hitter from Latrobe, Pa., watched his chances fade as he struggled to pars at 13, 14, 15 and 16.

Needing one birdie to force a sudden-death playoff, Palmer doubled his pleasure. He ran in a dramatic 37-foot putt on the 17th green to tie Venturi and then hit a magnificent 2-iron six feet from the pin on 18. When he dropped the putt for his final-round 70, he donned the Green Jacket for a second time.

Palmer, who had opened the day one stroke ahead of Venturi, finished the tournament with a 72-hole total of 282.

Sandy Lyle *celebrates after sealing his one-stroke Masters victory with a winning 10-foot putt.*

1992 Hockey Strike Ends

The first players' strike in National Hockey League history ended after 10 days when owners and Players Association officials agreed on a short-team contract that will last through the 1992–93 season.

The current season, which was interrupted with 30 regular-season games remaining, will resume immediately and the full slate of playoff games will begin next weekend. The New York Rangers already have clinched the overall regular-season championship and only a few teams still are jockeying for playoff position.

The players still must ratify a package that includes rights to revenue from the licensing of trading cards, more free-agent mobility and a regular-season schedule that increases from 80 to 84 games. The owners, who say they stand to lose $9 million this season, demanded the short-term contract.

April 10

A STAR IS BORN

1897: Ross Youngs, a .322 hitter for the New York Giants in a 10-year Hall of Fame career that was cut short in 1927 by Bright's disease.

★ ★ ★

1912: Clarke Hinkle, a football Hall of Fame fullback and linebacker who retired from Green Bay in 1941 with a then-record 3,860 rushing yards.

★ ★ ★

1938: Don Meredith, a Dallas Cowboys quarterback from 1960–68 who went on to greater fame as a member of the original Monday Night Football broadcast team and as an actor.

★ ★ ★

1950: Ken Griffey Sr., an outstanding hitter (2,143 hits) who finished his 19-year career in 1991 playing on the same Seattle team with his son, Ken Griffey Jr.

★ ★ ★

1988 Lyle Masters Calcavecchia

Sandy Lyle, recovering from a near-disastrous turn around Augusta National's infamous Amen Corner, birdied two of the final three holes and earned himself a one-stroke victory over Mark Calcavecchia in the 52nd Masters championship.

Lyle seemingly was in control when he three-putted No. 11 for a bogey 5, went in the water on the 12th and took a double bogey 5 and bunkered out for a par 5 on 13. That three-over-par nightmare dropped him a shot behind Calcavecchia, who was playing just ahead of him.

But Lyle, a 30-year-old from Scotland, would not die. He dropped a 15-foot putt on 16 that forced a tie and then set up his winning 10-footer on 18 with a spectacular 145-yard bunker shot. That gave him a final-round 71 for a 72-hole total of 281. Calcavecchia, who parred the 18th, finished the round with a 70.

The victory also gave Lyle the distinction of becoming the first English golfer to win the Masters. He won the British Open in 1985.

APRIL

11

A STAR IS BORN

1916: Dan Fortmann, a football Hall of Fame lineman who cut his eight-year career short in 1943 to become a doctor.

★ ★ ★

1956: Jim Breech, a current NFL placekicker.

★ ★ ★

1964: Bret Saberhagen, a current major league pitcher.

DEATH OF A LEGEND

1953: Kid Nichols (baseball).

★ ★ ★

1990: Harold Ballard (hockey).

★ ★ ★

1991: Walker Cooper (baseball).

1965

NICKLAUS IS THE MASTER

Jack Nicklaus, the 25-year-old rising star from Columbus, O., stormed around the difficult Augusta National Golf Club course with a final-round 69 and waltzed home with the most lopsided victory in the 29-year history of the Masters championship.

Nicklaus was nearly flawless as he completed his four-day victory cruise in a record 271 strokes. His final round included only one bogey and he finished nine strokes ahead of Arnold Palmer and South African Gary Player – the biggest victory margin in Masters history.

The keys to his record-setting performance were a third-round 64 that gave him a five-stroke advantage heading into the final day and a blazing putter. Nicklaus needed only 123 putts in the tournament's four rounds – 32, 31, 30 and 30. He made 19 birdies and went over par just five times.

Nicklaus, who also won the tournament in 1963, broke the four-round record of 274 set by Ben Hogan in 1953.

MILESTONES IN SPORTS

1962

The expansion New York Mets got off to a portentous start, dropping an 11–4 decision to the Cardinals at St. Louis in the first game in franchise history.

1966

Another barrier falls: Emmett Ashford worked an Opening Day game at Cleveland, becoming baseball's first black umpire.

1975

Lee Elder, the first black golfer to compete in a Masters Tournament, shot a second-round 78 and failed to make the cut with a two-round total of 152.

1981

WBC champion Larry Holmes successfully defended his heavyweight title with a unanimous 15-round decision over Trevor Berbick at Las Vegas.

1989

Philadelphia's Ron Hextall became the first goaltender in Stanley Cup playoff history to record a goal when he scored into an empty net in Game 5 of the Patrick Division final against Washington.

1976

FLOYD ENJOYS CRUISE

Raymond Floyd, rekindling memories of Jack Nicklaus' 1965 record-setting romp to the Masters championship, fired a final-round 70 over the unforgiving Augusta National Golf Club course and tied the Golden Bear's 11-year-old mark with a four-day victory total of 271.

Floyd's eight-stroke margin over second-place Ben Crenshaw was one short of Nicklaus' 1965 record margin over Gary Player and Arnold Palmer, but his four-day domination was no less impressive. He scorched to rounds of 65, 66, 70 and 70 and never was challenged in a pressure-free final round.

Whereas Nicklaus carved out his record-setting total with a hot putter, Floyd did it on Augusta National's four par-5 holes. He played those holes in 14-under with an eagle, 12 birdies and two pars.

Floyd's final 70 came while most golfers were struggling because of a stiff breeze that changed directions. Among the leaders going into the final day, Crenshaw's 67 was the only other sub-par round.

Record-setting Masters winner **Raymond Floyd.**

1977

WATSON TAMES GOLDEN BEAR

Tom Watson, looking for his first American major championship, fired a final-round 67 and held off the late charge of Jack Nicklaus for a two-stroke victory in the 41st Masters golf tournament.

In an extraordinary battle of wits and birdies, Watson dropped a 20-foot downhill putt on the 17th green to break a tie with the Golden Bear and then parred the 18th hole for a four-round total of 276. Nicklaus, who shot a final-round 66, bogeyed the 18th after a short second shot that landed in a bunker.

Watson spent the first half of the round matching birdies with playing partner Rik Massengale, who opened the day one stroke back. When Massengale fell out of contention on the back nine, Nicklaus suddenly appeared out of nowhere, catching Watson at 10 under par with a 13th-hole birdie.

The lead see-sawed until Watson finally took control on 17. He drilled a 9-iron to 20 feet, sank the curling putt and celebrated with a jig around the green. Nicklaus, hearing that he no longer was a co-leader, went for the pin on 18 and found the bunker instead, insuring Watson's victory.

Massengale finished the day four strokes back at 280 and tied for third with Tom Kite, who fired a final-round 67. The major title was Watson's second. He had previously captured the British Open.

1954 LAKERS KEEP ON WINNING

Jim Pollard scored 21 points and a rugged Minneapolis defense held Syracuse's offense in check as the Lakers rolled to an 87–80 seventh-game victory and claimed their third consecutive National Basketball Association championship and fifth in six years.

The powerful Lakers, who had struggled through the first six games against a team they were favored to beat handily, fought to a 17–14 first-quarter advantage before taking control of the game. They stretched their lead in the second quarter and the Nationals never were able to cut it below five again.

With Pollard, Slater Martin, Clyde Lovellette and big George Mikan doing most of the damage, the Lakers enjoyed a 27-point third quarter. Only Dolph Schayes (18 points) and Paul Seymour (16) could mount any offense for the Nationals, who had tied for second place in the Eastern Division.

MILESTONES • IN SPORTS •

1909

The Philadelphia Athletics christened new Shibe Park, baseball's first steel-and-concrete facility, with an 8–1 victory over the Boston Braves.

1955

The Athletics, who had called Philadelphia home for more than half a century, made their Kansas City debut a success with a 6–2 victory over Detroit at Municipal Stadium.

1966

A Brave new world: Pittsburgh spoiled the former Milwaukee Braves' debut in Atlanta with a 13-inning, 3–2 victory at new Civic Stadium.

1980

Shattering the dreams of hundreds of American athletes, the U.S. Olympic Committee endorsed President Jimmy Carter's call for a boycott of the Moscow Summer Games.

1992

Boston's Matt Young became the third pitcher in baseball history to pitch a complete-game, regulation no-hitter – and lose. The lefthander dropped a 2–1 decision to Cleveland.

APRIL 12

A STAR IS BORN

1880: Addie Joss, a Hall of Fame pitcher who died of meningitis after nine seasons and 160 victories.

★ ★ ★

1944: Mike Garrett, a Heisman Trophy-winning running back (1965) from Southern Cal who went on to play professionally with Kansas City and San Diego.

DEATH OF A LEGEND

1981: Joe Louis (boxing).

★ ★ ★

1989: Sugar Ray Robinson (boxing).

★ ★ ★

1958 HAWKS DEFEAT CELTICS

St. Louis forward Bob Pettit, providing the perfect capper for his record 50-point explosion, scored a basket with 16 seconds remaining that clinched the Hawks' 110–109 victory over Boston and their first National Basketball Association championship.

Bob Pettit, *St. Louis' 50-point scorer.*

Pettit was unstoppable in the Hawks' Game 6 title-clincher at St. Louis. He connected on 19 of 34 shots from the field and 12 of 19 free throws while setting a single-game record for a regulation NBA playoff game. And three of his field goals came in the closing minutes, each one stretching the St. Louis lead to three points after Boston had cut it to one.

St. Louis led after every quarter, 22–18, 57–52 and 78–77. But the Hawks never could shake the defending champions, who took a brief one-point lead in the final period. Boston, which was hampered by an ankle injury that limited center Bill Russell to 20 minutes, got 26 points from Bill Sharman and 23 from Tom Heinsohn.

Pettit scored 19 points in the final quarter, including the basket that put St. Louis ahead to stay, 95–93, with 6:16 remaining.

1954 SNEAD BEATS HOGAN

Masterful **Sam Snead** *outduelled Ben Hogan.*

Slammin' Sammy Snead conquered his sometimes-shaky putting problems and outdueled defending champion Ben Hogan by one stroke in an 18-hole playoff that produced his third Masters championship at the Augusta National Golf Club in Georgia.

Snead needed only 32 putts in his playoff-round 70, but it was a chip shot on 10 and an aggressive approach shot at the 470-yard 13th that turned the match in his favor.

After golf's top guns had played evenly through the front nine, Snead took a one-stroke lead at the 10th with a stunning 65-foot chip from the back of the green that dropped for a birdie 3.

Then, after Hogan had played up short of the creek that fronts the par-5 13th hole, Snead drove a daring 2-iron onto the green and two-putted for a birdie that broke another tie and gave him a lead that he never relinquished.

Hogan complicated his dilemma with a disappointing bogey on the 16th and that proved costly when Snead stumbled to a bogey at the 18th after hitting his second shot into a bunker.

Hogan and Snead had battled to a draw at 289 after the regulation 72 holes.

APRIL

13

A STAR IS BORN

1963: Mark Leiter, a current major league pitcher.

★ ★ ★

1966: Wes Chamberlain, a current major league outfielder.

★ ★ ★

MILESTONES IN SPORTS

1905

James J. Jeffries, citing lack of opposition, retired as undefeated heavyweight champion, relinquishing the crown he had held since 1899.

1954

New York Giants center fielder Willie Mays celebrated his return from a two-year hitch in the Army by belting a two-run, game-winning home run against Brooklyn.

1972

Baseball's first general strike ended after 13 days with players and owners agreeing not to make up any of the 86 cancelled games.

1975

Jack Nicklaus earned his record fifth Masters championship with a 72-hole total of 276 at Augusta National Golf Club.

1984

Montreal's Pete Rose joined Ty Cobb in baseball's 4,000-hit circle when he doubled off Philadelphia Phillies lefthander Jerry Koosman in the fourth inning of a 5–1 victory at Olympic Stadium.

1957

CELTICS WIN FIRST TITLE

Tom Heinsohn scored 37 points and big Bill Russell totaled 32 points and 19 rebounds as the young Boston Celtics recorded a dramatic 125–123 double-overtime victory over St. Louis in the seventh game of the National Basketball Association championship series.

Boston's first NBA title, earned before a national television audience and 13,909 fans at Boston Garden, did not come easily. The Celtics appeared on the verge of blowing the Hawks away through much of the game, but could not deliver the knockout punch.

The Hawks scrapped and clawed to stay close and Bob Pettit hit two free throws in the final seconds of regulation to tie the game at 103 and force overtime. Boston took a quick lead in the first extra period, but again St. Louis fought back, tying the score at 113 on a Jack Coleman shot.

When the Celtics jumped ahead in the second overtime, luck finally ran out on the Hawks. Again they closed the gap, but this time they couldn't force the tie. Jim Loscutoff's free throw proved to be the winner when Pettit's desperation shot with time running out rolled around the rim and dropped out.

Boston Coach **Red Auerbach** *with* **Bob Cousy** *(right) and* **Ed Macauley**, *the player he traded to get the rights to championship-securing center* **Bill Russell.**

1942

NELSON MASTERS HOGAN

Byron Nelson, playing an eight-hole stretch of the difficult Augusta National Golf Club course in an incredible five under par, scored an exciting one-stroke playoff-round victory over fellow Texan Ben Hogan and captured his second Masters championship.

The 30-year-old Nelson, forced into the playoff when Hogan birdied the final hole of regulation play a day earlier, dug himself an early hole when he hit a tree off the first tee and struggled to a double-bogey six. After dropping another stroke and trailing by three heading to the sixth tee, Nelson badly needed a lift and got it with a birdie 3.

After a par on 7, Nelson eagled 8 and birdied 11, 12 and 13. Hogan, who had been playing par golf, was staring at a three-stroke deficit and he could not recover. Only Nelson's final-hole bogey allowed Hogan to cut the final margin to one.

Hogan-beater **Byron Nelson.**

1986

NICKLAUS WINS SIXTH MASTERS

Jack Nicklaus, golf's 46-year-old Golden Bear, wrote a memorable ending to the 50th Masters championship when he recorded two birdies and an eagle on the final four holes in a dramatic charge that brought him the coveted Green Jacket for a record sixth time.

Nicklaus, who shot a final-round 65 for a total of 279, was four strokes behind co-leaders Seve Ballesteros and Tom Kite when he hit a 200-yard 4-iron over the water that fronts the par-5 15th. The ball landed pin high, 12 feet from the hole, and he sank the putt for an eagle.

Nicklaus then dropped a 40-foot putt on the par-3 16th for a birdie and took his first lead with a birdie at 17. When he completed his round, he had to wait as Kite and Australian Greg Norman stumbled. Kite barely missed a birdie putt to tie at 18 and Norman, who had pulled into a tie with four straight birdies, bogeyed the 18th after an errant approach shot.

In becoming the oldest golfer to win a Masters, Nicklaus won a major tournament for the 20th time and a PGA event for the 71st.

Nicklaus also has won five PGA Championships, four U.S. Opens, three British Opens and two U.S. Amateur titles.

MILESTONES IN SPORTS

1910

William Howard Taft became the first U.S. President to throw out a ceremonial first pitch when he attended Washington's home opener against Chicago.

1928

The New York Rangers, a 2-year-old expansion franchise, captured the Stanley Cup with a 2–1 Game 5 victory over the Maroons at the Montreal Forum.

1953

The former Boston Braves opened a new era in Milwaukee with a 3–2 victory over St. Louis, courtesy of a 10th-inning home run by Bill Bruton.

1955

The New York Yankees became the 13th of 16 major league teams to break the color barrier when Elston Howard singled in his first big-league at-bat in a game at Boston's Fenway Park.

1993

Although Pittsburgh's Joe Mullen scored with 1:06 remaining to salvage a 6–6 tie against New Jersey, the Penguins' NHL-record 17-game winning streak came to an end.

1960 CANADIENS TAKE FIFTH

Jean Beliveau scored a pair of goals and Henri Richard and Doug Harvey added one apiece as the methodical and relentless Montreal Canadiens earned their record fifth consecutive Stanley Cup championship with a 4–0 victory over the Toronto Maple Leafs.

The triumph at Maple Leaf Gardens completed a four-game title series sweep and an eight-game blitz through the playoffs. Only the 1951–52 Detroit Red Wings had performed such a double sweep in the 42 years of National Hockey League play and no other team had won as many as four straight Cups.

The Canadiens dominated the finale from the start. Beliveau connected on a long screened shot at 8:16 of the opening period and Harvey beat Toronto goalie Johnny Bower 29 seconds later. Richard notched the only second-period goal off a pass from his brother Maurice and Beliveau completed the scoring early in the third period.

The Canadiens also beat Toronto in a five-game 1959 Stanley Cup series. They were 20-5 in their five finals victories.

A STAR IS BORN

1941: Pete Rose, baseball's all-time hits leader (4,256) and a career .303 batter from 1963–86. He resigned as Cincinnati manager in 1989 under a cloud of accusations and later was issued a lifetime ban from baseball for alleged gambling violations.

★ ★ ★

1966: David Justice, a current major league outfielder.

★ ★ ★

1966: Greg Maddux, a current major league pitcher.

★ ★ ★

1970: Steve Avery, a current major league pitcher.

★ ★ ★

DEATH OF A LEGEND

1911: Addie Joss (baseball).

★ ★ ★

1922: Cap Anson (baseball).

★ ★ ★

1978: Joe Gordon (baseball).

★ ★ ★

APRIL 14

1968 MISTAKE PROVES COSTLY

Bob Goalby shot a final-round 66, but his victory in the 32nd Masters championship was decided in the scorer's tent, not on the Augusta National Golf Club course.

Goalby was declared the winner after millions of television viewers and thousands of spectators had watched Argentine Roberto de Vicenzo shoot a blazing 65 and apparently force a playoff for the Green Jacket. But when tournament officials discovered a mistake on de Vicenzo's scorecard, which he already had signed, his score was changed to 66 and 278 overall – good for second place.

The costly mistake was made on de Vicenzo's score for the 17th hole. Instead of a birdie 3, Tommy Aaron, de Vicenzo's playing partner and official "marker," had carded a 4. De Vicenzo, who was celebrating his 45th birthday, glanced at the card, signed it and left without discovering the mistake.

PGA rules are specific. If a golfer signs an incorrect card that adjusts the score in his favor, he is penalized. If he signs a card that gives him a higher score, that score stands.

The error ruined an amazing round that started with an eagle, two birdies and a "Happy Birthday" serenade from the gallery following the easy-going Argentine.

1969 EXPOS CAPTURE CANADA DEBUT

With several hundred reporters and numerous cameras focused on their every move, the expansion Montreal Expos passed their Opening Day test by defeating the St. Louis Cardinals, 8–7, in the first major league regular-season baseball game played on foreign soil.

True to expectations, the young Expos were a model of inconsistency. They jumped to a 6–0 lead, contributed four errors to the Cardinals' seven-run fourth-inning rally and then came back to win, scoring the decisive run in the seventh inning on winning pitcher Dan McGinn's single.

The 29,184 fans at Jarry Park got their own form of instant replay – everything in the pre-game ceremonies and introductions was done twice, in both French and English. When the game started, they watched the Expos explode to a quick lead, Mack Jones driving in five runs with a homer and a triple. But the Expos could not stand prosperity and let the defending National League-champion Cardinals come back in an ugly fourth inning.

Montreal fans welcome the expansion Expos to their new Canadian home.

APRIL

15

1958 WEST COAST OPENER

Home runs by Daryl Spencer and Orlando Cepeda backed the six-hit pitching of Ruben Gomez as the Giants, playing their first game at Seals Stadium, celebrated baseball's move to the West Coast with an 8–0 victory over the Los Angeles Dodgers.

It was a landmark occasion for both baseball and the two franchises, which had played for more than half a century in Brooklyn and New York City. The crowd of 23,448 that turned out to witness history in the making included numerous baseball and political dignitaries as well as former Detroit star Ty Cobb and Mrs. John McGraw, widow of the former New York Giants manager.

The game was all Giants. Jim Davenport's sacrifice fly and Jim King's run-scoring single netted two third-inning runs off Dodger righthander Don Drysdale and Spencer keyed a four-run fourth with the first West Coast home run – a solo shot. Willie Mays also contributed a two-run single and Cepeda hit his home run in the fifth.

A STAR IS BORN

1957: Evelyn Ashford, a five-time U.S. Olympian and the 1984 100-meter dash gold medalist. She has won three other Olympic golds in relay events.

★★★

1947 BASEBALL INTEGRATES

Jackie Robinson, a 28-year-old former college football and track star, began the great sociological experiment when he stepped onto Brooklyn's Ebbets Field and became baseball's first black major league player in more than six decades.

Robinson, making his long-anticipated debut as a first baseman, was the focal point of the Dodgers' season opener against the Boston Braves. He was hitless in three official at-bats against Johnny Sain, but he reached base on a seventh-inning error and came around to score the winning run in a 5–3 Brooklyn victory.

Receiving a warm reception from 25,623 fans, Robinson grounded out in his first two at-bats and hit a fly ball to left field in his third. In the seventh, Robinson made a sacrifice bunt and moved to second on a wild throw by Boston first baseman Earl Torgeson.

Robinson, the first black to play in the major leagues since 1884, was handpicked by Brooklyn President Branch Rickey to integrate the game.

Brooklyn rookie **Jackie Robinson** *hits a routine ground ball in his historic first major league at-bat.*

1985 HAGLER BEATS HEARNS

In one of the fiercest fights in boxing history, Marvelous Marvin Hagler scored a technical knockout over Thomas (Hit Man) Hearns at 2:01 of the third round and retained his undisputed middleweight championship.

The 16,034 fans at Caesar's Palace in Las Vegas were treated to a nonstop battle of fistic fury. The tone was set with the opening bell when Hearns raced to center ring and rocked Hagler with an overhand right and the champion responded with a staggering left.

Hearns spent much of the bout backpedaling under the fury of Hagler's rush. But that didn't stop him from landing some serious punches. He opened cuts over and under Hagler's right eye. The champion was a bloody mess when ringside doctors examined him between the second and third rounds and allowed him to continue.

That was bad news for Hearns. The challenger, trying to win a championship in his third weight division, was pounded to the canvas by a Hagler right. Hearns staggered to his feet by the count of eight, but the referee signaled the fight was over.

Marvin Hagler *was truly marvelous against Thomas Hearns.*

MILESTONES • IN SPORTS •

1909

Red Ames pitched a nine-inning Opening Day no-hitter, but the New York Giants' righthander surrendered a hit in the 10th and lost in the 13th when Brooklyn scored three times.

1954

The former St. Louis Browns celebrated their Baltimore debut with a 3–1 victory over the Chicago White Sox at Memorial Stadium.

1979

Fuzzy Zoeller dropped an 8-foot putt on the second hole of a sudden-death playoff to beat Tom Watson and Ed Sneed for the Masters championship.

1991

Los Angeles Lakers guard Magic Johnson recorded his NBA-record 9,888th assist in the second quarter of a game against Dallas.

A STAR IS BORN

1903: Paul Waner, a Hall of Fame outfielder who recorded a lofty .333 batting average over a 20-year major league career that ended in 1945.

★ ★ ★

1928: Dick (Night Train) Lane, a football Hall of Fame defensive back who intercepted 68 passes in a 14-year NFL career that ended in 1965.

★ ★ ★

1947: Kareem Abdul-Jabbar, the 7-foot-2 center who led UCLA to three college championships and then went on to lead Milwaukee and Los Angeles to six NBA titles before retiring in 1989 as the game's all-time leading scorer (38,387 points).

★ ★ ★

DEATH OF A LEGEND

1989: Jocko Conlan (baseball).

★ ★ ★

1940 FELLER PERFORMS A NO-HITTER FEAT

Cleveland's Bob Feller, a 21-year-old fireballer coming off a 24-victory season, became the first major league pitcher to throw an Opening Day no-hitter when he defeated the Chicago White Sox, 1–0, at Comiskey Park.

Cleveland's **Bob Feller**, *who has just completed the first Opening Day no-hitter in baseball history, gets a pat from teammate Hal Trosky.*

Feller, who had thrown three one-hitters, needed an outstanding play by second baseman Ray Mack to record the final out of his first career no-hitter. A lunging Mack knocked down Taft Wright's blistering ground ball, picked it up and threw him out.

Feller struck out eight and walked five, filling the bases in the second with two out before fanning White Sox rookie Bob Kennedy. But he settled down and retired 15 batters in a row from the fourth inning until he walked Luke Appling with two out in the ninth.

Feller got all the support he needed when batterymate Rollie Hemsley drove in a fourth-inning run with a triple – one of six hits surrendered by hard-luck loser Edgar Smith.

New York Giants pitcher Red Ames worked nine innings without allowing a hit in a 1909 opener against Brooklyn before surrendering a hit in the 10th.

1961 FLEMING SPARKS HAWKS

Reg Fleming fired up his Chicago teammates with a shorthanded goal in the second period and the inspired Blackhawks went on to beat Detroit, 5–1, and capture their first Stanley Cup championship in 23 years and third overall.

The victory in Game 6 of the final series at Detroit's Olympia Stadium capped the Blackhawks' run from a third-place regular-season finish.

The key was Fleming's goal, which tied the game midway through the second stanza and seemed to give the sagging Blackhawks new life.

Suddenly carrying play, Chicago took the lead on Ab McDonald's goal and then blitzed Red Wings' goalie Hank Bassen with goals by Eric Nesterenko, Jack Evans and Ken Wharram. Evans' goal was his first in two full seasons.

1949 LEAFS WIN 3RD STRAIGHT CUP

Cal Gardner's goal with 15 seconds remaining in the second period gave Toronto a lead it never relinquished en route to a 3–1 victory over Detroit and the Maple Leafs' record-setting third consecutive Stanley Cup title.

The victory before 14,544 ecstatic fans at Maple Leaf Gardens completed Toronto's second straight Stanley Cup series sweep of the Red Wings and gave the Leafs a 12–2 Cup series record in their three victories. No team had won more than two consecutive titles since the National Hockey League began play in 1917–18.

The verdict seemed inevitable, even after Detroit had taken a 1–0 lead on Ted Lindsay's goal in the opening minutes of the first period. Ray Timgren tied the score midway through the second stanza and Gardner shocked the Red Wings with his late-period score. Max Bentley capped the scoring late in the third period.

Ironically, the Maple Leafs' victory capped a regular season in which they had finished fourth in the overall standings and Detroit had finished first. The title was Toronto's fifth since 1940–41, when Hap Day took over as coach.

APRIL 16

MILESTONES • IN SPORTS •

1938

The St. Louis Cardinals shocked the baseball world when they traded former pitching ace Dizzy Dean, a 102-game winner from 1933–36, to the Chicago Cubs for pitchers Curt Davis and Clyde Shoun and outfielder Tuck Stainback.

1946

Baseball Commissioner A.B. (Happy) Chandler, trying to discourage defections to the renegade Mexican League, announced punitive suspensions of at least five years for any players who jumped American contracts.

1968

The Naismith Memorial Basketball Hall of Fame was dedicated in Springfield, Mass., on the Springfield College campus where Dr. James Naismith invented the game in 1891.

1976

Roy McMurtry, Ontario's attorney general, issued arrest warrants charging three Philadelphia Flyers – Don Saleski, Joe Watson and Mel Bridgman – with assault for their parts in several fights during a National Hockey League playoff game at Toronto.

1983

San Diego first baseman Steve Garvey passed the National League consecutive-games record of former Chicago Cub Billy Williams when he played in his 1,118th straight contest.

APRIL 17

A STAR IS BORN

1820: Alexander Cartwright, a baseball Hall of Famer and one of the pioneers of the game.

★ ★ ★

1852: Cap Anson, a pre-1900 Hall of Fame player and manager who batted .339 over 22 major league seasons.

★ ★ ★

1961: Boomer Esiason, a current National Football League quarterback.

★ ★ ★

1967: Marquis Grissom, a current major league outfielder

★ ★ ★

DEATH OF A LEGEND

1983: Dutch Leonard (baseball).

★ ★ ★

1976 SCHMIDT BLASTS CUBS

Mike Schmidt tied a major league record when he belted four consecutive home runs to help the Philadelphia Phillies recover from a 13–2 deficit and record a 10-inning 18–16 victory over the Chicago Cubs on a windy day at Wrigley Field.

Philadelphia's four-homer bomber **Mike Schmidt.**

Schmidt, the 10th player to homer four times in a game and only the fourth to hit them consecutively, went to work after two Rick Monday homers had sparked the Cubs to their 11-run lead after just four innings.

Schmidt belted a two-run shot in the fifth, a solo shot in the seventh, a three-run blast in the eighth and a two-run shot in the 10th that broke a 15–15 tie. The third baseman, the first to accomplish the four-homer feat since Willie Mays in 1951, also singled and drove in eight runs.

The Phillies tied the score at 13–13 on Bob Boone's leadoff ninth-inning home run and added two runs for a 15–13 lead. But Schmidt got his 10th-inning chance when the Cubs tied in the bottom of the ninth on Steve Swisher's two-run single.

The teams combined for 43 hits – 24 by the Phillies and 19 by the Cubs. They also combined for nine home runs, several helped by the gusty 20-mph wind.

MILESTONES IN SPORTS

1939

Heavyweight champion Joe Louis needed only one round to knock out Jack Roper in a title bout at Los Angeles.

1964

Pittsburgh spoiled the unveiling of New York's $25-million Shea Stadium by posting a 4–3 victory over the Mets.

1968

Baltimore 4, Oakland 1 in the first game at the Oakland-Alameda Coliseum.

1976

The NFL agreed to test instant replay as a means to assist officials at random games during the 1976 regular season.

1984

Oakland slugger Dave Kingman pounded three homers and drove in eight runs as the A's defeated Seattle, 9–6.

1953 MANTLE HAS A REAL BLAST

New York center fielder Mickey Mantle, enhancing his reputation as one of the greatest young power hitters baseball has ever produced, rocketed a 565-foot home run over the outer wall of Washington's Griffith Stadium that many veteran observers are calling the longest in history.

The switch-hitting Mantle was batting righthanded with teammate Yogi Berra stationed on first base when he connected with a fifth-inning Chuck Stobbs pitch for a two-run homer. The ball cleared the left-center-field wall 391 feet from the plate, continued to rise and ricocheted off the football scoreboard that sits atop a 50-foot outer wall, bounding into a yard where it was retrieved by a youngster.

The scoreboard rested 460 feet from the plate and the ball might have sailed farther than the measured 565 feet if it had managed to clear that barrier. The closest a ball had come to leaving Griffith Stadium in left field was a shot by former Yankee center fielder Joe DiMaggio that had a little help when it took a hop in the bleachers and bounced out.

Inspired by the 21-year-old Mantle's slugging feat, the Yankees went on to post a 7–3 decision over the Senators.

1963 NFL SUSPENDS TWO BIG STARS

National Football League Commissioner Pete Rozelle stated he will not tolerate gambling among either players or owners when he shackled two of the game's stars with indefinite suspensions that could end their careers.

Detroit defensive tackle Alex Karras and Green Bay halfback Paul Hornung were punished for betting on games and providing specific information to be used for betting purposes.

Green Bay star **Paul Hornung**, *who was suspended by NFL Commissioner* **Pete Rozelle.**

Rozelle, who fined five other Detroit players, cited Karras for making at least six large bets on games since 1958, but he stressed there was no evidence anybody had bet against his own team or tried to determine the outcome of a contest by poor play.

Hornung, the former Notre Dame Heisman Trophy winner who played on Packer championship teams in 1961 and '62, is best known for his NFL scoring feats. He holds the one-season record of 176 points (1960) and ranks third on the all-time list with 146 (1961). He also ranks third for points in one game with 33 (1961).

The Lions drawing $2,000 fines were John Gordy, Gary Lowe, Sam Williams, Joe Schmidt and Wayne Walker.

1966 CELTICS PICK BILL RUSSELL

The Boston Celtics, seeking their unprecedented eighth consecutive championship, took time out to announce that star center Bill Russell will become the National Basketball Association's first black coach, replacing Red Auerbach for the 1966–67 season.

The historic announcement came a day after the Celtics dropped a 133–129 decision to the Los Angeles Lakers in the NBA championship series opener.

Auerbach, Boston's coach for the last 16 seasons, had decided to concentrate his efforts on his duties as general manager and picked Russell as his successor.

The 6-foot-10 star will continue to play next season when he begins his one-year coaching contract. The outspoken 32-year-old, who joined the Celtics in the 1956–57 season and has led them to eight NBA titles, had previously denied having coaching aspirations, but Auerbach and Owner Marvin Kratter persuaded him to change his mind.

Russell, the fourth coach in Boston history, is the second black coach at the professional level. John McClendon served as coach of the Cleveland Pipers four years earlier in the unsuccessful American Basketball League.

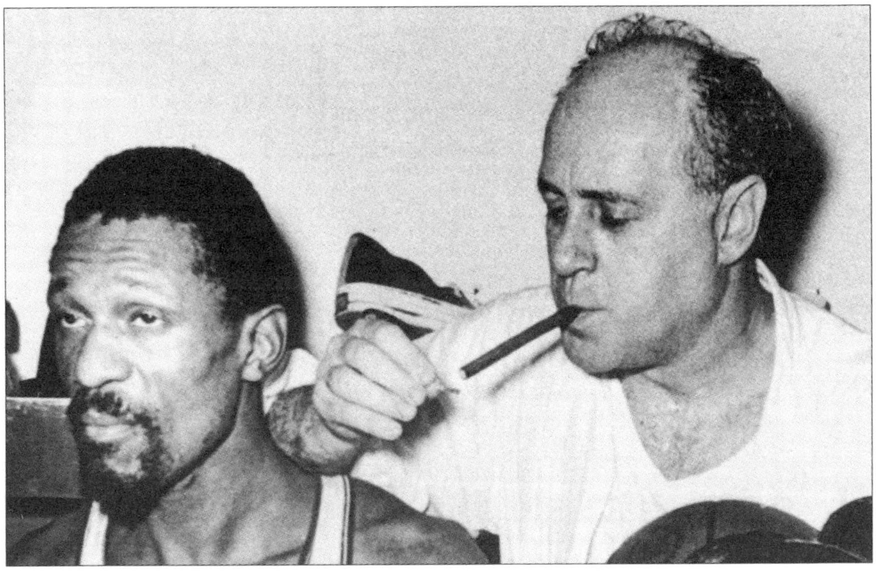

Boston Coach **Red Auerbach** *with his newly-named successor, star center* **Bill Russell.**

1942 LEAFS CLIP WINGS

Dave Schriner scored twice in a three-goal third period that lifted the Toronto Maple Leafs to a 3–1 victory over Detroit and completed the greatest Stanley Cup-series comeback in NHL history.

The Game 7 victory before 16,218 singing and celebrating fans at Maple Leaf Gardens capped Toronto's rebound from a 3–0 series deficit and gave the Maple Leafs their first Cup championship in 10 years. Not only were the Leafs down 3–0, they trailed the Red Wings, 3-2, entering the final period of Game 4 at Detroit.

But they fought back to win that game, 4–3, won the fifth game, 9–3, and shut out the Red Wings, 3–0, in Game 6. They needed one more comeback after entering the final period of Game 7 trailing 1–0.

That final comeback allowed Toronto to become the first team to recover from a three-game Stanley Cup final deficit.

A STAR IS BORN

1880: Sam Crawford, a Hall of Fame outfielder who batted .309 over an outstanding 19-year major league career that ended in 1917.

★ ★ ★

1948: Nate (Tiny) Archibald, a basketball Hall of Fame guard who scored 16,481 points over a 14-year NBA career that ended in 1984.

★ ★ ★

1962: Wilber Marshall, a current National Football League linebacker.

★ ★ ★

MILESTONES • IN SPORTS •

1923

New York's Yankee Stadium, the grandest ballpark ever constructed, was christened with a Babe Ruth home run and a 4–1 Yankee victory over Boston.

1945

Pete Gray, the St. Louis Browns' one-armed center fielder, made his Major League debut with a 1-for-4 performance during a 7–1 victory over the Detroit Tigers at Sportsman's Park.

1946

Jackie Robinson collected a home run and three other hits for the International League's Montreal Royals in his debut as Organized Baseball's first black player of the century.

1958

An N.L.-record crowd of 78,672 gathered at the massive Coliseum to witness the first major league game in Los Angeles – a 6–5 Dodger victory over the San Francisco Giants.

1959

It took the Montreal Canadiens only five games to defeat Toronto for their NHL-record fourth consecutive Stanley Cup championship.

1987

Philadelphia slugger Mike Schmidt made his milestone 500th career home run a dramatic one: a three-run ninth-inning shot that gave the Phillies an 8–6 victory over Pittsburgh.

1991

16–0: The home run-happy Detroit Tigers ruined the grand opening of Chicago's new Comiskey Park with a grand pounding of the White Sox.

APRIL 18

1962 BOSTON EARNS FOURTH STRAIGHT

The Boston Celtics, getting nine of their 10 overtime points from Sam Jones and Bill Russell, posted a 110–107 Game 7 victory over the Los Angeles Lakers and captured their National Basketball Association-record fourth consecutive championship.

Playing before a packed house of 13,909 screaming fans at Boston Garden after averting disaster with a Game 6 victory at Los Angeles, the Celtics controlled play until late in the fourth quarter when the Lakers came to life and forced the game into overtime.

The Lakers' comeback was triggered by Elgin Baylor (41) and Jerry West (35), who combined for 76 points. But the hero down the stretch was Frank Selvy, who scored Los Angeles' final two regulation baskets to tie the game at 100-100.

The Celtics regained control in the extra period, jumping to a 110–103 advantage that decided the issue. Russell's 30-point, 44-rebound effort helped the Celtics break the record of three straight NBA championships by the 1952–54 Minneapolis Lakers.

The Lakers had a chance to close out the Celtics' championship-record run in Game 6, but dropped a disappointing 119-105 decision on their home court.

APRIL

19

1986 SPINKS BEATS HOLMES

Michael Spinks survived the early-round rage of Larry Holmes and retained his International Boxing Federation heavyweight crown with an impressive 15-round split decision over the former champion at Las Vegas.

Holmes, who had lost his heavyweight crown to Spinks last September, rushed to center ring at the opening bell and wrestled the champion to the canvas, drawing a warning from the referee. He then attacked him furiously over the first four rounds, Spinks sitting back and biding his time.

Unable to score a quick knockout, the 36-year-old Holmes tired noticeably and the 29-year-old Spinks began taking control. Spinks dominated the fight from the eighth through the 13th rounds, landing his left hook at will and extending Holmes with an upbeat tempo.

Spinks suffered a scare near the end of the 14th round when he was staggered by a hard right, forcing him to retreat. But Holmes could not press the attack in the 15th and two of the three judges awarded the fight to Spinks.

The 29–0 champion entered the bout as an 8–5 underdog. Holmes, who had been undefeated before his first fight against Spinks, saw his record dip to 48-2.

After the fight, Holmes' handlers disclosed the challenger had broken his thumb in the third round.

1991 BATTLE OF THE AGES

Heavyweight champion Evander Holyfield beat 42-year-old George Foreman as expected in the "Battle of the Ages," but it took 12 grueling rounds and more than a few painful punches to accomplish the victory.

George Foreman *(left) and heavyweight champion* **Evander Holyfield,** *prior to their Battle of the Ages.*

Holyfield, giving away 49 pounds to the former champion, scored a unanimous decision in the fight at Atlantic City. But at the end, the crowd that had expected an early finish for the 257-pound, blubbery Foreman was chanting, "George, George, George."

Holyfield scored consistently through the fight with both hands and rocked Foreman near the end of the third round with a series of left hooks. But Foreman refused to go down and he kept blasting away, dealing some serious blows to the jaw and body of the 28-year-old champion. The victory was decisive, but Holyfield admitted it was not easy. "I couldn't just run over him," the champion said. "He hits hard and was able to move me around more than I wanted to." The win was the 26th in as many fights for Holyfield, who had recorded 21 knockouts. Foreman's record is 69-3.

1981 MARINERS SNAP A'S WIN STREAK

The Oakland A's set a major league record when they defeated Seattle, 6–1, in the first game of a doubleheader for their 11th consecutive season-opening victory, but the Mariners disappointed 29,834 fans at the Oakland Coliseum by claiming a streak-snapping 3-2 decision in the nightcap.

The doubleheader featured two bench-clearing battles, one of which forced Oakland ace Mike Norris out of the game. Norris, who earned his third victory in the opener, left with a shoulder injury after a sixth-inning fight that started when he brushed back Seattle's Lenny Randle.

But the A's survived that battle and passed the season-opening streaks of 10 games set by the 1955 Brooklyn Dodgers and matched by the 1962 Pittsburgh Pirates and the 1966 Cleveland Indians. But they could not extend their mark, thanks to a two-run, eighth-inning home run by Richie Zisk that gave the Mariners their nightcap victory.

The teams engaged in another bench-clearing incident in the second contest, precipitated by what the A's thought was a hard tag by Randle on Tony Armas during a rundown.

Oakland A's righthander **Mike Norris.**

A STAR IS BORN

1960: Andrea Mead Lawrence, an Olympic gold medal-winning skier in the 1950s.

★ ★ ★

1960: Frank Viola, a current major league pitcher.

★ ★ ★

1965: Keith Jackson, a current NFL tight end.

MILESTONES IN SPORTS

1907

Canadian Indian Tom Longboat trimmed more than five minutes off the Boston Marathon record with a winning time of 2:24.20.

1949

A granite monument dedicated to Babe Ruth and plaques honoring Lou Gehrig and Miller Huggins were unveiled in the center-field area of Yankee Stadium and dedicated during pregame ceremonies for New York's home opener.

1956

The Brooklyn Dodgers began their Jersey City home-away-from-home experiment with a 10-inning, 5–4 victory over Philadelphia in the first regular-season major league game ever played at Roosevelt Stadium.

1981

International League President Harold Cooper ordered suspension of the longest game in professional history after 8 hours, 7 minutes and 32 innings with Pawtucket and Rochester deadlocked, 2–2, at Pawtucket, R.I.

1986

High-scoring forward Dominique Wilkins riddled Detroit for 50 points in the Hawks' 137–125 first-round playoff victory at Atlanta.

1957 Kelley Wins at Boston

John Kelley, a 25-year-old school teacher from Connecticut, became the first American in 12 years to win the Boston Marathon, claiming the prestigious race with an impressive time of 2:20.05.

Kelley finally brought the title back to United States soil for the first time since 1945, when the race was won by another John Kelley (no relation). The 5-foot-5, 128-pound former Boston University student finished a half-mile ahead of second-place Veikko Karvonen, a former Boston Marathon winner.

Kelley took a 15-yard lead over his Finnish challenger at the 17-mile mark and used the course's three long hills to widen the gap. He had matters well under control at the end. Karvonen completed the 26-mile, 385-yard test in 2:23.54 and Korean runner Chong Woo Lim finished third.

The race was run in 70-degree temperature with a 25-mile per hour tailwind helping the times.

A STAR IS BORN

1892: Dave Bancroft, a Hall of Fame infielder who collected 2,004 hits from 1915–30.

★ ★ ★

1925: Ernie Stautner, a football Hall of Fame defensive tackle for 14 seasons (1950–63) with the Pittsburgh Steelers.

★ ★ ★

1961: Don Mattingly, a current major league first baseman.

★ ★ ★

DEATH OF A LEGEND

1908: Henry Chadwick (baseball).

★ ★ ★

1991: Bucky Walters (baseball).

1986 Jordan Scores 63 in a Losing Cause

Chicago superguard Michael Jordan scored a National Basketball Association playoff-record 63 points, but the Boston Celtics survived the barrage with a 135–131 double-overtime victory over the Bulls before a sellout crowd at Boston Garden.

Jordan made 22 of 41 shots and 19 of 21 free throws to top the previous playoff record of 61 points by Los Angeles Lakers forward Elgin Baylor in 1962 – against the Celtics. But Jordan's heroics were not enough as the Celtics took a 2–0 lead in the best-of-five first-round series.

Two of Jordan's points, his 53rd and 54th of the game, came on free throws with no time showing on the clock at the end of regulation and tied the game at 116–116. Boston guard Danny Ainge forced the second overtime with a layup that tied the score, 125–125, with 12 seconds remaining.

The game-winning shot was provided by guard Jerry Sichting, who hit a jumper from the top of the key to break a 131–131 tie. Hot-shooting Larry Bird was Boston's big gun with 36 points while teammate Kevin McHale scored 27 and grabbed 15 rebounds.

The 3-hour, 5-minute battle was physical. The teams were whistled for 66 fouls that resulted in 88 free throw attempts.

Japan's **Toshihiko Seko** *gives a smiling thumbs-up sign after winning the 1981 Boston Marathon.*

1981 Seko Wins Fast Race

Japan's Toshihiko Seko, aided by perfect weather, a fast early pace and a strong challenge from Americans Craig Virgin and Bill Rodgers, ran the fastest marathon in American history and captured the 85th Boston Marathon.

Seko pulled away from Virgin on the infamous "heartbreak hill" and sped to a 2:09.26 finish, one second better than Rodgers ran the 26-mile, 385-yard course in 1979. With 3.1 miles remaining, Seko increased his pace to a 4:40 mile and Virgin fell further back. The Lebanon, Ill., runner barely held off Rodgers for second place.

Seko, a 24-year-old Tokyo clerk, broke the string of three consecutive victories by the 33-year-old Rodgers, a four-time winner of the prestigious event. Ironically, Rodgers had outdueled Seko on "heartbreak hill" at the deciding point of his 1979 victory.

The women's winner was New Zealander Allison Roe, who ran the second-fastest women's marathon ever with her course-record 2:26.46.

Her victory helped ease bitter memories of the controversial finish of the previous year's marathon, when Rosie Ruiz was disqualified amid claims she had jumped into the race near its conclusion.

April 20

Milestones in Sports

1912

After two rainouts, the Boston Red Sox finally dedicated new Fenway Park with a 7–6 victory over the New York Highlanders.

1916

Cubs 7, Reds 6 in the first game at Chicago's new Wrigley Field.

1985

Portugal's Carlos Lopes shaved 54 seconds off the world marathon record with a blistering 2:07.11 performance at Rotterdam, the Netherlands.

1990

Dale Ellis connected on a National Basketball Association-record nine 3-point field goals and led Seattle to a 121–99 victory over the Los Angeles Clippers.

APRIL

21

1951 LEAFS WORK EXTRA HARD

Bill Barilko's 20-foot slapshot beat Montreal goaltender Gerry McNeil and gave the Toronto Maple Leafs a 3–2 victory over the Canadiens, bringing an end to an unprecedented all-overtime Stanley Cup final.

Barilko's winner came at 2:53 of overtime in Game 5 after the Maple Leafs had pulled their goalie and tied the game on a Tod Sloan goal with 32 seconds remaining in regulation. The Canadiens had taken their 2–1 lead on a Paul Meger goal at 4:47 of the final period.

The Maple Leafs' fourth Cup title in five years did not come easily. They won Game 1 on a Sid Smith goal at 5:51 of overtime and lost Game 2 when Montreal's Rocket Richard scored at 2:55 of an extra period. Ted Kennedy and Harry Watson scored overtime goals to win the third and fourth games.

Barilko, a defenseman, was set up for his series-clincher at Maple Leaf Gardens on a pass from Howie Meeker, who started the winning scramble with a shot that McNeil kicked aside. Harry Watson jumped on the rebound and slid the puck back to Meeker, who set up Barilko for his winner with McNeil out of position.

MILESTONES • IN SPORTS •

1972

The transplanted Washington Senators made their Major League debut as the Texas Rangers, defeating the California Angels, 7–6, at Arlington Stadium.

1976

Philadelphia third baseman Mike Schmidt connected for his seventh home run in four games, leading the Phillies to a 3–0 victory over the Pittsburgh Pirates.

1991

Notre Dame star Raghib (Rocket) Ismail spurned the National Football League and signed the richest contract in football history (four years, $18.2 million guaranteed) with the Canadian Football League's Toronto Argonauts.

A STAR IS BORN

1887: Joe McCarthy, a baseball Hall of Famer who recorded 2,126 victories as a manager and led the New York Yankees to seven World Series championships and eight A.L. pennants from 1931–46.

★★★

1898: Steve Owen, a former NFL player who went on to a Hall of Fame coaching career (1931–53) with the New York Giants.

★★★

1960: Michel Goulet, a current National Hockey League left winger.

★★★

1965: Ed Belfour, a current National Hockey League goaltender.

★★★

DEATH OF A LEGEND

1989: Tommy Thompson (football).

★★★

1980 RUIZ WINS... APPARENTLY

Bill Rodgers etched his name among the greats in the storied history of the Boston Marathon, but the spotlight for his most dramatic victory was stolen by a 26-year-old New Yorker who aroused a storm of controversy by claiming victory in the women's segment of the race.

Bill Rodgers *(above) won his third consecutive Boston Marathon, but New Yorker* **Rosie Ruiz** *(below) won nothing but heartache after her apparent victory in the women's segment of the race.*

Rodgers became the first runner in 56 years and only the second ever to capture three consecutive Boston Marathons. He did it with a time of 2:12.11, but most of the attention at the awards ceremony was focused on Rosie Ruiz, a Cuban-born American who had staggered home in 2:31.56 – in only her second marathon.

The controversy arose when race officials, several runners and fans questioned whether Ruiz had run the entire race. Her winning time was a dramatic 25-minute improvement on her New York Marathon time of 2:56.29 the previous October, a race in which she finished 24th among women contestants. And it was the third-fastest marathon time ever recorded by a woman.

There was no evidence that Ruiz had not run the entire course because the times of the leading women were not recorded at the six-mile checkpoints of the 26-mile, 385-yard course. Montreal marathoner Jacqueline Gareau and American Patti Lyons, the pre-race favorites, thought they had finished 1–2. Lyons said she saw Ruiz for the first time at the awards ceremony.

Race officials confirmed there were suspicions Ruiz had jumped into the race somewhere near the end and observers reported they had seen no women ahead of Gareau. Officials said they would investigate, using cameras, video equipment and interviews to form an opinion that, hopefully, would confirm or deny Ruiz's victory.

Six hours after the race at her Boston hotel room, Ruiz appeared shaken and insisted, "I ran the race. I really did. I feel like I went more than 26 miles."

Rodgers thought not. "The second I saw her, I was skeptical. I know a top runner when I see one. She didn't look tired. . . From 2:36 to beating Patti Lyons? I'm sorry."

MILESTONES IN SPORTS

1947

Cleveland righthander Bob Feller fired his record ninth career one-hitter, surrendering only a seventh-inning single to Al Zarilla in a 5–0 victory over the St. Louis Browns.

1969

Joe Frazier defended his heavyweight championship with a first-round knockout of Dave Zyglewicz in a tight fight at Houston.

1976

Toronto center Darryl Sittler tied an NHL playoff record with five goals as the Maple Leafs scored an 8–6 quarterfinal victory over Philadelphia.

1984

Montreal's David Palmer pitched baseball's fourth rain-shortened perfect game, retiring all 15 St. Louis Cardinals he faced in a 4–0 victory at Busch Stadium.

1984

Martina Navratilova ended Chris Evert Lloyd's 85-match clay winning streak in her home state of Florida with a 6–2, 6–0 victory in the Women's Tennis Association championship at Amelia Island, Fla.

1990

The San Antonio Spurs completed the biggest turnaround in NBA history (35 games) when they defeated Phoenix for their 56th victory and clinched the Midwest Division title on the final day of the regular season.

1970 SEAVER FANS 19 PADRES

New York Mets righthander Tom Seaver, inspired by the 1969 National League Cy Young Award he was presented during pre-game ceremonies, went out and humbled the San Diego Padres in one of the most dominating pitching performances in baseball history.

Seaver, a 25-game winner in 1969, was brilliant in a 19-strikeout performance that matched the nine-inning major league record set by St. Louis lefthander Steve Carlton last September. En route to that distinction, Seaver fanned a record 10 consecutive Padres to close out his 2–1 victory at Shea Stadium.

Seaver allowed only two hits and a fourth-inning walk. Al Ferrara accounted for San Diego's run with a second-inning home run, but a run-scoring triple in the fourth inning by Bud Harrelson gave the Mets a 2–1 lead they never relinquished.

Seaver had nine strikeouts when he faced Ferrara with two out in the sixth inning. He made the right fielder victim No. 10 and then fanned the next nine Padres, getting Ferrara again for his record-tying 19th. His 10 strikeouts in a row broke the previous mark of eight shared by four major leaguers.

APRIL 22

A STAR IS BORN

1918: Mickey Vernon, a .286 career hitter in a 20-year major league career that ended in 1960.

★ ★ ★

1938: Deane Beman, a former professional golfer who went on to greater fame as PGA commissioner, a post he has held since 1974.

★ ★ ★

1949: Spencer Haywood, a forward who scored 17,111 points in an outstanding ABA-NBA career that ended in 1983.

★ ★ ★

1959: Freeman McNeil, a current National Football League running back.

DEATH OF A LEGEND

1990: Bob Davies (basketball).

★ ★ ★

1947 WARRIORS WIN CHAMPIONSHIP

Joe Fulks scored 34 points and the Philadelphia Warriors completed their rise from a second-place regular-season finish to the first championship of the new Basketball Association of America with an 83–80 victory over the Chicago Stags.

The Warriors, who had finished the BAA's inaugural season 14 games behind the Washington Capitols in the Eastern Division, completed their title run with a four games to one edge in the championship series. Howie Dallmar's field goal and Ralph Kaplowitz's free throw with less than a minute remaining provided the Warriors' winning margin in the final game before 8,221 enthusiastic fans at Philadelphia's Arena.

But most of the firepower was provided by Fulks, the 11-team circuit's leading scorer with a 23.2-point average. The talented forward also was prominent in the Warriors' six-game playoff victory over the Washington Capitols.

Angelo Musi chipped in 13 points and George Senesky added 11 for Philadelphia. Tony Jaros kept Chicago in the game with a 21-point effort and teammate James Seminoff contributed 12.

1982 BRAVES' STREAK ENDS

Cincinnati pitchers Bruce Berenyi and Tom Hume combined on a six-hitter and Berenyi drove in the winning run with a fifth-inning single as the Reds posted a 2–1 victory over Atlanta and snapped the Braves' modern-record season-opening winning streak at 13 games .

Berenyi yielded five hits through six innings but gave way to Hume with the bases loaded and one out in the sixth. Hume got Glenn Hubbard on a short fly ball and Claudell Washington on a grounder to preserve the one-run lead and closed out the Braves in the eighth and ninth.

Cincinnati's **Bruce Berenyi** *helped halt the Braves' season-opening winning streak at 13 games.*

The 13-game streak was two games better than the 11-game season-opening run last season by the Oakland A's. And Braves righthander Bob Walk seemed intent on extending it to 14 when he cruised through the first four innings, allowing only one hit and nursing a 1–0 lead.

But consecutive fifth-inning singles by Larry Biittner, Paul Householder and Wayne Krenchicki plated one run and Berenyi gave the Reds the winner with a single to left.

APRIL

23

1950 WINGS SOAR IN OT

Detroit left winger Pete Babando fired a shot past New York goaltender Claude Rayner 8:31 into a second overtime period as the Red Wings claimed a tense 4–3 seventh-game victory over the Rangers and their first Stanley Cup title since 1943.

The Red Wings, expected to make short work of the upstart Rangers, needed all seven games and then some. The "then some" was made necessary by three-second-period goals that wiped out 2–0 and 3–2 New York advantages.

A packed house at Detroit's Olympia Stadium grew restless as first-period goals by Allan Stanley and Tony Leswick staked the Rangers to their early lead. But Babando and Sid Abel scored 21 seconds apart in the second period to tie the score.

New York regained the lead on a goal by Buddy O'Connor, but Jimmy McFadden answered for Detroit late in the period. The teams played through a scoreless third period and first overtime.

Rayner was spectacular in a losing cause, recording 39 saves. Detroit played the series without injured star Gordie Howe.

New York, a heavy underdog entering the playoffs, had dispatched the Montreal Canadiens in a suprising five-game first-round series.

1964 NO-HIT GAME IS WASTED

Houston righthander Ken Johnson made a strong pitch for hard-luck-player-of-the-year honors when he became the first pitcher in baseball history to lose a game in which he had pitched a complete-game no-hitter.

The 30-year-old knuckleballer baffled his former Cincinnati team through eight innings of the game at Houston's Colt Stadium. He retired the Reds without a hit, walked three batters and allowed just three balls to be hit out of the infield. But the game still was scoreless as he entered the ninth inning and Johnson contributed to his own downfall with an error.

When rookie Pete Rose bunted with one out, Johnson fielded the ball but threw wildly, allowing Rose to go to second. Rose moved to third on a grounder and scored when normally reliable second baseman Nellie Fox bobbled Vada Pinson's ground ball.

Houston's hard-luck no-hit man **Ken Johnson.**

Reds lefty Joe Nuxhall retired the Colt .45s in the bottom of the ninth and etched Johnson's name in infamy. Eight major leaguers had lost games in which they had no-hit opponents for nine innings, but all of them lost in extra innings.

MILESTONES IN SPORTS

1952

St. Louis lefty Bob Cain outdueled Cleveland's Bob Feller, 1–0, in a record-tying battle of one-hitters at Sportsman's Park.

1955

The Chicago White Sox tied the modern single-game scoring record when they blasted seven home runs out of Kansas City's windy Municipal Stadium and pounded the Athletics, 29–6.

1978

South African Gary Player rallied from a five-stroke final-round deficit to beat Andy Bean by one shot in the Houston Open and claim his third consecutive American tour victory.

1950 MIKAN POWERS LAKERS

Big George Mikan scored a playoff-record 40 points and the Minneapolis Lakers overpowered Syracuse, 110–95, to capture the first championship of the new National Basketball Association.

The Nationals had no answer for Mikan, who had averaged 27.4 points during the NBA's first regular season after the merger of the National Basketball League and Basketball Association of America. The six-game victory matched the Lakers' triumph in 1948–49 when they won the BAA championship.

The physical final game at Minneapolis was marred by three fights. Syracuse's Paul Seymour and the Lakers' Jim Pollard, who backed up Mikan with 16 points, tangled in a first-quarter skirmish that police had to break up. Lesser scuffles took place in a bitterly fought second quarter.

The Lakers held a commanding 81-56 lead after three quarters, but Syracuse was able to close the gap when four Minneapolis players fouled out.

Minneapolis big man **George Mikan** *hoists Coach* **John Kundla** *on his shoulders as* **Slater Martin** *(left) and* **Jim Pollard** *lend a hand.*

A STAR IS BORN

1900: Jim Bottomley, a Hall of Fame first baseman who batted .310 over a 16-year major league career that ended in 1937.

★ ★ ★

1915: Bud Wilkinson, the former Oklahoma coach who guided the Sooners to a record 47 straight victories (1953–57) and three national championships. He also coached St. Louis of the NFL.

★ ★ ★

1921: Warren Spahn, a Hall of Famer, the winningest lefthander in major league history (363) and a 13-time 20-game victor over a 21-year career that ended in 1965.

★ ★ ★

1943: Gail Goodrich, an outstanding NBA guard who scored 19,181 points from 1965–79.

★ ★ ★

1943: Tony Esposito, a hockey Hall of Fame goaltender who won three Vezina Trophies and played in 873 games over a 15-year National Hockey League career that ended in 1984.

★ ★ ★

1967 76ERS WIN NBA TITLE

Reserve forward Billy Cunningham scored 13 points in a fourth-quarter comeback that lifted the Philadelphia 76ers to a 125–122 victory over San Francisco and the first National Basketball Association championship to be won by a team other than the Boston Celtics since 1958.

The 76ers, who snapped Boston's string of eight consecutive titles by beating the Celtics in the semifinals, completed their victory over the Warriors in six games and their season with an unprecedented 79–17 record. They were a record 68–13 in the regular season, 11–4 in the playoffs while earning some votes as the greatest team in NBA history.

The 76ers' series-ending victory at San Francisco's Cow Palace featured a 27-point performance by guard Wally Jones and a 24-point, 23-rebound effort by center Wilt Chamberlain, who also blocked six shots. Philadelphia, with Cunningham providing the spark, overcame a five-point deficit entering the final quarter.

The 76ers also overcame a 44-point effort by Rick Barry, who averaged 41 points in the series. Jeff Mullins added 23 and Jim King 19 for the Warriors. The 76ers actually won the game at the free throw line, hitting 41 of 64. The Warriors shot only 29.

APRIL

24

A STAR IS BORN

1903: Mike Michalske, a football Hall of Fame lineman who played in the formative years of the NFL.

★ ★ ★

1954: Vince Ferragamo, a former National Football League quarterback

1963 COUSY'S LAST GAME

Boston guard Bob Cousy, bringing down the curtain on his 13th and final National Basketball Association season, scored 18 points and steadied the Celtics during a shaky stretch run that resulted in a 112–109 victory over the Los Angeles Lakers and their record fifth consecutive championship.

The 34-year-old Cousy, who already had announced his retirement, sat down with an ankle injury early in the final period with the Celtics holding a 92–83 lead. But the Lakers had trimmed their deficit to one point when the little guard returned to the Los Angeles Sports Arena floor with time running down.

Cousy steadied the sinking ship and the Celtics sealed another championship when Tom Heinsohn hit four key free throws in the final minute. Heinsohn led a balanced Boston attack with 22 points while Los Angeles got its typical production from Jerry West (32 points) and Elgin Baylor (28).

Cousy was the playmaker and guiding force on all six of Boston's NBA championships.

Flood waters of the Ohio River engulf Cincinnati's Crosley Field.

1940 OHIO'S FLOOD WATERS TURN CROSLEY INTO LAKE

Baseball took another day off in Cincinnati when flood waters from the Ohio River turned Crosley Field into a giant lake with grandstands.

A scheduled game against the St. Louis Cardinals was cancelled for the second consecutive day as the field disappeared from sight beneath the backwaters of the river, which was expected to crest at 60 feet – 8 above flood stage. It marked the third time a major league game had been washed out by a flood.

Players had visited the park a day earlier to participate in a brief throwing practice on some still-dry areas of the outfield, but everything soon was under water with no hope of resuming play for several days.

Once the water starts to fall, Cincinnati officials plan to speed the process with a giant siphon fashioned from a firehose and connected to the field's drains. The siphon cannot be used during the river's rise because of potential dangers to the park's sewer system. When the possibility of flooding became serious, five inches of sand was dumped on the diamond to protect the surface from inundation.

MILESTONES IN SPORTS

1951

The new American League, a major threat to the monopoly long enjoyed by baseball's National League, opened play with eight franchises located in Philadelphia, Boston, Chicago, Washington, Detroit, Cleveland, Baltimore and Milwaukee.

1945

Kentucky Senator Albert B. (Happy) Chandler was tabbed as baseball's second commissioner following the death of former Federal Judge Kenesaw Mountain Landis.

1971

Bob Foster, extended to 15 rounds for the first time in his career, defended his light heavyweight championship with a unanimous decision over Ray Anderson at Tampa, Fla.

1974

Tampa, Fla., interests were awarded the National Football League's 27th franchise, which would be known as the Tampa Bay Buccaneers and play its games in Tampa Stadium.

APRIL

25

A STAR IS BORN

1884: John Henry Lloyd, a Hall of Fame infielder who spent his professional career in the Negro Leagues before baseball's color barrier fell in 1947.

★ ★ ★

1952: Vladislav Tretiak, the outstanding Russian goalie who led the Soviet Union to Olympic gold medals in 1972 and '76.

DEATH OF A LEGEND

1983: Bob Waterfield (football).

★ ★ ★

1991: Laz Barrera (horse racing).

1964

LEAFS WIN 3RD IN ROW

Toronto scored three third-period goals and goaltender Johnny Bower turned in a superb 33-save shutout as the Maple Leafs posted a 4–0 victory over Detroit in Game 7 of the Stanley Cup finals and claimed their third consecutive championship.

The Maple Leafs, who had forced a seventh game on Bob Baun's overtime goal in Game 6 at Detroit, entered the final period with a 1–0 lead, courtesy of Andy Bathgate's first-period goal. But Dave Keon and Red Kelly gave Bower a cushion with goals 1:27 apart and George Armstrong iced the victory at 15:26 with his fifth goal of the playoffs.

Bower was outstanding in recording the first shutout of the playoffs and firing up Toronto 's largest crowd at Maple Leaf Gardens in three seasons. Detroit goalie Terry Sawchuk, who also finished with 33 saves, was solid through two periods before falling victim to the Leafs' third-period outburst. Bathgate's score came on a breakaway.

1989

MARIO GAINS REVENGE

Pittsburgh center Mario Lemieux, who left Game 4 of a Patrick Division final contest at Philadelphia after nearly being knocked unconscious, scored five goals in an eight-point masterpiece that carried the Penguins to a 10–7 Game 5 victory at the Pittsburgh Civic Center.

Lemieux, whose status was uncertain right up until game time, scored three goals before the game was seven minutes old and four by the end of the opening period before handing out three assists in a three-goal Pittsburgh second period that stretched the Penguins' lead to 9–3.

The Flyers fought back to 9–7 in the final period, but Lemieux capped his big performance with an empty-net goal that insured victory and gave Pittsburgh a 3–2 games advantage. The five goals, the four-goal first period and the eight-point game all matched National Hockey League playoff records.

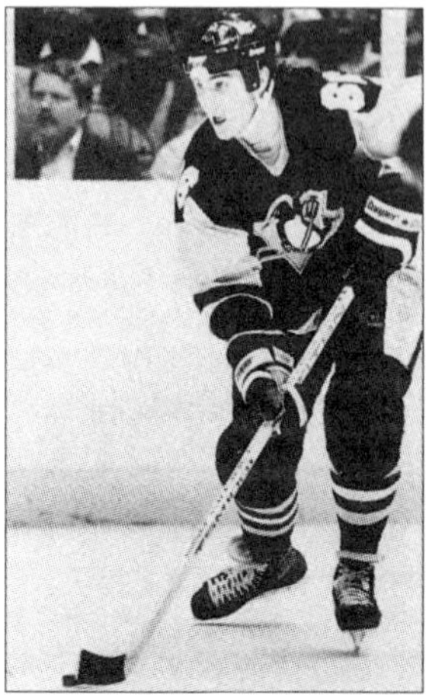

Pittsburgh Penguins sharpshooter **Mario Lemieux.**

MILESTONES •IN SPORTS•

1901

Amazing debut: The American League's new Detroit team opened its season by scoring 10 ninth-inning runs and defeating Milwaukee, 14–13.

1974

Two major National Football League rules changes: Sudden-death overtimes for regular-season games and goal posts moving to the back of the end zone.

1981

Thomas (Hit Man) Hearns defended his WBA welterweight boxing championship with a 13th-round knockout of Randy Shields at Phoenix.

1985

Former Detroit 31-game winner Denny McLain hit rock bottom when he was sentenced to 23 years in Federal prison after being found guilty on charges ranging from racketeering to drug trafficking.

1987

Cincinnati center fielder Eric Davis set a major league record for futility when he struck out against Houston Astros relief pitcher Dave Smith – his ninth whiff in a row over two games.

1976

MONDAY TO THE RESCUE

Chicago Cubs center fielder Rick Monday, celebrating the United States' bicentennial in his own special way, swooped down on two would-be protestors at Dodger Stadium and rescued an American flag they were trying to set on fire.

Monday was in position as the Los Angeles Dodgers were preparing to bat in the fourth inning of a Sunday afternoon game. The protestors jumped out of the stands, ran to a position in left field and spread out a large flag. When Monday saw one of them fumbling with a lighter, he went into action.

He ran over and snatched away the flag as security guards chased down the protestors. He was rewarded by 25,167 fans with a standing ovation as the Dodger Stadium message board flashed, "Rick Monday... You made a great play."

But that was just the tip of the iceberg. Monday's rescue made national headlines, he was buried by an avalanche of praise and was besieged by requests for interviews and appearances. He also received commendations from President Gerald Ford, Commissioner Bowie Kuhn, the Illinois legislature and the National League.

The Cubs even set aside May 4 as "Rick Monday Day" at Wrigley Field.

Chicago Cubs flag-saving hero **Rick Monday.**

MILESTONES IN SPORTS

1974

Another Hank Aaron record: Career home run No. 719 was his National League-best 15th grand slam and sparked Atlanta to a 9–3 victory over Chicago.

1981

Chris Evert Lloyd won her 49th straight clay-court match, dispatching Martina Navratilova, 6–0, 6–0, in the final of the Murjani tournament at Amelia Island, Fla.

1984

New York Nets 101, 76ers 98: Defending-champion Philadelphia was eliminated from the National Basketball Association playoffs in a stunning five-game, first-round upset.

1988

The Boston Bruins ended 45 years of frustration when they defeated Montreal, 4–1, in Game 5 of the Adams Division final for their first playoff series victory over the Canadiens after 18 consecutive losses.

A STAR IS BORN

1900: Hack Wilson, a muscular Hall of Fame outfielder who set the one-season RBI record in 1930 when he drove in 190 for the Chicago Cubs.

★ ★ ★

1918: Fanny Blankers-Koen, the outstanding Dutch athlete who won four gold medals at the 1948 Olympic Games.

★ ★ ★

1927: Harry Gallatin, a Hall of Fame forward who played in the formative years of the National Basketball Association.

★ ★ ★

1955: Mike Scott, a former N.L. Cy Young winner for the Houston Astros.

★ ★ ★

1952 BERG SHOOTS 64 IN 10-BIRDIE SHOW

Patty Berg, taking women's golf to a level that only men had previously reached, zoomed to a seven-stroke lead in the first round of the Richmond Open when she blazed around the course with a world-record 64.

Berg, the president and a co-founder of the Ladies' Professional Golf Association, was phenomenal in a 10-birdie, two-bogey performance that lowered the women's record by two strokes.

Using a new putter, Berg covered the front nine holes of the Richmond (Va.) Country Club course in a 30-stroke blitz that required only 11 putts. Four of her birdies were achieved on putts of 25, 15, 31 and 12 feet.

The previous best women's rounds on record, two 66s, belonged to Babe Didrikson Zaharias and Opal Hill. Amazingly, Berg's playing partner, Marlene Bauer, tied the previous course record with a 71 – and settled for a distant second place.

Berg has won more than 90 women's tournaments.

1964 CELTICS REACH NEW HEIGHTS

Bill Russell insured victory by emphatically slamming home a missed shot with 15 seconds remaining as the "too old" Boston Celtics claimed their sixth consecutive National Basketball Association championship with a 105–99 victory over the San Francisco Warriors at raucous Boston Garden.

The Celtics' Game 5 triumph put them a level above the great champions of team sports. Baseball's New York Yankees and hockey's Montreal Canadiens both had won five straight titles in their respective leagues, but never had a professional team captured six in a row. The Celtics' crown also was their seventh in eight years.

And it came in a season when everybody expected to see them wither and die, especially without retired playmaker Bob Cousy. They didn't. The final game was typical of the season and the series; the Celtics jumped to a lead and held on for dear life. Leading by as many as 11 points three times in the third period behind a Sam Jones scoring burst, Boston fought off a Philadelphia challenge that cut the margin to two.

But Russell, who did his usual sterling defensive job on Wilt Chamberlain, made his decisive dunk and the Celtics were champions again.

Happy Boston Celtics celebrate their sixth consecutive NBA championship.

1975 CONNORS EARNS GIANT PAYOFF

Jimmy Connors overpowered Australian John Newcombe, 6–3, 4–6, 6–2, 6–4, in an uninspired million-dollar tennis showdown choreographed by hungry promoters and staged at the glitzy Caesar's Palace in Las Vegas.

The event was a disappointment, both from an interest standpoint and artistically. There was little in the way of dramatics and the crowd was subdued and unresponsive. The 22-year-old Connors appeared to have prepared for the challenge, but his 30-year-old opponent played lethargically.

Newcombe, a three-time Wimbledon champion, could not get his big serve to work and he failed to win key points. Eleven times he worked Connors to break points in the first two sets, 10 times he failed. Connors took control in the third set by running off 10 consecutive points.

Connors, who collected $500,000, previously had defeated Australian Rod Laver in a similar match that paid him $150,000 and generated much more enthusiasm. If nothing else, the victory over Newcombe solidified Connors' status as the No. 1 player in the world.

Connors' victory lifted his four-year career winnings over the $1 million mark.

APRIL

27

The great **Rocky Marciano** *during his prime.*

1956 Marciano Retires

Rocky Marciano, the man criticized as too awkward and slow to be successful in boxing, announced his retirement after 49 consecutive professional victories and ended his 3½-year run as world heavyweight champion.

Marciano retires as boxing's first undefeated heavyweight champion. James Jeffries retired undefeated in 1905 but came back to fight, and lose, a title bout against Jack Johnson. Gene Tunney retired with the heavyweight crown in 1928, but he had lost an early-career fight.

Marciano achieved success with a plodding, aggressive, take-a-punch style that was successful, if not pretty. His jaw, like his fists, seemingly were made of iron and his rugged determination wore down opponents.

The Brockton, Mass., native won the crown from Jersey Joe Walcott in 1952 and defended it six times, the last against Archie Moore in September.

He was knocked off his feet only twice in his career – by Walcott in their first fight and by Moore in his last. He won 43 bouts by knockout.

1960 Lakers Go West to Los Angeles

The National Basketball Association expanded its horizons to the West Coast when the league's Board of Governors voted unanimously to allow the Minneapolis Lakers' owner, Bob Short, to shift his franchise to Los Angeles.

The Lakers, who won five NBA championships from 1949 to 1954 in Minneapolis, will begin play in Los Angeles in the 1960–61 season.

Short was given exclusive professional basketball rights in the new Memorial Sports Arena by the Los Angeles Coliseum Commission.

The Lakers, who finished third in the NBA's Western Division last year before bowing to St. Louis in the second round of the playoffs, will compete for fans with the Los Angeles franchise of the new American Basketball Association, which also will begin operation in 1960–61.

The Minneapolis-to-Los Angeles move will be the fourth franchise shift in NBA history. The Milwaukee Hawks moved to St. Louis, the Fort Wayne Pistons shifted to Detroit and the Rochester Royals went to Cincinnati in previous moves.

MILESTONES IN SPORTS

1944

Jim Tobin pitched the first Boston Braves no-hitter in 28 years and iced his 2–0 victory with a home run.

1968

Jimmy Ellis, staking his claim to a share of the heavyweight title stripped from Muhammad Ali, scored a 15-round majority decision over Jerry Quarry at Oakland.

1981

Los Angeles rookie sensation Fernando Valenzuela lowered his ERA to 0.20 with his fourth shutout of the season – a 5–0 victory over San Francisco.

1983

Houston's Nolan Ryan fanned Montreal's Brad Mills to pass Walter Johnson as baseball's all-time strikeout king. Mills was Ryan's 3,509th victim.

1947 Ruth Says Farewell

A thin, raspy-voiced Babe Ruth said a tear-jerking farewell to 58,339 fans at Yankee Stadium and thousands more who listened to his words at ballparks throughout the country as baseball took time to honor its most flamboyant and beloved superstar on "Babe Ruth Day."

The 53-year-old Ruth, who had retired in 1935 as holder of virtually every slugging record, looked weak and drawn as he accepted numerous awards and gifts before stepping to the microphone for a greeting that rocked the grandstands. His normal rollicking manner was subdued, his voice was scratchy from the series of operations he had undergone to combat throat cancer, but there was no mistaking baseball's Bambino.

An ailing **Babe Ruth** *is escorted to the dugout prior to 'Babe Ruth Day' festivities at Yankee Stadium.*

The smile was vintage Ruth and the words were upbeat and straight from the heart. He expressed his gratitude for the opportunity to play "the only real game in the world" and the "lovely things said about me" and then, with a final "thank you to everybody," Ruth smiled, waved to the crowd and walked into the Yankee dugout for the last time.

The former Boston and New York star carried with him lasting memories and a baseball legacy that included seven World Series championship rings, 714 career home runs, a .342 lifetime average and 2,204 career RBIs.

A STAR IS BORN

1896: Rogers Hornsby, a Hall of Fame second baseman who batted .358 over a 23-year career that ended in 1937. He set a one-season record when he hit .424 in 1924 for the St. Louis Cardinals.

★ ★ ★

1916: Enos Slaughter, a Hall of Fame outfielder who batted .300 over his 19-year career (1938–59) and became known for his hustling style of play.

★ ★ ★

1952: George Gervin, a sharpshooting forward who scored 20,708 points and won four NBA scoring championships over a 10-year career that ended in 1986.

DEATH OF A LEGEND

1981: Cliff Battles (football).

1966 CELTICS WIN EIGHTH IN ROW

Bill Russell scored 25 points and grabbed 32 rebounds as the Boston Celtics defeated Los Angeles, 95–93, in Game 7 of the National Basketball Association title series and ran their incredible string of championships to eight.

The victory, before 13,909 fans at Boston Garden, extended the longest championship reign in the history of major professional team sports. And it sent retiring Coach Red Auerbach out on a happy not – with his ninth title in 10 years.

Russell, who will take over as player-coach next season, was his usual rugged self against the Lakers as the Celtics rolled up a 19-point third-quarter lead and then held off a desperation Lakers' charge.

Russell got plenty of support from Sam Jones (22 points) and John Havlicek (16), but the real spark was provided by Tom Sanders and Don Nelson, who combined to hold high-scoring Los Angeles forward Elgin Baylor to 18 points – two in the first half. Jerry West led the Lakers with 36.

The Celtics, who had blown a three games to one lead in the series, also became the first team in 14 years to finish second in the regular-season Eastern Division race and still capture the championship.

Bill Russell, *the moving force behind the Boston Celtics' incredible NBA dynasty.*

1967 ALI'S TITLE TAKEN AWAY

The organizations that govern world boxing stripped Muhammad Ali of his heavyweight championship when the 25-year-old fighter, as expected, refused induction into the armed forces.

Ali, claiming exemption from the draft as an appointed minister of the Lost-Found Nation of Islam, an offshoot of the Black Muslim sect, said in a prepared statement: "I have searched my conscience and I find I cannot be true to my belief in my religion by accepting such a call."

Government action is sure to follow, a lengthy process of court hearings and an indictment that eventually could result in a five-year prison sentence and a $10,000 fine. But the boxing authorities wasted no time, taking away the title Ali, then known as Cassius Clay, earned in 1964 with a victory over Sonny Liston and defended nine times.

Ali's induction refusal became official when he appeared, as scheduled, at the U.S. Customs House in Houston with a battery of Civil Rights lawyers.

1974 TORRID MILLER WINS AGAIN

Johnny Miller continued his amazing blitz of the PGA Tour when he sank a five-foot par-saving putt on the 18th hole and recorded his fifth victory of the year – a one-shot decision over Buddy Allin and John Mahaffey in the Tournament of Champions held at Carlsbad, Calif.

Miller's final-round 69 over the LaCosta Country Club course was good enough to win a spirited three-way battle that was decided when Allin and Mahaffey bogeyed the 18th while Miller got his par. The three were tied after 17 and the par-4 18th played true to form – only one birdie the entire week.

Miller, who started the day two strokes behind leader Bob Charles and one behind Allin, claimed his victory after falling behind by four strokes on the front nine. He recovered with birdies on 10, 14 and 16, where he finally caught Allin.

The blazing Miller posted his 33rd subpar score in 44 rounds this year and dropped to 81 under par. He lifted his season winnings to $192,877–more than double anybody else.

Never had anybody won so many tournaments and so much money this early in a season. The blond-haired Californian swept to victories in the Crosley, Phoenix and Tucson events, the first three on the PGA Tour, and added a victory in the Heritage Classic. The Tournament of Champions triumph came one day before Miller's 27th birthday.

APRIL 28

A STAR IS BORN

1960: Tom Browning, a current major league pitcher.

★ ★ ★

1963: Mark Bavaro, a current National Football League tight end.

★ ★ ★

MILESTONES IN SPORTS

1974

Olga Morozova upset Billie Jean King, 7–6, 6–1, in the final of a Virginia Slims tournament at Philadelphia–the first victory for a Soviet woman in a major U.S. event.

1975

The NBA elected Larry O'Brien to succeed Walter Kennedy as its new commissioner.

1984

New York Islanders goaltender Billy Smith set an NHL record when he defeated Montreal, 5–2, for his 81st playoff victory.

1985

Hector (Macho) Camacho scored a unanimous 12-round decision over Roque Montoya and claimed the North American Boxing Federation's lightweight championship.

1988

Minnesota defeated Baltimore, 4–2, and dropped the Orioles to 0–21, an American League record for consecutive losses.

1988

Michael Jordan scored 50 points and the Chicago Bulls posted a 104–93 victory over Cleveland in the opener of a first-round NBA playoff series.

APRIL

29

A STAR IS BORN

1934: Luis Aparicio, a Hall of Fame shortstop who led the A.L. in stolen bases nine times.

★ ★ ★

1947: Johnny Miller, one of the hottest professional golfers in the 1970s. He won an incredible eight tournaments in 1974.

★ ★ ★

1947: Jim Ryun, an outstanding American distance runner who set two world records in the mile (1966 and '67) and one in the 1,500 meters (1967).

★ ★ ★

1952: Dale Earnhardt, an outstanding race car driver who has earned five NASCAR national championships and more than 50 career victories.

★ ★ ★

1967: Curtis Joseph, a current National Hockey League goaltender.

★ ★ ★

DEATH OF A LEGEND

1987: Gus Johnson (basketball).

★ ★ ★

1986

CLEMENS FANS 20 IN HISTORIC EFFORT

Roger Clemens, living up to his well-deserved nickname of "Rocket Man," fired his high-powered fastball past 20 Seattle Mariners in a record performance that produced a 3–1 Boston victory at Fenway Park.

Boston strikeout artist **Roger Clemens.**

Clemens claimed baseball's modern nine-inning strikeout mark with an amazing effort that topped the 19-strikeout performances of Steve Carlton (1969), Tom Seaver (1970) and Nolan Ryan (1974). Clemens was masterful in a three-hit, no-walk outing–only eight months after recovering from shoulder surgery.

The talented and resourceful righthander, consistently topping 95 miles per hour on the radar gun, struck out every member of the Seattle starting lineup at least once. Outfielder Phil Bradley went down four times, including a game-ending whiff that set the record.

Clemens fanned the side in three innings and matched the American League record of eight consecutive strikeouts from the fourth to sixth. Gorman Thomas accounted for Seattle's run with a seventh-inning homer.

1971

RANGERS BARELY STAY ALIVE

Pete Stemkowski slapped home a rebound off Ted Irvine's shot in the third overtime, giving the New York Rangers a do-or-die 3–2 victory over the Chicago Blackhawks in the sixth game of a National Hockey League semifinal playoff series at Madison Square Garden.

Stemkowski's goal, which came 1:29 into the third extra session, ended the Rangers' longest game since 1938 and forced a seventh game at Chicago.

It was the second goal of the series for the big New York center and both of them decided overtime games. The Rangers dominated play through most of the game, but couldn't solve Tony Esposito. The New Yorkers challenged the Chicago goalie 49 times, while Rangers netminder Ed Giacomin faced a mere 26 shots on his goal. The Blackhawks took a 2–0 lead on Dennis Hull and Chico Maki goals, but Rod Gilbert cut the deficit in half in the second period and Jean Ratelle tied the score in the third.

Neither team could break through in the next 40 minutes and Stemkowski brought a thankful roar from 17,250 fans when he knocked home the rebound off Irvine's shot at two minutes before midnight – 4 hours and 23 minutes after the start of the game.

The teams played a total of 101 minutes, 29 seconds – the Rangers' longest game since a 1938 loss to the New York Americans – 40 seconds into a fourth overtime.

It was the Rangers' fourth overtime battle in their last seven playoff games.

1988

ORIOLES FINALLY TRIUMPH

Mark Williamson and Dave Schmidt combined on a four-hitter and Cal Ripken and Eddie Murray blasted home runs as the Baltimore Orioles defeated Chicago, 9–0, and snapped their record season-opening losing streak at an amazing 21 games.

The sweet taste of victory ended a horrid nightmare in which the Orioles lost five times to Milwaukee, seven to Cleveland, six to Kansas City and three to Minnesota. Cal Ripken Sr., the manager when the season opened, gave way to Frank Robinson after only six games.

But it didn't matter who was calling the shots. Baltimore's 14th consecutive loss, 8–6 at Milwaukee, set a major league record for season-opening futility and their 21st, 4–2 at Minnesota, set the American League mark for consecutive losses.

When the Orioles beat the White Sox at Comiskey Park, they were just two losses shy of the major league record of 23 straight by the 1961 Phillies.

MILESTONES IN SPORTS

1978

Pete Rose, baseball's classic singles hitter, crashed three homers and drove in four runs as the Cincinnati Reds pounded the New York Mets, 14–7, at Shea Stadium.

1980

After reviewing photographs and conducting interviews for seven days, Boston Marathon officials stripped Rosie Ruiz of the women's title she allegedly won by entering the April 21 race near the end.

1981

Philadelphia's Steve Carlton became the first lefthander to surpass 3,000 career strikeouts when he fanned nine Montreal Expos in a 6–2 victory and finished the night with 3,006.

MILESTONES • IN SPORTS •

1922

Perfecto: Chicago White Sox rookie Charlie Robertson pitched baseball's third modern-era perfect game, beating the Tigers, 2–0, at Detroit's Navin Field.

1940

The Brooklyn Dodgers tied the major league record for most victories (nine) to open a season and they did it in style on Tex Carleton's no-hit, 3–0 victory over Cincinnati.

1944

New York first baseman Phil Weintraub drove in 11 runs, one short of the major league record, with four extra-base hits in a 26–8 Giants victory over Brooklyn at the Polo Grounds.

1967

Baltimore pitchers Steve Barber and Stu Miller combined on a nine-inning no-hitter–and lost, 2–1, to the Detroit Tigers.

1976

Muhammad Ali retained his heavyweight crown with a 15-round unanimous decision over Jimmy Young at Landover, Md.

A STAR IS BORN

1946: Don Schollander, an American swimmer who earned four gold medals at the 1964 Summer Olympic Games and added another in 1968 .

★ ★ ★

1961: Isiah Thomas, a current National Basketball Association guard.

★ ★ ★

1963: Al Toon, a current National Football League wide receiver.

★ ★ ★

1966: Jeff Brown, a current National Hockey League defenseman.

★ ★ ★

APRIL 30

1993 Assailant Stabs Tennis Star Seles

Monica Seles, the 19-year-old Yugoslavian-born tennis star ranked No. 1 in the world, was rushed to a hospital after a deranged spectator stabbed her in the back during a changeover in a Citizen Cup quarterfinal match at Hamburg, Germany.

Seles, who was leading, 6–4, 4–3, in her match against Bulgarian Magdalena Maleeva, was sitting in a chair at the side of the Rothenbaum Tennis Club court when a balding man dressed in a plaid shirt and jeans walked down the pedestrian aisle, stood at the waist-high barrier behind her and stabbed her between the shoulder blades with a nine-inch boning knife.

Seles jumped to her feet and staggered to mid-court, where she was assisted by tournament officials and her brother. Her assailant dropped his knife and was immediately restrained by security guards, who turned him over to police. The man was identified as a 38-year-old German citizen with a passion for Steffi Graf, a German tennis star ranked No. 2 behind Seles.

The knife left a two-centimeter wound, but Seles was fortunate it missed her spinal area. Doctors said it would be at least a month, maybe considerably longer, before Seles could resume playing tennis.

1961 Mays Blasts Four

San Francisco center fielder Willie Mays blasted his way into baseball's record books when he slugged a record-tying four homers and drove in eight runs in the Giants' 14–4 victory over Milwaukee at County Stadium.

Mays provided half of the Giants' offense in a record-tying eight-home run team performance. He became only the ninth player to perform the four-homer feat and he was waiting on deck in the ninth inning when Jim Davenport made the Giants' final out.

Mays, who homered in the first, third, sixth and eighth innings, belted his first two off Braves starter Lew Burdette and the others off relievers Seth Morehead and Don McMahon.

But Mays wasn't the only heavy basher of the day. Jose Pagan hit two homers and Orlando Cepeda and Felipe Alou one apiece for the Giants while Hank Aaron connected twice for the Braves.

San Francisco four-homer man **Willie Mays.**

1971 Bucks Claim NBA Title With Sweep

Oscar Robertson and Lew Alcindor, a little old and a little new, made 57 points between them and the Milwaukee Bucks completed a quick-and-easy National Basketball Association championship series sweep of the Baltimore Bullets with a convincing 118–106 victory at the Baltimore Civic Center.

The 32-year-old Robertson, playing his 11th NBA season and looking for his first championship, scored 30 points and handed out nine assists in the clinching victory. The 24-year-old Alcindor, the Bucks' 7-foot-2 second-year center, scored 27 and grabbed 12 rebounds. It was a match made in heaven–for Milwaukee fans.

Baltimore fans watched as the overmatched Bullets fell by margins of 10, 19, 8 and 12 points in the four losses. The Bucks dominated every game in becoming only the second NBA team to sweep a final series.

Baltimore's only satisfaction came from the 23-rebound effort of center Wes Unseld and the 28-point performance of Fred Carter in the final loss.

Oscar Robertson *was part of his first NBA championship team in Milwaukee.*

MAY 1

MILESTONES IN SPORTS

1948

Triple Crown hopeful Citation, with Eddie Arcaro in saddle, defeated Coaltown in the Kentucky Derby with a winning time of 2:05 2/5.

1959

Floyd Patterson defended his heavyweight crown with an 11th-round knockout of Brian London at Indianapolis.

1963

Walter Kennedy was selected as the NBA's second commissioner, succeeding Maurice Podoloff.

1969

Houston righthander Don Wilson pitched a 4–0 no-hitter against Cincinnati, the day after Reds righthander Jim Maloney had no-hit the Astros, 10–0, at Crosley Field. It marked the second time in big-league history back-to-back no-hitters had been thrown.

1971

A shocker: Gustavo Avila rode longshot Canonero II to an impressive Kentucky Derby victory over Jim French.

1973

The San Francisco Giants, down 7-1 with two out in the ninth inning, scored seven runs to stun the Pittsburgh Pirates, 8-7.

1975

Milwaukee's Hank Aaron raised his career RBI total to 2,211 and moved past Babe Ruth into first place on the all-time list when he drove in two runs in a 17–3 victory over Detroit.

1991 RYAN'S 7TH NO-HITTER

Nolan Ryan, showing that his 44-year-old arm still has plenty of juice, fired his record-extending seventh career no-hitter in a dominating 3–0 victory over the hard-hitting Toronto Blue Jays on Arlington Appreciation Night at Arlington Stadium.

Ryan, pitching in his 25th major league season, made career victory No. 305 a memorable one as he struck out 16, walked two and mesmerized the Blue Jays with an assortment of 95-plus mph fastballs, sharp curves and change-ups. The Jays, who entered the game with a .276 team average, did not hit a ball hard.

Ryan, who became the oldest pitcher in history to throw a no-hitter when he recorded No. 6 a year earlier against Oakland, walked Kelly Gruber on a 3–2 pitch in the first inning and Joe Carter on a 3–2 pitch in the seventh. With the crowd of 33,439 chanting his name, Ryan retired Manny Lee and Devon White on ninth-inning grounders and struck out Roberto Alomar to end the game.

Ryan, who has pitched a record 12 one-hitters in his amazing career, fanned at least one batter in every inning en route to his 26th game of 15 or more strikeouts.

1920 LONGEST GAME ENDS IN TIE

Righthanders Leon Cadore and Joe Oeschger matched pitches for 26 innings in the longest major league game ever played, but neither got a decision when the 1–1 marathon between the Brooklyn Dodgers and Boston was halted with darkness settling over Braves Field.

For 3 hours, 50 minutes Brooklyn's Cadore and Boston's Oeschger baffled hitters and snuffed out a succession of scoring chances. Cadore surrendered 15 hits and five walks but pitched out of numerous jams. Oeschger was in less danger, allowing nine hits and three walks. Both players managed to wriggle their way out of a bases-loaded, one-out situation with a game-saving double play.

Brooklyn scored its only run in the fifth inning on an Ivy Olson single and Boston tied the game an inning later on Tony Boeckel's single. The game remained scoreless for the next 20 innings as the teams battled in helpless frustration.

The previous longest game was a 24-inning affair between the Philadelphia Athletics and Boston in 1906. The A's eventually beat the Red Sox in that marathon, 4–1.

1991 RICKEY GETS RECORD

Oakland's Rickey Henderson, frustrated in a first-inning attempt to become baseball's all-time greatest basestealer, dove head-first into the record books three innings later when he swiped third base during the A's 7–4 victory over the New York Yankees at the Oakland Coliseum.

Henderson, who had tied Lou Brock's career record of 938 steals three days earlier, reached base in the first inning against starting pitcher Tim Leary. But Yankee catcher Matt Nokes gunned him down trying to swipe second. Henderson reached again in the fourth, advanced to second and took off on Leary's first pitch. Nokes' weak throw was late.

Henderson jumped to his feet, pulled the bag from its mooring and held it high over his head, saluting the crowd of 36,139. Brock joined Henderson in a brief ceremony that also included Henderson's mother, Bobbie.

Brock had retired in 1979 after 19 big-league seasons, most with the St. Louis Cardinals. Henderson, who also set the one-season record of 130 steals in 1982, recorded his 939th steal early in his 13th campaign.

Henderson got a chance to extend his record when he reached base again in the fifth, but he was thrown out for a second time by the inspired Nokes.

Oakland basestealing wizard **Rickey Henderson.**

A STAR IS BORN

1910: Cliff Battles, a football Hall of Fame halfback for six NFL seasons in the 1930s and the first to gain more than 200 yards in a single game.

★ ★ ★

1925: Chuck Bednarik, a football Hall of Fame center and linebacker in a 14-year career (1949–62) with the NFL's Philadelphia Eagles.

★ ★ ★

1930: Ollie Matson, a versatile football Hall of Fame halfback who ran, caught passes and returned kicks for 15 NFL seasons in the 1950s and '60s.

★ ★ ★

DEATH OF A LEGEND

1983: Norm Van Brocklin (football).

★ ★ ★

1987: Bobo Holloman (baseball).

★ ★ ★

MILESTONES
• IN SPORTS •

1923

New York Yankee shortstop Everett Scott played in his major league-record 1,000th straight game –a 3–0 loss to Walter Johnson and Washington.

1930

Des Moines defeated Western League rival Wichita, 13–6, at Des Moines, Iowa, in the first Organized Baseball game played under permanently-installed lights.

1964

A Kentucky Derby record: Bill Hartack rode Northern Dancer to a best-ever winning time of 2:00.

1981

Pleasant Colony and jockey Jorge Velasquez earned a pleasant victory in the Kentucky Derby with a time of 2:02.

1987

Alysheba edged Bet Twice by three-quarters of a length in the 113th Run for the Roses at Louisville's Churchill Downs.

1939 GEHRIG ENDS RECORD RUN

Yankee Manager **Joe McCarthy** *consoles* **Lou Gehrig,** *his suddenly inactive superstar.*

With iron-man first baseman Lou Gehrig sitting on the bench for the first time in 15 years, the New York Yankees clobbered the Detroit Tigers, 22–2, in an emotional game at Detroit's Briggs Stadium.

Gehrig, appearing weak, out of shape and listless in an early-season performance that defies explanation, voluntarily withdrew his name from the lineup, ending an incredible streak of 2,130 consecutive games that had started June 1, 1925. He told Manager Joe McCarthy he wanted to sit down "for the good of the team" and his boss reluctantly complied with the request.

Gehrig was coming off a .295, 29-homer, 114-RBI season that helped the Yankees win a third consecutive World Series championship. But the 35-year-old slugger reported to spring training feeling weak and never could get himself into top form. He was batting a meager .143 when he decided to sit down and end the streak.

Gehrig, the Yankee captain, carried the lineup to home plate as usual, but then took an unfamiliar seat on the bench. His replacement, Babe Dahlgren, had a homer, double and three RBIs.

Gehrig batted .340 with 493 homers and 1,976 RBIs during the streak.

MAY

2

A STAR IS BORN

1887: Eddie Collins, a savvy Hall of Fame second baseman who batted .333 over an outstanding 25-year American League career that ended in 1930.

★ ★ ★

1917 DOUBLE NO-HIT FEAT

Double no-hitter—1917 Cincinnati righthander Fred Toney and Chicago lefty Jim (Hippo) Vaughn hooked up for baseball's first double no-hitter, but Vaughn's effort went for naught when the Reds pushed across a 10th-inning run and earned a 1–0 victory at Chicago's Weeghman Park.

The amazing pitching duel unfolded on a raw, windy afternoon before 3,500 brave Chicago fans. Vaughn set down the Reds without a hitch for nine innings, allowing only three baserunners—two walks and an infield error. But Toney matched that feat, surrendering only a pair of walks to Chicago's Cy Williams.

Something had to give and it did in the top of the 10th. Cincinnati shortstop Larry Kopf opened the inning with the game's first hit, a clean single to right, and moved to third on an error by center fielder Williams. Kopf scored when Jim Thorpe's swinging bunt went for a single.

That's all Toney needed. He retired the Cubs in order in the bottom of the inning, completing his no-hit victory.

1954 MUSIAL BLASTS FIVE HOMERS

St. Louis slugger Stan Musial exploded for a major league-record five home runs in a Sportsman's Park doubleheader against the New York Giants, but the Cardinals could do no better than a split, winning the first game 10–6 and losing the nightcap 9–7.

Musial drove in six runs in a 4-for-4 first-game performance, three coming on an eighth-inning blast off Jim Hearn that made a winner of Al Brazle. Musial had walked in the first inning, homered in the third and fifth off Johnny Antonelli and singled in the sixth.

He came back in the second game with a 2-for-4 effort that included a two-run fifth-inning homer and a solo blast in the seventh. An eight-run Giants fourth inning kept the Cardinals froma sweep.

Musial, a six-time National League batting champion, finished his 6-for-8 afternoon with 21 total bases, two walks and nine RBIs. The teams combined for 12 home runs in the doubleheader.

Stan (The Man) Musial, *St. Louis' five-homer man.*

MAY

3

1986 17-1 Shot Wins Derby

Ferdinand, a 17–1 longshot with only two wins in his nine previous starts, shocked a Churchill Downs crowd of 123,891 by pulling away to a $2^1/_4$-length victory over Bold Arrangement in the 112th running of the Kentucky Derby.

Ferdinand's upset came under the direction of 54-year-old Bill Shoemaker, the oldest jockey to win a Kentucky Derby. He was handled by 73-year-old Hall of Fame trainer Charlie Whittingham, who had never won the prestigious race.

Shoemaker had to bring his colt from last place to first through heavy traffic and the result was the slowest time in 12 years – $2{:}02^4/_5$. Ferdinand was last around the first turn, moved into the pack on the backstretch and took his first lead with a furlong to go. He pulled away on the homestretch as Bold Arrangement fought a three-colt duel for second.

Snow Chief, the 2–1 favorite who had beaten Ferdinand by seven lengths in his last outing at Santa Anita, tired badly and finished 11th. Badger Land, the 5-2 second choice, finished a distant fifth after a poor start.

The victory was Shoemaker's 8,537th and his fourth in the Kentucky Derby.

1980 Filly Stuns Derby Field

Genuine Risk, making an improbable stretch dash that bolted her ahead of 12 straining colts, became the first filly in 65 years to win the prestigious Kentucky Derby at Louisville's Churchill Downs.

Genuine Risk *crosses the finish line at Churchill Downs, becoming the first filly in 65 years to win the Derby.*

The 106th Run for the Roses was a longshot dream for Genuine Risk owners Bert and Diana Firestone, who had watched their 3-year-old filly finish a disappointing third in the April 18 Wood Memorial—her first test against male horses. Trainer LeRoy Jolley had stated emphatically afterward that Genuine Risk would not run in the Derby against stronger colts.

Jolley was overruled, however, and jockey Jacinto Vasquez supported the decision with a brilliant ride. He brought Genuine Risk from well back on the home stretch and held off fast-closing Rumbo for a one-length victory, covering the $1^1/_4$-mile course in 2:02.

The victory was the first for a filly in a Kentucky Derby since 1915, when Regret performed the trick. No filly had even entered the Derby since 1959, when Silver Spoon finished fifth.

Boston's **Larry Bird** *launches a shot over Philadelphia defender* **Bobby Jones.**

1981 Celtics Catch Shaky 76ers

Larry Bird's 16-foot bank shot with 1:03 remaining capped a Boston comeback that produced a dramatic 91–90 victory over Philadelphia in Game 7 of the National Basketball Association's Eastern Conference championship finals at Boston Garden.

The victory, which advanced the Celtics into the NBA championship series, was Boston's third straight after losing three of the first four games. And none of them came easily. Boston had to wipe away deficits of 10, 17 and 11 points in the games and trailed, 89–82, with 5:23 remaining in the finale.

That's when the Celtics turned up the defensive tempo, put a blanket on Philadelphia's Julius Erving and began chipping away. Bird, who scored 23 points and grabbed 11 rebounds, sank two free throws to tie the game at 89 and then hit his bank shot to give Boston the lead.

Philadelphia guard Maurice Cheeks broke a 76er scoring drought by hitting one of two free throws with 29 seconds left, but the Celtics held on, becoming only the fourth NBA team to recover from a three games to one deficit.

Much credit for the win went to Boston forward Cedric Maxwell, who did an good defensive job on the high-scoring Erving and added 19 points.

A STAR IS BORN

1891: Eppa Rixey, a Hall of Fame lefthander who won 266 games in a 21-year career that ended in 1933.

★ ★ ★

1921: Sugar Ray Robinson, one of boxing's most successful and popular fighters from 1940–65. He recorded a 174–19–6 record and won the middleweight championship five times.

★ ★ ★

1921: Goode Tatum, a long-time Harlem Globetrotter.

★ ★ ★

1964: Ron Hextall, a current National Hockey League goaltender.

★ ★ ★

DEATH OF A LEGEND

1976: Ernie Nevers (football).

★ ★ ★

MILESTONES • IN SPORTS •

1936

Joe DiMaggio made his much-anticipated New York debut a memorable one, collecting a triple, two singles, three runs scored and an RBI in a 14–5 Yankee victory over the St. Louis Browns.

1941

Jockey Eddie Arcaro directed Whirlaway to a runaway Kentucky Derby victory over Staretor.

1970

The rivalry continues: Jack Nicklaus dropped a two-foot birdie putt on the first hole of a sudden-death playoff against Arnold Palmer to win the Byron Nelson Classic at Dallas.

1975

Foolish Pleasure and jockey Jacinto Vasquez outdueled Avatar in the 101st running of the Kentucky Derby.

1989 Soviet Hockey Star Defects

Soviet hockey prodigy **Alexander Mogilny,** *shortly after his defection to the United States.*

Alexander Mogilny, a 20-year-old hockey prodigy from the Soviet Union, arrived in the United States to begin his National Hockey League career with the Buffalo Sabres, one day after stunning the international hockey world with his defection to the West.

Mogilny slipped away from a banquet at Stockholm, Sweden, after helping the Soviet national team take its 21st world championship. He failed to show up for a team flight back to Moscow and instead was escorted by Buffalo General Manager Gerry Meehan on a flight to the U.S.

Meehan, who claimed the Sabres had nothing to do with Mogilny's decision, will benefit because Buffalo owns the NHL rights to the young winger. The defection came five weeks after one of Mogilny's former teammates, Sergei Priakin, became the first top-notch Russian player to receive permission to leave the USSR for the NHL.

Priakin's arrival signaled a new era of East-West cooperation that could suffer a setback with Mogilny's defection. Soviet officials accused the Sabres of piracy and portrayed Mogilny as money hungry and unpopular.

NHL teams, with the permission of Soviet authorities, have been negotiating with several other Russian players. But the Soviets have allowed Western teams to talk only to their aging stars, forbidding any contact with players in the prime of their careers. Mogilny is the first youthful Russian player to emigrate to the West.

A STAR IS BORN

1892: Jack Tobin, an outfielder who compiled a career .309 average in an 11-year Federal League and major league career that ended in 1927.

★ ★ ★

1928: Betsy Rawls, a winner of 55 women's tour events, including four U.S. Opens and two LPGA Championships in the 1950s and '60s.

★ ★ ★

DEATH OF A LEGEND

1986: Paul Richards (baseball).

★ ★ ★

1965 Alcindor Goes West

Lew Alcindor, the most highly recruited player in basketball history, ended several years of speculation and secrecy when he announced his decision to attend the University of California at Los Angeles.

The 7-foot-2 center, who was craved by more than 60 major colleges, selected a basketball-rich school more than 3,000 miles from his New York home. The Bruins have won consecutive NCAA Tournament championships under Coach John Wooden.

The announcement was made at Power Memorial High, the parochial school Alcindor has attended the last four years. The press conference was attended by several hundred reporters, photographers, television crews, radio broadcasters and curious students.

At 12:33 p.m., the 18-year-old Alcindor stepped to a microphone and said, "I have an announcement to make. This fall I'll be attending UCLA in Los Angeles." Nine minutes later, after answering numerous questions from the assembled reporters he said, "Excuse me, gentlemen, I have to go to class," and left the gym.

Alcindor, the son of a New York Transit Authority patrolman, led Power Memorial to 71 consecutive victories and set the city record by scoring an impressive 2,067 points and grabbing 2,002 rebounds.

MILESTONES IN SPORTS

1935

Omaha and jockey Willie Saunders overwhelmed Roman Soldier and the rest of the field in the Kentucky Derby.

1946

Aspiring Triple Crown winner Assault took a big first step with a plodding 2:06 3/5 victory in the Kentucky Derby.

1963

Jockey Braulio Baeza and Chateaugay captured the first leg of horse racing's Triple Crown with a 2:01 4/5 victory in the Kentucky Derby.

1985

The Edmonton Oilers tied a 41-year-old NHL playoff record when they scored 11 goals in an 11–2 romp past Chicago at Northlands Coliseum.

1991

Strike the Gold and jockey Chris Antley struck gold with a 2:03 victory in the Kentucky Derby.

MAY 4

1985 Cordero Rides Winner

Spend A Buck broke out of the gate quickly, ran the fastest first mile in the history of the Kentucky Derby and held on to win the annual Run for the Roses at Louisville's Churchill Downs.

Spend A Buck was never seriously challenged as he claimed a 5 1/4-length victory over Stephan's Odyssey – the biggest winning margin in a Derby since 1946.

His mile time of 1:34 4/5 was the fastest ever and his winning time of 2:00 1/5 was the third-fastest. Only Secretariat (1:59 in 1973) and Northern Dancer (2:00 in 1964) have run faster.

The victory was choreographed by trainer Cam Gambolati and executed by Angel Cordero Jr., who captured his third Kentucky Derby and became the oldest jockey to win the prestigious event. He broke Spend A Buck, a solid second choice behind Chief's Crown, to the front of the 13-horse field and never looked back.

Eternal Prince, a front-runner expected to fight Spend A Buck for the early lead, broke poorly out of the starting gate and never was a factor in the race.

Spend A Buck's victory, his eighth in 12 career starts, earned $406,800 for owners Dennis and Linda Diaz. The unfortunate Chief's Crown had won nine of his last 10 starts.

MAY

5

MILESTONES
IN SPORTS

1925

Detroit star Ty Cobb, not known for his power, muscled up for three home runs and tied a modern major league record with 16 total bases in the Tigers' 14–8 victory over the Browns at St. Louis.

1965

American Randy Matson knocked down a major track and field barrier when he heaved the shot put 70–7 1/4—the first time the 70-foot mark had been eclipsed—during a meet at Texas A&M University.

1978

Career hit No. 3,000: Cincinnati's Pete Rose reached the milestone with a single off Montreal righthander Steve Rogers.

1973 SECRETARIAT WINS DERBY

Secretariat, last out of the gate and still not a serious contender heading into the stretch turn, exploded past his 12 rivals with an incredible closing burst and won a dramatic Kentucky Derby with the fastest time in the event's 99-year history.

Jockey Ron Turcotte guided the Meadow Stable colt across the finish line in 1:59 2/5, bettering the 1964 record of 2:00 set by Northern Dancer. He beat Sham by 2 1/2 lengths and the remainder of the field by 10 1/2. The world record for 1 1/4 miles is 1:58 1/5.

The record crowd of 134,476 at Churchill Downs had made Secretariat the favorite and he lived up to that faith – but not without some pause. He fell behind early, ran unimpressively for a mile and then burst home with a closing kick never before seen in this prestigious race.

The victory was the 10th in 13 career starts for the Virginia-bred colt and it atoned for his third-place finish in the recent Wood Memorial. The son of Bold Ruler is the second consecutive Meadow Stable winner, following in the hoofsteps of 1972 winner Riva Ridge.

Unlike many of the spectators, Turcottle said he was never worried about Secretariat's early predicament. "My horse was perfectly relaxed," he said. "I wasn't worried coming out of the gate last. He went smoothly all the way, and when I asked him to go, why he just took off."

1904 YOUNG THROWS PERFECT GAME

Boston's 37-year-old Cy Young, already the winningest pitcher in baseball history, showed why in a game against Philadelphia when he retired all 27 Athletics he faced and recorded the first perfect game of the century.

Young, an eight-time 20-game winner and five-time winner of 30 or more, was in total command as he baffled and overpowered the Athletics en route to a 3–0 victory at Boston. No Philadelphia player came close to reaching base and eight went down on strikes. Only six balls were hit out of the infield.

The Red Sox managed 10 hits but could not do serious damage to starter Rube Waddell. They pushed across the only run Young needed in the sixth and added two more in the seventh.

Young's perfect game was only the third in major league history and the first from the 60-foot, 6-inch pitching distance. The two previous perfectos were recorded in the 1880s, when pitchers worked 45 feet from the plate.

Mr. Perfect, **Cy Young,.**

1979 DERBY VICTORY SPECTACULAR

Jockey **Ron Franklin** *and* **Spectacular Bid** *speed toward the finish line and a victory in the Kentucky Derby.*

Spectacular Bid, held back in the pack for three-quarters of a mile, turned on the burners and caught General Assembly on the upper stretch before pulling away to a 2 3/4-length victory in the Kentucky Derby at Churchill Downs.

With 19-year-old Ron Franklin calling the signals, Spectacular Bid was content to stay back and reserve strength in a slow and plodding Run for the Roses. When he finally made his challenge, General Assembly wilted under a strong stretch run.

The Kentucky-bred colt, a product of Hawksworth Farm, finished at 2:02 2/5 in winning his 11th consecutive stakes race. The victory was his 13th in 15 career starts and garnered a first prize of $228,650 for owners Teresa, Harry and Tom Meyerhoff.

The victory puts Spectacular Bid in the spotlight as he attempts to become the third Triple Crown winner in as many years, following Seattle Slew and Affirmed.

A STAR IS BORN

1884: Chief Bender, a Hall of Fame righthander who earned 208 victories and helped the Philadelphia Athletics win five A.L. pennants and three World Series between 1905 and 1914.

★ ★ ★

1905: Red Ruffing, a Hall of Fame righthander who earned 273 victories and helped the New York Yankees win seven American League pennants and six World Series between 1932 and 1942.

★ ★ ★

1919: Tony Canadeo, a football Hall of Fame halfback and defender who rushed for 4,197 yards in an 11-year career (1941–52) with the Green Bay Packers.

★ ★ ★

DEATH OF A LEGEND

1969: Ed Cicotte (baseball).

★ ★ ★

1975: Avery Brundage (Olympics).

★ ★ ★

1954 BANNISTER MAKES HISTORY WITH SUB-4-MINUTE MILE

MAY 6

England's **Roger Bannister,** *the mile barrier breaker.*

England's Roger Bannister tore down one of the most sacred barriers in sports when he ran the mile in a world-record 3:59.4 – the first sub-4-minute mile in track and field history.

Bannister, battling a stiff cross wind during a dual meet at Oxford University, swept through the first quarter of his historic race in 57.5 seconds, the second in 60.7, the third in 62.3 and the final in an explosive 58.9. Meet officials suggested Bannister might have run a 3:58 without the 15-mile per hour wind that made the record achievement even more remarkable.

The 25-year-old Bannister, running for the British Amateur Athletic Association in a meet against Oxford, followed the stiff pace set by teammates Chris Brasher and Chris Chataway. Brasher led through the first two laps and Chataway took over on the third. Chataway still led with 300 yards to go.

But Bannister, whose previous best effort was 4:02, sped down the stretch and broke the record of 4:01.4 set by Sweden's Gunder Haegg in 1945. His unofficial 1,500-meter time of 3:43 would have tied the world mark.

1972 RIVA RIDGE ROMPS

Ron Turcotte broke Riva Ridge into the early lead and the Meadow Stable colt recorded an impressive wire-to-wire victory over 15 rivals in the 98th running of the Kentucky Derby at Louisville's Churchill Downs.

Riva Ridge finished 3¼ lengths ahead of No Le Hace, but his biggest challenge came from Carlos Marquez aboard Hold Your Peace.

Marquez positioned Hold Your Peace just behind the fast-starting Riva Ridge out of the gate and they waged a dramatic two-horse battle until No Le Hace took second with an impressive stretch burst.

Riva Ridge finished the 1¼-mile test in a respectable 2:01⅘, earning $140,300 for Mrs. John Tweedy.

The victory was his third in four starts this year and 10th in 13 overall. Riva Ridge, trained by Lucien Laurin, was the betting favorite of the record Kentucky Derby crowd of 130,564. He didn't disappoint.

The wire-to-wire performance was the first in a Kentucky Derby since 1966, when Kauai King turned the trick and posted an impressive winning time of 2:02.

Riva Ridge, the son of First Landing, was not far off the all-time Kentucky Derby record time of 2:00, which had been set by the legendary Northern Dancer eight years earlier.

MILESTONES IN SPORTS

1925

New York shortstop Everett Scott, fighting a slump for the 5–11 Yankees, was surprisingly benched by Manager Miller Huggins after playing in a major league-record 1,307 consecutive games.

1978

Steve Cauthen rode Affirmed to a 2:01⅕ clocking and a 1½-length victory over Alydar in an intense Kentucky Derby duel at Churchill Downs.

1982

Righthander Gaylord Perry became the 15th member of baseball's 300-victory club when he pitched the Mariners to a 7–3 decision over New York at Seattle's Kingdome.

1953 BOBO'S NO-NO THROTTLES A'S

St. Louis Browns righthander Bobo Holloman became the first modern-era pitcher to throw a no-hitter in his first major league start when he handcuffed the Philadelphia Athletics, 6–0, before a sparse crowd of 2,473 at Sportsman's Park.

The 27-year-old Holloman, who also drove in three of the St. Louis runs with a pair of singles, struck out three batters and allowed five walks. He sailed through eight innings, walking two, before putting his masterpiece in danger with a temporary control loss in the ninth.

The nerve-wracking final inning opened with a pair of walks. But Holloman made a big pitch to Dave Philley and induced the outfielder to ground into a double play. One out away from a history-making achievement, Holloman walked Loren Babe before getting Eddie Robinson on a fly ball to right.

The no-hitter was the first for a Browns pitcher in 36 years and only the second in baseball history by a pitcher making his first big-league start. Charley Jones performed the feat for Cincinnati in 1892.

The Browns, who managed 13 hits, scored single runs in the second, third, fifth and sixth innings before securing victory with a two-run seventh.

A STAR IS BORN

1907: Weeb Ewbank, the football Hall of Fame coach who choreographed the biggest Super Bowl upset in history – the New York Jets' 1969 victory over Baltimore. He is the only man to coach champions in both the AFL and NFL.

★ ★ ★

1931: Willie Mays, a Hall of Fame center fielder who batted .302 and hit 660 career home runs, third highest on the all-time list . His outstanding 22-year career ended in 1973 with the New York Mets.

★ ★ ★

1953: Larry Andersen, a current major league pitcher.

★ ★ ★

1968: Clarence Jones, a current National Football League offensive tackle.

DEATH OF A LEGEND

1989: Earl (Red) Blaik (football).

MAY

7

1955 SHOEMAKER'S SWAPS WINS DERBY DUEL

Swaps, a 14-5 second choice with fast-rising jockey Bill Shoemaker in saddle, held off favored Nashua in an exciting stretch run and captured the 81st Kentucky Derby by 1 1/2 lengths at Louisville's Churchill Downs.

Shoemaker's first Derby was dramatic. He led Swaps to the front of the 10-horse pack right out of the gate and never relinquished the lead over the 1 1/4-mile test. But his resolve was tested. Eddie Arcaro, looking for his sixth Derby success, brought Nashua to within a half length on the final turn and the 3-year-olds barreled down the stretch in a breathtaking duel.

Just when it appeared Nashua would be able to catch his rival, however, Shoemaker gave Swaps the whip and he began pulling away. He had added a length to his lead when he hit the wire at a fast 2:01 4/5. The Kentucky Derby victory was only the second in history and first since 1922 for a California-foaled colt. Rex C. Ellsworth's Swaps entered the race undefeated in three 1955 races and the Belair Stud's Nashua was unbeaten in six races dating back to September.

A STAR IS BORN

1933: Johnny Unitas, a football Hall of Fame quarterback who led the Baltimore Colts to three NFL championships before retiring n 1973 as holder of virtually every league passing record.

★ ★ ★

1964: Leslie O'Neal, a current National Football League linebacker.

1968 IMAGE LOSES RACE AFTER WIN

Dancer's Image, the comeback colt that pulled off a startling victory in the May 4 Kentucky Derby, was disqualified by race officials after tests revealed he had run the prestigious race with an illegal drug in his system.

The disqualification, the first in 94 Kentucky Derby races at Louisville's Churchill Downs, provided a shocking conclusion to one of the most thrilling Run for the Roses in horse-racing history.

Calumet Farm's Forward Pass, the Derby favorite that had finished 1 1/2 lengths behind Dancer's Image, was declared the winner.

The presence of a pain-killing drug in a Dancer's Image urine sample was discovered in a routine post-race chemical test by the Kentucky State Racing Commission.

It seemed to mystify Dancer's Image owner Peter Fuller and his trainer Lou Cavalaris, who were forced to forfeit the $122,600 first prize.

With jockey Bobby Ussery swinging the whip, Dancer's Image had won the hearts of racing fans when he streaked along the rail from his last-place position in the 14-horse field to a stunning, if short-lived, victory.

MILESTONES IN SPORTS

1940

The Brooklyn Dodgers became the N.L.'s first air travelers when they flew from St. Louis to Chicago.

1957

The blooming career of Indians pitcher Herb Score was put on hold when the lefty was hit in the right eye by a line drive off the bat of New York Yankee Gil McDougald in a game at Cleveland's Municipal Stadium.

1959

Roy Campanella Night: 93,103 roaring fans at the Los Angeles Coliseum paid an emotional tribute to the wheelchair-bound former Brooklyn catcher before a Dodger-New York Yankee exhibition game.

1977

Jockey Jean Cruguet drove Seattle Slew to a 1 3/4-length victory over Run Dusty Run in the annual Run for the Roses at Louisville's Churchill Downs.

1992

Hall of Fame jockey Angel Cordero Jr., plagued by injuries in recent years, retired with 7,076 career victories, third on the all-time list.

1988 FILLY SHOWS TRUE COLORS

Winning Colors, a woman competing in what traditionally had been a man's race, led from start to finish and held off a stiff challenge by Forty Niner in becoming the third filly to win a Kentucky Derby at Churchill Downs.

Winning Colors, with jockey Gary Stevens whipping frantically, was wilting down the stretch as Forty Niner made up four lengths in the final furlong of the 1 1/4-mile race. But Forty Niner's mad dash came up a neck short in the closest Derby finish in 19 years.

It was a sentimental victory for the colt-sized filly, who went off as a second choice and followed in the hoofprints of previous female winners Regret (1915) and Genuine Risk (1980). The victory was shared by owner Eugene Klein and trainer D. Wayne Lukas, who won a Derby for the first time in 12 tries.

Winning Colors jumped into a quick lead and coasted until the homestretch, when Pat Day got Forty Niner to make his frantic run. Winning Colors' time was 2:02 1/5.

Jockey **Gary Stevens** *guides filly* **Winning Colors** *to the Churchill Downs finish line.*

MILESTONES
IN SPORTS

1907

Heavyweight champion Tommy Burns earned a referee's decision after battling Jack O'Brien for 20 rounds in a bout at Los Angeles.

1969

The Oakland Oaks posted a 135–131 overtime victory over Indiana and claimed the ABA's second championship in a Game 5 thriller at Oakland.

1971

Carlos Monzon scored a third-round technical knockout over Nino Benvenuti and retained his world middleweight title in a bout at Monte Carlo.

1973

St. Louis righthander Bob Gibson set a major league record when he started his 242nd straight game – a 9-7 loss to San Francisco.

1970

KNICKS WIN FIRST TITLE

Walt Frazier provided the firepower and Willis Reed the inspiration as the New York Knicks earned the first National Basketball Association championship in their 24-year history with a 113–99 Game 7 victory over the Los Angeles Lakers at Madison Square Garden.

Frazier scored a game-high 36 points, handed out 19 assists and played his usual chest-to-chest defense. Reed, who missed Game 6 in Los Angeles with a leg injury, played in pain and his presence, while not obvious in the box score, was critical to the Knicks' victory.

Thanks to several pain-killing injections, Reed was able to limp out for the center jump and he somehow made two quick baskets that sparked the Knicks to a 38–24 first-quarter lead. All Reed was really able to do was occupy Lakers center Wilt Chamberlain defensively, but that was enough.

The Knicks extended their lead to 51–31 and the margin remained 20 points or higher until the final minutes. Barnett contributed 21 points for New York while Dave DeBusschere scored 18 and grabbed 17 rebounds.

New York Knicks big man **Willis Reed.**

MAY

8

A STAR IS BORN

1893: Edd Roush, a Hall of Fame outfielder who batted .325 and won two N.L. batting championships over a 16-year career that ended in 1931.

★ ★ ★

1930: Doug Atkins, a football Hall of Fame defensive end and fierce pass rusher who retired in 1969 after 17 seasons in the NFL.

★ ★ ★

1932: Sonny Liston, the former world heavyweight champion (1962–64) who lost his title to a young challenger named Cassius Clay. He recorded a 50–4 record with 39 knockouts.

★ ★ ★

DEATH OF A LEGEND

1951: Leo Diegel (golf).

★ ★ ★

Oakland's **Catfish Hunter** *was perfectly marvelous in the game against Minnesota.*

1968

CATFISH FIRES PERFECT GAME

Oakland's Catfish Hunter became the first American League pitcher in 46 years to throw a regular-season perfect game when he retired all 27 Minnesota Twins he faced in a 4–0 Athletics victory at the Oakland Coliseum.

Hunter, a 22-year-old righthander who was 13–17 last year when the A's played their final season in Kansas City, struck out 11 and went to full counts on six batters. He flirted with danger in the second inning when he went to 3–0 on two-time A.L. batting champion Tony Oliva and came back to strike him out.

The Twins never came close to a hit. They hit only five balls out of the infield and went quietly in the ninth – pinch-hitter Rich Reese striking out on a 3–2 pitch to end the game.

Hunter, who joined the Athletics in 1965 at age 19, is the first pitcher to throw a perfect game since Los Angeles lefthander Sandy Koufax performed the feat in 1965. The last American Leaguer to do it was Yankee Don Larsen, who performed his masterpeice in the 1956 World Series against Brooklyn. The last to do it in the regular season was Chicago's Charlie Robertson in 1922.

1937

WAR ADMIRAL LIVES UP TO REPUTATION

War Admiral, living up to the reputation handed down by his famous sire, broke out of the gate with a vengeance and defeated Pompoon by two lengths in the 63rd running of the Kentucky Derby at Louisville's Churchill Downs.

War Admiral, the son of Man o'War, erased any doubts about his ability to run the 1 1/4-mile distance and he did it with apparent ease. He cruised ahead of the 20-horse field and, when challenged by a laboring Pompoon at the top of the stretch, pulled away with one crack of the whip from Charley Kurtsinger.

Kurtsinger, winning the prestigious event for a second time, directed War Admiral to a 2:03 1/5 time, the second fastest in Derby history. It was the Kentucky-bred colt's third victory in as many starts this year.

The victory was sweet for owner Samuel D. Riddle, who missed the race because of illness. Trainer George Conway accepted the trophy and the winner's check for $52,000.

MAY

9

MILESTONES
IN SPORTS

1930

Gallant Fox, a 3-year-old colt with Triple Crown aspirations, captured the Preakness Stakes by three-quarters of a length over Crack Brigade under the direction of Jockey Earl Sande.

1942

Alsab, with Basil James in saddle, won the Preakness Stakes by a length over dead-heat second-place finishers Requested and Sun Again.

1970

Alcorn A&M freshman Willie McGee, competing in a Southwestern Athletic Conference meet, tied the 100-yard dash world record of 9.1 seconds for the second consecutive night.

1976

South African Sally Little holed out on a 75-foot blast from a bunker in front of the 18th green, earning a dramatic one-stroke victory over Jan Stephenson in the Women's International tournament at Hilton Head Island, S.C.

1982

World welterweight champion Sugar Ray Leonard underwent two hours of surgery at Johns Hopkins Hospital in Baltimore to repair a partially detached retina in his left eye.

1985

Denis Savard scored a goal and assisted on two others as the Chicago Blackhawks ended Edmonton's 12-game playoff winning streak with a 5–2 victory in Game 3 of a Campbell Conference series.

1961 Gentile Slamfest Overpowers Twins

Free-swinging Baltimore first baseman Jim Gentile, becoming the fourth major leaguer to hit two grand slams in the same game, took his feat a step further by doing it in consecutive innings of a 13–5 Orioles victory over the Minnesota Twins.

After Twins starter Pedro Ramos had dug himself a first-inning hole by walking Whitey Herzog, surrendering a double to Jackie Brandt and walking Brooks Robinson, Gentile stepped to the plate and drove a pitch 425 feet over the center-field fence at Bloomington's Municipal Stadium. The fun was only just beginning.

In the second inning, walks to Herzog and Robinson sandwiched around an error on a ball hit by Brandt again set the stage for Gentile. This time he stroked a Paul Giel offering 370 feet over the right-field fence, capping a five-run inning and giving the Orioles a comfortable 9–0 lead.

The 6-foot-4 Gentile, a powerful left-handed hitter, also drove in a run with a sacrifice fly. He finished his big afternoon as the first player to hit grand slams in consecutive times at bat in the same game and the first to drive in eight runs in consecutive innings. His nine RBIs were three short of the major league record.

A STAR IS BORN

1928: Pancho Gonzales, an outstanding tennis player who won consecutive U.S. singles championships at Forest Hills in 1948 and '49.

★ ★ ★

1939: Ralph Boston, a successful long jumper who won a gold medal in the 1960 Olympic Games and a silver and bronze in the next two.

★ ★ ★

1948: Calvin Murphy, an NBA guard who scored 17,949 points over a 13-year career that ended in 1983.

★ ★ ★

1960: Tony Gwynn, a current major league outfielder.

★ ★ ★

1965: Steve Yzerman, a current National Hockey League center.

1975 McTear Equals Record

Houston McTear, a high school junior competing in the Florida Class-AA state championship meet, streaked to a 9.0-second clocking in the 100-yard dash, tying Ivory Crockett's world record.

The 18-year-old McTear was timed at 9.0 by all three judges in a preliminary heat at Winter Park, Fla. The wind gauge reading was 2 miles per hour, well within the allowable limit. The Baker High School star came back to win the final with a time of 9.3.

McTear's dash to glory tied the world record Crockett set last year in Knoxville, Tenn. It also broke the national high school record of 9.2 that McTear had set a week earlier and that Winter Park High's Mike Roberson had tied.

McTear already has competed against world-class sprinters.

1984 Long Battle Ends

Chicago's Harold Baines brought a merciful end to the first 8-hour game in major league history when he belted a Chuck Porter pitch over the Comiskey Park fence with one out in the bottom of the 25th inning, giving the White Sox a 7–6 victory over Milwaukee.

The home run brought the two-day marathon to an end after a record 8 hours, 6 minutes—43 minutes longer than the previous record-setter. The 25 innings tied the big-league record for a game played to a decision.

The contest had started the night before but was suspended after 17 innings with the score tied 3–3 because of a curfew. It was continued prior to the day's scheduled game.

Milwaukee appeared ready to claim victory in the 21st inning when Ben Oglivie blasted a three-run homer, but the White Sox retied the game in the bottom of the inning on a run-scoring single by Carlton Fisk and a two-run single by Tom Paciorek. The White Sox had pulled off a similar rally after trailing, 3–1, entering the ninth.

The victory went to Tom Seaver, who pitched one inning in his first relief appearance since 1976. Seaver also worked 8 1/3 innings in the 2-hour, 9-minute nightcap.

After more than 8 hours, Chicago's **Harold Baines** *ended a marathon against Milwaukee.*

MAY

10

MILESTONES
• IN SPORTS •

1970 BRUINS WIN STANLEY CUP

Boston defenseman Bobby Orr deflected an overtime pass from teammate Derek Sanderson past St. Louis goaltender Glenn Hall, giving the Bruins a 4-3 victory over the Blues and their first Stanley Cup championship in 29 years.

Orr's acrobatic goal, which he fired into the net as he was being tripped, came 40 seconds into the extra session and gave the Bruins a four-game sweep of the Blues. The Bruins' series victory was the Eastern Division's third straight, without a loss, since expansion and the loss was St. Louis' third straight, without a victory, in the same span.

The Blues did make the Bruins work in Game 4. Boston's Rick Smith and St. Louis' Red Berenson traded first-period goals, the Blues' Gary Sabourin and the Bruins' Phil Esposito scored in the second and Boston's John Bucyk scored at 13:28 of the third after Larry Keenan had given the Blues a 3–2 edge. That set the stage for Orr, who sent the 14,835 fans at Boston Garden into hysteria.

Boston Bruins defenseman **Bobby Orr** *did in the Blues with a Game 4 overtime goal.*

1974 NETS WIN ABA

Julius Erving and Larry Kenon, two preseason arrivals who helped turn New York from also-ran to title contender, combined for 43 points and the Nets captured their first American Basketball Association championship with a 111–100 victory over the Utah Stars at the Nassau Coliseum.

A sellout crowd cheered the Nets to their Game 5 triumph. It came hard as the Nets blew a 10-point third-quarter lead and trailed, 95–94, in the fourth before rallying.

The rally was sparked by Kenon, who scored 10 fourth-quarter points, and John Williamson, who scored 8. A 16–4 Nets spurt decided the issue.

The Nets claimed the championship with a team that averaged 23 years and less than three professional seasons per man. But the deciding factor was Erving, the acrobatic former Virginia forward who finished the game with 20 points and 16 rebounds.

New York Nets and ABA star **Julius Erving** *(32).*

A STAR IS BORN

1868: Ed Barrow, a Hall of Fame executive who joined the New York Yankees in 1920 and built the machine that would win 14 pennants and 10 World Series.

★ ★ ★

1957: Phil Mahre, a winner of three World Cup skiing championships (1981–83).

★ ★ ★

DEATH OF A LEGEND

1955: Tommy Burns (boxing).

1973 KNICKS WHIP LAKERS

Willis Reed scored 18 points, grabbed 12 rebounds and dished out seven assists, lifting the New York Knicks to a 102–93 victory over Los Angeles and their second National Basketball Association championship in 27 seasons.

The triumph at the Los Angeles Forum was New York's fourth straight after losing Game 1 of the title series. That matched the pattern of the previous year when the Lakers defeated the Knicks in five after losing the opener.

Reed, Earl Monroe (23 points) and Bill Bradley (20) provided the offensive spark, but it was the Knicks' typical chest-to-chest defense that ultimately wore down the Lakers. Most of the Laker points were posted by three players—Gail Goodrich with 28, Wilt Chamberlain, 23, and Jim McMillian, 19.

After trailing by two points at the half, New York spurted to a 71–59 third-quarter lead and held off two Los Angeles rallies. The Lakers pulled within four in the final minute before the Knicks could close them down.

1969

Pittsburgh, Cleveland and Baltimore agreed to move from the National Football Conference to the American Football Conference when the AFL-NFL merger becomes official in 1970.

1970

Well-traveled knuckleballer Hoyt Wilhelm, working for Atlanta in a 6–5 loss to St. Louis at Fulton County Stadium, became the first major league pitcher to appear in 1,000 games.

1973

The Montreal Canadiens earned their fourth Stanley Cup championship in six years with a 6-4 Game 6 victory at Chicago.

1975

Brian Oldfield unleashed three world record-breaking throws during shot put competition in an International Track Association meet at El Paso, Tex. The final throw of 75 feet was three feet farther than the old mark.

MAY

11

A STAR IS BORN

1903: Charlie Gehringer, Detroit's Hall of Fame second baseman who hit .320 and won an A.L. batting championship in a 19-year career that ended in 1942.

★ ★ ★

1934: Jack Twyman, a basketball Hall of Fame forward who scored 15,840 points and grabbed 5,421 rebounds in an 11-year NBA career that ended in 1966.

★ ★ ★

1939: Milt Pappas, a 209-game winner in a 17-year major league career that ended in 1973.

★ ★ ★

1950: Dane Iorg, a former major league outfielder and designated hitter.

★ ★ ★

1968

TOE LEAVES WITH TITLE

The Montreal Canadiens won their eighth Stanley Cup championship in 13 years, but they lost the most successful coach in the 51-year history of the National Hockey League. Moments after watching his team wrap up a 3–2 victory and a four-game sweep of the expansion St. Louis Blues, Toe Blake made an appearance on Canadian television to announce his retirement.

The 55-year-old Blake, whose run of success included a record five consecutive titles from 1956–60, said he no longer could stand the pressure. And the latest title, against a team stocked through an expansion draft a year earlier, contained plenty, despite its short duration. All four games were decided by a single goal and two went into overtime.

The finale went down to the wire, with third-period goals by Henri Richard and J.C. Tremblay wiping out a 2–1 St. Louis lead. Tremblay's 30-foot winner rattled off the post and settled behind 37-year-old Blues goalie Glenn Hall.

Montreal's **Toe Blake,** *the most successful coach in the history of the NHL..*

The Canadiens took a first-period lead on a goal by Dick Duff, but scores by Craig Cameron and Gary Sabourin in a 57-second span of the second period put the Blues on top – a lead they couldn't hold in the final 20 minutes.

MILESTONES IN SPORTS

1900

Heavyweight champion James Jeffries kept his record unblemished with a 23rd-round knockout of Gentleman Jim Corbett in a bout at Coney Island, N.Y.

1970

Montreal's Dan McGinn held the New York Mets to three singles while pitching a 3-0 shutout that ended Tom Seaver's two-season 16-game winning streak.

1970

The new Buffalo, Cleveland and Portland teams picked 33 players apiece in the NBA expansion draft.

1984

Dave Bergman drove in three runs and Milt Wilcox pitched a six-hitter as Detroit defeated California, 8–2, and lifted its record to 26–4—the best start in major league history.

1974

CROCKETT IS FASTEST HUMAN

Ivory Crockett , *the world's fastest human, hits the finish line.*

Ivory Crockett, a marketing representive for an Illinois computer firm, claimed the title "world's fastest human" when he became the first runner to cover 100 yards in 9 seconds during competition in the Tom Black Classic at the University of Tennessee.

Crockett, running for an Amateur Athletic Union club out of Philadelphia, shaved a tenth of a second off the world record set in 1963 by fellow American Bob Hayes and matched five times. He shaved two-tenths of a second off his previous best time of 9.2 seconds.

The 150-pounder ran on a wet track on a calm, windless day. The event was sanctioned by the National Collegiate Athletic Association and record confirmation was considered a formality.

1984

LEONARD WINS, RETIRES AGAIN

Popular Sugar Ray Leonard ended his 27-month retirement with a ninth-round technical knockout of Philadelphian Kevin Howard and then shocked the boxing world by retiring again.

Leonard, saying the old feeling just wasn't there, "officially retired for good" moments after the referee had stopped his difficult victory over Howard at 2:28 of the ninth round in a bout at Worcester, Mass. Leonard was ahead on all of the judges' cards, but a cut below his right eye and the reality of his first career knockdown convinced him to call it quits.

The knockdown came in the fourth round when the 27-year-old former welterweight champion got a little careless and Howard connected with a right to the chin. Leonard was on his feet by the count of three, but the psychological damage was done.

"I reached that decision when I was knocked down," Leonard said. "It just wasn't there."

Leonard had retired in November 1982 after undergoing an operation for a partially-detached retina, but the eye did not appear to be a problem during the fight. Leonard, who danced around the ring and delivered quick blows in his usual flashy style, retired with a professional record of 33–1.

1974 Celtics Get Back on Top

Boston center Dave Cowens scored 28 points and grabbed 14 rebounds while neutralizing Milwaukee counterpart Kareem Abdul-Jabbar as the Celtics defeated the Bucks, 102–87, and returned to the top of the National Basketball Association after a five-year absence.

The victory, Boston's third at Milwaukee Arena in a tough seven-game series, was the result of a hustling Celtic defense that threw a blanket over the 7-foot-2 Abdul-Jabbar in the second and third quarters. After Abdul-Jabbar notched 14 first-quarter points, he did not score another for 18 minutes as Boston took control.

Leading by two points after the first quarter, Boston stretched its advantage to 53–40 by halftime and led by 15 midway through the third quarter. Abdul-Jabbar (26 points) and Mickey Davis (15) led a Milwaukee comeback that cut the deficit to 71–68, but Cowens, John Havlicek and Jo Jo White sparked a counter-surge that put the game away.

Boston's first championship since 1969 also was its 12th in 18 years, thanks to a Bill Russell-led spurt from 1959–66 that produced eight in a row.

Milestones in Sports

1926

Washington great Walter Johnson joined Cy Young as baseball's only 400-game winners when he defeated the St. Louis Browns, 7–4.

1966

The St. Louis Cardinals christened new Busch Stadium with a 4–3 victory over the Atlanta Braves.

1973

Art Pollard, a 46-year-old veteran of 18 auto racing seasons, died in a morning accident while warming up his Eagle-Offenhauser for the Indianapolis 500.

1979

With six runners breaking 4 minutes, Villanova star Don Paige captured the Dream Mile at Philadelphia with a 3:56.3 clocking.

1985

Kathy Whitworth extended her professional golf-record victory total to 88 with a final-round 72 and a one-stroke victory over Amy Alcott in the United Virginia Bank Golf Classic.

1970 Banks Blasts 500th Homer

The familiar home run trot of Mr. Cub, Chicago's **Ernie Banks.**

Ernie Banks, Chicago's ever-popular Mr. Cub, lined a pitch from Atlanta pitcher Pat Jarvis into the left-field bleachers at Wrigley Field, joining eight other major leaguers in baseball's exclusive 500-home run club.

Banks' milestone blast came on a 1–1 second-inning pitch in a game eventually won by Chicago, 4–3, in 11 innings. It hit in a sparsely-populated bleacher section and bounced back onto the field, where it was retrieved and thrown to the Chicago dugout. The 39-year-old shortstop saluted the 5,264 fans with a tip of his cap while holding the ball high above his head.

Despite Banks' homer, the Cubs trailed, 3–2, in the ninth when Billy Williams tied the game with his 12th home run of the year. They won in the 11th when Ron Santo beat out an infield single with the bases loaded.

Braves outfielder Rico Carty extended his hitting streak to 30 games in a losing cause.

May 12

A Star Is Born

1925: Yogi Berra, a Hall of Fame catcher, three-time A.L. MVP and a fixture on New York Yankee teams that won 10 World Series from 1946–65.

★ ★ ★

1930: Pat McCormick, an American diver who won women's platform and springboard gold medals in both the 1952 and '56 Olympic Games.

★ ★ ★

1935: John Bucyk, a hockey Hall of Fame left winger who scored 556 career goals and helped the Boston Bruins win two Stanley Cup titles in the 1970s.

★ ★ ★

1956: Bernie Federko, a smooth-passing center who scored 1,130 points over a 14-year NHL career.

★ ★ ★

1957: Lou Whitaker, a current major league second baseman.

Death of a Legend

1971: Heinie Manush (baseball).

★ ★ ★

1992: Joe Burke (baseball).

★ ★ ★

1973 Pacers Earn 3rd ABA Title

George McGinnis scored 27 points and Indiana's stingy defense took care of the rest as the Pacers recorded an 88–81 victory over Kentucky and claimed their third American Basketball Association championship in four years.

The Pacers' Game 7 victory on the Colonels' home court, Louisville's Freedom Hall, was their third of the series. McGinnis' offensive heroics were vital to Indiana's cause, but the game really was decided by an outstanding third-quarter defensive effort.

The Colonels managed only 11 points in the period as Kentucky Coach Joe Mullaney desperately moved players in and out of his lineup in an attempt to change the momentum. Nothing worked.

A Walt Simon jumper and an Artis Gilmore basket at the beginning of the fourth quarter cut Indiana's lead to 66–56, but Gus Johnson extended Indiana's advantage and the Pacers never were threatened again. Three 3-point field goals by Rick Mount made the final score respectable.

Kentucky shot a cold 38 percent from the floor.

MAY 13

A STAR IS BORN

1914: Joe Louis, the former heavyweight champion who held his title for a record 11 years, 9 months before retiring in 1949. He recorded a career mark of 63–3.

★ ★ ★

1950: Bobby Valentine, a former major league infielder who went on to manage the Texas Rangers for eight seasons.

★ ★ ★

1961: Dennis Rodman, a current National Basketball Association forward.

★ ★ ★

1965: Jose Rijo, a current major league pitcher.

★ ★ ★

1973 RIGGS PULLS BIG HUSTLE

Bobby Riggs, a 55-year-old hustler who once ranked among the great players in the world, delivered a serious blow to women's tennis when he recorded a straight-sets victory over Margaret Court in a $10,000 battle-of-the-sexes match.

Riggs, who arranged the match with Court after Billie Jean King refused his challenge, had hyped it with unending putdowns of women's tennis. Before the nationally-televised event at Ramona, Calif., he played mind games with Court by presenting her with a Mother's Day bouquet of roses.

The match pitted Court's power game against Riggs' "soft attack." Every serve was slow, every shot was calculated and every move was well choreographed.

Riggs played with poise and confidence. Court, a winner in 89 of her last 92 women's matches, quickly lost rhythm and hope.

Riggs, who won both the Wimbledon and U.S. singles championships in 1939, four years before Court was born in Australia, served successive aces at 30-all for a 4–1 second-set lead. Court faulted on 19 of 37 first serves and made 10 return errors.

Riggs netted $12,500 for what he termed the greatest hustle of all time.

1958 MUSIAL MAKES 3,000

St. Louis star Stan (The Man) Musial, making an unexpected pinch-hitting appearance in a game at Chicago's Wrigley Field, lined a double down the left-field line off Cubs reliever Moe Drabowsky and entered the record books as baseball's eighth 3,000-hit man.

Musial, who was sitting out the game so he could get the historic hit in front of St. Louis fans in an upcoming homestand, was summoned by Manager Fred Hutchinson to bat for pitcher Sam Jones in the sixth inning with the Cardinals trailing, 3–1. Musial's opposite-field double drove in Gene Green and sparked a four-run rally that produced a 5–3 St. Louis victory.

The 37-year-old Musial is a seven-time N.L. batting champion and three-time MVP.

1976 NETS PULL OFF AMAZING RALLY

The New York Nets made a logic-defying comeback from a 22-point deficit in the final 17 minutes to record a 112–106 victory over the Denver Nuggets and claim the last American Basketball Association championship before its merger with the National Basketball Association.

The Nuggets had built its seemingly safe cushion behind a tight defense and the shooting of David Thompson, who scored a game-high 42 points. With five minutes remaining in the third quarter, the Nuggets led, 80–58, and 15,934 fans at the Nassau Coliseum were resigned to the idea the series would return to Denver for Game 7.

But that's when Coach Kevin Loughery unleashed his clawing, full-court defense. Instead of breaking the press for easy baskets, the Nuggets unraveled, turning the ball over and missing shots. By the end of the quarter, the lead was 92–78. The Nets outscored the Nuggets, 34–14, in the final period.

Julius Erving scored 31 points and made five fourth-quarter steals and John Williamson scored 24 of his 28 points in the second half to key the amazing comeback.

Fiery New York Nets Coach **Kevin Loughery.**

MILESTONES IN SPORTS

1942

Boston pitcher Jim Tobin, almost as good with a bat as he is with his strong right arm, became the first major league pitcher to hit three home runs in a game while pitching the Braves to 6–5 victory over Chicago at Braves Field.

1952

Nine innings, no hits, 27 strikeouts: Ron Necciai's formula for success while pitching for Bristol in a Class-D Appalachian League game against Welch. A third strike eluded the catcher, thus allowing one runner to reach first base, nullifying an otherwise perfect-perfect game.

1967

Mario Andretti, looking for his first victory in one of the world's most prestigious races, zipped through qualifying for the Indianapolis 500 with an average speed of 168.982 mph in a Ford-powered Hawk – the fastest laps ever recorded over the $2^1/_2$-mile Indianapolis Motor Speedway track.

1973

Bruce Crampton, needing a par 4 to win or a bogey 5 to tie, made a double-bogey 6 on the 18th hole of the Colonial National Invitation tournament at Fort Worth, Tex., and finished a stroke behind Tom Weiskopf.

1979

Tom Watson, reaffirming his growing reputation as one of the best golfers in the world, birdied the first hole of a sudden-death playoff against Bill Rogers and became the first three-time winner of the Byron Nelson Golf Classic at Dallas.

Boston's **Cedric Maxwell.**

1981 BIRD BOMBS ROCKETS

Larry Bird broke out of a shooting slump with 27 points, seven coming in a 2½-minute stretch when Boston broke open the game, as the Celtics defeated the Houston Rockets, 102–91, and earned their 14th National Basketball Association championship.

Bird, who had scored 28 total points in his previous three outings, took over Game 6 at the Summit after the Rockets had cut Boston's 84–67 advantage to 86–83. The second-year forward hit a 15-foot jump shot, an 18-footer and a 3-pointer that virtually sealed the victory.

Bird got plenty of help from Cedric Maxwell, who scored 19 points, and a strong Boston defense that held Houston under 50 percent shooting all six games. Robert Reid (27 points) and Moses Malone (23) got little help from their teammates.

The title-series victory was Boston's first since 1976. The Rockets were making their first appearance in the NBA Finals.

1972 MAYS MAKES METS DEBUT

Willie Mays, the Hall of Fame-bound center fielder who starred for 21 seasons with the New York and San Francisco Giants, made a triumphant return to New York as a member of the Mets and hit a game-winning home run against his old team.

Mays blasted a 3–2 pitch from San Francisco's Don Carrithers over the left-field fence in the fifth inning at Shea Stadium, snapping a 4-4 tie and sending the Mets on their way to a 5–4 victory. The home run, which came in Mays' first game and third at-bat for the Mets, was the 647th of his career and the first in a uniform other than that of the Giants.

The 41-year-old star, batting leadoff and playing first base, walked on five pitches from Sam McDowell to open the game. McDowell also walked Bud Harrelson and Tommie Agee, loading the bases, and Rusty Staub belted a grand slam home run to give the Mets a 4–0 advantage.

After the Giants had tied the game with four runs of their own in the fifth, Mays hit his home run in the bottom of the inning, making a winner of Ray Sedecki.

MAY 14

A STAR IS BORN

1881: Ed Walsh, a Hall of Fame righthander who won 40 games for the 1908 Chicago White Sox.

★ ★ ★

1899: Earle Combs, a Hall of Fame outfielder who batted .325 over a 12-year career in New York. He played for the 1927 Yankees, considered by many the greatest team in history.

★ ★ ★

1929: Gump Worsley, a hockey Hall of Fame goaltender who won two Vezina Trophies and played for four Stanley Cup winners in 24 seasons (1952–74).

★ ★ ★

1942: Tony Perez, a major league infielder who belted 379 home runs in a 23-year career that ended in 1986. He was a vital cog in Cincinnati's Big Red Machine of the mid-1970s.

★ ★ ★

DEATH OF A LEGEND

1987: Luke Sewell (baseball).

★ ★ ★

1992: Lyle Alzado (football).

1967 MANTLE HITS 500TH HOMER

Mickey Mantle became baseball's sixth 500-homer man when he connected with a seventh-inning pitch from Baltimore junk-baller Stu Miller and drove it into the lower right-field bleachers at Yankee Stadium.

Mantle's blast, which provided the winning run in New York's 6–5 victory over the Orioles, generated an emotional reaction from 18,872 fans who roared their approval through Elston Howard's ensuing at-bat and the between-innings interval that followed.

Mantle, in fact, was so unnerved by the salute that he committed a double-error in the eighth innning that gave Baltimore its final run. Playing first base, he dropped a throw that would have been the third out of the inning and made a bad throw to the plate as a run scored.

The Yankees, who once owned a 3–0 lead, had taken a 5–4 advantage in the sixth on Joe Pepitone's pinch-hit home run and Mantle provided the insurance. The home run lifted him into elite company with Babe Ruth, Willie Mays, Jimmie Foxx, Ted Williams and Mel Ott.

New York Yankee slugger **Mickey Mantle,** *the newest member of baseball's 500-homer club.*

MILESTONES · IN SPORTS ·

1919

Four days after winning the Kentucky Derby, Sir Barton captured the Preakness Stakes by four lengths.

1920

Washington fireballer Walter Johnson struggled to his 300th career victory, a 9–8 decision over Detroit.

1970

Four days after leading the Boston Bruins to their first Stanley Cup title in 29 years, Harry Sinden unexpectedly resigned as coach to go into the building business.

1972

Bobby Unser averaged an incredible 195.940 mph in his Eagle-Offenhauser during qualifying for the Indianapolis 500 – 17.244 mph faster than the previous qualifying record.

MAY

15

1971 MORE TRIPLE TALK

Canonero II, a surprise winner in the Kentucky Derby two weeks earlier, reinforced his credentials as a Triple Crown threat when he recorded a record-breaking victory in the Preakness Stakes at Baltimore's Pimlico Race Course.

The Venezuelan-bred colt quieted critics when he waged a spirited battle with Calumet Farm's Eastern Fleet and pulled away to a $1^{1}/_{2}$-length victory with a track-record time of 1:54 for $1^{3}/_{16}$ miles. The two contenders jumped to a quick lead and ran an easy 1-2, well ahead of the other nine entries.

Gustavo Avila, one of South America's leading jockeys, directed the victory that put Canonero II in position to become horse racing's ninth Triple Crown winner. Only the June 5 Belmont Stakes stands in the way of that goal.

Avila's front-running tactics were a departure from the come-from-behind strategy he employed in his Kentucky Derby upset. He hung stubbornly on Eastern Fleet's heels, pulled ahead at the top of the stretch and streaked to his eighth victory in 14 career starts.

The victory was worth a handsome $137,400 to Canonero II's Venezuelan owners and lifted his 1971 earnings to $302,212. He has failed to finish in the money only twice in his impressive career.

A STAR IS BORN

1940: Don Nelson, a former star forward for the Boston Celtics and current National Basketball Association coach.

★ ★ ★

1953: George Brett, the Kansas City Royals' star who retired after 1993, his 21st season, with 3,154 career hits and a .305 average.

★ ★ ★

1960: Joey Browner, a current National Football League safety.

★ ★ ★

1969: Emmitt Smith, a current National Football League running back.

★ ★ ★

DEATH OF A LEGEND

1969: Joe Malone (hockey).

★ ★ ★

1971: Goose Goslin (baseball).

★ ★ ★

1989: Joe Primeau (hockey).

★ ★ ★

1981 BARKER GETS PERFECTION

Len Barker, firing his 96-mile per hour fastball through the cold and mist at Cleveland Stadium, became the first major league pitcher in 13 years to throw a perfect game when he set down all 27 Toronto Blue Jays he faced in a 3–0 Indians victory.

Barker, growing stronger as the game progressed, struck out 11 and used pinpoint control to become the 10th perfect-game pitcher in big-league history, the first since Oakland's Catfish Hunter in 1968. Barker threw 84 strikes and he never threw more than five balls in an inning. Four balls were hit to the outfield and only one Blue Jay came close to getting a hit.

That was shortstop Alfredo Griffin, who led off the game with a sharp ground ball up the middle. Cleveland shortstop Tom Veryzer ranged far to his left, grabbed the ball and barely nipped the speedy Griffin on a close play at first base.

The 25-year-old Barker got all the support he needed when the Indians scored two first-inning runs and one in the eighth on Jorge Orta's home run. Barker retired pinch-hitter Ernie Whitt on a fly ball to end the game.

Cleveland's **Len Barker** *was king of baseball for one perfect night.*

1990 OILERS PREVAIL IN MARATHON

Edmonton's Petr Klima slipped a close-in shot through the legs of Boston goaltender Andy Moog 15 minutes and 13 seconds into the third overtime, giving the Oilers a 3–2 victory over Boston in a marathon beginning to the Stanley Cup final series.

Klima ended the longest game in Cup final history when he took a pass on a three-on-two Edmonton break and scored the Oilers' first goal against Moog in 72:13. The Oilers had taken a 2–0 lead early in the second period, but Boston forced overtime on two third-period goals by defenseman Ray Bourque.

The first overtime period was wide open, with both teams enjoying heart-stopping chances and the referees disallowing an apparent Edmonton goal by Esa Tikkanen. The second extra period was played with more caution.

Before Klima's winner, the game was stopped for 26 minutes when the lights dimmed and Boston Garden went dark. The problem was repaired and Klima quickly brought an end to the ninth-longest game in NHL playoff history.

The victory put the Oilers one step closer to their third Stanley Cup championship in four years. The Bruins, looking for their first cup in 18 years, last reached the final series in 1988 when they lost to Edmonton.

MILESTONES • IN SPORTS •

1937

War Admiral and jockey Charley Kurtsinger claimed the second jewel of the Triple Crown with a victory over Pompoon in the Preakness Stakes at Baltimore's Pimlico Race Course.

1941

An innocent-looking single off Chicago White Sox lefthander Edgar Smith launched New York Yankee Joe DiMaggio's record 56-game hitting streak.

1948

Citation and Eddie Arcaro followed their Kentucky Derby victory with a convincing win in the Preakness Stakes.

1953

Rocky Marciano's second heavyweight championship battle against Jersey Joe Walcott was decided quickly: a first-round knockout at Chicago.

1976

Elocutionist and jockey John Lively ruined the Triple Crown hopes of Kentucky Derby winner Bold Forbes with a victory in the Preakness Stakes.

MAY 16

A STAR IS BORN

1928: Billy Martin, a scrappy major league second baseman who went on to lasting fame as a manager. He managed five different major league teams, but was hired and fired by the New York Yankees five times.

★ ★ ★

1955: Olga Korbut, the diminutive Russian gymnast who captured the heart of America with her three gold medal-winning performance in the 1972 Olympics.

★ ★ ★

1955: Jack Morris, a current major league pitcher.

★ ★ ★

1957: Joan Benoit-Samuelson, a two-time Boston Marathon winner and the gold medalist in the first women's Olympic marathon in 1984.

★ ★ ★

1966: Thurman Thomas, a current National Football League running back.

★ ★ ★

1980 LAKERS USE MAGIC ACT

Magic Johnson, a 6-foot-8 point guard just one year removed from college, stepped into the center-position void created by an injury to Kareem Abdul-Jabbar and led the Los Angeles Lakers to a 123–107 victory in a shocking conclusion to the National Basketball Association championship series.

Johnson was supposed to plug the hole in the middle for Game 6 in Philadelphia while Abdul-Jabbar rested his sprained ankle for a seventh game in Los Angeles. But nobody bothered to describe the scenario to the former Michigan State star, who had led the Spartans to an NCAA Tournament title a year earlier as a sophomore.

Johnson was pure Magic, scoring 42 points and dominating players three inches taller while grabbing 15 rebounds and dishing out seven assists. Keith Wilkes added 37 points to the Lakers' cause and a 20–6 game-ending blitz settled the issue after the 76ers had pulled within two points.

Abdul-Jabbar had severely sprained his ankle while scoring 40 points in the Lakers' Game 5 victory.

Los Angeles point guard **Magic Johnson** *(32) became the center of attention and destroyed the 76ers in Game 6 of the NBA Finals.*

1976 CANADIENS END FLYER STREAK

Guy Lafleur and Peter Mahovlich scored 58 seconds apart in the third period and the Montreal Canadiens completed their four-game Stanley Cup final sweep of the defending-champion Flyers with a 5–3 victory at the Philadelphia Spectrum.

Montreal, which had lost just 11 regular-season games, completed its impressive playoff run in 13 contests and made short work of the infamous Broad Street Bullies, who had fought, scratched and clawed their way to consecutive NHL titles. It was Montreal's second championship in four years.

Spurred on by a frenzied capacity crowd, the Flyers jumped out quickly when Reggie Leach scored 41 seconds into the game on the first shot for either team. Then the game boiled down to a succession of power-play goals, the Canadiens getting three from Steve Shutt, Pierre Bouchard and Yvon Cournoyer and the Flyers getting two from Tom Bladon and Andre Dupont.

The score was 3–3 with 5:42 remaining when Lafleur and Mahovlich took over, pushing the Canadiens to their National Hockey League-record 18th Cup title.

Montreal Canadiens' standout **Guy Lafleur.**

1987 TRIPLE QUEST ALIVE

Alysheba continued to defy the oddsmakers and put himself in position to win an unlikely Triple Crown when he duplicated his Kentucky Derby victory with a half-length triumph over Bet Twice in the Preakness Stakes at Baltimore's Pimlico Race Course.

Alysheba, an 8–1 longshot despite his 3/4-length Derby victory over Bet Twice, rallied under the guidance of Chris McCarron when he caught Bet Twice at midstretch and barely outran him to the finish line. His 1:55 4/5 time in the 1 3/16-mile race was the slowest since 1975, just as his Derby-winning time of 2:03 2/5 for 1 1/4- miles was the slowest since 1974.

Believe it or not, the son of Alydar needs only a victory in the June 6 Belmont Stakes to become horse racing's 12th Triple Crown winner. His victory in the Preakness was only his third in 12 career starts, explaining why he went off as the fifth choice.

Alysheba is owned by the Clarence Scharbauer family and trained by Jack Van Berg.

MILESTONES IN SPORTS

1939

Philadelphia's Shibe Park played host to the first night game in A.L. history, but Cleveland spoiled the occasion with a 10-inning, 8–3 victory over the A's.

1955

Heavyweight champion Rocky Marciano continued his undefeated ways with a ninth-round technical knockout of Don Cockell at San Francisco.

1964

Bill Hartack added the Preakness Stakes to his Kentucky Derby victory when he rode Northern Dancer to a 2 1/4-length victory over The Scoundrel.

1977

Muhammad Ali, defending his heavyweight title for a ninth time, scored a unanimous decision over Alfredo Evangelista at Landover, Md.

1981

Pleasant Colony and jockey Jorge Valasquez grabbed the second leg of racing's Triple Crown with a one-length victory over Bold Ego in the Preakness Stakes.

MAY

17

A STAR IS BORN

1903: James (Cool Papa) Bell, a Hall of Famer who spent his professional years in the Depression-era Negro Leagues. He was known for his blazing speed.

★ ★ ★

1912: Ace Parker, a football Hall of Fame halfback whose NFL career was cut short by three years of military service in World War II.

★ ★ ★

1934: Earl Morrall, a 21-year NFL quarterback best remembered for his losing performance for Baltimore in Super Bowl III against the New York Jets and Joe Namath.

★ ★ ★

1956: Sugar Ray Leonard, an Olympic gold medalist (1976) who went on to win world championships in five different weight divisions as a professional. He compiled a career mark of 36–2–1 before retiring in 1991.

★ ★ ★

1963: Jon Koncjak, a current National Basketball Association center.

★ ★ ★

1966: Danny Manning, a current National Basketball Association forward.

★ ★ ★

1970: Chris Smith, a current National Basketball Association guard.

★ ★ ★

DEATH OF A LEGEND

1924: Candy Cummings (baseball).

★ ★ ★

1964: Steve Owen (football).

★ ★ ★

1982: Dixie Walker (baseball).

★ ★ ★

1983 ISLANDERS WIN 4TH CONSECUTIVE TITLE

Bryan Trottier, John Tonelli and Mike Bossy scored goals in a 97-second span of the opening period and the New York Islanders held on to claim a 4–2 victory over Edmonton and their fourth consecutive Stanley Cup.

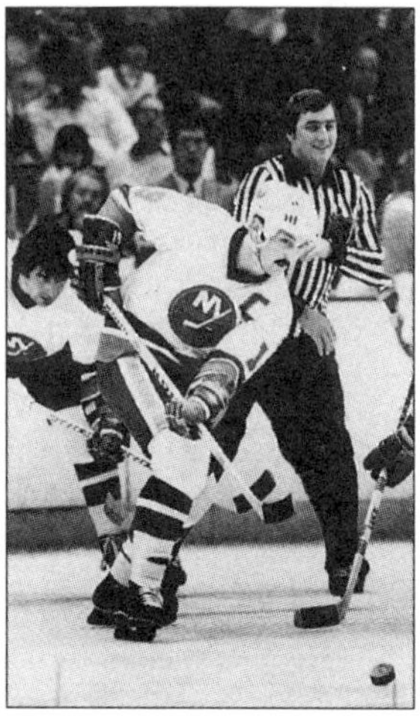

New York Islanders' star **Bryan Trottier.**

New York's four-game sweep in the Cup final put them in fast company with the Flying Frenchmen of Montreal, who enjoyed streaks of five consecutive Cups (1956–60) and four (1976–79). No other team had won more than three straight.

Game 4 at the Nassau Coliseum followed the same script as the earlier games: The Islanders shut down Gretzky and the vaunted Oilers offensive machine that had scored 424 regular-season goals. The Oilers managed just six in the series and Gretzky was limited to four assists with no goals. Trottier, Tonelli and Bossy gave New York its early lead and Edmonton answered with second-period goals by Jari Kurri and Mark Messier. But that was it for the Oilers. New York's Ken Morrow insured the victory with an empty-net goal 69 seconds before the final horn.

New York goaltender Billy Smith held Edmonton scoreless in seven of the 12 periods. The Islanders had finished sixth in the regular-season standings.

1979 PHILLIES WIN WINDY BATTLE AT WRIGLEY

Mike Schmidt's second home run of the game, a solo shot in the 10th inning off Bruce Sutter, gave the Philadelphia Phillies a 23–22 victory over Chicago in an 11-homer, 50-hit offensive deluge at Wrigley Field.

The 45 runs fell short of the major league record set 57 years earlier when the Cubs defeated the Phillies, 26–23, in another windy masterpiece at Wrigley. The 11 home runs tied a one-game record and the 50 hits fell two short of another.

Pitchers for both teams were terrorized by a stiff wind blowing toward left field. The Phillies built a seemingly safe 17–6 lead with a seven-run first inning and an eight-run third, but the Cubs scored six in the first and seven in the sixth before finally tying the game with a three-run eighth.

Schmidt and catcher Bob Boone, who drove in five runs, led the way for Philadelphia while Chicago slugger Dave Kingman blasted three homers and combined with Bill Buckner for 13 runs batted in.

Phillies reliever Rawly Eastwick, the team's fifth pitcher of the day earned the victory with two scoreless innings.

MILESTONES IN SPORTS

1925

Cleveland's Tris Speaker collected his 3,000th career hit off Washington lefthander Tom Zachary.

1939

Princeton 2, Columbia 1 in the first baseball game to be televised. The game was aired by New York experimental station W2XBS from Columbia's Baker Field.

1969

Majestic Prince defeated Arts And Letters in the Preakness Stakes, moving him one victory away from a Triple Crown.

1970

Atlanta's Hank Aaron reached the 3,000-hit milestone with a single off Cincinnati's Wayne Simpson at Crosley Field.

1975 BAYI SETS RECORD

Filbert Bayi of Tanzania, employing his familiar front-running strategy, lowered the mile world record by a tenth of a second in a blistering Kingston, Jamaica, race in which six runners broke the 4-minute barrier.

The 21-year-old Bayi led from start to finish in a 3:51 performance at the International Freedom Games. But he did not win without a challenge. He needed a strong stretch sprint to hold off American Marty Liquori (3:52.2) and Ireland's Eamonn Coghlan (3:53.3), who at one point pulled within a yard of the African.

Rounding out the field of sub-4-minute finishers was Rick Wohlhuter (3:53.8), Tony Waldrop (3:57.7) and Reg McAfee (3:59.5). Bayi, holder of the world 1,500-meter record, broke the 8-year-old mile mark of Jim Ryun. He ran a 59.6 opening quarter, 1:56.6 half mile and 2:55.3 three-quarter but could not shake Coghlan and Liquori.

Mile record-setter **Filbert Bayi** *in a familiar position—ahead.*

1963 Ernie Davis' Battle Ends

Former Syracuse star and Heisman Trophy winner **Ernie Davis.**

Former Syracuse star running back Ernie Davis, the 1961 Heisman Trophy winner who waged a valiant 10-month battle against leukemia, died in a Cleveland hospital at just 23 years of age.

The two-time All-America, college football's first black Heisman winner, led the Orangemen to the 1959 national championship as a sophomore and then proceeded to erase many of the school offensive records set by his predecessor, the great Jim Brown.

Davis rushed for 2,386 yards, 295 more than Brown, and outscored Brown, 220-187, in his varsity career. He signed an $80,000 contract to play with the National Football League's Cleveland Browns in July 1962, but doctors discovered his disease at a camp before the annual College All-Star Game.

The likeable youngster sat out the 1962 NFL season and was told in October that the leukemia was in remission. He even received permission to resume his training program, but his health suddenly deteriorated. He was admitted to the hospital May 15 – without having played a down of professional football.

A STAR IS BORN

1937: Brooks Robinson, Baltimore's Hall of Fame third baseman who led the A.L. in fielding 12 times and earned an MVP citation. He retired in 1977 after 23 years.

★ ★ ★

1946: Reggie Jackson, a Hall of Fame outfielder who blasted 563 career home runs and played on four World Series winners in a 21- year career that ended in 1987.

★ ★ ★

1960: Jari Kurri, a current National Hockey League right winger.

★ ★ ★

DEATH OF A LEGEND

1963: Ernie Davis (football).

1971 Canadiens Regain Cup

Veteran Henri Richard scored a pair of goals and rookie goaltender Ken Dryden capped his outstanding playoff performance with 31 saves as the Montreal Canadiens returned to the top of the National Hockey League mountain with a 3–2 victory over the Chicago Blackhawks in Game 7 of the Stanley Cup final.

The Canadiens, who failed to qualify for the playoffs in 1969–70 for the first time in 20 years, wiped out a 2–0 Blackhawks lead en route to their 11th Cup title in 19 years and 16th overall. A first-period goal by Dennis Hull and a second-period score by Denny O'Shea were matched late in the second period by Montreal's Jacques Lemaire and Richard.

Richard, playing on his 10th Stanley Cup winner, scored his game-winner on a 15-foot shot that evaded Tony Esposito early in the final stanza.

That made a winner of Dryden, who had not even played in an NHL game until the final two weeks of the season. Dryden played in six regular-season games and 20 playoff contests, often keeping Montreal in games with his spectacular saves. The playoff MVP made at least eight in the first period of the clincher.

1912 A's Bombard Fake Tigers

The Philadelphia Athletics pounded out 26 hits and handed the Detroit Tigers a 24–2 beating at Shibe Park. At least they looked like the Tigers.

The team doing battle against the powerful Athletics actually was a hastily-assembled group of Philadelphia semipros who were paid $25 to represent Frank Navin's team while the Tiger players were on strike.

Navin, knowing he would be liable for a $5,000 fine each day he failed to field a team, was pressed into the move when the Tigers, showing support for suspended teammate Ty Cobb, sent a telegram containing the signature of each player to A.L. President Ban Johnson in Chicago.

Manager Hughie Jennings secured a team and put hard-skinned Aloysius Travers on the mound to endure the inevitable beating. While the game was in progress, Johnson was traveling to Philadelphia.

The no-nonsense A.L. boss summoned the Detroit players to his hotel suite and threatened them with permanent suspensions. At the urging of Cobb, they agreed to return – each $100 poorer.

MAY 18

MILESTONES · IN SPORTS ·

1946

Triple Crown-bound Assault scored a neck victory over Lord Boswell in the Preakness Stakes.

1962

American Al Oerter became the world's first 200-foot discus man when he recorded a throw of 200–5 in a meet at Los Angeles.

1968

Big Frank Howard blasted two home runs in Washington's 8–4 victory at Detroit, giving him a major league-record 10 in six games.

1971

The Utah Stars captured the American Basketball Association's fourth championship with a 131–121 seventh-game victory over Kentucky.

1974

Little Current and jockey Miguel Rivera won the Preakness Stakes with a 1:54 3/5 clocking, the third fastest time in the race's long history.

1985

Pat Day rode Tank's Prospect to the fastest time (1:53 2/5) in Preakness history, but barely recorded a head victory over Chief's Crown.

1991

Hansel, with Jerry Bailey in saddle, won by a head over Corporate Report in the Preakness Stakes at Baltimore's Pimlico Race Course.

MAY

19

MILESTONES
•IN SPORTS•

1962

St. Louis Cardinals slugger Stan Musial, pinch-hitting against New York in a game at Busch Stadium, delivered his 3,516th career hit, a single that pushed him into second place on the all-time list.

1973

Jewel No. 2: Secretariat romped to a $2^1/_2$-length victory over Sham in the Preakness Stakes at Pimlico.

1979

Back to work: Major league umpires were back at work after the bitter six-week strike that forced baseball to employ amateur arbiters.

1984

A Preakness record: Gate Dancer completed the $1^3/_{16}$-mile race in an unprecedented $1:53^3/_5$.

1989

Kentucky, once considered the model for college basketball programs, was placed on three years probation by the NCAA for recruiting and other violations.

1990

Pat Day rode Summer Squall to a $2^1/_4$-length victory over Kentucky Derby winner Unbridled in Pimlico's Preakness Stakes.

1991

Willie T. Ribbs made auto racing history when he became the first black driver to qualify for an Indianapolis 500.

1984

Oilers Stop Islanders

Wayne Gretzky scored two goals and assisted on another as the Edmonton Oilers defeated New York, 5–2, and brought down the curtain on the Islanders' four-year reign as Stanley Cup champions.

Edmonton's Game 5 victory at the Northlands Coliseum denied an Islander bid to match Montreal's National Hockey League record of five consecutive Stanley Cup victories (1956–60).

The Oilers, the highest-scoring team in NHL history, won with a defensive effort that held the Isles to 12 goals – six in Game 2, their only victory.

The Oilers dominated the Game 5 finale, blowing to a 4–0 lead after two periods and then buckling down after allowing two Pat LaFontaine goals in the opening 35 seconds of the third. Dave Lumley provided a clincher when he slid the puck 160 feet into an empty net with 13 seconds remaining.

The Oilers, first-time Stanley Cup winners, were swept by the Islanders in 1983.

Key members of the **Edmonton Oilers,** *who ended the Islanders' four-year reign as Stanley Cup champions: (left to right)* **Charlie Huddy, Jari Kurri, Wayne Gretkzy, Paul Coffey** *and* **Jaroslav Pouzar.**

1979

Bid Wins No. 2

Spectacular Bid claimed the second jewel in horse racing's Triple Crown when he ran to a $5^1/_2$-length victory over Golden Act in the 104th running of the Preakness Stakes at Pimlico Race Course in Baltimore.

The charcoal gray colt, a recent winner of the Kentucky Derby and of 12 stakes races, was in exceptional form as he ran a slow track in the near-record time of 1:54 $^1/_5$ – one-fifth of a second off the Preakness record for $1^3/_{16}$ miles.

Spectacular Bid was next-to-last in the five-horse field when jockey Ron Franklin opened him up on the clubhouse turn and he blazed to the lead. By the time they reached the upper stretch, the Hawksworth Farm 3-year-old had a six-length advantage over Golden Act and was beginning to coast.

Spectacular Bid kept intact his record of never having lost at a distance of 7 furlongs or longer. The next test will come in the $1^1/_2$-mile Belmont Stakes, when he tries to become horse racing's 12th Triple Crown winner.

A STAR IS BORN

1928: Dolph Schayes, a basketball Hall of Fame forward who scored 19,249 points in a 16-year NBA career that ended in 1964.

★ ★ ★

1929: Curt Simmons, a lefthanded pitcher who won 193 games in a 20-year career that ended in 1967.

★ ★ ★

1957: Bill Laimbeer, a recently retired National Basketball Association center.

★ ★ ★

DEATH OF A LEGEND

1970: Ray Schalk (baseball).

1974

Flyers Make History

Goaltender Bernie Parent turned back 30 Boston shots and Rick MacLeish gave him all the support he needed with a first-period power play goal as the Philadelphia Flyers defeated the Bruins, 1–0, and became the first expansion team to win the Stanley Cup and the league title.

Shelving the rough-house tactics that had earned them the title "Broad Street Bullies," the smooth-skating Flyers touched off an emotional celebration at the Philadelphia Spectrum with a tight defensive effort and the sensational clutch play of Parent.

The Game 6 battle was decided in the opening session when MacLeish, being roughed up in front of the Boston net, had a shot by Andre Dupont bounce off his stick and past startled Bruins goalie Gilles Gilbert. Parent had to stop 16 first-period shots, but only 14 over the final two stanzas.

The game ended, fittingly, with Boston defenseman Bobby Orr sitting in the penalty box watching bedlam break out all around him. Orr had been penalized for tackling Bobby Clarke.

Philadelphia goalie **Bernie Parent** *and the* **Flyers** *were indeed No.1 after their victory over the* **Boston Bruins.**

A STAR IS BORN

1921: Hal Newhouser, a lefthander who won 207 major league games and consecutive MVP citations for Detroit (1944 and '45) in a 17-year career.

★ ★ ★

1931: Ken Boyer, a major league third baseman who batted .287 over a 15-year career that ended in 1969.

★ ★ ★

1940: Stan Mikita, a hockey Hall of Fame center who scored 541 goals and 1,467 points over a 22-year NHL career (1958–80) with the Chicago Blackhawks.

★ ★ ★

1940: Sadaharu Oh, the Japanese baseball first baseman who hit a world record 868 career home runs.

★ ★ ★

1946: Bobby Murcer, a major league outfielder who batted .277 over a 17-year career that ended in 1983.

★ ★ ★

DEATH OF A LEGEND

1971: Martin Dihigo (baseball).

★ ★ ★

1976: Syd Howe (hockey).

★ ★ ★

1990 SELES ENDS GRAF'S 66-MATCH STREAK

Monica Seles, a 16-year-old from Yugoslavia, ended the second-longest winning streak in tennis history when she defeated German-born Steffi Graf, 6–4, 6–3, in the final of the German Open at West Berlin.

Steffi Graf *went down to defeat after 66 consecutive victories.*

Seles lost the first two games before rebounding to hand the West German star her first setback in 67 matches – not far behind Martina Navratilova's all-time best winning streak of 74. Graf's last loss had come in June of 1989 to Arantxa Sanchez Vicario in the final of the French Open.

Graf was far from top form as she committed numerous unforced errors and suffered several tough service breaks after seemingly climbing back into the match. After closing out Graf in the opening set, Seles broke service for a 2–0 lead in the second and then broke Graf two more times.

The victory was Seles' first against Graf in four meetings and extended her own winning streak to 24 matches.

"This is just one match," a stoic Seles said after her victory. "I'm just happy to be playing well."

MAY 20

MILESTONES • IN SPORTS •

1978

Affirmed, with Steve Cauthen aboard, duplicated his Kentucky Derby victory over Alydar, this time by a neck in the Preakness Stakes.

1983

Larry Holmes retained his heavyweight championship, but he needed a 12-round split decision over Tim Witherspoon in a title bout at Las Vegas.

1983

Philadelphia lefty Steve Carlton fanned four Padres in a 5–0 loss to San Diego, moving past Walter Johnson and into second place (3,511) on the all-time strikeout list.

1985

Larry Holmes defended his heavyweight championship with a 15-round unanimous decision over Carl Williams at Las Vegas.

1989

Sunday Silence repeated his Kentucky Derby victory over Easy Goer, edging his rival by a nose in the Preakness Stakes.

1990

American Randy Barnes set a world record with a shot put heave of 75–10$\frac{1}{4}$ during competition in the Jack in the Box Invitational at UCLA's Drake Field.

1972 BEE BEE BEE PULLS SHOCKER

Bee Bee Bee ended the Triple Crown hopes of prohibitive favorite Riva Ridge with a mad dash around the $1\frac{3}{16}$-mile Pimlico Race Course en route to a stunning victory in the 97th running of the Preakness Stakes.

Bee Bee Bee, a long-shot given little consideration by Riva Ridge-mad bettors, took the lead early and held on to it, edging No Le Hace by $1\frac{1}{4}$ lengths. Riva Ridge, a 1–5 favorite after a convincing victory in the Kentucky Derby, faded on the stretch.

Riva Ridge, with Ron Turcotte holding the reins, appeared to be in perfect shape as he maneuvered into second place rounding the final turn. But the outstanding 3-year-old, a heavy favorite to become the first Triple Crown winner in 24 years, suddenly dropped back as No Le Hace and Key To The Mint sprinted into the money positions.

Bee Bee Bee, with 44-year-old Eldon Nelson aboard, covered the sloppy track in 1:55$\frac{3}{5}$.

1972 PACERS CLAIM 2ND ABA TITLE

Roger Brown scored 32 points and the Indiana Pacers wiped out a 12-point second-period deficit en route to a 108–105 victory over the New York Nets and their second American Basketball Association championship in three years.

The Pacers' Game 6 triumph at New York's Nassau Coliseum came at the expense of a Nets team that was severely hampered by injuries. John Roche, a 20-point scorer over the first five games, sat out with a sprained ankle and Rick Barry (ankle) and Ollie Taylor (wrist) performed in pain.

But that didn't diminish the sweet taste of victory for a team that had finished second in the ABA's Western Division, 14 games behind Utah. With Brown connecting on 10 of 17 two-point attempts and 3 of 6 three-pointers, the Pacers pulled to a 108–101 advantage and held off a late New York push.

Brown, who had scored 45 points in the final game of the Pacers' title-series victory over Los Angeles two years earlier, got 18-point support from Mel Daniels. Barry and Billy Melchionni led the Nets with 23 apiece.

MAY

21

A STAR IS BORN

1902: Earl Averill, a Hall of Fame outfielder who batted .318 in a 13-year career from 1929–41.

★ ★ ★

1912: Monty Stratton, a promising Chicago White Sox righthander who lost his leg in a hunting accident and came back to pitch in the minor leagues.

★ ★ ★

1923: Clarence (Bighouse) Gaines, the current basketball coach at Division II Winston-Salem State who ranks second on the all-time college victory list behind Adolph Rupp.

★ ★ ★

1960: Kent Hrbek, a current major league first baseman.

★ ★ ★

1952

Dodgers Score 15 Runs In Big First-Inning Blitz

Dodger pitcher **Chris Van Cuyk** *contributed four hits to a 19-1 blitz of the* **Cincinnati Reds.**

A not-so-funny thing happened to the Cincinnati Reds en route to a 19–1 loss to Brooklyn at Ebbets Field. They allowed a major league-record 15 first-inning runs – after retiring the first batter of the game.

Everything seemed normal enough when Reds third baseman Bobby Adams made a nice play on Billy Cox's game-opening grounder and threw him out.

But in a nightmare that will live on as an entry in baseball's record books, the next 19 Dodgers reached base on 10 hits, seven walks and two hit batsmen it was borderline unbelievable. The inning lasted for just under the hour (59 minutes) and records were set for batters coming to the plate (21) and runs scored with two out (12). Duke Snider, who blasted a two-run homer in his first at-bat, struck out against reliever Frank Smith to end the onslaught. Ewell Blackwell, the Cincinnati starter, was followed to the mound by Bud Byerly, Herm Wehmeier and Smith.

After the fateful first, offensive matters were turned over to Bobby Morgan, who blasted a pair of homers, and pitcher Chris Van Cuyk, who collected four hits.

1979

Canadiens Win Fourth in Row

Jacques Lemaire scored a pair of second-period goals and the Frenchmen of Montreal flew around the ice in recording a 4–1 victory over the New York Rangers that clinched their fourth consecutive Stanley Cup championship before an ecstatic home crowd at the Montreal Forum.

The Forum was electric through the entire scoreless third period as the Canadiens wrapped up their first Stanley Cup title before the home fans since 1968.

Montreal, which has claimed 18 championships since the Rangers last won in 1940, had clinched their last six on the road.

With Ken Dryden in the net, the Canadiens sealed the Game 5 victory with three second-period goals – two by Lemaire and another by Bob Gainey. The Rangers' Carol Vadnais and Montreal's Rick Chartraw had matched first-period goals. Dryden faced only seven New York shots over the final two periods.

When the final horn sounded, Scotty Bowman's Canadiens mobbed Dryden, paraded the Stanley Cup around the ice in hockey tradition and threw pieces of equipment to adoring fans in a wild celebration and happy that lasted well into the night.

1988

Risen Star Is A Rising Star

Risen Star took advantage of an early, strength-sapping duel between Kentucky Derby winner Winning Colors and Forty Niner and streaked to a 1 1/4-length victory over fast-closing Brian's Time in the 113th Preakness Stakes at Baltimore's Pimlico Race Course.

Eddie Delahoussaye guided Risen Star, a son of 1973 Triple Crown winner Secretariat, to victory along the rail after claiming the lead on the stretch turn.

Brian's Time, with Angel Cordero Jr. aboard, gave a valiant stretch run, making up seven lengths on Risen Star in the final half mile.

Risen Star's winning time was 1:56 1/5, the slowest Preakness winner in 18 years. The stage was set when Winning Colors broke into the early lead and Forty Niner followed, intent on not letting racing's third filly Kentucky Derby winner claim a second leg of the Triple Crown.

Winning Colors, with Gary Stevens in saddle, and Forty Niner, with Pat Day, bumped repeatedly along the backstretch as Risen Star rested in third place.

When Delahoussaye spotted the opening on the turn, he shot Risen Star into the lead he never relinquished.

MILESTONES IN SPORTS

1955

Nashua, a surprising loser to Swaps in the Kentucky Derby, ran to a one-length victory over Saratoga in the Preakness Stakes.

1977

Seattle Slew continued his romp toward a Triple Crown with a 1 1/2-length victory over Iron Constitution in the 102nd running of the Preakness.

1981

Butch Goring scored a pair of goals and the New York Islanders earned their second straight Stanley Cup with a 5-1 Game 5 victory over Minnesota at the Nassau Coliseum.

1977 A Female Qualifier

Janet Guthrie, building on the foundation she set last year when she became the first woman to officially enter the Indianapolis 500, became the first female to qualify for the Memorial Day race when she averaged 188.403 miles per hour on the last day of qualifications.

The 39-year-old barrier-breaker zipped her Lightning-Offenhauser around the $2^1/2$-mile oval Indianapolis Motor Speedway track on successive laps of 187.500, 188.363, 188.798 and 188.957 mph, earning a spot in the 33-car field.

Guthrie had been unable to make a qualifying attempt last year because her car was not fast enough.

With Rolla Vollstedt's sponsorship, that was not a problem this time. Guthrie posted the fastest speed (185.6 mph) on the opening day of practice and raised it to more than 191 before ramming the car into a wall.

Although the car was never the same after the accident, it was good enough to earn her a spot in the auto racing history books.

Auto racing barrier breaker **Janet Guthrie.**

1963 Mantle Flexes His Muscles

Yankee **Mickey Mantle,** *master of the gargantuan home run.*

Mickey Mantle, who came within inches of muscling the first fair ball out of Yankee Stadium in 1956, belted another gargantuan home run that gave the New Yorkers an 11-inning, 8–7 victory over the Kansas City Athletics.

Mantle, leading off the decisive 11th, connected with a two-ball pitch from righthander Bill Fischer, sending it soaring toward the right-field corner. The ball continued to rise and struck a facade that towers 108 feet above the field.

The drive was similar to the one Mantle hit off Washington's Pedro Ramos in a 1956 game. That one hit the facade and bounced back onto the field. This homer brought an end to a see-saw game that the Yankees appeared to have well in hand through seven innings.

Yankee starter Bill Stafford was protecting a seven-run lead and a three-hitter when he entered the eighth, but the A's struck for six runs and tied the game in the ninth on Ed Charles' home run.

Milestones in Sports

1915

Rhine Maiden became the third filly to win the Preakness Stakes when she held off Half Rock by a length and a half and finished in 1:58.

1963

Franchise shift: The Syracuse Nationals received permission from the NBA's Board of Governors to move operations to Philadelphia.

1976

Former heavyweight boxing contender Oscar Bonavena of Argentina was shot to death outside a legal house of prostitution near Reno, Nev. He was 33.

1983

Veteran Calvin Peete made up a seven-stroke deficit with a blazing final-round 63 and earned a two-stroke victory in the Atlanta Golf Classic.

A Star Is Born

1902: Al Simmons, a Hall of Fame outfielder who batted .334 and won a pair of A.L. batting titles during a 20-year career that ended in 1944.

★ ★ ★

1943: Tommy John, a lefthander who won 288 games in his 26-year career, more than half of them after undergoing rotator cuff surgery and missing the 1975 season.

★ ★ ★

1946: Jim Colborn, a former major league pitcher and one-time 20-game winner in the 1970s.

★ ★ ★

Death of a Legend

1954: Chief Bender (baseball).

★ ★ ★

1975: Lefty Grove (baseball).

★ ★ ★

1990: Rocky Graziano (boxing).

1975 Gilmore Sparks Title Victory

Artis Gilmore scored 28 points and set a playoff record with 31 rebounds as the Kentucky Colonels ended seven years of frustration by defeating the Indiana Pacers, 110–105, and securing their first American Basketball Association championship.

The Colonels' fifth-game victory at Louisville's Freedom Hall was choreographed and made possible by the 7-foot-2 Gilmore, who dominated the middle of the court and steadied his teammates every time the Pacers made a run. Indiana received plenty of firepower from its two-man arsenal of rookie Billy Knight, who scored 40 points, and George McGinnis, who added 31, but the Pacers couldn't handle the balanced Kentucky attack.

The Colonels never wavered as they forged a six-point first-half lead, led by four after three quarters and steadfastly refused to wilt at the end.

Gilmore got plenty of help from teammates Ted McClain, who scored 19 points, and Dan Issel, who added 16. Little Kentucky guard Louie Dampier handed out 12 assists.

The title-clinching victory was the 22nd for the Colonels in their last 25 games.

MAY

23

MILESTONES
· IN SPORTS ·

1941

Joe Louis, making his 17th title defense, defeated Buddy Baer on a seventh-round disqualification and retained his heavyweight championship in a fight at Washington D.C.

1976

Panama's Roberto Duran, generally considered the best boxer pound for pound in the world, defended his WBA lightweight championship with a 14th-round knockout of Lou Bizzarro at Erie, Pa.

1977

Los Angeles center Kareem Abdul-Jabbar joined former Boston great Bill Russell as the National Basketball Association's only five-time MVPs when he beat out Portland center Bill Walton in a lopsided vote, 159–29.

1980

Utah Jazz guard Terry Furlow died instantly when the Mercedes he was driving veered off Interstate 71 near Cleveland and crashed into a utility pole.

1981

Wilfred Benitez knocked out England's Maurice Hope in the 12th round of a fight at Las Vegas, claiming the world junior middleweight championship and becoming the fifth boxer to rule three different weight divisions.

1958 Chamberlain Leaves Kansas, Turns Pro

Abe Saperstein, *founder of the Harlem Globetrotters, poses with his newly signed prize* - **Wilt Chamberlain.**

Wilt Chamberlain, the University of Kansas' 7-foot-1 scoring machine, announced he is leaving school to go on a barnstorming tour of South America as a professional basketball player.

Wilt Chamberlain said he was giving up his senior year of eligibility because life as a touring pro would better prepare him for the type of basketball that is played in the National Basketball Association.

The NBA cannot take a player before his college class graduates and Chamberlain will have to wait a year before joining the Philadelphia Warriors, who own his rights.

Chamberlain said he was leaving because of the way Kansas opponents played against him – sometimes triple-teaming, other times running the clock. Such tactics, he said, forced him to neglect many facets of his game. He also said he wanted to make some money to help his family in Philadelphia.

Chamberlain, who was sought by more than 200 colleges before finally settling on Kansas, averaged 29.3 points as a sophomore and 30.1 last year when he led the Jayhawks to a runnerup finish in the NCAA Tournament. They lost the title game to North Carolina in triple overtime.

A STAR IS BORN

1888: Zack Wheat, a Hall of Fame outfielder who hit .317 and won an N.L. batting title for Brooklyn in 1918.

★ ★ ★

1943: John Newcombe, a 1960s and '70s Australian tennis star who won three Wimbledon titles and two U.S. and Australian championships.

★ ★ ★

1954: Marvin Hagler, a boxer who held the world middleweight championship from 1980–87 and ended his career with a 62–3–2 record.

★ ★ ★

DEATH OF A LEGEND

1990: Charlie Keller (baseball).

★ ★ ★

1972 Vaulters Match World Records

American Bob Seagren and Swede Kjell Isaksson waged a thrilling and crowd-pleasing pole vault duel in a special Amateur Athletic Union meet at the University of Texas-El Paso and then walked away as co-world record-holders in the prestigious event.

Isaksson entered the competition as the record-holder, thanks to an 18–2 vault two weeks earlier at Los Angeles. But Seagren took care of that with an 18–3 1/4 vault that Isaksson matched moments later.

The fun, however, was just beginning. On his third try at 18-4 1/4, Seagren sailed cleanly over the bar with what he called a "flawless jump" and reclaimed the world record. Moments later, also on his third try, Isaksson duplicated Seagren's feat again.

Both came up short in their three attempts at 18–6. All seven vaulters competing in the event were aided by a tailwind that gusted up to 20 miles per hour, but wind conditions only affect official records for running events. Isaksson said the wind did not help him anyway.

"In fact," he said, "I think I had a little headwind (on the record-tying jump)."

1977 Cauthen Hurt In Bad Spill

Little Steve Cauthen, the 17-year-old wonder jockey, was thrown and trampled in a three-horse accident in the fourth race at Belmont Park, suffering a concussion, a broken arm and a cracked rib.

Cauthen, the 95-pound apprentice who had won an incredible 252 races over the first five months, was aboard Bay Streak when the mishap occurred. The colt, in the lead as the horses turned for home, suddenly snapped a front leg and tumbled to the turf, throwing Cauthen and creating a serious obstacle for the rest of the field.

Volney, with Jorge Velasquez in saddle, hit Cauthen and tumbled to the ground. Then Low Return bumped into the fallen horses and tossed jockey Pat Day. Velasquez suffered a broken ankle and two horses had to be destroyed.

Cauthen, on his way to becoming the biggest single-season winner in horse racing history, also suffered a cut on his right hand that required 15 stitches and another above his right eye that needed 10.

Cauthen was making his Belmont Park debut. He failed to win in his first three races before the mishap.

MILESTONES
· IN SPORTS ·

1936

New York Yankee Tony Lazzeri hammered two grand slams and drove in an A.L.-record 11 runs in a 25–2 victory over the Philadelphia A's at Shibe Park.

1946

Joe McCarthy, who managed the New York Yankees to seven World Series championships, stepped down because of ill health and was replaced by catcher Bill Dickey.

1976

Muhammad Ali took his show to Munich, West Germany, and retained his heavyweight crown with a fifth-round technical knockout of Richard Dunn.

1980

Bob Nystrom's overtime goal gave the New York Islanders a 5–4 Game 6 victory over Philadelphia and their first Stanley Cup championship.

1992

Al Unser Jr.'s Galmer-Chevrolet roared to a half-car-length victory over Canadian Scott Goodyear in the tightest Indianapolis 500 finish in the 76 runnings of the Memorial Day race.

A STAR IS BORN

1899: Suzanne Lenglen, the French tennis legend who lost only one match from 1919 to her retirement in 1926. She won six Wimbledon singles titles.

★ ★ ★

1905: Martin Dihigo, a baseball Hall of Famer considered by many the greatest all-around star in Negro League history.

★ ★ ★

1963: Joe Dumars, a current National Basketball Association guard.

★ ★ ★

DEATH OF A LEGEND

1966: Jim Barnes (golf).

1935 Baseball Lights Up

Cincinnati's **Crosley Field** *during baseball's first night game.*

Through the wonders of technology, U.S. President Franklin D. Roosevelt pushed a button in Washington D.C. that transformed Cincinnati's Crosley Field into a beaming crescendo of lights, ushering in a bright new era for major league baseball.

The first night game in major league history, made possible through the pushing and prodding of Cincinnati General Manager Lee MacPhail, was a well-choreographed "happening" that attracted numerous baseball officials and political dignitaries. The game itself, featuring the Reds and Philadelphia Phillies, was nothing more than a sideshow.

After MacPhail entertained the 20,422 fans and special guests with a fireworks display and other pregame attractions, President Roosevelt pushed the button and everybody marveled as the players from both teams were given a special warmup. When play got under way, Cincinnati's Paul Derringer made two early runs stand up in a 2–1 victory.

With players from both teams saying they had no problem picking up the ball, the experiment was heralded as a success.

1987 Replacement Driver Unser Wins 4th Indy

Al Unser Sr. roared to a five-second victory over Roberto Guerrero in the Indianapolis 500—his record-tying fourth victory in the prestigious Memorial Day event.

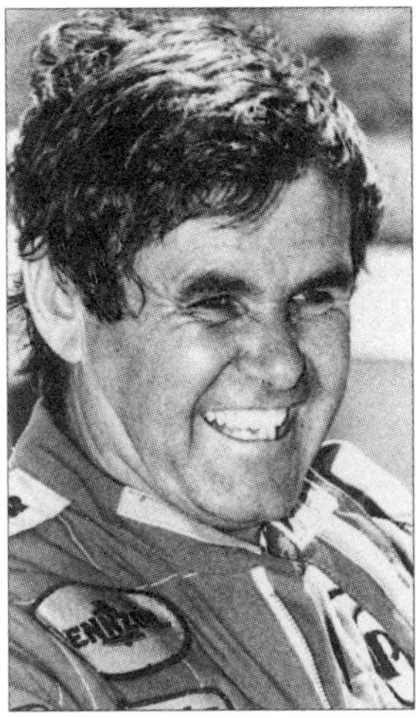

Four-time winner **Al Unser**.

Not only did the 47-year-old Unser match A.J. Foyt's record of four winners, he became the oldest driver to enter the winner's circle at the Indianapolis Motor Speedway. And all this happened because the Roger Penske team needed a replacement for Danny Ongais, who suffered a concussion in a practice accident.

It did not appear Unser would achieve any lofty goals as he settled his March-Cosworth into third place behind Mario Andretti's Lola-Ilmor Chevrolet and Guerrero's March-Cosworth. Andretti was in full control, leading for 170 laps, but his engine blew out on No. 180.

That moved Unser to second but he needed a break to make up the lap-plus lead Guerrero enjoyed with time running out. And he got it when the Colombian stalled his engine for almost a minute during his final pit stop. The mistake occurred when Guerrero kept his clutch engaged as the car was being released from the jack. The engine stalled as soon as the car hit pavement, allowing Unser to move into the lead.

Unser, who averaged 162.175 mph, had won in 1970, '71 and '78. Unser's 25-year-old son, Al Jr., finished in fourth place.

MAY

24

1990 New Oilers Return To Top

The Edmonton Oilers, playing just their second season after trading Wayne Gretzky to Los Angeles, completed their shocking rise to the Stanley Cup championship with a 4–1 victory over the Bruins at Boston Garden.

The Oilers' Game 5 triumph, built on a pair of two-goal periods and the sharp goaltending of Bill Ranford, silenced critics who had predicted the team would fall on hard times without Gretzky, who had led Edmonton to four Cup victories from 1984 to '88.

While this team will never be considered the equal of those champions, it was good enough to defeat the team that had finished with the best overall record in the NHL's regular season. And it did so convincingly, with superior speed, defense and goaltending.

After a scoreless first period, the Oilers took control on second-period goals by Glenn Anderson and Craig Simpson. Third-period scores by Steve Smith and Joe Murphy added to their advantage and only a late goal by Boston's Lyndon Byers kept Ranford from his shutout.

Ranford, who stopped 29 of 30 Boston shots, won the Conn Smythe Trophy as the most valuable player in the playoffs. Ranford played only because of an injury to Grant Fuhr.

MAY

25

MILESTONES
• IN SPORTS •

1906

Jesse Tannehill stopped Chicago on two hits and the Boston Red Sox snapped their A.L.-record 20-game losing streak with a 3–0 victory.

1935

Ruth's last hurrah: Babe slammed three homers and drove in six runs, but his Boston Braves dropped an 11–7 decision to Pittsburgh at Forbes Field.

1937

Detroit catcher Mickey Cochrane suffered a fractured skull when he was struck on the temple by a pitch from New York righthander Bump Hadley during a game at Yankee Stadium.

1975

Bobby Unser and his Jorgensen Eagle claimed first place in an Indianapolis 500 that was shortened to 435 miles by a heavy rainstorm.

1981

Bobby Unser was handed a one-lap penalty and fined $40,000 for violations in the previous day's Indianapolis 500, costing him an apparent victory and moving Mario Andretti into the winner's circle.

1989

The Flames brought a Stanley Cup championship to Calgary with an impressive six-game victory over the Montreal Canadiens.

1965 CLAY WINS REMATCH

Cassius Clay, trying to prove that his shocking 1964 upset of Sonny Liston was no fluke, scored the fastest knockout in heavyweight boxing history when he defeated the former champion again, this time with a controversial first-round punch that created a storm of protest.

Clay, who had defeated Liston 15 months earlier with a seventh-round technical knockout at Miami Beach, delivered his decisive blow, a short right, in a wild fight at Lewiston, Maine.

Referee Jersey Joe Walcott officially declared Clay a winner at 2:17, but Maine boxing officials scored the knockout at 1 minute even.

When the bout came to its sudden end, the fans at ringside took a few seconds to digest what they had just witnessed and then began yelling "Fake!"

The blow did not appear to be hard enough to knock anybody out and many in the arena felt it did not even connect with Liston's jaw.

But Liston certainly hit the deck and Clay danced over him, yelling and taunting like a madman.

The so-called "phantom punch" was viewed from many different angles on ABC-TV several days later, with no emphatic conclusion.

1991 MARIO LEADS CHARGE

Joe Mullen scored two goals and Pittsburgh scoring machine Mario Lemieux added a goal and three assists to his playoff ledger as the Pittsburgh Penguins pounded out an 8–0 victory over Minnesota and earned the first Stanley Cup championship in franchise history.

The Game 6 victory at the Met Center in Bloomington, Minn., ended the first all-American Stanley Cup final in 10 years. It was orchestrated by a swarming Pittsburgh attack that overwhelmed Minnesota goaltenders Jon Casey and Brian Hayward and the fine net work of Penguins goalie Tom Barrasso.

Barrasso stopped 39 shots and Pittsburgh gave him all the cushion he needed with three first-period goals – power-play shots by Ulf Samuelsson and Mullen and a short-handed effort by Lemieux. The Penguins' advantage increased to 6–0 after two periods and the final stanza was a Pittsburgh cruise.

The victory came in Pittsburgh's 24th season and in its first Stanley Cup final appearance. Lemieux finished the playoffs with 44 points, three below Wayne Gretzky's record.

A STAR IS BORN

1897: Gene Tunney, the former world heavyweight title holder (1926–28) who defeated Jack Dempsey twice.

★ ★ ★

1926: Bill Sharman, a basketball Hall of Fame player and coach. He played on four Boston Celtics championship teams from 1957 to '61 and later earned 466 victories as a coach in the ABA and NBA.

★ ★ ★

1932: K.C. Jones, a Hall of Fame guard who played on two college championship teams (San Francisco) and eight NBA title winners (Boston) in the '50s and '60s. He later coached ABA and NBA teams to 552 victories.

1975 WARRIORS DODGE BULLETS

Butch Beard scored the go-ahead basket with 1:45 remaining and added a pair of late free throws that clinched the Golden State Warriors' 96–95 victory over Washington and completed their four-game sweep of the National Basketball Association championship series.

The Warriors employed the same formula they had used through most of the playoffs to wrap up their first NBA title in 19 years – they fell behind early and roared back. In this case, their deficit was 14 points. In five of their previous six games, they had fallen behind by as many as 13.

Golden State caught the Bullets in the final quarter, fell behind again by eight points and finally took the lead for good on Beard's driving layup with less than two minutes remaining. Neither team was able to score through a succession of turnovers and Beard made a pair of late free throws that iced the victory.

Beard finished with 16 points, four behind Rick Barry's team-leading total. Washington's Phil Chenier led all scorers with 26. The sweep was only the third in the 29-year history of the NBA.

Golden State forward **Rick Barry** *reaches for a pass during the Game 4 NBA championship series clincher against Washington Bullets.*

MILESTONES · IN SPORTS ·

1956

Cincinnati pitchers Johnny Klippstein, Hersh Freeman and Joe Black combined for $9^2/_3$ innings of no-hit pitching, but the Milwaukee Braves pulled out a 2–1 victory on Frank Torre's 11th-inning single.

1970

The Indiana Pacers defeated the Los Angeles Stars, 111–107, and captured the ABA's third championship in a six-game final.

1972

Heavyweight champ Joe Frazier scored a fifth-round technical knockout of Ron Stander in a title bout at Omaha, Neb.

1974

Johnny Rutherford, driving a McLaren-Offenhauser, claimed his first Indianapolis 500 with a 23-second victory over Bobby Unser.

1984

Russian Sergei Bubka leaped into international consciousness with a world-record pole vault of $19–2^1/_4$ during competition at Bratislava, Czechoslovakia.

A STAR IS BORN

1947: Darrell Evans, a hard-hitting third baseman who finished his 21-year career in 1989 with 414 home runs.

★ ★ ★

1968: Willie Burton, a current NBA forward.

★ ★ ★

1970: Eric Anderson, a current NBA forward.

★ ★ ★

DEATH OF A LEGEND

1956: Al Simmons (baseball).

★ ★ ★

1959: Ed Walsh (baseball).

★ ★ ★

1959 HADDIX IS PERFECT

Pittsburgh lefthander **Harvey Haddix** *works against Milwaukee in his almost-perfect effort.*

Milwaukee first baseman Joe Adcock blasted a run-scoring double in the bottom of the 13th inning, turning the incredible 12-inning pitching masterpiece of Pittsburgh's Harvey Haddix into a heart-breaking 1–0 loss.

Haddix, a little lefthander with a sharp-breaking curveball and pinpoint control, was like a machine as he baffled Milwaukee batters and mesmerized a crowd of 19,194 fans at County Stadium. Three-up, three-down became the tension-mounting refrain as Braves hitters succumbed to his mastery inning after inning...

When Haddix sailed through the ninth, he became the sixth pitcher in modern baseball history to throw a regulation perfect game. When he threw his first pitch of the 10th, he became the first pitcher to take a perfecto into extra innings. And so it continued. The Braves went down quietly in the 10th, 11th and 12th.

But frustration turned to desperation as the Pirates tried in vain to get Haddix a single run. They managed 12 hits off Braves righthander Lew Burdette, but nobody crossed the plate. When Burdette retired the Pirates in the top of the 13th, the stage was set for a bizarre – and confusing – conclusion to the greatest pitching performance in baseball history.

Haddix's string of 36 consecutive outs was broken when leadoff batter Felix Mantilla reached base on third baseman Don Hoak's throwing error. After Mantilla moved to second on a sacrifice, Hank Aaron was walked intentionally, bringing Adcock to the plate. The big first baseman hit a drive that barely cleared the right-center-field fence for an apparent game-ending home run.

But nothing would come easily on this day. Aaron, apparently thinking the ball had hit the fence and that Mantilla had scored the winning run, left the basepath and joined a wild Braves celebration. Adcock circled the bases and was called out for passing his teammate. Adcock later was credited with a game-winning double and the final score was declared 1–0, not 3–0.

No matter. Haddix had pitched 12 perfect innings, $12^1/_3$ no-hit innings – and still lost.

1991 MEARS WINS FOURTH INDY

MAY 26

Rick Mears made a daring burst past Michael Andretti on the 188th lap and then held on for a 3.1-second victory in the Indianapolis 500 – his record-tying fourth in the Memorial Day classic.

Mears, who joined A.J. Foyt and Al Unser Sr. as four-time entrants into the Indianapolis Motor Speedway's winner's circle, was simply reclaiming what was rightfully his when he went high on the first turn in his Penske-Chevrolet and zipped past an unsuspecting Andretti, driving a Lola-Chevrolet.

Andretti had passed Mears at the same spot in precisely the same fashion one lap earlier and appeared headed for victory. Andretti's car had been running faster, only an earlier flat tire standing between him and an insurmountable lead. But after Mears passed and endured a seven-lap caution, he shocked everybody by outsprinting Andretti to the finish line.

Over the final three laps, he stretched a 1.8-second advantage to 3.1 and finished with an average speed of 176.460 mph. Mears previously had won in 1979, '84 and '88.

This Indy 500 will be remembered for an historical footnote. The field included its first black driver, Willy T. Ribbs, who dropped out after six laps with engine problems.

Rick Mears *joined the four-victory Indianapolis 500 club.*

MAY

27

A STAR IS BORN

1912: Sam Snead, the PGA's all-time top winner with 81 career victories. He won the Masters and PGA Championships three times each and the British Open once.

★ ★ ★

1956: Nick Lowery, a current National Football League placekicker.

★ ★ ★

1968: Frank Thomas, a current Major League first baseman.

★ ★ ★

DEATH OF A LEGEND

1953: Jesse Burkett (baseball).

★ ★ ★

1975

FLYERS WIN CUP AGAIN

Philadelphia's Bob Kelly and Bill Clement, a couple of journeymen forwards relegated to spot duty, scored third-period goals and netminder Bernie Parent made them stand up for a 2–0 victory at Buffalo that clinched the Flyers' second consecutive Stanley Cup championship.

Kelly broke a scoreless tie 11 seconds into the third period of Game 6 when he scrambled from a pileup behind the net and beat Sabres goaltender Roger Crozier. Clement gave the Flyers breathing room when he scored with 2:48 remaining. Parent faced 32 shots in recording his fourth shutout of the playoffs and the fifth for the defensive-minded Flyers.

The loss was tough for Crozier, who turned back 29 of 31 Philadelphia shots while working in place of Gerry Desjardins, Buffalo's No. 1 goalie. Crozier was outstanding for two periods before getting beat by Kelly's close-range game-winner and Clement's clincher.

Fred Shero's rough-and-tumble Flyers, known around the league as the Broad Street Bullies, matched their 1974 six-game Cup final victory over Boston.

1937

HUBBELL WINNING STREAK EXTENDS TO 24 GAMES

Giants lefthander **Carl Hubbell.**

New York right fielder Mel Ott blasted a ninth-inning home run and Giants lefthander Carl Hubbell retired all six Cincinnati batters he faced to claim a 3–2 victory over the Reds – his major league-record 24th consecutive triumph over two seasons.

Hubbell, making an unusual relief appearance, entered a 2–2 game in the bottom of the eighth inning and retired three Cincinnati batters on ground balls. In the top of the ninth, Ott belted a pitch from Reds lefty Lee Grissom 400-plus feet into the right-field bleachers.

When Hubbell retired three more Reds, all on fly balls, in the bottom of the inning, he raised his record to 8–0 and extended his big-league mark for consecutive victories. Hubbell's streak had started the previous year when he won his final 16 decisions.

Hubbell had set the record with his 22nd straight win, passing former Giant great Rube Marquard, who won 21 in a row in 1911–12. Marquard had set the major league record for consecutive one-season victories with 19. The relief victory was Hubbell's second during the streak.

The Giants and Hubbell were in position to win only because of the bat of Dick Bartell. His double in the third drove in New York's first run and his eighth inning-double tied the score.

The victory moved the Giants within a game of first-place Pittsburgh.

1972

FATE PLAYS HAND

Mark Donohue took his first lead with 13 laps remaining in the Indianapolis 500 when the two front-runners suffered car trouble and hung on to claim his first victory in the Memorial Day classic, beating Jerry Long by 47.1 seconds.

Donohue, driving one of Roger Penske's McLaren-Offys, was running third behind teammate Gary Bettenhausen's McLaren-Offy and Long's Eagle-Offy when fate played its unpredictable hand.

First Bettenhausen pulled out of the race with a malfunctioning ignition. Then Long had to pull into the pits, courtesy of a flat tire caused by a piece of metal debris. While Long was in the pits, Donohue took the lead and a subsequent spark plug problem kept Long from mounting a serious chase.

Donohue set a 500 record by finishing in 3 hours, 31.55 seconds with an average speed of 163.465 mph. He led just the final 13 laps, 103 fewer than Bettenhausen, who earned more than $20,000 in lap prizes.

Only fifteen of the 33 cars that started the race managed to finish.

Mark Donohue *(at the wheel) and his Indy-winning pit crew.*

MILESTONES · IN SPORTS ·

1968

Baseball took on an international flavor when officials announced National League expansion to Montreal and San Diego for the 1969 season.

1971

A hungry team of British golfers won four straight final-day singles matches in a 13–11 upset of the favored United States, clinching England's first Walker Cup victory since 1938 and second overall.

1981

Willie Shoemaker, already horse racing's winningest jockey, earned his 8,000th career victory when he rode War Allied in the first race at California's Hollywood Park.

1984

Rick Mears' Pennzoil Z-7 averaged an Indianapolis 500-record 163.612 mph, earning him a second victory in the prestigious Memorial Day race.

1990

In a clean and fast Indianapolis 500, Arie Luyendyk recorded an average winning speed of 185.981 mph – an Indy record.

1956 Long Extends Homer Streak

Pittsburgh slugger **Dale Long** *points to the Forbes Field seat where his record-breaking home run landed.*

Pittsburgh first baseman Dale Long drove a fourth-inning pitch from Brooklyn's Carl Erskine 375 feet over the right-field fence at Forbes Field, extending his own record for consecutive-game home runs and helping the Pirates to a 3–2 victory over the Dodgers.

Responding to the cheers of 32,221 fans, Long homered for the eighth straight game, a mark that should stand for many years. He had set the major league record for home runs in consecutive games when he connected with a May 26 pitch from righthander Ben Flowers in a contest at Philadelphia.

Long's record-setter, his only hit, tied the score at 2–2 after the Dodgers had taken a first-inning lead on Duke Snider's titanic two-run blast. But Pittsburgh's Bob Friend limited the Dodgers to one hit over the final eight innings and Pittsburgh scored its game-winner in the fifth on Bob Skinner's single.

Long's amazing streak started May 19 against Jim Davis of the Chicago Cubs and he also homered off Milwaukee's Warren Spahn and Ray Crone, St. Louis' Herman Wehmeier and Lindy McDaniel and Philadelphia's Curt Simmons and Flowers.

A STAR IS BORN

1888: Jim Thorpe, the Indian all-everything considered one of the greatest athletes of all time. He won Olympic gold medals and played both major league baseball and professional football.

★ ★ ★

1896: Warren Giles, the Hall of Fame executive who served as president of the National League from 1952–69.

★ ★ ★

1938: Jerry West, a basketball Hall of Fame guard who scored 25,192 points in a 14-year career (1960–74) with the Los Angeles Lakers.

★ ★ ★

1957: Kirk Gibson, a current major league outfielder.

★ ★ ★

1967: Glen Rice, a current National Basketball Association guard.

1957 West Coast Baseball

National League owners, opening the door for baseball expansion to the West Coast, voted unanimously to allow the Brooklyn Dodgers and New York Giants to shift their operations to Los Angeles and San Francisco – if they so desired.

The owners gave their permission with two conditions: The Dodgers and Giants must make their requests for a shift before October 1, and they must make the move together.

League approval gives Dodgers Owner Walter O'Malley and Giants Owner Horace Stoneham more leverage in their attempts to improve their baseball situations in New York. O'Malley has been upset over Brooklyn's inability to garner funds for a new stadium to replace tiny Ebbets Field, where his Dodgers have played since 1913. Stoneham has been concerned about the aging Polo Grounds and sagging attendance figures, which he claims are not enough to support a major league baseball team.

Before the N.L. action, West Coast talk had been regarded as an idle threat. Now New Yorkers must view seriously the attractive overtures being made to the two premier franchises by hungry Los Angeles and San Francisco officials.

1971 NBA Shines In Star Game

Oscar Robertson and Walt Frazier hit two free throws apiece in the final half minute as the National Basketball Association held on for a 125–120 victory over the American Basketball Association in a player-promoted all-star game at Houston's Astrodome.

Playing without 7-foot-2 Milwaukee center Lew Alcindor, who was married earlier in the day, the NBA held off a desperation ABA rally in the first-ever meeting between the rival leagues. The NBA was heavily favored in the nationally-televised contest, but the ABA stars simply would not go away.

The ABA, in fact, trailed by only a point at halftime and led 98–96 with just over nine minutes remaining. But two free throws by John Havlicek gave the NBA a 100–98 advantage and it never trailed again. The NBA stretched its lead to 10, but the ABA rallied to within a point on a Charlie Scott jumper with 58 seconds remaining, setting up Robertson and Frazier for the kill.

Frazier led the NBA with 26 points while Rick Barry scored 20 for the prestige-hungry ABA. The game was staged without the sanction of team owners.

MILESTONES IN SPORTS

1960

Jim Beatty shattered the American mile record with a 3:58 performance in the California Relays at Modesto, Calif.

1975

American Steve Smith set a world indoor pole vault record when he soared 18–5 during competition in an International Track Association meet at New York's Madison Square Garden.

1976

New York pitchers Ed Figueroa and Tippy Martinez combined to stop the 30-game hitting streak of Detroit's Ron LeFlore as the Yankees beat the Tigers, 9–5. The outfielder finished the game 0 for 4.

1978

Al Unser Sr. became the fifth man to win three Indianapolis 500s when he drove his Lola-Cosworth to an 8.19-second victory over Tom Sneva, averaging 161.363 mph. Unser joined a select circle of three-time winners which includes A.J.Foyt, Mauri Rose, Wilbur Shaw and Louis Meyer.

1983

American teenager Kathy Horvath ended top-seeded Martina Navratilova's winning streak at 36 matches with a shocking 6–4, 0–6, 6–3 victory in the fourth round of the French Open championships.

MAY

29

A STAR IS BORN

1932: Richie Guerin, an NBA guard who scored 14,676 points over a 13-year career that ended in 1970.

★ ★ ★

1939: Al Unser Sr., an outstanding race car driver who won four Indianapolis 500s and 39 CART victories in the 1970s and '80s.

★ ★ ★

1962: Eric Davis, a current major league outfielder.

★ ★ ★

DEATH OF A LEGEND

1966: Hippo Vaughn (baseball).

★ ★ ★

1977 FOYT SETS INDY MARK

A.J. Foyt, the grand old man of the Indy car racing circuit, took the lead on the 185th lap when Gordon Johncock dropped out and cruised to his record fourth Indianapolis 500 victory, beating Tom Sneva by 28 seconds.

Indianapolis 500 record-setter **A.J.Foyt.**

Johncock, who led 128 of the 200 laps, was 10 seconds ahead of Foyt and apparently in control when his Wildcat-DGS broke a valve spring on the fourth turn of the Indianapolis Motor Speedway track and began shaking. He pulled onto the infield grass and Foyt zoomed ahead in his Coyote-Foyt.

Foyt finished the race in 3 hours, 5 minutes and 57.70 seconds while averaging 161.331 mph. The victory was his first at Indianapolis since 1967 and it broke a deadlock with three-time winners Louis Meyer, Mauri Rose and Wilbur Shaw.

The race was especially notable for the debut of Janet Guthrie, the first woman driver in Indianapolis 500 history. Guthrie's Lightning-Offenhauser was plagued by engine trouble and completed only 27 laps, good for 29th place in the 33-car field.

MILESTONES IN SPORTS

1920

The great Man o'War streaked to an American mile record of 1:35 4/5 while winning the Withers Stakes at New York's Belmont Park.

1977

Blues defenseman Bob Gassoff was killed when the motorcycle he was riding crashed head-on with an automobile in St. Louis.

1982

The Indians ended the 14-game winning streak of Chicago righthander LaMarr Hoyt with a 5–2 victory over the White Sox.

1983

Tom Sneva drove his Penske March-Cosworth to an 11.1-second victory over Al Unser Sr. in the 67th Indianapolis 500, averaging 162.117 mph.

1988

Rick Mears again: The talented racer drove his Penske-Chevrolet V-8 to an average speed of 149.809 mph and a third Indianapolis 500 victory.

1971 AL UNSER GETS BIRTHDAY GIFT

Al Unser, celebrating his 32nd birthday behind the wheel of a blue and gold P.J. Colt-Ford known as the Johnny Lightning Special, won his second consecutive Indianapolis 500 with a record speed of 157.735 mph.

Unser set the speed mark despite a rash of accidents that wiped out nine cars and slowed the pace for 53 of the 200 laps around the Indianapolis Motor Speedway's $2^1/_2$-mile oval track. Unser led 102 laps and completed the race in 3 hours, 10 minutes and 11.56 seconds—22 seconds ahead of Peter Revson's McLaren M-16 Offenhauser.

Unser, who became only the fourth driver to win consecutive Indy 500s, actually won the race in the pits, completing four stops in 23 fewer seconds than it took Revson to make three stops. He also was aided by a late caution that slowed the race for 23 laps and allowed him to maintain an 18-second advantage when the green flag was restored on lap 189.

One of the four accidents occurred when the pace car driven by a local dealer struck a photographers' stand just as the race began.

The other three drivers to win consecutive Indianapolis 500s were Wilbur Shaw (1939-40), Mauri Rose (1947-48) and Bill Vukovich (1953-54). Vukovich died the next year in an Indy crash.

1990 RICKEY STEALS COBB THUNDER

Speedy Oakland left fielder Rickey Henderson swiped third base in the sixth inning of a game against Toronto at the Oakland Coliseum, breaking Ty Cobb's all-time American League stolen base record and putting him in position to challenge for the major league mark.

Henderson's 893rd career steal came on a 2–0 pitch from Toronto left-hander David Wells to Carney Lansford and he slid into third without even drawing a throw from catcher Greg Myers. Henderson pulled the base from its moorings, held it triumphantly over his head and accepted a rousing ovation from the appreciative crowd.

Ty Cobb *was a basestealing force in the early 1900s.*

The steal broke Cobb's 62-year-old A.L. record and left Henderson trailing only Lou Brock (938) and turn-of-the-century star Billy Hamilton (937) on the all-time list. Henderson set the record in his 11th season, 13 fewer than Cobb needed to steal 892 bases.

Henderson's record steal did not figure in the scoring and the Blue Jays went on to claim a 2–1 victory.

1955 VUKOVICH DIES AT INDY

Talented and determined Bill Vukovich, bidding to become the first race car driver to win three consecutive Indianapolis 500s, was killed in a fiery five-car smashup on the 141st lap of the Memorial Day classic at the Indianapolis Motor Speedway. He was 36 years old.

Vukovich, who had become the third driver to win consecutive races when he drove his Fuel Injection Special to victory in 1953 and '54, was leading after 140 laps when he became tangled in a four-car accident that occurred just in front of him on the backstretch. Vukovich veered away from the mass of cars, but he couldn't avoid the flying wreckage.

Driving at an estimated 150 mph, Vukovich hit another car, flipped and landed upside down. He was pinned in a fiery inferno as rescue workers rushed too late to his aid. Nobody else in the accident was seriously injured.

The tragedy, the worst at the track since 1939, took the enjoyment out of the race for the 175,000 fans and eventual winner Bob Sweikert. Sweikert averaged 128.209 mph in a John Zink Special.

1911 FIRST INDY RACE

Ray Harroun, averaging 74.602 miles per hour in his Marmon Wasp while other cars were falling by the wayside, captured the inaugural Indianapolis 500 before more than 80,000 racing enthusiasts at the Indianapolis Motor Speedway.

Harroun took the lead on the 190th lap of the 2 1/2-mile oval track and held off all challenges the rest of the way. He completed his grueling journey in 6 hours, 41 minutes and 8 seconds, pulling across the finish line 30 seconds ahead of Ralph Mulford's Lozier.

The 40-car race was marred by a series of accidents, one of which killed Arthur Greiner's mechanic at the 30-mile mark. Greiner's Amplex lost a front wheel, started twisting and hopping across the track and hurled both the driver and his mechanic, S.P. Dickson, from their seats. Dickson died when he was thrown against a fence 20 feet away and Greiner suffered a fractured arm.

Harroun collected a $10,000 first prize and another $5,000 in lap money. Only eight cars held the lead during the long race.

M

30

Drivers line up their cars for the start of the inaugural Indianapolis 500.

MILESTONES • IN SPORTS •

1936

An Indy first: Louis Meyer drove his Ring-Free Special to an unprecedented third Indianapolis 500 victory.

1951

Ezzard Charles' eighth defense of his heavyweight championship produced a unanimous 15-round decision over Joey Maxim at Chicago.

1956

New York slugger Mickey Mantle hit a titanic home run against Washington that bounced off a cornice high above Yankee Stadium's third deck, coming within 18 inches of leaving the park.

1982

Gordon Johncock drove his Wildcat-Cosworth across the finish line 16-hundredths of a second ahead of Rick Mears' Penske PC-10 in the closest Indianapolis 500 ever contested.

1987

On the same day in Las Vegas, heavyweight contenders Mike Tyson and Tony Tucker scored technical knockouts over Pinklon Thomas and Buster Douglas, setting up a title unification match.

1940 SHAW SURVIVES RAIN, REPEATS INDY VICTORY

Wilbur Shaw survived long odds and a driving rain to become the first driver to win consecutive Indianapolis 500s, completing the wet Memorial Day classic in 114.277 mph in his Boyle Special.

Shaw's record-tying third Indy victory, matching the feat accomplished by Louis Meyer in 1936, was achieved at well under the predicted pace because the final quarter of the race – 50 laps – was run under a yellow caution.

Shaw moved into the lead at the 250-mile mark, hurried through a pit stop and was still in first position 25 miles later when lightning and a relentless pelting rain dictated a caution that lasted the remainder of the afternoon.

Locked into position at 80 mph, Shaw literally cruised to his third triumph in four years. Only a second-place finish in 1938 separated him from an incredible four consecutive Indianapolis 500 victories.

Rex Mays, who had captured the pole in his Bowes Seal Fast Special, finished second.

A STAR IS BORN

1943: Gale Sayers, a Hall of Fame running back who gained 4,956 yards in a seven-year Chicago Bears career that was cut short by knee injuries.

★ ★ ★

1962: John Alt, a current National Football League offensive tackle.

★ ★ ★

1966: Brian Quinnett, a current NBA forward.

★ ★ ★

1972: Manny Ramirez, a current major league outfielder.

★ ★ ★

DEATH OF A LEGEND

1973: Swede Savage (auto racing).

★ ★ ★

1976: Max Carey (baseball).

★ ★ ★

1986 Rahal Wins Tight Indy

Bobby Rahal zipped past Kevin Cogan with two laps remaining and held off both Cogan and Rick Mears to win the Indianapolis 500 in the tightest three-car finish in the 75-year history of the Memorial Day classic.

Cogan, Rahal and Mears, all driving March-Cosworths, were locked in a spirited three-way duel with 15 miles remaining when a minor accident resulted in a yellow caution. If the race had ended under the caution, Cogan would have won with Rahal second and Mears third. But the green flag was restored with two laps remaining and the race was on – a race that nobody at the packed Indianapolis Motor Speedway would soon forget.

Rahal appeared destined for a second-place finish when he spotted an opening on the inside, made a bold move and shot past a stunned Cogan near the 2 1/2-mile oval track's start-finish line. He desperately held his slim advantage the rest of the way and finished 1.4 seconds ahead of Cogan. Mears was just four-tenths of a second behind Cogan when Rahal hit the finish line.

Rahal averaged 170.722 miles per hour, the fastest winning speed in history. The previous record was 163.612 mph by Rick Mears in 1984.

1983 76ers Zip Past Lakers

Moses Malone did the grunt work and Julius Erving soared to championship heights in the closing minutes as the Philadelphia 76ers earned their first National Basketball Association title in 16 years with a 115–108 victory that closed out a four-game sweep of the defending-champion Los Angeles Lakers.

The 30-year-old Erving, looking for his first NBA title, scored 21 points, seven coming in the crucial closing minutes at the Los Angeles Forum. The incomparable Dr. J made a dunk shot that tied the game at 106, scored on a three-point play that gave the 76ers their first lead since the opening minutes and connected on a top-of-the-key jumper with 24 seconds remaining.

Malone, the 6-foot-10 center who had signed a $13.2-million free-agent contract with Philadelphia before the season, scored 24 points and grabbed 23 rebounds. Malone was outstanding throughout the series, averaging 25.8 points and 18.5 rebounds.

The sweep was only the fourth in NBA Finals history and the 76ers completed the playoffs with an unprecedented 12–1 record. The Lakers got a 27-point, 13-assist effort from Magic Johnson in the finale.

76ers center **Moses Malone.**

1987 Oilers Again

Glenn Anderson's goal with 2:24 remaining put the finishing touch on a 3–1 Edmonton victory over Philadelphia and wrapped up the Oilers' third Stanley Cup championship in four years.

The Game 7 battle at Edmonton's Northlands Coliseum was dominated by the fast-skating Oilers, but Flyers' goaltender Ron Hextall held them in check with a 40-save performance that kept fans on the edge of their seats. The Oilers broke a 1–1 tie in the second period on a Jari Kurri goal and touched off a wild celebration when Anderson connected in the third period.

The defensive Oilers made life easy for goalie Grant Fuhr, who faced only 20 shots and spent most of the game watching Hextall sprawling at the other end of the ice. The underdog Flyers had reached a seventh game only because of Hextall's inspired play.

Edmonton had held a three games to one advantage in the series before losing Games 5 and 6.

Wayne Gretzky *(left) and goalie* **Grant Fuhr,** *key figures in Edmonton's third Stanley Cup championship.*

Milestones in Sports

1927

In an amazing twist of baseball fate, Detroit first baseman Johnny Neun pulled off a rare unassisted triple play – one day after Chicago Cub Jimmy Cooney turned the same trick.

1949

Sam Snead defeated Johnny Palmer, 3 and 2, in the final of the PGA Championship at Richmond, Va., becoming the first golfer to win PGA and Masters titles in the same year.

1954

Bill Vukovich became the third driver to win consecutive Indianapolis 500s when he averaged a record 130.840 mph in his Fuel Injection Special.

1967

A.J. Foyt earned his record-tying third Indianapolis 500 victory in a Coyote-Ford when Parnelli Jones' STP Oil Treatment Special broke down with three laps remaining in the Memorial Day race.

1980

Baltimore pitcher Scott McGregor held Minnesota's Ken Landreaux hitless in an 11–1 Oriole victory, ending his hitting streak at 31 games.

A Star Is Born

1871: Amos Rusie, a pre-1900 Hall of Fame pitcher and the man the New York Giants traded to get Christy Mathewson.

★ ★ ★

1943: Joe Namath, the football Hall of Fame quarterback who passed for 27,663 yards and 173 touchdowns in a 13-year career that ended in 1977.

★ ★ ★

Death of a Legend

1970: Terry Sawchuk (hockey).

★ ★ ★

1983: Jack Dempsey (boxing).

1975 Ryan's No-Hit Wonder

California righthander Nolan Ryan joined former Los Angeles great Sandy Koufax in a select circle when he pitched his fourth career no-hitter – a 1–0 decision over Baltimore at Anaheim Stadium.

Ryan struck out nine and walked four en route to matching the four-no-hitter feat Koufax carved out in the 1960s. Only two other modern-era players, Cleveland's Bob Feller and Cincinnati's Jim Maloney, had pitched three.

The 6-foot-2 Texan got a third-inning run on Dave Chalk's single and protected the lead masterfully – with some help from his friends. Second baseman Jerry Remy made an excellent defensive play in the seventh inning on Tommy Davis' chopping ground ball and outfielder Lee Stanton made a fine running catch in the fifth. But Ryan otherwise was in control.

When he struck out Bobby Grich to end the game, Ryan shook hands with third baseman Chalk and strolled off the mound like nothing unusual had happened. Ryan's first two no-hitters were pitched in 1973 and his third in 1974.

California Angels no-hit man **Nolan Ryan.**

A STAR IS BORN

1933: Alan Ameche, an NFL running back best remembered for scoring the winning overtime touchdown in Baltimore's 1958 championship game victory over the New York Giants.

★ ★ ★

1941: Dean Chance, a two-time 20-game winner who earned a Cy Young Award in 1964 when he finished 20–9 for the Los Angeles Angels.

★ ★ ★

1961: Paul Coffey, a current National Hockey League defenseman.

★ ★ ★

DEATH OF A LEGEND

1960: Lester Patrick (hockey).

★ ★ ★

1965: Curly Lambeau (football).

★ ★ ★

1980: Rube Marquard (baseball).

★ ★ ★

1992 Penguins Win Again

Mario Lemieux scored a goal and two assists as the Pittsburgh Penguins completed a four-game sweep of the Blackhawks and earned their second consecutive Stanley Cup championship with a 6–5 victory at Chicago Stadium.

Lemieux's strong work and a balanced Pittsburgh offense offset the combined five-goal production of Blackhawks Dirk Graham and Jeremy Roenick. Graham scored a hat-trick in the first period and Roenick added goals in the second and third periods, his final coming after the Penguins had grabbed a 6–4 lead.

The game was tied after one period, 3–3, and after two, 4–4. But Joe Murphy and Ron Francis gave Pittsburgh a 6–4 advantage early in the third and the Penguins weathered a late Chicago rush to seal their 11th consecutive victory.

The championship was Pittsburgh's second straight after 23 years of frustration and the first under Coach Scotty Bowman. Pittsburgh won its first title under Bob Johnson, who died of a brain tumor last November.

1946 Assault Gets Triple Crown

Assault, delivering an emphatic message to the lingering doubters who sent him off as a 7–5 second choice, roared down the stretch and posted a three-length victory over Natchez in the Belmont Stakes, completing his quest for horse racing's Triple Crown.

Assault, with Warren Mehrtens in saddle, poked his nose ahead of Natchez at the eighth pole on the homestretch and pulled away, adding the prestigious Belmont to his earlier victories in the Kentucky Derby and Preakness Stakes. The King Ranch 3-year-old joins Sir Barton, Gallant Fox, Omaha, War Admiral and Whirlaway in the very select circle of Triple Crown winners.

Assault drew a gasp from 43,599 Belmont Park fans when he stumbled out of the gate, but he quickly recovered and ran in fourth place down the backstretch and into the final turn. At that point the Texas-bred colt began making his move on the outside and he made the stretch run look easy.

Assault covered the $1^1/_2$-mile Belmont test in $2:30^4/_5$, well ahead of favorite Lord Boswell, a fifth-place finisher. Assault won for the fifth time in six 1946 outings and earned $77,400 for owner Robert J. Kleberg.

Assault won the Derby by eight lengths and the Preakness by a neck.

June 1

Milestones in Sports

1925

Young New York Yankee first baseman Lou Gehrig pinch-hit for Pee Wee Wanninger – his first appearance in an iron-man streak that would eventually grow to a record 2,130 consecutive games.

1957

University of California junior Dave Bowden became the first American to break the 4-minute mile barrier when he ran a 3:58.7 during competition in the Pacific AAU meet at Stockton, Calif. The previous best American time was the 4:00.5 clocking of Wes Santee during the 1954 Texas Relays.

1963

Willie Pastrano, who got his title shot only because two previous choices had suffered injuries, earned a shocking 15-round decision over Harold Johnson and claimed the world light heavyweight championship.

1972

American golf star Jane Blalock was suspended from tour play for one year by LPGA officials as the result of an investigation into "cheating" allegations.

1984

Livingstone Bramble scored a dramatic 14th-round knockout of popular Ray (Boom Boom) Mancini and claimed his World Boxing Association lightweight championship at Buffalo, N.Y.

JUNE

2

MILESTONES IN SPORTS

1949

Andy Seminick blasted two home runs and Del Ennis, Willie Jones and pitcher Schoolboy Rowe hit one apiece as Philadelphia tied a major league record with a five-homer eighth inning in a 12–3 victory over the Cincinnati Reds.

1973

Argentina's Carlos Monzon defended his middleweight crown for a second time against Emile Griffith, defeating the former champion in a unanimous 15-round decision at Monte Carlo.

1974

Chris Evert defeated 17-year-old Czech star Martina Navratilova, 6–3, 6–3, and captured the Italian Open – her first major international tennis title.

1984

In one of the great rounds in the history of women's golf, Patty Sheehan birdied eight of the first 13 holes and scored a dramatic eagle on 18 that gave her a third-round 63 and a nine-stroke lead in the LPGA Championship at Kings Island, O.

1990

Wisconsin's Suzy Favor completed an 800- and 1,500-meter double in the NCAA Track and Field championships at Duke, winning the 1,500 for the fourth straight year and claiming her NCAA-record ninth individual title.

1935

Ruth Leaves Game With 714 Homers

An overweight, underachieving Babe Ruth asked permission to go on baseball's voluntary retired list after receiving his unconditional release from the Boston Braves in the midst of his 22nd major league season.

Ruth was batting .181 in his first National League campaign after 21 glorious years with the Boston Red Sox and New York Yankees. His retirement, three days after a cameo appearance in a game against Philadelphia, was sparked by a dispute with Braves Owner Emil Fuchs and Manager Bill McKechnie.

Ruth, nursing a tender knee, had been denied permission to miss two games while attending a New York celebration as a representative of baseball. The Bambino demanded his release and Fuchs obliged.

Ruth retires as holder of every conceivable slugging record. He owns a .342 career average and he blasted 714 home runs, most of them in his 15 seasons with the Yankees. His most memorable season was 1927, when he hit a record 60 homers, drove in 164 runs and led the Yankees to a World Series championship.

Ruth did have some memorable moments with the Braves. He homered in his first N.L. game and blasted three in a May 25 contest at Pittsburgh.

Remaining true to his career-long style, Ruth saved his best for last. Home run No. 714 was a mammoth 600-foot blow that sailed over the right-field grandstand at Forbes Field.

Babe Ruth *hung up his uniform after one season with the Boston Braves.*

A STAR IS BORN

1864: Wilbert Robinson, a turn-of-the-century player who went on to a Hall of Fame managing career with the Brooklyn Dodgers.

★★★

1904: Johnny Weissmuller, a swimmer who won five gold medals at the 1924 and '28 Olympic Games and went on to greater fame in his movie role as "Tarzan."

★★★

1951: Larry Robinson, an NHL defenseman who helped Montreal to six Stanley Cup championships in a 20-year career that ended in 1992.

★★★

1953: Craig Stadler, a professional golfer who won the Masters in 1982.

★★★

DEATH OF A LEGEND

1941: Lou Gehrig (baseball).

★★★

1943: Nile Kinnick (college football).

★★★

1993: Johnny Mize (baseball).

★★★

1970

McLaren Dies In Test Run

Bruce McLaren, one of the world's top race car designers and drivers, was killed when the experimental MD8 racer he was driving on a test run crashed at about 180 miles per hour at the Goodwood circuit in Goodwood, England.

McLaren's car spun out of control and rammed into an earth bank, exploding on impact and breaking in two. McLaren was dragged free of the wreckage but died within minutes.

The 32-year-old New Zealand native, one of the wealthiest sports-racing enthusiasts in the world, had been at the top of the international racing profession for more than 10 years. He had reached the pinnacle of his career with Canadian-American Challenge Cup victories in 1967 and '69.

McLaren, who is survived by a wife and 4-year-old daughter, reportedly had been considering retirement from driving to devote more time to the business end of his operations.

1985

Lopez Coasts To LPGA Win

Nancy Lopez, overcoming a two-stroke first-round penalty for slow play, fired a final-round 65 and claimed a stunning eight-stroke victory over Alice Miller in the LPGA Championship at the Jack Nicklaus Sports Center in Mason, O.

Lopez, who also shot a seven-under-par 65 (including the penalty) in her opening round, entered the final day tied with Miller, but she posted three front-nine birdies and coasted to her 31st professional victory and second in two weeks. It was the sixth time the 28-year-old star had won successive tournaments.

In posting her second LPGA victory, Lopez was near perfect. She missed only one green in regulation, hit every fairway and birdied two of the four par-3s from within 14 feet. Only the first-day penalty kept her from tying Hollis Stacy's 72-hole tournament record of 271.

Lopez picked up $37,500 for her victory.

1932 Gehrig Hits 4 Homers

Lou Gehrig became the first player in modern baseball history to hammer four home runs in a single game, accomplishing his unprecedented feat in a seven-homer New York Yankee explosion that produced a 20–13 victory over the Philadelphia Athletics at Shibe Park.

Gehrig hit a two-run blast and three solo shots in his first four at-bats, joining pre-1900 stars Bobby Lowe (1894) and Ed Delahanty (1896) in baseball's select four-homer circle. The first baseman grounded out in the eighth inning and narrowly missed a fifth home run in the ninth, backing A's center fielder Al Simmons to the fence.

The Yankees also got home runs from Earle Combs, Babe Ruth and Tony Lazzeri, who completed his cycle with a ninth-inning grand slam. The New Yorkers collected 23 hits and set a major league record with 50 total bases.

Mickey Cochrane and Jimmie Foxx added to the fireworks with home runs for Philadelphia.

The classic batting stance of Yankee four-homer man **Lou Gehrig.**

1932 Giants Lose A Legend

Legendary New York Giants Manager **John McGraw.**

John J. McGraw, the man whose name was synonymous with New York Giants baseball for 30 years, shocked his friends, players, rivals and fans when he announced he was retiring as manager because of ill health.

McGraw's surprising decision became known when the team distributed a formal typewritten statement after a scheduled Polo Grounds doubleheader against Philadelphia had been postponed by rain.

McGraw was immediately replaced by star first baseman Bill Terry, who said he had been approached several days earlier. McGraw, a fiery, temperamental baseball genius who cut his teeth as a player for the pre-1900 Baltimore Orioles, managed briefly in the fledgling American League before taking the Giants job in 1902. Over the next three decades, he directed the team to 10 National League pennants and three World Series championships.

His managerial record shows 2,836 victories.

The 59-year-old McGraw, who will stay on in a front-office capacity, managed the Giants to an unprecedented four consecutive pennants from 1921–24.

1975 Pele Signs With Cosmos

Pele, the aging superstar of international soccer, became the richest player in team sports history when he agreed to leave his native Brazil and sign a three-year, $7-million contract with the New York Cosmos of the North American Soccer League.

The 34-year-old Pele, perhaps the best-known athlete in the world, will provide a heavy dose of credibility for the struggling American soccer scene. He had announced his retirement last October after scoring 1,216 goals in 1,253 games and leading Brazil to three championships in the four World Cups played between 1958 and 1970.

Pele, who had chosen to remain in retirement rather than play for Brazil in last year's World Cup, decided to join the Cosmos at the risk of offending his fans in Brazil. He will play about 85 games over the life of the contract, some of them overseas exhibitions. Warner Communications, owner of the Cosmos, also will be able to use Pele's name for advertising and marketing.

June 3

A Star Is Born

1943: Billy Cunningham, a basketball Hall of Famer who scored 13,626 points as a player and directed Philadelphia to 454 victories in eight seasons as a coach (1977–85).

★ ★ ★

1945: Hale Irwin, a current PGA Tour golfer who has three U.S. Open titles to his credit.

★ ★ ★

Milestones in Sports

1925

Chicago White Sox player-manager Eddie Collins collected career hit No. 3,000, a single, in his team's 12–7 victory at Detroit.

1952

An Olympic first: The powerful Soviet Union announced plans to send a team of athletes to compete in the Summer Games at Helsinki, Finland.

1961

Sherluck, a 65–1 longshot, scored a $2^1/_2$-length victory over Globemaster in the Belmont Stakes, ending Carry Back's bid for a Triple Crown.

1971

Chicago Cubs lefthander Ken Holtzman pitched his second no-hitter in three years, stopping the Reds, 1–0, at Cincinnati's Riverfront Stadium.

1974

Bjorn Borg, a 17-year-old Swede, surprised top-seeded Ilie Nastase, 6–3, 6–4, 6–2, and won the Italian Open singles championship.

JUNE 4

A STAR IS BORN

1862: Bob Fitzsimmons, a pre-1900 boxer who briefly held the heavyweight championship.

★ ★ ★

1943: Sandra Haynie, a former golfer who won two LPGA Championships and one U.S. Women's Open in the 1960s and '70s.

★ ★ ★

1963: Xavier McDaniel, a current National Basketball Association forward.

MILESTONES IN SPORTS

1972

Billie Jean King upset talented 20-year-old Evonne Goolagong, 6–3, 6–3, and captured her first career French Open championship.

1974

The National Football League awarded an expansion franchise to Seattle interests, with play to begin in 1976.

1974

Atlanta slugger Hank Aaron blasted his 16th career grand slam in a 7–3 victory at Philadelphia, breaking a tie with Willie McCovey atop the N.L.'s all-time list.

1980

Hockey great Gordie Howe retired at age 52, ending a career that spanned 32 active seasons in five decades.

1983

Chris Evert-Lloyd captured her fifth French Open and 15th Grand Slam title with a 6–1, 6–2 victory over Yugoslavia's Mima Jausovec.

1987 122: Moses Streak Ends

Danny Harris, a 21-year-old three-time NCAA champion, ended the incredible 122-race winning streak of Edwin Moses when he beat him in the 400-meter hurdles during international competition in a meet at Madrid.

Moses, who had not lost since August 26, 1977, ran a solid 47.69 final but could not catch Harris after hitting the last hurdle. Moses is the record-holder in the event and owns the 11 fastest times. Harris, who took the lead at the fifth of 10 hurdles, finished at 47.56, the best time of his career.

It was the second meeting between Moses and Harris, who finished 1–2 in the 1984 Olympic Games at Los Angeles.

Moses, 10 years older than his rival, had entered the race with 107 straight finals victories and 15 in preliminaries.

Moses ran a lap of honor after the race and the crowd of 11,000 still was chanting his name a half hour later. Harris shook Moses' hand and stepped aside, letting the veteran enjoy his moment in the sun.

Nate Page finished third, giving the U.S. a 1–2–3 sweep.

1964 Koufax Fires 3rd No-Hitter

Los Angeles lefthander Sandy Koufax pitched his record-tying third career no-hitter and faced the minimum 27 batters as the Dodgers defeated the Phillies, 3–0, at Philadelphia's Connie Mack Stadium.

Koufax struck out 12 in a dominating performance that allowed him to join former Cleveland great Bob Feller as the only modern-era pitchers to throw three no-hitters. Koufax lost his perfect game when he walked Richie Allen in the fourth inning, but Allen was cut down trying to steal.

Koufax, who has pitched no-hitters in three consecutive seasons, allowed just four balls to be hit out of the infield en route to his sixth victory in an injury-plagued campaign. Feller pitched his three no-hitters over an 11-year span.

Big Frank Howard gave Koufax all the support he needed with a three-run seventh-inning homer off Chris Short.

Sandy Koufax *celebrates his third career no-hitter.*

1976 Riotous Fans Help Celtics Eclipse Suns

Guard **Jo Jo White** *played a key role for the Celtics.*

The Boston Celtics, aided by thousands of riotous fans who ringed the Boston Garden court while harassing Phoenix players and referees, recorded a wild 128–126 triple-overtime victory over the Suns in Game 5 of the National Basketball Association championship series.

After regulation had ended 95–95 and the first overtime 101–101, the real drama unfolded. Boston's John Havlicek hit a running one-hander with two seconds remaining in the second extra session, giving the Celtics a 111–110 lead and setting off a wild celebration with fans pouring onto the court.

After 10 minutes of bedlam that included several fights and attacks on referees, the fans finally were pushed to the edge of the court so the game could be finished. The Suns were assessed a technical foul for an illegal timeout and Jo Jo White sank the free throw, giving Boston a two-point lead. But Phoenix inbounded the ball and Gar Heard sank a desperation jumper that tied the score and forced a third overtime.

This one was played in an ugly setting with fans running on and off the court, trying to touch players and snarling at referees. The Celtics took a six-point lead and held off the Suns for a 3–2 advantage in the best-of-seven final.

1937 War Admiral Wears Crown

War Admiral, ignoring a bloody front hoof that he must have torn in the starting gate, streaked to a track record while completing his quest for a Triple Crown with an easy victory in the Belmont Stakes.

War Admiral, the son of Man o'War, shattered the record set by his famous sire 17 years earlier when he ran the $1^1/2$-mile Belmont Park course in 2:28 3/5, beating Sceneshifter by a comfortable four lengths. Jockey Charlie Kurtsinger broke him from the gate on the outside and managed to secure the lead on the first turn – a lead he never relinquished.

The Glen Riddle product became the fourth horse to complete the Triple Crown, matching the feats of Sir Barton, Gallant Fox and Omaha in sweeping the Kentucky Derby, Preakness Stakes and Belmont.

The torn heel was not noticed until War Admiral was led into the winner's circle after the race.

The winning time also matched the American record for $1^1/2$ miles and War Admiral's clocking at $1^1/4$ miles was a full second faster than his winning time in the Kentucky Derby – a difficult two-length victory over Pompoon.

A STAR IS BORN

1874: Jack Chesbro, a turn-of-the-century Hall of Fame pitcher who set a still-standing record when he won 41 games in 1904 for the New York Highlanders.

★ ★ ★

1920: Marion Motley, a football Hall of Fame fullback who was a vital part of the Cleveland Browns incredible success from 1946–53.

★ ★ ★

1925: Art Donovan, a football Hall of Fame defensive tackle in a 12-year NFL career that ended in 1961.

★ ★ ★

1944: Tommie Smith, the Olympic gold medalist in the 200-meter sprint who was expelled from the Olympic Village for his part in a black-power protest during the awards ceremony.

★ ★ ★

DEATH OF A LEGEND

1953: Bill Tilden (tennis).

★ ★ ★

1943 Count Fleet Romps

In a stirring performance that gave new meaning to the term "rout," Count Fleet set a Belmont Stakes record and scored an incredible 30-length victory over Fairy Manhurst while grabbing the final leg of horse racing's Triple Crown.

The race was over almost as soon as the gate opened. Johnny Longden drove Count Fleet into a quick lead and the gap between him and the field seemed to widen with every stride. Mrs. John D. Hertz's son of Reigh Count exploded across the finish line in $2{:}28^1/5$, two-fifths of a second faster than fellow Triple Crown winner War Admiral ran the $1^1/2$ miles in 1937.

The victory was the sixth in as many 1943 starts for Count Fleet and the 16th in 21 career races. Not only did he become the sixth 3-year-old to win a Triple Crown, he also became the first to sweep all five spring specials – the Wood Memorial, Kentucky Derby, Preakness Stakes, Withers Mile and Belmont.

JUNE 5

MILESTONES • IN SPORTS •

1925

In an exciting 36-hole playoff for the U.S. Open championship, Willie Macfarlane prevailed over Bobby Jones, 75 and 72 to 75 and 73.

1971

Walter Blum rode Pass Catcher to an exciting victory in the Belmont Stakes, spoiling a bid by Canonero II to claim horse racing's ninth Triple Crown.

1976

Bold Forbes, with Angel Cordero in saddle, claimed the $1^1/2$-mile Belmont Stakes in 2:29, giving him victories in two of the three Triple Crown events.

1989

Toronto officials opened the wondrous new SkyDome to 48,378 fans, but the Blue Jays dropped a 5–3 decision to the Milwaukee Brewers.

1989

Michael Chang, a 17-year-old American, pulled a shocking upset when he fought back from a two-set deficit and defeated top-seeded Ivan Lendl, 4–6, 4–6, 6–3, 6–3, 6–3, in a quarterfinal match of the French Open.

1977 Walton Keys Blazer Win

Bill Walton anchored a solid team effort that wore down the Philadelphia 76ers and the 7-year-old Portland Trail Blazers completed their unlikely run to the National Basketball Association championship with a 109–107 Game 6 victory at Portland.

Walton dominated the middle, scoring 20 points, grabbing 23 rebounds, blocking eight shots and handing out seven assists. His effort throughout the series enabled Portland to pull off an NBA first – four consecutive victories in the championship series after losing the first two games.

The Game 6 triumph did not come easily. The Trail Blazers held a 12-point advantage with six minutes remaining, but Julius Erving and George McGinnis led a Philadelphia charge that cut their deficit to three with 51 seconds to go. After Portland's Maurice Lucas hit a free throw, a McGinnis basket cut the lead to two with 27 seconds on the clock.

After the 76ers regained possession on a jump ball, Erving, Lloyd Free and McGinnis all missed final shots.

Erving finished the contest with 40 points and McGinnis scored 28. Their combined 68 points accounted for 62 per cent of Portland's scoring

Bill Walton, *the driving force in Portland's National Basketball Association championship run.*

JUNE

6

1981 CROWN HOPES DASHED

Pleasant Colony, making a bid to become the 12th Triple Crown winner in horse racing history, fell short in his stretch run at the Belmont Stakes and finished third behind Summing and Highland Blade.

Pleasant Colony, jittery before, during and after the race, broke last out of the gate and finally reached contention status at the top of the stretch.

But the Johnny Campo-trained colt had used up too much too soon and was unable to make a serious charge at the leaders.

Summing, an 8–1 longshot with George Martens in saddle, completed the 1½-mile test in 2:29 and edged Highland Blade by a neck in an exciting finish that was overshadowed by Pleasant Colony's Triple Crown failure. The dirt-colored colt came home 1½ lengths behind Highland Blade.

Summing had not finished in the money in either the Kentucky Derby or Preakness Stakes, both Pleasant Colony victories. Pleasant Colony had gone off as a 4–5 betting favorite among the 61,106 fans at Belmont Park.

"You can't be sorry, that's the name of the game," Campo said after the race.

"I'm disappointed but I have no excuse," said Pleasant Colony jockey Jorge Velasquez.

1987 BET TWICE STEALS ALYSHEBA'S CROWN

Bet Twice, an agonizingly-close runner-up in both the Kentucky Derby and Preakness Stakes, emphatically avenged those losses with a 14-length romp in the Belmont Stakes and ruined Alysheba's Triple Crown hopes.

Craig Perret *rides* **Bet Twice** *across the Belmont finish line.*

Bet Twice, with Craig Perret in saddle, left no doubt about his superiority on this afternoon. After losing to Alysheba by three-quarters of a length in the Kentucky Derby and by a half length in the Preakness, the son of Sportin' Life roared down the stretch to a 2:28⅕ clocking.

Bet Twice took a five-length lead over second-place Cryptoclearance at the 1¼-mile mark and extended it by nine over the next quarter. Alysheba, never even in contention, finished fourth after being sent off as a 4–5 favorite.

Bet Twice's margin of victory was the fifth largest in Belmont history and his triumph broke the five-year winning streak of trainer Woody Stephens.

1967 NHL EXPANSION TEAMS STOCKED

The National Hockey League, celebrating its 50th anniversary, officially doubled in size when it stocked six new entries with a 120-player expansion draft.

The proceedings at New York's Queen Elizabeth Hotel began with league President Clarence Campbell drawing the Los Angeles Kings' name out of the Stanley Cup and ended six hours later with the Kings, Philadelphia Flyers, Pittsburgh Penguins, St. Louis Blues, Minnesota North Stars and California Seals fully stocked and ready to play their first seasons in 1967–68.

The Kings used their first pick to select veteran Toronto goaltender Terry Sawchuk and the other new teams followed suit, picking goalies Glenn Hall (St. Louis), Bernie Parent (Philadelphia), Joe Daley (Pittsburgh), Cesare Maniago (Minnesota) and Charlie Hodge (California).

Each new entry, which paid a fee of $2 million, went on to select 20 players and the general feeling after the draft was that the six original franchises had not been overly generous. Most of the available players were journeymen and untried youngsters with marginal skills.

The six existing franchises are the Boston Bruins, New York Rangers, Montreal Canadiens, Toronto Maple Leafs, Chicago Blackhawks and Detroit Red Wings.

Glenn Hall, *the first draft selection of the expansion St. Louis Blues.*

MILESTONES IN SPORTS

1939

A major league-record five New York Giants – Harry Danning, Frank Demaree, Burgess Whitehead, Manuel Salvo and Joe Moore – pounded home runs in the fourth inning of a 17–3 victory over Cincinnati at the Polo Grounds.

1944

Most sports canceled schedules as the Allied forces began their D-day invasion of mainland Europe.

1946

The Basketball Association of America, forerunner to the NBA, was founded and Maurice Podoloff was named the league's first president.

1957

A thick fog at Brooklyn's Ebbets Field forced postponement of a game between the Dodgers and Chicago Cubs with Brooklyn leading, 1–0, in the second inning.

1964

Northern Dancer's bid for a Triple Crown came up short when he finished third behind Quadrangle and Roman Brother in the Belmont Stakes.

A STAR IS BORN

1907: Bill Dickey, a Hall of Fame catcher who batted .313 and helped the New York Yankees win seven World Series from 1932–43.

★ ★ ★

1935: Bobby Mitchell, a football Hall of Fame running back and wide receiver in an 11-year career that ended in 1968.

★ ★ ★

1956: Bjorn Borg, an outstanding Swedish tennis star who won five straight Wimbledon titles (1976–80) and six French Opens.

★ ★ ★

MILESTONES
· IN SPORTS ·

1960

Nat Holman, the 63-year-old dean of college basketball coaches, retired after 43 years at the helm of City College of New York.

1969

Majestic Prince, looking for the final jewel on his Triple Crown, finished $5^{1/2}$ lengths behind Arts and Letters in the Belmont Stakes.

1970

Australian champion Margaret Court reached the halfway point of her quest for a tennis grand slam when she defeated Helga Niessen, 6–2, 6–4, in the final of the French Open.

1975

Avatar and Bill Shoemaker turned the tables on Kentucky Derby winner Foolish Pleasure and Jacinto Vasquez, winning the Belmont Stakes by a neck in 2:28$^{1}/_{5}$.

1980

Eddie Maple rode 53–1 longshot Temperence Hill to a shocking two-length victory over filly Genuine Risk in the 112th running of the Belmont Stakes.

1980

Chris Evert-Lloyd captured her fourth French Open title with an easy 6–0, 6–3 victory over Virginia Ruzici.

A STAR IS BORN

1922: Rocky Graziano, a former world middleweight boxing champion (1946–47) who retired with a 67–10–6 record.

★ ★ ★

1947: Thurman Munson, a former Yankee.catcher and A.L MVP who was killed in a plane crash in 1979.

★ ★ ★

DEATH OF A LEGEND

1992: Bill France (auto racing).

1930 GALLANT FOX ENDS QUEST

Gallant Fox overcame drizzling rain, a muddy track and the frantic challenge of Whichone to post an impressive Belmont Stakes victory and claim the final jewel in his Triple Crown.

The William Woodward colt, with Earl Sande aboard, was up to all three challenges while adding the Belmont to his Kentucky Derby and Preakness Stakes victories and joining Sir Barton (1919) in the select circle of Triple Crown winners. And he made believers out of 40,000 Belmont patrons, who sent Harry Payne Whitney's Whichone off as a prohibitive favorite.

Critics claimed Gallant Fox had beaten weak fields in the Derby and Preakness while pointing out that Whichone had defeated him in their only other confrontation – the 1929 Futurity. But Sande rushed Gallant Fox into the early lead and he led wire to wire.

Whichone made a move on the final turn and pulled close on the stretch. But Gallant Fox suddenly burst forward and hit the finish line pulling away. His time was 2:31$^{3}/_{5}$ and his victory margin was four lengths. It was the fastest Belmont time since the race was lengthened to $1^{1}/_{2}$ miles in 1926.

1978 BULLETS BEAT SONICS

Wes Unseld sank two free throws with 12 seconds remaining and Bob Dandridge added a breakaway layup at the buzzer as the Washington Bullets defeated Seattle, 105–99, and claimed the franchise's first National Basketball Association championship in 30 years.

The Game 7 victory at the Seattle Coliseum did not come easily. The veteran Bullets held the lead from late in the opening quarter and owned a 13-point advantage going into the final stanza, but the young Sonics refused to die.

They pulled within 101–97 with 26 seconds remaining and fouled Unseld, the veteran center playing his last NBA season. Unseld missed two free throws and Paul Silas scored for Seattle off a rebound, cutting the Sonics' deficit to two. Unseld quickly was fouled again with 12 seconds left.

This time, however, he was up to the task, hitting two of three free throws. Dandridge's basket iced the victory that gave the Bullets their first NBA title since 1948, when the team was in Baltimore, and erased memories of four-game NBA Final losses in 1971 and '75. The Bullets also became the third NBA team to win a seventh game on the road.

Dandridge and Charley Johnson led Washington with 19 points apiece and Marvin Webster topped Seattle with 27.

JUNE 7

1941 WHIRLAWAY WINS CROWN

Jockey Eddie Arcaro unexpectedly pushed Whirlaway to a big lead at the half-mile mark and the Calumet Farm colt responded with a solid three-length victory over Robert Morris in a Belmont Stakes battle that provided the final jewel for his Triple Crown.

Whirlaway, a prohibitive favorite but a back-of-the-pack runner in his Kentucky Derby and Preakness Stakes victories, suddenly shot into the lead and opened an eight-length advantage down the backstretch. Robert Morris made his move at the start of the far turn and pulled close, but Whirlaway had plenty left for an inspiring stretch run that secured victory.

That run started on the turn when Whirlaway pulled wide and Robert Morris followed. The stretch chase was no contest, Whirlaway holding on for a 2:31 clocking and a victory that put him in Triple Crown company with Sir Barton, Gallant Fox, Omaha and War Admiral.

Warren Wright, owner of Whirlaway and Calumet Farms, was not on hand to witness the historic victory. He remained home to watch his son's graduation. Still, Wright gained $39,770 for the victory.

Wes Unseld, *center of attention for the Washington Bullets.*

JUNE

8

MILESTONES IN SPORTS

1950

29–4: The Boston Red Sox set major league records for runs and total bases (60) in their relentless pounding of the St. Louis Browns at Fenway Park.

1965

The Kansas City Athletics made Arizona State outfielder Rick Monday the No. 1 selection in baseball's first free-agent draft.

1974

Miguel Rivera coaxed Little Current to an impressive seven-length victory over Jolly Johu in a slow and one-sided Belmont Stakes. Little Current was clocked at 2:29 1/5.

1980

Sweden's Bjorn Borg posted a 6–4, 6–1, 6–2 victory over Vitas Gerulaitis and became the first five-time winner of the French Open tennis championship.

1980

South African Sally Little fired a final-round 73 and became the fourth non-American to win a major women's tournament, beating Jane Blalock by three strokes in the LPGA Championship at Mason, O.

1985

Creme Fraiche, with Eddie Maple in saddle, edged Stephan's Odyssey by half a length in the 117th running of the Belmont Stakes. Creme Fraiche's winning time was 2:27.

1966 AFL, NFL WILL MERGE

Peace was restored to football when the 47-year-old National Football League and the 7-year-old American Football League agreed to a merger that will be fully implemented in 1970, when the lucrative television contracts for both circuits run out.

The accord will result in a single league of at least 26 teams in 25 cities with the 15 existing NFL franchises joining forces with the nine AFL franchises and two new ones that will be added as soon as practical. Until 1970, the leagues will continue to operate in their present form.

They will, however, move toward the merger. The winners of each league will meet in a world championship game next January and inter-league preseason play will begin in 1967. The most important move will be a common draft that will eliminate the costly bidding wars for players – a major driving force behind the decision to merge.

The agreement requires the present AFL teams to pay the NFL clubs $18 million in principal and interest over a 20-year period and the NFL teams will receive the fees paid by the two new franchises.

NFL Commissioner Pete Rozelle will preside over the unified league.

1935 OMAHA WINS TRIPLE CROWN

Omaha, challenged in a grueling stretch duel by Firethorn, pulled away at the sixteenth pole to a 1 1/2-length victory in the Belmont Stakes—a Triple Crown-clinching triumph that allowed him to match the feat of his famous sire.

Omaha, the son of 1930 Triple Crown winner Gallant Fox, became the third horse to win the Kentucky Derby, Preakness Stakes and Belmont in the same year. And he did it on a raw, windy, wet day and on a sloppy track that was more to the liking of his chief rival.

The race was a tactical chess game, Willie Saunders keeping Omaha back in the pack until the final turn. But suddenly he turned the chestnut colt loose and he shot past leader Rosemont. Firethorn followed and pulled even with a quarter to go.

The colts ran neck and neck for a furlong before Firethorn began to tire and Omaha pulled away. He finished the 1 1/2-mile test in a respectable 2:30 3/5, thanks in large part to a blazing final quarter that was clocked in 0:25 3/5 and spelled doom for Firethorn backers.

Omaha earned $35,480 for owner William Woodward, who has bred two of the three Triple Crown winners.

1968 PHILLIES END DRYSDALE RUN

Don Drysdale *(right), who set a major league record with 58 consecutive scoreless innings, poses with fellow Los Angeles Dodger ace* **Sandy Koufax.**

A sacrifice fly by Philadelphia's Howie Bedell scored Tony Taylor in the fifth inning of a game at Dodger Stadium, ending Los Angeles righthander Don Drysdale's incredible record-setting scoreless-innings streak at 58.

Drysdale had received a standing ovation from 50,060 Dodger fans two innings earlier when he moved past the mark of 55 2/3 scoreless innings set by former Washington great Walter Johnson in 1913. He pitched a scoreless fourth before surrendering fifth-inning singles to Taylor and Clay Dalrymple and Bedell's RBI fly ball.

Drysdale had started his string on May 14 with a 1–0 shutout of the Chicago Cubs and then proceeded to blank St. Louis, Houston twice, San Francisco and Pittsburgh. The Phillies, buoyed by their fifth-inning success, went on to score two more runs off Drysdale before he was relieved in the seventh, but he received credit for a 5–3 victory – his eighth against three losses.

A STAR IS BORN

1912: Walter Kennedy, a former National Basketball Association commissioner.

★ ★ ★

1917: Byron (Whizzer) White, a college and professional football star who went on to a career in 1962 as a Supreme Court justice.

★ ★ ★

1939: Herb Adderley, a football Hall of Fame cornerback who intercepted 48 passes in a 12-year career t\hat ended in 1972.

★ ★ ★

DEATH OF A LEGEND

1982: Satchel Paige (baseball).

★ ★ ★

JUNE 9

MILESTONES • IN SPORTS •

1906

Boston 6, St. Louis 3: The Beaneaters' losing streak ended at 19 N.L. games.

1966

Five home runs in one inning: Rich Rollins, Zoilo Versalles, Tony Oliva, Don Mincher and Harmon Killebrew connected for Minnesota in a 9–4 victory over Kansas City.

1978

Larry Holmes claimed the World Boxing Council's heavyweight championship with a split decision over Ken Norton at Las Vegas.

1984

Laffit Pincay rode Swale to a four-length victory over Pine Circle in the Belmont Stakes, giving the Woody Stephens-trained colt two-thirds of a Triple Crown.

1990

Go And Go, with Michael Kinane in saddle, covered the $1\frac{1}{2}$-mile Belmont course in 2:27 $\frac{1}{5}$ and recorded an eight-length victory over Thirty Six Red.

1991

The London Monarchs scored a 21-0 victory over Barcelona at London's Wembley Stadium and captured the first World League of American Football championship.

A STAR IS BORN

1893: Emil (Irish) Meusel, a .310 hitter over 11 major league seasons from 1918–27.

★ ★ ★

1951: Dave Parker, a major league outfielder who batted .290 and collected 2,712 hits over a 19-year career that ended in 1991.

★ ★ ★

1973 SECRETARIAT GETS CROWN

Secretariat, running away from his Belmont Stakes competitors almost like they were standing still, streaked to a spine-tingling 31-length victory that earned him the first Triple Crown in a quarter of a century and left 69,138 fans gasping in amazement.

Without a challenge from the other 3-year-olds or much prodding from jockey Ron Turcotte, Secretariat roared down the stretch, widening his lead with every powerful stride. He crossed the finish line in 2:24, a track record and the fastest $1\frac{1}{2}$ miles ever run on an American dirt course.

The 31 lengths were the largest margin of victory ever posted in the Belmont and the victory gave him a sweep of the Kentucky Derby, Preakness Stakes and Belmont – the first Triple crown since Citation turned the trick in 1948. The victory also was Big Red's 12th in 15 career races.

The Meadow Stable product, a son of Bold Ruler, got only a brief challenge from Sham, the second-place finisher in both the Derby and Preakness. He took control of the race at the three-quarter pole and really turned on the jets. Twice A Prince finished a distant second.

1979 BID'S BID FAILS

Disconsolate jockey **Ron Franklin.**

Spectacular Bid, attempting to become the third Triple Crown winner in three years and 12th overall, sagged to a disappointing third-place finish in the Belmont Stakes behind upset villains Coastal and Golden Act.

Spectacular Bid had not lost in 10 months and had won 14 of 16 career races, leaving disappointed backers to point fingers at 19-year-old jockey Ron Franklin. Franklin, who had held the colt back and used late surges to win the Kentucky Derby and Preakness, ran him out to an early lead in the $1\frac{1}{2}$-mile Belmont and couldn't hold on at the end.

Spectacular Bid took the lead with more than a mile to go and held it until one-eighth mile remained. That's when Coastal, undefeated in four races as a 3-year-old, surged past him on the rail and Golden Act followed, nosing him out for second-place money.

Ruben Hernandez brought Coastal home in 2:28$\frac{3}{5}$.

1985 LAKERS SNAP JINX

Kareem Abdul-Jabbar scored 29 points and James Worthy added 28 as the Los Angeles Lakers wiped out 26 years of frustration against arch-rival Boston with a 111–100 victory that gave them their second National Basketball Association championship in four years.

The Game 6 triumph at Boston Garden completed the Lakers' first NBA Finals victory over the Celtics in nine tries dating back to 1959. It also denied Boston its chance to become the NBA's first repeat champion since 1969. The loss was only the second for the Celtics in a total of 17 championship series.

Despite an off shooting night by its guards and center Robert Parish, Boston played the Lakers to a 55–55 halftime deadlock. But the Lakers took control after intermission by hitting six straight shots. The 38-year-old Abdul-Jabbar foiled the Celtics' comeback attempt with three crucial baskets in the final $2\frac{1}{2}$ minutes.

The Celtics were able to stay in the game on the shooting of Kevin McHale (32 points) and Larry Bird (28).

Los Angeles Lakers forward **James Worthy.**

JUNE

10

A STAR IS BORN

1951: Dan Fouts, a National Football League quarterback who passed for 43,040 yards and 254 touchdowns during a 15-year San Diego career that ended in 1987.

★ ★ ★

DEATH OF A LEGEND

1946: Jack Johnson (boxing).

★ ★ ★

1977 GEIBERGER SHOOTS 59

Veteran Al Geiberger, performing in his typical slow-moving, take-things-as-they-come manner, wrote his name into the golf record books when he carded an amazing 59 during the second round of the Memphis Golf Classic – the first sub-60 round in a PGA-sponsored event.

Geiberger was unconscious as he cruised around the 7,193-yard Colonial Country Club course with 11 birdies and an eagle, breaking the previous professional mark of 60 shared by six golfers. He shot a front-nine 30 and a back-nine 29, dropping an eight-foot birdie putt on 18 for the record.

The lanky 39-year-old played one incredible seven-hole stretch in 8-under par – six birdies and an eagle. He missed a 12-foot putt following that string that would have tied Bob Goalby's professional record of eight consecutive birdies. His hot streak included a pitch-in and putts of 18 and 20 feet.

Several golfers had shot 59s, but never in a PGA event. Six golfers, including the great Sam Snead, had shot 60s in PGA events, but they were all on shorter courses in the 1950s. Geiberger's 13-under-par effort, coupled with his first-round 72, gave him a six-stroke advantage over Keith Fergus, who shot a 67.

1978 AFFIRMED JOINS SELECT CIRCLE

Affirmed, never in control but usually in first place at the finish line, scored his third straight narrow victory over arch-rival Alydar in the Belmont Stakes and claimed the 11th Triple Crown in horse racing history.

Affirmed had beaten Alydar by 1$^{1}/_{2}$ lengths in the Kentucky Derby and by a neck in the Preakness Stakes, setting up an interesting showdown in the Belmont. And true to form, the outstanding 3-year-olds pulled away from the rest of the pack on the backstretch and ran side by side the rest of the way, jockey Steve Cauthen pushing Affirmed forward by a head at the finish line.

Affirmed covered the 1$^{3}/_{16}$-mile course in 2:26$^{4}/_{5}$, the third fastest time in Belmont history. As he hit the finish line, Cauthen stood triumphantly in the stirrups and waved to the crowd.

Affirmed scored his seventh victory over Alydar in nine career meetings – most of them in similar fashion to his Belmont victory. Affirmed's Triple Crown was the third in six years after a stretch of 25 years without one.

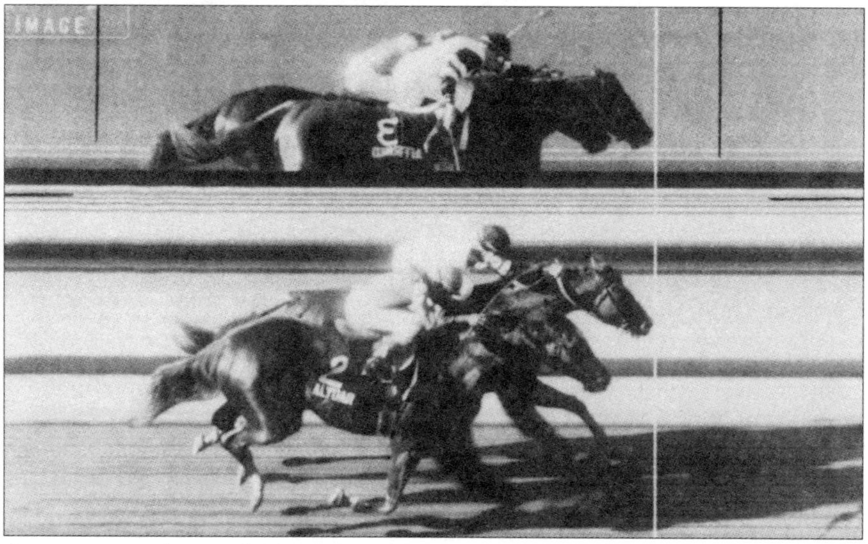

A mirror image photograph (above) shows how close **Affirmed's** *victory over* **Alydar** *really was.*

1989 GRAF'S STREAK ENDS

Arantxa Sanchez, a 17-year-old Spaniard looking for her first major tennis title, shocked two-time defending champion Steffi Graf, 7–6, 3–6, 7–5, in the final of the French Open and derailed the West German's hopes of winning a second straight Grand Slam.

Graf had not lost a Grand Slam match since falling to Martina Navratilova in the U.S. Open 21 months earlier. She appeared too much for Sanchez when she got to set point (6–5) in the opening set tiebreaker.

But the youngster fought gamely, evening the count at 6–6, and winning the tiebreaker, 8–6. And then, after being dominated in the second set, Sanchez fought back from 5–3 with a pair of third-set service breaks and claimed an unlikely victory over the best female player in the world while becoming the youngest winner in the event's history.

MILESTONES • IN SPORTS •

1944

St. Louis showed no mercy to Cincinnati lefthander Joe Nuxhall, who became the youngest player in major league history (15 years, 10 months) when he pitched 2/3 of an inning in an 18–0 loss to the Cardinals.

1948

Former middleweight champion Tony Zale regained his lost title when he knocked out Rocky Graziano in the third round of a fight at Newark, N.J.

1959

Cleveland's Rocky Colavito became the eighth major leaguer to blast four home runs in one game, hitting his consecutively in an 11–8 victory over the Orioles at Baltimore's Memorial Stadium.

1972

Atlanta's Hank Aaron moved into second place on baseball's all-time list with home run No. 649 – his N.L. record-tying 14th grand slam. The Braves beat Philadelphia, 15–3.

1981

Great Britain's Sebastian Coe ran 800 meters in a world-record time of 1:41.72 in an international track meet at Florence, Italy.

1989

Sunday Silence and jockey Pat Valenzuela fell eight lengths short in their bid for a Triple Crown, finishing second to Easy Goer in the Belmont Stakes.

1991

Denver and Miami interests became proud owners of major league baseball franchises, which were scheduled to begin National League play in 1993.

A STAR IS BORN

1879: Roger Bresnahan, a Hall of Fame catcher from 1897–1915 and the man credited with introducing shin guards.

★ ★ ★

1903: Ernie Nevers, a football Hall of Fame fullback who set the long-standing NFL record of 40 points in one game. He played only five NFL seasons, from 1926–31.

★ ★ ★

1913: Vince Lombardi, the football Hall of Fame coach who guided Green Bay to three NFL championships and consecutive Super Bowl victories in the 1960s while compiling a 106–36–6 mark.

★ ★ ★

1939: Jackie Stewart, a Scottish race car driver who ranks second on the all-time list for Formula 1 victories.

★ ★ ★

1956: Joe Montana, a current National Football League quarterback.

★ ★ ★

1977

UNDEFEATED SLEW WINS TRIPLE CROWN

Seattle Slew, attempting to become the first undefeated Triple Crown champion in horse racing history, romped to a four-length victory over Run Dusty Run in the 109th running of the Belmont Stakes.

Jean Cruguet *and* **Seattle Slew** *lead the pack around the final turn en route to a Triple Crown-clinching victory in the Belmont Stakes.*

Jockey Jean Cruguet broke Seattle Slew into a quick lead on the muddy track and, for all intents and purposes, the race was over. An extremely slow early pace that didn't produce any challengers worked in his favor and the fast-closing son of Bold Reasoning had no problem coasting to a 2:29 3/5 clocking – the slowest winning time since 1971.

With 70,229 Belmont Park fans cheering him on, Cruguet stood up in the stirrups 20 yards before the finish and began celebrating the 10th Triple Crown in racing history.

The victory was Seattle Slew's ninth in as many outings in a career carefully planned and executed by owners Karen and Mickey Taylor and trainer Billy Turner.

JUNE

11

MILESTONES IN SPORTS

1919

First Triple Crown winner: Johnny Loftus rode Sir Barton to a five-length victory over Sweep On, completing their sweep of the Kentucky Derby, Preakness Stakes and Belmont Stakes.

1960

Celtic Ash, an English-bred longshot with Bill Hartack in saddle, captured the 92nd Belmont Stakes in 2:29 3/5, beating Venetian Way by 5 1/2 lengths.

1977

Edwin Moses ran the 400-meter hurdles in a world-record 47.45 during competition in the AAU national championships at Los Angeles.

1990

Texas' Nolan Ryan added to his growing legacy with his record sixth no-hitter – a 5–0 victory at Oakland. He became the oldest pitcher (43) to throw a no-hitter and the first to do it for three different teams.

1950

'NEW' HOGAN WINS OPEN

Ben Hogan, defying the odds and predictions he would never play golf again, completed his amazing comeback from a near-fatal 1949 automobile accident with a playoff-round 69 that earned him a second U.S. Open championship.

Hogan sealed his inspirational victory when he rolled in a 50-foot birdie putt on 17, opening a four-stroke lead over Lloyd Mangrum (73) and George Fazio (75). His victory was aided by a two-stroke penalty assessed Mangrum on the 16th green when, trailing by a stroke, he lifted his ball to get rid of a bug.

Hogan had nearly clinched the victory in regulation, but the double round over the Merion Golf Club course in Ardmore, Pa., took its toll and he lost a three-stroke lead over the final six holes.

After the accident, Hogan had undergone an abdominal operation in which doctors tied off blood vessels in his legs. He had not walked 36 holes since his January return and he was tired and in obvious pain when he reached the clubhouse.

But Hogan appeared refreshed and relaxed when he teed off the next day and he left no doubt he still was the No. 1 player in the world.

Open champion **Ben Hogan.**

1989

CHANG PULLS UPSET

Michael Chang completed his uphill climb to a first major professional championship when he rallied to defeat Stefan Edberg, 6–1, 3–6, 4–6, 6–4, 6–2, in the final of the French Open, becoming the first American to win the Grand Slam event since 1955.

The 17-year-old Chang also was the youngest man ever to win a Grand Slam title and he did it with a string of upsets after entering the tournament as the 15th seed. His earlier victory over Ivan Lendl probably was more dramatic, but beating the third-seeded Edberg was the crowning blow.

As he did through the entire tournament, Chang rallied from a seemingly impossible deficit. This time he trailed two sets to one and needed several crucial rallies in the fourth set to stave off elimination. But in the end, his passing shots and hard service returns outclassed Edberg's serve-and-volley strategy in a 3-hour, 41-minute endurance test.

JUNE

12

1930 FOUL! A NEW CHAMP

Max Schmeling, who had to be carried from the ring by his handlers after being felled by a low blow from Jack Sharkey, was awarded the world heavyweight championship – the first time the prestigious title ever was claimed on a foul.

The conclusion of the bout at New York's Yankee Stadium, staged to decide a successor to retired champion Gene Tunney, left 80,000 fans confused and upset. Sharkey had appeared to be well on his way to victory as the fourth round came to a close, but Schmeling suddenly tumbled to the canvas – courtesy of an obvious below-the-belt shot from Sharkey.

As the German writhed in pain, referee Jim Crowley consulted with judge Harold Barnes, who said the blow indeed was a foul. Crowley hesitated as the bell signaled the end of the round and then checked again with Barnes as Schmeling's handlers pleaded for a call.

When Sharkey finally was disqualified, he sat disconsolately in his corner as pandemonium broke out. Schmeling became the first European to win a heavyweight championship.

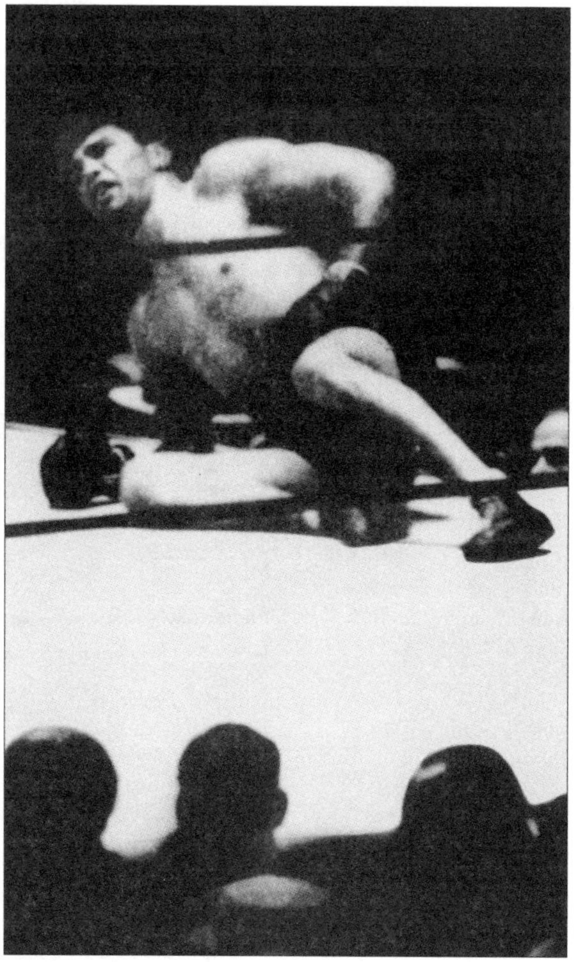

Heavyweight challenger **Max Schmeling** *writhes in pain after being felled by a low blow from* **Jack Sharkey.**

1991 BULLS EARN NBA TITLE

Michael Jordan and Scottie Pippen combined for 62 points and the Chicago Bulls ended 25 years of frustration by beating Los Angeles, 108–101, and claiming their first National Basketball Association championship.

The Game 5 victory at the Los Angeles Forum was Chicago's fourth straight after losing the series opener and it culminated a 15–2 playoff run that featured a smothering defensive effort and some dazzling offense.

Jordan scored 30 points and added 10 assists in the clincher while Pippen enjoyed a 32-point, 13-rebound, seven-assist, five-steal night. But the biggest thorn in the Lakers' side was guard John Paxson, who made 9 of 12 shots, finished with 20 points and scored five baskets in the final six minutes to seal the verdict.

After the Lakers had tied at 93–93, Paxson made two jump shots and a layup to put the Bulls up by six. He made another jumper from the top of the key with 1:58 remaining and an 18-footer that stretched the Bulls' lead to 105–101 after Los Angeles had crept within two.

The Lakers, who played without injured starters James Worthy and Byron Scott, got a 16-point, 20-assist, 11-rebound effort from Magic Johnson.

1948 CITATION WINS TRIPLE CROWN

Calumet Farm's Citation, emphatically justifying his status as a 1–5 favorite, ran away from the field in the 80th running of the Belmont Stakes and claimed the eighth Triple Crown in horse racing history.

Citation stumbled out of the starting gate, but that was the only mistake he made. Eddie Arcaro quickly urged him into the lead where he ran neck and neck with Faraway before surging ahead to stay at the seven-furlong pole. From there it was a race against the clock and again Citation won.

He finished at 2:28 1/5, matching the fastest-ever time for the 1 1/2-mile Belmont – Triple Crown-winner Count Fleet's 1943 record. His final victory margin was eight lengths over Better Self.

The victory was Arcaro's fourth in the Belmont Stakes and the Triple Crown was the second for Calumet Farm owner Warren Wright. The first Calumet Farm colt to win the Kentucky Derby, Preakness Stakes and Belmont was Whirlaway in 1941.

The victory was Citation's 18th in 20 career starts and earned Wright $77,700.

MILESTONES • IN SPORTS •

1920

The great Man o'War, with Clarence Kummer in saddle, set a world record for 1 3/8 miles (2:14 1/5) while scoring a wire-to-wire victory in the Belmont Stakes.

1939

Baseball dignitaries and fans gathered in Cooperstown, N.Y., to induct the Hall of Fame's first class and dedicate its newly-constructed museum and Doubleday Field. Baseball Commissioner Kenesaw Mountain Landis presided over the festivities.

1948

Ben Hogan earned his first U.S. Open championship with a two-shot victory over Jimmy Demaret at Los Angeles' Riviera Country Club.

1981

Major league players brought the baseball season to a skidding halt when they went on strike against owners who refused to budge on the sticky free-agent compensation issue.

1981

Larry Holmes defended his heavyweight crown with an easy third-round technical knockout of former champion Leon Spinks in a fight at Detroit.

1990

Baltimore shortstop Cal Ripken moved into second place on baseball's all-time iron man list, playing in his 1,308th consecutive game and passing Everett Scott.

A STAR IS BORN

1956: Mario Soto, a righthanded pitcher who won 100 games from 1977–88 for the Cincinnati Reds.

★ ★ ★

1935 Braddock Pulls Major Upset

Max Baer *and* **James J. Braddock** *trade blows during their heavyweight championship fight in New York.*

James J. Braddock, a down-and-out fighter who was on the New Jersey relief rolls a year earlier, pulled off a stunning upset of heavyweight champion Max Baer with a unanimous 15-round decision at New York's Madison Square Garden Bowl.

The 29-year-old Braddock, a journeyman fighter who had worked briefly as a longshoreman before launching his comeback, entered the fight as one of the heaviest underdogs in heavyweight title-fight history. And his plodding, awkward performance against Baer did little to win over opinion on his abilities as a fighter.

But courage and determination, qualities Braddock does possess, were enough to overcome Baer, who spent much of the fight clowning and little of it acting like a heavyweight champion.

Baer was lethargic for the first six rounds and Braddock plodded his way to a decisive edge. Baer picked up the pace in the seventh and launched a vicious body attack in the late rounds, but it was too little too late.

Milestones in Sports

1912

New York Giants righthander Christy Mathewson earned his 300th career victory when he handcuffed the Chicago Cubs, 3–2.

1924

The New York Yankees were awarded a 9–0 forfeit victory over the Tigers when Detroit fans rioted in response to a Yankee-Tiger beanball fight.

1953

Native Dancer claimed two-thirds of a Triple Crown with a neck victory over Jamie K. in the Belmont Stakes.

1970

Billie Jean King led the United States to a 4-3 Wightman Cup victory over England – the Americans' 35th in 42 Cup competitions.

1991

A bolt of lightning killed Bill Fadell, a 27-year-old spectator, during the first round of the U.S. Open at Chaska, Minn.

1953 Hogan Wins Fourth Open

Ben Hogan, winning for the fourth time in five 1953 outings, tamed the difficult Oakmont (Pa.) Country Club course with a final-round 71 and claimed his fourth U.S. Open championship with a six-stroke victory over Sam Snead.

Hogan, who shot a final-day 73–71 for a 283 total, became only the third golfer to win the prestigious event four times and the first since Bobby Jones won his fourth in 1930. Starting the final round with a one-shot lead over Snead, he carved out a magnificent back-nine 33 that produced the runaway.

Hogan closed the day with a birdie 3 that brought a roar of approval from the gallery. That added the U.S. Open to 1953 victories in the Masters, the Pan-American and the Colonial in his home state of Texas. His only loss of the year was in the Greenbrier Open – to Snead.

While Hogan was distancing himself from the field, Snead was struggling to a final-round 76.

The 40-year-old Hogan previously had won U.S. Opens in 1948, '50 and '51.

June 13

A Star Is Born

1897: Paavo Nurmi, the Finnish distance runner who won nine gold medals at the 1920, '24 and '28 Olympic Games.

★ ★ ★

1903: Red Grange, a football Hall of Fame halfback for Illinois who became a major attraction for the NFL during its formative years.

★ ★ ★

1915: Don Budge, the tennis great best remembered for his unprecedented 1938 grand slam feat – victories in the Australian, Wimbledon, French and U.S. championships in the same year.

★ ★ ★

Death of a Legend

1989: Judy Johnson (baseball).

1989 Pistons Claim NBA Crown

Backup center James Edwards scored 13 fourth-quarter points as the Detroit Pistons rallied for a 105–97 victory over the Los Angeles Lakers and captured their first NBA championship, ending four decades of frustration dating back to the franchise's days in Fort Wayne, Ind.

The four-game sweep, the fifth in the history of NBA Finals play, ended the two-year championship reign of the Lakers and the brilliant career of 42-year-old center Kareem Abdul-Jabbar.

When the NBA's all-time leading scorer was removed with 19 seconds remaining, the crowd of 17,505 at the Los Angeles Forum gave him a rousing ovation.

By then, the Pistons were ready to do a little celebrating of their own. They had rallied from a 16-point first-quarter deficit with the same formula that had carried them through the season – a smothering defense and outstanding guard play.

Joe Dumars, Isiah Thomas and Vinnie Johnson combined for 51 points and the Pistons completed their playoff run with a record for fewest points allowed – 92.9 per game. James Worthy scored 40 for the Lakers, who played without injured Magic Johnson and Byron Scott.

The NBA champion **Detroit Pistons.**

JUNE

14

1991 BURRELL SETS RECORD

Leroy Burrell, shooting out of the starting blocks like a well-timed rocket, streaked to a world-record clocking of 9.90 in the 100-meter dash and further entrenched himself as the world's fastest human.

Burrell, running in the Mobil national track and field championships at Randalls Island, N.Y., edged fellow American and Santa Monica Track Club teammate Carl Lewis by a foot in the exciting final at Downing Stadium.

Lewis, who set the previous world record of 9.92 in the 1988 Olympic Games at Seoul, South Korea, was timed at 9.93.

With a slight tail wind aiding his run, the 24-year-old Burrell broke out of the blocks like a shot and established a lead in the first 10 meters. He stretched it to about 4 meters halfway through the race and then held off Lewis' patented big kick at the finish line.

"It's hard to explain how I feel," Burrell said after the race.

"I'm so overwhelmed by the whole thing. there are so many emotions flowing through me right now that I can't describe the feeling."

The victory was Burrell's third in nine races against Lewis, but his third in the last four. Burrell, who was ranked No. 1 in the world for most of last year, had a previous best time of 9.94.

1990 PISTONS DO IT AGAIN

Vinnie Johnson hit a 14-foot jump shot with less than one second remaining and the Detroit Pistons joined an elite list of National Basketball Association champions with a 92–90 victory over the Trail Blazers at Portland.

The five-game victory gave the Pistons back-to-back titles and allowed them to join the Celtics and Lakers as the only franchises to win two or more consecutive championships. And this one ended dramatically, thanks to the clutch final-quarter play of Johnson and Isiah Thomas.

The Pistons trailed, 90–83, with two minutes remaining when Johnson went to work. He hit a 12-foot jumper, added a free throw and sank a 10-footer to cut Detroit's deficit to 90–88. Thomas tied the score with 36 seconds to go on an 18-foot jumper.

After an errant Portland pass put the Pistons in position to win, Johnson scored the last of his 15 fourth-quarter points to seal the victory. Thomas led the Pistons with 29.

Hot-shooting Detroit guard **Vinnie Johnson.**

MILESTONES IN SPORTS

1934

Max Baer claimed Primo Carnera's heavyweight title when he scored an 11th-round technical knockout over the big Italian in a fight at Long Island, N.Y.

1965

Cincinnati's Jim Maloney no-hit New York for 10 innings and struck out 18, but the Mets won in the 11th when Johnny Lewis touched the righthander for a game-winning home run.

1980

Hubert Green, competing in the third round of the U.S. Open at Baltusrol Golf Club in Springfield, N.J., fired a PGA-record eight consecutive 3s – five birdies and three pars.

1981

Donna Caponi scored a dramatic victory in the LPGA Championship when she dropped an 18-foot birdie putt on the 18th hole and beat Jerilyn Britz and Pat Meyers by one stroke at Kings Island, O.

1992

The Chicago Bulls, down by 15 points in the fourth quarter, rallied for a 97–93 victory over Portland and claimed their second consecutive NBA championship in six games.

1987 LAKERS DEFEAT CELTICS

The Los Angeles Lakers, trailing old nemesis Boston by five points at intermission, outscored the Celtics, 30–12, in an inspired third quarter and claimed their fourth National Basketball Association title of the decade with a 106–93 win at the Forum.

The third period of the Game 6 showdown was a personal showcase for Lakers point guard Magic Johnson, who contributed 14 points, 4 assists and 4 rebounds to the critical surge. The Lakers carried an 81–68 margin into the final quarter and turned matters over to 40-year-old Kareem Abdul-Jabbar, who scored 14 of his 42 points while grabbing six rebounds and blocking four shots.

The game was decided by the third-quarter aggressiveness of the younger and quicker Lakers. Four high-scoring Celtics – Larry Bird, Kevin McHale, Robert Parish and Danny Ainge – combined for two points in the period and Boston missed 24 of its first 32 shots in the second half.

Dennis Johnson scored 33 for Boston, but Bird was held to 16 and missed 9 of 12 shots in one stretch.

A STAR IS BORN

1926: Don Newcombe, a righthander who won 149 games for the Brooklyn and Los Angeles Dodgers from 1949–60.

★ ★ ★

1958: Eric Heiden, a three-time world champion speed skater who set an Olympic Winter Games record by winning five gold medals in 1980.

★ ★ ★

1969: Steffi Graf, a current tennis star and a 1988 winner of the women's grand slam.

MILESTONES IN SPORTS

1902

Nig Clarke blasted a professional-record eight home runs as his Corsicana team destroyed Texarkana, 51–3, in a Class B Texas League game.

1925

The Philadelphia Athletics, trailing Cleveland 15–4 after seven innings, pulled off one of baseball's greatest comebacks when they scored 13 runs in the eighth and claimed a 17–15 victory.

1948

An A.L. last: Detroit defeated Philadelphia, 4-1, in the first night game at Briggs Stadium.

1953

The St. Louis Browns snapped their 14-game losing streak and New York's 18-game winning run with a 3–1 victory.

1992

Boston reliever Jeff Reardon became baseball's all-time save leader when he recorded No. 342 in the Red Sox's 1–0 victory over New York.

1938 He's Johnny On the Spot

Cincinnati double no-hit ace **Johnny Vander Meer.**

Cincinnati lefty Johnny Vander Meer, battling his control and an emotional group of Dodgers in the first night game at Brooklyn's Ebbets Field, stunned the baseball world by firing his second consecutive no-hitter.

In a feat that may never even be challenged, much less equaled, Vander Meer struck out seven and extended his hitless-innings streak to $18\frac{1}{3}$ as he pitched the Reds'to a 6-0 victory. Five days earlier, in the daylight of Cincinnati, the fireballing 22-year-old had no-hit the Boston Bees, 3–0.

His only hurdle in the first night game outside of Cincinnati was his own wildness.

He took a 4–0 lead and a no-hitter into the seventh and pitched around two walks. He carried his gem into the ninth and again had problems finding the strike zone, walking the bases loaded with one out.

But with his shutout and his shot at baseball immortality on the line, Vander Meer buckled down. He induced Ernie Koy to bounce into a force at the plate and completed his no-hit deuce by getting Dodger's shortstop Leo Durocher on a fly ball.

Before Vander Meer's stunning feat, no pitcher had ever thrown more than one no-hitter in a single season.

JUNE 15

A STAR IS BORN

1938: Billy Williams, a Hall of Fame outfielder who batted .290, collected 2,711 hits and blasted 426 home runs in an 18-year career that ended in 1976.

★ ★ ★

1957: Brett Butler, a current major league outfielder.

★ ★ ★

1958: Wade Boggs, a current major league third baseman.

★ ★ ★

DEATH OF A LEGEND

1968: Sam Crawford (baseball).

★ ★ ★

1976: Jimmie Dykes (baseball).

★ ★ ★

1991: A.B. (Happy) Chandler (baseball).

★ ★ ★

1992: Eddie Lopat (baseball).

★ ★ ★

1980 Jack Wins Again

Ending whispers that he no longer could win on the PGA Tour, 40-year-old Jack Nicklaus fired a final-round 68 and claimed his record-tying fourth U.S. Open golf championship, beating Japan's Isao Aoki by two strokes and breaking his own tournament record with a four-round total of 272.

Nicklaus, who opened the event with a record-tying 63, either led or shared the lead all four rounds en route to his record 18th major tournament victory. The triumph was his first since 1978, when he won the British Open and Philadelphia Classic in back-to-back weeks.

Nicklaus and Aoki were tied entering the final round at the Lower Course of the Baltusrol Golf Club in Springfield, N.J., but Aoki's ninth-hole bogey gave Nicklaus a two-stroke lead and he maintained that advantage to the end. Not, however, without a major challenge.

Nicklaus had to birdie both the 17th and 18th holes, matching Aoki, to seal the victory that allowed him to join Willie Anderson, Bobby Jones and Ben Hogan as the only other four-time Open winners.

1949 Fan Shoots Eddie Waitkus

A 19-year-old Chicago typist who told police she wanted to do something exciting in her life shot and seriously wounded Philadelphia first baseman Eddie Waitkus in a bizarre incident at a local hotel where the Phillies were staying during a series with the Cubs .

Ruth Steinhagen, who reportedly has had a crush on Waitkus dating back to his three full seasons with the Cubs, lured him to a room at the Edgewater Beach Hotel with an urgent note and then shot him with a rifle at close range as he sat in a chair.

Waitkus was rushed to a hospital where doctors removed the bullet and stopped the bleeding. His condition was described as serious, but stable.

Steinhagen's mother and friends described her as "obsessive" about Waitkus, to the point of threatening to move to Philadelphia in the offseason when he was traded by the Cubs. She had written him letters and visited two psychiatrists about her obsession.

Eddie Waitkus *meets the press in Philadelphia.*

JUNE

16

1951 HOGAN TAMES OPEN MONSTER

Ben Hogan, finally taming "the hardest course I have ever played," stormed back from a two-stroke final-round deficit with a 67 and claimed his second consecutive U.S. Open golf championship – a two-stroke victory over Clayton Heafner that added another chapter to his amazing comeback story.

Hogan's 18th-hole birdie completed a final round that produced the tournament's first sub-par score over the 6,927-yard Oakland Hills Country Club course in Birmingham, Mich. Coupled with his 71 earlier in the day, Hogan finished with a 287 that secured his third U.S. Open triumph.

It also gave him a second straight title after a near-fatal 1949 automobile accident had threatened his career. The talented Texan had opened with a 76 and 73 that left him discouraged and five strokes behind co-leaders Bobby Locke and Jimmy Demaret.

But Hogan was in top form in Saturday's double round and his opening 71 threatened par and served notice something special was about to transpire. His front-nine 32 shot him into the lead and he waited an hour and a half after his final putt as Heafner and Locke fell short in their comeback bids.

MILESTONES
·IN SPORTS·

1934

Glenn Cunningham posted the fastest mile in history when he ran 4:06.7 at Princeton's Palmer Stadium.

1960

The Cleveland Indians signed lefthander Sam McDowell, who pitched 40 no-hitters in his high school career, for a reported bonus of $75,000.

1985

Andy North posted a final-round 74, for a 72-hole 279 and a one-stroke victory in the U.S. Open at Birmingham, Mich.

1989

Doug Weaver, Mark Wiebe, Jerry Pate and Nick Price all scored second-round holes-in-one off the sixth tee at the Oak Hill Country Club in Rochester, N.Y.

1975 LAKERS GET A BIG MAN

The Los Angeles Lakers, coming off a last-place finish in the National Basketball Association's Pacific Division, turned from pretenders to contenders when they traded four players to Milwaukee for 7-foot-2 center Kareem Abdul-Jabbar and backup center Walt Wesley.

The deal gives Los Angeles a major force in the middle of its lineup and puts the Lakers on track to contend for their first NBA title since 1972. They had to give up veterans Elmore Smith and Brian Winters and youngsters Dave Meyers and Junior Bridgeman to obtain the 28-year-old Abdul-Jabbar, who led the Bucks to a 1970–71 championship.

Abdul-Jabbar, approaching free agency and unhappy in Milwaukee, had requested a trade to either the New York Knicks or the Lakers. He grew up and played his high school basketball in New York. He played collegiately at UCLA.

Abdul-Jabbar missed 17 games with an injury in 1974–75 and the Bucks finished at 38–44.

New Los Angeles Lakers acquisition **Kareem Abdul-Jabbar.**

A STAR IS BORN

1916: Hank Luisetti, the former Stanford All-America basketball star who is credited with introducing the one-hand shot.

★★★

1951: Roberto Duran, a Panamanian boxer who held titles in four weight divisions from 1972-90. He finished with an 86–9–0 record.

★★★

1958: Darrell Griffith, a high-flying forward who led Louisville to the 1980 NCAA Tournament championship before playing eight seasons with the NBA's Utah Jazz.

★★★

1961: Steve Larmer, a current National Hockey League right winger.

★★★

1962: Wally Joyner, a current major league first baseman.

★★★

1968 TREVINO TAKES MAJOR STEP

Lee Trevino, the self-professed Merry Mexican with a quip for every occasion, shot a final-round 69 and earned his first PGA Tour victory – a four-stroke triumph over Jack Nicklaus in the U.S. Open at Rochester, N.Y.

The former $30-per-week assistant pro at a course in Horizon City, Tex., broke a final-round tie with Bert Yancey when he parred the ninth hole of the Oak Hill Country Club course and he steadily stretched his lead over the back nine en route to his $30,000 payday.

He compiled his record-matching total of 275 with four sub-par rounds – the first time in 68 years of U.S. Open play that anybody had broken par four times. The 28-year-old Trevino joined Nicklaus and Jack Fleck as golfers to score their first victories in the Open.

Yancey had set the pace over the first three rounds, but the former West Pointer soared to a final-round 76 and finished third. Nicklaus, the defending champion, concluded with a 67.

U.S. Open champion **Lee Trevino.**

A STAR IS BORN

1923: Elroy (Crazylegs) Hirsch, a football Hall of Fame halfback and end for 12 NFL seasons from 1946–57.

★ ★ ★

1940: Bobby Bell, a football Hall of Fame linebacker who played from 1963–74 with the Kansas City Chiefs in the AFL and NFL.

★ ★ ★

1948: Dave Concepcion, a smooth-fielding shortstop who collected 2,326 hits in his 19-year career (1970–88) with the Cincinnati Reds.

★ ★ ★

DEATH OF A LEGEND

1987: Dick Howser (baseball).

★ ★ ★

1989: John Matuszak (football).

1973 Miller Fires 63, Captures U.S. Open

Johnny Miller, six strokes behind the leaders and apparently out of contention after a third-round 76, blazed around the Oakmont (Pa.) Country Club course with a U.S. Open-record 63 and claimed the prestigious title by one stroke over John Schlee.

Miller's nine-birdie, 29-putt performance produced one of the most dramatic conclusions in the storied history of the event. He had opened play six strokes behind co-leaders Julius Boros, Jerry Heard, Arnold Palmer and Schlee, but one by one they fell by the wayside.

Mostly it was a case of the blond Californian taking control. He birdied the first four holes, bogeyed No. 8 and birdied 9, 11, 12 and 13. Pars at 14 through 18 capped the lowest round ever recorded in 70 years of Open play.

When he finished, Miller had to wait as the various contenders came up short in their bids to catch him. Schlee provided the best challenge, but a two-stroke penalty on a first-hole unplayable lie ended up costing him a victory.

JUNE 17

MILESTONES • IN SPORTS •

1943

Boston Red Sox player-manager Joe Cronin performed an unprecedented double when he pinch-hit three-run homers in both ends of a doubleheader against Philadelphia at Fenway Park.

1954

Rocky Marciano made his third successful heavyweight title defense, scoring a unanimous decision over Ezzard Charles at New York's Yankee Stadium.

1960

Boston's Ted Williams became the fourth major leaguer to hit 500 home runs when he connected off Wynn Hawkins in a 3–1 victory at Cleveland.

1987

Less than two years after managing the Royals to their first World Series championship, Dick Howser died of brain cancer in a Kansas City hospital. He was 51.

1991

Payne Stewart struggled to a playoff-round 75 at the Hazeltine National Golf Club in Chaska, Minn., but that was good enough for a two-stroke U.S. Open victory over Scott Simpson.

1976 NBA, ABA Merge

The American Basketball Association, plagued by bad debts, lawsuits, unstable ownerships and fast-moving franchises, ended its colorful nine-year existence when it agreed to merge with the rival National Basketball Association.

Peace came to professional basketball when four teams were absorbed into the expanding NBA and two were dismantled. With the addition of the three-time ABA-champion Indiana Pacers, New York Nets, Denver Nuggets and San Antonio Spurs, the NBA becomes a 22-team circuit for the 1976–77 season.

The move will cost the Nets, Pacers, Nuggets and Spurs \$3.2 million apiece with the Kentucky Colonels and St. Louis Spirits agreeing to discontinue operations. Those six teams were all that was left of the 11-team circuit that began play in 1967–68.

1962 Young Nicklaus Defeats Palmer in Open Playoff

Arnold Palmer, *in a not-so-victorious moment.*

Young Jack Nicklaus, cooly fending off Arnold Palmer and his vociferous, taunting fans, fired a playoff-round 71 and became the first PGA Tour rookie to win a U.S. Open championship.

The 22-year-old Ohioan refused to let either the Palmer mystique or the shouts of "Come on Arnie" from the 11,000-strong gallery at the Oakmont Country Club rattle him. Palmer, a former Open winner from nearby Latrobe, Pa., had matched shots with his young adversary through the first four rounds, both finishing at 283 to set up the playoff.

The husky Nicklaus set a fast pace in the extra round, grabbing a four-stroke lead after six holes. But Palmer made one of his patented charges, recording birdies on 9, 11 and 12 that cut his deficit to one. Nicklaus, however, was unfazed. He fought back with a birdie at 13 and never was seriously threatened again en route to his three-stroke victory.

Nicklaus, the second player to make the U.S. Open his first tour victory, finished the 90-holes with one three-putt green. Palmer had three in the playoff round, 10 overall.

JUNE

18

A STAR IS BORN

1924: George Mikan, a basketball Hall of Fame center who dominated the NBA during its formative years. He led the Minneapolis Lakers to five of the first eight NBA championships.

★ ★ ★

1939: Lou Brock, a Hall of Fame outfielder who led the N.L. in stolen bases eight times and collected 3,023 hits in a 19-year career that ended in 1979.

★ ★ ★

1961: Andres Galarraga, a current major league first baseman.

★ ★ ★

1960

ARNIE WINS IN A RUSH

Arnold Palmer, staging the most incredible closing rush in major tournament history, fired a final-round 65, wiped out a seven-stroke deficit and claimed an unlikely U.S. Open victory at Cherry Hills Country Club in Denver.

Palmer was seven strokes behind third-round leader Mike Souchak when he opened the afternoon round by driving the green at the first hole. He carded a birdie three and followed that by chipping in from 30 feet for another birdie at hole No. 2.

Two more birdies followed en route to a front-nine 30 that put him back into the thick of a wild scramble. With 10 golfers creeping to within two strokes of each other with nine holes to play, the Open came down to a survival of the fittest.

One by one the others faded, especially Souchak, who ballooned to a 75. One who refused to wilt was 20-year-old Jack Nicklaus, who carded a final-round 71 and 282 total – the lowest amateur score ever recorded in a U.S. Open.

After his early birdie binge, Palmer settled down to par the last seven holes and came home with a two-stroke victory over Nicklaus.

1941

LOUIS SURVIVES CONN CHALLENGE

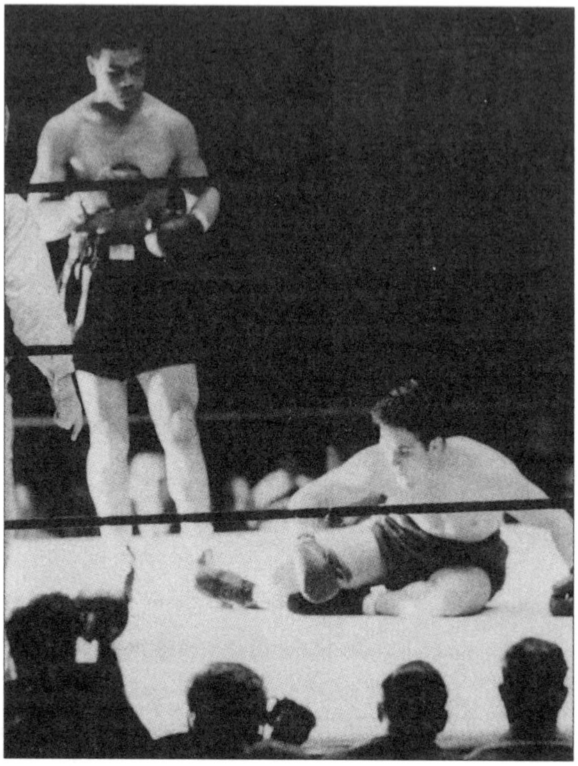

Heavyweight champion **Joe Louis** *stands over the fallen* **Billy Conn** *after a nip-and-tuck 13-round battle.*

Heavyweight champion Joe Louis, apparently on the brink of losing his long-held title to a former light heavyweight champion, knocked out Billy Conn in a suddenly-inspired 13th round at New York's Polo Grounds.

After 12 even rounds, Conn was within striking distance of dethroning one of the greatest champions in boxing history. But with the crowd cheering his every move, the challenger changed tactics. Admitting later he was feeling a little cocky, Conn began trading blows with Louis in the 13th round – and quickly regretted his decision.

Louis, making his 18th defense of the title he won in 1937, caught Conn with a blow to the jaw that buckled his knees. Sensing victory, Louis delivered a series of savage blows that sent the challenger down for the count.

1984

ZOELLER CATCHES THE GREAT WHITE SHARK

Fuzzy Zoeller, who watched Australian Greg Norman catch him on the final hole of regulation with a 40-foot putt, blazed around the West course at Winged Foot with a playoff-round 67 and carved out a whopping seven-stroke victory in the U.S. Open championship at Mamaroneck, N.Y.

Zoeller got sweet revenge on the second hole of the playoff when he sank a 68-foot putt for a birdie 3 that set the tone for the day. Norman three-putted the second green for a double bogey and he suddenly trailed by three strokes, a deficit that would only get larger.

Norman, golf's white shark, also three-putted at 3 and 5 en route to a 75. The match was so one-sided that Norman, resigned to his fate by the 18th hole, pulled a white towel out of his bag and waved it at Zoeller as a sign of surrender. Zoeller had done the same on the 18th fairway the day before.

Zoeller's 67 was the lowest score ever recorded in a U.S. Open playoff round. His eight-stroke margin was the largest in an 18-hole playoff.

U.S. Open golf champion **Fuzzy Zoeller.**

MILESTONES IN SPORTS

1975

Boston rookie Fred Lynn crashed three homers, a triple and a single and drove in 10 runs in the Red Sox's 15-1 victory over Detroit.

1986

California righthander Don Sutton defeated Texas, 3-1, and became the 19th pitcher to record 300 career victories.

1989

Curtis Strange fired a final-round 70 at Pittsford, N.Y., and became the first golfer to win consecutive U.S. Open champion ships since Ben Hogan in 1950–51.

1986 Basketball Star Bias Dies at 22

Maryland All-America forward Len Bias, the man touted as the heir-apparent to three-time National Basketball Association Most Valuable Player Larry Bird in Boston, collapsed and died from cocaine intoxication – two days after being selected by the Celtics as the second overall pick in the NBA draft.

The 6-foot-8 Bias, the Atlantic Coast Conference's Player of the Year as a senior, was celebrating his recent good fortune with teammates David Gregg and Terry Long at his College Park, Md., residence when he suddenly collapsed.

He was rushed to the hospital where it later was determined that he had been sniffing cocaine, probably minutes before his death. The autopsy report stated that the intoxication had caused his heart to beat irregularly, triggering seizures and cardiac arrest.

During the 48 hours before his death, the 22-year-old Bias had followed a stressful schedule that took him from Washington to New York to Boston to Washington. He had been introduced to the local media and fans in Boston and his whirlwind tour had been filled with parties, meetings and interviews. The celebration continued after his return.

Bias averaged 23.2 points per game and pulled down 224 rebounds as a senior. He finished his career with a school-record 2,149 points.

Milestones in Sports

1971

UCLA lefthander Jimmy Connors became the first freshman to win an NCAA tennis championship when he defeated Stanford's Roscoe Tanner, 6–3, 4–6, 6–4, 6–4, at South Bend, Ind.

1972

Curt Flood's long legal battle against the reserve clause came to an end when the United States Supreme Court extended baseball's unique exemption from the nation's antitrust laws.

1983

Carl Lewis pulled off the first post-1900 triple in track and field history, winning the 100 and 200-meter dashes and the long jump in the USA/Mobil championships at Indianapolis.

1989

Oklahoma football Coach Barry Switzer resigned under a cloud of scandal after 16 seasons that produced 157 victories and three national championships.

1992

Evander Holyfield made his third heavyweight title defense with a unanimous 12-round decision over 42-year-old Larry Holmes at Las Vegas.

1973 Howes Join Forces

Gordie Howe, the most prolific scorer in National Hockey League history and one of the game's brightest stars, ended his two-year retirement and signed a four-year, $1 million contract to play with sons Marty and Mark for the World Hockey Association's Houston Aeros.

The 45-year-old Howe, who holds NHL career records for games (1,687), goals (786) and points (1,023), couldn't resist the chance to form a unique combination with his sons. And it's conceivable all three could play at the same time – Gordie is a right wing and 19-year-old Marty a left wing and 18-year-old Mark a defenseman.

The move was a public relations natural for the WHA, which is badly in need of gate attractions and recognition in its long uphill battle with the established NHL. Before his retirement, Howe provided the NHL and the Detroit Red Wings plenty of both for 25 outstanding seasons.

June 19

A Star Is Born

1884: Ed Cicotte, a righthander who won 210 games before being banished from baseball as part of the 1919 World Series scandal involving members of the Chicago White Sox.

★ ★ ★

1903: Lou Gehrig, the New York Yankees' Hall of Fame first baseman who batted .340, hit 493 home runs and played in a record 2,130 consecutive games before his 17-year career was cut short in 1939 by a fatal disease.

★ ★ ★

1924: Leo Nomellini, a football Hall of Fame defensive tackle who played in 266 straight games during a 14-year NFL career that ended in 1963.

★ ★ ★

1940: Shirley Muldowney, the first woman drag racer to win the Top Fuel Championship. She won the title three times.

★ ★ ★

Death of a Legend

1986: Len Bias (basketball).

★ ★ ★

1955 Longshot Fleck Upsets Hogan

Jack Fleck, an unknown Iowan looking for his breakthrough victory on the PGA Tour, shot a playoff-round 69 and pulled off a stunning upset of Ben Hogan in the final round of the U.S. Open at the Olympic Country Club in San Francisco.

Fleck raised eyebrows in the final round of regulation when he birdied the 18th hole to catch the four-time Open champion at 287, and force the extra session. Then a gallery of more than 10,000 watched in shock as he matched shots with the man generally regarded as the best golfer in the world.

Fleck not only matched shots with Hogan, he forged a three-stroke lead after 10 holes and still led by one when the competitors teed off on 18. That's when disaster struck Hogan and fate smiled on the man who had won but two minor Tour victories.

Hogan, hitting first, slipped on sand and dribbled his tee shot into some long grass. His next swing moved the ball about two feet, his third about three more. His fourth swing finally got the ball back on the fairway and Hogan played out to a 6, sinking a 30-foot putt. Fleck got his par for a three-stroke advantage that completed the upset.

The WHA's Houston Aeros reunited the Howe family, (left to right) **Marty, Mark** *and* **Gordie.**

JUNE

20

MILESTONES IN SPORTS

1940

Joe Louis ran his successful string of heavyweight title defenses to 11 when he scored an eighth-round technical knockout of challenger Arturo Godoy at New York's Yankee Stadium.

1966

Billy Casper, who forced a playoff by wiping out a seven-stroke final-round deficit on the back nine, scored a four-stroke victory over Arnold Palmer and won the U.S. Open championship at San Francisco.

1970

Brigham Young junior Ralph Mann broke a 10-year-old world record when he ran the 400-meter hurdles in 48.8 seconds during competition in the NCAA outdoor championships at Drake University.

1980

Panamanian slugger Roberto Duran handed crowd-pleaser Sugar Ray Leonard his first professional loss and took away his welterweight title with a unanimous decision at Montreal's Olympic Stadium.

1988

An overtime thriller: Curtis Strange earned his first U.S. Open title with a four-stroke playoff victory over British rival Nick Faldo at the Brookline (Mass.) Country Club.

1993 BULLS GET THREE-TEAT

John Paxson connected on a 3-point jump shot with 3.9 seconds remaining, giving the Chicago Bulls a dramatic 99–98 victory over Phoenix and their third consecutive National Basketball Association championship.

The Game 6 triumph at Phoenix allowed the Bulls to join elite company – only the Minneapolis Lakers (1952–54) and Boston Celtics (1959–66) had won as many as three straight titles. And the Bulls won the finale despite a 5-for-18 fourth-quarter shooting performance that put the Suns in position to win.

The Bulls held an 87–79 advantage heading into the final period, but Phoenix scored seven straight points and eventually took the lead. The Suns, however, couldn't stand prosperity and went into a scoring slump of their own, making only 5 of 21 shots over the final 12 minutes.

Still, they led 98–94 when Michael Jordan drove for a basket, cutting the margin to two. When Phoenix missed a shot, the Bulls got the rebound and their final chance. The ball was pushed inside to Horace Grant, who kicked it back out to Paxson for the winner.

The incomparable Jordan finished the game with 33 points and the series with a playoff-record 41-point average. Charles Barkley led Phoenix with 21 points and 17 rebounds.

1960 PATTERSON REGAINS TITLE FROM SWEDE JOHANSSON

Floyd Patterson, atoning for his loss to Ingemar Johansson a year earlier, dropped the Swede in the fifth round of their Polo Grounds rematch and became the first boxer to win a heavyweight championship twice.

The victory was sweet revenge for the 25-year-old Patterson, who was knocked down seven times in the decisive third round of their first fight at Yankee Stadium. Patterson carefully avoided Johansson's powerful right hand and controlled the fight from the opening bell.

Floyd Patterson *(left) and* **Ingemar Johansson** *pose for photographers during their weigh-in.*

A crowd of 31,892 sensed Patterson's dominance early and cheered wildly in the fifth round when he connected with a left hook to the chin that put the undefeated champion down. Johansson was up by the count of 9, but Patterson methodically moved in for the kill, finally connecting with another left hook at 1:51 of the round. This time Johansson could not get up.

Patterson, obviously sensing Johansson was finished, leaped in joy as the count was taking place and then was mobbed by happy handlers and ecstatic fans climbing into the ring. The victory was Patterson's 36th in 38 fights. Johansson is 22–1.

The fight was the first for both fighters since their previous matchup. Johansson, a heavy underdog in the first fight, had entered this one as the solid favorite.

1964 VENTURI HEATS IT UP

Ken Venturi, overheated and on the verge of collapse after firing a morning-round 66, revived for an afternoon 70 that earned him an impressive four-stroke victory over Tommy Jacobs in the U.S. Open championship at the Congressional Country Club in Washington D.C.

Venturi, who started the day six strokes behind Jacobs, staggered at the 16th tee of the morning round and barely made it to the clubhouse, where he was examined by a doctor. He rested for the allotted 45 minutes, took salt tablets and pronounced himself ready to play.

Trailing by two heading into the final 18 holes, Venturi caught Jacobs at the second and owned a two-stroke advantage after nine. Playing slowly with a doctor at his side in the 100-degree heat, Venturi pulled away as Jacobs struggled to a 76.

The victory was Venturi's first as a professional after four lean years on the PGA Tour. He collected $17,000 – five times as much as he had earned in his 27 previous starts.

A STAR IS BORN

1903: Glenna Collett-Vare, a golfer who won the women's U.S. Amateur title a record six times in the 1920s and '30s.

★★★

1925: Doris Hart, an outstanding women's tennis player who won all four major singles championships at least once from 1949–55.

★★★

1935: Len Dawson, a football Hall of Fame quarterback who passed for 28,507 yards and 237 TDs in a 19-year career.

★★★

MILESTONES IN SPORTS

1932

Journeyman fighter Jack Sharkey pulled a shocking upset at Long Island, N.Y., when he earned a split decision over Max Schmeling and claimed the heavyweight championship.

1938

Boston third baseman Pinky Higgins set a major league record when he collected his 12th straight hit, a single against Detroit, over a two-day, four-game period.

1954

Australian John Landy ran an unofficial 3:58 mile, topping the 3:59.4 run by Roger Bannister a month earlier when he shattered the 4-minute barrier.

1963

Bullet Bob Hayes, a 20-year-old college freshman, shattered the world record for the 100-yard dash with a 9.1-second clocking in the AAU championships at St. Louis.

1970

Detroit shortstop Cesar Gutierrez collected six singles and a double in the Tigers' 12-inning 9–8 victory at Cleveland, becoming the first modern major leaguer to get seven hits in a game.

1979

The NBA approved the 3-point field goal for a one-year trial, setting distances ranging from 22 feet at the baseline to 23–9 at the top of the key.

1986

Spurning a $7.6-million contract from the NFL's Tampa Bay Buccaneers, Auburn Heisman Trophy winner Bo Jackson signed a three-year, $1.066-million baseball deal with the Kansas City Royals.

1992

Tom Kite, 42, won his first major championship when he beat Jeff Sluman by two shots in the U.S. Open at Pebble Beach, Calif.

Jim Bunning, *Philadelphia's Mr. Perfect.*

1988 LAKERS WIN 2ND IN ROW

James Worthy scored the first triple-double of his career and the Los Angeles Lakers became the first National Basketball Association team to win back-to-back titles since 1969 with a 108–105 Game 7 victory over Detroit at the Los Angeles Forum.

Fulfilling the bold "I'll guarantee it" promise made last June by Coach Pat Riley when asked if his team could repeat, the Lakers needed 24 playoff games, the most in NBA history, to seal the championship. After finishing the regular season with a league-best 62–20 mark, the Lakers were extended to seventh games in series against Utah and Dallas.

Worthy scored 36 points, grabbed 16 rebounds and handed out 10 assists in the finale. After trailing by five points at halftime, Los Angeles took control with a 25–3 third-quarter spurt and led, 94–79, with 7:44 remaining.

The Pistons, playing without injured Isiah Thomas, made it close with a 17–4 run of their own, but a Worthy basket and two Magic Johnson free throws in the final minute sealed the victory.

JUNE 21

Los Angeles Coach **Pat Riley** *fulfilled his prediction of a Lakers championship repeat.*

1964 BUNNING HAS PERFECT DAY

Philadelphia righthander Jim Bunning retired all 27 New York Mets he faced in a 6–0 victory at Shea Stadium – the major leagues' first regular-season perfect game in 42 years.

Bunning struck out 10 and needed only 86 pitches and two good defensive plays to become the eighth pitcher in baseball history and the first modern-era National Leaguer to throw a perfecto. The last N.L. pitcher to accomplish the 27-batter feat was John Montgomery Ward, who did it in 1880.

The last American Leaguer to turn the trick was New York Yankee righthander Don Larsen, who did not permit a Brooklyn Dodger to reach base in Game 5 of the 1956 World Series. The last regular-season perfect game was pitched by the Chicago White Sox's Charlie Robertson in 1922.

By the seventh inning of the doubleheader opener at Shea, the Phillies owned a commanding 6–0 lead and the New York crowd had switched allegiance. When Bunning struck out rookie John Stephenson to end the game, the fans began chanting his name and teammates mobbed him near the pitcher's mound.

Bunning also became the first pitcher to throw no-hitters in both leagues. He pitched one in 1958 for the American League's Detroit Tigers.

A STAR IS BORN

1902: Howie Morenz, a fast-skating Hall of Fame center who reigned as the most popular player in the NHL during a 14-year career that ended in 1937.

★ ★ ★

1918: Ed Lopat, a lefthanded pitcher who won 166 games from 1944–65.

★ ★ ★

1959: Tom Chambers, a current National Basketball Association forward.

★ ★ ★

1967: Derrick Coleman, a current National Basketball Association forward.

★ ★ ★

DEATH OF A LEGEND

1969: Maureen Connolly (tennis).

★ ★ ★

1973: Frank Leahy (football).

★ ★ ★

JUNE

22

1947 EWELL'S NEAR MISS

Cincinnati righthander Ewell Blackwell, within two outs of matching Johnny Vander Meer's 1938 consecutive no-hitter feat, surrendered singles to Eddie Stanky and Jackie Robinson before settling down to complete his 4–0 victory over the Brooklyn Dodgers in the first game of a doubleheader at Crosley Field.

With 31,204 fans cheering him on, Blackwell entered the ninth with a no-hitter intact – four days after holding the Boston Braves hitless in a 6–0 Reds victory at Cincinnati. He retired pinch-hitter Gene Hermanski on a fly ball and then faced leadoff man Stanky, a pesky righthanded batter.

On Blackwell's second pitch, Stanky hit a sharp grounder that skipped over the mound, through the pitcher's legs and into center field. Blackwell retired Al Gionfriddo on a fly ball, but Robinson dumped a looper into right field for another hit. Carl Furillo was retired for the final out.

Ironically, Blackwell's near miss came against the same teams that Cincinnati lefthander Vander Meer had pitched his no-hitters against in 1938 – Boston and Brooklyn. The key blow for the Reds was a bases-clearing eighth-inning double by Eddie Miller.

1938 LOUIS GETS REVENGE

Heavyweight champion Joe Louis, avenging the only loss on his 39-fight ledger, knocked out German slugger Max Schmeling at 2:04 of the opening round in a quick-and-easy title fight at New York's Yankee Stadium.

The 80,000-plus fans had barely settled into their seats when the champion unleashed a vicious attack on the man who had knocked him out in the 12th round of a 1936 fight – a year before Louis had ascended to the heavyweight throne. A powerful right hand sent Schmeling sprawling, an act that would be repeated two more times.

Schmeling was up by the count of three and Louis promptly sent him down again, with another right. Schmeling bounced up quickly, only to be greeted by another Louis right that knocked him down for a final time. Schmeling's handlers threw in the towel – literally.

The 32-year-old Schmeling, who held the heavyweight title in 1930 and '31, failed in his bid to become the first fighter in boxing history to win the crown twice. Louis was defending his championship for the fourth time.

Cincinnati righthander **Ewell Blackwell.**

1937 YOUNG LOUIS WINS TITLE

Joe Louis battered James J. Braddock for seven rounds and knocked him out with a powerful right to the jaw in the eighth, becoming boxing's first black heavyweight champion since Jack Johnson lost to Jess Willard in 1915.

The fight at Chicago's Comiskey Park was supposed to be a romp for the 23-year-old Louis. Braddock, a journeyman 31-year-old who had pulled a monumental upset in beating Max Baer two years earlier, was making his first title defense and was seemingly overmatched by the Brown Bomber out of Detroit.

And the early moments of the match seemed to support that notion as the younger, more agile Louis danced around the slow, plodding champion and fired several short punches.

But 60,000 screaming fans watched in amazement as Braddock suddenly connected with a punch that sent Louis to the canvas. The shock was only temporary, however. Louis jumped up and, after shaking away the cobwebs, proceeded to pound the champion into bloody submission.

The end came in the eighth round when Louis connected with a right that sent Braddock sprawling. The champion made no attempt to get up and eventually was carried out of the ring as Louis celebrated his coronation as the first black champion in 22 years. Jack Johnson ruled the boxing world as heavyweight champion from 1908-1915.

MILESTONES IN SPORTS

1949

Ezzard Charles claimed the heavyweight crown vacated by Joe Louis with a unanimous 15-round decision over Jersey Joe Walcott at Chicago.

1962

St. Louis' Stan Musial became baseball's all-time total bases leader when he collected a home run and three singles in a doubleheader at Philadelphia and raised his career total to 5,866 – three more than Ty Cobb.

1979

Larry Holmes retained his World Boxing Council heavyweight title with a 12th-round technical knockout of Mike Weaver at New York's Madison Square Garden.

1982

Philadelphia's Pete Rose passed Hank Aaron and moved into second place on the all-time hit list with a third-inning double against St. Louis – his 3,772nd career safety.

A STAR IS BORN

1903: Carl Hubbell, a Hall of Fame lefthander who recorded five consecutive 20-victory seasons for the New York Giants in the 1930s and finished his 16-year career with 253 wins.

★ ★ ★

1947: Pete Maravich, a basketball Hall of Fame guard who scored 15,948 points in a 10-year NBA career (1970–80) after setting NCAA season and career scoring records for Louisiana State.

★ ★ ★

1962: Clyde Drexler, a current National Basketball Association guard.

★ ★ ★

June 23

1967 Ryun Leads Parade

Jim Ryun, the gifted 20-year-old sophomore at the University of Kansas, led a parade of sub-4-minute milers to the finish line in the Amateur Athletic Union meet at Bakersfield, Calif., and lowered his own world record by two-tenths of a second.

Ryun finished the race in 3:51.1, just under the recognized world mark of 3:51.3 that he set a year earlier at Berkeley, Calif. He was followed by six other runners who broke the once-sacred 4-minute barrier: Jim Grelle, 3:56.1; Dave Willborn, 3:56.2; Tom von Ruden, 3:56.9; Roscoe Divine, 3:57.2; Sam Bair, 3:58.6, and Marty Liquori, 3:59.8.

Despite the bunching of the field under 4 minutes, the race for first was never really close. Ryun took the lead quickly and won by 40 yards. He ran quarters of 59.2 seconds, 59.8, 58.6 and a sprinting 53.5 that gave him the record.

Young distance-running sensation **Jim Ryun.**

1981 Pawtucket Wins Marathon Finish

Dave Koza's bases-loaded single in the bottom of the 33rd inning gave Pawtucket a 3–2 victory over the Rochester Red Wings, ending the longest professional game and most-publicized minor league contest in baseball history.

The one-inning conclusion to the marathon took just 18 minutes – a stark contrast to the 8-hour, 7-minute battle that was fought April 18 before play was suspended with the teams tied 2–2 after 32 innings. That decision was made at 4:07 a.m. by International League President Harold Cooper.

It was a good move from a public relations standpoint. With major league baseball crippled by a long players' strike, the game drew national headlines and little McCoy Stadium at Pawtucket, R.I., was crammed with 5,756 fans, 54 newspaper representatives and numerous television and radio crews, including broadcasters from Great Britain and Japan, when the game was continued.

The outcome was decided quickly. Lefthander Bob Ojeda retired Rochester in order in the top of the 33rd and the Red Sox loaded the bases with nobody out in the bottom of the inning, setting up Koza's winning hit.

Miami and St. Petersburg of the Florida State League played 29 innings (1966) in the previous longest professional game.

A Star Is Born

1895: George Weiss, a Hall of Fame baseball executive who, as general manager, helped guide the New York Yankees to 10 A.L. pennants in 13 years.

★ ★ ★

1940: Wilma Rudolph, the American track star who won three gold medals at the 1960 Olympic Games.

★ ★ ★

Death of a Legend

1976: Lon Warneke (baseball).

★ ★ ★

Milestones in Sports

1922

Walter Hagen scored a one-stroke victory over Jim Barnes and George Duncan at Royal St. George's Golf Club in Sandwich, England, becoming the first American-born winner of the British Open.

1950

Texas 3, Washington State 0 in the championship game of the first College World Series played at Omaha, Neb.

1963

Jimmy Piersall, the New York Mets' eccentric outfielder, belted his 100th career home run in a game against Philadelphia and celebrated by running the bases backward.

1971

Philadelphia's Rick Wise pitched a 4–0 no-hitter against Cincinnati and drove in three of the runs with two homers.

1917 Ernie Shore Is Perfect In 27-Out Relief Stint

Boston righthander Ernie Shore, called into the pitch when starter Babe Ruth was ejected from the game after walking the first batter, set down 27 consecutive Washington Senators in a "perfect" 4–0 victory in the first game of a Fenway Park doubleheader.

While it's arguable whether Shore's effort constitutes a perfect game because of the walk, there's no doubt the performance ranks among the greatest in baseball history. Only Boston's Cy Young (1904) and Cleveland's Addie Joss (1908) had recorded perfectos since the turn of the century.

Shore's effort was even more impressive considering he wasn't expecting to pitch. But when Ruth walked Washington's Ray Morgan to open the game, he got into a heated argument with home-plate umpire Brick Owens, who sent him packing. Shore was summoned and catcher Sam Agnew replaced Pinch Thomas.

That was a critical move because Agnew threw out Morgan trying to steal and contributed three hits. Shore struck out only two but otherwise handcuffed the Senators.

Boston's **Ernie Shore** *turned in a perfect relief performance against the Washington Senators.*

JUNE 24

A STAR IS BORN

1895: Jack Dempsey, the former world heavyweight champion (1919–26).

★ ★ ★

1928: Larry Foust, an early-NBA forward who scored 11,198 points in his 12-year career.

★ ★ ★

1931: Billy Casper, a professional golfer who won two U.S. Opens and one Masters championship from 1959–70.

★ ★ ★

1933: Sam Jones, a basketball Hall of Fame guard who scored 15,411 points and played on 10 Boston Celtics championship teams in 12 NBA seasons (1957–69).

★ ★ ★

DEATH OF A LEGEND

1984: Clarence Campbell (hockey).

1977 MANAGER FOR A DAY

Eddie Stanky, homesick and lonely for his Alabama lifestyle, resigned his post as manager of the Texas Rangers, one day after replacing Frank Lucchesi and guiding the team to a 10–8 victory over the Minnesota Twins.

Eddie Stanky *as coach at South Alabama.*

The 60-year-old Stanky watched his new team defeat the Twins in a night game at Minneapolis and then boarded a plane the next morning for Mobile, Ala., where he was met by his wife, Dickie, and a group of officials from the University of South Alabama, where he had coached since 1968.

Stanky, a pepperpot second baseman known as The Brat during an 11-year career in the 1940s and '50s, said he had started to have second thoughts as he was flying to Minneapolis. He said he went back to the hotel room after the game and couldn't sleep. "I called my wife around 5 after 6 (in the morning) and told her I was coming home," he said.

Stanky, who managed the St. Louis Cardinals and Chicago White Sox after his playing career ended, immediately was reinstated as the coach at South Alabama, the school he built into a national baseball power. The shocked Rangers named coach Connie Ryan interim manager.

MILESTONES IN SPORTS

1960

American high jumper John Thomas continued his assault on the record book when he soared 7–2 in the AAU championships at Bakersfield, Calif., breaking his own world mark of 7–1 3/4.

1961

Villanova's Frank Budd shaved a tenth of a second off the world 100-yard dash record with a 9.2-second clocking in an AAU meet at Randalls Island, N.Y.

1963

Joey Giardello battered 43-year-old Sugar Ray Robinson for 10 rounds and won a unanimous decision in his hometown of Philadelphia.

1968

In a quick-and-easy heavyweight title defense, Joe Frazier stopped Manuel Ramos in the second round at New York's Madison Square Garden.

1962 REED RUINS TIGERS

Jack Reed, a utility outfielder who had entered the game in the 13th inning for defensive purposes, stroked his first major league home run in the 22nd inning of a game at Detroit, giving the New York Yankees a 9–7 victory over the Tigers and ending the longest game (timewise) in baseball history.

The 7-hour marathon, 1:41 longer than the previous longest major league contest, came to a merciful end when Reed followed a walk to Roger Maris with a blast into the lower left-field stands off Phil Regan, Detroit's seventh pitcher. Jim Bouton, New York's seventh hurler, retired the Tigers in the bottom of the inning and picked up the victory.

The Yankees opened the game with a vengeance against old nemesis Frank Lary, scoring six runs in a first inning that was capped by Clete Boyer's three-run homer. The Yankees added a second-inning run, but that was it. They wouldn't score again over the next 19 innings.

The Tigers scored three runs in the first, three in the third and tied the game in the sixth. But Tex Clevenger, Bud Daley and Bouton combined to pitch shutout ball over the next 16 innings for the Yankees and Reed made their effort pay dividends.

1968 NORTHRUP SLAMS INDIANS

Detroit outfielder Jim Northrup joined five major leaguers in an exclusive slugging fraternity when he blasted two grand slams in a 14–3 Tiger victory over the Indians at Cleveland Stadium.

Northrup became only the second player to hit slams in consecutive innings, connecting off Eddie Fisher in a six-run Tiger fifth and off Bill Rohr in a five-run sixth. Only Baltimore's Jim Gentile had previously performed the consecutive-innings feat (1961).

Ironically, Northrup had struck out with the bases loaded in the first inning facing Cleveland starter Mike Paul. But he didn't fan against Fisher in the fifth, breaking open a 3–2 game and sending Denny McLain on the way to his 13th victory in 15 decisions.

The homers were the ninth and 10th of the season for Northrup, who finished his big day with just the two hits and eight RBIs.

The home run swing of Detroit Tiger slammer **Jim Northrup.**

1932 CLOSING RUSH LIFTS SARAZEN

Golfer **Gene Sarazen,** *a man of many trophies.*

Gene Sarazen, staging the greatest closing rush ever witnessed in a major golf championship, covered his last 27 holes in an amazing 98 shots and captured the U.S. Open golf championship by three strokes over Phil Perkins and Bobby Cruickshank.

Sarazen opened the final day trailing leaders Perkins and Jose Jurado by five strokes. But he closed the gap with a morning round of 70 that was capped by a back-nine 32 and then tore up the difficult Fresh Meadow Country Club course in Long Island, N.Y., with a U.S. Open-record 66.

It was an unexpected finish to a tournament Perkins seemingly had in hand. The former British Amateur champion fired a final-round 70 and was in the clubhouse with a 72-hole total of 289 when Cruickshank posted a scorching 68 that tied for the lead.

Then news circulated that Sarazen was on fire.

He finished the front nine with a 32 and came home with a 34 that prompted the large gallery to rush the 18th green and carry him off like a triumphant warrior.

Sarazen, who earlier had won the British Open, joined Bobby Jones as the only golfers to win two major tournaments in the same year.

1948 LOUIS BEATS WALCOTT

Joe Louis, trailing on two of the three judges' cards after 10 rounds in his last professional fight, stormed back with an 11th-round knockout of Jersey Joe Walcott and retained his world heavyweight championship in a bout at New York's Yankee Stadium.

Louis, who had announced that his 25th title defense would be his last, win or lose, was on the verge of surrendering the crown he had held for more than 11 years when he suddenly caught Walcott with a right to the jaw. Sensing victory, Louis pressed his advantage with a series of combinations that backed Walcott against the ropes.

Louis finally landed another right to the jaw that sent Walcott to the canvas. The 34-year-old challenger gamely tried to reach his feet, but the referee counted him out.

Walcott had built his advantage with a dancing, jabbing style that infuriated the jeering crowd of 42,667 and prompted the referee to warn both fighters to step up the pace. Walcott knocked Louis down with a right in the third round, but the champion jumped up, unhurt.

JUNE 25

A STAR IS BORN

1942: Willis Reed, a basketball Hall of Fame center who led the New York Knicks to NBA championships in 1970 and '73.

★ ★ ★

1959: Alejandro Pena, a current major league pitcher.

★ ★ ★

1963: Doug Gilmour, a current National Hockey League center.

★ ★ ★

1964: Dell Curry, a current National Basketball Association guard.

★ ★ ★

DEATH OF A LEGEND

1918: Jake Beckley (baseball).

★ ★ ★

MILESTONES • IN SPORTS •

1965

The NHL voted to expand from six teams to 12 by 1968 and awarded franchises to interests in St. Louis and Los Angeles.

1981

Sugar Ray Leonard, surviving a stiff challenge from Ayub Kalule, scored a ninth-round technical knockout and added the WBA's junior middleweight championship to his WBC welterweight title.

1981

Magic Johnson signed a 25-year, $1 million-per-season contract with the Los Angeles Lakers – the longest and richest in sports history.

1992 EAGLES' STAR BROWN KILLED IN ACCIDENT

Jerome Brown, the Philadelphia Eagles' All-Pro defensive tackle, was killed instantly along with his 12-year-old nephew when the car he was driving skidded out of control on wet pavement and crashed into a palm tree in his hometown of Brooksville, Florida. He was 27.

A witness said that Brown, a former All-America at the University of Miami, was driving his 1992 Corvette when the car suddenly veered out of control, skidded off the left side of the road and hit the tree before overturning. He said the car was destroyed.

The flamboyant Brown, the Eagles' No. 1 draft pick in 1987, had played six professional seasons, earning Pro Bowl berths in 1990 and last year.

He had combined with Reggie White, Clyde Simmons and Mike Pitts to form one of the most ferocious defensive fronts in professional football history. That unit had lifted the Eagles' defense to a No.1 ranking on the National Football League's total defense charts.

JUNE

26

A STAR IS BORN

1903: Babe Herman, a sweet-swinging outfielder who batted .324 over a 13-year career that ended in 1945.

★ ★ ★

1914: Babe Didrikson Zaharias, generally considered the greatest female athlete of all time. She won two gold medals at the 1932 Olympics and went on to a record-setting career in women's golf.

★ ★ ★

1936: Hal Greer, a basketball Hall of Fame guard who scored 21,586 points in a 15-year NBA career that ended in 1973.

★ ★ ★

1961: Greg LeMond, a three-time winner of the Tour de France and the only American to win the prestigious cycling championship.

★ ★ ★

DEATH OF A LEGEND

1993: Roy Campanella (baseball).

1959 JOHANSSON PULLS UPSET

Ingemar Johansson, who had bragged to American writers about the speed and power in his right hand, gave them a first-hand exhibition of those qualities when he knocked heavyweight champion Floyd Patterson to the canvas seven times in the third round before claiming his crown at New York's Yankee Stadium.

Swede **Ingemar Johansson** *stands over fallen* **Floyd Patterson** *after one of his seven knockdown punches in the third round.*

The shocking upset was witnessed by 30,000 fans who alternately cheered and groaned as Patterson would regain his feet, only to be knocked down again by the determined Swede. There were 57 seconds remaining in the round when referee Ruby Goldstein ended the massacre.

Patterson, a heavy favorite in his fifth title defense, dropped his guard early in the third round and Johansson dropped him for the first time with a looping right to the jaw. Patterson was up at the count of nine and back down even faster. The pattern continued until the referee made his decision.

The 26-year-old Johansson, the first Scandinavian-born boxer to win a heavyweight title, kept his professional record perfect with his 22nd victory. He is the first non-American heavyweight champion since Italy's Primo Carnera won the title in 1934 and the third in history. German Max Schmeling was the first in 1930.

1970 ROBINSON JOINS SELECT CIRCLE

Frank Robinson, battling severe pain from a back injury he suffered the day before, blasted two grand slams in Baltimore's 12–2 victory at Washington, joining a select club that includes only six other major leaguers.

Robinson had hurt his back while making a game-saving catch in the 13th inning of a game against Boston. The pain was so severe he had to take pain-killing injections between innings and he bunted rather than swing away when batting in the 14th.

But Robinson was inflicting most of the pain against the Senators – connecting for bases-loaded homers in the fifth and sixth innings against pitchers Joe Coleman and Joe Grzenda.

Both Baltimore rallies started with pitcher Dave McNally drawing a walk, Don Buford singling and Paul Blair walking. The 34-year-old Robinson took care of the rest, depositing Coleman's pitch over the right-field fence and Grzenda's into the upper stands in left-center field.

Robinson, who was on deck in the ninth when Blair flied out with the bases full, joined Jim Gentile and Jim Northrup as the only players to hit grand slams in consecutive innings.

Frank Robinson *muscled up in a big game at Washington.*

MILESTONES IN SPORTS

1962

Boston Red Sox righthander Don Wilson pitched a no-hitter against the Los Angeles Angels and punctuated his 2–0 victory with a third-inning home run.

1971

American John Smith streaked to a world-record clocking of 44.5 seconds in the 440-yard dash during competition in the National AAU championships at Eugene, Ore.

1911 OPEN JINX ENDS

John McDermott, battling two talented opponents, the elements and a 16-year British jinx, recorded a two-stroke victory in a three-way playoff round and became the first American-born golfer to win a U.S. Open championship.

The 21-year-old from Atlantic City, N.J., showed resilience and determination over the difficult 6,636-yard Chicago Golf Club course. He played in heavy rain over his final 18 holes of regulation and carded a 79, tying Mike Brady and George Simpson with a 72-hole total of 307.

When play started in the playoff, the golfers had to contend with intense heat, gusting winds and wet greens – problems that were reflected in their scores. McDermott came home with an 80, two strokes better than Brady and five better than Simpson.

McDermott had flirted with the possibility of becoming the event's first American winner in 1910, when he lost in a playoff to Great Britain's Alex Smith. The Britons had dominated throughout the 16-year history of the tournament.

MILESTONES
· IN SPORTS ·

1914

Jack Johnson strengthened his hold on the heavyweight division with a 20-round referee's decision over Frank Moran at New York's Madison Square Garden.

1958

Chicago lefthander Billy Pierce, one out away from baseball's first regular-season perfect game since the Chicago White Sox's Charlie Robertson turned the trick in 1922, surrendered a looping double to Washington pinch-hitter Ed Fitzgerald before closing out his 3–0 victory.

1971

JoAnne Carner fired a final-round 73 and cruised home with a whopping seven-stroke victory over Kathy Whitworth in the U.S. Women's Open at Erie, Pa.

1972

Chicago star Bobby Hull shocked the hockey world when he signed a $2.5-million contract and jumped to the Winnipeg Jets of the fledgling World Hockey Association.

1992

Dan O'Brien, the reigning world decathlon champion, failed to qualify for the American Olympic team when he no-heighted during pole vault competition at the U.S. trials.

1975

Lightning Strikes Lee Trevino, Two Other Golfers

Golfers Lee Trevino, Jerry Heard and Bobby Nichols, competing in the second round of the Western Open at Oak Brook, Ill., were rushed to the hospital after being struck by lightning on the Butler National Golf Club course.

Trevino and Heard were sitting under an umbrella near the 13th green when a bolt of lightning apparently struck the bag against which Trevino was leaning. He was burned across his back and Heard suffered burns on his upper right leg. Both were rushed by ambulance to the hospital, where their injuries were diagnosed as minor.

Nichols fell down on the fourth green when lightning flashed, got up and went directly to the clubhouse. He asked to be taken to the hospital about an hour later, complaining of a severe headache and a bad taste in his mouth. Nichols suffered minor burns on his head.

Half the field of 156 already had completed their rounds when the storm moved through. Three other players, including Arnold Palmer, told of lightning bolts knocking clubs out of their hands.

1988

Iron Mike KOs Spinks

Mike Tyson, the iron-fisted slugging machine from New York, repaired the division within the heavyweight ranks with an emphatic first-round knockout of Michael Spinks in a title-deciding fight at Atlantic City, N.J.

Tyson laid undisputed claim to the heavyweight championship when he sent Spinks sprawling to the canvas for a second time at 1:31 of the opening round – the fourth fastest knockout in heavyweight title history. He had set up the knockout with an earlier left hook that dropped Spinks for the count of 3.

For 21,785 fans, it was over that quickly. Tyson had opened the battle of unbeatens by relentlessly stalking his adversary and striking with speed and raw power. Unable to evade his relentless stalker, Spinks chose to stand and fight – and quickly paid the price.

The victory was Tyson's 35th in a row, his 31st by knockout. Spinks had never even been knocked down in his previous 31 fights. Tyson, who collected $22 million, was defending the recognized heavyweight championship that Spinks had surrendered for not fighting a prescribed line of challengers.

Iron-fisted heavyweight champion **Mike Tyson.**

JUNE
27

1959

Wright Rush Is All Right

Mickey Wright, surviving a late rush by Louise Suggs and a late collapse of her own, became the first woman to win consecutive U.S. Open championships with a two-stroke victory over Suggs at Pittsburgh.

Wright took the lead with a one-under-par 69 in the morning round and closed with a 71, despite some erratic play on the last three holes. She missed the green on 16, hit into a creek and a sand trap on 17 and three-putted on 18.

No matter. The tall blonde had built a big lead by that point, thanks to a six-stroke swing in the morning. Suggs, who enjoyed a two-stroke advantage at the halfway point, ballooned to a morning 75 and could never recover. Her afternoon 69 simply made it close.

Wright's 287 total was a women's record and was one stroke better than her winning 1958 score.

A STAR IS BORN

1964: Chuck Person, a current National Basketball Association forward.

★ ★ ★

DEATH OF A LEGEND

1992: Sandy Amoros (baseball).

★ ★ ★

JUNE 28

A STAR IS BORN

1893: Ken Williams, a .319 career hitter who won the A.L. home run (39) and RBI (155) titles in 1922 for the St. Louis Browns.

★★★

1949: Don Baylor, a 19-year major leaguer (1970–88) who belted 338 home runs and collected 2,135 hits. Baylor is a current major league manager.

★★★

1960: John Elway, a current National Football League quarterback.

★★★

1964: Mark Grace, a current major league first baseman.

★★★

DEATH OF A LEGEND

1962: Mickey Cochrane (baseball).

★★★

1963: Frank (Home Run) Baker (baseball).

★★★

1957 Frick Overrules All-Star Voters

Baseball Commissioner Ford Frick, upset about the ballot-stuffing antics of over-zealous Cincinnati fans, overruled the will of the people by replacing three of the eight potential Reds starters for the National League All-Star team with players he deemed more worthy.

Baseball Commissioner **Ford Frick** *moved swiftly on the All-Star ballot-stuffing antics of Cincinnati fans*

Frick was reacting to an avalanche of votes from the Cincinnati area that could have resulted in an all-Cincinnati starting lineup of George Crowe (first base), Johnny Temple (second), Don Hoak (third), Roy McMillan (shortstop), Ed Bailey (catcher), Frank Robinson (left field), Gus Bell (center field) and Wally Post (right field).

Frick opened two spots in the outfield with the elimination of Bell and Post and dropped Crowe at first base. He replaced Crowe with St. Louis' Stan Musial and filled the outfield openings with New York's Willie Mays and Milwaukee's Hank Aaron.

A half-million-vote surge had lifted Bell from third place to first, Post from second to first and Crowe from nowhere to first. Frick made his decision before the tabulations for the July 9 classic at St. Louis were even complete.

MILESTONES IN SPORTS

1939

Joe Louis retained his heavyweight title with a fourth-round technical knockout of Tony Galento at New York's Yankee Stadium.

1939

The New York Yankees hit a one-game-record eight home runs and a doubleheader-record 13 in a 23–2 and 10–0 sweep of the Philadelphia Athletics.

1947

California 8, Yale 7 in the championship game of the first College World Series at Kalamazoo, Mich.

1966

Ernie Terrell retained his World Boxing Association title with a unanimous 15-round decision over Doug Jones at Houston.

1970

The Pittsburgh Pirates completed their 62-year tenure at Forbes Field with a 3–2 and 4–1 doubleheader sweep of the Chicago Cubs.

1976 The Bird Flies

Detroit Tigers mound groomer and pitching ace **Mark (The Bird) Fidrych.**

Detroit rookie Mark (The Bird) Fidrych continued his eye-catching run of success through the American League when he charmed a national-television audience with a charismatic 5–1 victory over the East Division-leading New York Yankees before 47,855 jubilant fans at Tiger Stadium.

The talented right-hander dispatched the New Yorkers on seven hits and raised his record to 8–1 before making two curtain calls after the game. The large crowd refused to leave, chanting, "Bird! Bird! Bird!" for 10 minutes before Fidrych returned with a cap-doffing smile. The crowd went wild and started the chant again.

Fidrych's success is only partly responsible for his popularity. The nation got a good look at the youngster against the Yankees – complete with his constant discussions with the ball, between-innings mound grooming and ever-ebullient presence. The Yankees certainly got an eyeful of his talent.

Their only breakthrough came on a solo home run by Elrod Hendricks. Fidrych was supported by Rusty Staub's two-run homer and Aurelio Rodriguez's solo shot.

1981 Pate Takes Dive

Jerry Pate, winless on the PGA Tour for most of the last three years, dropped a birdie putt on the 18th hole to secure a two-stroke victory in the Danny Thomas-Memphis Classic and then celebrated by diving, fully clothed, into the lake next to the green.

Pate, a former U.S. Open champion who had finished second eight times since his last victory, did not even bother to sign his scorecard before fulfilling his victory promise. When his final putt dropped for a 72-hole total of 274, he grinned, handed his putter and sun visor to his caddy and ran for the water.

Pate had entered the final round over the 7,249-yard Colonial Country Club course with a one-stroke lead. He fell to second place with a double-bogey on 6, but he regained the top spot for good with a 10th-hole birdie. Tom Kite and Bruce Lietzke made late bids, but both came up two strokes short and tied for second.

Pate picked up $54,000 for his victory.

A STAR IS BORN

1936: Harmon Killebrew, a powerful Hall of Fame infielder who blasted 573 home runs in a 22-year career that ended in 1975.

★ ★ ★

1956: Pedro Guerrero, a 15-year major leaguer who finished his career in 1992 with a .300 average and 215 home runs.

★ ★ ★

1964: Pepper Johnson, a current National Football League linebacker.

★ ★ ★

1968: Theoren Fleury, a current National Hockey League center.

DEATH OF A LEGEND

1960: Frank Patrick (hockey).

★ ★ ★

1967: Primo Carnera (boxing).

★ ★ ★

1968: Paddy Driscoll (football).

★ ★ ★

1983: Joe Delaney (football).

★ ★ ★

1986: Jack Christiansen (football).

1956

DUMAS TOPS HIGH JUMP BARRIER

Charley Dumas, defying the laws of gravity like nobody before him, broke a major track and field barrier when he leaped over a bar positioned at 7 feet, 1/2 inch and took a well-earned spot on the United States Olympic team during trials at the Los Angeles Coliseum.

Dumas, a freshman at Compton Junior College in California, broke the 7-foot barrier on his second attempt as 50,000 stunned fans looked on. After missing badly on his first try, Dumas cleared the height easily on his second and then declined to make any higher attempts. Once the shock wore off, the appreciative crowd saluted the remarkable achievement of the new record-holder.

Dumas' effort came as a shock because his previous best jump was 6–10 1/4, a mark he reached in a 1955 Amateur Athletic Union meet at the Coliseum. His best effort so far this year had been 6–10.

MILESTONES IN SPORTS

1956

American Glenn Davis tore down a major track barrier when he broke 50 seconds in the 400-meter hurdles, posting a 49.5 clocking in a meet at Los Angeles.

1960

Gene Fullmer retained his National Boxing Association middleweight championship with a bloody 12-round technical knockout of Carmen Basilio at Salt Lake City.

1970

The National Hockey League gave controversial Oakland Athletics Owner Charles O. Finley permission to buy the financially-strapped Oakland Seals.

1983

Kansas City Chiefs back Joe Delaney, a 1,000-yard rusher two years earlier, drowned in his hometown of Monroe, La., while trying to rescue three young swimmers.

1983

Angel Cordero joined Johnny Longden, Laffit Pincay and Bill Shoemaker in the exclusive 5,000-win club when he rode Another Rodger to victory in the ninth race at Belmont Park.

1933

PRIMO CARNERA KOs SHARKEY

Italian giant **Primo Carnera** *hovers over* **Jack Sharkey** *after knocking down the heavyweight champion in the sixth round of a fight at New York.*

Italian giant Primo Carnera ended Jack Sharkey's one-year reign as heavyweight champion when he connected with a powerful uppercut to the chin in the sixth round of a title bout at the Long Island City Bowl.

Sharkey was making his first and last defense of the championship he had claimed last June with a 15-round decision over Max Schmeling. And the Boston fighter looked good in the early going, scoring decisive victories in four of the first five rounds with his quickness and evasive tactics.

But Carnera, 6 inches taller and 60 pounds heavier than the champion, was a time bomb waiting to explode – and he did so in the sixth round with an uppercut that nearly decapitated the unsuspecting Sharkey. The champ tumbled to the canvas, limp and without movement, as the referee counted him out.

The crowd of 40,000 watched in shock as the scenario unfolded and boxing crowned its first Italian champion. Sharkey was quickly revived by his handlers and escorted from the ring as bedlam broke loose.

In addition to becoming the first Italian heavyweight champion, Carnera became the sport's second non-American champion. The first was Germany's Max Schmeling.

JUNE

29

1990

FIRST NO-HIT DOUBLE

Oakland righthander Dave Stewart and Los Angeles lefty Fernando Valenzuela, working at different ballparks 3,000 miles apart, combined to make baseball history when they became the first major league pitchers to throw complete-game no-hitters on the same day.

Stewart, a 20-game winner in each of the last three seasons, performed his feat at the SkyDome in Toronto, striking out 12 Blue Jays and walking three in a 5–0 victory. Valenzuela struck out seven St. Louis Cardinals and walked three in a 6–0 victory at Dodger Stadium in Los Angeles.

Stewart needed only one good defensive play to secure his first career no-hitter – a diving stop by first baseman Mark McGwire. Valenzuela needed three, two by shortstop Alfredo Griffin on ground balls.

Valenzuela was fortunate in the ninth after walking Willie McGee. Cardinal star Pedro Guerrero hit a smash up the middle that the pitcher deflected. The ball went right to second baseman Juan Samuel, who turned a double play.

The only thing close to the Stewart-Valenzuela no-hit duet was the 1917 double no-hitter thrown by Chicago's Hippo Vaughn and Cincinnati's Fred Toney – at each other. Vaughn gave up a hit in the 10th and lost, 1–0.

JUNE

30

A STAR IS BORN

1912: Daniel Reeves, a football Hall of Famer who stretched the NFL into a coast-to-coast operation when he moved the Cleveland Rams to Los Angeles in 1946.

★ ★ ★

1957: Roy Green, a former National Football League wide receiver.

★ ★ ★

1965: Mitch Richmond, a current National Basketball Association guard.

★ ★ ★

1966: Mike Tyson, the youngest heavyweight champion in history when he claimed the title in 1986. After suffering his first defeat and losing the crown, he was convicted of rape and sentenced to prison.

1984 USFL Teams Set Record

Los Angeles back Mel Gray ran 24 yards for a touchdown 3:33 into a third overtime period, giving the Express a 27–21 United States Football League playoff victory over the Michigan Panthers and ending the longest game in professional football history.

Los Angeles Express running back **Mel Gray.**

The game at the Los Angeles Memorial Coliseum lasted 93 minutes, 33 seconds, 10:53 longer than the previous record-setter – Miami's 27–24 Christmas Day victory over the Kansas City Chiefs in a 1971 National Football League playoff contest.

Los Angeles quarterback Steve Young forced overtime with a two-point conversion run after Kevin Nelson had scored on a one-yard touchdown with 52 seconds remaining in regulation. Michigan placekicker Novo Bojovic had two opportunities to win the game, but missed a 37-yard field goal attempt in the first overtime period and a 36-yarder in the second.

Los Angeles broke on top with a five-yard Nelson run and a 32-yard Tony Zendejas field goal, but Michigan fought back on a pair of Bobby Hebert touchdown passes that gave the Panthers temporary 14–10 and 21–13 advantages.

MILESTONES IN SPORTS

1909

Cubs 3, Pirates 2 in the first game at Pittsburgh's $2-million Forbes Field.

1965

The National Football Legue awarded its 15th franchise to Rankin M. Smith, a life insurance executive in Georgia.

1970

Braves 8, Reds 2 in the first game at Cincinnati's new Riverfront Stadium.

1978

San Francisco's Willie McCovey became the 13th player to hit 500 career home runs when he connected off Atlanta's Jamie Easterly in the second inning of a 10–9 loss at Fulton County Stadium.

1979

The incredible Mary Decker set an American record for the women's mile with a 4:23.5 clocking in the Brooks Meet of Champions at Philadelphia.

1985

The new professional basketball Hall of Fame dedicated its three-story, $11.5- million museum in ceremonies at Springfield, Mass.

1978 White Sox Name Doby Second Black Manager

Larry Doby, the second modern-era black to play major league baseball, became the game's second black manager when the Chicago White Sox selected him to replace the fired Bob Lemon.

The 53-year-old Doby follows in the history-making footsteps of former Baltimore manager Frank Robinson, just as he followed Jackie Robinson into the major leagues in 1947, breaking the American League color barrier. Robinson became baseball's first black manager – in Cleveland – in 1975 and lasted two-plus seasons.

Doby got his chance when the White Sox fired Lemon, who had guided the team to a 90–72 record in 1977 and a 34–40 mark so far this year. Chicago Owner Bill Veeck is the same man who signed Doby as a player for Cleveland in 1947.

Doby was an outfielder who appeared in six All-Star Games and played in two World Series. He had worked as a coach and batting instructor under Lemon, his former teammate with the Indians.

New Chicago White Sox Manager **Larry Doby** *(left).*

1908 Young Does It Again

Cy Young, the grand old man of baseball, pitched his record third career no-hitter and added insult to injury by driving in four runs in Boston's 8–0 victory over the Highlanders at New York's Hilltop Park.

The 41-year-old Young struck out two and walked one, allowing one Highlander to reach base. Young pitched his first career no-hitter in 1897 for Cleveland and became the first modern-era pitcher to throw a perfect game in 1904 for the Red Sox. Only a walk to Harry Niles kept him from matching that feat against the Highlanders.

Young helped his own cause with three hits, including two-run singles in the third and ninth innings. The 18-year veteran righthander enjoyed a comfortable 5–0 lead after four innings.

Young's no-hitter was the major leagues' first since last September. It allowed him to match the three-no-hitter feat of former Chicago pitcher Lawrence Corcoran, who performed the triple in the 1880s.

1951 FELLER SAYS NO-NO AGAIN

Cleveland righthander Bob Feller added to his ever-growing list of pitching milestones when he fired his record-tying third career no-hitter and defeated the Detroit Tigers, 2–1, in the first game of a doubleheader at Cleveland Stadium.

The 32-year-old fireballer was far from top form, but he was good enough to match the career no-hit feats of Lawrence Corcoran, a pitcher from the 1880s, and the venerable Cy Young, who did most of his damage in the first decade of the century. In addition to his three no-hitters, Feller has pitched 10 one-hitters and managed to reach the 20-victory plateau five times.

Feller treated 48,891 Indians fans to a three-walk, five-strikeout masterpiece that lifted his season record to 11–2. Detroit touched him for a fourth-inning run when Johnny Lipon reached base on shortstop Ray Boone's error, stole second, moved to third on a wild throw and scored on a sacrifice fly.

Luke Easter drove in both Cleveland runs with a first-inning groundout and an eighth-inning single.

A smiling **Bob Feller** *accepts congratulations from his Cleveland teammates after firing his third career no-hitter.*

MILESTONES IN SPORTS

1910

The Chicago White Sox unveiled $750,000 Comiskey Park, but the St. Louis Browns spoiled the occasion by posting a 2–0 victory.

1960

Neale Fraser captured the Wimbledon singles championship when he defeated Rod Laver, 6–4, 3–6, 9–7, 7–5, in an all-Australian battle of lefthanders.

1975

Muhammad Ali defended his heavyweight championship with a unanimous 15-round decision over Joe Bugner at Kuala Lumpur, Malaysia.

1977

With Queen Elizabeth II watching from the Royal Box, Great Britain's Virginia Wade recorded an emotional 4–6, 6–3, 6–1 Wimbledon victory over Betty Stove of The Netherlands.

1977

East Germany's Margit Oelsner became the first woman to break 11 seconds in the 100-meter dash when she streaked to a 10.88 clocking in the East German national track and field championships at Dresden.

1980

Great Britain's Steve Ovett, winning his 42nd straight race, lowered the mile world record to 3:48.8 in an international track and field meet at Oslo, Norway.

1960 THOMAS TOPS OWN RECORD

John Thomas, a 19-year-old Boston University student, soared to world high jump records on consecutive leaps in an amazing effort of self one-upmanship during competition in the United States Olympic trials at Stanford Stadium in Palo Alto, Calif.

With 41,000 spectators watching the action, Thomas bettered the listed world record of 7-foot–1 when he cleared 7–2 1/2 on his first attempt at that height. But he wasn't finished. When the bar was moved to 7–3 3/4, he easily cleared that height and then went for 7–4 1/2, missing for the first time.

Before the record-setter, Thomas had cleared 7-foot and 7–1 on first attempts and his record-setters brought his career total of 7-foot jumps to 34. Thomas already had broken Russian Yuri Stepanov's world record with a 7–2 leap, but it had not yet been certified as a record.

A STAR IS BORN

1941: Rod Gilbert, a hockey Hall of Fame right winger who scored 1,021 points over a long career with the New York Rangers.

★ ★ ★

1958: Nancy Lieberman, a college All-America basketball player at Old Dominion and in 1986 the first woman to play in a men's professional league (USBL).

★ ★ ★

1961: Carl Lewis, a world record-setting sprinter and long jumper who captured four gold medals at the 1984 Los Angeles Olympic Games and two more in 1988 at Seoul.

★ ★ ★

JULY 1

1990 NO-HIT EFFORT WASTED

New York righthander Andy Hawkins entered the record book when he pitched a no-hitter against Chicago, but his post-game feeling was not jubilation. Hawkins, victimized by some brutal eighth-inning fielding by the Yankees, lost a 4–0 decision to the White Sox.

The complete-game no-hitter loss put Hawkins in select company. Only Houston's Ken Johnson in 1964 had previously suffered such an indignity, losing a 1–0 decision to Cincinnati on a ninth-inning throwing error. Hawkins' eighth inning against Chicago was nothing short of a nightmare.

It started with two out when third baseman Mike Blowers mishandled Sammy Sosa's ground ball. Hawkins followed by walking Ozzie Guillen and Lance Johnson, loading the bases. But Chicago third baseman Robin Ventura lifted a harmless-looking fly ball to left field, an apparent rally-killer.

Not so. Rookie Jim Leyritz, fighting a swirling wind, dropped the ball and three runners raced home. Ivan Calderon followed with another harmless-looking fly ball to right that Jesse Barfield dropped, allowing Ventura to score.

Dan Pasqua popped out to end the inning and the Yankees, held to four hits by three Chicago pitchers, were retired in the ninth, sealing the final verdict.

JULY

2

A STAR IS BORN

1905: Rene Lacoste, one of France's "Four Musketeers" of the 1920s who won seven Grand Slam tennis titles.

★ ★ ★

1931: Larry Costello, a 13-year NBA star who became a college and professional coach. His NBA teams won 430 games.

★ ★ ★

1937: Richard Petty, the king of the NASCAR racing circuit with more than 200 career victories and a seven-time winner of the prestigious Daytona 500.

★ ★ ★

1964: Jose Canseco, a current major league outfielder.

★ ★ ★

DEATH OF A LEGEND

1903: Ed Delahanty (baseball).

★ ★ ★

1964: Glenn (Fireball) Roberts (auto racing).

★ ★ ★

1973: Chick Hafey (baseball).

★ ★ ★

1993: Don Drysdale (baseball).

Heavyweight champion
Jack Dempsey.

1977 Borg Aces Connors

Bjorn Borg dramatically brought down the curtain on Wimbledon's first hundred years when he outlasted Jimmy Connors in an exhausting five-set marathon that crowned him as the top male player in the game.

Borg's second straight Wimbledon title was accomplished in a 3-hour, 14-minute battle under a hot afternoon sun that produced a 3–6, 6–2, 6–1, 5–7, 6–4 victory. It was a heavyweight match that went the distance, Connors blasting away with his relentless power and the 21-year-old Borg counter-punching with his pace-changing repertoire of ground strokes.

The best was saved for last when the aggressive, emotional Connors made a spirited comeback from an 0–4, 30–40 fifth-set deficit. He held service and broke Borg twice to square the set at four games, all the while shaking his fist and exhorting himself to go, go, go.

And then, just as suddenly as he had recovered his momentum, he lost it. He won the first point of the ninth game and then double-faulted. When the crowd cheered, Connors responded with an obscene gesture. His concentration broken, he dropped the next three points and Borg held service to close out his third triumph against Connors in 11 matches.

Swedish tennis champion
Bjorn Borg.

1903 Delahanty Dies In Bridge Fall

Ed Delahanty, a .346 career hitter for 16 outstanding seasons with Philadelphia and Washington and one of baseball's brightest stars, plunged to his death off a railroad bridge that crosses the Niagara River between Fort Erie, Ontario, and New York state.

While the circumstances surrounding Delahanty's death remained a mystery, some reports said it was the result of a drunken binge. Others called it a simple accident. Still others suggested Delahanty might have committed suicide.

What is known for sure is that the 34-year-old Delahanty, the 1902 American League batting champion, had inexplicably jumped the Senators and boarded a Michigan Central Railroad train headed for New York. After consuming five drinks, he became rowdy and trainmen forced him off at Fort Erie.

Delahanty started walking across the draw bridge, which was preparing to open. Warned to return to the Canadian side, he refused and plunged to his death. His mangled body, found 20 miles south of the bridge, was identified by dental records.

MILESTONES
IN SPORTS

1933

New York Giants lefty Carl Hubbell, striking out 12 and walking none, pitched all 18 innings of a 1–0 six-hit victory over the St. Louis Cardinals.

1938

Helen Wills-Moody earned her record eighth Wimbledon singles title when she defeated old rival Helen Jacobs, 6–4, 6–0.

1941

Joe DiMaggio extended his consecutive-game hitting streak to 45 and moved past Willie Keeler on the all-time list when he homered off Boston's Dick Newsome.

1954

Egyptian Jaroslav Drobny, a 32-year-old Wimbledon favorite for 16 years, captured the coveted singles title on his 11th attempt with a 13–11, 4–6, 6–2, 9–7 victory over Australian Ken Rosewall.

1966

California lefthander Billie Jean King captured her first major tournament when she defeated three-time champion Maria Bueno, 6–3, 3–6, 6–1, in the Wimbledon singles final.

1972

Bob Seagren, the 1968 Olympic pole vault champion, soared to a world-record height of 18–5 3/4 during competition in the Olympic trials at Eugene, Ore.

1921 Dempsey Knocks Out Frenchman Carpentier

Jack Dempsey, performing before the largest crowd in boxing history in the so-called "battle of the century," knocked out Frenchman Georges Carpentier in the fourth round and retained his world heavyweight title at Jersey City, N.J.

With 90,000 fans packed into a wooden arena, Dempsey stalked his lighter opponent from the opening bell and worked the body at every opportunity. That strategy appeared sound as Carpentier did most of his damage from long range.

Dempsey brought the crowd to its feet in the fourth round when he connected with a left to the face and a right just above the ear, knocking Carpentier to the canvas. The Frenchman jumped up but Dempsey resumed the attack. Another left followed by rights to the ribs and jaw put Carpentier down to stay.

The match produced several firsts. It was the first to feature a legitimate European challenger, the first to be broadcast on radio and the first with a million-dollar purse.

1954 Babe Shows Old Form In Victory

Babe Didrikson Zaharias, who is acknowledged as the "greatest woman athlete" of all time, capped her courageous comeback from a cancer operation with an emotional and heart-warming victory in the U.S. Women's Open – a victory she offered as inspiration to cancer victims around the world.

Zaharias, obviously tired but still as overpowering as ever, recorded a 12-stroke triumph over Betty Hicks at the Salem Country Club in Peabody, Mass. The Open championship was her third and the victory was her fourth since undergoing a potential career-ending operation only last spring.

"When I was in the hospital, I prayed that I could play again," Zaharias said after her victory. "Now I'm happy because I can tell people not to be afraid of cancer."

Babe finished her final 36-hole test with a 72-hole total of 291.

Babe Didrikson Zaharias, *culminating her comeback from a cancer operation, displays her U.S. Women's Open trophy.*

1912 Giants Lefty Extends Mark

Young New York left-hander Rube Marquard extended his major league record for consecutive victories to 19 and the Giants extended their winning streak to 16 when he out-dueled Brooklyn lefty Nap Rucker, 2–1, in the first game of a doubleheader sweep at the Polo Grounds.

But Marquard's record-setter did not come easily. The talented Frenchman allowed nine hits and the Dodgers had baserunners in all but one inning. Marquard allowed only one to score, however, and the Dodgers finished their frustrating effort by stranding 14.

Rucker was much sharper. He allowed only four New York hits and was in control most of the way. But the Giants scored a fourth-inning run when shortstop Bert Tooley dropped Beals Becker's popup, allowing Red Murray to score. And they notched their winning run in the seventh when Murray doubled, moved to third on a bunt and scored on Chief Meyers' sacrifice fly.

That was all Marquard needed. Twice Brooklyn had the bases loaded and failed to score. The Dodgers managed two baserunners in the ninth, but Marquard ended matters on a strikeout and fly ball.

The previous record for consecutive victories in a season, 16, was shared by American League righthanders Smokey Joe Wood and Walter Johnson.

1966 Pitcher Cloninger Becomes Slugger

In a history-making performance that might stand the test of time, Atlanta's Tony Cloninger became the first National League player to hit two grand slams in the same game and topped off his offensive heroics by pitching the Braves to a 17–3 victory over San Francisco.

The once-in-a-lifetime performance, witnessed by 27,002 fans at Candlestick Park, put Cloninger in the company of such active and former American Leaguers as Tony Lazzeri (1936), Jim Tabor (1939), Rudy York (1946) and Jim Gentile (1961). Cloninger, a 24-game winner last season, added a run-scoring single in his nine-RBI effort that set a major league record for a pitcher.

Cloninger hit his first slam to right-center field off Bob Priddy, climaxing a seven-run Atlanta first inning. He connected again in the fourth off Ray Sedecki, a shot over the right-field fence, and capped his slugging spree with a single.

Cloninger, who pitched a seven-hitter, enjoyed a two-homer, five-RBI game against the New York Mets on June 16.

A STAR IS BORN

1916: John Kundla, a 423-game winner as an NBA coach. He led the Minneapolis Lakers to five championships in the 1940s and '50s.

★ ★ ★

1953: Frank Tanana, a current major league pitcher.

DEATH OF A LEGEND

1985: Frank Selke (hockey).

JULY 3

MILESTONES • IN SPORTS •

1931

Max Schmeling officially dedicated Cleveland's new Municipal Stadium when he recorded an exciting 15th-round technical knockout of Young Stribling and retained his world heavyweight boxing championship.

1977

Seattle Slew, horse racing's first undefeated Triple Crown winner, lost his first race when J.O. Tobin and jockey Bill Shoemaker beat him by 16 lengths in the Swaps Sweepstakes for 3-year-olds at Hollywood Park.

1980

Edwin Moses lowered his 3-year-old world record in the 400-meter hurdles with a time of 47.13 in a track and field meet at Milan, Italy.

1983

In a 15-minute span, Evelyn Ashford streaked to a world-record clocking of 10.79 in the women's 100 meters and Calvin Smith dashed to a men's world record of 9.93 in the National Sports Festival at Colorado Springs.

1983

John McEnroe claimed his second Wimbledon championship when he downed New Zealand's Chris Lewis, 6–2, 6–2, 6–2, in 1 hour, 25 minutes.

1985

A Wimbledon shocker: South African Kevin Curren defeated top seed and defending champion John McEnroe, 6–2, 6–2, 6–4, in a quarterfinal match.

JULY

4

1981 Borg's Streak Finally Ends

John McEnroe, keeping his volatile temper and off-colored antics under tight rein, earned his first Wimbledon singles title and ended Bjorn Borg's five-year championship reign with a 4–6, 7–6, 7–6, 6–4 victory at the All-England Tennis Club.

McEnroe's victory was decisive and subdued. After a week filled with tantrums, verbal abuse of referees and arguments, he entered the final playing under the threat of a $10,000 fine and suspension. The 22-year-old left-hander showed there is more to his game than the controversy and theatrics that have made him an international villain.

The key was a sometimes-erratic first serve that was steady and controlled on this day. McEnroe won 82 of 104 points played off his first serve and used it to dominate both tiebreakers, which he won 7–1 and 7–4.

Borg, who entered the action with a 41-match Wimbledon winning streak, took McEnroe to four set points in the third set, but couldn't produce the winner.

McEnroe's victory, which came on the heels of several volatile outbursts during a semifinal match against Rod Frawley, gave the United States a Wimbledon singles sweep. Chris Evert-Lloyd upheld the honor of the American women with a triumph over Hana Mandlikova.

MILESTONES • IN SPORTS •

1919

Jack Dempsey, giving away 50 pounds to 6-foot-7 Jess Willard, knocked the champion down six times in the first round and claimed his heavyweight crown with a fourth-round technical knockout in a fight at Toledo, O.

1932

New York Yankee catcher Bill Dickey, who broke the jaw of Washington's Carl Reynolds in a one-punch fight after a collision at home plate, was fined $1,000 and suspended 30 days.

1939

Boston slugger Jim Tabor tied the major league record when he belted two grand slams in the second game of a doubleheader sweep of Philadelphia. Tabor hit four homers and drove in 11 runs in the twin-bill.

1948

The Boston Red Sox matched the major league record when they exploded for 14 runs in the seventh inning of a 19–5 victory over Philadelphia.

1975

Billie Jean King, winning the Wimbledon singles championship for a sixth time, rolled past Australian Evonne Goolagong-Cawley, 6–0, 6–1.

1982

Jimmy Connors ended his frustrating seven-year Wimbledon drought with a 4-hour 3–6, 6–3, 6–7, 7–6, 6–4 victory over defending champion John McEnroe.

1992

Steffi again: West German lefthander Steffi Graf captured her fourth Wimbledon championship in five years with a quick-and-easy 6–2, 6–1 victory over Monica Seles.

1939 Gehrig Says Farewell

In a gala pageant attended by 61,808 fans and members of the 1927 Yankee championship team, former first baseman Lou Gehrig said an emotional farewell to New Yorkers between games of a doubleheader against Washington.

The "Lou Gehrig Day" festivities were to honor the Yankee "Iron Horse," who was forced out of the lineup two months ago for the first time in 2,130 games by a debilitating form of infantile paralysis. Such members of the 1927 Yankees as Babe Ruth, Tony Lazzeri and Bob Meusel were escorted around the field by the Seventh Regiment Band and they formed a human rectangle around the home plate area along with all the current Yankees and Senators.

When Gehrig emerged from the dugout, the crowd roared. Speaker after speaker delivered glowing tributes and gifts were presented before Gehrig moved to the microphone. Looking haggard and tired, he choked back emotion and spoke, as always, from his heart.

"What young man wouldn't give anything to mingle with such men as I have for all these years?" he said. "You've been reading about my bad break for weeks now. But today I think I'm the luckiest man on the face of the earth."

Former Yankee great **Lou Gehrig,** *trying to hold back the tears.*

A STAR IS BORN

1880: George Mullin, a righthander who won 212 games in 12 seasons in the early 1900s.

★ ★ ★

1930: George Steinbrenner, the owner of the New York Yankees.

★ ★ ★

1941: Digger Phelps, a college basketball coach who compiled 393 victories in 20 years at Notre Dame.

★ ★ ★

1910 Johnson Pounds Jeffries

Jack Johnson, the black heavyweight champion with the taunting smile, pounded out a convincing 15-round victory over former champion James J. Jeffries and silenced the cries for a "Great White Hope" to bring sanity back to the boxing world.

It was a one-sided victory that sparked race riots around the country and reaffirmed Johnson's place as the greatest champion of the century. Johnson worked over the 35-year-old challenger from the opening bell and dropped him three times in the decisive 15th round, the last time for good.

The large crowd at Reno, Nev., sat in stunned silence, realizing its hope of crowning a white champion had vanished. Jeffries, who had retired as the undefeated champ in 1905, was a last resort. Heeding the pleas of the white community, he had returned to an intensive training regimen and tried to revive the fire that had driven him to seven successful title defenses during his six-year reign.

But the fire just wasn't there and Jeffries was admittedly overmatched. "I could never have whipped Jack Johnson at my best," he said after the knockout.

Heavyweight champion **Jack Johnson** *stands over knockdown victim* **James Jeffries** *en route to a shockingly easy victory.*

1980 Borg Wins Fifth Wimbledon in Row

In a grueling test of wills that ranks among the greatest tennis matches ever played, Sweden's Bjorn Borg outlasted American John McEnroe in five sets and captured his fifth consecutive Wimbledon singles championship.

The 3-hour, 53-minute thriller at the All-England Tennis Club was "electrifying." Borg triumphed, 1–6, 7–5, 6–3, 6–7, 8–6, to stretch his Wimbledon winning streak to 35 matches. But it was the 21-year-old McEnroe who provided most of the excitement, stretching the 24-year-old defending champ to the very edge of his game.

Seven times McEnroe fought off match point in the incredible fourth set, five times in the 34-point tiebreaker. Both players dove, lunged and fought their way through the excruciating tiebreaker that McEnroe finally claimed, 18–16.

Then it was up to Borg to show his championship mettle and reclaim lost momentum. He lost the first two points, but then won 19 straight off his serve through nine games. McEnroe continued his bulldog imitation, but Borg's consistency and determination finally wore him down.

The end came swiftly in the 14th game. From 15-all, Borg hit three straight winners and claimed the $50,000 first prize.

The barrier breakers: Brooklyn's **Jackie Robinson** *(left) and Cleveland's* **Larry Doby.**

1947 Doby Makes Debut

It lacked the fanfare and public interest that Jackie Robinson's history-making Brooklyn Dodgers debut generated three months earlier, but Larry Doby's first American League appearance was no less significant. The former Negro League star broke another baseball color barrier when he pinch-hit for the Cleveland Indians in the seventh inning of a game against the White Sox at Chicago's Comiskey Park.

Doby, whose contract was purchased from the Newark Eagles by Indians Owner Bill Veeck, became the century's second black major leaguer when he batted for pitcher Bryan Stephens with one out and runners on first and third base. After getting an enthusiastic reception from more than 18,000 White Sox fans, the 185-pound lefthanded batter worked the count to 2–2 before going down swinging on a pitch from Earl Harrist. The White Sox went on to record a 6–5 victory.

Doby's debut capped a whirlwind day in which he signed his contract and was driven to Comiskey Park by Veeck. Doby, a .415 hitter for Newark, received a very cordial welcome from surprised Cleveland teammates when he was introduced by Veeck in the Indians' locker room.

Milestones in Sports

1904

The Philadelphia Phillies brought the Giants back to earth when they recorded a 6–5 victory in 10 innings, ending the New Yorkers' winning streak at 18 games and dropping their record to 53–18.

1970

Donna Caponi dropped a 4-foot putt on the final hole and earned her second straight U.S. Women's Open championship with a one-stroke victory over Sandra Haynie and Sandra Spuzich at Muskogee, Okla.

1974

Chris Evert, the 19-year-old wunderkind from Florida, earned her first Wimbledon championship with a 6–0, 6–4 cakewalk past Russian Olga Morozova.

1975

Arthur Ashe confused Jimmy Connors with his change-of-pace attack and became the first black male to win a Wimbledon singles title with an historic 6–1, 6–1, 5–7, 6–4 victory.

1992

American teen idol Andre Agassi scored his first major tournament victory when he defeated Goran Ivanisevic, 6–7, 6–4, 6–4, 1–6, 6–4, in the finals of the Wimbledon championships.

July 5

1968 Wilt Is Traded To L.A.

In a major trade that could change the balance of power in the National Basketball Association, the Philadelphia 76ers sent 7-foot-1 scoring machine Wilt Chamberlain to the Los Angeles Lakers for three players and cash.

Chamberlain, who averaged 24.3 points and 23.8 rebounds last season, will join a talented Lakers cast that includes Elgin Baylor and Jerry West. Los Angeles officials have been looking for a big man and Philadelphia Owner Irv Kosloff was upset by what he considered unreasonable demands by Chamberlain.

Chamberlain had led Philadelphia to its first championship two years ago, but the 76ers were upset last year in the playoffs. When Alex Hannum resigned as coach, the seven-time scoring champion demanded a million-dollar contract and a say in naming a replacement.

What he got was a ticket to the West Coast. Coming to Philadelphia were Darrell Imhoff, Archie Clark and Jerry Chambers.

A Star Is Born

1923: John McKay, the college and pro football coach who led Southern California to five Rose Bowls in the 1960s and '70s.

★ ★ ★

1956: James Lofton, a current National Football League wide receiver.

JULY

6

A STAR IS BORN

1948: Brad Park, a hockey Hall of Fame defenseman who scored 896 points in 17 seasons with the New York Rangers, Boston and Detroit.

★ ★ ★

MILESTONES IN SPORTS

1929

The St. Louis Cardinals, getting grand slam homers from Chick Hafey and Jim Bottomley, erupted for a modern one-game record 28 runs in a 28–6 pounding of Philadelphia at the Baker Bowl.

1938

Brooklyn shortstop Leo Durocher, with the aid of two American League throwing errors, circled the bases on a seventh-inning sacrifice bunt attempt to highlight the National League's 4–1 All-Star Game victory at Cincinnati.

1968

Three in a row: Billie Jean King claimed her third Wimbledon title with a 9–7, 7–5 victory over Judy Tegart.

1974

Jimmy Connors, matching the accomplishment of fiance Chris Evert the day before, won his first Wimbledon title with a 6–1, 6–1, 6–4 victory over Australian Ken Rosewall.

1983

Boston's Fred Lynn blasted the first grand slam in All-Star Game history and the A.L. ended its embarrassing 11-game losing streak to the N.L. with an emphatic 13–3 victory at Chicago's Comiskey Park.

1933 BABE STEALS STAR SHOW

The crowds were enthusiastic in anticipation of baseball's first All-Star Game at Chicago's Comiskey Park.

It was billed as the "Game of the Century" and that was Babe Ruth's cue to take center stage. Ever the showman, the New York Yankees' Bambino belted the first home run in baseball's first All-Star Game and propelled the American League to a 4–2 victory over the National League.

The extravaganza, staged at Comiskey Park in conjunction with Chicago's Century of Progress Exhibition, was the brainchild of Chicago Tribune sportswriter Arch Ward. The top players from both leagues were on hand and 47,595 enthusiastic fans turned out to salute the greatest collection of baseball talent ever assembled on one field.

The A.L. grabbed a 1–0 lead in the second inning when Yankee pitcher Lefty Gomez, a notoriously weak hitter, singled home Chicago 's Jimmie Dykes. The lead increased when Ruth pounded a third-inning pitch from St. Louis' Wild Bill Hallahan into Comiskey Park's right-field stands for a two-run homer.

St. Louis player-Manager Frank Frisch got one of the runs back with a sixth-inning home run, but Philadelphia ace Lefty Grove finally slammed the door with three shutout innings that secured the A.L.'s historic victory.

1986 HORNER BLASTS 4

Atlanta first baseman Bob Horner joined an elite club of baseball sluggers when he muscled up and blasted four home runs in a single game – an 11–8 loss to the Montreal Expos at Atlanta's Fulton County Stadium.

Horner became only the 11th player to accomplish the feat and the first in 10 years. Nobody had done it in the regulation nine innings since 1961, when San Francisco's Willie Mays belted four out of Milwaukee's County Stadium.

Horner's long-ball barrage began in the second inning with a solo blast and he added another solo shot in the fourth and a three-run drive in the fifth. All came off Montreal starter Andy McGaffigan. The record-tying blow came with two out in the ninth inning when he connected with a pitch from reliever Jeff Reardon.

The standing ovation accorded the muscular 200-pounder was just dying down when Reardon recorded the final out.

1935 WILLS-MOODY WINS 7TH WIMBLEDON

Helen Wills-Moody, showing the indomitable will that has made her the greatest female champion in tennis history, recovered from a 5–2 third-set deficit against old foe Helen Jacobs and captured her record-tying seventh Wimbledon singles championship.

The 29-year-old Wills-Moody treated 19,000 fans at the All-England Club's Centre Court to the greatest rally the prestigious tournament had ever produced. After splitting the first two sets, 6–3, 3–6, Wills-Moody trailed 5–2 and faced match point in the third when she went on the attack.

Suddenly going to the net with reckless abandon, she rattled off five straight games and claimed victory, matching the Wimbledon title record of Dorothea Lambert Chambers.

The triumph was especially impressive because Wills-Moody was coming off a two-year layoff and had been playing competitively for only a month.

Seven-time Wimbledon champion **Helen Wills-Moody.**

MILESTONES · IN SPORTS ·

1912

Jim Thorpe won four of the five events and scored an easy victory for the United States in the pentathlon competition at the Stockholm Summer Olympic Games.

1924

Great Britain's Harold Abrahams outdueled American Jackson Scholz with a 10.6-second clocking in the final of the 100-meter dash at the Paris Olympic Games – a race that inspired the 1981 movie "Chariots of Fire."

1936

After three straight losses, the National League broke through for its first All-Star Game victory – a 4–3 decision at Braves Field in Boston.

1937

All-Star casualty: St. Louis righthander Dizzy Dean suffered a broken toe when he was hit by a line drive off the bat of Cleveland's Earl Averill in the midsummer classic at Washington.

1973

Winning for the fifth time in eight years, Billie Jean King humbled 18-year-old Chris Evert with a 6–0, 7–5 victory in the Wimbledon singles final.

1978

Martina Navratilova rallied from a first-set loss and a 2–4 final-set deficit to win her first Wimbledon championship with a 2–6, 6–4, 7–5 victory over Chris Evert.

1990

A Wimbledon record: Martina Navratilova captured her ninth title with a 6–4, 6–1 victory over Zina Garrison.

1986 HEPTATHLON MARK FALLS IN MOSCOW

JULY 7

American Jackie Joyner, making her bid for the title of "world's greatest female athlete," gave new meaning to the word "detente" when she set a women's world record in the heptathlon and won the hearts of Russian fans with her performance in the Goodwill Games at Moscow.

Joyner received a wild ovation when she turned in a 2:10.02 time in the 800-meter race that closed the seven-pronged, two-day event. That gave her 7,148 points, 202 more than the previous heptathlon mark. The crowd had been alerted that Joyner needed a 2:24.64 clocking in the 800 meters to set a record and it cheered her to victory.

That race culminated an impressive showing by the East St. Louis native. She set a first-day record with 4,151 points and opened her second day by setting a heptathlon world mark with a 23-foot leap in her favorite event – the long jump.

World heptathlon champion **Jackie Joyner** *captured the hearts of Russian fans with her record-setting Goodwill Games effort in Moscow.*

1975 RUFFIAN BREAKS A LEG

A much-publicized $350,000 match race between unbeaten filly Ruffian and Kentucky Derby winner Foolish Pleasure turned into a nightmare at Belmont Park when Ruffian broke her leg early in the race and had to be destroyed.

Ruffian was unbeaten in 10 races and went off against her more experienced opponent as a 2–5 betting favorite. And jockey Jacinto Vasquez guided her to a slight lead in the first 3 1/2 furlongs of the 1 1/4-mile test before disaster struck.

When the Kentucky-bred 3-year-old suddenly pulled up lame, Vasquez directed her to the side of the track and Braulio Baeza rode Foolish Pleasure to an uncontested victory and the $225,000 first prize.

But that was the least of Ruffian owner Stuart Janney's concerns. A team of doctors operated on Ruffian's right ankle for 3 1/2 hours and then fitted it with a cast and special shoe. But eight hours after the race, Ruffian awoke from the anesthesia and managed to kicked off the fitting. Janney had no choice but to have her put to sleep.

Fittingly, Ruffian was buried the following day on the infield area at Belmont Park.

1964 CALLISON BLAST DESTROYS A.L.

Philadelphia right fielder Johnny Callison drilled a three-run, ninth-inning shot into the right-field seats at New York's Shea Stadium, giving the National League a dramatic 7–4 All-Star Game victory over the American League.

Callison's first-pitch blast off Boston relief ace Dick Radatz capped a four-run N.L. rally that wiped out a 4–3 deficit entering the final frame. The Nationals had tied the game when San Francisco's Willie Mays walked, stole second and came around on a wild throw by New York Yankee first baseman Joe Pepitone after a bloop single by the Giants' Orlando Cepeda. Callison's two-out blow followed an intentional walk to Cincinnati catcher Johnny Edwards.

The victory, the N.L.'s second straight and sixth in seven years, finally evened the overall series at 17–17–1. But it did not appear that would be the case when the A.L. scored two sixth-inning runs on a triple by Baltimore's Brooks Robinson and took a 4–3 lead on California shortstop Jim Fregosi's seventh-inning sacrifice fly.

Two of the N.L.'s runs came on fourth-inning homers by Chicago's Billy Williams and St. Louis' Ken Boyer.

A STAR IS BORN

1905: Satchel Paige, a Hall of Famer generally regarded as one of the great pitchers of all time. He spent his best seasons in the old Negro League before reaching the majors late in his career.

★ ★ ★

1909: Billy Herman, a Hall of Fame second baseman who batted .304 over 15 seasons in the National League from 1931–47.

★ ★ ★

1960: Ralph Sampson, a former 7-foot-4 center in the National Basketball Association.

★ ★ ★

DEATH OF A LEGEND

1982: Joe Dugan (baseball).

★ ★ ★

1983: Vic Wertz (baseball).

★ ★ ★

1992: Clint Frank (football).

★ ★ ★

JULY

8

MILESTONES IN SPORTS

1947

Washington pinch-hitter Stan Spence delivered a run-scoring single in the seventh inning that gave the American League a 2–1 All-Star Game victory over the National League – its 10th win in 14 midsummer classics.

1950

Louise Brough, beating Margaret Osborne du Pont in the final for the second straight year, captured her third consecutive Wimbledon singles title with a 6–1, 3–6, 6–1 victory.

1952

A two-run homer by Chicago's Hank Sauer was the big blow in the National League's 3–2 All-Star Game victory over the American League – a game shortened to five innings by rain.

1941 Williams Has a Blast

Young Boston slugger Ted Williams drove a two-out, ninth-inning pitch from Chicago's Claude Passeau off the upper right-field parapet of Detroit's Briggs Stadium for a three-run homer, giving the American League a dramatic 7–5 victory over the National League in baseball's ninth All-Star Game.

Williams' monster blow capped a four-run uprising that sent the stunned Nationals down to defeat in the midsummer classic for the sixth time. Williams was batting only because Brooklyn second baseman Billy Herman made a bad throw to first on a double-play grounder by New York's Joe DiMaggio that could have ended the game.

The N.L. appeared to be in control until the fateful ninth. That's because of the offensive work of Pittsburgh shortstop Arky Vaughan – normally a light hitter. Vaughan muscled up for two home runs and four RBIs that helped the N.L. carry a 5–2 lead into the bottom of the eighth inning.

The A.L. got one back when DiMaggio doubled and scored on brother Dominic's single. The Americans loaded the bases with one out in the ninth on two singles and a walk. DiMaggio's grounder was handled by Boston shortstop Eddie Miller, but Herman's relay to first was wide.

American League Manager Del Baker congratulates All-Star Game hero **Ted Williams.**

1935 A.L. Stars Do The Foxx Trot

The powerful American League team continued its domination of the All-Star Game series when Philadelphia slugger Jimmie Foxx blasted a two-run homer and drove in three runs in a 4–1 victory over the National League at Cleveland Stadium.

Foxx, playing third base instead of his regular first base position, belted his two-run shot in the first inning off St. Louis' Bill Walker. The Americans added a third run in the second on a sacrifice fly by Boston's Joe Cronin and Foxx drove in the final run in the fifth.

New York Yankee ace Lefty Gomez, who has started all three All-Star Games for the A.L., pitched six innings of three-hit ball before giving way to Cleveland's Mel Harder. The righthander allowed one hit in three innings.

The Nationals, still looking for their first midsummer classic victory, scored their only run in the fourth on a double by Pittsburgh's Arky Vaughan and a single by New York's Bill Terry.

1967 Ryun Lowers 1,500 Record

Kansas University sophomore Jim Ryun added another world record to his impressive resume when he streaked to a 35-yard victory over Kenyan Kip Keino in the 1,500-meter competition of the United States-British Commonwealth track and field meet at the Los Angeles Coliseum.

Ryun completed his "metric mile" in 3:33.1, topping the 7-year-old record of Australian distance king Herb Elliott. Elliott ran his record-setting 3:35.6 in the 1960 Summer Olympic Games at Rome.

Ryun's performance came on the heels of his greatest career feat – a world record in the mile. The talented 20-year-old had lowered his own mile mark to 3:51.1 in an Amateur Athletic Union meet two weeks ago. His 1,500-meter time was the equivalent of a 3:48 mile.

Ryun set the 1,500-meter record with an amazing 38.1-second kick after covering his lap fractions in 60.9, 1:57.5 and 2:55.

A STAR IS BORN

1923: Harrison Dillard, the only man in Olympic Games history to win gold medals in both the 100-meter dash (1948) and the 110-meter hurdles (1952).

★ ★ ★

1952: Jack Lambert, a football Hall of Fame linebacker who anchored Pittsburgh's "Steel Curtain" defense and helped the Steelers win four Super Bowl championships in the 1970s.

★ ★ ★

DEATH OF A LEGEND

1981: Wild Bill Hallahan (baseball).

★ ★ ★

Two-time British Open champion **Tom Watson.**

1977 WATSON CAPTURES 2ND BRITISH OPEN

Tom Watson, hungrily eyeing Jack Nicklaus' status as the world's greatest golfer, defeated the Golden Bear in a dramatic head-to-head shootout that produced his second British Open championship in three years.

In a no-holds-barred battle of indomitable wills and spectacular shots, Watson prevailed by one stroke. But he needed birdies on three of the last four holes at the Turnberry, Scotland, course to finish with a 65 and four-round total of 268.

Watson and Nicklaus had pulled away from the rest of the field with third-round 65s that left them in a dead-heat entering the final round. When they approached the 15th tee, Nicklaus held a two-stroke advantage and appeared ready to avenge a tough loss to Watson in the recent Masters tournament at Augusta.

But the 27-year-old Missourian had other ideas. Watson chipped in from the fringe of the green for a birdie on 15 and then dropped a dramatic 60-foot putt on 16 for a tying birdie. When he dropped another birdie putt on No.17, he was in control.

JULY 9

A STAR IS BORN

1918: Nile Kinnick, a University of Iowa halfback who captured the Heisman Trophy in 1939.

★ ★ ★

1922: Jim Pollard, a basketball Hall of Famer and member of the Minneapolis team that won five NBA titles in the 1940s and '50s.

★ ★ ★

1947: O.J. Simpson, a former Heisman Trophy winner from Southern Cal and a pro football Hall of Fame running back who rushed for 11,236 yards in his 10-year NFL career.

★ ★ ★

DEATH OF A LEGEND

1951: Harry Heilmann (baseball).

★ ★ ★

1976: Tom Yawkey (baseball).

MILESTONES · IN SPORTS ·

1922

Johnny Weissmuller of the Illinois Athletic Club became the first swimmer to break the 1-minute barrier in the 100-meter freestyle when he covered the distance in 58.6 seconds at Alameda, Calif.

1940

The National League posted the first shutout in All-Star Game history when it blanked the American League, 4–0, at St. Louis' Sportsman's Park.

1963

San Francisco's Willie Mays dominated the A.L. in every way possible – hitting, baserunning, defense – and the N.L. recorded a 5–3 All-Star Game victory at Cleveland's Municipal Stadium.

1968

Three All-Star firsts: a 1–0 decision, an indoor contest and a game played on artificial turf. The National League won the history-making battle at Houston's Astrodome.

1991

Baltimore's Cal Ripken provided the big blow, a three-run homer, and the A.L. cruised to its fourth straight All-Star Game victory over the N.L. at Toronto's SkyDome.

1957 MINOSO RESCUES A.L. ALL-STARS

Chicago left fielder Minnie Minoso, an eighth-inning defensive replacement, threw a runner out at third base in the ninth and ended the contest with a spectacular running catch as the American League held on for a 6–5 victory over the National League in the All-Star Game at St. Louis.

The outcome was decided in a wild final inning after the A.L. completed eight frames with a 3–2 lead. The Americans seemed to have things under control in the top of the ninth when Detroit's Al Kaline delivered two more runs with a single and Minoso doubled home another.

But it wouldn't be that easy. St. Louis' Stan Musial walked to open the inning and San Francisco's Willie Mays tripled and scored moments later on a wild pitch. When Pittsburgh's Hank Foiles singled and Cincinnati's Gus Bell walked, things got sticky.

Milwaukee's Eddie Mathews struck out, but Chicago's Ernie Banks singled to left. Minoso fielded the drive and fired a strike to third base, cutting down Bell trying to take an extra base.

With Banks at second, Brooklyn's Gil Hodges ripped a drive toward left-center. Minoso raced into the gap, extended his glove and pulled down the ball to end the game.

A.L. All-Star sluggers (left to right) **Luke Appling, Dom DiMaggio, Rudy York, Ken Keltner, Ted Williams** *and* **Stan Spence.**

1946 WILLIAMS WINS 'EPHUS' BATTLE

Boston's Ted Williams belted two home runs in a 4-for-4, five-RBI explosion that keyed the American League's 12–0 All-Star Game victory over the National League at Fenway Park. But the real story was an eighth-inning confrontation between Williams and Pittsburgh pitcher Rip Sewell.

The outcome already had been decided when the Red Sox's Splendid Splinter stepped to the plate to face the Pirates righthander. The A.L. owned a 9–0 lead and its ninth midsummer classic victory was all but assured. The only remaining question was whether Sewell would dare throw his infamous "ephus pitch" to the game's top hitter.

It did not take long to get the answer. On Sewell's first pitch, he wound up like he was going to throw a fastball and delivered a high-arcing blooper that dropped toward the plate. Williams took a wild swing and fouled the ball.

Again Sewell wound up and delivered the blooper, this one outside for a ball. When Sewell threw a fastball down the middle, Williams was caught by surprise. But he wasn't by Sewell's third "ephus," which he rocketed out of the park for a three-run homer and the icing for the A.L. victory.

JULY

10

A STAR IS BORN

1943: Arthur Ashe, a former tennis great and the first black man to win the U.S. Open, Wimbledon and Australian singles titles. He had a long association with the U.S. Davis Cup team, both as a player and its captain.

★ ★ ★

1954: Andre Dawson, a current major league outfielder.

★ ★ ★

MILESTONES · IN SPORTS ·

1951

Stan Musial, Bob Elliott, Gil Hodges and Ralph Kiner connected for an All-Star Game-record four home runs as the N.L. won consecutive midsummer classics for the first time with an 8–3 victory over the A.L. at Detroit.

1971

California Angels slugger Tony Conigliaro, the victim of a severe beaning in 1967 when he played for Boston, ended his comeback attempt because of failing eyesight.

1984

Los Angeles' Fernando Valenzuela and New York's Dwight Gooden combined to strike out an All-Star Game-record six straight A .L. batters, highlighting the N.L.'s 3–1 victory at San Francisco.

1989

Rumanian Paula Ivan, the 1988 Olympic 1,500-meter champion, lowered the world record in the women's mile to 4:15.61 during competition in a Grand Prix meet at Nice, France.

1934 HUBBELL'S STRIKEOUT ACHIEVEMENT

Four of **Carl Hubbell's** *All-Star-record strikeout victims: (left to right)* **Al Simmons, Lou Gehrig, Babe Ruth** *and* **Jimmie Foxx.**

The American League recorded a come-from-behind 9–7 victory in baseball's second All-Star Game, but the 48,363 fans who attended the battle at New York's Polo Grounds left the park talking about a great pitching performance.

The memorable effort was turned in by the Giants' Carl Hubbell, who worked three scoreless innings. But that wasn't why the fans were talking. It was how he worked them – and against whom.

After surrendering a single to Detroit's Charlie Gehringer to open the game and a walk to Washington's Heinie Manush, Hubbell settled down and began turning over his vaunted screwball. Before the A.L. could do any damage, he struck out Yankees Babe Ruth and Lou Gehrig and also Philadelphia's Jimmie Foxx.

After the N.L. had taken a 1–0 lead in the bottom of the inning on a home run by St. Louis second baseman Frank Frisch, Hubbell struck out Chicago's Al Simmons and Washington's Joe Cronin. Five of the best hitters in the game, all down on strikes – consecutively. After Yankee Bill Dickey broke the spell with a single, Hubbell fanned Yankee pitcher Lefty Gomez.

Hubbell's pitching and a three-run homer by St. Louis' Joe Medwick boosted the National League to a 4–0 lead. But the N.L. pitchers could not stand prosperity. The American League scored eight runs off Chicago's Lon Warneke and Brooklyn's Van Lingle Mungo and held on for its second straight All-Star victory.

1971 TREVINO EARNS BRITISH TITLE

Lee Trevino, playing with his usual poise and carefree confidence after taking a near-disastrous 7 on the 17th hole, drilled home a birdie putt on 18 and claimed the 100th British Open championship with a one-stroke victory over Liang Huan Lu at the Royal Birkdale course in Southport, England.

Trevino's problems in the tall rough on 17 turned a three-stroke lead into a slim one-stroke advantage. Lu put on the pressure with a final-hole birdie, but Trevino responded with a birdie of his own.

The victory gave the self-described Merry Mex a four-week sweep of the U.S., Canadian and British championships. He became only the fourth golfer to win the U.S. and British titles in the same year and the first since Bobby Jones turned the trick in 1930. Trevino beat Jack Nicklaus in a U.S. Open playoff June 21 and followed with a playoff win over Art Wall in the Canadian Open.

1936 KLEIN'S POWER SHOW

Philadelphia slugger Chuck Klein led off the 10th inning with a line drive into the right-field stands at Pittsburgh's Forbes Field, giving him a record-tying four home runs in a single game and sparking the Phillies to a 9–6 victory over the Pirates.

Klein's outburst put him in select company. He became only the second modern-era (post–1900) player to accomplish the feat and fourth overall. New York Yankee first baseman Lou Gehrig did it in 1932, hitting all four of his homers in the regulation nine innings .

Klein started his barrage with a three-run first-inning blast and then drove Pittsburgh's Paul Waner to the fence with a second-inning drive. He hit solo shots in the fifth and seventh innings to set the stage for his game-winner in the 10th.

Klein finished his record-trying afternoon with six RBIs.

Philadelphia Phillies masher **Chuck Klein.**

1950 Schoendienst Delivers Big

St. Louis second baseman Red Schoendienst, an 11th-inning defensive replacement, blasted a 14th-inning pitch from Detroit's Ted Gray into the left-field stands at Chicago's Comiskey Park, giving the National League a 4–3 victory over the American League in the longest All-Star Game ever played.

Schoendienst's blast snapped a four-game National League losing streak and rewarded an outstanding pitching performance by Philadelphia's Jim Konstanty, New York's Larry Jansen and Cincinnati's Ewell Blackwell. Those pitchers combined for nine innings of two-hit shutout ball after the Americans had taken a 3–2 fifth-inning lead.

But the A.L. pitchers were almost as good. Before Schoendienst's homer, the Nationals had managed only one run in 11 innings off Cleveland's Bob Lemon, Detroit's Art Houtteman, New York's Carl Reynolds and Gray. That run came in the form of a ninth-inning bazooka shot by Pittsburgh's Ralph Kiner that tied the game and forced extra innings.

1924 Liddell Makes Dash to Glory

Eric Liddell, a 22-year-old Scottish divinity student, became the third runner in 24 hours to set a world record in the 400-meter sprint when he dashed to Olympic gold in 47.6 seconds during competition in the Summer Games at Paris.

Liddell, saving the best for last, set a torrid pace out of the blocks and somehow managed to hold off American Horatio Fitch and Great Britain's Guy Butler. He beat Fitch by five meters and topped the world-record mark of 47.8 set by Fitch only hours earlier in a semifinal heat.

Fitch had broken the mark of 48 seconds set in a quarterfinal heat by Switzerland's Josef Imbach, who took a head-over-heels tumble in the final and failed to finish. American J. Coard Taylor had third place clinched until he stumbled a few feet from the finish line.

Liddell, normally a 100-meter man, decided to forego that event when he found out the finals would be held on a Sunday – his day of worship. He trained hard in the 200- and 400-meter events and captured a bronze in the 200 before his gold medal-winning effort.

July 11

A Star Is Born

1944: Lou Hudson, an NBA guard who scored 17,940 points over his 13-year career in the 1960s and '70s.

★ ★ ★

1934: Bob Allison, a 13-year major leaguer who belted 256 home runs for the Washington Senators and Minnesota Twins from 1958–70.

★ ★ ★

1963: Al MacInnis, a current National Hockey League defenseman.

★ ★ ★

1973 Crowd-Pleaser Stones Sets World Record

Dwight Stones, a 19-year-old crowd-pleaser who leaped into world track consciousness with a medal-winning performance in last year's Summer Olympic Games, set a world record in the high jump when he cleared 7 feet 6 1/2 inches during a dual United States-West Germany track and field meet held at Munich.

Stones' record-setting leap was made before 25,000 West German fans in the same stadium where he won his Olympic bronze medal. And true to form, the young Californian milked the moment for everything he could get.

Stones already had won the competition with a second jump of 7–5 1/2, but he asked the officials to raise the bar a full inch. He made a looping approach, threw himself into the air with all the strength he could muster and brushed the bar on his descent, making it wobble precariously for a few tense moments.

Stones quickly jumped to his feet, clenched his fists triumphantly and watched the bar intently. When it stopped wobbling, Stones streaked onto the track and took a fist-pumping victory lap – much to the delight of the roaring crowd.

The 6-foot-5 Stones broke the world record of 7–6 1/4 set by Pat Matzdorf in 1971.

Record-setting high jumper **Dwight Stones** *put on quite a show for West German fans at Munich.*

Milestones in Sports

1971
West German Hildegard Falck became the first woman to break the 2-minute barrier in the 800-meter run when she was clocked in 1:58.3 in a meet at Stuttgart, West Germany.

1971
Jane Blalock fired a final-round 68 and claimed a two-stroke victory over JoAnne Carner in the George Washington golf tournament at Horsham, Pa.

1973
Gene Sarazen, 71 years old and playing just for fun, scored a hole-in-one at the par 3 eighth hole during first-round action in the British Open golf championship at Troon, Scotland.

1985
Houston righthander Nolan Ryan fanned New York's Danny Heep in the sixth inning of the Astros' 4–3 victory, becoming baseball's first 4,000-strikeout man.

1989
Kansas City's Bo Jackson and Boston's Wade Boggs hit back-to-back home runs to open the game, highlighting the A.L.'s 5–3 All-Star Game victory over the N.L. at Anaheim Stadium.

JULY

12

A STAR IS BORN

1938: Ron Fairly, a major league outfielder and first baseman who batted .266 over a 21-year career that ended in 1978.

★ ★ ★

1943: Paul Silas, a 16-year NBA star who scored 11,782 points and grabbed 12,357 rebounds from 1964–80.

DEATH OF A LEGEND

1892: Alexander Cartwright (baseball).

1967 PEREZ CATCHES CATFISH

Cincinnati's Tony Perez drove a pitch from Oakland's Catfish Hunter over the left-field fence in the 15th inning, ending the longest All-Star Game in history and giving the National League its fifth straight victory.

Perez's blow at Anaheim Stadium gave the National League a 2–1 victory over the American League and ended a stretch of eight scoreless innings. The Nationals had scored their first run on a second-inning homer by Philadelphia's Dick Allen and the Americans had tied on a homer by Baltimore's Brooks Robinson in the sixth.

The teams combined for just 17 hits and 12 pitchers recorded 30 strikeouts while issuing two walks. The N.L. failed to score for 12 consecutive innings, the A.L. was blanked for nine straight. Hunter gave up the winner in his fifth inning of four-hit pitching.

1955 MUSIAL HAS A BLAST

St. Louis slugger Stan Musial pounded his record-breaking fourth All-Star Game home run over the wall at Milwaukee's County Stadium, giving the National League a come-from-behind 12-inning 6–5 victory over the American League in the second-longest midsummer classic ever played.

Musial's blast off Boston pitcher Frank Sullivan completed the N.L.'s rally from a 5-0 seventh-inning deficit and electrified a pumped-up Milwaukee crowd of 45,643 that had roared its approval throughout the top of the inning when Braves righthander Gene Conley struck out the side.

The Nationals appeared to be in for a long day when the A.L. erupted for four first-inning runs off Philadelphia righthander Robin Roberts – before anybody had been retired. One run scored on a wild pitch and three more on a long home run by New York Yankee Mickey Mantle.

After the A.L. had increased its lead to 5–0 in the sixth, the Nationals fought back. Milwaukee's Johnny Logan singled home a seventh-inning run and another scored on an error. Chicago's Randy Jackson and Milwaukee's Hank Aaron singled home eighth-inning runs and the tying run scored on another error.

1964 MICKEY HAS WRIGHT STUFF

Mickey Wright fired a playoff-round 70 and recorded a two-stroke victory over Ruth Jessen in the U.S. Women's Open championship – her record-tying fourth triumph in the showcase event of the women's professional golf tour.

Wright joined Betsy Rawls as the only four-time winners of the event played annually at different courses around the country. Jessen had forced the playoff when she birdied the 18th hole at the San Diego Country Club while Wright was struggling to a bogey. Both finished the 72 holes at 290.

Both golfers played consistently in the playoff, Jessen recording 17 pars and one bogey and Wright getting four birdies to go along with her only bogey. Wright's birdie at the 10th gave her a two-stroke advantage and this time she protected it on an uneventful 18th hole.

Wright previously had won Opens in 1958, '59 and '61. She also won the prestigious LPGA Championship four times in a successful seven-year span.

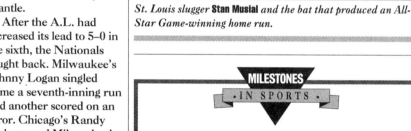

St. Louis slugger **Stan Musial** *and the bat that produced an All-Star Game-winning home run.*

MILESTONES • IN SPORTS •

1921

New York slugger Babe Ruth became baseball's all-time home run leader when he belted No. 137 and passed 19th Century star Roger Connor.

1945

Chicago righthander Hank Wyse pitched a three-hitter and stopped Boston outfielder Tommy Holmes' N.L.-record 37-game hitting streak in the first game of a doubleheader at Wrigley Field.

1949

Brooklyn's Jackie Robinson, Roy Campanella and Don Newcombe and Cleveland's Larry Doby became the first black players to compete in All-Star Game competition – an 11–7 A.L. victory at Brooklyn's Ebbets Field.

1954

Major league players formally organized into a group called the Major League Baseball Players Association and hired J. Norman Lewis to represent the group in negotiations with the owners.

1966

A 10th-inning single by Los Angeles shortstop Maury Wills gave the N.L. a 2–1 All-Star Game victory over the A.L. in the 105-degree heat at St. Louis' Busch Stadium.

1979

Bill Veeck's Disco Demolition Night promotion at Chicago's Comiskey Park went awry when unruly fans refused to leave the field between games of a doubleheader and forced the White Sox to forfeit the nightcap to Detroit.

1943 Starry, Starry Night

Boston second baseman Bobby Doerr blasted a three-run second-inning home run and the American League went on to record its eighth victory in 11 All-Star Games – a 5–3 decision over the National League at Philadelphia's Shibe Park.

The game, however, carried a lot more significance than the final score. It was the first All-Star Game played at night and the A .L. achieved its victory without any New York Yankees in its lineup. Yankee Manager Joe McCarthy, thumbing his nose at critics who suggested the A.L. could not win the annual contest without his Yankees, refused to play any of the five New Yorkers selected to the team.

No problem. The A.L. wiped out a 1–0 deficit on Doerr's home run and added single runs in the third and fifth innings. Washington 's Dutch Leonard, Detroit's Hal Newhouser and Boston's Tex Hughson scattered 10 hits and were never really challenged.

The Nationals got a home run from Pittsburgh's Vince DiMaggio.

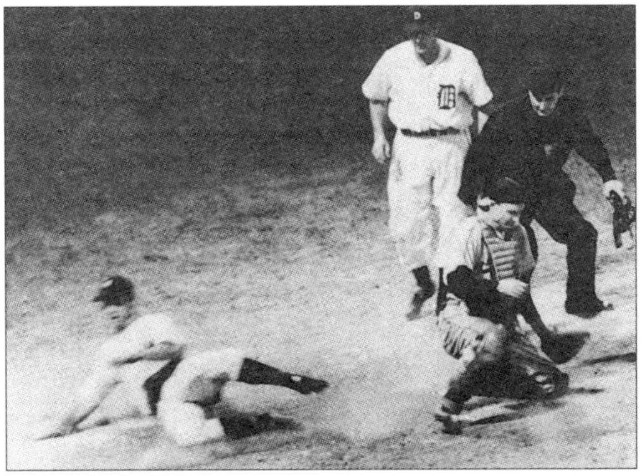

American Leaguer **George Case** *slides safely across the plate as N.L. catcher* **Walker Cooper** *misses connections with a low throw during action in the 1943 All-Star Game.*

1934 Amazing Ruth Hits 700th Home Run

Babe Ruth, nearing the end of his storied career, blazed another baseball trail when he smashed his 700th career home run to help the New York Yankees record a 4–2 victory over the Detroit Tigers.

The 39-year-old Ruth, holder of the one-season home run mark and virtually every other power-hitting record imaginable, connected for his milestone blast off Tigers righthander Tommy Bridges in the third inning. The two-run shot over the right-field wall at Navin Field drove in Earle Combs and gave the Yankees a 2–0 lead.

The New Yorkers went on to victory when catcher Bill Dickey belted a two-run eighth-inning double to support the six-hit pitching of Red Ruffing.

Ruth's 21-year record is likely to stand for a long time. Only two players, teammate Lou Gehrig and Rogers Hornsby, have topped the 300-homer barrier.

A STAR IS BORN

1890: Stan Coveleski, a Hall of Fame righthander who won 215 games over 14 seasons from 1912–28.

★ ★ ★

1935: Jack Kemp, the quarterback who directed Buffalo to two AFL championships in the 1960s before trading in his cleats for a seat in the U.S. House of Representatives.

★ ★ ★

1954: David Thompson, the high-flying forward who led North Carolina State to an NCAA championship in 1974 and went on to score 11,264 points in eight NBA seasons.

★ ★ ★

1963: Spud Webb, a current NIBA guard.

DEATH OF A LEGEND

1954: Grantland Rice (sportswriter).

★ ★ ★

1992: Alex Wojciechowicz (football).

1971 A.L. Stars Snap Loss Streak at 8

Three heavyweight sluggers brought a merciful end to the American League's embarrassing eight-game All-Star losing streak when they provided the muscle for a 6–4 victory over the National League at Detroit's Tiger Stadium.

The long-ball heroics of Oakland's Reggie Jackson, Baltimore's Frank Robinson and Minnesota's Harmon Killebrew accounted for all the A.L. scoring and offset a three-home run barrage by Cincinnati's Johnny Bench, Atlanta's Hank Aaron and Pittsburgh's Roberto Clemente.

The A.L., loser in 12 of the last 13 midsummer classics, appeared to be in trouble early when Bench hit a two-run second-inning shot and Aaron connected in the third, giving the N.L. a 3–0 lead. But Jackson brought the Americans to life – emphatically.

Batting for teammate Vida Blue in the bottom of the third with a man on base, Jackson made solid contact with a delivery from Pittsburgh's Doc Ellis and sent a towering shot toward no-man's land. The ball hit a light tower on the roof in right-center field, an estimated 520 feet from home plate. Jackson admired his work from the batter's box before beginning his home run trot.

Robinson drove his two-run homer later in the inning and Killebrew hit his in the sixth.

Reggie Jackson *watches his home run sail into the outer reaches of Tiger Stadium.*

July 13

Milestones in Sports

1963

Early Wynn, making his eighth attempt to reach the lofty 300-victory plateau, finally succeeded when he pitched five innings of Cleveland's 7–4 victory in the second game of a doubleheader against Kansas City.

1965

Willie Mays, Joe Torre and Willie Stargell hit home runs and the National League took its first-ever lead in the All-Star Game series with a 6–5 victory over the American League at Minnesota's Metropolitan Stadium.

1972

In an unprecedented maneuver, Carroll Rosenbloom traded his NFL Baltimore Colts franchise to Robert Irsay for his Los Angeles Rams – with the teams remaining in their cities and the ownerships changing places.

1982

A two-run homer by Cincinnati's Dave Concepcion sparked the N.L. to its 11th straight All-Star Game victory – a 4–1 decision over the A.L. in the first midsummer classic played on foreign soil (Montreal).

1991

Four Baltimore pitchers – Bob Milacki, Mike Flanagan, Mark Williamson and Gregg Olson – teamed up to pitch a 2–0 no-hitter against Oakland.

1993

Champion race car driver Davey Allison died from a head injury a day after the helicopter he was piloting crashed at Talladega (Ala.) Superspeedway.

JULY

14

A STAR IS BORN

1898: A.B. (Happy) Chandler, baseball's second commissioner who served from 1945-51.

★ ★ ★

1967: Robin Ventura, a current major league third baseman.

★ ★ ★

DEATH OF A LEGEND

1908: Lord Stanley (hockey).

★ ★ ★

1982: Jackie Jensen (baseball).

1966 JIM BROWN RETIRES FOR ACTING CAREER

Cleveland running back Jim Brown, given a report-or-else ultimatum by Browns Owner Art Modell, announced his retirement from professional football to pursue a second career as a movie actor.

Brown, who gained an NFL-record 12,312 yards and scored a record 126 touchdowns during his outstanding nine-year career, made his surprise announcement from Elstree, England, where he is filming the movie "The Dirty Dozen." The Browns are preparing for training camp in Hiram, O.

Brown had asked Modell to excuse him from camp while he finished filming. But Modell announced in mid-June that his star would be fined and suspended if he failed to report by July 17 – the starting date for all regulars. The 30-year-old Brown, who had hinted the coming season might be his last anyway, told reporters there was no chance he would reconsider. The man who posted a career average of 5.2 yards per carry and ran for a record 1,863 yards in 1963 is giving up an estimated $80,000 salary, the highest in the NFL.

Cleveland running back great **Jim Brown.**

1991 MALLON WINS OPEN

Meg Mallon, a non-winner on the LPGA Tour for four seasons, shot a near-flawless final-round 67 and claimed the United States Women's Open championship – her second major title in three weeks.

Mallon, who captured the LPGA Championship two weeks ago at Bethesda, Md., outdueled veterans Pat Bradley and Amy Alcott in the 98-degree heat of Fort Worth, Tex. She broke a three-way tie when she drilled home birdie putts at 14 and 15 on the Colonial Country Club's back nine and then held for a two-stroke victory over Bradley.

Bradley, who held or shared the lead through three rounds, managed only one birdie all day and suffered bogeys on 9 and 10. Mallon hit 17 of 18 greens and 10 of 12 fairways in regulation and used her hot putter to wipe out a two-stroke deficit entering the final round.

1970 ROSE CRUSHES FOSSE

Cincinnati's Pete Rose, delivering another serious blow to the already-bruised ego of the American League, crushed Cleveland catcher Ray Fosse in a violent 12th-inning collision at home plate and scored the winning run in a 5–4 National League All-Star Game victory at Cincinnati.

Rose scored from second base on a two-out single by Chicago's Jim Hickman. The throw from Kansas City center fielder Amos Otis was on the money and when Rose and ball arrived at the same time, Fosse never had a chance. He lay dazed on hands and knees, his head resting on the ground, as triumphant National Leaguers celebrated their eighth straight All-Star victory.

Once again, the Americans seemed to have victory in hand. They entered the ninth with a 4–1 lead and New York ace Catfish Hunter on the mound.

But the pattern of N.L. comebacks continued when the Nationals scored three times and forced extra innings. San Francisco catcher Dick Dietz hit a home run, teammate Willie McCovey singled home a run and Pittsburgh right fielder Roberto Clemente tied the game with a sacrifice fly, forcing extra innings.

The winning rally started with two out when Rose and Los Angeles' Bill Grabarkewitz singled.

MILESTONES IN SPORTS

1946

Cleveland Manager Lou Boudreau unveiled his "Williams Shift" against Boston. All defenders except the third baseman and left fielder were shifted to the right side of the field when the Red Sox's Ted Williams batted.

1967

Houston's Eddie Mathews became the seventh member of baseball's 500-homer club when he connected off Juan Marichal in an 8–6 Astros' victory over San Francisco at Candlestick Park.

1968

Another "500" man: Atlanta's Hank Aaron hit the first of several milestone blasts off San Francisco lefty Mike McCormick at Atlanta's Fulton County Stadium.

1968

Houston righthander Don Wilson tied Bob Feller's one-game strikeout record with 18, but dropped a 5–4 decision at Cincinnati.

1987

A two-run 13th-inning triple by Montreal's Tim Raines broke the longest scoreless tie in All-Star Game history and gave the N.L. a 2–0 victory over the A.L. at Oakland.

1987

Going back on earlier statements that he would play only baseball, Kansas City outfielder Bo Jackson took up a new "hobby" when he signed a five-year contract to play for the NFL's Los Angeles Raiders during the "offseason."

1992

The American League struck early and fast en route to its fifth straight All-Star Game victory – a one-sided 13–6 decision over the National League at San Diego's Jack Murphy Stadium.

MILESTONES IN SPORTS

1912

Jim Thorpe firmly established himself as the "world's greatest athlete" when he completed the Olympic decathlon with a world-record 8,412 points at the Summer Games in Stockholm.

1923

Bobby Jones captured his first major golf championship when he defeated Robert A. Cruickshank by two strokes in an 18-hole playoff to decide the U.S. Open at Long Island, N.Y.

1972

Lee Trevino saved par by sinking a chip shot on the 17th hole and went on to win his second straight British Open title with a one-stroke decision over Jack Nicklaus at Muirfield, Scotland.

1973

California's Nolan Ryan became only the fourth pitcher to throw two no-hitters in a season when he struck out 17 and stopped Detroit, 6–0, at Tiger Stadium.

1975

Chicago's Bill Madlock drilled a two-run ninth-inning single to break a 3–3 tie and the N.L. recorded a 6–3 All-Star Game victory over the A.L. – its 12th win in 13 years.

1978

Jack Nicklaus won another British Open title and became the first golfer to win all four majors at least three times.

A STAR IS BORN

1935: Alex Karras, an outstanding defensive tackle for the Detroit Lions in the 1960s who went on to greater fame as a television and movie actor.

★ ★ ★

DEATH OF A LEGEND

1986: Billy Haughton (harness racing).

★ ★ ★

JULY 15

1961 PALMER WINS BRITISH OPEN

Arnold Palmer, making his overpowering presence felt overseas, fired a double-round 69–72 over England's rain-soaked Royal Birkdale course and became the first American to capture a British Open championship since Ben Hogan in 1953.

Palmer's four-round total of 284 was one stroke better than Dai Rees, a Welshman who shot a final-day 71–72. The morning round was played in a steady rain, the afternoon portion in off-and-on sunshine.

Weather played havoc with the tournament throughout and wrecked the scores of many of the world's top golfers. After a sunny opening round, heavy rain and strong wind did heavy damage to the course and third-round play was even postponed for a day.

But Palmer did not let that get in the way of victory. He ignored the rain and soggy conditions to shoot a blazing front-nine 32 on the morning round and zipped into a lead he never relinquished.

1952 DROPO GETS 12 STRAIGHT HITS

Detroit's Walt Dropo, a big, lumbering first baseman known for his run-producing skills, tied a 14-year-old major league record when he delivered his 12th consecutive hit during the second game of a doubleheader against Washington at Griffith Stadium.

Dropo's fifth-inning double allowed him to tie the 1938 consecutive-hits mark of Boston's Pinky Higgins. His shot at the record came up short in the seventh when he stood helplessly at home plate and watched Senators catcher Mickey Grasso snare his foul popup near the stands. He came back in the ninth, however, to single home two runs in the Tigers' 9–8 loss.

Dropo's improbable streak began a day earlier when he banged out five straight singles in a game against the New York Yankees. In the opener of the twin-bill against Washington (an 8–2 loss), he drilled four more singles in as many at-bats. He tripled home three runs in the first inning of the nightcap and then singled in the third, setting the stage for his record-tying double.

Walt Dropo, *the Detroit Tigers' unlikely hit man.*

Betsy King *roared from behind to win the U.S. Women's Open.*

1990 KING CATCHES PATTY SHEEHAN

Betsy King, playing a solid but unspectacular double round on the final day of the U.S. Women's Open, made up 11 shots on Patty Sheehan over the last 32 holes and claimed her second straight victory in the most prestigious event on the LPGA Tour.

It was more a case of Sheehan collapsing than King making a stirring comeback. After building a six-stroke advantage with a blazing 66 and 68 through the rain-plagued opening rounds, Sheehan birdied two of the first three holes in the weather-forced double round.

At that point, she had an eight-stroke advantage over her nearest pursuer – 10 strokes over King. But then she came unraveled. Over a 21-hole stretch from the 43rd hole of the tournament to the 63rd, she was nine over par, losing 11 strokes to King. She rebounded with two birdies to force a tie with two holes remaining, but she slid back to finish 75–76 – 285. King's final 70–71 gave her a one-stroke victory.

That made her the fifth player to win consecutive Women's Opens.

JULY

16

A STAR IS BORN

1888: Shoeless Joe Jackson, an outstanding hitter who batted .356 over 13 major league seasons before being banned from baseball for his part in the 1919 Black Sox World Series scandal.

★ ★ ★

1942: Margaret Smith-Court, the women's tennis star who won a record 26 Grand Slam singles titles and recorded a one-season Grand Slam in 1970.

★ ★ ★

1960: Terry Pendleton, a current major league third baseman.

★ ★ ★

1968: Barry Sanders, a current National Football League running back.

★ ★ ★

DEATH OF A LEGEND

1992: Buck Buchanan (football).

1988

FloJo Zips To Record

Speed was the order of the day during the U.S. Olympic trials at Indianapolis, but only two of the four world records set on the blistering afternoon qualified under international guidelines because of a swirling wind that aided performances.

Florence Griffith-Joyner, sister-in-law Jackie Joyner-Kersee, Carl Lewis and Willie Banks amazed 11,567 spectators at the Indiana University Track Stadium with the best performances in the history of their events. But Lewis' record 9.78 clocking in the men's 100-meter dash final and Banks' record 59–8 1/2 leap in the triple jump final were struck down by strong wind readings.

An amazing performance by Griffith-Joyner, however, was a point of controversy. In her 100-meter heat, FloJo streaked to a world record of 10.60, far faster than Evelyn Ashford's 1984 record of 10.76. But a 3.2-meter following wind wiped it out.

No problem. Griffith-Joyner came back 2 1/2 hours later and ran an astounding 10.49 quarterfinal, this time with the wind meters showing 0.0. The next heat also was recorded at 0.0 before the wind reading jumped to 5 meters. Disbelieving officials complained, but the record stood.

Joyner-Kersee capped the day by shattering her own world record in the women's heptathlon with 7,215 points.

MILESTONES IN SPORTS

1924

New York Giants first baseman George Kelly became the first player to hit home runs in six consecutive games – connecting a record seven times during that span.

1970

The Pittsburgh Pirates unveiled new Three Rivers Stadium, but Cincinnati spoiled the festivities by recording a 3–2 victory .

1971

New England quarterback Joe Kapp, refusing to sign his name to a standard players' contract because of the controversial reserve clause, walked out of the Patriots' training camp and returned to his home near Boston.

1985

Great Britian distance king Steve Cram added the metric mile to his growing list of world records when he covered the 1,500-meter race in 3:29.67 at a Grand Prix track and field meet at Nice, France.

1982

Tabb Adds World Mark

Mary Decker-Tabb, running in an all-comers meet she saw advertised in her hometown newspaper at Eugene, Ore., set a world record in the 10,000-meter run when she was clocked in 31:35.30.

Running on a lark, the talented 23-year-old streaked to victory in an event that had been dominated in the past by Soviet women. The previous mark of 32:17.19 was held by Yelina Sipatova and Russians had recorded the next nine fastest times, although Loa Olafsson of Denmark had run an impressive 31:45.04 race in 1978 against a field of men. That hand-timed mark was never accepted as a record.

Decker-Tabb had just arrived home after a record-setting tour of Europe and saw the ad. "It's a small meet and I thought I'd give them some support," she explained. "It's the first time I've ever run the 10,000 on a track. I'm surprised the record was so easy."

The meet was held on Hayward Field track, where she had already set a world record in the 5,000-meter run in the June Prefontaine Classic. Decker-Tabb had smashed the world mile record (4:18.08) the previous Friday in a Paris meet.

To say her 10,000-meter record was decisive is an understatement. Debbe Eide, running out of the Oregon Track Club, was a distant second at 33:14.6 while Universty of Oregon runner Eryn Forbes placed third at 33:31.7.

1971

Prefontaine Wins Shocker

American Steve Prefontaine, taking advantage of a bizarre misjudgement by an Ethiopian rival, scored a lopsided 5,000-meter victory during a Pan Africa-United States dual track meet at Durham, N.C.

Prefontaine and Ethiopian soldier Mirus Ifter were engaged in a thrilling battle heading into the final two laps when Ifter suddenly sprinted to a 100-meter lead and continued the frantic pace as 18,000 spectators at Duke University watched in stunned silence.

But as the gun sounded announcing the final lap, the African suddenly slowed and then stopped as Prefontaine passed him on the first turn. Prefontaine went on to record an easy victory while Ifter watched in amazement, evidently thinking he had won the race.

After a 15-minute consultation, it was determined that Ifter, who did not speak English, had simply miscalculated and run his sprint lap too soon. Prefontaine, with a winning time of 13:57.6, was declared the winner.

Oregon long-distance champion **Steve Prefontaine.**

MILESTONES IN SPORTS

1961

Baseball Commissioner Ford Frick issued his infamous "asterisk ruling," in effect telling New York's Roger Maris that he would not be recognized as the one-season home run champion unless he broke Babe Ruth's record in the first 154 games of his 162-game schedule.

1974

St. Louis righthander Bob Gibson joined former pitching great Walter Johnson as baseball's only 3,000-strikeout pitchers when he fanned Cincinnati's Cesar Geronimo during a game at Busch Stadium.

1979

New York's Lee Mazzilli tied the score with an eighth-inning homer and forced in the winning run with a ninth-inning walk as the N.L. recorded its eighth straight All-Star Game victory, 7-6, at Seattle.

1970:

Great Britain's Sebastian Coe, who set a world record in the 800-meter run 12 days earlier, lowered the mile world record to 3:49 during competition at Oslo, Norway.

1983

The Michigan Panthers defeated the Philadelphia Stars, 24–22, in the first championship game of the new United States Football League.

Cleveland righthander **Jim Bagby Jr** *(above) helped end the record 56-game hitting streak of New York Yankee star* **Joe DiMaggio** *(below).*

1941 DiMaggio's Streak Ends

They say all good things must come to an end and that certainly was the case for New York Yankee Clipper Joe DiMaggio and his major league-record 56-game hitting streak – with, of course, a little help from Cleveland players Al Smith, Jim Bagby Jr. and Ken Keltner.

DiMaggio's amazing run of success, which started May 15 against Chicago, carried into the game at Cleveland's Municipal Stadium. And it looked like the streak would go to 57 in the first inning when DiMaggio smashed a Smith delivery down the third-base line. Keltner, however, made a nice backhand stop, wheeled and threw him out.

After DiMaggio drew a walk in the fourth, he batted against Smith in the seventh and hit another smash–right at Keltner. The third baseman calmly fielded the ball and fired to first. Down to his last chance in the eighth inning with the bases loaded and the Yankees leading 3–1, DiMaggio hit a Bagby pitch up the middle. Shortstop Lou Boudreau grabbed the grounder, stepped on second and threw to first for a double play. The streak had ended.

Over the two months, DiMaggio batted .408 with 15 home runs and 55 RBIs.

JULY 17

A STAR IS BORN

1917: Lou Boudreau, a Hall of Fame infielder who batted .295 over 15 seasons (1938–52) and compiled 1,162 victories as a player-manager and manager.

★ ★ ★

1941: Daryle Lamonica, a former Oakland Raiders quarterback known as the "mad bomber"

★ ★ ★

1956: Bryan Trottier, a 17-year center who scored 520 goals and 1,410 points and helped the New York Islanders win four straight Stanley Cup titles (1979–83).

★ ★ ★

1963: Matti Nykanen, an outstanding Finnish ski jumper and thtree-time Olympic gold medalist.

DEATH OF A LEGEND

1961: Ty Cobb (baseball).

★ ★ ★

1974: Dizzy Dean (baseball).

★ ★ ★

1987: Travis Jackson (baseball).

1966 Ryun Runs 3:51.3

Jim Ryun carved his name ahead of the greatest runners in track and field history when he blazed to a 3:51.3 clocking in the mile, knocking more than two seconds off the world record held by Frenchman Michel Jazy.

Ryun's record-breaking effort highlighted action at the All-America invitational meet at Berkeley, Calif. The 19-year-old Kansas University freshman ran the quarter in 57.7, the half mile in 1:55.4 and the three-quarters in 2:55 before sprinting home with a 56.3 final lap that secured the record. He topped his previous best time of 3:53.7.

Ryun was paced by Texas runners Tom von Ruden and Richard Romo and did not take the lead until about the three-quarters mark. His 1,500-meter time was 3:36.1, about a half second off the world record.

Ryun is the first American to hold the prestigious mark since another Kansan, Glenn Cunningham, in 1934.

1983 Watson Wins Again

Tom Watson sank a curling 20-foot putt on the 16th hole, breaking a three-way tie and putting him in position to win his fifth British Open championship.

After his dramatic tie-breaking putt, Watson parred the 17th and 18th holes of the Royal Birkdale Golf Club. That concluded his final-round 70 and gave him a four-round total of 275, one stroke better than Hale Irwin and Andy Bean.

In one of the tightest championships of modern time, eight players held or shared the lead at one point in the final round. When Watson was on the 12th hole, five shared first place. When he teed up for 16, he was one of three tied on the crowded leader board.

But not for long. Watson caught the edge of the rough on his drive, hit an 8-iron 20 feet from the cup and curled in his putt. He had the lead for good.

The British Open title was Watson's second straight and first on an English course. The others had come in Scotland.

JULY

18

A STAR IS BORN

1929: Dick Button, a five-time world champion figure skater who won the men's title at the 1948 and 1952 Winter Olympic Games.

★ ★ ★

1935: Tenley Albright, a two-time world champion figure skater who won a gold medal at the 1956 Winter Olympic Games.

★ ★ ★

1957: Nick Faldo, a current British golfer, who has won three British Opens and two Masters.

★ ★ ★

1972: Anfernee Hardaway, a current National Basketball Association guard.

1987 MATTINGLY'S HOMER BINGE

Don Mattingly, a hard-hitting New York Yankee first baseman not known for his power hitting, completed an unlikely charge into the record books when he blasted a home run for the record-tying eighth consecutive game.

Mattingly tied the 31-year-old record set by Pittsburgh's Dale Long – a mark many thought would stand forever. The 26-year-old connected with a pitch from Texas righthander Jose Guzman during a 7–2 Rangers victory at Arlington Stadium.

Mattingly, who started his streak July 8 against Minnesota pitcher Mike Smithson, had set the stage for the record-matcher the night before when he homered off Texas lefty Paul Kilgus, breaking the American League record of home runs in six straight contests. His fourth-inning blow off Guzman brought a mighty roar from the 41,871 Texas fans – many there to see if Mattingly could make history.

The home run was Mattingly's 18th of the season and his 10th in the record-tying stretch.

MILESTONES • IN SPORTS •

1927

Philadelphia veteran Ty Cobb collected his 4,000th career hit when he doubled against his former Detroit teammates and pitcher Sam Gibson.

1947

Detroit righthander Fred Hutchinson ended New York's A.L.-record 19-game winning streak when he shut out the Yankees, 8–0.

1962

The Minnesota Twins recorded an A.L. first when Bob Allison and Harmon Killebrew connected for grand slam home runs in an 11-run first inning against Cleveland.

1982

A broken record: Tom Watson earned his fourth British Open championship at the Royal Troon course in Scotland.

1991

Former Notre Dame star Raghib (Rocket) Ismail made his Canadian Football League debut for Toronto a memorable one: 213 all-purpose yards in the Argonauts' 39–18 victory over Hamilton at the SkyDome.

1951 WALCOTT STUNS CHARLES

Jersey Joe Walcott, a 21-year veteran and a four-time loser in heavyweight championship fights, pulled a stunning upset when he knocked out Ezzard Charles with a powerful left hook in the seventh round of a title bout at Pittsburgh's Forbes Field.

Heavyweight champion **Jersey Joe Walcott.**

The 37-year-old Walcott, a heavy underdog to the younger, speedier Charles, became the oldest champion in heavyweight boxing history when his wild blow sent Charles to the canvas. He watched from a neutral corner as the champion got to his knees, tried to rise and finally fell backward as many of the 28,272 fans stormed the ring.

Charles, who called the knockout blow a "lucky punch," was behind on all cards when the scheduled 15-round fight abruptly ended. He took the first round, but Walcott fought cleverly the rest of the way and dished out most of the punishment. He caught Charles with three solid left hooks in the sixth before the big one connected a round later.

The victory ended Charles' 24-fight winning streak and gave Walcott his first triumph over the defending champion in three bouts.

1948 SEEREY GOES WILD

Pat Seerey, a roly-poly outfielder who batted .171 and hit 11 home runs last season for Cleveland, joined an elite baseball fraternity when he blasted four home runs during the Chicago White Sox's 11-inning 12–11 victory over Philadelphia in the first game of a doubleheader at Shibe Park.

Seerey became only the third modern-era player to accomplish the four-homer feat and the fifth overall. The righthanded hitter drove in six runs with homers in the fourth, fifth and sixth innings, helping the White Sox recover from a 5–0 deficit.

When a three-run seventh-inning shot by the Athletics' Eddie Joost forced extra innings, Seerey settled matters with a solo blast in the 11th.

Seerey, a five-year veteran, was acquired from Cleveland earlier in the season. His best year came in 1946 when he hit 26 home runs. He joined Lou Gehrig (1932) and Chuck Klein (1936) as the only modern-era players (post–1900) to hit four homers in a game.

Klein hit his fourth home run in the 10th inning of a game for the Philadelphia Phillies while Gehrig, a former New York Yankee first baseman, performed his four-homer feat in the regulation nine innings.

Pat Seerey, *Chicago's four-homer man, is congratulated by Boston slugger* **Ted Williams.**

MILESTONES IN SPORTS

1960

A near-perfect debut: San Francisco righthander Juan Marichal shut out Philadelphia, 2–0, while allowing only one harmless single.

1964

Unheralded Bobby Nichols fired a four-round PGA Championship-record 271 and posted a shocking three-stroke victory over Arnold Palmer and Jack Nicklaus at the Columbus (O.) Country Club.

1970

Billy Casper won the $30,000 first prize in the Philadelphia Golf Classic and moved into second place behind Arnold Palmer on the career money-winning list with $1,084,732.

1986

Tim Witherspoon defended his WBC heavyweight championship with an 11th-round technical knockout of Frank Bruno in Wembley, England.

1992

Nick Faldo rallied for two birdies on the last four holes and captured his third British Open championship in six years with a one-stroke victory over John Cook at Muirfield, Scotland.

A STAR IS BORN

1898: Bob Meusel, a career .309 hitter in 11 major league seasons and an outfielder on the vaunted 1927 New York Yankee World Series championship team.

★ ★ ★

1916: Phil Cavarretta, a first baseman-outfielder who batted .293 over 22 major league seasons from 1934–55.

★ ★ ★

1923: Alex Hannum, an outstanding professional basketball coach who won 649 games in the ABA and NBA combined.

★ ★ ★

1990 Rose Gets Jail Term

Pete Rose continued his difficult slide from the pedestal he once occupied atop the baseball world when a U.S. District judge sentenced him to five months in prison after pleading guilty for failure to report income from the sale of baseball memorabilia.

Rose, the game's brightest star only five years ago when he broke baseball's all-time hits record (4,256), was told to report to a minimum-security Correctional Institution Camp at Marion, Ill., by August 10, or as soon as he recovers from arthroscopic knee surgery. Judge S. Arthur Spiegel also fined Rose $50,000, ordered him to spend three additional months in a halfway house after his release and ordered him to spend 1,000 hours doing community service.

The ever-cocky, never-give-an-inch Rose was uncharacteristically contrite in the courtroom. "I hope no one has to go through what I went through the last year and a half," he said. "I lost my dignity, I lost my self-respect, I lost a lot of dear fans and almost lost some very dear friends."

Rose's slide started last August when he was handed a lifetime ban from baseball by Commissioner A. Bartlett Giamatti for his alleged gambling involvement.

1910 Young Wins 500th Game

Cleveland's Cy Young, the 43-year-old genius who holds just about every pitching record imaginable, became baseball's first – and possibly last – 500-game winner when he defeated the Senators, 5–2, in the first game of a doubleheader at Washington.

It took the venerable righthander 11 innings to earn his milestone win, but he went the distance and allowed only four hits. The Indians scored three times in the top of the frame to help Young lift his record to 500–302.

Young, who began his major league career in 1890 in the old National League with Cleveland, compiled 287 victories in the senior circuit and 213 with Boston and Cleveland after the American League was formed in 1901. Making his record even more impressive is the fact that Kid Nichols and Pud Galvin are tied for second on the all-time victory list – with 361.

Young is a five-time 30-game winner and a 16-time 20-game winner.

1947 Babe Wins 17th In Row

JULY 19

The incomparable Babe Didrikson Zaharias, reinforcing her reputation as the world's greatest female athlete, stretched her phenomenal string of golf victories to 17 when she overpowered Dot Kielty, 9 and 8, on the final 18 holes of the Broadmoor golf tournament at Colorado Springs.

Zaharias, who had set the course record with a 68 earlier in the event, was simply too much for Kielty. Babe roared to a five-hole lead on the Los Angeles native in the morning round and continued her assault in the afternoon, never getting a challenge. She ended the scheduled 36-hole final on the 28th hole.

Zaharias has won the Broadmoor three straight times, including a 6-and-4 final victory over Kielty in 1945. Her 17-match streak is unprecedented in golf, men or women, and she adds that accomplishment to her recent victories in the British Ladies Championship and the U.S. Women's Amateur. She was the first American ever to win the British tournament. Zaharias also is a three-time winner of the Western Open.

Sweet-swinging **Babe Didrikson Zaharias** *continued her assault on the golf record books with her unprecedented 17th consecutive victory.*

JULY

20

A STAR IS BORN

1901: Heinie Manush, a Hall of Fame outfielder who batted .330 in 17 major league seasons in the 1920s and '30s.

★ ★ ★

1930: Chuck Daly, a current NBA coach who has compiled more than 500 career victories.

★ ★ ★

1940: Tony Oliva, a .304 hitter over 15 major league campaigns in the 1960s and '70s with Minnesota and a three-time American League batting champion.

★ ★ ★

DEATH OF A LEGEND

1988: John Galbreath (football).

★ ★ ★

1985

Slaney Wins In Rematch

In a much-anticipated rematch of Olympic proportions, Mary Decker-Slaney recorded a lopsided 3,000-meter victory over Zola Budd during the Peugeot Talbot Games at Minneapolis.

The race brought together the principals in the controversial 3,000-meter collision that wrecked Decker-Slaney's medal hopes at the 1984 Los Angeles Olympic Games. Decker-Slaney, who was tripped up by her barefooted rival and sent sprawling to the track's infield, had bitterly chastised Budd while blaming her for the accident.

This race was to be the great grudge match and ABC television went so far as to show it live. But if there was any remaining bitterness, it didn't show.

Decker-Slaney shook Budd's hand before the race and the competitors ran shoulder to shoulder through five laps of the $7^1/_2$-lap duel. When Decker-Slaney accelerated the pace on the backstretch of the sixth lap, Budd fell back.

The 26-year-old Decker-Slaney finished in 8:32.91, 40 meters ahead of second-place Cornelia Burki of Switzerland. Budd finished fourth.

1983

Hall Board Shoots Down Billy Cannon

Billy Cannon, the two-time All-America running back from LSU and a 10-year professional who went on to a post-football career as an orthodontist, was denied a spot in the college Hall of Fame because of his recent guilty plea in a counterfeiting case.

The 45-year-old former Heisman Trophy winner (1959) was elected to the elite fraternity in February and was to be inducted in December. But when he pleaded guilty to the felony charge in Baton Rouge, La., the National Football Foundation and Hall of Fame's 18-member board unanimously voted to deny Cannon the honor – explaining that Hall of Fame candidates must be "great football players but also good citizens."

Cannon was arrested in Baton Rouge July 9 as part of a $6 million counterfeiting ring. Cannon's plea bargain resulted in a lesser charge of conspiracy to possess and deal in counterfeit $100 bills. In return for his testimony, he was granted immunity from further prosecution.

Cannon is best known for his 89-yard punt return that gave LSU a 7–3 victory over Mississippi in a 1959 battle of undefeated teams.

1937

Budge Needs Big Comeback In Davis Final

Don Budge, a prohibitive favorite in his match against lightly regarded Baron Gottfried von Cramm, had to stage a remarkable rally to defeat the determined German, 6–8, 5–7, 6–4, 6–2, 8–6, and give the United States a 3–2 victory in its inter-zone Davis Cup final at Wimbledon.

Budge dug himself into a hole when he dropped the first two sets and had to really turn it on the rest of the way. He began attacking ferociously in the third and took control, evening the match with the kind of domination spectators had expected to see.

But just as quickly as the momentum shifted to Budge, it shifted back to von Cramm. The German took a 4–1 lead in the fifth set and put his team in position for a major Davis Cup upset. Again Budge had to dig deep. He rattled off three straight games, including a key service break, to even matters at 4–all and the match carried on to the 14th game, when Budge converted his fifth match point with a forehand to von Cramm's backhand.

That ended a great tennis battle and put a relieved U.S. team into the challenge round against England.

MILESTONES • IN SPORTS •

1958

Detroit righthander Jim Bunning joined baseball's no-hit fraternity when he struck out 12 Boston Red Sox batters and pitched the Tigers to a 3–0 victory.

1976

The curtain falls: Milwaukee slugger Hank Aaron hit the 755th – and last – home run of his record-setting career off California righthander Dick Drago.

1980

Tom Watson, continuing his startling overseas dominance, earned a third British Open championship with a four-round total of 271 over the demanding Muirfield course in Scotland.

Detroit pitcher **Jim Bunning** *wipes away the sweat after firing a no-hitter against the Boston Red Sox.*

1973 AARON HITS No. 700

All eyes turn toward the left-field fence as **Hank Aaron** *sends home run No. 700 into the record books.*

Atlanta slugger Hank Aaron reached another milestone in his incredible career when he bashed home run No. 700 in a game against Philadelphia and moved within 14 of Babe Ruth's all-time record.

Aaron connected for his milestone blast off left-hander Ken Brett in a game at Atlanta's Fulton County Stadium. The third-inning blow came with a man aboard and sailed 400 feet into the left-center field bleachers, giving the Braves a 4–2 lead.

As the left-center field scoreboard flashed a larger-than-life "700," Aaron circled the bases to a standing ovation. The crowd wouldn't stop until the unassuming 39-year-old had been pushed out of the dugout for two curtain calls.

An 18-year-old Atlantan retrieved the ball and earned 700 silver dollars when he returned it to Aaron. But the uncooperative Phillies spoiled the occasion by recording an 8–4 victory.

Ironically, Aaron was only 5 months old when Ruth connected for No. 700 in July 1934.

1959 RED SOX PLAY FIRST BLACK

Pumpsie Green, a 6-foot stringbean infielder, broke another of baseball's longstanding color barriers when the Boston Red Sox inserted him into a game at Chicago as a pinch-runner.

Green, who had been recalled from Minneapolis earlier in the day, made history when he became the first black player for the last major league team to break the color barrier. He remained in the game and played one inning at shortstop before getting a starting assignment the next day.

Green had been the subject of controversy since spring training, when the Red Sox shipped him to their American Association affiliate for more seasoning. The National Association for the Advancement of Colored People (NAACP) didn't like the decision and cried discrimination, even going so far as to launch a full investigation into the Red Sox's policy.

Boston had stood alone since June of last year when the Detroit Tigers broke their color barrier by playing Ozzie Virgil for the first time.

Pumpsie Green, *Boston's second baseman and the Red Sox's first black major league player.*

1952 O'BRIEN WINS OLYMPIC GOLD

Parry O'Brien, a curly-haired student at the University of Southern California, threw the shot put an Olympic-record 57 feet, 1 1/2 inches and outdueled two other Americans for the gold medal in the Summer Games at Helsinki, Finland.

O'Brien, who uses an unusual new style, beat Darrow Hooper by three-quarters of an inch and world record-holder James Fuchs by more than an inch. Fuchs was hindered by a pulled ligament in a finger on his throwing hand, an injury he suffered 10 days earlier.

A healthy Fuchs would have produced an even more lively competition. Fuchs had won 88 consecutive meets before falling to the 20-year-old O'Brien in the 1951 Amateur Athletic Union championships and O'Brien was beaten by Hooper at the recent Olympic trials. Both O'Brien and Hooper shattered the Olympic mark with their best throws.

O'Brien uses a new technique in which he starts with his back to the front of the circle and unwinds into the throw with every bit of momentum he can muster. The technique has attracted interest in track-and-field circles around the world.

JULY 21

A STAR IS BORN

1881: Johnny Evers, a Hall of Fame second baseman who batted .270 in an 18-year career from 1902–29.

★ ★ ★

1961: Henry Ellard, a National Football League wide receiver.

★ ★ ★

DEATH OF A LEGEND

1967: Jimmie Foxx (baseball).

★ ★ ★

1976: Earle Combs (baseball).

★ ★ ★

MILESTONES • IN SPORTS •

1945

Detroit's Les Mueller pitched 19 2/3 innings, but his Tiger teammates could do no better than a 24-inning 1–1 tie with the Philadelphia Athletics.

1972

Bart Starr, who quarterbacked the Green Bay Packers to five NFL championships and two Super Bowl victories, announced his retirement because of recurring pain in his passing arm and shoulder.

1976

Nadia Comaneci, a 14-year-old Rumanian, received her fourth and fifth perfect scores of the competition and won the women's all-around gymnastics gold medal in the Summer Olympic Games at Montreal.

1989

Mike Tyson was his usual efficient self when he recorded a first-round technical knockout of Carl Williams and retained his heavyweight championship at Atlantic City.

JULY

22

1990 LeMond First Again

American Greg LeMond joined an elite group of riders who have won the Tour de France three or more times when he cruised into Paris with his third career victory in bicycling's most prestigious race.

LeMond, unlike his dramatic come-from-behind victory last year, was the frontrunner all the way as the 156-man field completed the last leg of its three-week, 2,122-mile journey with a 113-mile run from Bretigny-sur-Orge to Paris. Belgian Johan Museeuw captured the final leg, but LeMond won the overall honors with a final time of 90 hours, 43 minutes and 20 seconds.

LeMond, riding for the American Z team, finished 2 minutes, 16 seconds ahead of Italy's Claudio Chiappucci. Victory was sweet for the man who had to drop out of a minor race three months ago because of undertraining and a viral infection. There was no such problem in France.

The victory was LeMond's third in five years and put him in a tie with Belgian Philippe Thys and Frenchman Louison Bobet, other three-time winners. Jacques Anquetil, Eddie Merckx and Bernard Hinault all won the prestigious event five times.

Italy's Adriano Baffi finished second on the race's final stage.

1990 Faldo Wins British Open

Nick Faldo, laying his claim as the world's best golfer, fired an unspectacular final-round 71 over the venerable St. Andrews course in Scotland and recorded a five-stroke victory over American Payne Stewart and Zimbabwe's Mark McNulty in the British Open.

The victory was Faldo's second in golf's oldest major championship and his fourth major victory in as many years. That's the best such streak since Tom Watson won five majors from 1980–83.

The victory also was Faldo's second major of this year (he won the Masters earlier), a feat last accomplished by Watson in 1982.

Faldo's 18-under-par 270 was the second-lowest British Open score ever, two strokes higher than Watson's 1977 total. He averaged one birdie for every three holes over the first three rounds, but played the finale more conservatively, protecting his five-stroke margin.

For a while it appeared the strategy might backfire. Stewart birdied the fifth, sixth, 10th and 12th holes to pull within two of Faldo. But a crucial mistake halted his momentum on 13 and he bogeyed three of the last six holes for a final 71. McNulty shot a closing 65.

1963 Sonny Liston KOs Patterson

Scowling, intimidating Sonny Liston, proving that his first-round knockout of Floyd Patterson last September was no fluke, repeated his performance in a bout at Las Vegas and retained his world heavyweight championship.

In a mirror image of his victory at Chicago, Liston stepped in quickly and sent the former champion to the canvas with a sledgehammer right. Patterson jumped up by the count of two, but went back down even faster. He rose again and was greeted by another right that ended the mismatch before many of the 7,816 fans at Convention Hall had even settled into their seats.

The end came at 2:10 of the opening round, 4 seconds slower than the knockout at Chicago. The victory, Liston's 35th against one loss, probably ended Patterson's hopes of winning the championship for a record third time.

A STAR IS BORN

1893: Jesse Haines, a Hall of Fame pitcher who won 210 games over 19 major league seasons with St. Louis in the 1920s and '30s.

★ ★ ★

1949: Lasse Viren, an outstanding Finnish distance runner who captured 5,000 and 10,000-meter gold medals in consecutive Olympic Games (1972, '76).

★ ★ ★

DEATH OF A LEGEND

1979: J.V. Cain (football).

★ ★ ★

1982: Lloyd Waner (baseball).

MILESTONES • IN SPORTS •

1923

Washington's Walter Johnson stepped into uncharted territory when he notched his 3,000th career strikeout in a 3–1 victory over Cleveland.

1973

Susie Maxwell Berning fired a final-round 72 and earned her third U.S. Women's Open golf championship with a five-stroke victory over Gloria Ahret and Sally Hamlin at Rochester, N.Y.

1976

East German Kornelia Ender won her third and fourth gold medals of the Montreal Olympic Games – 27 minutes apart. She tied the world record in the 100-meter butterfly and set a world mark in the 200-meter freestyle.

1979

St. Louis Cardinals tight end J.V. Cain collapsed during a summer camp workout and died two hours later – on his 28th birthday. Cause of death was unknown.

1984

Kathy Whitworth surpassed Sam Snead in career victories (85) when she defeated Rosie Jones in a sudden-death playoff for the Rochester (N.Y) International golf title.

Kathy Whitworth, *the all-time winningest player in the professional golf ranks.*

Oakland shortstop **Bert Campaneris,** *known for his speed and baserunning, broke into the major leagues with a two-home run first game.*

1989 CALCAVECCHIA SNEAKS IN

July 23

American Mark Calcavecchia, seemingly a third party to a British Open battle between two Australians, came out of nowhere to claim his first major victory in a four-hole playoff at the Royal Troon Golf Club in Troon, Scotland.

It appeared honors would go to either Wayne Grady, who led from the second round until the 17th hole of the final round, or Greg Norman, who opened the day six strokes behind Grady and birdied the first six holes en route to a course-record 64.

But Grady bogeyed two of the last five holes to drop into a tie with Norman while Calcavecchia sneaked home with birdies on two of the last three holes. His 68 forced a three-way tie at 13-under 275.

The 10th playoff in British Open history was the first under a four-hole format instituted in 1985. The three golfers played the first, second, 17th and 18th holes, with low score deciding the championship.

Calcavecchia had two pars and two birdies for 13 strokes, three better than Grady. Norman picked up on 18 after going into two bunkers and out of bounds.

British Open champion **Mark Calcavecchia.**

A STAR IS BORN

1918: Pee Wee Reese, a Hall of Fame shortstop for the Brooklyn Dodgers in the 1940s and '50s.

★ ★ ★

1936: Don Drysdale, a Hall of Fame pitcher who won 209 games over 14 seasons in the 1950s and '60s with the Brooklyn and Los Angeles Dodgers.

★ ★ ★

DEATH OF A LEGEND

1975: Emlen Tunnell (football).

MILESTONES IN SPORTS

1964

Kansas City shortstop Bert Campaneris became the second modern-era player to hit two home runs in his first major league game – a 4–3 A's victory over Minnesota.

1969

San Francisco first baseman Willie McCovey provided the muscle with two home runs as the N.L. won its seventh straight All-Star Game with a 9–3 decision over the A.L. at RFK Stadium in Washington.

1970

Marilyn Neufville, a 17-year-old London schoolgirl from Jamaica, set a world record for the 400-meter run with a 51-second clocking during competition in the British Commonwealth Games.

1972

Belgian great Eddy Merckx won his record-tying fourth consecutive Tour de France, the crown jewel on the world bicycle racing tour.

1976

The Pittsburgh Steelers were awarded a 24–0 victory in the annual College All-Star Game when fans flooded onto Chicago's Soldier Field during a second-half downpour and tore down both goal posts.

1960 RAWLS WINS AGAIN

Betsy Rawls roared back from a seven-stroke third-round deficit with a sparkling 68 and then came home with a final-round 75 that gave her a record-setting fourth U.S. Women's Open golf championship.

Rawls' 68, which tied the Women's Open record set by Fay Crocker in 1958, was fashioned over the 6,137-yard Worcester (Mass.) Country Club course. It wiped out the big advantage Mickey Wright had built over 36 holes and left the women tied going into the final round.

Wright, who fired a morning 75, continued her downward slide in the afternoon, but Joyce Ziske jumped into the picture and actually took a two-stroke advantage on the front nine. When Rawls putted out in the group just ahead of her, Ziske needed an 18th-hole par to tie, a birdie to win.

She got neither. Ziske missed a four-foot par putt that could have forced a playoff and Rawls had achieved her one-stroke victory with a four-round total of 292.

1989 LEMOND PULLS OFF COMEBACK

They said it couldn't be done, but Greg LeMond thought otherwise. And the talented American proved it by racing from Versailles to Paris in an incredible 26 minutes, 57 seconds to win the Tour de France bicycle race for a second time.

LeMond began the day 50 seconds behind overall leader Laurent Fignon of France. The Tour already had covered 2,000 miles in three weeks and everybody wrote off Fignon as uncatchable. Everybody except LeMond.

The 28-year-old blazed through the 15-mile time trial like a man possessed. His speed translated into 34 miles per hour, faster than anybody had ever traveled in the event. When he hit the finish line on the Champs-Elysees, he waited for Fignon, who had started two minutes behind him. When it became evident Fignon was not going to finish in time, LeMond pumped his fist in the air.

Fignon finished the final leg 58 seconds behind LeMond, resulting in a winning margin of 8 seconds – the lowest in history. Fignon and LeMond dominated the race, the American leading after eight stages, the Frenchman after nine.

JULY

24

1978 YANKEE SKIPPER MARTIN RESIGNS

Billy Martin, the fiery, intense New York manager and keeper of the "Bronx Zoo," ended his stormy three-year association with equally volatile Yankee Owner George Steinbrenner when he submitted a tearful resignation on a balcony at Kansas City's Crown Center Hotel.

Martin's decision brought an end to a stormy half-season that included celebrated run-ins with Steinbrenner and slugger Reggie Jackson. The last straw was an off-hand quip Martin made about the pair as he got off a plane in Chicago. He told a reporter, "The two of them deserve each other. One's a born liar, the other's convicted."

The reference was to a two-year suspension Steinbrenner served after being convicted of making illegal political campaign contributions. Jackson is coming off a five-game suspension for failure to follow Martin's orders in a recent game.

Martin's resignation comes on the heels of a five-game winning streak after the Yankees had dropped 14 games behind American League East Division-leading Boston.

Martin tearfully told reporters that he wished the Yankees luck in their pennant quest under new manager Bob LeMon.

1983 'PINE TAR' STEALS SHOW

In one of baseball's more bizarre and controversial conclusions to a game, George Brett's apparent two-run ninth-inning home run was disallowed by umpires and New York was granted a 4–3 victory over Kansas City at Yankee Stadium.

At the center of the controversy was Brett's bat and the sticky substance called pine tar that he uses to enhance his grip. According to the rules, no foreign substance may extend more than 18 inches up the handle, a distance clearly violated by Brett. When the Yankees protested after his home run, the umpires examined the bat and Tim McClelland voided the homer, declaring Brett out and the game over.

Brett flew out of the dugout in a rage and had to be restrained. In the confusion, Royals pitcher Gaylord Perry picked up the bat and tried to take it into the clubhouse. He was intercepted by a uniformed guard. The Royals filed a protest that will be heard by American League President Lee MacPhail.

The controversy started when Brett drilled a two-out, two-run home run over the right-field wall off Yankee reliever Goose Gossage, giving the Royals an apparent 5–4 advantage.

MILESTONES IN SPORTS

1950

Commissioner A.B. (Happy) Chandler presided over the dedication of a new $175,000 wing at the Hall of Fame museum at Cooperstown, N.Y.

1968

The Bionic Man: Chicago knuckleballer Hoyt Wilhelm made his record-setting 907th career appearance, but lost a 2–1 decision to Oakland.

1976

American John Naber captured his fourth gold medal and became the first person to break the 2-minute barrier in the 200-meter backstroke at the Montreal Summer Olympic Games.

1976

Jerry Pate fired a course-record 63 and captured the Canadian Open golf tournament by four strokes over fellow American Jack Nicklaus.

1987

The Salt Lake City Trappers tied the longest winning streak (27 games) in Organized Baseball history when they beat the Pocatello Giants, 7–2, in a Pioneer League contest.

West German tennis champion **Boris Becker.**

1987 BECKER OUTLASTS 'OLD' MCENROE

In a marathon that pitted youth against determination and guile, West Germany's Boris Becker outlasted American John McEnroe in a 6-hour, 38-minute endurance test that put West Germany on the brink of upset in a Davis Cup relegation match.

The battle at Hartford, Conn., believed to be the longest ever played in American Davis Cup competition, was decided more by stamina than by talent. The younger Becker held up for a 4–6, 15–13, 8–10, 6–2, 6–2 victory when the 28-year-old McEnroe simply ran out of gas.

The decisive set was the second. It lasted a grueling 2 hours, 35 minutes with neither player willing to give an inch through 28 exhausting games. Only a mishit in the 20th by McEnroe came between him and a straight-sets victory.

It was obvious from the beginning Becker was the stronger player, but McEnroe kept him off balance with every trick in the book – including the usual arguments with linesmen, displays of temper and incessant talking.

But just as McEnroe refused to yield, Becker refused to be distracted. He gave West Germany a 2–0 lead in the best-of-five series when McEnroe couldn't continue the early pace and went down quietly in the last two sets.

A STAR IS BORN

1934: Willie Davis, a football Hall of Fame defensive end for the Cleveland Browns and Green Bay Packers from 1958–69.

★ ★ ★

1939: Walt Bellamy, an outstanding center who scored 20,941 points over 14 NBA seasons.

★ ★ ★

1963: Karl Malone, a current National Basketball Association forward.

★ ★ ★

1964: Barry Bonds, a current major league outfielder.

★ ★ ★

1972 N.L. WINS LATE AGAIN

A 10th-inning single by Cincinnati's Joe Morgan drove home San Diego's Nate Colbert and helped the National League extend the American League's All-Star Game woes with a 4–3 victory at Atlanta's Fulton County Stadium.

The N.L.'s ninth win in 10 years was orchestrated with another patented ninth-inning rally that snatched away another apparent A. L. victory.

This time the Americans held a 3–2 ninth-inning advantage when Chicago's Billy Williams singled, moved to third on a single by Pittsburgh catcher Manny Sanguillen and scored the tying run on a ground ball by Houston slugger Lee May.

Despite all of the late-game N.L. theatrics, the most exciting moment belonged to Atlanta slugger Hank Aaron. Playing before his home fans, the man with 659 career home runs pounded a two-run blast in the sixth inning that wiped away a 1-0 A.L. lead.

But that didn't hold up for long. Kansas City second baseman Cookie Rojas belted a two-run shot in the eighth inning to put his team on the brink of victory.

1941 GROVE GETS 300TH

The third attempt was a charm for 41-year-old Boston veteran Lefty Grove, who staggered into the select 300-victory circle with a hard-fought 10–6 victory over the Cleveland Indians in a game at Fenway Park.

It wasn't pretty, but that did not diminish the accomplishment of the talented lefthander who recorded 195 wins as the ace of a powerful Philadelphia Athletics team from 1925–33 and 105 more over the last eight campaigns with the Red Sox. Eight times Grove topped the 20-win plateau and he still ranks as the last American Leaguer to win 30 games in a season (1931).

His seventh victory of the year was decided by a four-run eighth-inning rally after the Red Sox already had overcome 4–0 and 6–4 deficits. Jimmie Foxx, Grove's teammate in both Philadelphia and Boston, fittingly provided the go-ahead run with a two-run triple in the eighth and Jim Tabor added a homer and four RBIs.

Lefty Grove *completed his 300-victory major league tour in Boston.*

MILESTONES IN SPORTS

1902

Unbeaten James Jeffries defended his heavyweight boxing championship with an eighth-round knockout of Bob Fitzsimmons at San Francisco.

1962

St. Louis slugger Stan Musial claimed another National League record when he drove in his 1,862nd run in a 5–2 Cardinal loss to Los Angeles.

1970

In a revolutionary scoring change for the normally traditional sport of tennis, the U.S. Open championships at Forest Hills , N.Y., instituted a nine-point tiebreaker.

1971

Arnold Palmer fired a Westchester Classic-record 270 and recorded an easy five-stroke victory over Hale Irwin and Gibby Gilbert.

1976

American Jim Montgomery became the first swimmer to crack the 50-second barrier in the 100-meter freestyle when he finished the race at 49.99 and captured gold at the Montreal Olympic Games.

1976 MOSES GRABS GOLD

Edwin Moses, a 20-year-old college senior who had never competed in the 400-meter hurdles before this year, earned Olympic gold in the event when he raced to a world-record clocking of 47.64 during action in the Summer Games at Montreal.

Moses covered the one-lap, 10-hurdle race eight meters ahead of American silver medalist Mike Shine and six more ahead of Russian Yevgeny Gavrilenko. The winning time broke the 1972 Olympic world record (47.82) of Uganda's John Akii-Bua, who was denied a chance to face Moses when African nations decided to boycott the Olympic Games.

Moses, basically self-coached, had entered only one 400-meter hurdles race before March and he had never run the event in an international meet. The 6-foot-1 Morehouse College student displayed the speed and strength that could carry him to great heights for years to come.

Edwin Moses *earned a surprising gold medal at Montreal.*

JULY 25

A STAR IS BORN

1941: Nate Thurmond, a basketball Hall of Fame center who scored 14,437 points and grabbed 14,464 rebounds over a 14-year NBA career.

★ ★ ★

1954: Walter Payton, a pro football Hall of Fame running back who set the career record for rushing yardage (16,726) over a career that ended in 1987.

★ ★ ★

1962: Doug Drabek, a current major league pitcher.

★ ★ ★

DEATH OF A LEGEND

1986: Ted Lyons (baseball).

★ ★ ★

JULY

26

A STAR IS BORN

1920: Bob Waterfield, a pro football Hall of Fame quarterback in a career that spanned from 1945–62.

★ ★ ★

1923: Hoyt Wilhelm, a Hall of Fame pitcher from 1952–72 who set the major league record for games pitched with 1,070.

★ ★ ★

1956: Dorothy Hamill, the Olympic gold medalist and world-champion figure skater in 1976.

1964 2 BEARS DIE IN CRASH

The defending National Football League-champion Chicago Bears, preparing for a new season at their training camp in Rensselaer, Ind., were shocked by the news that running back Willie Galimore and end John Farrington had been killed in an automobile crash not far from the facilities at St. Joseph's College.

The players, both starters last season, died instantly when the Volkswagen driven by Galimore went off the road, threw them out of the car and pinned them. They were driving about 55mph at 10:25 p.m., evidently trying to beat curfew.

In Galimore, the Bears lose a 29-year-old who gained 2,985 yards over seven seasons. The 29-year-old Farrington owns the Chicago record for longest touchdown catch – 98 yards in 1961. He caught 21 passes for 335 yards last year.

1952 MATHIAS STILL HAS HIS GOLDEN TOUCH

Californian Bob Mathias, a bandage covering a painful leg injury, ran the 1,500-meter race in 4:50.8 and finished off his world record-setting performance in the decathlon at the Summer Olympic Games in Helsinki.

Bob Mathias, *Olympic decathlon champion, throwing the discus.*

Mathias' gritty effort lifted his two-day point total to 7,887, well beyond the second-place total (6,975) of fellow American Milton Campbell. It also allowed him to defend the championship he had won first as a 17-year-old schoolboy in London four years earlier.

When he suffered his muscle injury while broad jumping on the opening day of competition, it seemed unlikely that he would approach the world record of 7,825 points he had set in the Olympic trials. And with three events remaining, he was 99 points behind his world-record pace.

But suddenly Mathias came to life. He soared 13–1 1/2 in the pole vault, 9 3/4 inches higher than he had gone in the Olympic trials. When he followed with a career-best 194–10 3/8 javelin throw, the record was within his grasp.

Mathias ran his 1,500 meters in near darkness, the track illuminated only by the electric scoreboard lights.

MILESTONES • IN SPORTS •

1928

Heavyweight champion Gene Tunney scored an 11th-round technical knockout of Tom Heeney in a title fight at New York.

1933

Joe DiMaggio, an 18-year-old playing in his first professional season, saw his 61-game hitting streak come to an end during a Pacific Coast League game against Oakland.

1971

Muhammad Ali scored a 12th-round technical knockout of former sparring partner Jimmy Ellis in a non-title fight at the Houston Astrodome.

1976

Yugoslavia stunned the defending-champion Soviet Union basketball team, 89–84, and wrecked the much-anticipated grudge match with the United States at the Montreal Olympic Games.

1981

Renaldo Nehemiah tied his own world record with a wind-aided 13-second run in the 110-meter hurdles at the National Sports Festival in Syracuse, N.Y.

Pat Bradley *with her U.S. Women's Open championship trophy.*

1981 BRADLEY WINS OPEN

Pat Bradley, a long hitter with a knack for finishing second, fired a U.S. Women's Open-record 279 over four rounds and captured the LPGA Tour's top prize at the La Grange (Ill.) Country Club.

Bradley, a second-place finisher 24 times in her professional career, shot an Open-record 66 to wipe out a three-stroke deficit and claim the $22,000 first prize. She needed a birdie on the final hole to edge Beth Daniel by a stroke.

The final round was a two-way struggle between Bradley and Daniel after they had forged a two-way tie on the fifth hole. Bradley did not lead by herself until the 15th, where she rolled in a monster 70-foot putt. She held on to that precarious advantage through 17 and both golfers birdied the 18th to close out their exciting battle.

The 30-year-old Bradley had entered the final day trailing Kathy Whitworth by three strokes.

MILESTONES IN SPORTS

1946

Boston's Rudy York matched the feats of Tony Lazzeri and Jim Tabor when he blasted two grand slams during a 13–6 Red Sox victory over St. Louis.

1950

Philadelphia's Del Ennis hit a bases-loaded double in the seventh inning and a grand slam homer in the eighth, accounting for seven RBIs and helping the Phillies defeat Chicago, 13–3.

1972

The WHA's Quebec Nordiques dipped into the NHL's rich history when they tabbed former Montreal great Maurice (Rocket) Richard as their new coach.

1973

Walter Blum became the sixth jockey to win 4,000 races when he rode Student Lamp to victory in the seventh race at Monmouth Park in New Jersey.

1983

Veteran righthander Gaylord Perry, pitching for Kansas City in a 5–4 victory over Cleveland, became the third pitcher of the season and fourth overall to reach 3,500 career strikeouts.

1985

Great Britain's Steve Cram took more than a second off the mile world record when he was clocked at 3:46.31 in the "Dream Mile" at a Grand Prix track and field meet at Oslo, Norway.

1952

Czech Does Triple Duty

Emil Zatopek, a 30-year-old Czechoslovakian Army major with super-human endurance, completed an amazing and unprecedented Olympic "triple" when he added the marathon to his 5,000 and 10,000-meter victories in the Summer Games held at Helsinki, Finland.

The amazing Zatopek set an Olympic record in an event that he had never run before. He completed the marathon in 2:23.3, a half mile in front of his nearest competitor. Zatopek already had set Olympic records in winning his first two gold medals.

The marathon victory came three days after he had won the 5,000 and a week after his 10,000 victory. His time for the 26-mile, 385-yard event was 6 minutes and 16 seconds faster than it had ever been run in Olympic competition.

When Zatopek came through the tunnel and entered the Olympic stadium, 70,000 people cheered his every step. The little hunch-back runner dashed across the finish line like a sprinter completing the 100-meter race. The crowd roar continued for several minutes and then broke out all over again after he received his medal and circled the track in a victory lap.

JULY

27

A STAR IS BORN

1889: Joe Tinker, a Hall of Fame shortstop who batted .264 over 13 seasons from 1902–16.

★ ★ ★

1905: Leo Durocher, a former shortstop for the St. Louis Gashouse Gang and a long-time major league manager who compiled 2,008 career victories.

★ ★ ★

1948: Peggy Fleming, a three-time world-champion figure skater and the 1968 Olympic gold medalist.

★ ★ ★

DEATH OF A LEGEND

1948: Joe Tinker (baseball).

★ ★ ★

1985: Smokey Joe Wood (baseball).

★ ★ ★

1993

Celtics' Lewis Dies

Reggie Lewis, a 27-year-old forward who averaged 20.8 points for the Boston Celtics last season, died at a Waltham, Mass., hospital after collapsing while shooting baskets at the team's Brandeis University training center.

Lewis, who had collapsed with a heart ailment during a playoff game against Charlotte last April, fell to his back gasping for air during his light workout. He was rushed to the hospital where he died of apparent cardiac arrest.

Lewis had been warned by a team of cardiologists after his April collapse that he suffered from a severe form of heart disease that threatened his life if he continued to play basketball. But Lewis had later received conflicting diagnoses and was undecided about retirement. He had not participated in any official team workouts since the diagnosis.

Lewis, a six-year professional out of Northeastern University, carried a 17.6-point career average and played in the 1991–92 NBA All-Star Game.

Former Boston Celtics star **Reggie Lewis.**

1987

Long Streak Finally Ends

Eddie Taubensee blasted a three-run homer to cap a six-run first inning and Billings went on to record a 7–5 Pioneer League victory over Salt Lake City, ending the Trappers' Organized Baseball-record winning streak at 29 games.

The loss, Salt Lake's first in July, ended a month of near-perfect baseball – and fun. The Trappers had set the record of 28 two days earlier when they defeated Pocatello, 13–3, at Derks Field in Salt Lake City and they also added another victory over Pocatello the next afternoon for good measure.

The loss to Billings came after the Trappers had scored a pair of first-inning runs. But the Mustangs rallied for their streak-snapping victory that ended the rookie league team's brief brush with celebrity status.

The Trappers had made national headlines and drawn large crowds when they approached, and finally surpassed, the 85-year-old record winning streak of 27 games set by the 1902 Corsicana Oilers of the Texas League and tied in 1921 by the International League's Baltimore Orioles.

JULY

28

A STAR IS BORN

1943: Bill Bradley, a three-time college basketball All-America, a member of two NBA championship teams with the New York Knicks and currently a U.S. Senator from New Jersey.

★ ★ ★

1949: Vida Blue, a 209-game winner over 17 major league seasons from 1969–86.

★ ★ ★

DEATH OF A LEGEND

1986: Joe Oeschger (baseball).

MILESTONES IN SPORTS

1913

After 11 years of frustration and disappointment, the United States recovered the Davis Cup with a 3–2 victory over Great Britain at Wimbledon.

1983

A.L. President Lee MacPhail overruled the umpires' decision in the "Pine Tar" game played four days earlier at Yankee Stadium. The decision restored Kansas City third baseman George Brett's home run and ordered the game resumed at a later date with the Royals leading the Yankees, 5–4.

1987

Angel Cordero rode winners in both divisions of the Colleen Stakes at Monmouth Park and became the fourth jockey to record 6,000 career victories.

1989

St. Louis master thief Vince Coleman finally was caught by Montreal catcher Nelson Santovenia, ending his major league-record streak of 50 consecutive steals.

1958 Everybody Wins In Historic Track Meet at Moscow

It was the type of competitive reaction that officials from both the Soviet Union and United States could only dream about before the countries got together for an historic two-day dual track and field meet at Moscow.

After American Rafer Johnson had reclaimed his title "world's greatest athlete" with a world record-setting victory over Vasily Kuznetsov in the decathlon, he was affectionately being mobbed by appreciative Russians. That was the spirit of the entire competition.

That's not to say the competition was not intense. The program was divided into men's and women's segments and final scores were carefully kept. The American men won 13 of the 21 events and outpointed the Russians, 126–109. But the American women fell to their Soviet counterparts, 63–44.

The Russians unofficially recorded a 172–170 overall victory, but the countries had agreed not to combine the scores. The highlight of the competition was the decathlon duel between Johnson and Kuznetsov. Johnson was the recognized world record-holder in the event (7,985 points), but Kuznetsov had recently broken that mark with an 8,013 total that was awaiting official acceptance.

As expected, the 30,000-plus crowd at Lenin Stadium was solidly behind its star. But its exhortations seemed to have more effect on Johnson than Kuznetsov. With his status as the best decathlete in the world hanging precariously in the balance, Johnson answered the call and posted a world record with 8,302 points.

1993 Young's Streak Ends

Ryan Thompson singled home the tying run in the bottom of the ninth inning and New York Mets teammate Eddie Murray doubled home the winner, bringing a long-awaited end to Anthony Young's major league-record 27-game losing streak with a 5–4 victory over the Florida Marlins at Shea Stadium.

The victory was the first for Young since April 19, 1992 – a span of 74 appearances. He appeared headed for his 28th straight loss when he surrendered a ninth-inning run, giving the Marlins a 4–3 advantage.

"The guys treated it like I had won a World Series game for them," said Young, who was given a bottle of champagne by Manager Dallas Green. Young (1–13) had broken the previous record of 23 straight losses set by Cliff Curtis of the Boston Braves in 1910–11.

Montreal pitcher **Dennis Martinez** *was perfect for one night against the Dodgers.*

1991 Martinez Has Perfect Night

Montreal righthander Dennis Martinez, working off the same mound from which Sandy Koufax threw his perfect game 26 years earlier, retired all 27 Los Angeles batters he faced in a 2–0 victory at Dodger Stadium.

Martinez struck out five and outdueled Dodger righthander Mike Morgan while pitching the 13th perfect game in baseball history. It was the second at Dodger Stadium – the first since Koufax shut down Chicago, 1–0, in 1965.

Martinez, the National League earned-run average leader, had been matched pitch for pitch by Morgan through five innings. But Montreal's Ron Hassey ended the double perfecto with a leadoff sixth-inning single and the Expos scored twice in the seventh when shortstop Alfredo Griffin made two errors and Larry Walker drove a triple to right-center field.

Martinez, a 36-year-old Nicaraguan, brought the 45,560 fans to their feet in the ninth when he retired Mike Scioscia on a fly ball, pinch-hitter Stan Javier on strikes and pinch-hitter Chris Gwynn on a game-ending fly.

Seattle home run streaker **Ken Griffey Jr.**

1993

Griffey Has Close Call

JULY

29

Young Seattle slugger Ken Griffey Jr. fell short of breaking a long-standing major league record when he failed to hit a home run during the Mariners' 4–3 victory over Minnesota at the Kingdome.

The 23-year-old Griffey had tied the record shared by Dale Long and Don Mattingly when he homered in his eighth consecutive game the night before off Minnesota righthander Willie Banks. The 404-foot shot, Griffey's 30th homer of the season, prompted a three-minute ovation and put him in position to break a record many predicted would never be approached after Long first recorded his feat for Pittsburgh in 1956.

But Mattingly duplicated it for the New York Yankees in 1987 and Griffey almost broke it in his second-at-bat against the Twins' Scott Erickson. After singling in his first at bat, Griffey hit a long shot to center that hit off the base of the wall for a double. He grounded out in the fifth inning and popped up against relief pitcher Larry Casian in the seventh.

1983

Garvey Streak Ends

San Diego first baseman Steve Garvey's National League-record iron man streak ended at 1,207 games when he suffered a dislocated thumb in a home plate collision against Atlanta and sat out the second game of a doubleheader.

Garvey, who had not missed a game since September 2, 1975, was injured in the first inning of the twin-bill opener at Jack Murphy Stadium when he tried to score from third on a wild pitch by the Braves' Pascual Perez. He was tagged out on the throw from catcher Bruce Benedict to Perez covering the plate and jammed his left thumb, an injury that required an elbow-length cast.

That ended the 34-year-old Garvey's streak 100 games short of former New York Yankee Everett Scott's second-place mark of 1,307 and 923 behind former Yankee great Lou Gehrig's all-time record of 2,130.

Steve Garvey's *iron man streak ended at San Diego.*

1976

Cuban Runner Doubles Pleasure

Cuban Alberto Juantorena zipped past American Fred Newhouse with 30 meters remaining and captured the 400-meter final at the Montreal Summer Games, becoming the first runner ever to win both the 800- and 400-meter races in one Olympics.

The unprecedented double appeared to be in jeopardy when Newhouse broke out fast and maintained a good lead for 200 meters. But Juantorena, who had set a world record while winning the 800 four days earlier, made his move around the last turn. As they hit the straightaway and headed for home, the powerfully built Cuban turned on the jets and won by a yard.

Juantorena's time of 44.26 was the third fastest in history and the fastest at sea level. Lee Evans and Larry James both ran faster in 1968 in the thinner air of Mexico City.

The 400-meter victory completed the double that had eluded four previous runners. Mel Sheppard (1908), Ted Meredith (1912), Arthur Wint (1948) and Mal Whitfield (1948 and '52) all won one of the races but lost the other.

Juantorena's record time in the 800 was 1:43.50.

A STAR IS BORN

1887: Tim Mara, the founder of the NFL's New York Giants and a charter member of the pro football Hall of Fame.

★ ★ ★

DEATH OF A LEGEND

1992: Bunny Larocque (hockey).

★ ★ ★

MILESTONES • IN SPORTS •

1909

National League President Harry Pulliam, unable to cope with personal and professional problems, died from a self-inflicted gunshot.

1957

Floyd Patterson solidified his hold on the world heavyweight boxing championship when he recorded a 10th-round technical knockout of Tommy Jackson in New York.

1981

The United States used a 31-point effort by Kevin Magee to post a 93–87 victory over the Soviet Union in the basketball final of the World University Games at Bucharest, Romania.

1991

Jack Nicklaus fired a playoff-round 65 over the tough Oakland Hills Country Club course in Birmingham, Mich., and defeated Chi Chi Rodriguez by four strokes in the United States Senior Open.

JULY

30

MILESTONES
• IN SPORTS •

1928

Canadian sprinter Percy Williams came out of nowhere to win gold medals in the 100- and 200-meter events in the Summer Olympic Games at Amsterdam.

1933

St. Louis ace Dizzy Dean struck out a major league-record 17 Chicago batters during an 8–2 Cardinal victory in a doubleheader opener at Sportsman's Park.

1936

A major league first: The Boston Red Sox, accompanied by American League President Will Harridge, were transported by airplane from St. Louis to Chicago.

1968

Washington lost a 10–1 decision to Cleveland, but the Senators took consolation in an unassisted triple play by shortstop Ron Hansen – the eighth in major league history.

1969

An era ends: Bill Russell, who led the Boston Celtics to an unprecedented 11 NBA championships in 13 years as both a player and coach, announced his retirement.

1990

Saying he had acted in a manner "not in the best interests of baseball," Commissioner Fay Vincent banned ever-controversial New York Yankee Owner George Steinbrenner indefinitely from further involvement with the team.

1976 JENNER WINS DECATHLON

American Bruce Jenner completed a four-year obsession when he hit the finish line of the 1,500-meter run, raised his arms and officially declared himself the world's best athlete during decathlon competition in the Summer Olympic Games at Montreal.

Jenner's world record-setting victory in the grueling two-day, 10-event test provided a much-needed boost for an American track and field team that was falling well short of expectations at Montreal. Jenner had entered the competition as a slight favorite, but Germany's Guido Kratschmer and Russian Nikolai Avilov offered serious competition.

Jenner's strategy was simple. Since most of his weaker events would be run on the first day, he simply wanted to stay within striking distance (maybe 200 points) of Kratschmer and Avilov. Jenner knew he was in control when the first day ended and he trailed Kratschmer by 35 and Avilov by 17.

The second day was Jenner's showcase. He took control early and accelerated the pace toward the first-ever 8,500-point finish. When he ran the 1,500-meter in 4:12.6, he checked in with a whopping 8,617 points – 206 more than second-place Kratschmer.

American decathlon champion **Bruce Jenner.**

1980 HOUSTON'S RICHARD SUFFERS A STROKE

Houston ace J.R. Richard, the powerful 6-foot-8 righthander who has averaged more than 15 victories in his seven-plus major league seasons, underwent surgery to correct a blocked artery in his neck only a few hours after collapsing during a team workout at the Astrodome.

Richard, who had been complaining about a tired arm for months, was rushed away in an ambulance after suddenly collapsing while playing catch. Surgery was performed immediately when a blood clot was detected in a main artery that provides circulation for the upper limbs. Without that circulation, Richard suffered a stroke.

Richard, a 20-game winner in 1976 and a career 107-game winner with a 3.15 earned-run average, had undergone four days of tests a week earlier. Doctors, unable to find anything wrong, had suggested that Richard's problems could be emotional rather than physical

The big fireballer had pitched two scoreless innings for the National League in the July 6 All-Star Game.

Houston righthander **J.R. Richard** *before his 1980 stroke.*

1989 SOTOMAYOR SOARS TO GREAT HEIGHTS

Javier Sotomayor, a 21-year-old jumping jack from Cuba, surpassed another track and field barrier when he became the first high jumper to clear 8 feet in the Carribean Championships at San Juan, Puerto Rico.

The 6-foot-4 Sotomayor broke his own world record of 7–11 1/2 when he soared over the bar on his second attempt at the historic height. He had jumped 7–4 1/4, 7–5, 7–6 1/2, 7–8 1/4 and 7–10 1/2 before asking for the bar to be moved up to 2.44 meters, or 8 feet.

Sotomayor, who had set his previous world record last year in Spain, brushed the crossbar with his left leg on the first attempt, barely missing the barrier breaker. He made it cleanly on the next jump as officials of the International Amateur Athletic Federation – the sport's governing body – watched.

Sotomayor's jump came 33 years after American Charley Dumas became the first 7-foot high jumper.

A STAR IS BORN

1890: Casey Stengel, a former major league outfielder who became manager of the New York Yankees and New York Mets. He guided the Yankees to 10 pennants and seven World Series championships from 1949–60.

★ ★ ★

1958: Daley Thompson, the British decathlete who won gold medals in consecutive Olympic Games (1980 and '84).

★ ★ ★

1963: Chris Mullin, a current National Basketball Association forward.

DEATH OF A LEGEND

1941: Mickey Welch (baseball).

★ ★ ★

MILESTONES • IN SPORTS •

1932

Fans witnessing the first game at Cleveland's new Municipal Stadium were treated to a pitching duel: Philadelphia's Lefty Grove recorded a 1–0 victory over the Indians and Mel Harder.

1961

An All-Star first: The second midsummer classic of the season, tied 1–1 after nine innings, was ended by a Boston downpour.

1976

Sugar Ray Leonard (light welterweight), Michael Spinks (middleweight) and Leon Spinks (light heavyweight) turned in impressive gold medal-winning performances in the Summer Olympic Games at Montreal.

1983

Australian Jan Stephenson braved 100-degree temperature to shoot a final-round 74 and post a one-stroke victory over JoAnne Carner and Patty Sheehan in the 38th U.S. Women's Open at Tulsa, Okla.

1990

Rubber-armed Texas fireballer Nolan Ryan became baseball's 20th 300-game winner when he pitched $7^{2}/_{3}$ innings of an 11–3 victory over the Brewers at Milwaukee's County Stadium.

A STAR IS BORN

1951: Evonne Goolagong, an Australian tennis champion who won six Grand Slam titles in the 1970s.

★ ★ ★

1969: Andre Ware, a current National Football League quarterback.

★ ★ ★

DEATH OF A LEGEND

1970: Jimmy Conzelman (football).

★ ★ ★

1981 BASEBALL STRIKE ENDS

The 50-day strike that shut down baseball and forced the cancellation of 706 games came to a merciful end when players and owners announced agreement on the free-agent compensation issue that had dragged out a settlement.

The seven-week work stoppage, the longest in American sports history, forced cancellation of 38 percent of the schedule and forced a creative plan to restructure the season. Teams that were in first place as of June 11 were declared first-half winners and the remainder of the schedule will be played to determine second-half champions. The two "half" winners will meet in a special series to determine division champions.

The agreement came with the season teetering on the edge of collapse. The solution was a complicated pooling system for free-agent compensation and two compromises – one from each side. The owners agreed to restore service credit to the players for strike time and the players agreed to add a year onto the 1980 Basic Agreement that was signed without resolution of the sticky compensation issue.

The second half of the season will kick off with the August 9 All-Star Game in Cleveland.

1954 ADCOCK BLASTS FOUR, SETS TOTAL BASE MARK

Big Milwaukee first baseman Joe Adcock muscled his way into the baseball record books when he blasted four home runs against the Brooklyn Dodgers and added a double for a major league-record 18 total bases.

Adcock's explosion keyed a 15–7 Braves victory over the Dodgers at Ebbets Field and tied the record for most home runs in a single game. His 18 total bases topped the four-homer, one-single (17 total bases) efforts of pre-1900 stars Ed Delahanty and Bobby Lowe and current Brooklyn first baseman Gil Hodges. Hodges performed his feat in 1950.

Adcock, the seventh player to hit four home runs in a game, connected off four different Brooklyn pitchers. He touched Don Newcombe for a solo blast in the second inning, Erv Palica for a three-run shot in the fifth, Pete Wojey for a two-run blast in the seventh and Johnny Podres for a solo belt in the ninth. His double came off Palica in the third and he finished his big day with seven RBIs.

Milwaukee slugger **Joe Adcock** *(9) is greeted at the dugout after one of his four home runs.*

JULY 31

1984 U.S. CAPTURES 1ST TITLE

A fired-up group of American gymnasts, refusing to give in to pressure or the reigning world-champion Chinese squad, earned the country's first-ever men's team gold medal in Olympic competition during a shocking upset at the Los Angeles Summer Games.

The Americans, up by 1.05 points after the compulsory exercises, held off the Chinese, 591.40 to 590.80. The competition was not decided until the Americans performed their final venue, the horizontal bar, before 9,356 chanting fans at UCLA's Pauley Pavilion.

The Americans faced a tough decision entering that final exercise – take out their risky moves and play it safe or go for broke? The lead was down to .60 of a point and any mishap could prove disastrous. Still, they did not back down.

The pressure mounted when Scott Johnson landed badly at the conclusion of his routine and received a 9.50 score. With the team allowed to drop only one score at the end of its exercise, there was no margin for error.

Mitch Gaylord set the tone for a big finish when he superbly performed his dangerous "Gaylord II" somersault-twist maneuver and received a 9.95. Tim Daggett hit his triple back somersault dismount and got a perfect 10. Peter Vidmar capped the victory with a 9.95.

AUGUST

1

1978 ROSE STREAK ENDS AT 44

Two Atlanta pitchers, a 24-year-old rookie and a tough veteran, brought a well-publicized end to Pete Rose's 44-game hitting streak as the Braves rolled to a 16–4 rout of the Cincinnati Reds in a game at Fulton County Stadium.

Rose had tied Willie Keeler's National League record the night before when he singled off Atlanta knuckleballer Phil Niekro. Next up – former New York Yankee center fielder Joe DiMaggio's 1941 mark of 56 consecutive games. But that drive never really got off the ground.

Facing McWilliams, a young lefthander, Rose walked on a 3–2 count in the first inning, hit a line drive that the pitcher snared ankle high in the second and grounded out in the fourth. He hit the ball hard against Garber in the seventh, but third baseman Bob Horner turned his line drive into a double play.

As chance would have it, Rose got to the plate one more time – with two out in the ninth inning.

After listening to a long ovation from the aroused Braves fans, Rose bunted Garber's first pitch foul, took two balls and foul-tipped the next pitch. On Garber's fifth de livery, he took a full cut and missed for strike three.

1972 COLBERT'S EXPLOSION

San Diego slugger Nate Colbert went on a record offensive binge, punishing Atlanta with five homers and 13 runs batted in during the Padres' 9–0 and 11–7 doubleheader sweep of the Braves at Atlanta's Fulton County Stadium.

Colbert's 7-for-9 performance earned him several entries in baseball's record book. The five homers matched Stan Musial's 1954 doubleheader feat and the 13 RBIs were a doubleheader record. So were his 22 total bases, which were achieved on five home runs and two singles.

The 6-foot-1, 200-pounder belted a pair of first-game homers and drove in five runs. His first-inning three-run shot came off Ron Scheuler and a solo blast in the seventh came off Mike McQueen.

Colbert came back to hit three homers in the nightcap, one a second-inning grand slam off Pat Jarvis that accounted for half of his second-game RBIs. Two-run blows in the seventh and ninth closed out his big day and also gave him an N.L.-leading 30 home runs and 82 RBIs.

Colbert entered the game batting .233.

1928 TUNNEY RETIRES

Gene Tunney, two-time vanquisher of Jack Dempsey and ruler of the heavyweight boxing world since September 1926, retired as undefeated champion, five days after scoring an 11th-round technical knockout over Tom Heeney.

The Heeney bout was only the second defense of the heavyweight crown Tunney took from Dempsey in a 1926 unanimous decision at Philadelphia. Tunney and Dempsey hooked up again a year later in Chicago and produced one of the classic bouts in the history of boxing

Fighting before a record crowd, Dempsey floored the champion in the seventh round but failed to go immediately to a neutral corner as the rules specified. The delay allowed Tunney to beat the "long count" and he came back to record another unanimous decision.

Although not the most active heavyweight champion in history, the 30-year-old Tunney will go down as the sport's most successful. The only other champ to retire undefeated was James Jeffries in 1904 and he later was lured back for a bout against black champion Jack Johnson – which he lost.

Heavyweight champion **Gene Tunney** *during his prime.*

MILESTONES IN SPORTS

1945

New York Giants slugger Mel Ott became baseball's third 500-homer man when he connected off Boston's Johnny Hutchings during a 9–2 victory over the Braves at the Polo Grounds.

1965

The Soviet men recorded their first-ever victory over a United States track team, 118-112, and the Russian women managed an easy $63^{1/2}$–$43^{1/2}$ triumph in the annual Russian-American meet at Kiev.

1987

Mike Tyson gained undisputed possession of the world heavyweight boxing crown with a unanimous 12-round decision over IBF champion Tony Tucker in a title bout at Las Vegas.

1990

The University of Arkansas cut its 75-year ties with the Southwest Conference to become a member of the Southeastern Conference.

1992

Great Britain's Linford Christie streaked to a 9.96 clocking and American Gail Devers was timed at 10.82 seconds in 100-meter gold-medal performances at the Barcelona Summer Olympic Games.

A STAR IS BORN

1921: Jack Kramer, an American tennis star who won the U.S. singles championship in 1946 and both the Wimbledon and the U.S. championships in 1947.

★ ★ ★

1967: Gregg Jefferies, a current major league infielder.

★ ★ ★

DEATH OF A LEGEND

1991: Chris Short (baseball).

★ ★ ★

1979 Munson Dies In Crash

New York Yankee catcher Thurman Munson, the team's captain and moving force for 10 solid seasons, died in a fiery crash when the small plane he was flying went down short of the runway at the Akron-Canton Airport in Ohio.

The 32-year-old Munson, a veteran pilot who often flew to his Canton home to be with his wife and three children, was making an approach when his Cessna Citation twin-engine jet clipped the top of some trees and crashed a few hundred feet short of the runway.

Passengers David Hall and Jerry Anderson escaped when the plane burst into flames, but their efforts to rescue Munson were thwarted by the intense heat. Both survivors were reported in fair condition at a local hospital.

The sometimes-gruff, always-intense Munson was a career .292 hitter who topped the .300 level five times. He was the American League Rookie of the Year in 1970 and its Most Valuable Player in 1976. He helped the Yankees capture three A.L. pennants and also keyed two World Series championships.

1963 College Stars Upset Packers

Wisconsin quarterback Ron VanderKelen fired a 74-yard touchdown strike with 3 minutes remaining and a team of college players recorded an astounding 20-17 upset of the two-time defending National Football League-champion Green Bay Packers in the annual College All-Star Game at Chicago's Soldier Field.

The shocker, ending a five-year string of NFL victories, was made possible by an opportunistic defense that shut down Green Bay's running attack and an offense that controlled the ball. Green Bay, a one-time loser in 1962 and favored by two touchdowns, looked disinterested and lackadaisical at times.

The Packers jumped ahead early on Jim Taylor's two-yard run, but the collegians fought back on a field goal and Larry Ferguson's six-yard run. The teams then traded field goals, setting the stage for VanderKelen's late heroics.

With the All-Stars clinging to their three-point lead, VanderKelen threw a short out pattern to Badger teammate Pat Richter. He caught the pass, made a move on Green Bay cornerback Jesse Whittenton, broke free and rambled 74 yards.

Taylor scored a meaningless one-yard touchdown with 8 seconds remaining to at least make the final score respectable for Green Bay fans.

Former New York Yankee catcher **Thurman Munson.**

1992 Jackie Again

Jackie Joyner-Kersee, reestablishing herself as the greatest woman athlete of the 1980s and '90s, captured her second straight Olympic heptathlon championship with a 7,044-point performance at the Summer Games in Barcelona.

Joyner-Kersee, the first woman to win the seven-pronged event in back-to-back Olympics, dominated the field as she rolled to a 199-point victory over Irina Belova of the United Team. The 30-year-old champion would have been competing for a third straight Olympic title if not for a hamstring injury that led to a five-point loss in the 1984 Games held at Los Angeles.

She took the Barcelona lead with a victory in the first event, the 100-meter hurdles, and built on it the rest of the way. When she started the second day with a 23–3 1/2 long jump, she virtually wrapped up the championship. She concluded the grueling two-day competition with a 2:11.78 time in the 800 meters, insuring her sixth 7,000-point effort – a level that only one other woman has achieved.

Heptathlon hurdler **Jackie Joyner-Kersee.**

August 2

A Star Is Born

1937: Billy Cannon, a former Heisman Trophy-winning running back for LSU and a 10-year professional in the AFL and NFL.

★ ★ ★

1932: Lamar Hunt, the founder of the American Football League and the Kansas City Chiefs.

★ ★ ★

Death of a Legend

1979: Thurman Munson (baseball).

★ ★ ★

Milestones in Sports

1938

Brooklyn recorded a 6–2 victory over St. Louis in the first game of a doubleheader at Ebbets Field – a game best remembered for its experimental yellow baseball.

1948

The incredible Fanny Blankers-Koen of Holland covered 100 meters in 11.9 seconds, winning one of her four gold medals in the Summer Olympic Games at London.

1960

The eight-team Continental League expired without a pitch being thrown when major league baseball agreed to expand by four teams, with ownership groups to come from Continental members.

1991

Texas reliever Mike Jeffcoat, batting for the first time in the major leagues, doubled in a 15–1 victory over Milwaukee and became the first pitcher to drive in a run since the 1973 designated hitter rule.

AUGUST

3

A STAR IS BORN

1894: Harry Heilmann, a four-time A.L. batting champion and career .342 hitter in a Hall of Fame career that spanned 17 seasons.

★ ★ ★

1940: Lance Alworth, a football Hall of Fame wide receiver from 1962–72 with the San Diego Chargers and Dallas Cowboys.

★ ★ ★

1951: Marcel Dionne, a hockey Hall of Fame center who scored 1,771 points in a long career with Detroit, Los Angeles and the New York Rangers.

★ ★ ★

1956: Todd Christensen, an outstanding tight end for the Los Angeles Raiders.

★ ★ ★

DEATH OF A LEGEND

1932: Dan Brouthers (baseball).

★ ★ ★

1957: Nels Stewart (hockey).

1984

RETTON: A PERFECT 10

Mary Lou Retton, her back planted firmly against the wall and needing nothing short of perfection to claim the first-ever gymnastics gold medal for an American woman, performed a flawless vault and provided a stunning conclusion to the all-around competition at the Los Angeles Olympic Games.

Gymnastics all-around gold medalist **Mary Lou Retton** *competing on the uneven bars.*

With 9,023 nervous fans watching in tense silence at UCLA's Pauley Pavilion, the 4-foot-9, 94-pound Retton sprinted into action, needing a 9.95 score to tie Rumania's Ecaterina Szabo, a perfect 10 to win. She hit the springboard, went into her twisting, somersaulting maneuver and "stuck" the landing, triggering a big smile from Retton and a roar from the crowd.

The scoreboard confirmed all suspicions. Mary Lou indeed had her 10 and a gold medal. As if to punctuate her gigantic victory, Retton went ahead with a meaningless second vault and earned another 10.

Her 79.175 to 79.125 victory over Szabo capped an evening-long battle with the competitors matched in pairs – each able to see what the other was doing. Szabo earned a perfect score on the balance beam, Retton answered with a 10 on the floor routine. The lead see-sawed back and forth before Mary Lou's dramatic finish.

"I had goosebumps going up and down me," Retton said after her victory. "I knew from the takeoff, I knew from the run – I just knew it."

MILESTONES IN SPORTS

1928

The U.S. team, surprisingly shut out in track races at the Amsterdam Olympic Games, finally broke through on the sixth day of competition when Ray Barbuti edged Canada's James Ball in the 400-meter final.

1940

Cincinnati catcher Willard Hershberger, apparently despondent over recent poor play, committed suicide by cutting his throat with a razor blade in his Boston hotel room prior to a Reds game against the Braves.

1946

Historian, a 5-year-old gelding, tied Man o'War's 26-year-old world record for $1^5/_8$ miles when he won the Sunset Handicap at Hollywood Park in $2:40^4/_5$ with Ovie Scurlock in saddle.

1960

In an unprecedented trade of major league managers, Cleveland's Joe Gordon was given control of the Detroit Tigers and Jimmie Dykes moved into the Indians' dugout.

1921

CHICAGO PLAYERS BANNED

Judge Kenesaw Mountain Landis, baseball's new commissioner, handed eight members of the Chicago White Sox a lifetime ban from the game for their parts in trying to "fix" the 1919 World Series.

With one fell swoop of his newly acquired dictatorial powers, Landis delivered a clear message that gambling and other miscreant behavior no longer will be tolerated within his baseball jurisdiction.

"Regardless of the verdict of juries, no player that throws a ballgame, no player that undertakes or promises to throw a ballgame, no player that sits in a conference with a bunch of crooked players and gamblers . . . and does not promptly tell his club about it, will ever play professional baseball," Landis said in a far-reaching statement.

The eight White Sox – pitchers Eddie Cicotte and Lefty Williams, infielders Chick Gandil, Swede Risberg, Buck Weaver and Fred McMullin and outfielders Joe Jackson and Happy Felsch – had been pronounced not guilty by a Chicago jury the night before. But that's because the prosecution's case had been destroyed by the mysterious disappearance of all paperwork on the fix.

The White Sox lost the World Series to Cincinnati.

Chicago ace **Eddie Cicotte.**

1936

OWENS ENJOYS GOLD RUSH

American sprinter Jesse Owens, putting a dent in Adolf Hitler's theories on Aryan superiority, streaked to a world record-tying victory in the 100-meter dash, just minutes before Der Fuhrer entered his box at Reich Sports Field Stadium during track and field competition in the Berlin Olympic Games.

Owens, a black Ohio State student, shot out of the starting blocks and was well ahead by his first two strides. He never was seriously challenged in his 10.3-second burst, finishing a yard ahead of Ralph Metcalfe – another black American sprinter.

The record-tying performance, saluted heartily by 110,000 East German fans, came on the heels of Owens' apparent world-record run 24 hours earlier in a semifinal heat. But his 10.2 mark in that race was disallowed because of a following wind. Owens did not learn the record had been disallowed until he returned the next day.

MILESTONES IN SPORTS

1976

American Dwight Stones, a disappointing bronze medalist in the Montreal Olympic Games four days earlier, broke his own high jump world record when he cleared 7-7$1/4$ in the Bicentennial Meet of Champions at Philadelphia.

1982

Joel Youngblood became the first major league player to collect hits for two teams on the same day. Youngblood singled as a member of the New York Mets in Chicago and, after being notified that he had been traded to Montreal, flew to Philadelphia and singled in his Expos debut against the Phillies. His hits came against two potential Hall of Fame pitchers – Chicago's Ferguson Jenkins and Philadelphia's Steve Carlton.

1984

American Evelyn Ashford zipped to a gold medal in the 100-meter final of the Los Angeles Summer Games with an Olympic-record clocking of 10.97.

1984

Young Jackie Joyner-Kersee, hobbled by a hamstring injury suffered on the first day of competition, finished five points behind Austrian Glynis Nunn's Olympic-record total of 6,390 in the heptathlon event at the Los Angeles Summer Games.

1989

Hard-luck Toronto pitcher Dave Stieb, one out away from a perfect game, surrendered a two-out, ninth-inning double to New York's Roberto Kelly. Stieb had lost two 1988 no-hit bids with two out in the ninth inning, one on a bad-hop single and another on a bloop single.

1985 TWO STAR RISE AGAIN

AUGUST 4

On a wonderfully nostalgic day that featured two milestones achieved a continent apart, Chicago White Sox righthander Tom Seaver earned his 300th career victory and California's Rod Carew collected his 3,000th hit.

Never before had two such performances occurred on the same day. The 40-year-old Seaver, a three-time Cy Young Award winner, became the 17th pitcher to join the "300 club" when he defeated the Yankees, 4–1, in New York. The 39-year-old Carew, a seven-time American League batting champion, became the 16th member of the "3,000 club" when he singled off Minnesota's Frank Viola in a game at Anaheim Stadium.

Chicago righthander **Tom Seaver**, *a new member of baseball's 300-victory club.*

Seaver, performing in the city where he pitched the first 11 seasons of his 19-year career, struck out seven Yankees, walked one and allowed only a run-scoring single to Ken Griffey in the third inning. He concluded his 145-pitch effort by retiring Don Baylor on a fly ball with two runners on base.

Carew, performing against the team for which he had played the first 12 seasons of his 19-year career, sliced a third-inning pitch from Viola into left field.

1932 DIDRIKSON CROSSES OLYMPIC HURDLES

Babe Didrikson, who single-handedly won the team title for the Employers Casualty Insurance Company of Dallas during the July Olympic trials, earned her second gold medal of the Los Angeles Summer Games with a world-record clocking of 11.7 seconds in the 80-meter hurdles.

Didrikson, who earlier set a world record in winning the javelin throw, defeated fellow American Evelyn Hall by a nose with a magnificent closing burst. Didrikson won on sheer speed. Hall stayed with her because she has a much sounder hurdling technique.

Hall actually touched ground before Didrikson after the last hurdle, but Babe's closing burst and stretch at the tape gave her a half-inch victory. It also added to her growing reputation as the world's greatest female athlete.

During the Olympic trials at Evanston, Ill., Didrikson won six of the eight events she entered and scored 30 points, more than any team. But she was limited to three events in the Olympic Games and settled on the javelin, hurdles and high jump.

A STAR IS BORN

1890: Dolf Luque, a righthanded pitcher who compiled a 193–179 record in 20 National League seasons from 1914–35.

★★★

1921: Maurice (Rocket) Richard, a Hall of Fame right winger for 18 NHL seasons with the Montreal Canadiens and one-time holder of the all-time record for career goals (544).

★★★

1958: Mary Decker-Slaney, the queen of American distance running during the 1970s and '80s who at one time held seven different American and world records.

★★★

1962: Roger Clemens, a current major league pitcher.

★★★

1986 USFL SUSPENDS 1986 OPERATION

United States Football League owners, rallying behind the old Brooklyn cry "Wait until next year," suspended operation for the 1986 season and said they would attempt to bring back a larger, more powerful league in 1987.

The decision to suspend what would have been the circuit's first fall campaign was made six days after the USFL's lengthy antitrust suit against the National Football League netted only a $1 award in damages. The USFL, claiming among other things that the NFL had acted to keep it from getting a network television contract, had sought as much as $1.69 billion.

Without a major damage award or a network TV deal, the eight-team league was in trouble. Commissioner Harry Usher made the announcement in New York – with the promise the USFL would be back in 1987 when the NFL's television contracts and collective bargaining agreement with the players expire.

The USFL, which started as a 12-team spring league in 1983, expanded to 18 in 1984 before dropping back to 14 and finally eight for the fall campaign.

AUGUST

5

MILESTONES IN SPORTS

1921

Harold Arlin wrote his name into the history books as baseball's first radio broadcaster when he described the Pittsburgh Pirates' 8–5 victory over Philadelphia over station KDKA in Pittsburgh.

1967

A football first: The Denver Broncos defeated the Detroit Lions, 13–7, in a preseason matchup of AFL and NFL teams. The victory was the AFL's first over its rival league in two tries.

1984

The incomparable Edwin Moses stretched his 400-meter hurdles winning streak to 103 while earning his second Olympic gold medal in the event with a 47.75 clocking at the Los Angeles Summer Games.

1986

New San Francisco Giants pitcher Steve Carlton joined Nolan Ryan as baseball's second 4,000-strikeout pitcher while being pounded by Cincinnati for seven runs in a $3^1/_3$-inning stint.

1987

Gene Fullmer retained his NBA middleweight title at Ogden, Utah, with a 15-round split decision over Cuban Florentino Fernandez – despite fighting the last two rounds with a broken right arm.

1991

Paul Brown, the legendary coach who founded the Cleveland Browns and later helped build Cincinnati into an NFL power, died of complications from pneumonia at age 82.

1991 Bubka Hits 20-Footer

Russian Sergei Bubka, the most prolific record-setter in the history of track and field, became the first pole vaulter to reach 20 feet outdoors when he cleared 20–0$^1/_4$ on his final attempt during competition in a Grand Prix meet at Malmo, Sweden.

Bubka won the competition with a 19–2$^1/_4$ effort, but asked officials to raise the bar with the announcement he would try for the record height just once. He failed, but 20,000 fans chanting "Bubka! Bubka! Bubka!" changed his mind.

He missed again on his second attempt, but added another notch to his blazing pole with his record-setting third vault. It was the 13th world record the amazing Russian has set outdoors since 1984 and his 28th overall, one behind former Finnish distance king Paavo Nurmi, who stretched his success in a number of events across a full decade.

Bubka had cleared the 20-foot barrier three times indoors earlier in the year.

A STAR IS BORN

1962: Patrick Ewing, a current National Basketball Association center.

★ ★ ★

DEATH OF A LEGEND

1964: Art Ross (hockey).

★ ★ ★

1978: Jesse Haines (baseball).

★ ★ ★

1978: Dutch Clark (football).

★ ★ ★

1991: Paul Brown (football).

★ ★ ★

New York Yankee slugger **Dave Winfield.**

1983 Watch The Birdie

New York outfielder Dave Winfield, stunned by reaction in Toronto a day earlier when he was arrested for killing a seagull with a thrown ball, breathed a sigh of relief when a Canadian attorney said he would push to have cruelty to animal charges dropped.

The 6-foot-6 slugger was put in jail by Canadian police after the Yankees' 3–1 victory over the Blue Jays at Exhibition Stadium. The incident occurred in the middle of the fifth inning when Winfield threw a warmup ball to a ball boy near the Yankee bullpen in right-center field. The ball skipped past him, hitting a sleeping seagull on the head and killing the visitor from nearby Lake Ontario.

When the boy returned with a towel to remove the bird, Winfield, unaware seagulls are on Canada's list of endangered species, stood with his cap over his heart in a mocking tribute. Fans immediately began hurling debris and insults in his direction.

If convicted, Winfield could have paid a $500 fine and spent up to six months in jail.

1984 Benoit Stars In Marathon

American Joan Benoit recorded an emphatic victory in her first showdown with Norway's Grete Waitz and easily captured the gold medal in the first women's marathon ever run during Olympic competition.

Benoit, the world record-holder who underwent arthroscopic knee surgery in April, completed the 26-mile, 385-yard course during the Los Angeles Summer Games in 2:24.52, about 400 meters ahead of Waitz. It marked the first time Waitz had lost a marathon that she finished.

Benoit's strategy was simple. She pulled away from the pack at the 3-mile mark and never looked back. Waitz, who seemed unconcerned by Benoit's aggressive move, began her kick too late and could not catch up. Benoit made her triumphant appearance from the Los Angeles Coliseum tunnel and was greeted by 77,083 fans who began a long, sustained victory celebration.

The fever pitch increased when Switzerland's Gabriela Andersen-Schiess made a different kind of appearance from the tunnel. Staggering and weaving, she struggled around the track, flanked by two members of the medical unit, as numerous runners passed her by. She finally managed to cross the finish line and collapsed, suffering from heat exhaustion and dehydration.

Joan Benoit, *winner of the first women's marathon in Olympic competition.*

MILESTONES IN SPORTS

1926

New Yorker Gertrude Ederle made double history when she became the first woman to swim the English Channel and accomplished the feat in a record time of 14 hours, 31 minutes.

1952

Former Negro League star Satchel Paige became the oldest pitcher (47) to throw a complete game or a shutout when he pitched the St. Louis Browns to a 1–0, 12-inning victory over Detroit.

1972

South African Gary Player, ignoring rainy conditions, fired a final-round 72 and captured his second PGA Championship by two strokes at the Oakland Hills Country Club in Birmingham, Mich.

1978

John Mahaffey dropped a birdie putt on the second hole of a sudden-death playoff at Oakmont (Pa.) Country Club and defeated Jerry Pate and Tom Watson for the PGA Championship.

1981

Baseball owners and players, ready to reopen play after a seven-week strike that forced cancellation of 706 games, agreed on a format that will divide the season into halves and necessitate an extra round of divisional playoffs.

1988

Chicago reliever Goose Gossage joined Rollie Fingers as the only members of baseball's 300-save club when he produced the final out of the Cubs' 7–4 victory over Philadelphia.

1992

American Kevin Young set the only track and field world record of the Barcelona Olympic Games when he blazed to a 46.78 clocking in the 400-meter hurdles.

1948 Mathias Captures Rugged Decathlon

Bob Mathias, a 17-year-old boy competing against the best athletes from 19 countries, became the youngest person ever to win a decathlon when he piled up 7,139 points under difficult conditions in the Summer Olympic Games at London.

Mathias' victory came as the clock approached midnight in a Wembley Stadium illuminated by floodlights. It was witnessed only by his parents, two brothers and a few hundred spectators. And it was achieved in the rain that had made competition slippery and treacherous throughout the two-day, 10-event battle.

Mathias sloshed to the finish line in the final event, the 1,500-meter run, in 5:11, well behind Ignace Heinrich of France and American Floyd Simmons. But he already had piled up a big lead and beat Heinrich by 165 points. Amazingly, he did it while pole vaulting in semi-darkness, throwing the javelin in total darkness and running the 1,500 meters around a dark, somber track. He needed a flashlight to illuminate markers for his javelin run.

But nothing fazed the recent California high school graduate who walked away with the title "world's greatest athlete."

Bob Mathias *sails over the bar during pole vault competition in the 1948 Olympic decathlon.*

1958 Elliott Wins Dreamy Mile

Australian Herb Elliott, benefitting from a furious pace set by five of the world's greatest distance runners, knocked almost 3 seconds off the mile record in an incredible race in Dublin, Ireland.

Elliott's time of 3:54.5 broke the 4-year-old 3:58 record of fellow Australian John Landy. But even more amazing, three other runners also broke Landy's record and another finished under 4 minutes – the first time five runners had broken the once-sacred barrier in the same race.

Australian Merv Lincoln finished second at 3:55.9, Ireland's Ron Delany was third at 3:57.5, New Zealand's Murray Halberg was fourth at 3:57.5 and Australia's Albert Thomas was fifth at 3:58.6. Halberg broke the world record but couldn't even finish among the top three.

Thomas set a fast early pace and Lincoln moved in front on the third lap. Elliott made his move when the bell sounded for the final lap and opened up a lead on the backstretch. He finished 15 yards ahead of Lincoln.

A STAR IS BORN

1906: Ken Strong, a football Hall of Fame halfback and placekicker with the Staten Island Stapletons, New York Yankees and New York Giants in the formative years of the NFL from 1929–47.

★ ★ ★

1908: Helen Jacobs, a former tennis star who captured the Wimbledon singles championship in 1936 and four U.S. titles from 1932 through '35.

★ ★ ★

1962: Tony Fernandez, a current major league shortstop.

★ ★ ★

1965: David Robinson, a current National Basketball Association center.

★ ★ ★

AUGUST 6

1962 Mexico Shocks U.S.

Rafael Osuna, down and almost out in the heat and altitude of Mexico City, reached deep and pulled out an amazing burst of energy that spurred him to a fifth-set victory over Jon Douglas and the Mexican Davis Cup team to a stunning upset of the United States.

Osuna's 9–7, 6–3, 6–8, 3–6, 6–1 victory was an unpredictable roller-coaster of domination. The young Mexican stormed out quickly, but Douglas fought back to win a tight third set. Osuna suddenly ran out of gas in the fourth, gulping oxygen on the sideline and appearing to be near collapse at times on the court.

The United States team appeared to be on the verge of dodging an upset bullet.

Osuna, however, seemed to draw energy from the wild cheering of the partisan fans and literally overpowered the startled Douglas in the decisive set. With the crowd saluting his every move, he finally provided the clincher.

Osuna had provided easy pickings in his first-round match for Chuck McKinley, but Douglas lost to Mario Llamas. The most serious blow was delivered by an underdog Mexican doubles team of Osuna and Antonio Palafox, which defeated the world-renowned team of McKinley and Dennis Ralston in five sets.

AUGUST 7

A STAR IS BORN

1887: Bill McKechnie, a baseball Hall of Fame manager who directed five major league teams to 1,899 victories and four World Series championships over 25 seasons from 1915–46.

★ ★ ★

1929: Don Larsen, a major league pitcher who won 81 games but is best remembered for his perfect game in the 1956 World Series.

★ ★ ★

1932: Abebe Bikila, an Ethiopian who became the first runner to win consecutive Olympic marathons (1960 and '64).

★ ★ ★

1942: Carlos Monzon, the Argentine middleweight champion who compiled a career record of 89–3–9 from 1963-77. He held the middleweight crown for a record 6 years, 9 months.

★ ★ ★

1945: Alan Page, a football Hall of Fame defensive tackle from 1967–81 with the Minnesota Vikings and Chicago Bears.

★ ★ ★

DEATH OF A LEGEND

1960: Luis Firpo (boxing).

★ ★ ★

Olympic tennis gold medalist **Jennifer Capriati.**

1954 BANNISTER BEATS LANDY

If it wasn't the greatest head-to-head battle ever staged, it was close. Roger Bannister versus John Landy. The Englishman versus the Australian. A major showdown between the only two sub-4-minute milers in history.

The hype that preceded this duel at the British Empire Games at Vancouver called it the "Mile of the Century." Even an American. television network got in on the act, combining with a Canadian company to make it the most widely viewed event in sports history.

The fascination was over Bannister, the first man to break 4 minutes on May 6 when he was clocked at 3:59.4, and Landy, who was clocked at 3:58 on June 21. It appeared to be a race made in heaven – one of those "great matchups" that so often fall short of expectations. But not this time.

When the starting gun sounded, Landy bolted into the lead and Bannister stayed on his heels. Pride was at stake and the fast pace never wavered. Landy maintained his lead as the runners hit the homestretch, but Bannister suddenly made his move. With a wild sprint to the tape, the Englishman won and collapsed into the arms of waiting friends.

Both runners finished under 4 minutes, Bannister at 3:58.8 and Landy at 3:59.6.

MILESTONES IN SPORTS

1952

74-year-old Bion Shively drove Sharp Note to a three-heat victory in the Hambletonian Stakes, one of the premier events for 3-year-old trotters, at Good Time Park in Goshen, N.Y.

1982

25-year-old Tommy Haughton directed Speed Bowl to a straight-heat victory in the Hambletonian Stakes, becoming the youngest driver to win trotting's premier event.

1983

Hal Sutton survived three straight bogeys on the back nine and held on for a one-stroke victory over Jack Nicklaus in the PGA Championship at the Riviera (Calif.) Country Club.

1983

Norway's distance queen Grete Waitz was clocked in 2:28.09 while winning the women's marathon in the inaugural world track and field championship at Helsinki, Finland.

1985

Baseball players and owners reached agreement and ended the sport's second midseason players' strike in five years after two days and 25 game cancellations.

1992

LSU center Shaquille O'Neal, the top pick in the NBA draft, signed a seven-year contract with the Orlando Magic for a reported $40 million.

1992 UPSETS SPICE OLYMPIC PLAY

It was a day of shocking defeats for three expected gold medalists at the Barcelona Olympic Games. West German Steffi Graf was vanquished on the tennis court, American Jackie Joyner-Kersee finished third in the long jump and Ukrainian champion Sergei Bubka failed to even clear a height in the pole vault.

The most surprising of these developments was the failure of Bubka, the most dominant pole vaulter in history. Bubka, a 30-time world record-setter and the first vaulter to clear 20 feet, missed twice at heights of 18–8 1/4 and once at 18–10 1/4 – and was gone.

Graf, attempting to defend the gold medal she won in 1988 at Seoul, ran into an American buzzsaw in 16-year-old Jennifer Capriati . The youngster dropped the first set and then roared back for a 3–6, 6–3, 6–4 victory before an approving and enthusiastic crowd at Vall d'Hebron.

Joyner-Kersee, also a 1988 gold medalist, could manage only a 23–2 1/2 long jump and had to settle for winning a bronze medal behind German gold medalist Heiki Drechsler and the Unified Team's Inessa Kravets.

1956 WILLIAMS FINED

Ted Williams, showing contempt and anger for catcalling Boston fans, drew a $5,000 fine from Red Sox General Manager Joe Cronin for his spitting gestures and disrespectful "conduct on the field."

Williams, known for his on and off-field temper tantrums, reacted to jeering fans during an exciting 1–0 Red Sox victory over New York at Fenway Park. Williams became the target of disaffection when he dropped an 11th-inning fly ball.

The crowd reaction worked Williams into a frenzy. He responded by making an outstanding catch to end the inning and then, as he returned to the dugout, he emphatically spit toward the crowd and the press box, prompting another chorus of boos.

In the bottom of the 11th, Williams walked with the bases loaded, forcing in the winning run. As he headed for first base, he flipped his bat high into the air. Immediately after the game, Cronin announced the disciplinary action.

Ted Williams – *a gesture that cost him $5,000.*

1988 OLD WRIGLEY LIGHTS UP

In an emotional, exciting and disappointing end to an era, the Chicago Cubs finally gave up on their 53-year holdout and turned on the lights at 74-year-old Wrigley Field.

The last bastion of day-only baseball gave way to progress when a 91-year-old Chicago fan flipped the switch that turned on 540 lights resting in six banks on the park's roof. With 36,399 fans and more than 500 media representatives taking part in what was presented as a gala occasion, mixed emotions flooded out as tradition was wiped away and Wrigley, unaccustomed to change, became a glittering wonderland.

The occasion also was marked by fireworks. In the first inning of the game against Philadelphia, Phillies leadoff man Phil Bradley belted Rick Sutcliffe's fourth pitch over the left-field fence. In the bottom of the inning, Chicago's Ryne Sandberg returned the favor. But both of those lightning bolts were quickly overshadowed by the real thing.

After $3^1/2$ innings of baseball, fans watched as rain, lightning, thunder and gusting winds turned the game into an historical footnote. The home runs and the Cubs' 3–1 lead were wiped away when officials announced they would call the game "light up" all over again the next night against the New York Mets.

Chicago's **Wrigley Field** *shows off its newly erected light stands.*

AUGUST 8

1992 DREAM TEAM ROLLS

The American Dream Team made official what everybody knew way before the Barcelona Olympics championship basketball game. It was head and shoulders above the competition, both literally and figuratively.

With a 117–85 victory over Croatia, the Who's Who collection of high-priced National Basketball Association talent ended its double mission of bringing gold back to the United States and conquering the world. The recent decision to allow professionals to compete in what had been an amateur-only format spelled doom for other gold medal contenders.

With such names as Michael Jordan, Magic Johnson, Patrick Ewing, Larry Bird, David Robinson and Charles Barkley running the floor, the Americans blitzed the opposition, often winning by 40 or more points. The Croatians, beaten by 33 in their first meeting with the Dream Team actually played well in the final.

With 9:44 remaining in the half, Croatia had a 25-23 lead. But Barkley's three-point basket and three straight assists sparked the U.S. on one of its patented runs – and turned the contest into an inevitable rout.

The Croats could come no closer than 72–53 in the second half and the U.S. took care of that with an 8–0 run.

MILESTONES • IN SPORTS •

1902

Great Britain's Reggie and Laurie Doherty recorded a final-day doubles victory over Americans Holcombe Ward and Dwight F. Davis, but the U.S. recorded a 3–2 overall triumph and won its second straight Davis Cup battle.

1920

Detroit's Howard Ehmke allowed three hits and stopped the New York Yankees, 1–0, in the fastest game in A.L. history – 1 hour, 13 minutes.

1982

California third baseman Doug DeCinces connected for three home runs in the Angels' 9–5 victory over Seattle – the second time in six days he had performed the feat.

1982

Ray Floyd, looking for his second PGA Championship title, struggled to a final-round 72 but held on for a three-stroke victory over Lanny Wadkins at the Southern Hills Country Club in Tulsa, Okla.

1991

Thomas Weaver, a 39-year-old spectator at the PGA Championship in Carmel, Ind., died when he was struck by lightning.

A STAR IS BORN

1913: Cecil Travis, an infielder who batted .314 over a 12-year career in the 1930s and '40s with the Washington Senators.

★ ★ ★

1936: Frank Howard, a powerful 6-foot-7 outfielder who belted 382 home runs for four major league teams in a 16-year career from 1958–73.

★ ★ ★

1947: Ken Dryden, a hockey Hall of Fame goaltender who led Montreal to six Stanley Cup championships in the 1970s and compiled an outstanding 2.24 career goals-against average.

★ ★ ★

DEATH OF A LEGEND

1934: Wilbert Robinson (baseball).

★ ★ ★

1990 PETE ROSE ENTERS PRISON FACILITY

Former baseball great Pete Rose, just five years removed from becoming the game's all-time hits leader, entered a Federal work camp in Marion, Ill., to begin serving a five-month sentence for income tax evasion.

Rose became a "convict" when he checked into the Southern Illinois Prison Camp to begin serving the sentence imposed July 20 by United States District Court Judge S. Arthur Spiegel. Rose checked into the facility two days before the court-ordered deadline that allowed him time to recover from knee surgery.

Rose is scheduled for release from the minimum-security camp on January 7, at which time he will serve three more months at a Cincinnati halfway house. He will perform one of about 35 prison jobs and he has said he will not grant interviews during his incarceration.

The 49-year-old former Cincinnati player and manager, who was banned from baseball last August for his alleged gambling activities, later pleaded guilty for failing to report income from gambling and memorabilia sales.

AUGUST

9

1988 SHOCKER: GRETZKY BECOMES A KING

Wayne Gretzky, *as a pre-trade Oiler and post-trade King.*

In a trade that shook the very foundations of the National Hockey League and left Edmonton fans and thousands of Canadians fighting emotions ranging from shock to gloom, Oilers center Wayne Gretzky was dealt to the Los Angeles Kings.

If it wasn't the most sensational trade in sports history, it was close. The Great One, considered a national treasure throughout Canada and a step above royalty in Edmonton, was sent to the Kings along with Marty McSorley and Mike Krushelnyski for highly regarded youngsters Jimmy Carson and Martin Gelinas, three No. 1 draft picks and $10 million in American money.

But the biggest slap in the face to Edmonton fans might have been the news that Gretzky asked Owner Peter Pocklington to make the deal. He said he had sought the trade for personal reasons, "for the benefit of Wayne Gretzky, my new wife and our expected child in the new year."

Gretzky had been married in July to American actress Janet Jones, a Los Angeles native who was welcomed into the Canadian community as a national heroine. But when the trade was announced, she quickly received blame for Gretzky's desire to go Hollywood.

But Edmonton's loss was clearly Los Angeles' gain. What the fans of Tinsel Town were "gaining" was the greatest offensive player in hockey history. In nine seasons with the Oilers, Gretzky won Most Valuable Player honors eight times and eight scoring championships while leading his team to four Stanley Cup titles.

He also piled up an amazing 43 NHL scoring records, including most goals (92) and assists (163) in a season and most assists (1,086) in a career.

Although Gretzky is only 27 years old, he is just 219 goals and 182 points away from Gordie Howe's once-sacred career marks.

When news of the trade broke, the Edmonton office was swamped with calls from irate fans who threatened to cancel their season tickets.

Conversely, the Kings could not handle all the calls offering congratulations and seeking tickets. The Kings, owned by Bruce McNall, have managed just five winning seasons in 21 years.

A STAR IS BORN

1928: Bob Cousy, a basketball Hall of Fame playmaker who helped lead the Boston Celtics to six NBA championships in the 1950s and '60s.

★ ★ ★

1938: Rod Laver, the Australian tennis champion who ranks as the only person to complete two single-season grand slams.

★ ★ ★

1967: Deion Sanders, a current major league outfielder and National Football League defensive back.

★ ★ ★

DEATH OF A LEGEND

1969: George Preston Marshall (football).

1953 INCREDIBLE EAGLE LIFTS WORSHAM TO VICTORY

Lew Worsham called it a lucky shot. Everybody else called it amazing. When Worsham dropped his 140-yard approach to the 18th green at Chicago's Tam o'Shanter course for an eagle, he became an instant winner of $25,000 – the richest prize ever offered for a golf tournament.

The most amazed spectator of all might have been Chandler Harper, who had finished his play in the World Championship of Golf with a 279 and figured to walk away with the big payoff. Worsham, 140 yards down the fairway, needed to get down in two to force a playoff. He appeared to be a likely candidate for $10,000 second-place money.

As Worsham stood over his ball, he looked toward a green surrounded by fans who outlined a horseshoe-shaped path down the middle of the fairway. He swung his wedge and the ball hit on the front of the green, bounced three times and curled into the hole. After a brief pause, as if trying to grasp what it had just witnessed, the crowd roared its approval and hailed the amazed Worsham as he walked toward the green.

Adding to the excitement were the television cameras that broadcast Worsham's instant victory to a national audience – a first ever for golf.

MILESTONES · IN SPORTS ·

1900

The first Davis Cup: An American team of Malcolm D. Whitman, Dwight F. Davis and Holcombe Ward defeated a British team, 3–0, at the Longwood Cricket Club near Boston.

1916

Joe Bush pitched Philadelphia to a 7–1 victory at Detroit, snapping the A's A.L. record-tying 20-game losing streak.

1936

The amazing Jesse Owens captured his fourth gold medal of the Berlin Summer Olympic Games when he ran the opening leg for America's world record-setting 4 X 100-meter relay team.

1963

Jim Hickman's two-out, bases-loaded home run in the ninth inning gave the New York Mets a dramatic 7–3 victory over Chicago and ended pitcher Roger Craig's 18-game losing streak one short of the major league record.

1969

Southern California running back and Heisman Trophy winner O.J. Simpson signed a four-year contract with Buffalo, ending speculation the Bills would not be able to meet the rookie's lofty demands.

1981

Baseball kicked off its "second season" following the seven-week players' strike with the All-Star Game in Cleveland. Montreal catcher Gary Carter's two home runs led the N.L. to a 5–4 victory over the A.L.

1988

The Chicago Cubs recorded a 6–4 victory over New York in the first official night game at Wrigley Field. The Cubs had played 3½ innings the night before against Philadelphia before rain forced a postponement.

1929

Alex Wins 373rd

It wasn't as easy as it used to be, but St. Louis veteran Grover Cleveland Alexander earned his record-tying 373rd career victory when he pitched four shutout innings against Philadelphia and the Cardinals rallied for an 11–9 decision in 11 innings at Shibe Park.

Old Pete took over in the eighth and watched as the Cardinals rallied for a ninth-inning run to force a 9–9 tie. Relying on savvy and experience rather than his once-feared fastball, Alexander coaxed three more scoreless innings out of his 42-year-old arm, shutting down the Phillies in the 11th after St. Louis had scored twice in the top of the inning.

The victory tied the one-time Philadelphia star with former New York Giants great Christy Mathewson as the top National League winner of all time. It also tied him for third place on the all-time victory list behind former American Leaguers Cy Young (511 wins) and Walter Johnson (416).

Alexander is a three-time 30-game winner and a nine-time 20-game winner.

1984

Collision Dashes Decker Gold Rush

Mary Decker, trying to add Olympic gold to her long list of running achievements, tumbled along with her dream to the infield of the Los Angeles Coliseum track after a mid-race collision with Zola Budd during the 3,000-meter final of the Summer Games.

Everything was rosy for **Mary Decker** *before her Olympic Games collision with Zola Budd.*

Decker, the world record-holder in the event, was leading with a little more than three laps remaining when disaster struck. Budd , a South African running under the colors of Great Britain, passed on the outside and appeared to cut to the inside ahead of Decker. The runners were too close and Decker tripped on Budd's foot, falling to the infield.

As the race continued, Decker sat on the grass, unable to get up. Rumania's Maricica Puica went on to win in 8:35.96 while the bare-footed Budd, obviously shaken, dropped to seventh. Decker eventually was carried off the track by her fiance, British discus thrower Richard Slaney.

Decker, who suffered a minor hip injury, blamed the 18-year-old Budd for the mishap, stating flatly, "She tripped me." Other runners suggested that Decker, not Budd, might have been to blame for the accident.

Budd was disqualified immediately after the race but later was reinstated.

1980

Nicklaus Wins Fifth PGA

It wasn't exciting and it wasn't dramatic. But nobody was complaining as the Golden Bear made his triumphant stroll up the 18th fairway. Just watching Jack Nicklaus at the top of his game was worth the price of admission.

Nicklaus was closing out the fifth PGA Championship victory of his storied career. When he dropped his final putt for a 69 and a four-round total of 274 over the Oak Hill Country Club course in Rochester, N.Y., he finished off his record-setting seven-stroke victory over Andy Bean. It was the largest margin of victory ever for the tournament – by three strokes.

It also was Nicklaus' record 19th victory in a major tournament and second of the year. It gave him five PGA titles, five Masters, four U.S. Opens, three British Opens and two U.S. Amateurs. It was his 68th career win, second only to Sam Snead (84). Bobby Jones ranks second on the career 'majors' list with a total of 13 victories.

Nicklaus had entered the day with a three-stroke advantage after a third-round 66.

A Star Is Born

1920: Red Holzman, a basketball Hall of Famer who coached three NBA teams to 696 victories over 18 seasons.

★ ★ ★

1933: Rocky Colavito, a former major league outfielder who hit 374 home runs over 14 seasons in the 1950s and '60s.

Death of a Legend

1970: Joe Lapchick (basketball).

★ ★ ★

1990: Cookie Lavagetto (baseball).

Milestones in Sports

1928

American Johnny Weissmuller broke his own Olympic record and earned his second 100-meter freestyle gold medal with a 58.6-second performance in the Summer Games at Amsterdam.

1932

American Buster Crabbe set an Olympic record with a 4:48.4 clocking in the 400-meter freestyle during swimming competition at the Los Angeles Summer Games.

1944

It took Boston's Red Barrett just 58 pitches and 1:15 to dispatch Cincinnati, 2–0, in a game at Crosley Field.

1949

Ezzard Charles, making his first defense of the heavyweight championship, scored an impressive eighth-round technical knockout of Gus Lesnevich at New York's Yankee Stadium.

1971

Minnesota slugger Harmon Killebrew belted career homers 500 and 501 off Baltimore lefthander Mike Cuellar, but the Twins dropped a 10-inning, 4–3 decision to the Orioles.

1981

Philadelphia first baseman Pete Rose celebrated baseball's return from the 50-day players' strike with a single in a game against St. Louis, making him the National League's all-time hit leader (3,631).

AUGUST

11

1986 Tway Shocks Norman

Bob Tway wrote a shocking closing script for the PGA Championship when he holed a 25-foot bunker shot and claimed the prestigious title as an incredulous Greg Norman stood near his ball on the fringe of the 18th green.

The incredible tournament-winning shot capped Tway's comeback from a four-stroke deficit after 10 holes at the Inverness Country Club in Toledo, O. After watching Tway jump up and down in celebration of his amazing shot, an obviously shaken Norman needed three strokes to finish off his round.

The birdie gave Tway a final-round 70 and his first victory in a major event.

Norman, who had blown final-round leads earlier in the year in the Masters and U.S. Open, finished with a 76, thanks to a double bogey on 11 and bogeys on 14 and 18.

The 27-year-old Tway completed his four rounds in 276, two better than Norman. They had teed off on 18 deadlocked at 7 under par.

A STAR IS BORN

1907: Bobo Newsom, a 211-game major league winner in a 20-year career that ended in 1953.

★ ★ ★

1938: Vada Pinson, a .286 career hitter in an 18-year career that spanned from 1958–75.

1984 Lewis Earns Fourth Gold

Carl Lewis, doing a pretty fair impression of the late Jesse Owens, earned his fourth gold medal of the Los Angeles Olympic Games when he anchored the American 400-meter relay team to a world record on the final day of track and field activity.

Lewis, whose gold medals were in the same events Owens dominated in the 1936 Olympic Games at Berlin, helped the relay team post a time of 37.83 seconds before an appreciative crowd of 96,400 at the Los Angeles Coliseum. The team that also included Sam Graddy, Ron Brown and Calvin Smith beat the Jamaican team by a solid 7 meters.

Lewis' previous medals had come in the 100-meter dash, the 200-meter and the long jump. He said he plans to give his long jump medal to Ruth Owens, Jesse's widow, because that was Owens' favorite event.

After the medal-presentation ceremony, Lewis was carried off the field by his relay teammates – a surprising reaction to many observers. Throughout the Olympics, stories had circulated about tension between Lewis and other athletes because of what they deemed preferential treatment for the star.

1991 Daly Wins PGA

Long-hitting, crowd-pleasing rookie John Daly, the final man accepted into the field for the PGA Championship, completed a Cinderella four-day run that gave him an inspiring three-stroke victory in one of golf's most prestigious tournaments.

Daly, averaging better than 300 yards off the tee on the long Crooked Stick Golf Club course in Carmel, Ind., won the hearts of the gallery with his go-for-broke style. He wasn't perfect, but while everybody else was hitting long irons on the par 4 holes, Daly was pitching into birdie situations. And he played the par 5s in 12 under par for the tournament.

Daly, expected to wither under final-round pressure, shot a solid 71. Bruce Lietzke, who never could mount a serious charge, finished with a 70, missing several easy birdie opportunities.

Daly, a 5-foot-11, 190-pound blond-haired slugger, became only the sixth golfer to get his first tour victory in a major tournament. He was a late replacement when Nick Price had to drop out and he drove all night to make his first-round tee time.

Long-hitting **John Daly** *vaulted to the top of the golf world with his shocking victory in the PGA Championship.*

MILESTONES IN SPORTS

1929

Babe Ruth broke new ground when he belted his 500th career home run off Willis Hudlin at Cleveland's League Park, but it wasn't enough as the New York Yankees lost to the Indians, 6–5.

1949

The warring National Basketball League and Basketball Association of America merged into a 17-team circuit that stretched from Boston to Denver and adopted the name National Basketball Association.

1950

North Carolina's Charlie (Choo Choo) Justice rambled for 133 yards and a touchdown, leading an inspired college team to a stunning 17–7 victory over the defending NFL-champion Philadelphia Eagles in the College All-Star Game at Chicago's Soldier Field.

1961

Milwaukee lefthander Warren Spahn turned a six-hit performance into his 300th career victory – a 2-1 decision over the Chicago Cubs.

1969

Don Drysdale, the Dodgers' last player link to their Brooklyn roots, retired because of a bad shoulder. The big righthander compiled a 209–166 record and 2.95 ERA in 14 seasons in Brooklyn and Los Angeles.

1987

Oakland first baseman Mark McGwire tied the major league rookie home run record shared by former National Leaguers Frank Robinson and Wally Berger when he blasted No. 38 in an 8–2 loss to Seattle.

1991

Making only his second major league start, 21-year-old Chicago lefty Wilson Alvarez pitched a no-hitter and defeated Baltimore, 7–0.

MILESTONES IN SPORTS

1948

With a major league-record 14 players hitting safely, the Cleveland Indians piled up 29 hits and defeated the St. Louis Browns, 26–3, in the second game of a doubleheader at St. Louis.

1964

New York Yankee center fielder Mickey Mantle belted home runs from both sides of the plate during a 7–3 victory over Chicago, the record 10th time he had accomplished the feat.

1966

Cincinnati's Art Shamsky, who entered the game as a defensive replacement in the eighth inning, belted three home runs in a 14–11, 13-inning loss to Pittsburgh.

1984

In a wild baseball melee that centered around Atlanta pitcher Pascual Perez, umpires ejected 13 players, managers and coaches before the Braves mercifully posted a 5–3 victory over San Diego at Fulton County Stadium.

1986

Boston dropped a doubleheader to Kansas City, but Don Baylor set a dubious one-season record when he was hit by a pitch for the 25th time.

1978 STINGLEY PARALYZED

Darryl Stingley, New England's leading receiver in 1977 with 39 receptions, suffered a paralyzing injury when he was hit by Oakland defensive back Jack Tatum while trying to catch a pass during a National Football League exhibition game at the Oakland Coliseum.

Stingley was the target on a second-quarter pass over the middle from Patriots quarterback Steve Grogan. As he dived for the low toss, he was smashed by Tatum and fell to the ground, motionless. After about five minutes, Stingley was carried off the field.

The 26-year-old former Purdue star was rushed to an Oakland hospital where a one-hour operation was performed on what was described as a "fracture dislocation of his cervical spine." Doctors attempted to realign Stingley's vertebrae and reduce pressure on his spine, but came out of the operating room with fears he might be permanently paralyzed from the head down.

The 6-footer had caught 110 passes for 1,883 yards and 14 touchdowns in his five-year professional career.

AUGUST 12

Darryl Stingley, *10 years after his crippling football injury.*

1974 RYAN FANS 19, TIES RECORD

California righthander Nolan Ryan, who missed a no-hitter by two outs in his previous start, tied the major league single-game strikeout record when he fanned 19 Boston hitters during a 4–2 Angels victory at Anaheim Stadium.

Ryan was his usual dominating self as he blew away hitter after hitter en route to his 15th victory. A mighty roar from the 9,345 fans went up when he notched No. 18 and a youngster ran out to the mound to shake Ryan's hand. When he struck out Bernie Carbo in the ninth for his record-tying 19th, a young woman ran out to the mound and kissed him.

Ryan tied the major league mark set by Philadelphia's Steve Carlton in 1969 and matched a year later by the New York Mets' Tom Seaver. He broke the American League record of 18 strikeouts set by Cleveland's Bob Feller in 1938.

Ryan also matched the record of 32 strikeouts in consecutive games set by Boston's Luis Tiant.

The strikeout form of California Angels righthander **Nolan Ryan.**

1975 WALKER BREAKS 3:50

John Walker, a tall New Zealander who had always come up a little short in his bids for recognition, lopped more than a second off the mile world record and became the first person to break the 3:50 barrier during competition in a meet at Goteborg, Sweden.

Walker finished in 3:49.4, breaking the 3:51 record held by Tanzanian Filbert Bayi. The 23-year-old was more than 5 seconds ahead of Australian Ken Hall and took almost 3 seconds off his best time.

Walker had lost to Bayi in three head-to-head matches this season. His most memorable meeting with Bayi was in the 1974 British Commonwealth Games in the 1,500-meter race. Bayi won that metric mile encounter with a world-record 3:32.2 time.

The 6-foot-1 Walker ran his first three laps in 56.3, 59.2 and 58 before closing with a blistering 55.9.

A STAR IS BORN

1880: Christy Mathewson, a Hall of Fame pitcher who won a National League record-tying 373 games, all but one with the New York Giants, in a 17-year career that ended in 1916.

★ ★ ★

1892: Ray Schalk, a Hall of Fame catcher who played 18 major league seasons (1912–29), 17 with the Chicago White Sox.

★ ★ ★

1915: Alex Wojciechowicz, a football Hall of Fame center and linebacker from 1938–50 with the NFL's Detroit Lions and Philadelphia Eagles.

★ ★ ★

1950: George McGinnis, a high-scoring forward who tallied 17,009 professional points with the ABA's Indiana Pacers (1971–75) and three NBA teams (1975–82).

AUGUST

13

A STAR IS BORN

1912: Ben Hogan, an outstanding golfer who won 62 career PGA titles and nine majors from 1946–53.

★ ★ ★

1949: Bobby Clarke, a hockey Hall of Fame center who amassed 1,210 points over 15 NHL seasons with the Philadelphia Flyers.

★ ★ ★

1949: Andre Thornton, a 14-year major league first baseman in the 1970s and '80s who hit 253 home runs for three teams.

★ ★ ★

DEATH OF A LEGEND

1988: Edward Bennett Williams (football).

1936 JESSE OWENS GETS LONG JUMP GOLD

Jesse Owens, shaking off a controversy that threatened to knock him out of his best event, soared to an Olympic-record leap of 26–5 1/2 in the long jump and captured his second gold medal in the Berlin Summer Games.

American sensation **Jesse Owens** *soars to his second Olympic gold medal in the long jump.*

Owens, the world record-holder at 26–8 1/4, was still dressed in his sweatsuit when he took a practice run down the runway and into the pits. To his surprise, the officials counted it as his first of three attempts in the qualifying round. When he fouled on his second, he was in jeopardy of missing the cut.

But Owens took a safe third jump, qualified and then waged an exciting battle with German Luz Long in the final. Owens opened with an Olympic-record leap of 25–5 1/2 and then upped the mark to 25–10. But in the fifth of the six rounds, Long matched Owens' record. Owens responded with a 26–3 3/4 jump and stretched it again with his final leap.

MILESTONES IN SPORTS

1906

Chicago Cubs righthander Jack Taylor was knocked from the box in the third inning by Brooklyn, ending a streak of 187 complete-game performances.

1948

Former Negro League great Satchel Paige fired his first major league shutout and complete game at the age of 42, pitching Cleveland to a 5–0 victory over Chicago before 51,013 fans at Comiskey Park.

1979

St. Louis outfielder Lou Brock joined baseball's 3,000-hit club when he managed an infield single off Chicago righthander Dennis Lamp during a 3–2 victory over the Cubs.

1986

Running back Herschel Walker, the USFL's brightest star for three seasons, signed a five-year contract with the NFL's Dallas Cowboys that will play him a reported $1 million per year.

1987

Jackie Joyner-Kersee became the first American woman to hold or share the world long jump record when she soared 24–5 1/2 and tied Heike Drechsler's mark during competition in the Pan American Games at Indianapolis.

1989 STEWART WINS PGA

Payne Stewart, getting an assist from normally steady Mike Reid, charged to a one-stroke victory in the PGA Championship and earned his first major tournament title.

PGA Championship winner **Payne Stewart.**

Stewart birdied four of his last five holes at the Kemper Lakes Golf Course in Hawthorn Woods, Ill., and then watched as Reid struggled home. Reid, who owned a three-stroke lead after 15 holes, took a bogey at 16 and a shocking double bogey at 17 before missing a 5-foot birdie putt at 18 that could have forced a playoff.

Reid's collapse was Stewart's gain. Stewart's final-round 67 vaulted him over 10 golfers and left him a stroke ahead of Reid, Curtis Strange and Andy Bean. His 276 total was 12 under par and he completed the back nine in 31.

Reid's collapse began when he pushed his drive into the water on 16. He recovered for a bogey, but really butchered the par-3 17th. He hit his tee shot to the back fringe, chipped up short, missed a par putt and missed a 2-footer coming back.

1919 UPSET PULLS UPSET

It was only fitting that Man o'War's first career loss should come against a horse named Upset. It also was fitting that even in losing, the 2-year-old thoroughbred showed that he clearly was the superior horse.

Racing in the Sanford Memorial at Saratoga, N.Y., undefeated Man o'War was given a horrible start and recovered to catch Upset at the wire, losing by a neck. Starter C.H. Pettingill had problems getting the horses lined up and Man o'War's chief rivals, Upset and Golden Broom, were four lengths ahead before Johnny Loftus could even get him started.

Golden Broom set a furious pace and Man o'War started making up ground on the backstretch. By the final turn, the Glenn Riddle Farm colt had moved up to third and was pressuring the leaders.

On the homestretch, Upset suddenly passed Golden Broom and Man o'War followed. With 100 feet to go, Man o'War was three-quarters of a length back and at the wire, he was down by a neck.

MILESTONES IN SPORTS

1936

The United States defeated Canada, 19–8, and won the basketball gold medal in the Berlin Summer Games. It was the first time the sport was played as an official Olympic event.

1937

The Detroit Tigers set an A.L. record by scoring 36 runs in a doubleheader sweep of St. Louis. The Tigers pounded the Browns, 16–1 and 20–7.

1968

World Boxing Association heavyweight champion Jimmy Ellis retained his title with a 15-round decision over Floyd Patterson at Stockholm, Sweden.

1971

St. Louis righthander Bob Gibson added another feather to his illustrious career when he no-hit the Pirates, 11–0, at Pittsburgh's Three Rivers Stadium.

1982

Philadelphia's Pete Rose reached another milestone when he moved past Hank Aaron on the career at-bat list in a 15–11 Phillies victory at Montreal. Rose's first at-bat was his 12,365th.

1987

Oakland's Mark McGwire set a one-season major league rookie home run record when he blasted No. 39 off Don Sutton during a 12-inning, 7–6 victory over California.

1988

Little Jeff Sluman fired a record-tying final-round 65 and earned a surprising three-stroke victory over Paul Azinger in the PGA Championship at Edmond, Okla.

1959 NFL Faces A Challenge

A new six-team professional football league, which will compete with the long-established National Football League, was introduced by the circuit's founder, Texas millionaire Lamar Hunt, during a press conference in Chicago.

The American Football League will begin play in 1960 with franchises in Dallas, Houston, Minneapolis-St. Paul, Denver, New York and Los Angeles. Hunt said two more teams could be added with possible sites including Seattle, Buffalo, San Francisco, Kansas City and Miami.

The new owners, which include oilman K.S. (Bud) Adams of Houston and Barron Hilton of Los Angeles, will meet in two weeks to draw up a constitution. The group also will make plans for a college draft and other financial matters.

The NFL has had a monopoly on the professional football business since 1949, when the 4-year-old All-America Football Conference reached a merger agreement with the league that lifted its membership to 12 teams.

August 14

A Star Is Born

1952: Debbie Meyer, the first swimmer to win three individual gold medals at one Olympics competition (1968, Mexico City).

★ ★ ★

1954: Mark (The Bird) Fidrych, an eccentric and lovable pitcher who captured the hearts of baseball fans in 1976 when he won 19 games for Detroit before suffering a career-shortening arm injury.

★ ★ ★

1959: Earvin (Magic) Johnson, the slick-passing, high-scoring guard who led the Los Angeles Lakers to five NBA titles in the 1980s. Johnson, a three-time MVP, retired as the NBA's all-time assist leader (9,921) in 1991 when he tested HIV-positive for AIDS.

★ ★ ★

Death of a Legend

1943: Joe Kelley (baseball).

★ ★ ★

1960: Fred Clarke (baseball).

1977 Wadkins Beats Littler

Lanny Wadkins sank a par putt on the third hole of a sudden-death playoff with Gene Littler and captured his first PGA Championship after recovering from a five-stroke deficit on the back nine of regulation.

Wadkins' victory was more a case of Littler's demise. The veteran with 29 tournament titles to his credit had a five-stroke lead with nine holes to play on the tough Pebble Beach course and appeared to be headed for his first PGA title. But suddenly "the wheels fell off."

Littler bogeyed five holes on the back nine and came back to the pack. When he parred 18, he found himself in a tie at 282 with the 27-year-old Wadkins. They halved the first two holes of the playoff and Littler missed the green on the third. When he settled for a bogey, Wadkins had his championship.

Wadkins shot a final-round 70 that included a pair of front-nine eagles. It was his first victory since 1973. Four-time PGA winner Jack Nicklaus shot a final-round 73 and fell just short with a four-day total of 283.

1903 Jeffries Whips Jim Corbett

James J. Jeffries, the burly, apparently invincible heavyweight champion, successfully defended his title for the sixth time when he knocked out Gentleman Jim Corbett in the 10th round of a fight at San Francisco.

A determined and stalking Jeffries finally caught up with the dancing Corbett early in the final round, sending the former champion to the canvas with a big left hook to the stomach. Corbett was up by the count of nine, but Jeffries continued the attack with an other shot to the stomach and a right to the jaw that sent him down for a final count.

With 10,000 fans, the largest crowd ever assembled in the United States for a prize fight, watching the action at the Mechanics Pavilion, Corbett and Jeffries opened cautiously. But Jeffries, 30 pounds heavier and convinced that Corbett could not hurt him, began stalking him like a determined bulldog.

Jeffries knocked Corbett down for a nine count in the sixth round and Corbett made his only serious flurry in the eighth. The pro-Corbett crowd was resigned to the inevitable as the knockout approached.

The victory was Jeffries' second over Corbett. He knocked him out in the 23rd round of a May 1900 bout at New York's Coney Island.

Jim Corbett *might have been a gentleman, but he was no match for heavyweight champion James J. Jeffries.*

AUGUST

15

MILESTONES
IN SPORTS

1948

Babe Didrikson Zaharias captured her first U.S. Women's Open golf championship when she fired a final-round 78 and overpowered Betty Jameson by eight strokes at the Atlantic City (N.J.) Country Club.

1950

Heavyweight champion Ezzard Charles defended his crown for a third time with a 14th-round technical knockout of Freddie Beshore in a fight at Buffalo.

1966

Light heavyweight champion Jose Torres retained his title with a unanimous decision over Eddie Cotton at the Las Vegas Convention Center.

1975

Fiery Baltimore Manager Earl Weaver, ejected from the first game of a doubleheader against Texas by umpire Ron Luciano, was tossed out of the nightcap by Luciano during a heated pregame lineup exchange.

1982

Juergen Hingsen, a 24-year-old West German, set a world decathlon record when he compiled 8,723 points during competition in the all-West German track and field championships at Ulm, West Germany.

1990

Philadelphia's Terry Mulholland fired a 6–0 no-hitter at the San Francisco Giants – the major leagues' record eighth no-hitter of the season.

1993

Azinger Wins PGA

Greg Norman watched incredulously as his 4-foot par putt on the second sudden-death playoff hole lipped out, giving Paul Azinger a victory in the PGA Championship at the Inverness Club in Toledo, O.

Azinger's first major title came at the expense of the snake-bit Australian who won last month's British Open at Royal St. George's. Norman has had more than his share of bad luck, including playoff losses in each of the four major championships and a 1986 PGA loss when Bob Tway sank an incredible 18th-hole bunker shot – on the same Inverness course.

Norman carried a one-stroke lead into the final round and shot a 69, barely missing an 18th-hole birdie putt that could have ended the competition. Azinger's final-round 68 forced the playoff that started on the 18th tee.

Both golfers missed makable birdie putts on 18 and both hit the 10th green in regulation, Norman 20 feet away and Azinger 7. Norman's putt came up four feet short and Azinger barely missed his, tapping in for par. When Norman's second putt lipped out, the seventh playoff in PGA history was over.

Hard-luck San Francisco Giants lefthander **Dave Dravecky.**

1989

Dravecky Career In Doubt

San Francisco's Dave Dravecky, the talented lefthander who underwent cancer surgery in his pitching arm 10 months earlier, saw his dramatic comeback end prematurely when he broke his arm while throwing a pitch during a game against Montreal.

Dravecky, making his second comeback start, was pitching to Tim Raines in the sixth inning when one of his pitches went wild and he fell to the ground. He was conscious as he was taken off the field, holding the arm from which a cancerous tumor had been removed.

"It was a sharp, painful pop," Dravecky told his trainers. "It was the strangest experience I've ever felt." The pitcher was taken to a hospital where X-rays revealed a fracture in the upper arm near the surgical scar. The injury ended his season and most likely his career.

He had won his first comeback start against Cincinnati, pitching into the eighth inning. He carried a 3–0 lead into the sixth against Montreal and was eventually credited with a 3–2 victory.

1965

Marr Pulls Upset

Dave Marr, a 31-year-old Texan who did not figure to challenge in the prestigious PGA Championship, fired a final-round 71 and walked away with a heady two-stroke victory over Jack Nicklaus and Billy Casper while claiming the tournament's $25,000 first prize

Marr, who preceded his closing 71 with rounds of 70, 69 and 70 over the 7,090-yard Laurel Valley Golf Club course in Ligonier, Pa., was tied with Casper until he birdied 10 and 11. He added a birdie 3 at 15 with an 18-foot putt and sealed victory with an approach on 18 that rolled to within three feet of the cup.

Nicklaus and Casper both shot final 71s to finish at 282, but much of the attention was on Arnold Palmer, who was trying to win his first PGA in his own backyard. Huge galleries followed Palmer and cheered his shots throughout the event, but he finished at 294 – tied for 33rd.

It was Marr's first major victory and first tour triumph since 1962.

A STAR IS BORN

1859: Charles Comiskey, a baseball Hall of Famer who played and managed for 13 seasons in the pre-1900 major leagues and then founded the Chicago White Sox as an original team owner in the American League.

★ ★ ★

1936: Lionel Taylor, an outstanding receiver who set most of the career pass-catching records in the AFL while playing for the Denver Broncos.

★ ★ ★

DEATH OF A LEGEND

1983: Earl Averill (baseball).

★ ★ ★

MILESTONES
IN SPORTS

1948

Babe Ruth, the New York Yankees' Sultan of Swat who changed the course of baseball with his home run-hitting prowess over a 23-year career that produced more than 50 slugging records, died of throat cancer at age 53.

1965

The city of Miami, Fla., under the dual partnership of Joe Robbie and entertainer Danny Thomas, was awarded an AFL franchise with play scheduled to begin in 1966.

1976

Dave Stockton calmly sank a 14-foot par putt on the 18th green to close out a final-round 70 that gave him a one-stroke victory over Don January and Ray Floyd in the PGA Championship at Bethesda, Md.

1980

Niatross, driven by Clint Galbraith, sped to a world pace record for a mile with a time of 1:52$\frac{4}{5}$ in a special race at the State Fairgrounds in Syracuse, N.Y. Niatross eclipsed the record he had shared with Abercrombie.

1989

American Roger Kingdom ran the 110-meter high hurdles in a world-record 12.92 seconds during competition in an international meet at Zurich.

1989

Tom Drees became the first pitcher in baseball history to throw three no-hitters in a season when he pitched Vancouver of the Pacific Coast League to a 5–0 seven-inning victory over Las Vegas.

1992

Nick Price captured his first major title when he shot a final-round 70 over St. Louis' Bellerive Country Club course and earned a three-stroke victory in the 74th PGA Championship.

AUGUST 16

1920 Indians' Shortstop Dies After Beaning

Cleveland shortstop Ray Chapman, a 29-year-old veteran of nine seasons, was hit on the head by a pitch from New York Yankee righthander Carl Mays and became the first major league player to die as a result of injuries suffered during a game.

Chapman, a career .278 hitter and a key performer for the pennant-bound Indians, was struck during a Cleveland-Yankees game at New York's Polo Grounds. He suffered massive head trauma and was rushed to the hospital where two operations were performed, but he died the next day.

Chapman, leading off the fifth inning of a game the Indians led, 3–0, was crouching over the plate in his usual batting style when a Mays fastball suddenly rose toward his head. Chapman froze and the ball hit his skull, bouncing toward the mound. Mays picked it up and threw to first, thinking the ball had hit Chapman's bat.

Mays, a two-time 20-game winner who throws with a submarine delivery, is known around the American League as a pitcher who will knock down aggressive hitters.

Carl Mays, *whose pitch caused Ray Chapman's death.*

1984 Rose Returns To Cincinnati

Like the prodigal son returning home to his adoring family, Pete Rose was embraced by Cincinnati fans as the Reds new player-manager.

Rose, 130 hits away from passing Ty Cobb as baseball's all-time leader, was acquired from the Montreal Expos for a minor league player and immediately named to replace Vern Rapp, who had led the Reds to a 50–70 record in his first season as manager. Rose will be given the chance to revive a franchise he helped lead to four National League pennants as a player in the 1970s.

The 43-year-old Rose, who picked up his 4,000th career hit four months earlier for Montreal, will see occasional action at first base and pinch-hit regularly. Reds officials are hoping he can infect the team with the enthusiasm and hustle he used to build a career that includes three N.L. batting championships and one Most Valuable Player citation.

Rose, a native of Cincinnati, spent his first 16 seasons with the Reds and was a vital cog in the Big Red Machine of the mid-1970s that won consecutive World Series. He later played on a Series winner with Philadelphia.

Pete Rose *in his combination job as Cincinnati first baseman and manager.*

1970 Stockton Wins PGA Title

Dave Stockton, who said "I'll bury the course" before the final round of the PGA Championship, fell short in his prediction but did manage a 73 that was good enough for a two-stroke victory at the Southern Hills Country Club in Tulsa, Okla.

The confident Stockton cruised to his first major victory after building a six-stroke lead over Arnold Palmer and an eight-stroke advantage over Bob Murphy through nine holes. Stockton stumbled down the stretch, but neither Palmer nor Murphy, who shot a final-day 70 and 66, could make a serious challenge and finished tied for second at 281.

Stockton, who entered the final round with a three-stroke lead, was the only golfer to break par over the 72 holes. The shot that put him in control was a 120-yard wedge that dropped in for an eagle 2 on the seventh hole.

The second-place tie was the third for Palmer in this prestigious event, the only major he has failed to win.

A STAR IS BORN

1862: Amos Alonzo Stagg, a college football Hall of Famer who recorded 314 career victories over an amazing 55 seasons as coach at the University of Chicago and College of the Pacific from 1892–1946.

1930: Frank Gifford, a football Hall of Fame halfback for 12 seasons with the New York Giants and later a member of ABC's Monday Night Football broadcast team.

★ ★ ★

1961: Christian Okoye, a current NFL running back.

★ ★ ★

DEATH OF A LEGEND

1948: Babe Ruth (baseball).

★ ★ ★

AUGUST

17

1968 CARNER WINS FIFTH AMATEUR

Long-hitting JoAnne Carner overcame soggy conditions at the Birmingham (Mich.) Country Club and a persistent effort from close friend and rival Ann Quast Welts to record her fifth victory in the prestigious Women's Amateur championship.

Carner, consistently outdriving her smaller opponent by 40 yards, built a two-hole lead on the front nine of the morning round before letting it slip away on the second hole in the afternoon. She fought back, however, to win the next two holes and insured her 5 and 4 victory with birdies on 12 and 13.

Morning play was delayed 30 minutes while officials tried to dry off the course after torrential overnight thunderstorms. The rain turned sand traps into water hazards, pools of water dotted all the fairways and the 18th green was submerged briefly when the River Rouge overflowed its banks.

But the course was pretty well dried by mid-afternoon and both golfers said the water did not interfere with the match play. The victory moved Carner up to one behind Glenna Collett, the outstanding champion who captured six Amateur titles in the 1920s and 1930s.

1988 REYNOLDS STEALS SHOW

Carl Lewis won his pre-Olympic 100-meter sprint showdown with Canada's Ben Johnson, but fellow American Butch Reynolds stole the spotlight when he shattered Lee Evans' 20-year-old world record in the 400 meters during a meet at Zurich, Switzerland.

Reynolds brightened a muggy night of competition when he streaked to a shocking 43.29-second clocking, breaking one of track and field's oldest marks. He shot past fading Nigerian Innocent Egbunike with about 100 meters remaining and outsprinted Danny Everett to the finish line.

"I finally did it," said a jubilant Reynolds as the crowd at Letzigrund Stadium chanted his name. Shortly after Reynolds' victory, the 100-meter contestants lined up for the duel that would feature Lewis and Johnson for the first time this year. Johnson had won the last five meetings, but Lewis still held an 11–8 career advantage.

True to form, Johnson surged out of the blocks, but Lewis didn't panic. He caught his rival with 30 meters remaining and won the race at 9.93 seconds – the second fastest 100 ever run.

400-meter world record-holder **Butch Reynolds.**

MILESTONES IN SPORTS

1947

Led by Californians Louise Brough and Margaret Osborne, the American women's tennis team rolled to its 11th straight Wightman Cup victory – a 7–0 triumph over Great Britain at Forest Hills.

1966

San Francisco center fielder Willie Mays moved into second place on baseball's all-time home run list when he connected for career shot No. 535 off St. Louis' Ray Washburn.

1973

New York Mets slugger Willie Mays blasted his 660th – and last – major league home run off Cincinnati lefthander Don Gullett.

1989

Baltimore shortstop Cal Ripken played in his 1,208th consecutive game, moving past Steve Garvey into third place on baseball's all-time iron man list.

1990

Chicago's Carlton Fisk broke Johnny Bench's career home run record for catchers when he blasted No. 328 in a game against Texas.

1933 GEHRIG BREAKS SCOTT'S RECORD

Former Yankee shortstop **Everett Scott** *fell to No. 2 on baseball's iron man list.*

New York Iron Horse Lou Gehrig made baseball history when he played in his 1,308th consecutive game and passed former Yankee shortstop Everett Scott's major league record. But the St. Louis Browns put a damper on the occasion with a 10-inning 7–6 victory over the New Yorkers at Sportsman's Park.

Gehrig was the center of attention when he was called to the home plate area after the first inning and, surrounded by players from both teams, presented with a silver statuette by American League President Will Harridge. When play resumed, the Yankees jumped to a lead they held until Browns Manager Rogers Hornsby blasted a game-tying homer off Lefty Gomez in the ninth inning.

The Browns went on to win in the 10th when Oscar Melillo singled and eventually scored on Jim Levey's double. The second-place Yankees got home runs from Babe Ruth and Bill Dickey and Gehrig was 2 for 5 in his historic contest.

Gehrig's streak started on June 1, 1925, when he appeared as a pinch-hitter and he hasn't missed a game since, including spring training, exhibition or World Series.

Yankee Manager Joe McCarthy, who was ill in his hotel room, missed the festivities.

A STAR IS BORN

1913: Rudy York, a slugging first baseman who hit 277 home runs over a 13-year career with four American League teams in the 1930s and '40s.

★ ★ ★

1941: Boog Powell, a big, slugging first baseman who belted 339 home runs and helped the Baltimore Orioles win five A.L. pennants in a 17-year career that ended in 1977.

★ ★ ★

1952: Guillermo Vilas, an Argentine tennis star who won four major titles in the 1970s.

★ ★ ★

1964: John Offerdahl, a current National Football League linebacker.

AUGUST

18

1992 CELTICS STAR BIRD DECIDES TO RETIRE

Larry Bird, the man who carried Indiana State University to the NCAA Tournament final, the Boston Celtics to three championships and the National Basketball Association to new heights of prosperity, ended his outstanding 13-year professional career because of a chronic back problem.

Former Boston Celtics' superstar **Larry Bird.**

The 35-year-old Bird made his announcement after playing for the United States "Dream Team" during the Olympic Games in Barcelona. He said he was in pain the entire time and finally decided that enough was enough. During his career, he earned three NBA Most Valuable Player citations and played in 11 All-Star Games.

But more than anything, he combined with Los Angeles Lakers guard Magic Johnson to help lift the NBA into a new era of prosperity. After Indiana State had lost to Johnson's Michigan State team in the NCAA Tournament final, the two stars moved into the NBA and triggered the league's enormous rise in popularity. Over the years, the Johnson-Bird rivalry was as intense as the battles between the teams they represented.

The 6-foot-9 forward, finished with 21,791 points and a 24.3 average.

1962 BEATTY SETS RECORD

The once-sacred 4-minute mile barrier continued to take a beating as Californian Jim Beatty set an American record with four other runners nipping at his heels during the Elmsley Carr invitation mile at London's White City Stadium.

Beatty crossed the finish line in 3:56.5, recording the sixth fastest mile ever run and breaking Dyrol Burleson's 3:57.6 American record. Fellow Californian Jim Grelle also beat the record at 3:56.7 with England's Stanley Taylor and American Bob Seaman next at 3:58 and Great Britain's Michael Berisford fifth at 3:59.2.

Seaman carried the pace through a 57.9-second first quarter and Grelle led through a 1:58.3 half mile before the 130-pound Beatty moved into the lead. Grelle inched ahead on the final turn, but Beatty spurted on the homestretch and flung himself at the tape just ahead of his American teammate.

Only four runners have recorded faster times, including world record-holder Peter Snell of New Zealand at 3:54.4.

A STAR IS BORN

1893: Burleigh Grimes, a Hall of Fame pitcher who won 270 games over a 19-year career from 1916–34. He was the last of the legal spitballers.

★ ★ ★

1934: Roberto Clemente, a baseball Hall of Fame outfielder who won four N.L. batting titles and collected 3,000 hits over an 18-year career with the Pittsburgh Pirates before being killed in a 1972 plane crash.

★ ★ ★

1935: Rafer Johnson, an outstanding American decathlete who won the gold medal in the 1960 Olympic Games at Rome.

★ ★ ★

1923 WILLS WINS OPEN

It took 17-year-old Californian Helen Wills only 33 minutes to send a message to the other top women tennis players around the world. That message came in the form of a 6–2, 6–1 blitz of defending champion Molla Mallory in the final of the U.S. singles championship.

Mallory, in fact, had won seven of the last eight U.S. titles and was considered the country's top player. She had defeated a 16-year-old Wills, 6–3, 6–1, in the 1922 final, but that extra year of experience made the difference.

Wills, much quicker and more mobile, simply overpowered Mallory in every facet of the game. Her decisive victory was viewed by 6,000 fans at the West Side Tennis club, the new stadium at Forest Hills, N.Y. Ironically, Wills had helped dedicate the new facility a week earlier when she defeated English star Kathleen McKane in the opening match of the inaugural Wightman Cup series – the women's version of the Davis Cup.

MILESTONES • IN SPORTS •

1915

More than 50,000 Boston fans got their first official look at new Braves Field and the Braves rewarded them with a 3–1 victory over the St. Louis Cardinals.

1931

New York first baseman Lou Gehrig became the third major leaguer to play in 1,000 straight games, but the Yankee iron man went hitless in an 11-inning, 5–4 loss at Detroit.

1958

Floyd Patterson successfully defended his heavyweight championship with a 13th-round technical knockout of Roy Harris at Los Angeles.

1973

Atlanta slugger Hank Aaron edged closer to Babe Ruth's all-time home run mark when he belted No. 704 in a game at Montreal and set a major league record for career extra-base hits (1,378).

1980

Kansas City third baseman George Brett, bidding to become baseball's first .400 hitter since 1941, collected three singles in a game at Texas, extending his hitting streak to 30 and raising his average to .404.

1983

Kansas City relief ace Dan Quisenberry brought down the curtain on the July 24 "Pine Tar Game" when he retired the New York Yankees without incident in the bottom of the ninth inning to complete a 5–4 Royals victory.

AUGUST

19

A STAR IS BORN

1931: Bill Shoemaker, the most successful jockey in horse racing history with 8,833 wins during his outstanding 41-year career. Shoemaker rode five winners in the Belmont Stakes, four in the Kentucky Derby and two in the Preakness Stakes.

★ ★ ★

1936: Al Oerter, an outstanding American discus thrower who captured gold medals in four consecutive Summer Olympics Games (1956–68), an unprecedented feat.

★ ★ ★

1958: Anthony Munoz, a current National Football League offensive tackle.

★ ★ ★

1960: Morten Andersen, a current National Football League placekicker.

★ ★ ★

DEATH OF A LEGEND

1975: Mark Donohue (auto racing).

★ ★ ★

1951

Veeck Has Last Laugh

St. Louis Browns Owner Bill Veeck, pulling off the greatest promotional stunt in the history of baseball, sent a 3-foot-7 midget to the plate during the second game of a doubleheader against the Detroit Tigers, raising the wrath of several humorless major league officials.

Veeck's stunt followed a between-games birthday bash celebrating the A.L.'s 50th anniversary. At the end of his carnival-like presentation, midget Eddie Gaedel, dressed in a Browns uniform bearing the number "one-eighth," popped out of a 7-foot papier-mache cake to the delight of 20,000 fans.

But the best was yet to come. With the Browns batting in the bottom of the first inning of the nightcap, Gaedel suddenly popped out of the dugout, swinging three toy bats. When the announcer introduced Gaedel as a pinch-hitter for Frank Saucier, umpire Ed Hurley immediately called Browns Manager Zack Taylor for a conference. Taylor came out armed with an official A.L. contract bearing Gaedel's name and Hurley had no choice but to continue play.

Detroit pitcher Bob Cain, trying not to laugh, looked at the crouching Gaedel and tried to negotiate the smallest strike zone in history. He wasn't successful. Cain fired four straight balls to the first-time batter and Gaedel waddled to first base as the crowd roared. He was replaced by pinch-runner Jim Delsing. The rest of the game was uneventful as the Tigers completed their sweep with a 6–2 victory.

But the next day wasn't. As his long-time critics accused Veeck of making a mockery of the National Pastime, unamused A. L. President Will Harridge ordered him to release Gaedel, saying the use of a midget was not in the best interests of baseball.

St. Louis Browns' midget **Eddie Gaedel** *popped out of a papier-mâché cake (above) and got some help from friends (below).*

1965

Maloney Gets His No-Hitter

If at first you don't succeed, try, try again. Cincinnati's Jim Maloney put that philosophy to good use in a game at Chicago's Wrigley Field and completed his first "official" career no-hitter – a 10-inning 1–0 decision that was decided by shortstop Leo Cardenas' home run.

Maloney had not been so fortunate a month earlier when he fired a 10-inning no-hitter, but lost to the last-place New York Mets when Johnny Lewis hit an 11th-inning homer. Maloney was outstanding in that contest, striking out 18 batters and walking only one at New York's Shea Stadium.

By comparison, Maloney's second no-hit effort was just plain ugly. The fireballing righthander needed 187 pitches and walked 10 batters, pitching out of numerous jams. He went to a three-ball count 15 times and hit a batter. The Cubs loaded the bases in the third and ninth innings but came up empty.

Maloney was not all bad, however. He also struck out 12 batters and outdueled Chicago righthander Larry Jackson. The tough-luck Cubs pitcher suffered a jolt when Cardenas drove his 10th-inning pitch off the left-field foul pole.

The 10 walks were a record for a no-hitter.

MILESTONES IN SPORTS

1921

Detroit's 34-year-old Ty Cobb became the youngest member of baseball's 3,000-hit club when he connected off Boston pitcher Elmer Myers.

1922

Molla Mallory won her third straight U.S. women's singles championship and seventh overall when she dispatched 16-year-old Californian Helen Wills, 6–3, 6–1, in the final.

1958

The Douglas Copper Kings of the Arizona-Mexico League broke new ground when all nine members of their starting lineup homered in a 22–8 victory over Chihuahua.

1975

American auto racer Mark Donohue died from brain injuries he suffered during a practice-run accident before the Austrian Grand Prix.

1981

American Renaldo Nehemiah shattered the 13-second barrier in the 110-meter hurdles when he was clocked in 12.93 seconds in a meet at Zurich.

1993

Great Britain's Sally Gunnell set a world record when she covered the 400-meter hurdles in 52.74 seconds in the World Track and Field Championships at Stuttgart, Germany.

1955 Palmer Gets 1st Victory

Arnold Palmer, a tour rookie looking for his first professional victory, fired a final-round 70 and captured the Canadian Open with a near-record four-round total of 265.

Palmer, who had shot 64-67-64 in the first three rounds at the Weston Club in Toronto, finished four strokes ahead of Jack Burke Jr. and five ahead of Fred Hawkins. His 23-under-par total was two strokes above the tournament record and he walked away with the $2,400 first prize.

Palmer, last year's U.S. Amateur winner, had one brief scare in the final round. Hawkins went birdie-eagle-birdie on the second through fourth holes and Palmer stumbled with a double bogey on five, cutting his five-stroke advantage to two.

But the youngster from Latrobe, Pa., hit his second shot 12 feet from the pin on the par-5 seventh en route to a birdie and then rolled in a 40-foot putt on the ninth for another birdie. The rest was easy.

Milestones in Sports

1944

Robert Hamilton pulled off a major upset when he defeated Byron Nelson, 1-up, to win the PGA Championship.

1961

An underdog American team pulled off a surprising 6–1 victory over Great Britain, giving the U.S. its 27th Wightman Cup victory in 33 tries.

1974

California fireballer Nolan Ryan recorded his third 19-strikeout performance of the season in an 11-inning, 1–0 loss to Detroit.

1991

Miami quarterback Dan Marino became the highest paid player in NFL history when he agreed to a five-year contract worth a reported $25 million.

1993

Great Britain's Colin Jackson streaked over the 110-meter hurdles in the world-record time of 12.91 seconds in the World Track and Field Championships at Stuttgart, Germany.

1961 Phillies Stop Slide

John Buzhardt scattered nine Milwaukee hits and the Philadelphia Phillies ended the longest modern-era losing streak in baseball history when they defeated the Braves, 7–4, in the second game of a doubleheader at County Stadium.

The Phillies had lost their 23rd consecutive game, 5–2, on a first-game five-hitter by Warren Spahn. That added to the modern record they had set two days earlier when they dropped their 21st straight game. But the nightcap victory left them one short of the all-time mark – 24 consecutive losses by the 1899 Cleveland Indians.

Buzhardt, the last pitcher to win a game before the streak started on July 28, lifted his record to 4–13. He was clinging to a 3–2 lead when his teammates scored four runs in the eighth inning, a rally he capped with a squeeze bunt.

Wes Covington contributed a home run to the Philadelphia cause.

New York Yankee **fans** *put a humorous touch on the Yogi Berra-Phil Linz harmonica incident.*

1964 Linz Versus Yogi

Normally mild-mannered New York Manager Yogi Berra, showing the strain of the Yankees' recent slump, blew up at reserve infielder Phil Linz over his harmonica playing on the team bus as it headed for Chicago's O'Hare Airport.

The second-place Yankees had just dropped a 5–0 decision to the White Sox at Comiskey Park and Linz, sitting in the back of the bus, took out his harmonica and began to play. Berra, sitting in the front, turned around and shouted at him, "Put that thing in your pocket ."

After momentary silence, Linz blew the harmonica again and an irate Berra rushed toward him and yelled, "I said to put it away. You'd think you just won four straight."

Instead of putting it away, Linz flipped the harmonica toward Berra and the first-year manager angrily swatted it away, hitting first baseman Joe Pepitone on the knee. When Linz told Berra he should be allowed to do what he wants off the field, Berra replied, " Play it in your room."

After Berra sat down, coach Frank Crosetti began yelling at Linz, who told him to mind his own business.

A Star Is Born

1908: Al Lopez, a Hall of Fame catcher over a 19-year major league career that ended in 1947

★ ★ ★

1944: Graig Nettles, a fine defensive third baseman who blasted 390 home runs over a 22-year career that ended in 1988.

★ ★ ★

1960: Mark Langston, a current major league pitcher.

★ ★ ★

AUGUST

21

A STAR IS BORN

1912: Hector (Toe) Blake, a hockey Hall of Fame coach who guided the Montreal Canadiens to eight Stanley Cup championships in the 1950s and '60s after a 15-year career as a left winger.

★★★

1936: Wilt Chamberlain, a basketball Hall of Famer and one of the NBA's original 7-foot centers. He was a four-time MVP, a seven-time scoring champion and an 11-time rebounding champ. He scored 31,419 points in a career that ended in 1973.

★★★

1945: Willie Lanier, a football Hall of Fame middle linebacker known for his fierce hitting over 11 seasons with the Kansas City Chiefs (1967–77).

★★★

1954: Archie Griffin, the only two-time Heisman Trophy winner in college football history and later a professional footballer.

★★★

1959: Jim McMahon, a current National Football League quarterback.

★★★

1914 HAGEN WINS U.S. OPEN

Walter Hagen, a colorful young golfing sensation out of New York, established himself as a national force when he fired a final-day 75–73 for a record-tying 290 and scored a one-stroke victory in the U.S. Open championship at Chicago's Midlothian Country Club.

Hagen, an eye-catching gallery favorite in his multi-colored shirt and red bandana, had set a fast pace with a record-shattering first-round 68 and entered the second day with a one stroke lead over Tom McNamara. But while McNamara was fading, Chicagoan Chick Evans was making a belated rush that gave the 22-year-old Hagen a few anxious moments.

Evans, playing with a bothersome ankle injury, nevertheless enjoyed the best final day of the tournament. He shot a 71–70 and missed three makable birdie putts that could have swung the final result his way. Spectators surrounding the 18th green stood on their tiptoes to watch Evans miss a 30-foot putt that could have forced a playoff.

With the victory, Hagen became the third American-born golfer to win the prestigious event. American Francis Ouimet had become the first amateur winner in 1913.

MILESTONES IN SPORTS

1947

The Maynard Midgets of Williamsport, Pa., captured the first Little League World Series, played appropriately in Williamsport.

1963

Pittsburgh's Jerry Lynch hit his major league-record 15th pinch-hit home run to give the Pirates a 7–6 victory at Chicago.

1975

A baseball first: Chicago Cubs brothers Rick and Paul Reuschel combined on a 7–0 shutout of the Los Angeles Dodgers.

1982

Saving grace: Milwaukee reliever Rollie Fingers became baseball's first 300-save man when he closed out a 3–2 Brewers victory over Seattle.

1989

Cincinnati ended Chicago outfielder Jerome Walton's 30-game hitting streak during a 6–5, 10-inning victory at Wrigley Field .

Two of baseball's premier pinch-hitters: **Pirates Smoky Burgess** *(left) and* **Jerry Lynch.**

1985 DECKER-SLANEY LOWERS MILE WORLD RECORD

Rumanian Maricica Puica was good enough to break her own mile world record during competition in the Weltklasse track and field meet at Zurich, Switzerland. But she wasn't good enough to beat Mary Decker-Slaney.

Decker-Slaney, undefeated in outdoor meets this season, continued her domination with a record-setting time of 4:16.71. But her victory did not come easily. Puica challenged late and pulled close on the homestretch, but she didn't have quite enough to catch Decker-Slaney.

Puica, who had set the mile record (4:17.44) two years ago, finished at 4:17.33. Zola Budd, the bare-footed South African running under the flag of Great Britain, was right behind Puica at 4:17.52. Puica had not lost an outdoor competition this year.

Decker-Slaney, who normally likes to lead from the beginning, digressed from her normal pattern. Diana Richburg set the early pace and Decker-Slaney did not move ahead until the halfway mark. She never trailed again.

1931 RUTH BLASTS 600TH

New York slugger Babe Ruth, adding yet another feather to his record-filled cap, blasted his 600th career home run in the Yankees ' 11–7 victory over the St. Louis Browns at Sportsman's Park – the site of several other historic Bambino blasts.

Ruth connected off Browns righthander George Blaeholder in the third inning of a game the Yankees already led, 1–0. The ball cleared the stadium and bounced off a car parked on the street.

Ruth's heroics were nothing new to the baseball fans of St. Louis. In both the 1926 and '28 World Series against the Cardinals, Ruth had muscled up for record-setting three-home run games at Sportsman's Park.

Ruth's 600th blast – and 35th of the season – was followed by Lou Gehrig's 34th home run and the Yankees went on to score five runs in the inning.

AUGUST

22

MILESTONES • IN SPORTS •

1957

Heavyweight champion Floyd Patterson defended his title with a sixth-round knockout of challenger Pete Rademacher during a title fight in Seattle.

1960

Chicago Cubs pitcher Jim Brewer, whose cheek bone was fractured when Cincinnati's Billy Martin charged the mound and slugged him in an August 4 game, filed suit against the hot-tempered second baseman for $1,040,000.

1964

Barbara McIntire captured her second U.S. Amateur golf title with a 3-and-2 victory over three-time winner JoAnne Gunderson at Hutchinson, Kan.

1961

New York Yankee Roger Maris, making a serious bid to wipe out Babe Ruth's one-season home run record, became the first player to reach the 50 plateau in August when he connected off Los Angeles Angels righthander Ken McBride.

1970

Former Southern Cal running back and Heisman Trophy winner O.J. Simpson was named the greatest college football player of the 1960s in a poll conducted by the National Collegiate Sports Services.

1989 RYAN FANS 5,000TH

Texas righthander Nolan Ryan, going where no pitcher had previously dared to go, fanned Oakland's Rickey Henderson on a 3–2 fastball and became the first player to reach the almost-magical 5,000-strikeout plateau.

Ryan started the Arlington Stadium game needing six strikeouts to reach the milestone and Ranger fans cheered virtually every pitch. The big Texan did not make them wait long, striking out Jose Canseco in the first inning, Dave Henderson and Tony Phillips in the second and Rickey Henderson and Ron Hassey in the third. That put him in milestone position at 4,999.

Ryan, working in 101-degree heat, went to a full count on Rickey Henderson leading off the fifth. Henderson fouled off two pitches before swinging and missing at the third. The crowd of 42,869 went into a long roar and the 42-year-old Ryan showed his appreciation with a tip of his cap.

He went on to strike out 13 and finished the night with 5,007. But the Rangers dropped a 2-0 decision to the A's – Ryan's 261st career loss. Steve Carlton, who retired last year, ranks second on the all-time strikeout list with 4,136.

1965 MARICHAL ATTACKS ROSEBORO

In an ugly incident that stunned players, managers, 42,807 fans at Candlestick Park and thousands more watching the game on television in Los Angeles, San Francisco pitcher Juan Marichal attacked Dodger catcher John Roseboro with a bat, cutting open his head and touching off a 14-minute brawl.

Marichal was batting in the third inning against Los Angeles lefthander Sandy Koufax when he suddenly wheeled around and swung at Roseboro, hitting him twice before peacemakers could arrive. As Marichal was restrained, both benches emptied onto the field, although fighting was minimal as most players seemed horrified by the sight of blood trickling down Roseboro's face.

Marichal, who said the incident was triggered by return throws from Roseboro to Koufax that came perilously close to his ear, was ejected from the game while Roseboro received stitches for a two-inch gash that could have been a lot worse.

The game had started as a duel between the National League's most glamorous pitchers and its top two teams. But that was quickly forgotten. The rest of the contest was uneventful, with the Giants posting a 4–3 victory on Willie Mays' three-run homer.

Los Angeles catcher **John Roseboro** *(left) and San Francisco pitcher* **Juan Marichal** *(right), the principals in the horrifying bat-swinging attack.*

A STAR IS BORN

1909: Mel Hein, a football Hall of Fame center who never missed a game in 15 seasons for the New York Giants. He was All-Pro eight consecutive seasons (1933–40) and the NFL's first official MVP.

★ ★ ★

1939: Carl Yastrzemski, a Hall of Fame outfielder who earned three batting titles, won a Triple Crown (1967) and belted 3,419 hits and 452 home runs over 23 seasons with the Boston Red Sox.

★ ★ ★

1956: Paul Molitor, a current major league infielder and designated hitter.

1973 U.S., CUBAN TEAMS BRAWL

In a brawl that made international headlines, United States and Cuban basketball players threw chairs, traded punches and delivered kicks near the end of a quarterfinal contest dominated by the Americans in the World University Games at Moscow.

The United States owned a big lead and the game appeared to be proceeding smoothly when 7-foot-3 North Carolina State center Tom Burleson and Cuba's Juan Domeco scrambled for a loose ball near the Cuban bench with less than 2 minutes remaining. Inexplicably, Cuban bench players suddenly raced onto the Central Army Sports Club floor and the battle was on.

It lasted for five minutes before Soviet police could swarm the court and restore some sort of order. The police ringed the court as the Americans went on to finish off their 98–76 victory without further incident. During the fracas, Cuban Coach Ernesto Diaz was seen kicking American Coach Ed Badger in the stomach.

Amazingly, nobody was seriously injured in the melee, although Virginia guard Wally Walker needed three stitches to close a cut from a bottle that was thrown onto the court.

AUGUST

23

1957 5-Foot Angel Perfect

Angel Macias, a pint-sized, ambidextrous Mexican with a big heart, punctuated the championship game of the Little League World Series by pitching a perfect game and leading his underdog Monterrey team to a 4–0 victory over a squad from La Mesa, Calif.

The 5-foot, 88-pounder struck out 11 of the 18 batters he faced and did not permit a ball to be hit out of the infield. The Mexicans, giving away 35 pounds and 5 inches per player, scored all of their runs in the fifth inning on two hits, two walks, two fielder's choices and a pair of La Mesa errors.

Monterrey's path to Williamsport, Pa., was long and hard. In becoming the first non-American team to win the 11-year-old World Series, Monterrey started with a 150-mile trek to McAllen, Tex., and then made subsequent stops at Corpus Christi, Tex., Fort Worth, Tex., and Louisville, Ky., compiling an 11–0 record. The youngsters edged Bridgeport (Conn.), 2–1, in the semifinal round.

To celebrate the success of their conquering heroes, Monterrey citizens took the day off and listened to game progress reports via loudspeakers installed in public squares. When the final score became official, pandemonium broke loose and the celebration lasted far into the night.

1936 Feller Records 15 Strikeouts in Debut

Firing a blazing fastball that is sure to terrorize American League hitters for years to come, Cleveland righthander Bob Feller struck out 15 batters in his first major league start and stopped the St. Louis Browns, 4–1.

Young and talented, Cleveland's **Bob Feller** *burst upon the major league scene with a 15-strikeout performance.*

Feller, a 17-year-old phenom from Van Meter, Iowa, came within two strikeouts of matching Dizzy Dean's modern major league single-game record (1933) and within one of Rube Waddell's A.L. mark (1908). He allowed just six hits and the Browns scored their only run in the sixth inning on back-to-back doubles by Lyn Lary and Roy Bell.

But the Indians gave their young hurler all the runs he needed with a three-run burst in the bottom of the sixth and added another in the seventh. Hal Trosky collected four hits and two RBIs for Cleveland.

Feller had burst into the national consciousness when he struck out eight St. Louis Cardinals in three innings of a July 6 exhibition game.

1931 Grove Falls Short

Philadelphia's Lefty Grove, bidding to set an American League record for consecutive victories, saw his 16-game streak come to an end when he dropped a heart-breaking 1–0 decision to Dick Coffman and the St. Louis Browns.

Pitching in the first game of a doubleheader at Sportsman's Park, Grove allowed seven hits, struck out six and did not permit a walk. Coffman, however, was even better. The righthander permitted just three singles and walked one in outdueling the hottest pitcher in baseball.

To make matters worse, the Browns scored their only run on a third-inning misplay by left fielder Jimmy Moore, who was filling in for regular Al Simmons. After Fred Schulte singled, Moore misjudged a fly ball by Oscar Melillo, allowing it to fall for a double.

The loss, Grove's third in 30 decisions, kept the lefthander from breaking the A.L. consecutive-wins record of 16 set in 1912 by Joe Wood and tied that season by Walter Johnson.

Philadelphia's **Lefty Grove** *fell short in his bid for the A.L. consecutive-victory record.*

MILESTONES IN SPORTS

1961

Five San Francisco Giants – Orlando Cepeda, Felipe Alou, Jim Davenport, Johnny Orsino and Willie Mays – belted home runs in a 12-run ninth inning as the Giants cruised to a 14–0 victory over Cincinnati. It was the third time the feat had been accomplished.

1970

Pittsburgh's Roberto Clemente enjoyed his second straight five-hit game in an 11–0 victory over Los Angeles, becoming the first modern major leaguer to collect 10 hits in two consecutive games.

1980

Controversial Oakland A's Owner Charles O. Finley made a graceful exit from baseball when he sold the team to the Haas family of San Francisco for $12.7 million.

1989

A leadoff home run in the 22nd inning by Los Angeles catcher Rick Dempsey gave the Dodgers a 1–0 victory over Montreal in the second-longest shutout in major league history.

1992

The Houston Astros, plagued by home scheduling conflicts, completed a marathon 26-game road trip with a 3–1 victory over Philadelphia and a respectable 12–14 record.

A STAR IS BORN

1922: George Kell, a Hall of Fame third baseman who compiled a .306 average during a 15-year career that ended in 1957.

★ ★ ★

1934: Sonny Jurgensen, a football Hall of Fame quarterback who passed for 32,224 yards and 255 touchdowns over an 18-year career that ended in 1974.

★ ★ ★

1961: Julio Franco, a current major league designated hitter.

1989 GIAMATTI HANDS ROSE LIFE BAN

Cincinnati Manager Pete Rose, baseball's all-time hits leader and one of the most popular players in the game for more than three decades, was handed a lifetime ban from the National Pastime by Commissioner A. Bartlett Giamatti in a monumental ruling that rivaled the 1919 Black Sox scandal.

Commissioner **A. Bartlett Giamatti**, *the man who banned Pete Rose from baseball.*

In 1919, eight members of the Chicago White Sox were handed lifetime bans by Commissioner Kenesaw Mountain Landis for their parts in "fixing" the outcome of the World Series against the Cincinnati Reds. Rose's ban, the result of a mountain of evidence that had been gathered to chronicle his gambling activities and associations with known bookmakers, followed months of legal maneuvering between the commissioner and the game's top personality.

In announcing his decision at a New York press conference, Giamatti told reporters that Rose had accepted his lifetime suspension, acknowledged that he had been treated fairly and waived his right to a hearing. Giamatti also said he believed Rose had bet on games involving his own team, a statement Rose vigorously denied at his own nationally televised press conference later in the day.

The ban was a compromise in the battle the 51-year-old Giamatti had waged against Rose since replacing Commissioner Peter V. Ueberroth on April 1. Rose in effect signed a carefully-worded agreement that allowed him to continue denying guilt publicly while giving him the right to apply for reinstatement annually. Giamatti got the suspension he wanted and reestablished the authority of baseball's highest office.

Rose, who also agreed to dismiss a civil suit against the commissioner, compiled his record 4,256 hits in a 24-year career that began in 1963 with Cincinnati. Known as "Charlie Hustle" for his never-give-an-inch style of play, he served as the catalyst for Cincinnati teams that won four World Series and the Big Red Machine of the mid-1970s that ranks among the game's all-time best teams. He later helped Philadelphia into two World Series.

He played briefly for Montreal before completing his career as a player-manager with the Reds in 1986 and was Cincinnati's manager at the time of his banishment. He is the 15th major leaguer to receive a lifetime ban.

A STAR IS BORN

1887: Harry Hooper, a Hall of Fame outfielder who batted .281 over a 17-year career that ended in 1925 with the Chicago White Sox .

★ ★ ★

1890: Duke Kahanamoku, a swimmer who won three gold medals and two silvers at the 1912, 1920 and 1924 Olympic Games.

★ ★ ★

1960: Cal Ripken Jr., a current major league shortstop.

★ ★ ★

1963 PENNEL TOPS 17-FOOT POLE VAULT BARRIER

John Pennel, scaling a track and field mountain that seemed out of reach only two years earlier, became the first pole vaulter to clear 17 feet when he broke his own world record while competing in the Florida Gold Coast Amateur Athletic Union meet at Miami.

Pennel's 17–0 3/4 vault came only a year and a half after Marine John Uelses had cleared 16 feet for the first time. Pennel set a world record in March when he vaulted 16–3 and has broken the record six times en route to his barrier-breaking 17-footer.

The big moment, fittingly, occurred in Pennel's hometown before friends and family. Using a fiberglass pole and obviously fired up, Pennel soared over the record-breaker on his first try, but missed three times at 17–3 7/8. His previous world mark was 16–10 1/4.

AUGUST 24

MILESTONES IN SPORTS

1908

Heavyweight champion Tommy Burns, making his 10th successful title defense, knocked out challenger Bill Squires for the second time in 10 weeks, this time in the 13th round of a bout at Sydney, Australia.

1943

The Philadelphia A's, who had tied the A.L. record for futility when they lost their 20th straight game (6–5) in the opener of a doubleheader against Chicago, exploded for eight runs in the third inning of the nightcap and coasted to an 8–1 victory.

1945

Rapid Robert Feller, celebrating his return to baseball after almost four years in the Navy, struck out 12 Detroit Tigers and pitched Cleveland to a 4–2 victory before a roaring home crowd of 46,477.

1973

Avenging last year's controversial Olympic basketball loss to the Soviet Union at Munich, an American men's team recorded a 75–67 win over the Russians in the final of the World University Games at Moscow.

1975

Montreal catcher Gary Carter threw out Los Angeles' Dave Lopes trying to steal in the 12th inning of a game eventually won by the Expos in 14, 5–3. The play ended Lopes' record string of 38 consecutive successful steals.

AUGUST

25

A STAR IS BORN

1927: Althea Gibson, the first black tennis player to win both the Wimbledon and U.S. singles titles. She won both tournaments in 1957 and '58.

★ ★ ★

1946: Rollie Fingers, a Hall of Fame relief pitcher who won both the A.L. MVP and Cy Young awards in 1981. He was the first to record 300 career saves.

★ ★ ★

1966: Cornelius Bennett, a current National Football League linebacker.

★ ★ ★

1966: Albert Belle, a current major league outfielder.

★ ★ ★

DEATH OF A LEGEND

1984: Waite Hoyt (baseball).

★ ★ ★

1988: Art Rooney (football).

★ ★ ★

1991

CARL LEWIS BREAKS 100-METER RECORD

The amazing Carl Lewis, a six-time gold medalist in two Olympic Games as a sprinter and long jumper, set a world record in the 100-meter final of the world championships at Tokyo with a blistering time of 9.86 seconds.

Sprinter **Carl Lewis,** *the world's fastest human.*

Lewis led the fastest 100-meter field ever assembled across the finish line with a late burst that barely edged out fellow American Leroy Burrell. Burrell, the previous record-holder at 9.90, also broke the existing mark with a 9.88 time.

Amazingly, six of the eight runners finished under 10 seconds. American Dennis Mitchell was third at 9.91, Britain's Linford Christie fourth at 9.92 and Namibia's Frank Fredericks and Jamaica's Ray Stewart tied for fifth at 9.96. Only twice previously had as many as three runners finished under 10 seconds.

Lewis' feat sent the 75,000 spectators at National Stadium into an uproar. He had run a 9.93 (third fastest in history) only two hours earlier in a semifinal heat.

Lewis is 30 years old.

MILESTONES • IN SPORTS •

1904

Heavyweight champion James Jeffries, making his seventh successful title defense, made short work of Jack Munroe with a second-round technical knockout in San Francisco.

1952

Detroit's Virgil (Fire) Trucks became the third pitcher in major league history to throw two no-hitters in one season when he blanked New York, 1–0, in a memorable game at Yankee Stadium.

1967

Minnesota righthander Dean Chance, who had recorded a rain-shortened five-inning perfect game earlier in the month, pitched his first career nine-inning no-hitter as the Twins defeated the Cleveland Indians, 2–1.

1985

New York Mets righthander Dwight Gooden, at 20 years, nine months and nine days, became the youngest pitcher to win 20 games when he defeated the San Diego Padres, 9–3.

Big **Hack Miller** *contributed a pair of home runs to Chicago's wild 26–23 victory over Philadelphia.*

1922

26–23: LIFE AT WRIGLEY

Cliff Heathcote banged out five hits and Hack Miller pounded a pair of home runs to lead the Chicago Cubs to a 26–23 victory over Philadelphia in the highest-scoring game in major league history.

The three-hour battle at windy Wrigley Field featured a modern-record 51 hits – 27 by the Cubs and 24 by the Phillies. Chicago owned a 25–5 lead after $3^1/2$ innings, but the Phillies threw a scare into the Wrigley faithful by scoring 14 runs in the final two innings.

The Cubs used two big innings to forge their seemingly insurmountable lead and then held on for dear life. They scored 10 runs in the second frame and tied a modern record with a 14-run fourth. The Phillies chipped away with three runs in the second, two in the third, one in the fourth, three in the fifth, eight in the eighth and six in the ninth.

Russ Wrightstone and Curt Walker led the Philadelphia attack with four hits apiece. Battered Phillies pitchers Jimmy Ring and Lefty Weinert allowed all 26 of the Chicago runs.

1946

HOGAN WINS FIRST MAJOR

Little Ben Hogan, looking for his first major tournament victory, registered a blistering 30 over the front nine holes of the afternoon round and defeated Ed (Porky) Oliver, 6 and 4, in the final of the PGA Championship at the Portland (Ore.) Country Club course.

The 135-pound Hogan, trailing his 207-pound opponent by three holes after the morning round, turned on the jets after the break. He dropped birdie putts on holes 20 through 23 and finished the front nine with another birdie. When he scored birdies on the 28th and 29th, he held a 4-up advantage and the match was all but over.

Hogan, the year's leading money-winner, was poised for another birdie on the 32nd hole when Oliver missed his putt and conceded the match. It marked the first time Hogan had made it past the quarterfinal round of the match-play event and the victory earned him $3,500.

Oliver had built his 3-up morning lead with a consistent 70.

1939 W2XBS Televises 1st Baseball Game

With 33,535 fans watching at Ebbets Field and considerably fewer watching on the estimated 400 television sets in New York state, history was made when Red Barber handled play-by-play and postgame interviews for the first telecast of a major league baseball game.

The historic contest, which pitted Cincinnati and Brooklyn in the opener of a Saturday afternoon doubleheader, was broadcast live by W2XBS, the station that had televised a college game between Columbia and Princeton three months earlier. W2XBS used two cameras, one at ground level near home plate and another in the upper deck near third base.

Barber, who had sold Dodgers General Manager Larry MacPhail on the idea, was positioned in the upper deck and worked without a monitor, having to watch the cameras and guess what they were showing.

The Reds won the game, 5–2, as Bucky Walters picked up his 21st victory, but the Dodgers captured the non-televised nightcap, 6–1 . After the opener, Barber rushed to the field and interviewed managers Bill McKechnie of Cincinnati and Leo Durocher of the Dodgers.

Ground-breaking broadcaster **Red Barber** *interviews Dodgers Manager* **Leo Durocher** *after the first televised game in baseball history.*

Milestones in Sports

1947

Brooklyn's Dan Bankhead, making his debut as baseball's first black pitcher, fared better at the plate than on the mound. He homered in his first at-bat but surrendered 10 hits and six earned runs to Pittsburgh in 3 1/3 innings.

1961

Anne Quast-Decker overwhelmed Phyllis Preuss, 14 and 13, at Tacoma, Wash., in the most one-sided U.S. Amateur golf final ever played.

1961

The Hockey Hall of Fame, built in Toronto with funds donated by the NHL's six member teams, was dedicated by Canadian Prime Minister John G. Diefenbaker and Livingston T. Merchant, the U.S. ambassador to Canada.

1973

An American team led by the Evert sisters, Chris and 15-year-old Jeanne, captured its fifth straight Wightman Cup and 38th in 50 years with a 5–2 victory over Great Britain at Brookline, Mass.

1990

Taiwan cruised to a 9–0 victory over an American team from Shippensburg, Pa., and captured its 14th victory in 17 trips to the Little League World Series in Williamsport, Pa.

August 26

1989 American Team Triumphs

An upstart team of American Little Leaguers from Trumbull, Conn., temporarily pulled down the curtain on foreign domination when they defeated a heavily favored Kaohsiung Taiwan team, 5–2, in the 43rd Little League World Series championship game.

With 5-foot-1, 126-pound Chris Drury pitching a five-hitter and driving in two runs, Trumbull became the first American team to win the title since 1983 and just the fifth in the last 23 years. Teams from Taiwan have won 13 World Series during that span.

Drury, who struck out two and walked four, was in command all the way. His two-run bases-loaded single in the fourth inning gave Trumbull a 4–1 cushion and Ken Martin added an insurance run in the fifth with a solo home run. Martin drove in three of Trumbull's runs.

The title game, televised nationally and viewed by a crowd of 40,000, was the culmination of about 12,250 tournament games worldwide involving about 7,000 teams 11- and 12-year olds.

1987 Paul Molitor's Streak Ends After 39 Games

Cleveland rookie John Farrell, making his second major league start, put the brakes on Milwaukee designated hitter Paul Molitor's 39-game hitting streak, but the Brewers scored a 10th-inning run to eke out a 1–0 victory at County Stadium.

Molitor, trying to match the fourth-longest streak in modern baseball history, a 40-game effort by Detroit's Ty Cobb in 1911, never got the ball out of the infield against Farrell, who pitched the first nine innings.

Molitor struck out in his first at-bat, grounded into a third-inning double play, grounded out to shortstop in the sixth and reached base in the eighth on an error. He was on deck in the 10th when Milwaukee pinch-hitter Rick Manning singled home the winning run.

The streak, longest in the majors since 1978 when Cincinnati's Pete Rose hit in a National League-record 44 games, started July 16 against California. During the streak, Molitor was 68 for 164, a .415 average. He is batting .365 for the season.

The streak was the longest in the American League since 1941, when Yankee Clipper Joe DiMaggio set the major league record by hitting in 56 consecutive games.

A STAR IS BORN

1934: Tom Heinsohn, a basketball Hall of Famer who was a member of eight Boston Celtics championship teams as a player from 1956–65 and two more as Boston coach from 1969–78.

★ ★ ★

AUGUST

27

Record-breaking basestealer **Rickey Henderson** *caught and passed Lou Brock.*

1982

Henderson Runs Wild

Oakland speedster Rickey Henderson planted his feet firmly in baseball's record books when he stole four bases during a 5–4 loss at Milwaukee and became the greatest one-season base thief of all time.

Henderson electrified the County Stadium crowd in the third inning when he drew a walk off Doc Medich. The righthander threw to first four times and then pitched out, but Henderson still ran and slid safely into second under catcher Ted Simmons' accurate throw with steal No. 119, one more than Lou Brock managed for St. Louis in 1974.

American League President Lee MacPhail, Brock and players from both teams joined Henderson on the field for a brief ceremony. Henderson pulled the second-base bag from its mooring and held it high as the Milwaukee crowd saluted his feat.

Henderson further celebrated by stealing three more bases, giving him 122 with more than a month remaining in the season.

1973

NHL Expands Again

The National Hockey League, a six-team circuit through the first half century of its existence, will add four teams to increase its membership to 20 by 1976 and realign into a four-division format for the 1974–75 campaign.

The expansion and format change will be accompanied by a new playoff formula that allows the top three clubs from the five-team divisions to qualify for postseason play. Under the formula, first-place teams will draw a first-round bye while other teams battle in best two-of-three series.

The current 16-team circuit will expand to 18 for 1974–75 with the addition of teams in Kansas City and Washington and to 20 in 1976 with teams yet to be determined.

Under the new format, the two New York teams will join Philadelphia, Atlanta and a 1976 expansion club in Division I. Detroit, Pittsburgh, Los Angeles, Montreal and Washington will compete in Division II. Division III will include Chicago, Kansas City, Minnesota, St. Louis and Vancouver while Division IV will be made up of Boston, Buffalo, California, Toronto and the other 1976 expansion team.

A Star Is Born

1931: Joe Cunningham, a .291 career hitter over 12 major league seasons (1954–66).

★ ★ ★

1952: Buddy Bell, a smooth-fielding third baseman who compiled a .279 average over an 18-year career that ended in 1989.

★ ★ ★

1962: Adam Oates, a current NHL center.

Milestones • In Sports •

1960

Joseph Mormello, a 12-year-old fireballer, pitched a no-hitter to lead Levittown, Pa., to a 5–0 victory over Fort Worth, Tex., in the Little League World Series title game at Williamsport, Pa.

1971

Boston Bruins defenseman Bobby Orr signed what is believed to be the richest contract in NHL history: $1 million over five years.

1972

Jack Nicklaus became the greatest one-season money winner in golf history when he captured the $40,000 first prize in the U.S. Match-Play Championship and lifted his 1972 earnings to $280,481.

1977

Texas teammates Toby Harrah and Bump Wills combined for a rare baseball feat when they connected for inside-the-park home runs on consecutive pitches during an 8–2 victory over New York at Yankee Stadium.

1978

Cincinnati's Joe Morgan hit his 200th career home run and became the first major leaguer to compile 200 homers while stealing 500 bases.

1980

Great Britain's Steve Ovett shattered the 1,500 meter world record with a 3:31.4 clocking in Koblenz, West Germany.

The controversial and talented **John McEnroe** *avoided an early U.S. Open dismissal.*

1985

McEnroe Wins, Avoids Upset

John McEnroe, valiantly fighting to stave off one of the biggest upsets in U.S. Open history, won a fifth-set tie-breaker, 9–7, from unseeded Shlomo Glickstein in a grueling four-hour first-round match at the National Tennis Center in Flushing Meadows, N.Y.

McEnroe's 6–1, 6–7, 2–6, 6–3, 7–6 victory over the stubborn Israeli was anything but easy. Suffering lapses of concentration, the defending champion easily won the first set before running into trouble. Seemingly anticipating McEnroe's every move, Glickstein, the 175th-ranked player in the world, won a tight second set and then sent shockwaves through the complex with a third-set triumph that put him in position for an improbable victory.

But the top-seeded McEnroe fought back to take the fourth set and broke Glickstein for a 3-1 lead in the finale. Glickstein returned the favor by holding service in the fifth game and breaking McEnroe in the sixth to even the match. The players traded breaks in both the seventh and eighth games.

McEnroe got to match point (6–3) in the tie-breaker, but Glickstein recovered to tie at 6–6 and 7–7 before McEnroe could close him out and advance to the second round.

MILESTONES • IN SPORTS •

1963

Speedy Scot, bidding to become the second horse to win a trotting triple crown, completed the second leg of that goal with a three-heat victory in the prestigious Hambletonian at Du Quoin, Ill.

1970

Ever-controversial Detroit righthander Denny McLain, a 31-game winner in 1968, was suspended by the Tigers without pay for a clubhouse incident in which the pitcher doused a sportswriter with water.

1971

Cathy Calhoun, a 13-year-old Californian, shattered the world record in the 1,500-meter freestyle with a 17:19.20 clocking in the AAU swimming championships at Houston.

1971

Philadelphia pitcher Rick Wise knocked in five runs with a grand slam and a solo home run as the Phillies defeated San Francisco, 7–3, in the second game of a doubleheader at Philadelphia.

1987

Philadelphia's Mike Schmidt passed both Willie McCovey and Ted Williams on the career list when he blasted his 522nd home run in an 8–1 Phillies victory over San Diego.

A STAR IS BORN

1943: Lou Piniella, a .291 hitter in an 18-year career that stretched from 1964–84 and currently a major league manager.

★ ★ ★

1950: Ron Guidry, a 170-game winner over 14 seasons with the New York Yankees. The lefthander was 25–3 with a 1.74 ERA in 1978.

★ ★ ★

1971: Janet Evans, an outstanding swimmer who won three individual gold medals at the 1988 Olympic Games and another in 1992.

★ ★ ★

1954 Battling Palmer Wins U.S. Amateur

Arnold Palmer, a 24-year-old battler from Latrobe, Pa., wiped out a two-hole morning-round deficit with an afternoon 70 and recorded a 1-up victory over 43-year-old Robert Sweeny in a thrilling conclusion to the U.S. Amateur championship in Detroit.

The match was not decided until Palmer rolled a 40-foot putt to within three inches of the cup on the 36th hole of the day, forcing Sweeny to concede. Palmer had not taken his first lead until the 32nd hole after tying his veteran opponent three times.

Palmer went 2-up with a 10-foot birdie putt on 33 and the players halved the 34th. Sweeny got back within striking distance on 35 when Palmer three-putted, but he ruined his chance on the final hole when he pushed his drive into the rough and failed to hit the green with his second shot.

Sweeny putted well in the morning when he fired a 70, but he could do no better than 74 in the afternoon.

The victory was Palmer's first in five U.S. Amateur appearances.

1981 Coe Lowers Mile Record

Sebastian Coe, one of the two British runners currently dominating the ever-changing world of distance running, covered the mile in 3:47.33 and lowered the world record by a remarkable 1.07 seconds during an international track and field meet in Brussels.

It marked the third time in 10 days that the prestigious mark had been broken. Coe broke fellow countryman Steve Ovett's record with a 3:48.55 clocking on August 19 in Zurich and Ovett came back one week later with a 3:48.40 mile in West Germany.

Coe's latest effort was helped by perfect weather conditions (71-degree temperature) and a crowd of 50,000 at Heysel Stadium cheering him on. Tom Byers of the United States paced Coe through a 54.92-second first lap and a 1:52.67 half mile. Kenyan Mike Bolt also benefited from the fast pace, finishing second in 3:49.45 – 2.12 seconds behind Coe's fast lead.

The versatile Coe also holds the world records in the 800- and 1,000-meter events.

England's **Sebastian Coe** *hits the finish line and completes his record-setting mile in a meet at Brussels, knocking a remarkable 1.07 seconds off the previous mark set by fellow countryman Steve Ovett two days earlier.*

AUGUST 28

1960 Olympic Protest Denied

A United States protest claiming victory for American Lance Larson in the 100-meter freestyle final was disallowed by the International Amateur Swimming Federation, which reaffirmed Australian John Devitt as gold medalist in the event at the Rome Summer Olympic Games.

The protest stemmed from an exciting battle waged by Larson and Devitt over the final 25 meters of the race. Devitt caught Larson and edged ahead, but Larson made a dramatic surge at the end and appeared to have touched home first.

The three automatic timers, used strictly for backup in case of a close call, showed Larson with clockings of 55, 55.1 and 55.1 seconds, and Devitt with three 55.2s. Devitt was credited with a winning time of 55.2, an Olympic record.

But the six judges who pick first and second place split their votes evenly between the contestants and the chief judge, who normally collects the judges' cards and correlates votes, broke the tie – an unusual procedure. R. Max Ritter, treasurer of the U.S. Olympic Committee and a member of the protest panel, called the decision method "trickery" and said the tie-breaker should have been based on the timing devices and film that showed Larson winning the race.

AUGUST

29

Young and talented Utah center **Moses Malone.**

1974 Moses Aims For Stars

Moses Malone, a 19-year-old recent high school graduate from Petersburg, Va., found his own version of the Promised Land when he signed a contract with a potential value of $3 million to play for the American Basketball Association's Utah Stars.

The 6-foot-11 phenom, who had committed to play for the University of Maryland, changed his mind at the bidding of Utah President Jim Collier. In becoming the first basketball player to go directly from high school to the professional ranks, Malone will make between $150,000 and $200,000 per season while competing for a number of incentive bonuses.

But the good news does not stop there. Malone, who was pursued by more than 300 colleges before settling on Maryland, also will get a $120,000 scholarship fund for use during the offseason and receive $30,000 for every year of college he completes.

The signing was called a major coup for the ABA in its continuing war against the more established National Basketball Association. The Stars had drafted Malone last spring, but many considered it a publicity stunt.

MILESTONES IN SPORTS

1934

The Philadelphia Athletics knocked Detroit pitcher Schoolboy Rowe from the box during a 13–5 victory at Shibe Park, ending the youngster's A.L. record-tying 16-game winning streak.

1960

Fast-punching Davey Moore retained his world featherweight boxing crown with a unanimous 15-round decision over Kazuo Takayama in a title bout at Tokyo.

1965

Colorful Casey Stengel ended his 56-year baseball career with the announcement that he was retiring as New York Mets manager for health reasons.

1965

San Francisco's Willie Mays connected for his 17th home run of the month, surpassing Ralph Kiner's one-month N.L. record of 16. The Giants beat the New York Mets, 8–3, at Shea Stadium.

1971

Hank Aaron made another mark in the N.L. record book when he blasted a two-run homer against Chicago and reached the 100-RBI plateau for the 11th time in his 18-year career.

1988 L.J. Violates Drug Policy

New York Giants star Lawrence Taylor, the premier linebacker in the National Football League and a self-admitted drug abuser in recent years, was handed a 30-day suspension by the National Football League for violating its substance-abuse policy.

NFL spokesman Joe Browne said Taylor failed to pass a routine drug test administered between mid-July and mid-August. As a result, the former North Carolina star will miss the Giants season-opener Monday night against Washington and subsequent regular-season games against the San Francisco 49ers, Dallas Cowboys and Los Angeles Rams.

Taylor's positive drug test constituted a second violation of the NFL's drug policy. A third violation would result in a permanent suspension, a penalty recently handed Indianapolis running back Tony Collins. Such a suspension would be subject to appeal based on good behavior. The Giants also could suspend Taylor without pay – a move that would cost him $250,000.

Taylor, the NFL's 1986 Most Valuable Player after helping lead the Giants to a Super Bowl victory, acknowledged in last year's autobiography, "LT: Living on the Edge," that he had become addicted to cocaine in 1985. He underwent treatment at a drug rehabilitation center in February 1986.

A STAR IS BORN

1945: Wyomia Tyus, the first woman to win consecutive Olympic gold medals in the prestigious 100-meter dash (1964, '68).

★ ★ ★

1946: Bob Beamon, the American long jumper who startled the world during the 1968 Summer Olympic Games at Mexico City when he soared 29 feet, 2 1/2 inches to break the world record by almost 2 feet.

★ ★ ★

1961: Rodney McCray, a former National Basketball Association forward.

★ ★ ★

1962: Carl Banks, a current National Football League linebacker.

★ ★ ★

DEATH OF A LEGEND

1965: Paul Waner (baseball).

★ ★ ★

1977 Brock Steals Record

St. Louis Cardinals speedster Lou Brock ended his chase of Ty Cobb's ghost when he swiped a pair of bases in a game at San Diego and became the greatest career basestealer in modern baseball history.

Brock, who set the single-season steal record with 118 in 1974, swiped second after a game-opening walk to tie Cobb's record of 892 and passed Cobb in the seventh when he stole second after reaching on a fielder's choice.

The record-setter, which came on the first pitch by San Diego starter Dave Freisleben and beat the wide throw of catcher Dave Roberts, was followed by a mob scene and a brief ceremony during which Brock was presented the second-base bag. He was removed from the lineup in a game which was eventually won by the Padres, 4–3.

Lou Brock *slides safely with one of his 893 stolen bases.*

MILESTONES
· IN SPORTS ·

1905

Detroit rookie Ty Cobb doubled off New York Highlanders pitcher Jack Chesbro in his major league debut – a 5–3 Tigers victory.

1918

It took just 56 minutes for the New York Giants to post a 1–0 victory over the Brooklyn Dodgers at the Polo Grounds.

1937

Joe Louis, making his first defense of the heavyweight crown he won five weeks earlier, scored a unanimous 15-round decision over Tommy Farr in a bout at New York's Yankee Stadium.

1974

George Steinbrenner, the principal owner of the New York Yankees who had pleaded guilty to two federal charges of violating campaign contribution laws, was fined $15,000 by a federal judge for his involvement in the campaign of former President Richard Nixon.

1992

Russian sensation Sergei Bubka soared 20–1 during a meet in Padua, Italy, and smashed his pole vault world record for the 31st time.

1991

Powell's Mighty Leap Tops Beamon

They said it couldn't be done. But Californian Mike Powell, who had spent his eight-year long jumping career in the imposing shadow of Carl Lewis, thought otherwise. And with one gigantic leap in the world track and field championships at Tokyo, Powell wiped away years of frustration and a cherished record that had stood unchallenged for more than two decades.

Mike Powell *takes a giant leap into the record books.*

Powell soared 29 feet, 4 1/2 inches – 2 inches beyond the 29-2 1/2 Bob Beamon had posted in 1968 in the rarefied air of Mexico City during the Olympic Games. Not only did the fourth-round jump wipe out the oldest record in track and field history, it also gave Powell his first victory over Lewis in 15 competitions.

Powell's feat was a shocker for Lewis, who had recorded long jump victories in 65 consecutive meets over 10 years while topping 28 feet 56 times with a personal best of 28–10 1/4. And just 15 minutes before Powell's historic leap, Lewis had soared 29–2 3/4, a world-record distance negated by an excessive tailwind.

Before the competition ended, Lewis would top his personal best jump four times and the 29-foot barrier three times.

AUGUST

30

A STAR IS BORN

1899: Kiki Cuyler, a Hall of Fame outfielder who batted .321 over an 18-year career that ended in 1938.

★ ★ ★

1918: Ted Williams, a Hall of Fame outfielder who is considerd one of the best hitters in history. The Boston star was a six-time batting champion, a two-time Triple Crown winner and a two-time MVP. He played 19 years, batting .344 and hitting 521 home runs.

★ ★ ★

1943: Jean-Claude Killy, a French Alpine skier who captured three gold medals in the 1968 Olympic Games and two World Cup titles.

★ ★ ★

1944: Tug McGraw, a relief pitcher over 19 major league seasons (1965–84).

★ ★ ★

1953: Robert Parrish, a current NIBA center.

★ ★ ★

DEATH OF A LEGEND

1952: Arky Vaughan (baseball).

★ ★ ★

1989: Joe Collins (baseball).

1970

Nichols Gets Rich

Bobby Nichols, the surprising 1964 PGA Championship winner who lists himself as a club professional, watched in amazement on the 18th green as his 14-foot birdie putt hesitated on the rim of the cup and then dropped to give him a one-stroke victory in the rich Dow Jones Open at Clifton, N.J.

The putt, which appeared to stop an inch short, suddenly fell into the hole, giving the 34-year-old Nichols a closing 69, a victory over Labron Harris Jr., and a $60,000 first-place check.

Harris, who closed with a 70, had dropped a seven-foot birdie putt moments earlier on the same hole to set up the possibility of a playoff. The final round had been a two-way battle between Nichols, the club professional at Firestone Country Club in Akron, O., and Harris.

1987

Johnson Sets Sprint Record

Canadian sprinter Ben Johnson, exploding out of the starting blocks like a greyhound chasing a rabbit, blazed to the fastest 100-meter clocking in track and field history and a decisive victory over rival Carl Lewis in the world championships at Rome.

Johnson, establishing himself as the world's fastest human, covered the 100 meters in an incredible 9.83 seconds, a full tenth of a second better than Calvin Smith's 4-year-old record of 9.93. Incredibly, Lewis tied Smith's mark with a 9.93 clocking, but finished a full meter behind Johnson.

With the crowd of 64,500 at Stadio Olimpico primed for a classic battle, Johnson surged out of the blocks in breathtaking fashion. Clearly ahead of Lewis, running in the adjoining lane, after a few strides, he never relinquished the lead en route to a time many considered impossible.

Entering the competition, Johnson had beaten Lewis five straight times after Lewis had prevailed in their first seven meetings. Lewis was the 100-meter gold medalist in the 1984 Los Angeles Olympic Games.

AUGUST

31

MILESTONES
IN SPORTS

1934

With 79,432 fans cheering them on at Soldier Field, the NFL-champion Chicago Bears could do no better than a scoreless tie against a team of graduated college seniors in football's first College All-Star Game.

1935

Glenna Collett-Vare earned her record sixth U.S. Women's Amateur title with a 3 and 2 victory over young Patty Berg.

1937

Detroit rookie Rudy York capped the most prolific home run-hitting month in baseball history when he connected for his 17th and 18th of August during a 12–3 Tigers victory over Washington.

1972

In an embarrassing snafu, American sprinters Rey Robinson and Ed Hart were disqualified from the Olympic 100-meter event when they failed to appear for the quarterfinal heats of the Summer Games in Munich. The runners were given the wrong time by a U.S. coach.

1990

Forming the first father-son combination in baseball history, Ken Griffey Sr. and Ken Griffey Jr. played side by side in Seattle's outfield during a Kingdome game against Kansas City.

1992

In a trade that shocked the baseball world, Oakland sent slugging outfielder Jose Canseco to Texas for outfielder Ruben Sierra and pitchers Bobby Witt and Jeff Russell.

1969

Rocky Marciano Killed in Crash

Rocky Marciano, the former heavyweight boxing champion who retired undefeated in 1956, was one of three persons who died when a single-engine plane crashed near Newton Airport about 30 miles east of Des Moines, Iowa.

Marciano, a Brockton, Mass., native who won all 49 of his professional fights, 43 of them by knockout, was on his way to Des Moines to visit friends when the plane went down in a wooded area about two miles from the airport. Contractor Glenn Bells, believed to be the pilot, had radioed for landing instructions about 10 p.m., but nothing was heard from the plane again.

Marciano, a ring bulldog who won the heavyweight title in 1952 with a 13th-round knockout of Jersey Joe Walcott, was one day short of his 46th birthday. The third victim was insurance executive Frank Farrell.

Marciano had retired at age 31 to devote more time to his family.

Former heavyweight champion **Rocky Marciano.**

1955

Nashua Outduels Swaps

William Woodward's Nashua, whipped into a frenzy by Eddie Arcaro, streaked to a six-length victory over Swaps and Bill Shoemaker in a 1¼-mile $100,000 winner-take-all match race at Chicago's Washington Park.

It was sweet revenge for Nashua and Arcaro, who had finished second to Swaps and Shoemaker in their only previous meeting – the prestigious Kentucky Derby at Louisville Downs. Nashua had gone on to win the Preakness Stakes and Belmont Stakes, but the victories were hollow because Swaps was not entered in either race.

Swaps, the California-bred pride of the West Coast, entered the match race as the favorite, but Arcaro whipped Nashua, the pride of the East, into an early lead and Swaps could never pull closer than a neck at the half-mile marker.

The race was witnessed by 35,262 and millions more watched on national television or listened to a radio description.

1950

Hodges Joins 4-Homer Club

Brooklyn first baseman Gil Hodges became the fourth player in modern major league history to hit four home runs in a game and just the second to accomplish the feat in a nine-inning contest as the Dodgers blitzed the Boston Braves, 19–3, before a crowd of 14,226 at Ebbets Field.

Hodges connected in the second, third, sixth and eighth innings off four different Braves pitchers. His third-inning blast off Normie Roy came with two teammates aboard and his other three – off Warren Spahn, Bob Hall and Johnny Antonelli – were two-run shots, giving him nine runs batted in for the day.

Hodges also grounded out in the fourth inning and singled in the seventh. His 17 total bases tied one-game records set by Bobby Lowe and Ed Delahanty prior to 1900. Both Lowe and Delahanty hit four home runs and a single.

Only New York Yankee Lou Gehrig (1932) had hit four homers in a nine-inning game since 1900. The Philadelphia Phillies' Chuck Klein had accomplished the feat in 10 innings (1936) and the Chicago White Sox's Pat Seerey did it in 11 (1948).

Brooklyn basher **Gil Hodges** *celebrates his four-home run barrage.*

A STAR IS BORN

1875: Eddie Plank, a Hall of Fame lefthander who recorded 327 victories over 17 seasons from 1901–17.

★ ★ ★

1913: Ray Dandridge, a Hall of Fame infielder who played in the old Negro Leagues.

★ ★ ★

1931: Jean Beliveau, a hockey Hall of Fame center who scored 507 goals and played on 10 Stanley Cup championship teams in 18 seasons with the Montreal Canadiens (1950–71).

★ ★ ★

1935: Frank Robinson, a Hall of Fame outfielder who batted .294 and belted 586 home runs over a 21-year playing career that ended in 1976. He was the first player to win MVP awards in both leagues and baseball's first black manager.

★ ★ ★

1955: Edwin Moses, the outstanding American hurdler who won 122 consecutive races from 1977–87. He won gold medals in the 400-meter hurdles in both the 1976 and '84 Olympic Games.

★ ★ ★

DEATH OF A LEGEND

1969: Rocky Marciano (boxing).

★ ★ ★

1990: Nat (Sweetwater) Clifton (basketball).

MILESTONES
IN SPORTS

1906

The Philadelphia Athletics scored three runs in the top of the 24th inning and held on for a 4–1 victory over Boston in the longest game in major league history.

1967

San Francisco's Dick Groat drew a bases-loaded walk in the 21st inning to give the Giants a 1–0 victory over Cincinnati in a game that matched the previous major league record for longest scoreless tie.

1972

Shane Gould, a 15-year-old Australian, earned her third Olympic gold medal and set her third world record when she was clocked at 2:03.56 in winning the 200-meter freestyle at the Munich Summer Games.

1973

George Foreman retained his heavyweight boxing crown with a first-round knockout of Puerto Rican Joe (King) Roman at Tokyo.

1985

Bill Elliott drove his Ford Thunderbird to victory in the Southern 500 at Darlington, N.C., claiming his 10th Grand National victory in 20 starts this year.

SEPTEMBER 1

1989

Baseball Head Dies Of Heart Attack

A. Bartlett Giamatti, the scholarly baseball commissioner who dared take on superstar Pete Rose, suffered a heart attack and died at his summer home on Martha's Vineyard, eight days after handing Rose a lifetime ban from the game.

Giamatti, a former professor of English and comparative literature and president of Yale University, collapsed at his Cape Cod retreat and was rushed to Martha's Vineyard Hospital, where he was pronounced dead at age 51.

Giamatti had succeeded Peter V. Ueberroth as commissioner on April 1 and spent most of his time in office dealing with the sticky Rose situation. As evidence mounted that the Cincinnati manager had bet on baseball games, perhaps even those of his own team, Giamatti stepped up the pressure.

After months of legal maneuvering, the situation was resolved when the commissioner and Rose agreed on the lifetime ban. A week and a day after that announcement, Giamatti died.

Giamatti previously had spent nine years as the youngest president in Yale history before leaving to take the post as National League president. He served two years in that role before being elected to the commissioner's job.

1946

Patty Berg Wins 1st Open

Patty Berg, the hard-hitting shotmaker from Minneapolis, captured the richest purse in the history of women's golf when she overpowered Betty Jameson, 5 and 4, in the 36-hole final of the inaugural United States Women's Open golf tournament, played at Spokane, Wash.

Berg took a big step toward the $5,600 first prize when she broke the 18-hole morning deadlock by winning five of the first six holes in the afternoon round. She started her streak with a 25-foot birdie putt on 19 and then won the 20th, 22nd, 23rd and 24th holes to take a 4-up lead.

After the women traded birdies on 28 and 30, Berg closed out the match on the 32nd hole when she parred and Jameson missed a 7-foot putt for a bogey.

The tournament, which the Women's Professional Golfer's Association hopes to turn into its annual showcase event, was medal play for the first two rounds and match play the rest of the way. Berg also managed to walk away with medal honors with a 72–73—145.

Patty Berg, *winner of the inaugural Women's Open.*

1983

Frenchman Vaults 19-1½

High-flying Frenchman Thierry Vigneron sailed over the bar at 19 feet, 1½ inch, setting a world pole vault record during competition in the Golden Gala track and field meet before 40,000 fans at the Rome Olympic Stadium.

Vigneron made his record pole vault on his third attempt after just missing on his first two. He broke the 19–1 record set by another Frenchman, Pierre Quinon, five days earlier during a track and field competition in Cologne, West Germany.

Vigneron stole the spotlight from Louise Ritter, whose high jump of 6–7¾ broke her own American mark of 6–6¾. Ritter took three shots at a world record height of 6–8¾, but came up short on each one. She made her record-setting jump after barely clearing a preliminary height of 6–6 on her final attempt.

Edwin Moses was another headliner, winning his 86th consecutive final in the 400-meter hurdles competition.

A STAR IS BORN

1866: Gentleman Jim Corbett, a turn-of-the-century boxer and a one-time world heavyweight champion.

★ ★ ★

1904: Ray Flaherty, a football Hall of Fame player and coach from 1926–49 in the AFL, NFL and AAFC.

★ ★ ★

1923: Rocky Marciano, the world heavyweight boxing champion who retired undefeated in 1956 after a three-year reign.

★ ★ ★

1935: Guy Rodgers, a 1960s National Basketball Association star who handed out 6,917 career assists and scored 10,415 points.

★ ★ ★

1960: Karl Mecklenburg, a current National Football League linebacker.

★ ★ ★

1966: Tim Hardaway, a current National Basketball Association guard.

★ ★ ★

DEATH OF A LEGEND

1989: A. Bartlett Giamatti (baseball).

★ ★ ★

SEPTEMBER

2

A STAR IS BORN

1901: Adolph Rupp, the former Kentucky college basketball coach who holds the NCAA record for career victories (875).

★ ★ ★

1943: Glen Sather, an outstanding hockey coach who led Edmonton to four Stanley Cup titles from 1979–89.

★ ★ ★

1948: Terry Bradshaw, the football Hall of Fame quarterback who directed Pittsburgh to four Super Bowl titles .

★ ★ ★

1948: Nate Archibald, a basketball Hall of Fame guard who scored 16,481 points in his 14-year NBA career.

★ ★ ★

1952: Jimmy Connors, the all-time leader in men's tennis singles titles (109) and a five-time winner of the U.S. Open.

★ ★ ★

1960: Eric Dickerson, a current National Football League running back.

1960 WILMA GETS SWEET WIN

Wilma Rudolph, culminating a lifelong battle against illness and adversity, ran away with the title "world's fastest female" when she captured the 100-meter final in the Summer Olympic Games at Rome.

Rudolph, the 20th of 22 children who grew up in rural Tennessee, blitzed to a clocking of 11.0, a world-record time that was not recognized because of a 2.752-meter tailwind. But that didn't matter because the gold-medal victory was sweet enough.

Rudolph had to overcome numerous obstacles en route to that victory. A premature baby that weighed just 4 1/2 pounds at birth, she suffered through bouts with polio, double pneumonia and scarlet fever that cost her the use of her left leg. As a child she wore a brace, but daily leg rubbings by her mother and other forms of rehabilitation worked wonders. By the time she reached high school, she was a talented athlete.

Now a mother and a student at Tennessee State University, Rudolph dominated the 100-meter competition. She won her semifinal in a world record-tying 11.3 seconds before becoming the first American gold medalist in the event since Helen Stephens in 1936.

1972 WOTTLE'S SURGE NETS SURPRISING GOLD MEDAL

American Dave Wottle, who wasn't supposed to challenge for a gold medal because of recent knee problems, leaned into the tape less than a foot ahead of Russian favorite Yevgeny Arzhanov and captured the 800-meter Olympic final in the Summer Games at Munich, West Germany.

Wottle's major upset seemed unlikely as late as 50 meters from the finish line. Running well behind at that point, the 22-year-old had virtually conceded victory to the Soviet star who had not lost an outdoor 800 race in two years. But suddenly he found himself alongside the staggering Russian and Arzhanov lunged desperately for the finish line, losing his balance and sprawling onto the synthetic track. Wottle's final acceleration carried him to the line and he leaned in for the victory. Both runners were timed at 1:45.9.

MILESTONES IN SPORTS

1918

Baseball's regular season came to an early conclusion because of restrictions forced by World War I.

1952

A sparkling major league debut: Washington righthander Mike Fornieles pitched a one-hitter and defeated Philadelphia, 5–0.

1962

St. Louis veteran Stan Musial moved into second place on the all-time hit list when he singled as a pinch-hitter in a 4–3 loss to the New York Mets for No. 3,516.

1979

Atlanta's James Mayberry, playing in his first NFL game, intercepted a desperation overtime pass by New Orleans punter Russell Erxleben after a wild snap and returned it six yards for the winning score in a 40–34 victory.

1982

The NBA's Philadelphia 76ers signed 6-foot-10 free-agent center Moses Malone to a six-year deal worth $13.2 million.

Toronto ace **Dave Stieb** *finally overcame his no-hit jinx.*

1990 STIEB SHAKES OFF JINX, PITCHES 1ST NO-HITTER

The ninth-inning jinx is history. Toronto righthander Dave Stieb finally won his long battle against bad luck when he pitched the Blue Jays to a 3–0 victory over Cleveland and notched baseball's record ninth no-hitter of the season.

It was a long time coming. Four times Stieb had entered the ninth inning of games with no-hitters and four times opposing teams had broken them up – three times with two out. This time he made it through the final inning with only a two-out walk raising any concern. He retired the Indians' Chris James on a fly ball, Candy Maldonado on strikes and Jerry Browne on a line drive to right.

Stieb's 17th victory also was the first no-hitter in Toronto history. Not that Stieb hadn't tried. He carried a no-hitter into the ninth against Cleveland late in the 1988 season and was disappointed by a two-out bad-hop single. Six days later, he had Baltimore down to one out when an opposite-field bloop single spoiled his day.

The 33-year-old lost a bid for a perfect game against New York in August 1989 on a two-out double, and he lost another ninth-inning no-hit bid in 1989.

1977 Oh My: A New King

The successful form of Japanese home run king **Sadaharu Oh.**

Japanese star Sadaharu Oh became the most prolific slugger in professional baseball history when he blasted a third-inning pitch into the right-field stands of Tokyo's Korakuen Stadium and passed the career home run total of former American great Hank Aaron.

Oh, the 37-year-old first baseman of the Yomiuri Giants, hit a full-count pitch from Yakult pitcher Yasumiro Suzuki for home run No. 756, one more than Aaron managed in his 23-year major league career with the Milwaukee and Atlanta Braves and Milwaukee Brewers. The 328-foot shot touched off a national celebration and talk of Oh's next goal – the never-achieved 800-homer barrier.

Oh, who has said he wouldn't fare as well in American baseball, reached the milestone in his 19th season. Japanese parks are generally smaller than those in the United States and the pitching is not considered of equal quality, but Oh achieved his record while playing in considerably shorter seasons.

Oh, a lefthanded hitter, knew the instant he hit the historic ball where it was going. So did the 55,000 screaming fans who rose to their feet. Oh circled the bases slowly with arms raised and jumped with both feet on home plate, where he was mobbed by his teammates.

The first-place Giants recorded an 8–1 victory over the Swallows.

1972 Viren Falls, Wins

Lasse Viren, the latest in a long line of flying Finns, recovered from the brink of disaster and raced to a stunning world record-setting victory in the 10,000-meter final of the Summer Olympic Games at Munich, West Germany.

Viren was running comfortably in fifth place midway through the grueling competition when he suddenly stumbled on the backstretch and tumbled to the track, tripping up Tunisia's Mohamed Gammoudi in the process. Both runners got up, but Gammoudi, bruised and discouraged, quickly dropped out.

Not Viren. About 50 yards behind the leaders, he quickly made that up and, with 9 1/2 laps to go, he even took the lead. Spaniard Mariano Haro reclaimed the lead briefly, but Viren took control on the final lap and fought Belgium's Emiel Puttemans down the home stretch.

The Finn extended his lead to eight yards at the finish and posted a world record time of 27:38.3. Viren celebrated his noble triumph with a flag-waving victory lap, much to the delight of the fired-up German crowd.

1990 Thigpen Saves Chicago

Chicago White Sox reliever Bobby Thigpen set a one-season major league record when he recorded his 47th save in a victory over Kansas City – and, amazingly, he did it with 29 games remaining on the schedule.

Thigpen pitched the ninth inning and retired Kevin Seitzer on a grounder, gave up a single to Brian McRae and got a double-play grounder from George Brett to close out Chicago's 4–2 victory at Comiskey Park. His 47th save in 54 save opportunities put him one ahead of the mark New York Yankee reliever Dave Righetti set in 1986.

The victory went to White Sox reliever Wayne Edwards, who benefited from Carlton's Fisk's tie-breaking sixth-inning home run. The homer was Fisk's 330th as a catcher, also a major league record. The veteran backstop has 351 total homers, tying him for 41st on the all-time list.

Thigpen appears to be a shoe-in to reach the once-considered impossible barrier of 50 saves in a season.

Chicago White Sox save master **Bobby Thigpen**

September 3

Milestones in Sports

1917

Philadelphia's Grover Cleveland Alexander made life easy for the Phillies' bullpen when he pitched both ends of a 5–0 and 9–3 doubleheader sweep of the Brooklyn Dodgers.

1928

Longtime Detroit and Philadelphia Athletics star Ty Cobb collected a double and closed out his career with 4,191 hits.

1957

Milwaukee ace Warren Spahn set a major league record for lefthanders when he pitched his 41st career shutout, an 8–0 decision over Chicago at Wrigley Field.

1970

Chicago Cubs outfielder Billy Williams, saying he was "pooped," took himself out of the lineup and ended his N.L.-record iron man streak at 1,117 games.

1974

Basketball great Oscar Robertson, who recently severed ties with the NBA's Milwaukee Bucks, announced his retirement to accept a broadcasting job with CBS.

A Star Is Born

1916: Eddie Stanky, a pepperpot second baseman who batted .268 over his 11-year career in the 1940s and '50s.

★ ★ ★

Death of a Legend

1970: Vince Lombardi (football).

★ ★ ★

SEPTEMBER

4

A STAR IS BORN

1937: Dawn Fraser, an Australian swimmer who set a record by winning a gold medal in the same event at three straight Olympic Games (1956, '60, '64).

★ ★ ★

1949: Tom Watson, an outstanding golfer who captured five British Opens, two Masters and one U.S. Open.

★ ★ ★

1963: John Vanbiesbrouck, a current NHL goaltender.

★ ★ ★

DEATH OF A LEGEND

1980: Hank Greenberg (baseball).

★ ★ ★

1972

SPITZ ENDS GOLD RUSH

Mark Spitz completed his amazing Olympic blitz when he swam the butterfly leg for the American 400-meter medley relay team and earned his unprecedented seventh gold medal at the Munich Summer Games.

Not only did the amazing Californian win more gold medals than anybody in the history of the Olympics, every one was earned by a world-record performance. He captured the 100- and 200-meter freestyle and 100- and 200-meter butterfly for individual golds and participated in three winning relays.

The 22-year-old Spitz was the deciding factor in the 400-meter medley, which closed out the swimming competition. Handling the third leg, Spitz turned a tight battle against the East Germans into an American rout. He blitzed through his butterfly 100 meters two body lengths ahead of his nearest competitor and made life easy for anchorman Jerry Heidenreich.

The freestyle specialist touched home at 3:48.16, giving the American team its 10th victory in a total of 15 events.

Seven-time gold medalist **Mark Spitz** *gets a little lift from his friends after the American Olympic victory in the 4x100-meter medley relay.*

1972

IOC'S RULING STUNS DEMONT

Rick DeMont, a 16-year-old high school student from California, was disqualified from the 1,500-meter freestyle race he was favored to win and stripped of the 400-meter gold medal he already had won when doping tests turned up positive because of a prescription he was taking for an asthmatic condition.

The stunned youngster was informed of the disqualification just moments before the 1,500 final and watched the race in tears from poolside. It was a sad conclusion to a situation that was beyond his control.

DeMont had taken the prescription Marex since childhood. But Marex contains an ephedrine that is included on the International Olympic Committee's list of banned drugs that can affect an athlete's performance. DeMont had listed the prescription on his official Olympic forms, but American team doctors apparently failed to clear the prescription with the medical committee. There is some doubt whether anybody even had a copy of the IOC drug-control manual.

As a result, DeMont was stripped of the 400-meter gold he had won in an earlier upset and a chance to compete in his best event.

The fateful decision was made after a recheck of his urinalysis and a second meeting of the IOC Medical Committee.

1976

STEVE LOBELL WINS, LOSES

Steve Lobell, having survived a lost shoe, a cut foreleg and more than five hours in the blazing sun to win the prestigious Hambletonian, fought a different kind of battle three hours after the race when he collapsed and almost died from heat exhaustion.

In a wild afternoon of racing at the Du Quoin (Ill.) State Fairgrounds, Billy Haughton drove Steve Lobell to victory in the second heat and in the fourth-heat runoff to claim the second jewel on trotting's triple crown.

With 18 3-year-olds in the crowded field, gaining the required two-heat victory needed for first place figured to be difficult – and it was. Zoot Suit, driven by Vernon Dancer, won the first heat, Steve Lobell tied a world record over the mile course (1:56²/5) in winning the second and Armbro Regina, with Joe O'Brien in sulky, took the third. That forced a grueling runoff, which Steve Lobell won easily.

But three hours later, the colt collapsed in the stable after going into shock. He was revived after two hours of intensive care by a veterinarian, who pronounced him all right – with rest.

Steve Lobell wasn't the only near casualty of the day. In the second heat, Stanley Dancer's Nevele Thunder, a winner in 22 of 36 starts, tripped and broke a bone in a leg, ending his career.

MILESTONES IN SPORTS

1920

The incredible Man o'War set a world record for a mile and five furlongs when he ran 2:40⁴/5 to win the Lawrence Realization Stakes at Belmont Park.

1969

The 31-game hitting streak of Los Angeles center fielder Willie Davis came to an end during a 3–0 loss to San Diego.

1971

Chris Evert, a 16-year-old tennis phenom, pulled off a shocking upset over Mary Ann Eisel in the second round of the U.S. Open, 4–6, 7–6, 6–1.

1991

Major league baseball announced that it will remove the controversial asterisk from Roger Maris' 1961 record of 61 home runs.

MILESTONES
• IN SPORTS •

1949

Pancho Gonzales overcame a heart-breaking first-set loss and rebounded for a 16–18, 2–6, 6–1, 6–2, 6–4 victory over Ted Schroeder and his second straight U.S. singles championship.

1960

Young and brash Cassius Clay scored a unanimous decision over three-time European champion Zbigniew Pietrzykowski of Poland to win the gold medal in the light heavyweight division at the Rome Olympic Games.

1979

The Indiana Pacers signed four-time All-America Ann Meyers to a $50,000 no-cut contract, making her the first female player in NBA history.

1979

Oakland righthander Matt Keough pitched the Athletics to a 6–1 victory over Milwaukee, ending his two-year 18-game losing streak and his record-tying 14-game streak to open a season.

1992

Dan O'Brien, who surprisingly failed to make the U.S. team during the Olympic trials, set a world decathlon record of 8,891 points in a meet at Talence, France.

World decathlon record-holder **Dan O'Brien.**

1972 Terrorists At Munich

Eleven Israeli athletes were among 17 people who died in a 22-hour drama that began with a terrorist invasion of the Olympic Village at Munich, West Germany, and ended with a wild shootout at a military airport 15 miles away.

In a gripping saga of death and bloodshed that shut down the Summer Olympic Games and dominated the international spotlight for almost one full day, the well-organized Palestinians climbed a fence surrounding the lightly guarded compound that houses more than 10,000 athletes and began the ordeal with their invasion of the Israeli quarters.

They were met by a coach who, seeing their machine guns and recognizing the danger, held the door shut and screamed for everybody to get out. Several athletes managed to escape, but two Israelis were killed and nine were taken hostage.

With the immediate area cleared and the building surrounded by German police, the long, intense hours of negotiation opened. First the commandos demanded the release of 200 Arab prisoners in Israel. Then they requested helicopters to take them to an airport and a plane to fly them to Cairo.

The Israeli government would not relent to the prisoner demands, but the Germans promised them their helicopters and plane. After more than 20 hours, the terrorists and their hostages boarded a bus inside the compound and drove to the helicopters. They then flew to the airport, where a Boeing-707 was waiting.

When the helicopters landed, two terrorists walked the 170 yards from the helicopter to the plane. As they walked back, German sharpshooters suddenly opened fire and the commandos fired back. During the resulting confusion, one of the terrorists threw a grenade into the helicopter holding the hostages.

When the final toll was taken, 11 Israelis, five terrorists and one German policeman had been killed. Three more terrorists were taken captive.

The Olympic Games were suspended for 34 hours and a memorial service was held at the main Olympic stadium.

SEPTEMBER

5

A STAR IS BORN

1875: Napoleon Lajoie, a baseball Hall of Fame infielder who won three American League batting championships and finished his 21-year major league career with a .339 average.

★ ★ ★

1936: Bill Mazeroski, a former Gold Glove second baseman best remembered for his ninth-inning seventh-game home run that gave Pittsburgh a 1960 World Series victory over the New York Yankees.

★ ★ ★

DEATH OF A LEGEND

1971: George Trafton (football).

★ ★ ★

1992: Billy Herman (baseball).

★ ★ ★

1989 Evert Retires After Losing

Chris Evert, the classy queen of tennis for much of the last 18 years, dropped a 7–6, 6–2 decision to Zina Garrison in a quarterfinal match of the U.S. Open and then called it a career.

Evert, who jumped into the tennis spotlight in 1971 when she advanced to the semifinal of the U.S. Open as a 16-year-old phenom, retired with one of the great overall records in the history of the sport. She finished with a 1,304–145 match record, 18 major championships, a U.S. Open record of 101–12 and almost $9 million in winnings. Evert won 157 singles titles, more than any player in history.

The end came suddenly. The 34-year-old Evert had played well in the early rounds and she jumped to a 5–2 first-set lead against Garrison. But her 25-year-old opponent suddenly began attacking the net and took control. She ran down everything Evert hit and made Chris chase down her drop shots and lobs. The final result was a stark reminder of why the former champion had decided to retire.

When the final winner was hit, Evert calmly went to the sideline, waved a final goodbye to the crowd and put her arm around Garrison's neck as they walked off the court.

Chris Evert, *pictured above after her victory in the 1978 U.S. Open, retired after competing in the 1989 championship.*

SEPTEMBER

6

A STAR IS BORN

1862: Thomas Burns, a major league outfielder in the pre-1900 National League who batted .310 over 18 seasons.

★ ★ ★

1888: Red Faber, a Hall of Fame pitcher who won 254 games in his 20-year major league career.

★ ★ ★

1929: Dow Finsterwald, a professional golfer who claimed victory in the 1958 PGA Championship.

★ ★ ★

1946: Ron Boone, a former professional basketball guard who scored 17,437 points in his combined ABA and NBA careers.

★ ★ ★

1960

RAFER WINS DECATHLON

Rafer Johnson, extended to the limits of his endurance by young C.K. Yang of Taiwan, held on to win the Olympic decathlon by 58 points and claim the title "world's greatest athlete."

Olympic decathlon champion **Rafer Johnson** *zips across the finish line in the 100-meter dash.*

Johnson, the world record-holder in the grueling 10-event test, finished with an Olympic-record 8,392 points during the two-day competition in the Rome Summer Games. But the Californian was defeated in seven of the 10 events by Yang and survived only because of his superiority in the field competitions – the shot put, javelin and discus.

Entering the final event, the tough 1,500-meter race, Yang had a chance to win. He needed a resounding victory and he had the speed advantage over his bigger opponent. But Johnson doggedly stayed with Yang, refusing to let him gain more than a five-yard advantage, and both crossed the finish line on wobbly legs.

Johnson had beaten Yang by 258 points in a pre-Olympic AAU meet. But that decisive score could be attributed to an injury that plagued Yang in the final event.

MILESTONES IN SPORTS

1924

St. Louis Browns righthander Urban Shocker defeated the Chicago White Sox, 6–2, in both ends of a doubleheader.

1960

Former Oregon student Otis Davis flew to victory in the 400-meter race at the Rome Olympic Games, knocking three-tenths of a second off the world record with a clocking of 44.9 seconds.

1960

Australian Herb Elliott completed the 1,500-meter race in a world-record 3:35.6 during competition in the Rome Olympic Games.

1992

The 1,500-meter world record fell again, this time to Algerian Noureddine Morceli, who ran a 3:28.86 in a meet at Rieti, Italy.

1975

EVERT CLAIMS 1ST U.S. OPEN

Chris Evert, who as a 16-year-old shocked the tennis world by reaching the semifinal of the U.S. Open, finally won the event on her fifth try when she rallied to defeat arch-rival Evonne Goolagong, 5–7, 6–4, 6–2, at the West Side Tennis Club in Forest Hills, N.Y.

But Evert, who stretched her winning streak on clay to 84 matches over $2^1/_2$ years, needed every ounce of energy and patience she could muster in winning a match that her 24-year-old Australian opponent seemed destined to dominate. Goolagong, beating Evert at her own baseline game, won the battle of long rallies in a marathon first set that set the tone for the match.

The 20-year-old Floridian refused to buckle, however, and came back to win the second set on the only service break. Then, leading 3–2 in the third, Goolagong inexplicably ran out of patience and Evert rattled off four straight games to close her out with little resistance.

It was Evert's 12th victory over Goolagong in 21 matches and her fourth major championship. It also was her first appearance in a U.S. Open final, ending five years of frustration.

Evert collected $25,000 for her victory, bringing her season winnings to $280,027.

1920

TILDEN EARNS TITLE

Bill Tilden, fighting off tenacious Bill Johnston in one of the most grueling tennis matches ever witnessed, captured his first U.S. singles championship and staked his claim as the world's greatest player.

Tilden, coming off a victory at Wimbledon, needed everything he could muster to hold off the man who had defeated him in last year's U.S. final at Forest Hills, N.Y. His 6–1, 1–6, 7–5, 5–7, 6–3 victory was accomplished after numerous twists and turns had left the 10,000-plus fans at the West Side Tennis Club gasping in appreciation.

The first two sets were tradeoffs, but the real fun began in the third. Playing outstanding back-and-forth tennis, the players traded service breaks before Tilden broke for set in the 12th game. But Johnston fought back in an amazing fourth set during which he recovered three times from match point and made Tilden dig deep. The Philadelphian was up to the task, breaking Johnston's service three times while closing out the final set.

Tilden's powerful serve produced 20 aces.

United States singles champion **Bill Tilden.**

SEPTEMBER 7

A STAR IS BORN

1908: Paul Brown, the former coach and general manager who built the Cleveland Browns into an NFL power in the 1950s and later the coach and a front-office official with the Cincinnati Bengals.

★ ★ ★

1923: Louise Suggs, a women's professional golf great who won 11 major championships and 50 LPGA titles from 1949–62.

★ ★ ★

1951: Bert Jones, a former National Football League quarterback.

★ ★ ★

1965: Bruce Armstrong, a current National Football League offensive tackle.

★ ★ ★

DEATH OF A LEGEND

1954: Pop Warner (football).

★ ★ ★

1954: Ken Boyer (baseball).

★ ★ ★

1984: Joe Cronin (baseball).

★ ★ ★

1953 CONNOLLY OPENS UP, SECURES GRAND SLAM

Maureen Connolly, *the first woman to capture a tennis grand slam.*

It took 18-year-old Maureen Connolly only 43 minutes and a minimum of energy to defeat Doris Hart for her third straight U.S. singles championship and nail down the first grand slam in the history of women's professional tennis.

The blonde Californian was the irresistible force in her 6–2, 6–4 victory over Hart, a four-time U.S. finalist but never a winner Connolly simply had too much speed for her veteran opponent, who used every trick in the book to slow down her young nemesis – without much success.

Hart also had lost to Connolly in the final at Wimbledon, another of Connolly's Big Four victories that comprise the grand slam. Little Mo earlier captured the Australian and French championships to join former men's star Don Budge (1938) as the only players to win all four majors in the same year.

To illustrate her dominance, Connolly matched men's winner Tony Trabert by going through the 10-day tournament without losing a set. Trabert, winning his first U.S. Open title, defeated Vic Seixas in a straight-sets Forest Hills, N.Y., final, 6–3, 6–2, 6–3.

1993 WHITEN JOINS ELITE CLUBS

St. Louis Cardinals outfielder Mark Whiten, hitless in the first game of a doubleheader at Cincinnati, came back in the nightcap to hit four homers and drive in 12 runs in a one-for-the-books performance that tied two of baseball's premier records.

Whiten's four-homer assault matched the single-game feats of 11 previous major leaguers, the most recent being Atlanta's Bob Horner in 1986. The 12 RBIs matched the 69-year-old one-game record of another Cardinal, Sunny Jim Bottomley, who did it in 1924. The RBI total was the most since 1975, when Boston's Fred Lynn drove in 10 in a game against Detroit.

Whiten's power surge, which lifted his season home run total to 22, started in the first inning when he blasted a grand slam off rookie Larry Luebbers. After fouling out in the fourth, Whiten hit three-run homers off rookie Mike Anderson in the sixth and seventh. He capped the Cardinals' 15–2 victory with a two-run blast off reliever Rob Dibble in the ninth.

Ironically, Whiten was 0 for 4 in St. Louis' 14–13 opening-game loss but did drive in a run. He finished his memorable day with a doubleheader record-tying 13 RBIs.

1970 SHOEMAKER MAKES HISTORY

Bill Shoemaker rewrote horse racing history when he guided favorite Dares J to a 2 1/2-length victory in the fourth race at Del Mar, the record 6,033rd winner of his storied career.

The 39-year-old Shoemaker passed Johnny Longden as the world's winningest jockey on his 24,534th mount. He had tied the record two days earlier at the same California track.

With 20,000 fans and Longden himself watching from the stands, Shoemaker broke on top early and never looked back in the six-furlong race. When he reached the winner's circle on the 2-year-old filly, a blanket of white flowers was thrown around his neck, he was greeted by Longden and he was also presented with a gold bowl and some other trophies.

Longden rode 6,032 winners in a legendary career that ended in 1966 when he won the San Juan Capistrano Handicap aboard George Royal at age 59.

After the ceremonies, Shoemaker posed for photographs with Longden, his arm draped over his shoulders. He told his predecessor, "I knew you'd be rooting all the way and be waiting for me when I got back."

MILESTONES IN SPORTS

1915

It took Bill Johnston four sets to defeat Maurice McLoughlin in the first U.S. singles championship held at Forest Hills, N.Y.

1963

In festivities at Canton, O., pro football dedicated its new Hall of Fame building and inducted 17 charter members, including such names as George Halas, Red Grange, Bronko Nagurski and Jim Thorpe.

1975

A shocking upset: Manuel Orantes overpowered Jimmy Connors in straight sets to win the U.S. Open tennis championship.

1980

Green Bay 12, Chicago 6 in overtime: The Packers win when Chester Marcol has his 35-yard field goal blocked, but picks up the loose ball and runs for a touchdown.

1985

Another upset: Hana Mandlikova needed two tiebreakers to defeat Martina Navratilova in the U.S. Open final, 7–6, 1–6, 7–6.

1991

Brigham Young quarterback Ty Detmer became the NCAA career passing leader with 11,606 yards, but the Cougars dropped a 27–23 decision to UCLA.

1992

Fay Vincent, after receiving a no-confidence vote from the league owners, resigned as baseball commissioner.

SEPTEMBER 8

A STAR IS BORN

1907: Buck Leonard, a Hall of Fame first baseman and one of the great stars of the old Negro Leagues from 1934–50.

★★★

1956: Maurice Cheeks, a current National Basketball Association guard.

★★★

MILESTONES IN SPORTS

1939

Bob Feller, Cleveland's 20-year-old fireballer, became the youngest modern-era 20-game winner when he pitched the Indians to a 12–1 victory over the St. Louis Browns.

1965

In a promotion dreamed up by Charles O. Finley, Kansas City shortstop Bert Campaneris became the first player in modern baseball history to play all nine positions in one game – a 13-inning 5–3 loss to California. Campaneris had to leave the game in the ninth inning after a collision at home plate while he was playing catcher.

1990

Brigham Young quarterback Ty Detmer passed for 406 yards and three touchdowns to lead the Cougars to a 28–21 upset victory over No. 1-ranked Miami at Provo, Utah.

1990

Gabriela Sabatini pulled off a 6–2, 7–6 upset of Steffi Graf in the U.S. Open final at Flushing Meadow, N.Y.

Rocket Rod Laver, *tennis' double grand slammer.*

1969 LAVER EARNS SECOND SLAM

Rod Laver, 31 years old and no longer able to rely on his rocket serve, out-finessed and out-hustled his younger opponent in the final of the U.S. Open championship, becoming the first player ever to achieve two tennis grand slams.

Laver's 7–9, 6–1, 6–2, 6–2 victory over fellow Australian Tony Roche was the perfect conclusion to a season that already had produced Wimbledon, Australian and French championships – the other three legs of the tennis grand slam. He matched his own grand slam performance of 1962 and the 1938 accomplishment of Don Budge. Maureen Connolly (1953) is the only woman to win all four majors in the same year.

In Roche, Laver was facing a 24-year-old who had defeated him in five of seven matches. And true to form, Roche came out firing on all cylinders and captured a first-set tie-breaker that would have disheartened many opponents.

But Laver was not about to let his slam slip away. He took control in a quick-and-easy second set, waited out a 30-minute rain delay and then coasted through the third and fourth sets to claim the $16,000 first prize – and his singular place in the history books.

1988 OWNERS PICK BART GIAMATTI

Baseball's 26 owners, who seldom are able to agree on anything, banded together long enough to select National League President A . Bartlett Giamatti as the sport's new commissioner to succeed Peter V. Ueberroth.

Ueberroth had announced that he would not serve a second term as the high priest of baseball and the owners, impressed with Giamatti's law-and-order, no-nonsense style in dealing with tough N.L. problems, had little trouble picking him as successor to Ubberoth during a meeting in Montreal.

The 50-year-old Giamatti, a former professor of literature and president of Yale University, will begin his five-year term on April 1, six months before Ueberroth's five-year reign is scheduled to end. Ueberroth was brought in to straighten out baseball's financial difficulties and now the owners were looking for a more issue-oriented leader.

If Giamatti does have a deficiency, it's in the business area that Ueberroth strengthened during his tenure. Giamatti answered that criticism by saying he plans to hire a deputy commissioner with a strong business acumen to serve as his aide.

1957 GIBSON BEATS BROUGH

Althea Gibson, completing her breakthrough season, became the first black winner of the U.S. singles championship when she overwhelmed Louise Brough, 6-3, 6–2, at Forest Hills, N.Y.

Gibson, who earlier had become the first black Wimbledon champion and first black to represent the United States in the Wightman Cup, completed her historic journey without losing a set. The most games she surrendered in any set was four.

Brough, a four-time Wimbledon champion and one-time U.S. winner, was simply overpowered. Both players started slowly, cautiously probing the other for weaknesses. But after an error-filled five games, Gibson, trailing 2–3, suddenly began showing her superiority .

She won four straight games to close out the first set and then destroyed Brough with her powerful forehand in the second. Brough continued to make errors and Gibson cruised to victory.

Althea Gibson *shows off her U.S. singles trophy.*

A STAR IS BORN

1877: Frank Chance, a Hall of Fame first baseman and long-time player-manager of the Chicago Cubs. He was part of the Cubs' legendary Tinker-to-Evers-to-Chance infield.

★ ★ ★

1898: Frank Frisch, a Hall of Fame infielder and manager who batted .316 over his 19-year major league career.

★ ★ ★

1899: Waite Hoyt, a Hall of Fame pitcher who won 237 games over his 21-year major league career.

★ ★ ★

1949: Joe Theismann, a former National Football League quarterback who played his college football at Notre Dame.

★ ★ ★

1954: Walter Davis, a former National Basketball Association guard.

★ ★ ★

1964: Brett Hull, a current National Hockey League right winger.

★ ★ ★

DEATH OF A LEGEND

1915: Al Spalding (baseball).

★ ★ ★

1970: Cy Denneny (hockey).

★ ★ ★

1972 RUSSIANS STUN U.S.

American basketball players sit dejectedly on the bench after losing a controversial championship game to the Soviet Union.

In a bizarre and chaotic conclusion to the gold medal basketball game, the Soviet Union snapped the 63-game Olympic winning streak of the United States with a 51–50 victory that touched off international controversy.

The controversy surrounded the final seconds of the championship contest in the Summer Games at Munich, West Germany. The Russians, given a second chance on an inbounds play after the Americans apparently had won, threw a full-court pass that resulted in a last-second basket – and the first American basketball loss in Olympic history.

The result, officially protested by irate U.S. Coach Hank Iba, was nothing short of incredible. The game, which started at 11:30 p.m. Munich time because of television considerations, was controlled most of the way by the Russians. They carried a five-point lead into halftime and owned a 10-point advantage (38–28) with 10 minutes remaining. They still led by eight with 6:07 left when the U.S. made its move.

A full-court American press began forcing turnovers and Kevin Joyce hit a pair of baskets that cut the Soviet lead to 44–42. The Russians managed to carry a one-point lead into the final moments, but Doug Collins picked up a loose ball with six seconds remaining and drove for what could have been a go-ahead basket. He was fouled and calmly sank both free throws.

This is where the fun began. On Collins' second free throw, the horn sounded just as he was releasing the ball – for no apparent reason. But the shot went in and the Russians hurriedly inbounded the ball, which was deflected away as the clock ran out. The American players began jumping excitedly, thinking they had won.

But their mood changed quickly. Robert Jones, secretary-general of the International Amateur Basketball Federation, ruled courtside that the Soviets would get another chance with the clock reset to three seconds. Jones apparently believed the Soviets should have been granted a timeout before their first inbounds pass. Iba stomped and snorted, but the decision stood.

This time the desperation throw-in traveled the length of the court, toward 6-foot-8 Aleksander Belov. The burly Russian bulled over defenders Joyce and James Forbes, grabbed the ball and laid it in the basket as pandemonium broke loose.

1968 ASHE CAPTURES FIRST 'OPEN'

Arthur Ashe, a 25-year-old Army lieutenant, held off the stiff five-set challenge of Dutchman Tom Okker and recorded a number of firsts while winning the U.S. singles championship at Forest Hills, N.Y.

Ashe is the first black winner in the long history of the event, the first winner of the U.S. championship as an "open" tournament and the classic's first American winner since 1955. As an amateur, Ashe had to turn down the $14,000 first prize, the richest ever in tennis history.

The bespectacled Ashe needed 2 hours, 40 minutes to win his 25th consecutive singles match. The determined Okker gave him everything he could handle in a 14–12, 5–7, 6–3, 3–6, 6–3 thriller that was played at the West Side Tennis Club.

Ashe used a scorching serve that produced 26 aces, he changed pace consistently and he threw lots of clever lobs at his opponent. Okker countered with a tenaciousness that pushed Ashe into an extended first-set tie-breaker and carried through to the final set before Ashe took control with a second-game service break.

The match might have been decided in the 64-minute first set that seemed to set the tone for the rest of the match. Every time Okker would fire his best shot and seemingly gain the advantage, Ashe would have the answer. Ashe survived the set by scoring 15 aces.

SEPTEMBER 9

MILESTONES · IN SPORTS ·

1960

Denver Broncos 13, Boston Patriots 10 in the first AFL regular-season game before 21,597 fans at Boston.

1971

Gordie Howe retired after playing 25 seasons with the Detroit Red Wings and scoring an NHL career-record 786 goals.

1970

Denny McLain, who won 31 games for Detroit in 1968, was suspended for the third time this season by Commissioner Bowie Kuhn, allegedly for carrying a gun.

1974

Jimmy Connors captured his first U.S. Open championship when he defeated Australian Ken Rosewall in straight sets.

1979

Two young lions claimed their first U.S. Open titles – John McEnroe with a victory over Vitas Gerulaitis and Tracy Austin with a surprise win over Chris Evert Lloyd.

1989

West German Steffi Graf claimed her seventh major title in two years when she beat Martina Navratilova, 3–6, 6–4, 6–2, in the U.S. Open final.

1992

Milwaukee's Robin Yount became baseball's 17th 3,000-hit man when he singled on a seventh-inning pitch from Cleveland's Jose Mesa during a 5–4 loss at Milwaukee's County Stadium.

SEPTEMBER

10

MILESTONES
• IN SPORTS •

1926

The powerful combination of Bill Tilden and Bill Johnston was too much for the French as the United States captured its seventh straight Davis Cup with a 4–1 victory at Philadelphia.

1967

Lefthander Billie Jean King captured her first U.S. singles championship and ended a six-year drought for American women when she defeated Ann Haydon Jones, 11–9, 6–4, at Forest Hills, N.Y.

1971

Billie Jean King ended the fairy tale run of 16-year-old Chris Evert when she recorded a straight-set victory in the semifinal round of the U.S. Open.

1978

The New York Yankees, closing in on first-place Boston in the A.L. East, concluded their "Boston Massacre" weekend in which they outscored the Red Sox, 42–9, and outhit them, 67–21, in four games at Fenway Park.

1983

Another first-time U.S. Open winner: Martina Navratilova defeated Chris Evert Lloyd, 6–1, 6–3.

1992

An all-woman jury in Minneapolis ruled in favor of the players in the "Freeman McNeil" antitrust suit, declaring professional football's Plan B free agency system too restrictive.

1988 GRAF SLAMS SABATINI

Steffi Graf, dominating the women's tour with her intimidating forehand, became the fifth player to complete a grand slam when she defeated Gabriela Sabatini, 6–3, 3–6, 6–1, in the U.S. Open final at the National Tennis Center.

Graf joined Maureen Connolly and Margaret Court as the only women to win the Wimbledon, Australian, French and U.S. championships in the same year. Don Budge was the first man to accomplish the feat and Australian Rod Laver did it twice. But Graf's 60th victory in 62 matches was not easy.

The 19-year-old broke her 18-year-old opponent's service twice to take the first set, but Sabatini fought back with breaks of her own in the fourth and eighth games of the second.

With her powerful forehand in top form in the deciding set, Graf broke Sabatini at love in the second game and broke again in the sixth on a double-fault. The West German produced her slam-clinching point on a backhand that almost took the racket out of Sabatini's hand.

Dominating **Steffi Graf** *completed her grand slam with a victory over Gabriela Sabatini in the U.S. Open.*

1974 BROCK RUNS TO RECORD

Baseball crowned its second basestealing king in 12 years when St. Louis speedster Lou Brock swiped his 104th and 105th bases in a game against Philadelphia and erased the one-season record of former Los Angeles shortstop Maury Wills.

Brock, the Cardinals' 35-year-old outfielder, tied the record in the first inning when he singled off Phillies starter Dick Ruthven and quickly took off, delighting the 27,285 Redbird fans at Busch Stadium. He slid safely under Bob Boone's throw.

With the crowd chanting, "Lou, Lou, Lou" in the seventh, Brock singled again and Ruthven made two throws to first. Brock set sail on his second pitch and again beat Boone's throw, sparking a wild mob scene around second base as players from both teams rushed to congratulate him.

Brock's first steal gave him 740 for his career, one more than Max Carey, the former all-time National League leader. Lost in the confusion was the 8–2 Phillies victory

1962 LAVER MAKES HISTORY

Rod Laver, the lefthanded Rocket from Australia, used a big serve and outstanding ground strokes to overpower fellow countryman Roy Emerson in the final of the U.S. championships, completing the first men's tennis grand slam in 24 years.

Laver, already winner of the Wimbledon, Australian and French championships, defeated Emerson, 6–2, 6–4, 5–7, 6–4, at Forest Hills, N.Y. The only other men's slam had been earned by Don Budge in 1938, the year Laver was born.

Laver, having early problems with his vaunted first service, chipped and stroked his way to easy victories in the first two sets. He was ruthless at the net and his overhead was devastating.

But Laver seemed to tire in the third set and Emerson took his cue. With the crowd cheering him on, Emerson broke service in the eighth game and won with two good backhands in the 12th. It was only the second set Laver had lost in the tournament.

Regaining his momentum with a service break in the fifth game of the finale, Laver quickly closed out the man who had conquered him in the U.S. singles final the previous year.

A STAR IS BORN

1929: Arnold Palmer, one of the world's outstanding golfers during a career that produced four Masters titles, two British Opens, one U.S. Open and one U.S. Amateur.

★ ★ ★

1934: Roger Maris, the former New York Yankee star outfielder who broke Babe Ruth's one-season home run record when he blasted 61 in 1961.

★ ★ ★

1940: Buck Buchanan, a football Hall of Fame defensive end who played his entire 13-year NFL career (1963–75) for the Kansas City Chiefs.

★ ★ ★

1948: Bob Lanier, a former NBA center who scored 19,248 points in his 14-year career.

★ ★ ★

1963: Randy Johnson, a current major league pitcher.

★ ★ ★

1966: Joe Nieuwendyk, a current National Hockey League center.

★ ★ ★

MILESTONES
• IN SPORTS •

1946

The Brooklyn Dodgers and Cincinnati Reds battled to the longest scoreless tie in baseball history in a game at Ebbets Field.

1956

Cincinnati's Frank Robinson tied Wally Berger's major league rookie record when he belted home run No. 38 in an 11–5 victory over New York.

1966

Brazilian star Maria Bueno captured her fourth U.S. singles championship with a 6–3, 6–1 victory over Nancy Richey.

1976

After a 12-year retirement, Minnie Minoso went 0 for 3 for Chicago in a game against California, making him a four-decade major leaguer.

1991

Atlanta hurlers Kent Mercker, Mark Wohlers and Alejandro Pena pitched the first combined no-hitter in National League history, beating the San Diego Padres, 1–0.

A STAR IS BORN

1913: Paul (Bear) Bryant, the legendary Alabama college football coach who compiled the most victories (323) in Division I-A competition.

★ ★ ★

1924: Tom Landry, the original Dallas Cowboys coach. He led the team to 271 victories (1960–88) and two Super Bowl championships.

★ ★ ★

1958: Don Slaught, a current major league catcher.

★ ★ ★

1964: Ellis Burks, a current major league outfielder.

★ ★ ★

SEPTEMBER

11

1985 ROSE BREAKS HIT RECORD

Jubilant Cincinnati teammates and son Petey mob **Pete Rose** *after record-breaking hit No. 4,192.*

Cincinnati player-manager Pete Rose, culminating a career-long dream and covering himself with a cloak of immortality, slashed a pitch from San Diego's Eric Show into left-center field and became baseball's all-time hit leader.

Rose's record-breaking hit No. 4,192 came on a 2–1 pitch before a capacity crowd at Riverfront Stadium and a national television audience. It ended his long chase of Ty Cobb's record, a mark many thought would stand forever.

The entire scenario was vintage Rose. Basking in the spotlight that he has craved throughout his career, the 44-year-old star drove his record-breaker over the infield and rounded first base with his usual gusto. As he paused and retreated back to the bag, flashing cameras turned the stadium into a dazzling light show and pandemonium broke loose.

Leading the charge of players from the dugout was Rose's 15-year-old son Petey, and ceremonies followed in which Rose was congratulated and presented with a new red Corvette by the Marge Schott, the owner of the reds.

Then, suddenly, Rose was left alone, fighting back tears as a monstrous ovation rocked the stadium. When the game finally resumed, Rose scored both of the Reds runs in a 2–0 victory and added a triple to his 23-year hit total.

1955 TONY'S TENNIS TRIPLE

American Tony Trabert, completing the best one-season performance since Don Budge captured his tennis grand slam in 1938, beat Australian Ken Rosewall in the final of the U.S. championships and walked away with his third major title of the year.

Trabert, who earlier had won the French and Wimbledon championships, cruised past Rosewall, 9–7, 6–3, 6–3, in a short-but-sweet final at the West Side Tennis Club in Forest Hills, N.Y. After fighting off Rosewall in a first-set tie-breaker, Trabert was in command.

The victory also was sweet revenge for the recent humiliation suffered by the American Davis Cup team against the Australians. Rosewall and Lewis Hoad played major roles in the Australian sweep and Trabert recorded straight-set victories over both en route to his U.S. title.

In addition to his victories in the three majors, Trabert has also won the National Clay Courts tournament.

1959 FACE FINALLY LOSES

The Los Angeles Dodgers scored a pair of ninth-inning runs for a 5–4 victory over Pittsburgh, removing all doubt that Pirates reliever Elroy Face is mortal.

That had not appeared to be the case over a 98-game span dating back to May 30, 1958. Face had recorded 22 consecutive victories, including 17 in a row this season. He needed only two more to tie the one-year record of former New York Giant Rube Marquard.

But the Dodgers, playing in the first game of a doubleheader before their home fans at the Los Angeles Coliseum, took care of that.

Face entered the game in the eighth inning with Pittsburgh leading, 4–3, and a man on first. He pitched out of that jam but quickly got into trouble in the ninth when Maury Wills singled and Jim Gilliam tripled to tie the game. Charlie Neal produced the winner with a single.

Face's 22 straight wins also were two short of the two-season record set by Carl Hubbell, another Giants pitcher, in 1936 and '37.

Pittsburgh Manager **Danny Murtaugh** *with 'fireman'* **Elroy Face.**

SEPTEMBER

12

1951 SUGAR RAY'S SWEET REVENGE

Sugar Ray Robinson, seeking revenge for the worst beating of his career, scored a 10th-round technical knockout over British middleweight Randy Turpin and reclaimed the crown he had lost last in July in London.

Looking like the Sugar Ray of old before 61,370 doting fans at New York's Polo Grounds, Robinson worked over his opponent with the same quick jabs and lightning combinations he used to build his reputation as the "best fighter pound for pound" in the world.

Robinson was well ahead on points by the 10th round, but he suddenly caught Turpin with a right to the jaw that sent him spinning to the canvas. Turpin struggled to his feet at the count of nine and Robinson unleashed a vicious attack that rendered the champion helpless.

No longer able to defend himself, Turpin was saved by the referee, who stepped in with eight seconds remaining in the round.

Victory was sweet for Robinson, who had been battered by Turpin during their first match. So was the record purse, 30 percent of which went to Robinson. The fight set middleweight division records for both attendance and receipts.

1981 AUSTIN WINS SECOND OPEN

Tracy Austin, dominated and overwhelmed in a quick-and-easy first set, rebounded to claim her second U.S. Open championship with a shocking 1–6, 7–6, 7–6 victory over Martina Navratilova.

Two-time U.S. Open champion **Tracy Austin.**

The 18-year-old Austin, the youngest U.S. Open winner ever two years ago when she defeated Chris Evert Lloyd, became the first player in the long history of the event to win the title on a final-set tie-breaker. She treated the 18,892 fans at the National Tennis Center to one of the most exciting finishes in years while denying Navratilova her first U.S. championship.

It did not appear excitement was in the cards when Navratilova stormed through the first set with a devastating combination of overheads, volleys, drop shots and ground strokes, sweeping the first five games and making it look very much like a mismatch.

But Martina's momentum did not carry over. Austin, as has been her style, dug in and fought back and the two players were virtually even the rest of the way. The difference was the two tie-breakers, which Austin won, 7–4 and 7–1.

Austin could have avoided the second, squandering three 12th-game match points. But she regained her composure and stormed to a 6–1 tie-breaker advantage before winning on a double fault.

1962 CHENEY MAKES MARK

Washington righthander Tom Cheney, forced to work a little overtime in his battle against the Baltimore Orioles, turned his extra effort into a major league record that could stand for many years.

Cheney struck out 21 Orioles in the 16-inning contest at Baltimore's Memorial Stadium, the most ever for a game of any duration. His record-setting performance also was a victory, thanks to a solo home run by Bud Zipfel that broke a 1–1 tie.

Cheney did not appear to be on course for anything out of the normal when he finished the regulation nine innings with 13 strikeouts. But as the game dragged on, his strikeout totals mounted – two in the 10th, two in the 11th, two more in the 14th.

When the 19th Oriole went down, Cheney owned the modern major league record. When he got No. 20 in the 15th, he shattered the all-time mark. His final strikeout came in the bottom of the 16th after the Senators had taken their 2–1 lead.

Former Cleveland fireballer Bob Feller and Los Angeles Dodger lefty Sandy Koufax share the modern nine-inning record of 18 strikeouts.

Tom Cheney *worked overtime to get his record.*

MILESTONES IN SPORTS

1947

Pittsburgh slugger Ralph Kiner continued his amazing home run streak in a victory over Boston, blasting Nos. 48 and 49 and raising his record four-game total to eight.

1951

The St. Louis Cardinals played the first two-opponent major league doubleheader of the century, beating the New York Giants, 6–4, and losing to the Boston Braves, 2–0.

1976

Going 1 for 3 as a designated hitter for the Chicago White Sox, 53-year-old Minnie Minoso became the oldest player to get a hit in a regulation major league game.

1979

Boston slugger Carl Yastrzemski opened a new club when he became the first A.L. player to get 3,000 career hits and 400 home runs. Hit No. 3,000 was a single off New York's Jim Beattie in a 9–2 Red Sox victory.

1992

Monica Seles won her sixth grand slam title in two years with a straight-set victory over Arantxa Sanchez Vicario in the U. S. Open final.

A STAR IS BORN

1913: Jesse Owens, the track and field star who earned four gold medals at the 1936 Berlin Olympic Games.

★ ★ ★

1940: Mickey Lolich, the Detroit lefthander best remembered for his three victories in the Tigers' 1968 World Series conquest of St. Louis.

★ ★ ★

1959: Deron Cherry, a former National Football League defensive back.

★ ★ ★

1981 LEONARD RALLIES TO DEFEAT HEARNS

Sugar Ray Leonard, down but not quite out in his title fight against Thomas (Hit Man) Hearns, pulled off a shocking rally that resulted in a 14th-round technical knockout and gave him control of both factions of the welterweight division.

Thomas Hearns *holds onto the ropes after a series of* **Sugar Ray Leonard** *punches sent him down in the 13th round of their welterweight championship fight.*

Leonard, his eye almost swollen shut and apparently on his last legs against a younger and fresher Hearns, suddenly caught his opponent with a right cross in the 13th round. The shot staggered Hearns and Leonard followed with a flurry of punches that knocked him to his knees. Hearns went down again later in the round, but made it to the bell with victory hopes still alive.

But Leonard wasn't about to let go of his newfound momentum. He charged in quickly with three lefts to open the 14th round and stalked the dazed Hearns around the ring the rest of the way. The fight was stopped at 1:45.

The stunning rally by the popular Leonard delighted the large Las Vegas crowd. The loss was Hearns' first in 33 fights while Leonard won for the 31st time in 32 bouts. But more importantly, the victory gave Leonard control of both the WBC and WBA welterweight crowns, making him the first common division champion since Roberto Duran won the lightweight championship in 1978.

1970 COURT EARNS SLAM

Margaret Court, matching the feat performed by Maureen Connolly 17 years earlier, swept past Rosemary Casals in the final of the U.S. Open tennis championship and completed the second women's grand slam.

Court's 6–2, 2–6, 6–1 victory at Forest Hills, N.Y., capped a brilliant season that included triumphs in the Wimbledon, Australian and French championships, the other three legs of tennis' Big Four. Court had won three of the four on three different occasions.

The talented 5-foot-9 Australian coasted through the first set against her 21-year-old opponent as expected, but Casals fought back in the second, becoming the first U.S. Open player to win a set from her in two years.

Court broke Casals in the second and sixth games of the final set and concentrated her attack on her backhand volley, forcing numerous errors.

Besides Connolly, who performed her feat as an amateur in 1953, Court joined two men in the elite grand slam club – Don Budge (1938) and fellow Australian Rod Laver (1962 and 1969).

1989 DAY'S DAY: 8 WINNERS IN 9 ARLINGTON RACES

Jockey Pat Day, working a sloppy track on a gloomy Chicago day, rode eight winners in nine mounts on the program at Arlington International Race Course – the most remarkable one-day performance in horse racing history.

Day's 8-for-9 effort was the best percentage day ever for a rider at a North American track, topping the 8-for-10 efforts of Dave Gall (1978), R.D. Williams (1984) and Chris Loseth (1984).

Chris Antley rode a total of nine winners in 1987, but they came on 14 mounts in day and night programs at two different tracks.

Day's only loss came in the third race when he finished a close second on Wayne's By George, $1^1/_4$ lengths behind Speed Tells, the fans' betting favorite.

Day's eight first-place finishers won by a total of 37 lengths and only two of the horses were the betting favorites.

"I'm still in a little bit of a shock," Day said after his day's work. "The reality of what I've done hasn't quite sunk in. Something like this you can't ever put into words."

SEPTEMBER 13

A STAR IS BORN

1897: Eddie Rommel, a righthanded pitcher for the Philadelphia Athletics powerhouses of the 1920s and '30s and a 171-game winner in his 13-year career.

★ ★ ★

1926: Rick Wise, a righthanded pitcher who won 188 games in his 18-year major league career.

★ ★ ★

MILESTONES IN SPORTS

1936

Bob Feller, Cleveland's 17-year-old flamethrower, tied the major league record for strikeouts in a game when he fanned 17 Philadelphia batters in a two-hit, 5–2 victory.

1965

A 500-homer man: San Francisco's Willie Mays connected off Houston's Don Nottebart in a 5–1 victory.

1971

Another 500-homer man: Frank Robinson's victim was Detroit pitcher Fred Scherman in a 10–5 loss at Baltimore.

1989

The baseball owners, meeting in Milwaukee, made Fay Vincent the unanimous choice to succeed A. Bartlett Giamatti as commissioner.

1992

Stefan Edberg earned his second straight U.S. Open championship with a four-set victory over Pete Sampras.

SEPTEMBER

14

A STAR IS BORN

1869: Kid Nichols, a Hall of Fame pitcher from the turn of the century. He won 361 games in a 15-year career.

★ ★ ★

1924: Jerry Coleman, a second baseman on the New York Yankee powerhouse teams of the 1950s and later a baseball announcer.

★ ★ ★

1940: Larry Brown, a former college championship coach and a current coach in the National Basketball Association.

★ ★ ★

1957: Tim Wallach, a current major league third baseman.

★ ★ ★

1965: Troy Neel, a current major league outfielder and designated hitter.

★ ★ ★

1968 McLain's 30th Win

Detroit righthander Denny McLain completed his impossible journey to the prestigious 30-win plateau when his Tiger teammates rallied for two ninth-inning runs and edged the Oakland Athletics, 5–4, in a dramatic contest at Tiger Stadium.

The old and the new: **Dizzy Dean**, *a 30-game winner in 1934, with Detroit's* **Denny McLain**, *the first man to reach the plateau since.*

McLain, who allowed a pair of Reggie Jackson home runs and struck out 10 in his bid to duplicate the feat last achieved 34 years ago by St. Louis' Dizzy Dean, no longer had control of his own destiny when he went to the dugout for the bottom of the ninth. The A's held a 4–3 advantage and McLain, scheduled to bat in the inning, would give way to a pinch-hitter. It was now or never.

No problem. Al Kaline batted for McLain and drew a leadoff walk. One out later, Mickey Stanley singled Kaline to third. Jim Northrup's grounder to first base was handled by Danny Cater, but his throw to the plate was off target and Kaline scored to tie the game. Willie Horton then lined a drive over a drawn-in outfield to score Stanley and win the game.

A wild celebration ensued as McLain and his Tiger teammates rushed out of the dugout. The victory lifted McLain to 30–5 and made him the first American League pitcher to win 30 games since Philadelphia's Lefty Grove turned the trick (31–4) in 1931.

MILESTONES IN SPORTS

1923

Jack Dempsey continued his reign of terror over the heavyweight division with a second-round knockout of Luis Firpo in a title bout at New York.

1923

Boston first baseman George Burns joined an exclusive club when he pulled off an unassisted triple play against the Cleveland Indians.

1947

Jack Kramer recovered from a two-set deficit and defeated Frank Parker in a Forest Hills thriller, giving him his second straight U.S. singles championship.

1987

The Toronto Blue Jays, led by three Ernie Whitt home runs, muscled up to hit a major league-record 10 during an 18–3 victory over Baltimore.

1990

A major league first: The Griffeys, 20-year-old son Ken Jr. and 40-year-old father Ken Sr., hit back-to-back home runs in the first inning of Seattle's 7–5 loss to California.

1991

Fifteen-year-old Kim Zmeskal became the first American woman to win the all-around gold medal at the world gymnastics championship.

1951 Nieman Debut Is Spectacular

St. Louis rookie Bob Nieman made the most spectacular debut in baseball history, but the Browns could not stand prosperity and dropped a 9–6 decision to the Boston Red Sox.

With Fenway Park's "Green Monster" left-field wall beckoning to the 24-year-old, Nieman obliged and sent a Mickey McDermott second-inning pitch out of the park for a two-run homer – on his first major league swing. An inning later, again with a teammate on base, Nieman took his second swing and blasted another McDermott pitch over` the wall.

It was the first time any player had homered in his first two at-bats and he added a bunt single in the ninth inning to cap a 3-for-5 performance. Despite the rookie's outburst, Boston persevered behind the home run hitting of Walt Dropo, Ted Williams and Dom DiMaggio.

Nieman was leading the Class-AA Texas League in hitting when his contract was purchased.

1991 Faulk Runs Wild

San Diego State record-setter **Marshall Faulk.**

Marshall Faulk, a freshman playing in his second collegiate game, set an NCAA single-game rushing record when he bolted for 386 yards and seven touchdowns during San Diego State's 55–34 victory over Pacific.

Faulk's phenomenal performance bettered the record of 377 yards set by Indiana's Anthony Thompson in 1989 and fell one touchdown short of the NCAA record of eight scored by Illinois' Howard Griffith last year. In addition to his seven TDs, Faulk also ran for a two-point conversion, giving him 44 points – four short of Griffith's record.

The youngster broke just about every freshman rushing and scoring record possible. And he didn't even get his first carry until 10:05 into the game – when starter T.C. Wright suffered a thigh bruise.

But time was not a factor. He had 323 yards by the end of the third quarter, bettering the single-game freshman rushing record of 322. He scored on touchdown runs of 9, 5, 61, 7, 47, 2 and 25 yards.

Faulk's 386 yards were gained on 37 carries.

SEPTEMBER 15

A STAR IS BORN

1938: Gaylord Perry, a righthanded pitcher who won 314 games in his 22-year major league career.

★ ★ ★

1940: Merlin Olsen, a football Hall of Fame defensive tackle who went on to later fame as a broadcaster and actor.

★ ★ ★

1961: Dan Marino, a current National Football League quarterback.

★ ★ ★

DEATH OF A LEGEND

1924: Frank Chance (baseball).

★ ★ ★

1991: Smoky Burgess (baseball).

MILESTONES IN SPORTS

1912

Boston's Smokey Joe Wood pitched the Red Sox to a 2–1 victory over the St. Louis Browns, tying Walter Johnson's record of 16 straight wins.

1963

The three Alou brothers, Felipe, Matty and Jesus, played together in the same San Francisco outfield as the Giants posted a 13–5 victory over Pittsburgh.

1973

Secretariat roared to a world record-setting victory in the Marlboro Cup Invitational Handicap, finishing the 1 1/8-mile course in 1:45 2/5.

1985

JoAnne Carner, at 46 years, five months and nine days, became the oldest woman to win an LPGA championship when she captured the Safeco Classic by two shots.

1990

Chicago bullpen ace Bobby Thigpen became baseball's first 50-save reliever in a 7–4 victory over Boston.

1978 ALI AVENGES TITLE LOSS

Muhammad Ali, considerably more serious and businesslike than he was in his previous bout with Leon Spinks, dominated his 25-year-old opponent in every way possible and claimed the world heavyweight championship for a record third time.

Fighting before a large New Orleans crowd that chanted his name and roared every time he connected with a punch, Ali danced, jabbed and fended off Spinks with left hooks and sharp rights that kept him at arm's length. He was in total control of his young opponent and walked away from the ring with a unanimous 15-round decision.

Ali was helped by Spinks' lack of tenacity – something that was not lacking when the former Marine upset Ali in Las Vegas. In that February 15 shocker, Spinks stalked Ali relentlessly and slugged it out with the champion in a wild and desperate 15th round. This time the 36-year-old Ali was the one doing the stalking.

1969 CARLTON GETS 19 STRIKEOUTS

It appears the New York Mets, the one-time bumblers who lost 120 games in their first major league season eight years ago, are not about to let anything interfere with their march toward a first National League championship.

St. Louis lefthander Steve Carlton discovered that when he turned in the performance of his life against the Mets – and lost. Carlton struck out a major league-record 19 batters but surrendered a pair of two-run homers to Ron Swoboda and dropped a 4-3 decision at Busch Stadium.

The talented 24-year-old struck out the side in the first, second and fourth innings and entered the dramatic ninth with 16 strikeouts, two short of the big-league record shared by Sandy Koufax, Bob Feller and Don Wilson. He struck out pitcher Tug McGraw to open the inning, got Bud Harrelson to tie and finished on a high note, getting rookie Amos Otis for the fourth time.

But as overpowering as Carlton was, he couldn't handle Swoboda – and that cost him. The Mets right fielder hit his two-run shots in the fourth and eighth-innings, wiping out one-run deficits on both occasions and helping the Mets raise their league-leading margin to 4 1/2 games over Chicago.

Carlton, whose record dropped to 16–10, faced 38 batters, allowed nine hits and walked two in his amazing performance.

1971 KING, SMITH WIN

Stan Smith and Billie Jean King returned to the winner's circle at Forest Hills and New York tennis fans cheered the first American sweep of the U.S. Open championship in 16 years.

The second-seeded Smith, taking time out from his two-year Army hitch, put down the challenge of unseeded Czechoslovakian Jan Kodes in a 3–6, 6–3, 6–2, 7–6 victory before a crowd of 12,879 at the West Side Tennis Club. The 6-foot-4 Smith, who had won the tournament as an amateur in 1969, used his power serve to keep Kodes off balance and struck numerous winners off Kodes' serves.

Smith put Kodes away in the fourth-set tie-breaker when he recovered from a 1–3 deficit.

King, a three-time Wimbledon winner who captured her first U.S. title in 1967, had little trouble beating Rosemary Casals, 6–4, 7–6, in the women's final. Casals took King into a second-set tie-breaker, but Billie Jean won that, 5–2, and easily closed out her victory.

U.S. Open champion **Stan Smith,** *one half of an American sweep.*

SEPTEMBER

16

A STAR IS BORN

1934: Elgin Baylor, a basketball Hall of Fame forward who scored 23,149 career points for the National Basketball Association's Minneapolis and Los Angeles Lakers.

★ ★ ★

1955: Robin Yount, a former major league shortstop and outfielder who retired in 1994 after becoming a member of baseball's 3,000-hit club.

★ ★ ★

1958: Orel Hershiser, a current major league pitcher.

★ ★ ★

DEATH OF A LEGEND

1951: Bill Klem (baseball).

★ ★ ★

1974: Phog Allen (basketball).

★ ★ ★

1924 BOTTOMLEY DRIVES IN 12

The St. Louis Cardinals unleashed a one-man wrecking crew on Brooklyn and the result wasn't pretty – a 17–3 thrashing of the Dodgers before their home fans at Ebbets Field.

St Louis' **Jim Bottomley,** *a one-man wrecking crew.*

Most of the damage was done by first baseman Jim Bottomley, who collected six hits and drove in a one-game major league-record 12 runs. To call Bottomley a wrecking crew might be an understatement.

Bottomley singled home two first-inning runs, doubled home a second-inning run, blasted a fourth-inning grand slam, belted a two-run sixth-inning homer, singled home two more runs in the seventh and broke Wilbert Robinson's previous record of 11 RBIs with a ninth-inning single.

Bottomley's two home runs and the six RBIs they produced came off Brooklyn pitcher Art Decatur. Rube Ehrhardt and Tex Wilson surrendered two RBIs apiece and Jim Roberts and Bonnie Hollingsworth one each.

Robinson, who had set the previous record for Baltimore in 1892, watched Bottomley's explosion from a choice seat – as Dodger manager. Pitcher Willie Sherdel took advantage of the explosion and gained credit for the victory.

1975 HIT RECORD FALLS

Rennie Stennett, collecting a record-tying two hits in two different innings, became the first modern-era major leaguer to get seven hits in a nine-inning game when he keyed Pittsburgh's 22–0 romp over Chicago at Wrigley Field.

Stennett's incredible outburst tied the all-time record set by Baltimore's Wilbert Robinson in 1892 and it surpassed anything that had been seen in this century. The second baseman had four singles, two doubles and a triple to lead a 24-hit Pittsburgh charge that produced the most lopsided shutout in baseball history.

Stennett singled and doubled in the first inning, singled in the third, doubled and singled in the fifth, singled in the sixth and tripled in the eighth, at which point he gave way to a pinch-runner. He raised his average nine points and scored five runs.

Pittsburgh's **Rennie Stennett.**

1988 BROWNING HAS PERFECT FORM

It was as simple as 1–2–3. Cincinnati lefthander Tom Browning used that tried-and-true formula to perfection in his 1–0 victory over Los Angeles and pitched the 12th perfect game in baseball history.

Working before a small but excited crowd (16,591) at Cincinnati's Riverfront Stadium, Browning set down the Dodgers on 102 pitches and never went to a three-ball count on any batter. Just to show how masterful Browning was, he recorded first-pitch strikes on 22 of the 27 Dodgers he faced and struck out seven. He required nothing beyond routine defensive plays.

The Reds scored their only run on a sixth-inning throwing error. Rick Dempsey was retired on a fly ball to open the ninth, Steve Sax grounded out and pinch-hitter Tracy Woodson struck out.

The perfect game was the first in the major leagues since 1984, when California's Mike Witt retired all 27 Texas Rangers he faced on the final day of the season.

Browning's gem snapped a streak of six no-hit bids that were broken up in the ninth inning.

MILESTONES • IN SPORTS •

1926

Bill Tilden, fighting a knee injury, lost to Frenchman Henri Cochet, 6–8, 6–1, 6–3, 1–6, 8–6, in a quarterfinal match of the U.S. championship. The loss ended Tilden's six-year reign as U.S. singles king.

1927

Frenchman Rene Lacoste captured his second straight U.S. singles title with an 11–9, 6–3, 11–9 victory over Bill Tilden.

1950

In its first game as a member of the NFL, the four-time AAFC-champion Cleveland Browns whipped defending NFL champion Philadelphia, 35–10, at Philadelphia.

1959

Chicago became an official member of the NBA when the league expanded its membership to nine.

1960

Venerable Milwaukee lefthander Warren Spahn pitched his first career no-hitter, a 4–0 decision over Philadelphia, and became a 20-game winner for the 11th time.

1961

Young Jack Nicklaus captured his second U.S. Amateur golf title in three years, beating H. Dudley Wysong, 8 and 6.

1977

The Seattle Mariners, behind the pitching of Doc Medich, snapped Kansas City's 16-game winning streak, baseball's longest in 28 years.

1989

Raghib (Rocket) Ismail ran back two kickoffs for touchdowns and No. 2-ranked Notre Dame used them to defeat No. 1 Michigan, 24–19, in a classic battle at Ann Arbor, Mich.

A STAR IS BORN

1879: Rube Foster, a former player, manager, league president and founder of the Negro American and National leagues. He was the 10th Negro League player elected to the baseball Hall of Fame.

★ ★ ★

1927: George Blanda, a football Hall of Fame quarterback and placekicker for four AFL and NFL teams.

★ ★ ★

1934: Maureen Connolly, the first woman to win a tennis Grand Slam (1953). Little Mo's career ended prematurely the next year because of a horse riding accident.

★ ★ ★

1937: Orlando Cepeda, a National League MVP first baseman who collected 2,351 hits and 379 home runs in 17 major league seasons.

★ ★ ★

1960: Anthony Carter, a current National Football League wide receiver.

★ ★ ★

1960: John Franco, a current major league relief pitcher.

★ ★ ★

1922 SISLER STRETCHES HIT STREAK TO 41

St. Louis Browns' hit man **George Sisler** *(right) with New York Yankee great* **Babe Ruth.**

St. Louis Browns first baseman George Sisler drove a sixth-inning single to center field off Waite Hoyt, extending his hitting streak to a modern-record 41 straight games and keying a rally that led to a 5–1 victory over the New York Yankees.

Playing before 31,000 boisterous fans at New York's Polo Grounds, the Browns won their second straight game from the Yankees and pulled to within a half game of the American League leaders with 10 to play. Hub Pruett allowed five hits in his complete-game effort, but the big story of the day was the torrid Sisler.

Hitless in his first two at-bats, he belted a Hoyt pitch up the middle to supplant Ty Cobb's modern-record 40-game streak and pull within three of Willie Keeler's all-time mark. He came around to score on a Hank Severeid single as the Browns tallied three times to wipe out a 1–0 deficit.

Sisler started his streak July 27 against the Yankees' Joe Bush and, ironically, Bush ended it at 41 games September 18 when the New Yorkers handed the Browns a 3–2 defeat that severely damaged St. Louis' A.L. pennant hopes.

SEPTEMBER 17

MILESTONES IN SPORTS

1935

Former outfielder Len Koenecke, evidently despondent about being cut by the Brooklyn Dodgers, died during a brawl he started with the pilot and co-pilot aboard a charter plane headed for Buffalo, N.Y.

1954

Rocky Marciano defended his heavyweight championship with an eighth-round knockout of Ezzard Charles during a title fight at New York.

1967

Rookie John Gilliam returned the opening kickoff 94 yards for a touchdown, but the National Football League's expansion New Orleans Saints lost their first-ever regular-season game to the Los Angeles Rams, 27–13.

1988

Minnesota's Jeff Reardon became the first reliever to save 40 games in both leagues when the Twins beat Chicago, 3–1.

1990

Arbitrator George Nicolau awarded baseball players $102.5 million in damages after finding that the owners violated their collective bargaining agreement in 1987 and '88 by acting in collusion against free agents.

1992

Little League baseball stripped the Philippines of its 1992 World Series championship for use of ineligible players.

1984 JACKSON BLASTS 500TH

California's Reggie Jackson put the icing on his 18-year major league career when he belted a Bud Black pitch into the right-field seats at Anaheim Stadium for his 500th career home run.

Jackson's seventh-inning blow saved the day for 28,862 fans, who were watching the Kansas City Royals deliver a 10–1 beating to their Angels. When the 38-year-old veteran sent one of his patented towering drives out of the park, the crowd roared to life.

Jackson, who has played with Oakland, Baltimore, New York and California, became the 13th member of baseball's 500-home run club and the first newcomer since San Francisco slugger Willie McCovey joined in 1978. Jackson, alias Mr. October, is renowned for his post-season heroics, which include six American League Championship Series home runs and 10 in World Series play.

The loss dropped the Angels a game and a half behind the first-place Royals and a half game behind Minnesota.

1920 NFL FORMED

The American Professional Football Association, the product of 10 dreamers meeting in a Hupmobile showroom, was organized in Canton, O., with the announced goal of bringing order out of chaos.

The new circuit, the forerunner of the National Football League, was the brainchild of George Halas, coach and founder of the Decatur Staleys, and Ralph Hay, manager of the Canton Bulldogs. It was in Hay's automobile dealership that the team owners gathered, sitting on the running boards and fenders of cars while discussing their plans.

Joining Halas and Hay were representatives of the Akron Pros, Dayton Triangles, Cleveland Tigers, Rock Island Independents, Chicago Cardinals, Hammond Pros, Muncie Flyers and Rochester Jeffersons.

Each team was charged an admission fee of $100 and the legendary Jim Thorpe was named league president. It was decided the league would use the same playing rules as college football and everybody agreed not to tamper with players on the other teams' rosters.

SEPTEMBER

18

A STAR IS BORN

1925: Harvey Haddix, the 14-year major league pitcher who threw a 12-inning perfect game for Pittsburgh in 1959, only to lose to Milwaukee in the 13th.

★ ★ ★

1954: Dennis Johnson, a former National Basketball Association star who scored 15,535 points and handed out 5,499 assists in a 14-year career.

★ ★ ★

1950: Darryl Sittler, a 15-year National Hockey League center and a member of the NHL's 1,000-point club.

★ ★ ★

1956: Peter Stastny, a current National Hockey League center.

★ ★ ★

1959: Ryne Sandberg, a former major league second baseman.

★ ★ ★

1968 CONSECUTIVE NO-HITTERS

St. Louis righthander Ray Washburn, matching the performance of San Francisco's Gaylord Perry less than 24 hours earlier in the same ballpark, threw his first career no-hitter and beat the Giants, 2–0.

San Francisco's **Gaylord Perry** *after his no-hit feat.*

The back-to-back no-hitter feat at San Francisco's Candlestick Park was a baseball first. The 30-year-old Perry had worked his magic in a 1–0 victory over the Cardinals and Washburn was simply returning the favor.

Spotting his fastball and mixing in an outstanding slow curve and occasional slider, the veteran Washburn was in full control after pitching around two first-inning walks. He struck out Willie Mays and Dick Dietz to get out of that jam and then coasted the rest of the way without incident.

The 30-year-old veteran struck out eight and walked five in his 138-pitch masterpiece and got all the support he needed when Mike Shannon doubled home a seventh-inning run to break up a pitching duel against San Francisco's Bob Bolin.

Perry needed only 101 pitches and 100 minutes to outduel Bob Gibson in his first career no-hitter. Ron Hunt's first-inning homer accounted for the game's only run. Perry lifted his record to 15–14, Washburn to 13–7.

MILESTONES IN SPORTS

1939

Bobby Riggs and Alice Marble added U.S. singles championships to the Wimbledon titles they captured earlier in the year.

1963

A disappointing crowd of 1,752 showed up to see Philadelphia beat the New York Mets, 5–1, in the last game at the historic Polo Grounds.

1967

The United States yacht Intrepid beat the Australian yacht Dame Pattie in four straight races to successfully defend the America's Cup at Newport, R.I.

1977

In another four-straight victory over the Australians, the United States yacht Courageous, skippered by Ted Turner, held on to the America's Cup in action at Newport, R.I.

1984

The Detroit Tigers, becoming only the fourth team to lead from start to finish in a season, clinched the A.L. East Division championship with a 3–0 victory over Milwaukee.

1987

Detroit's Darrell Evans became the first 40-year-old to hit 30 home runs in a season when he connected in a game against Milwaukee.

1990

The International Olympic Committee selected Atlanta over Athens and four other cities to play host to the 1996 Summer Olympic Games.

1988 LARGENT BREAKS JOINER'S RECORD

Seattle wide receiver Steve Largent broke the National Football League record for career receiving yardage, but the moment was diminished by the Seahawks' 17–6 loss to San Diego at Jack Murphy Stadium.

Largent, competing in his 13th NFL campaign, moved past former San Diego star Charlie Joiner when he caught a 19-yard pass in the second quarter from quarterback Dave Krieg. That gave him 12,148 yards, two more than Joiner managed during his outstanding 18-year career. Ironically, Joiner, a Chargers coach, was watching Largent's historic performance from the press box.

Largent finished the day with four catches for 71 yards. But he did not have much effect on the outcome of a game the Chargers dominated from the opening kickoff. Gary Anderson rushed for 120 yards and linebacker Keith Browner returned an interception 55 yards for a touchdown as the Chargers defeated the Seahawks and snapped their losing streak at eight.

1966 UNITAS PASSES TITTLE

Baltimore QB **Johnny Unitas.**

Johnny Unitas completed the first phase of his Y.A. Tittle chase when he fired four touchdown passes to lead Baltimore to a come-from-behind 38–23 victory over the Minnesota Vikings.

Unitas passed Tittle on the National Football League's career touchdown list when he threw a 26-yard third-quarter strike to John Mackey, giving the Colts their first lead. The scoring toss gave him 213 for his 10-year career, one more than Tittle, and he added a four-yard TD pass to Tom Matte in the final quarter.

Baltimore needed Unitas' record-setting heroics as the Vikings thrilled 47,426 home fans by jumping to a 16–0 first-half lead. But Unitas threw an 83-yard bomb to Mackey in the second quarter and a four-yarder to Raymond Berry in the third before his record-setter to Mackey.

Unitas should pass Tittle on the career passing yardage charts later this season.

A STAR IS BORN

1922: Emil Zatopek, a Czechoslovakian distance runner who won an unprecedented Olympic triple (the 5,000-meter, 10,000-meter and marathon) at Helsinki in 1952.

★ ★ ★

1922: Willie Pep, a two-time world featherweight boxing champion who compiled a 230–11–1 career record in the 1940s and '50s.

★ ★ ★

1926: Duke Snider, a Hall of Fame outfielder who hit 407 career home runs, most of them with the Brooklyn and Los Angeles Dodgers from 1948–62.

★ ★ ★

1943: Joe Morgan, a Hall of Fame second baseman best remembered as the two-time MVP for Cincinnati's Big Red Machine of the mid–1970s.

★ ★ ★

1957: Dan Hampton, a former National Football League defensive tackle.

★ ★ ★

1962: Randy Myers, a current major league relief pitcher.

★ ★ ★

1967: Jim Abbott, a current major league pitcher.

★ ★ ★

1951 Owners Select Frick

Ford Frick, the long-time president of the National League and a man well-versed in the problems facing baseball, was elected as the sport's third commissioner, replacing A.B. Happy Chandler.

Frick finally received the support of the 12 major league owners during a marathon meeting in Chicago. He had battled Cincinnati General Manager Warren Giles through at least 50 ballots without either getting the required three-fourths majority.

When Giles took his name off the candidates list, Frick quickly was elected to a seven-year term. Frick follows first commissioner Kenesaw Mountain Landis, the former federal judge who died in office, and Chandler, a former governor of Kentucky and U.S. Senator who was forced to resign last December. Frick is a former teacher, sportswriter and radio commentator.

1925 Tilden Hex Continues

Big Bill Tilden, seemingly on the brink of losing the United States singles championship for the first time in six years, rallied to win a marathon second set and went on to claim a 4–6, 11–9, 6–3, 4–6, 6–3 victory over long-time whipping boy Bill Johnston.

Tilden, who had defeated Johnston four previous times for the U.S. title after losing to him in 1919, had his hands full this time. Johnston played spectacular tennis in capturing the first set and then took the world's greatest player to three set points in the second.

But Tilden, who seems to thrive when his back is against the wall, rallied to win the long tie-breaker, recovered from a third-set deficit and came back in the final set after Johnston had come back to win the fourth.

It was an exciting conclusion to the championship tournament at the West Side Tennis Club in Forest Hills, N.Y., and the 14,000 fans who expected an easy Tilden victory got their money's worth. Tilden, a two-time Wimbledon champion, had crushed Johnston in both the 1923 and '24 finals – his fourth and fifth straight U.S. victories.

Pittsburgh Pirates slugger **Ralph Kiner**, *the National League's first two-time 50-homer man.*

1959 A New Force In Golf

Jack Nicklaus, a talented 19-year-old junior at Ohio State University, became the second youngest winner in the long history of the U.S. Amateur golf championships when he dropped in an eight-foot birdie putt on the final hole.

The putt broke a tie with defending champion Charley Coe and gave Nicklaus a dramatic 1-up victory at the Broadmoor Golf Club in Colorado Springs. The golfers were even going into the par 4 36th hole and Nicklaus put his second shot eight feet from the pin. Coe , just off the fringe, chipped up short and the youngster sealed his first major victory with a dead-center putt.

The husky Nicklaus trailed Coe 2-up after the morning round, but recovered for an afternoon 69 that included a number of pressure shots. He took the lead for the first time on the 32nd hole and let Coe come back to tie on 35 before pulling out the victory.

Nicklaus, at 19 years, 8 months, was 3 months older than Robert A. Gardner when he won back in 1909.

September 19

Milestones in Sports

1949

Pittsburgh slugger Ralph Kiner became the first National League to hit 50 home runs in two different seasons.

1955

Chicago shortstop Ernie Banks blasted his record fifth grand slam of the season, but the Cubs dropped a 12-inning 6–5 decision to St. Louis.

1968

Mickey Mantle belted his 535th career home run, but he couldn't stop Detroit righthander Denny McLain from notching his 31st victory with a 6–2 decision over the Yankees.

1981

North Carolina back Kelvin Bryant rushed for four touchdowns and added another through the air as the Tar Heels rolled past outmanned Miami of Ohio, 49–7.

1985

Minnesota quarterback Tommy Kramer passed for 436 yards and three touchdowns in a 33–24 loss to the Chicago Bears.

1988

American diver Greg Louganis, a double gold winner in the 1984 Olympic Games, hit his head on the board during preliminary-round competition in the 3-meter springboard, seriously jeopardizing his chances for another two-gold medal performance in the Summer Games at Seoul, South Korea.

SEPTEMBER 20

MILESTONES IN SPORTS

1958

Baltimore knuckleballer Hoyt Wilhelm, making a rare start, pitched a 1–0 no-hitter against the New York Yankees.

1969

Sophomore quarterback John Reaves made his first collegiate game a memorable one, firing five touchdown passes in Florida's 59–34 victory over Houston.

1980

Kansas City's George Brett went 0 for 4 in a 9–0 loss to Oakland, dropping his average below .400 for the final time.

1992

Philadelphia second baseman Mickey Morandini turned the first unassisted triple play in the N.L. since 1927, but the Phillies dropped a 3–2 decision to Pittsburgh.

A STAR IS BORN

1917: Red Auerbach, the coach who guided the Boston Celtics to eight consecutive NBA titles and won more games (938) than anybody in league history. He currently is the Celtics' general manager.

★★★

1935: Jim Taylor, a football Hall of Fame fullback and star for the great Green Bay teams of the 1960s. He rushed for 8,597 yards in 10 seasons.

★★★

1951: Guy Lafleur, a dazzling hockey Hall of Fame center who scored 560 career goals and 1,353 points in 17 NHL seasons.

★★★

1973 BILLIE JEAN IS THE KING

Billie Jean King, a long-time standard-bearer for both tennis and equality, struck a major blow for women everywhere when she recorded a crushing victory over 55-year-old Bobby Riggs in the so-called "Battle of the Sexes" at Houston's Astrodome.

Bobby Riggs *and* **Billie Jean King***: Friendly enemies.*

Playing amid a circus atmosphere in a match that attracted 30,492 paying customers and worldwide attention, the 29-year-old King crushed the former men's champion, 6–4, 6–3, 6–3, in 2 hours, 4 minutes. The match was viewed by a national television audience and in 36 foreign countries via satellite.

The winner-take-all match was the brainchild of Riggs, the brash tennis hustler who goaded Margaret Court into a Mother's Day confrontation on national television and then proceeded to humiliate her, 6–2, 6–1. King, who at first had resisted Riggs' putdowns of women's tennis and his sexist remarks, took up the mantle after Court's embarrassing loss.

And after months of incredible publicity and buildup, it quickly became clear that this would be no ordinary tennis match. Spectators in the courtside seats, some paying as much as $100 per ticket, sipped champagne and were entertained by a brassy band and costumed characters from Astroworld. Banners, not usually seen at tennis matches, hung everywhere and fans were loud and vociferous – even before the first serve.

King, a five-time Wimbledon and three-time U.S. champion, entered the stadium on a gold litter held aloft by four muscular athletes. Riggs was pulled in on a gold-wheeled rickshaw by six models in tight outfits, affectionately dubbed "Bobby's Bosom Buddies."

Riggs presented King with a large candy sucker; King gave her tormentor a brown baby pig. It was all in fun – until play began. Then Billie Jean quickly became the tormentor. Using the serve-and-volley game that is most prominent in men's tennis, King got to everything Riggs hit and won 26 of her 34 first-set points with outright winners – shots Riggs never touched. As the match wore on, Riggs' game deteriorated and the outcome was never in doubt.

American gold medal diver **Greg Louganis.**

1988 STITCHED-UP LOUGANIS WINS

American Greg Louganis, showing no ill effects from a potentially serious accident in a preliminary round, came back to win the 3-meter springboard diving championship and became the first man ever to win the event in consecutive Olympic Games.

Louganis, sporting a small bandage on the crown of his head, was consistently spectacular in his 11 final-day dives as he held off China's Tan Liangde in the competition at Seoul, South Korea. The 27-year-old Louganis, who also had finished ahead of Tan in the 1984 Los Angeles Olympic Games, completed the competition with 730.80 points to Tan's 704.88.

The bandage was the result of a ninth dive gone awry in the previous day's preliminary. On a reverse $2^1/2$ somersault pike, Louganis hit his head on the board, creating a gash that required five stitches. He fought off nerves going into the second round and was leery before his ninth dive – the same one he had missed the day before.

"I was a little nervous going into the ninth," Louganis admitted later, but he executed flawlessly and coasted through his final two dives.

1934 Deans Put on Show

It was showtime at Ebbets Field and the St. Louis Dean brothers were doing most of the "showing" to the mesmerized Brooklyn Dodgers.

First, Dizzy Dean showed the Dodgers plenty of his vaunted fastball and recorded a 13–0 victory in the opener of a doubleheader. His three-hit shutout was his 27th win of the season and helped the Cardinals keep pace with the first-place New York Giants in the National League pennant race.

But that stellar performance by Ol' Diz was nothing compared to what brother Paul did in the nightcap. The younger Dean went out and pitched his first career no-hitter, allowing only one baserunner (a first-inning walk) and leading the Redbirds to a 3–0 victory.

The win was the 18th of the season for Paul, a rookie righthander. When he had retired Ralph Boyle on a ground ball to end his masterpiece, excited Dodger fans stormed out onto the field to help him celebrate.

The three hits were the fewest ever managed by one team in a doubleheader. But Dizzy said, only half-jokingly, that he and Paul could have done better. "If 'n Paul had told me he was gonna pitch a no-hitter, I'd of throwed one, too," he said.

St. Louis' Dean brothers, **Dizzy** *(left) and* **Paul,** *were the centers of attention as the Cardinals drove to the 1934 pennant.*

A Star Is Born

1938: Doug Moe, who has won more than 600 games as a National Basketball Association coach.

★ ★ ★

1942: Sam McDowell, a lefthanded pitcher in the 1960s and '70s known as "Sudden Sam" because of his blazing fastball and strikeout ability.

★ ★ ★

1949: Artis Gilmore, a 7-foot-2 center who scored 24,041 points in his combined 17-year ABA-NBA career.

★ ★ ★

1957: Sidney Moncrief, a five-time NBA all-star guard who scored 11,931 points over his 11-year career.

★ ★ ★

1958: Rick Mahorn, a current National Basketball Association forward/center.

★ ★ ★

1959: Danny Cox, a current major league pitcher.

★ ★ ★

1963: Cecil Fielder, a current major league first baseman.

★ ★ ★

1985 Holmes' Reign Ends

Michael Spinks, the light heavyweight titleholder looking to move up in class, brought a shocking end to Larry Holmes' seven-year reign as heavyweight champion when he recorded a unanimous 15-round decision in a shocking title bout at Las Vegas.

It was a lackluster Holmes against a hungry Spinks and the result was clear-cut – Spinks claimed the title his brother (Leon) had held briefly in 1978 and Holmes missed in his bid to tie former heavyweight champion Rocky Marciano's record of 49 consecutive professional victories.

Spinks was not exactly dominant in his first heavyweight fight, but he was a lot closer than Holmes. The champion looked disinterested, fending the challenger off with weak jabs and seldom throwing his right.

Spinks never hurt Holmes, but he at least put together some good combinations.

The loss gave Holmes the distinction of becoming the first champion to be dethroned by a light heavyweight. And the loss came exactly 30 years to the day when Marciano recorded his record 49th straight win – against light heavyweight champion Archie Moore.

1955 Marciano Gets Past Moore

Rocky Marciano, surviving a second-round knockdown and a determined effort from challenger Archie Moore, successfully defended his heavyweight championship with a ninth-round knockout in a savagely-fought bout at New York's Yankee Stadium.

The unbeaten Marciano, who has won a record 49 consecutive fights, got all he could handle from the light heavyweight champion. Using his boxing skill and finesse to negate Marciano's punching power, the challenger shocked the crowd of 61,574 when he dropped the champion to his knees in the second round.

Dazed but not in serious trouble, Marciano survived the round and opened a relentless attack on Moore. The crowd gasped through a wild sixth round when both fighters forgot about boxing and slugged it out. When the bell sounded, both staggered to their corners, exhausted.

Marciano, making his sixth title defense of the crown he won three years earlier, dropped the 38-year-old Moore twice in that round, once in the eighth and for the final time in the ninth.

September 21

Milestones in Sports

1970

Keith Jackson, Howard Cosell and Don Meredith described the action as Cleveland defeated the New York Jets, 31–21, in the first of ABC-TV's Monday Night Football telecasts.

1971

Washington owner Bob Short received A.L. approval to move his financially troubled franchise to the Dallas-Fort Worth area, ending 71 years of continuous major league baseball in the nation's capital.

1980

New York quarterback Richard Todd completed an NFL-record 42 passes for 447 yards and three touchdowns, but the Jets still dropped a 37–27 decision to San Francisco.

1981

Philadelphia lefty Steve Carlton became the N.L.'s all-time top strikeout pitcher when he made Andre Dawson his 3,118th victim in a 1–0, 17-inning loss to the Montreal Expos.

1986

San Diego youngster Jimmy Jones fired a one-hit, 5–0 shutout at the Houston Astros in his major league debut.

1990

The U.S. Olympic "Dream Team" became a reality when 10 NBA stars were named to the elite squad: Charles Barkley, Larry Bird, Patrick Ewing, Magic Johnson, Michael Jordan, Karl Malone, Chris Mullin, Scottie Pippen, David Robinson and John Stockton.

SEPTEMBER

22

A STAR IS BORN

1889: Hooks Dauss, an early century major league pitcher who won 222 games in 15 seasons for Detroit.

★ ★ ★

1920: Bob Lemon, a Hall of Fame pitcher who won 207 games over a 13-year career in the 1940s and '50s and later managed in the major leagues.

★ ★ ★

1927: Tom Lasorda, the long-time manager of the Los Angeles Dodgers who has compiled more than 1,300 career victories.

★ ★ ★

1932: Ingemar Johansson, the Swedish boxer who beat Floyd Patterson for the world heavyweight championship in 1959 and lost it back to him the next year.

★ ★ ★

1942: David Stern, the current commissioner of the National Basketball Association.

★ ★ ★

1961: Vince Coleman, a current major league outfielder.

★ ★ ★

1927

LONG COUNT AIDS TUNNEY

Gene Tunney, making his first defense of the heavyweight championship he had won a year earlier from Jack Dempsey, retained his crown with a unanimous 10-round decision over Dempsey in what forever will be remembered as "the long-count fight."

With a fight-record crowd of 150,000 watching at Chicago's Soldier Field, the champion rallied from a controversial seventh-round knockdown to record a convincing victory. Dempsey claimed he was robbed of the championship by either the referee or the timekeeper – or both.

Dempsey was upset about a seventh round in which he stood on the brink of victory. Unfortunately for him, he also stood over the fallen Tunney too long, ignoring the attempts of referee Dave Barry to get him to a neutral corner.

When Dempsey finally realized the situation, he moved to the opposite corner and the count began. Tunney, given the benefit of an extra five or six seconds, began regaining his senses and struggled to his feet at the count of nine. He made it through the round and controlled the rest of the fight.

Dempsey's complaints were in vain. Under Illinois State Athletic Commission boxing rules, Barry handled the situation correctly.

Gene Tunney *is declared heavyweight champion as a sullen* **Jack Dempsey** *looks on.*

MILESTONES IN SPORTS

1911

Venerable Boston Braves pitcher Cy Young defeated Pittsburgh, 1–0, for his 511th – and final – major league victory.

1954

An outstanding major league debut: Brooklyn lefthander Karl Spooner struck out 15 New York Giants in a 3–0 shutout.

1968

Minnesota's Cesar Tovar, following the lead of Kansas City's Bert Campaneris three years earlier, played all nine positions for the Twins in a 2–1 victory over Oakland.

1974

The Pittsburgh Steelers and Denver Broncos played to a 35–35 tie – the first in the NFL since the overtime rule was adopted before the season.

1987

The National Football League Players Association began its 24-day work stoppage after the completion of the New York Jets' 43–24 Monday night victory over New England.

1991

Pat Bradley became the LPGA's first $4 million career winner when she captured the Safeco Classic in a playoff against Rosie Jones.

1991

Miami's 16–13 victory over Green Bay was the 300th win of Dolphins Coach Don Shula's illustrious career.

1969

MAYS HAS A BLAST

Willie Mays inched his way a little bit closer to baseball immortality when he drilled his 600th career home run in the San Francisco Giants' 4–2 victory over San Diego at Jack Murphy Stadium.

"Baseball immortality" can be defined in this case as former New York Yankee slugger Babe Ruth, the only previous player to reach the 600 plateau. Mays' milestone blast came in the seventh inning when he pinch-hit for Giants rookie George Foster and blasted a two-run shot over the left-center field fence off Mike Corkins, breaking a 2–2 tie.

Mays' lucky 13th home run prompted a big ovation from the San Diego crowd and he was accorded a hero's welcome at home plate by ecstatic teammates. The ball was retrieved and presented to him in the dugout.

The 38-year-old slugger is playing in his 19th big-league season.

1990

8 TDs BREAK RECORD

Illinois fullback Howard Griffith, atoning for a first-quarter fumble that cost his team seven points, stormed through the Southern Illinois University-Carbondale defense for 208 yards and scored an NCAA-record eight touchdowns in a 56–21 Illini victory at Champaign, Ill.

Playing on the same Memorial Stadium field that Red Grange dedicated with a five-touchdown effort in 1924, Griffith scored on runs of 5, 51, 7 and 41 yards as Illinois turned a 21–7 deficit into a 28–21 halftime lead.

Griffith picked up right where he left off in a 28-point Illini third quarter, scoring on runs of 5, 18, 5 and 3 yards. He didn't play in the fourth period and finished the day with all of Illinois' points – excluding the conversion kicks.

Griffith's outburst produced three major NCAA records. His 48 points were five more than the great Jim Brown scored for Syracuse in a 1956 game, the eight touchdowns were one more than Arnold (Showboat) Boykin scored for Mississippi in 1951 and the eight rushing TDs also broke Boykin's record.

MILESTONES · IN SPORTS ·

1926

The seven-year heavyweight reign of Jack Dempsey came to an end when former Marine Gene Tunney recorded a unanimous 10-round decision over the champion in a fight at Philadelphia.

1957

Hank Aaron drilled a two-run 11th-inning homer to give the Braves a 4–2 victory over the St. Louis Browns and their first Milwaukee pennant.

1978

California Angels outfielder Lyman Bostock was tragically killed by a shotgun blast meant for somebody else while riding in an automobile on the streets of Gary, Ind.

1979

St. Louis star Lou Brock stole his 938th and final base, breaking a tie with 19th century speedster Billy Hamilton and taking over first place on the all-time basestealing charts.

1983

A milestone: Philadelphia lefthander Steve Carlton recorded a 6–2 victory over his old team, the St. Louis Cardinals, for career victory No. 300.

1986

Houston's Jim Deshaies set a major league record by striking out the first eight batters he faced en route to a two-hit, 4–0 victory over the Los Angeles Dodgers.

1992

History was made when the Tampa Bay Lightning put goaltender Manon Rheaume in the nets during an NHL exhibition game against St. Louis. Rheaume, who gave up two goals in one period, became the first female to play in one of the four professional team sports.

1908 MERKLE'S MISTAKE

Fred Merkle's *'boner' cost the Giants a 1908 N.L. pennant.*

In a bizarre end to a game that could potentially decide the National League pennant, the Chicago Cubs benefited from a baserunning blunder by New York first baseman Fred Merkle and claimed a 1–1 tie in a contest the Giants apparently had won.

Whether or not the Cubs' claim will be upheld by the N.L. president remains to be seen, but umpire Hank O'Day ruled the game a tie and his decision probably will stand. "Merkle's Boner" occurred with two out in the bottom of the ninth inning when Al Bridwell singled home Moose McCormick from third base, giving the Giants an apparent 2–1 victory.

Not so. Merkle, the runner at first, did not bother to touch second base after the hit, sprinting directly to the center-field locker room at the Polo Grounds to avoid the inevitable crush of fans rushing onto the field. Chicago second baseman Johnny Evers, noticing Merkle's indiscretion and well versed in the rule book, frantically called for the ball, tagged second and appealed to O'Day.

The umpire signaled "out," nullifying the run. But with the field flooded by celebrating fans and most players already retired to their locker rooms unaware of the confusing turn of events, there was no way to continue the game. So he ruled it a tie and turned the matter over to the league office.

SEPTEMBER 23

A STAR IS BORN

1966: Tony Mandarich, a current National Football League offensive lineman.

★ ★ ★

1952 ROCKY GAINS TITLE

Bruised, bleeding and behind on all the judges' cards, 28-year-old Rocky Marciano ended the one-year reign of heavyweight champion Jersey Joe Walcott with a powerful right to the jaw in the 13th round of a battle at Philadelphia's Municipal Stadium.

The powerful but plodding Marciano had been dominated in the early rounds by the quicker Walcott, who floored the unbeaten challenger in the opening minutes. But Marciano stayed true to form and continued stalking the 38-year-old champion, taking punishment but steadily wearing him down with his relentless pursuit.

His determination finally paid off after 43 seconds of the 13th round.

Obviously down and needing a valiant rally, the popular Marciano connected with his big shot, knocking Walcott back against the ropes and onto the canvas. After Walcott was counted out and dragged to his corner, it took several minutes for him to regain his senses.

Marciano had his 43rd consecutive victory (38 by knockout) and boxing had its first white champion since 1937.

1962 WILLS PASSES COBB

Los Angeles shortstop Maury Wills ran into the record books when he swiped his 96th and 97th bases during a 12–2 loss at St. Louis, breaking a 47-year-old modern record that many thought would stand forever.

Wills, who had stolen headlines as well as bases during his assault on Ty Cobb's 1915 record, tied the former Detroit Tiger great after he singled in the third inning. With 20,743 Cardinal fans chanting "Go, go, go," the speedy Wills took off for second on a Larry Jackson pitch and Carl Sawatski's throw bounced past Dal Maxvill into center field.

Wills singled again in the seventh and quickly set sail for the record-breaker, sliding safely under Sawatski's high throw. When he was thrown out moments later trying to go to third on a ground ball, he left the field to a standing ovation.

Dodgers shortstop **Maury Wills,** *safe with another steal.*

SEPTEMBER

24

A STAR IS BORN

1910: Dixie Walker, an outstanding major league batter who compiled 2,064 hits during his 18-year career in the 1930s and '40s.

★ ★ ★

1946: Mean Joe Greene, a football Hall of Fame defensive tackle who helped the Pittsburgh Steelers capture four Super Bowl victories in the 1970s.

★ ★ ★

1956: Hubie Brooks, a current major league outfielder.

★ ★ ★

1964: Rafael Palmeiro, a current major league first baseman.

★ ★ ★

DEATH OF A LEGEND

1980: Ernie Shore (baseball).

★ ★ ★

1938

BUDGE WINS GRAND SLAM

Don Budge completed the greatest one-year performance in the history of tennis when he recorded a 6-3, 6–8, 6–2, 6–1 victory over doubles partner Gene Mako in the final of the United States championships at the West Side Tennis Club in Forest Hills, N.Y.

The victory gave the red-headed Californian one-year victories in the Wimbledon, Australian, French and U.S. championships for tennis' first grand slam. He also won in doubles at Wimbledon and Forest Hills, he helped the U.S. defend its Davis Cup title against Australia and he gained possession of the Newport Casino Challenge Cup. He was dominating, winning every singles tournament he entered.

Nobody expected the U.S. final to be anything more than an exhibition for the talented Budge. And indeed it appeared to be exactly that as he rolled to an easy first-set win over Mako before inexplicably losing concentration after building a 5–2 second-set lead. Mako fought back valiantly to hand the 23-year-old Budge his only set loss of the prestigious tournament.

But that was it. Using his splendid placements and power, he rolled confidently through the final two sets and claimed the historic victory.

1988

JACKIE GRABS GOLD

Jackie Joyner-Kersee, battling an injured knee and memories of a slim five-point loss in the 1984 Olympics, laid claim to the title of "world's greatest female athlete" when she captured the seven-pronged heptathlon event at the Summer Games in Seoul, South Korea.

Joyner-Kersee opened a big lead on the first day of competition, even though she was competing on a knee she twisted in the day's second event – the high jump. She still managed personal bests in the 100-meter race (12.69 seconds) and the shot put (51–10) before undergoing therapy for the injury.

It was still bothering her on the second day when she prepared for her best event, the long jump. Pushing off her right foot instead of the normal left foot to save stress on her knee, Joyner-Kersee amazingly soared 23–10¼, an Olympic heptathlon record. The knee cost her points in the javelin throw, but she finished in a blaze of glory, setting a personal best (2:08.51) in the 800 meters.

That gave her 987 points and a world-record total of 7,291.

MILESTONES IN SPORTS

1938

In a record 22 minutes, American Alice Marble destroyed Australian Nancye Wynne, 6–0, 6–3, in the women's U.S. singles championship at Forest Hills, N.Y.

1950

Chicago quarterback Jim Hardy set an NFL record for futility when he threw eight interceptions in the Cardinals' season-opening 45–7 loss to Philadelphia at Comiskey Park.

1957

End of an era: A disappointing Brooklyn crowd of 6,702 watched the Dodgers and lefthander Danny McDevitt beat Pittsburgh, 2–0, in the last game at Ebbets Field.

1967

St. Louis kicker Jim Bakken set an NFL record when he booted seven field goals in the Cardinals' 28–14 victory at Pittsburgh.

1974

Detroit right fielder Al Kaline joined baseball's exclusive 3,000-hit club when he doubled off Baltimore lefty Dave McNally in a 5–4 Tiger victory.

1988

Surprising Janet Evans outdueled East German Astrid Strauss in the 800-meter freestyle final and captured her third swimming gold medal of the Seoul Summer Olympic Games.

1940

FOXX JOINS ELITE 500 HOMER CLUB

Boston slugger Jimmie Foxx joined the elitest of baseball clubs when he hit his 500th career home run in a 16–8 Red Sox victory over Philadelphia. And he did it in style, connecting during a four-home run sixth-inning salvo in the city where he began his illustrious career 15 years earlier.

The muscular righthanded slugger joined former New York Yankee immortal Babe Ruth as the only players to reach the magical 500-homer barrier when he drove a pitch from Athletics righthander George Caster out of Shibe Park in the first game of a doubleheader. His blast followed a Ted Williams homer and teammates Joe Cronin and Jim Tabor connected later in the inning.

It was only fitting that Foxx should reach his milestone against the team for which he hit 302 home runs in 11 seasons – including 58 in one year (1932). But the three-time Most Valuable Player still trails the mighty Ruth on the all-time list by an incredible 214.

Boston's **Jimmie Foxx,** *baseball's second 500-homer man.*

MILESTONES
• IN SPORTS •

1920

Molla Bjurstedt Mallory earned her fifth U.S. singles championship in six years with a 6–3, 6–1 victory over Marion Zinderstein.

1926

The National Hockey League expanded its membership to 10 with the addition of three American franchises – the New York Rangers, Chicago Blackhawks and Detroit Red Wings.

1932

Philadelphia slugger Jimmie Foxx blasted his 58th home run in a 2–1 final-day loss to the Washington Senators, falling two short of Babe Ruth's one-season record.

1954

Early Wynn lost his no-hit bid and shutout in the ninth inning, but the Cleveland Indians cruised past Detroit, 11–1, for their American League-record 111th victory of the season.

1965

It was supposed to be a publicity stunt, but 60-year-old Satchel Paige baffled Boston batters on one hit during a scoreless three-inning stint for Kansas City in a game eventually won by the Red Sox, 5–2.

1982

Ricky Edwards rushed for 177 yards and four touchdowns as Northwestern ended its 34-game losing streak with a 31–6 victory over Northern Illinois.

1989

Uncharted territory: A 4-for-5 performance against the New York Yankees gave Boston third baseman Wade Boggs his seventh consecutive 200-hit season.

1988 Biondi Strikes Gold

Swimmer **Matt Biondi,** *winner of five Olympic gold medals.*

Matt Biondi, completing the greatest American medal rush since Mark Spitz 16 years earlier, captured his fifth Olympic gold and seventh medal overall when he swam the butterfly segment for the United States' world record-setting 400-meter medley relay team at the Summer Games in Seoul, South Korea.

Biondi's seven total medals matched the number won by Spitz at the 1972 Games at Munich, but all of Spitz's were gold. Biondi won individual golds in the 100-meter freestyle and 50-meter freestyle and three more in relays. He also captured individual silver and bronze medals.

Biondi teamed with David Berkoff (backstroke), Rich Schroeder (breaststroke) and Chris Jacobs (freestyle) in the world-record medley relay performance on the final day of swimming competition. They won by 5 meters and finished in 3:36.93, breaking the 3:38.28 mark set in the previous Olympic Games by a team anchored by Biondi.

Another notable final-day winner was East Germany's Kristin Otto, who captured the 50-meter freestyle for her sixth gold medal in six events – a record for women.

1986 Great Scott Says No-No

When Houston righthander Mike Scott retired San Francisco slugger Will Clark on a soft ground ball, he brought down the curtain on a double dose of baseball immortality – a no-hitter and a 2–0 National League West Division-clinching victory for his Astros.

Mike Scott *gets a champagne bath from Manager* **Hal Lanier.**

Never in the long history of baseball had a division title or pennant been clinched by a no-hitter. And he performed his memorable feat before 32,808 delirious home fans at the Astrodome, further cementing his chances for the N.L. Cy Young Award.

The 31-year-old master of the split-finger fastball needed only 102 pitches to clinch the Astros' second division title and first since 1980. He struck out 13 Giants, bringing his N.L.-leading total to 298, and allowed only three balls to be hit out of the infield. Two Giants reached base on walks and another was hit by a pitch, but otherwise the big righthander was in full control.

Scott, who raised his record to 18–10, got all the support he needed from teammate Denny Walling, who belted a solo home run.

September 25

1962 Liston Takes Title

Big, bad Sonny Liston dropped one of his righthanded bombs on the jaw of Floyd Patterson and claimed the world heavyweight championship with a first-round knockout in a surprisingly quick fight at Chicago's Comiskey Park.

Liston, a 214-pound fighting machine with an unsmiling, no-nonsense disposition, made short work of his 189-pound opponent, putting him on the canvas with a devastating right just 2:06 after the opening bell. He doubled Patterson over with a body shot, straightened him with a left and dropped him with the big right. And just like that, it was over.

Patterson, the only man to win the heavyweight championship twice, was simply overmatched. He tried to stay away from his powerful challenger early, but Liston stalked and waited for an opening. When he found it, he made the champion his 24th knockout victim in a nine-year career that has produced a 34–1 record.

Patterson won the title in 1956, lost it to Ingemar Johansson in 1959 and won it back in 1960.

A STAR IS BORN

1905: Red Smith, a Pulitzer Prize-winning sportswriter in Philadelphia and New York from 1936–82.

★ ★ ★

1917: Phil Rizzuto, a New York shortstop in the 1940s and '50s who went on to additional fame as a Yankee broadcaster.

★ ★ ★

1951: Bob McAdoo, an NBA forward-center who scored 18,787 points over a 13-year career that ended in 1976..

★ ★ ★

DEATH OF A LEGEND

1929: Miller Huggins (baseball).

★ ★ ★

1976: Red Faber (baseball).

SEPTEMBER

26

A STAR IS BORN

1925: Bobby Shantz, a little lefthanded pitcher who won 24 games for the Philadelphia Athletics in 1952 and 119 over his 16-year major league career.

★ ★ ★

DEATH OF A LEGEND

1977: Ernie Lombardi (baseball).

★ ★ ★

1988 LEWIS LEADS SWEEP

Amazing Carl Lewis, the long jump gold medalist in the 1984 Olympics at Los Angeles, became the first athlete to repeat as winner of that event four years later when he led a 1–2–3 American sweep in the Summer Games at Seoul, South Korea.

Not only did Lewis win gold, he recorded the four longest jumps of the day – shortly after running two heats of the 200-meter sprint and qualifying for the semifinals.

Lewis was listed as the first of the 12 long jump finalists, but Olympic officials, in deference to his 200-meter races, allowed him to jump last. It probably did not matter. He won the medal with a leap of 28–7 1/2 but also posted one jump at 28–1 and two at 27–11 1/2. Mike Powell won the silver medal with a 27–10 1/4 effort and Larry Myricks won bronze with 27–1 3/4.

Lewis ran his two 200-meter heats 70 minutes apart and made his first jump 55 minutes later.

1981 RYAN TAKES THE FIFTH

It took Nolan Ryan almost two years, but the fireballing Houston righthander finally gave the National League a dose of his no-hit magic when he shut down the Los Angeles Dodgers in a 5–0 victory at the Astrodome.

Nolan Ryan *acknowledges an ovation from appreciative Houston fans after pitching his record fifth career no-hitter.*

The no-hitter was the record-setting fifth of Ryan's illustrious career, moving him past former Dodger lefthander Sandy Koufax on the career list. Koufax pitched his four no-hitters in consecutive seasons (1962–65) and made his last one the most memorable – a perfect game against the Chicago Cubs.

Ryan's first four no-hitters were pitched in the 1970s as a member of the California Angels. Against the Dodgers, the 34-year-old struck out 11 and overcame an early problem with wildness. He threw 65 pitches through the first three innings and issued all three of his walks during that span.

But he had no such problem the rest of the way, retiring the last 19 Dodgers in a row. He struck out pinch-hitter Reggie Smith to open the ninth and recorded the last two outs on easy ground balls.

1971 FOUR ORIOLE HURLERS WIN 20

Righthander Jim Palmer, following the lead of teammates Dave McNally, Mike Cuellar and Pat Dobson, fired a three-hitter and pitched Baltimore to a 5–0 victory over Cleveland, giving the Orioles a one-season record-tying four 20-game winners.

Palmer was overpowering in his easy victory at Cleveland's Municipal Stadium – Baltimore's eighth straight triumph and 98th overall. He contributed a run-scoring double to a three-run seventh-inning rally that snapped a scoreless tie and helped him lift his ledger to 20–9.

That makes him just one of the boys on the talented Baltimore staff. McNally is 20–5, Cuellar 20–9 and Dobson 20–8. McNally and Cuellar are lefthanders, Palmer and Dobson righthanders. Cuellar's 20th win two days earlier had clinched Baltimore's third consecutive American League East Division championship.

The Oriole foursome joins an elite club. The only other time in baseball history that a team produced four 20-game winners in one season was 1919 – the infamous Chicago Black Sox team that featured a staff of Ed Cicotte, Urban Faber, Lefty Williams and Dickie Kerr. That quartet, half of which later was banned from baseball for its part in helping to fix the World Series against the Cincinnati Reds, combined for 87 wins.

Cicotte and Williams played major roles in baseball's most shameful scandal.

MILESTONES • IN SPORTS •

1908

Chicago's Ed Reulbach shut out Brooklyn, 5–0 and 3–0, in both ends of a doubleheader.

1925

Walter Hagen won his second PGA Championship with a 6-and-5 victory over William Melhorn at Olympia Fields III.

1954

Willie Mays collected three final-day hits and captured his first N.L. batting title with a .345 average – three points better than New York Giants teammate Don Mueller and four ahead of Brooklyn's Duke Snider.

1961

New York's Roger Maris tied Babe Ruth's 34-year-old record when he belted a pitch from Baltimore's Jack Fisher into the right-field seats at Yankee Stadium for his 60th home run – in his 159th game of the season.

1965

The Green Bay Packers held Baltimore star Lenny Moore without a touchdown catch in an NFL game at Milwaukee, ending his record 18-game TD-catching streak.

1981

No. 1-ranked Southern Cal held off No. 2 Oklahoma, 28–24, in a battle of the titans at the Los Angeles Coliseum.

1981

North Carolina back Kelvin Bryant completed a touchdown-scoring binge with four in a 56–14 rout of Boston College for an NCAA-record 15 in three games.

1987

San Diego catcher Benito Santiago extended his hitting streak to a rookie-record 28 games, but the Padres dropped a 3–1 decision to Los Angeles.

MILESTONES
IN SPORTS

1914

A baseball milestone: Cleveland's Nap Lajoie collected career hit No. 3,000 in the Indians' 5–3 victory over New York.

1930

The highlight of Chicago's 13–8 victory over Cincinnati at Wrigley Field was two home runs by Hack Wilson – his National League-record 55th and 56th of the season.

1940

Floyd Giebell, a 30-year-old Detroit rookie, outdueled Cleveland ace Bob Feller and pitched the Tigers to a 2–0 A.L. pennant-clinching victory at Cleveland Stadium.

1950

Ezzard Charles retained his heavyweight crown and ruined the comeback attempt of Joe Louis, battering the former champion in a 15-round unanimous decision at New York's Yankee Stadium.

1973

California fireballer Nolan Ryan fanned 16 Minnesota Twins in 11 innings during a season-ending 5–4 victory and finished with a one-season record 383 strikeouts.

1975

Kansas' Nolan Cromwell ran for 294 yards, an NCAA record for a quarterback, in the Jayhawks' 20–0 victory over Oregon State. Cromwell, normally a safety, was making his first collegiate start at the position.

1988

American Greg Louganis made a near-perfect final dive to win the 10-meter platform competition and his second gold medal in the Summer Olympic Games at Seoul, South Korea.

SEPTEMBER 27

1930 JONES WINS GOLF SLAM

Bobby Jones *pulled off an unprecedented golf sweep in 1930.*

Bobby Jones pulled off the greatest one-year feat in golf history when he closed out Gene Homans, 8 and 7, in the United States Amateur and completed golf's first grand slam.

Jones, who earlier had won the British Open, British Amateur and U.S. Open tournaments, turned the U.S. Amateur final into his own personal victory parade.

Displaying the outstanding shotmaking that has made him the most feared golfer in the world and acknowledging the cheers of 18,000 spectators after almost every swing, the 27-year-old Georgian assaulted the Merion Cricket Club course at Ardmore, Pa., and closed out Homans with a par putt on the 29th hole.

With victory in hand, a Marine escort helped Jones fight through delirious well-wishers and make his way back to the clubhouse. The victory was his fifth in the prestigious U.S. Amateur tournament and 13th in what are classified as major tournaments.

Jones' amazing feat was accomplished over a five-month period.

1935 CUBS' STREAK HITS 21

Bill Lee *won 20 games for the fast-closing Cubs.*

The Chicago Cubs completed their long journey from nowhere when they stretched their winning streak to 21 games and claimed the National League pennant during a doubleheader sweep of the St. Louis Cardinals.

The 6–2 first-game victory at Sportsman's Park officially put the Cubs into the World Series, an unlikely scenario before the All-Star break when they were in fourth place, 10 1/2 games behind the New York Giants. But a 20–3 stretch followed by the long winning streak turned them into runaway winners.

The Cubs battered Dizzy Dean in the opener, collecting 15 hits and handing big Bill Lee his 20th victory of the season. Then, as if to punctuate their accomplishment, they posted a 5–3 triumph in the nightcap.

The streak, the second longest in baseball history behind the New York Giants' 26-game run of 1916, began September 4 with a victory over Philadelphia. It lasted 24 days during which the Cubs won 18 home games and three in St. Louis.

A STAR IS BORN

1919: Johnny Pesky, a pepperpot major league infielder for three American League teams in the 1940s and '50s. He collected 1,455 hits in a career interupted by World War II.

★ ★ ★

1939: Kathy Whitworth, a seven-time LPGA player of the year who won seven major titles and 88 career tournaments – more than anybody in LPGA or PGA history.

★ ★ ★

1949: Mike Schmidt, the 18-year Philadelphia Phillies third baseman who blasted 548 career home runs.

★ ★ ★

DEATH OF A LEGEND

1956: Babe Didrikson Zaharias (track, golf).

★ ★ ★

1978: Neil Johnston (basketball).

★ ★ ★

1990: Larry O'Brien (basketball).

1988 GOLD MEDAL DENIED

Sprinter Ben Johnson, a conquering hero just three days earlier, was sent home in disgrace by Canadian Olympic officials after it was announced he had tested positive for a performance-enhancing steroid.

Johnson's roller-coaster ride from glory to oblivion began during the 100-meter final in the Summer Olympic Games at Seoul, South Korea. Johnson, in a much-ballyhooed battle with American Carl Lewis for the title of world's fastest human, literally exploded out of the blocks and made a near-supernatural dash into the record book. He was timed in an incredible 9.79 seconds, well ahead of Lewis' 9.92.

After the race, however, a routine test on his urine sample found traces of an anabolic steroid called stanozolol. After deliberation, the International Olympic Committee declared Johnson's victory null, stripped him of his gold medal and awarded it to Lewis.

The Canadian Olympic Committee followed that lead. It ordered the Jamaican-born sprinter to return home and then banned him from competing on its national team for life.

Lewis thus became a double gold medal winner (he also won the long jump) at Seoul and a six-time gold medalist in his two Olympic Games.

SEPTEMBER

28

MILESTONES IN SPORTS

1920

The Chicago White Sox, one game behind Cleveland with three games remaining in the A.L. season, were stunned when a Cook County (Ill.) grand jury returned indictments against eight players suspected of fixing the 1919 World Series. All eight were immediately suspended.

1951

Los Angeles quarterback Norm Van Brocklin opened the season with a bang: an NFL-record 554 passing yards and five TD passes in the Rams' 54–14 victory over the New York Yanks.

1951

Yankee righthander Allie Reynolds clinched at least a tie for the A.L. pennant when he pitched his record-tying second no-hitter of the season, beating Boston 8–0 in the first game of a doubleheader.

1969

Minnesota's Joe Kapp joined an exclusive club when he became the fifth NFL quarterback to throw seven touchdown passes in one game. He also threw for 449 yards in the Vikings' 52–14 victory over Baltimore.

1975

Oakland's Vida Blue, Glenn Abbott, Paul Lindblad and Rollie Fingers shut out California 5–0 in baseball's first-ever four-pitcher no-hitter.

1976

Muhammad Ali held onto his heavyweight crown by beating Ken Norton in a unanimous 15-round decision.

1988 Hershiser Extends Scoreless Streak

Los Angeles Dodger righthander Orel Hershiser, completing one of the greatest runs of pitching perfection in the history of baseball, lifted his consecutive scoreless-innings streak to 59 and broke the 20-year-old record held by former Dodger Don Drysdale.

Los Angeles Dodger record-setter **Orel Hershiser.**

Hershiser, making his final start of the regular season in a game at San Diego, needed nine scoreless innings to tie Drysdale's 1968 mark. And sure enough, he matched zeroes for nine innings with the Padres' Andy Hawkins. Given an unexpected chance to break the record, Hershiser pitched a scoreless 10th before leaving the contest that eventually was won by San Diego, 2–1, in 16 innings.

That completed Hershiser's incredible run that started August 30 when he held the Expos scoreless for the final four innings of a game at Montreal. Over the streak, he shut out Atlanta twice and Cincinnati, Houston and San Francisco once each. He finished his impressive season with a 2.26 earned-run average and National League-leading totals in victories (23) and shutouts (8).

He also led the Dodgers to an N.L. West Division championship and a pennant.

A STAR IS BORN

1913: Alice Marble, an outstanding woman tennis player who won four U.S. singles titles and a Wimbledon championship in the 1930s' and '40s.

★ ★ ★

1919: Tom Harmon, a Heisman Trophy-winning halfback from Michigan (1940) who played professional football before beginning a distinguished career as a sports broadcaster.

★ ★ ★

1941: Charley Taylor, a football Hall of Fame wide receiver who held the NFL record for career receptions when he retired in 1977 .

★ ★ ★

1954: Steve Largent, a former Seattle wide receiver who ranks second on the NFL's all-time lists for receptions (819) and reception yardage (13,089).

★ ★ ★

1962: Grant Fuhr, a current National Hockey League goaltender.

1938 Hartnett Blasts Homer in Gloom

Chicago Manager Gabby Hartnett, his team just one or two pitches away from having to settle for a tie with Pittsburgh, belted a Mace Brown curve into the thickening darkness that enveloped Wrigley Field and gave the Cubs a dramatic 6–5 victory and first place in the tight National League standings.

It was obvious by the crack of the bat where Hartnett's two-out, ninth-inning blast was headed, but few saw it land. The victory, which touched off a mob scene, capped a comeback-filled afternoon and gave the Cubs a half-game lead over the stunned Pirates, who had held first place since July 12.

The victory was important because a tie would have necessitated a next-day doubleheader, seriously strapping the Cubs' already-overextended pitching staff. A loss would have been even more serious, dropping the Cubs $1^1/2$ games back with three days left in the season.

Chicago twice had to fight back from two-run deficits, the last time in the eighth. When Charlie Root retired the Pirates in order in the ninth, darkness already was descending over Wrigley. Brown quickly retired the first two Cubs in the bottom of the inning and got two strikes on Hartnett. With the umpires ready to call for play stoppage, Hartnett belted Brown's next pitch into the night.

1941 Ted Tops .400

Boston's Ted Williams, saying "I don't care to be known as a .400 hitter with a lousy average of .39955," remained in the Red Sox lineup for a final-day doubleheader and turned in a spectacular 6-for-8 performance that gave him a final mark of .406.

Williams, refusing Manager Joe Cronin's offer to let him sit out the games against Philadelphia at Shibe Park and thus maintain his .400 average (rounded off), went 4 for 5 in the opener, collecting three singles and a home run. Batting .4039 going into the nightcap, he collected a single and double in three at-bats. The Red Sox won the first game, 12–11, and the second, 7–1.

The 23-year-old Williams became baseball's first .400 hitter since the New York Giants' Bill Terry batted .401 in 1930 and the first in the American League since Detroit's Harry Heilmann batted .403 in 1923. He also finished with A.L.-leading totals in home runs (37), runs scored (135) and walks (145) while driving in 120 runs.

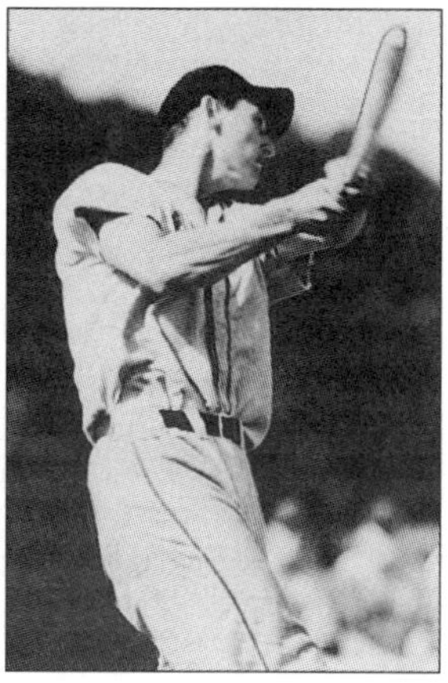

The classic batting form that made **Ted Williams** *a .406 hitter in 1941.*

1965 Koufax Is Perfecto

San Francisco's **Dusty Rhodes** *(left) and Cleveland's* **Vic Wertz** *– two important World Series figures.*

It was only a matter of time. Los Angeles lefthander Sandy Koufax became the first major league pitcher to record four career no-hitters and he added a little icing to his cake by retiring all 27 Chicago Cubs he faced in recording baseball's eighth perfect game – a 1–0 victory at Dodger Stadium.

In one of the most dominant performances ever witnessed, the Dodger southpaw struck out 14, including the last six he faced, and required only routine defensive help. His final strikeout victim was Harvey Kuenn, a former A.L. batting champion.

The unfortunate victim of this masterpiece was Cubs lefty Bob Hendley, who retired the first 12 batters he faced and finished with a one-hitter. The only Dodger run came in the fifth when Lou Johnson walked and came around to score on a wild throw. Johnson's seventh-inning double was the game's only hit.

The perfecto was only the second of modern-era N.L. history.

September 29

Milestones in Sports

1913

Washington righthander Walter Johnson capped his 36-victory season by pitching the Senators to a 1–0 victory over the Philadelphia Athletics.

1923

Gene Sarazen defeated Walter Hagen on the second hole of a dramatic playoff and captured his second straight PGA Championship.

1953

Bill Veeck sold controlling interest of the St. Louis Browns to a syndicate that received quick A.L. approval to move the team to Baltimore.

1974

St. Louis speedster Lou Brock completed the greatest single season of baseball larceny when he stole his 118th base in a 7–3 victory over Chicago.

1976

Walter Alston ended his 23-year career as Dodger manager, retiring with 2,040 victories, four World Series championships and seven N.L. pennants to his credit.

1984

Western Michigan's Mike Prindle etched his name into the NCAA record book when he kicked seven field goals in a 42–7 victory over Marshall.

1987

New York first baseman Don Mattingly hit his major league-record sixth grand slam of the season off Boston lefty Bruce Hurst to key a 6–0 Yankee victory.

A Star Is Born

1953: Warren Cromartie, a former major league outfielder.

★ ★ ★

1956: Sebastian Coe, an outstanding British distance runner in the 1970s and '80s who held world records in the 800 meters, 1,500 meters and the mile.

★ ★ ★

1963: Dave Andreychuk, a current National Hockey League left winger.

★ ★ ★

1965: Hersey Hawkins, a current National Basketball Association guard.

★ ★ ★

Death of a Legend

1937: Ray Ewry (track and field).

★ ★ ★

1975: Casey Stengel (baseball).

★ ★ ★

1982: Monty Stratton (baseball).

★ ★ ★

1989: August A. Busch (baseball).

★ ★ ★

1954 Mays Robs Indians

Vic Wertz hit a vicious 460-foot line drive that was caught. Dusty Rhodes hit a lazy 271-foot fly ball that wasn't. And that spelled the difference in the New York Giants' exciting 5–2 first-game World Series victory over the heavily-favored Cleveland Indians.

The contest, a pitching duel between the Giants' Sal Maglie and Cleveland's Bob Lemon, entered the eighth inning tied, 2–2. But then the fun began. Indians' leadoff batter Larry Doby walked and Al Rosen singled. Don Liddle, a lefthander, was brought in to face the dangerous Vic Wertz, who had tripled home Cleveland's first two runs in the opening inning.

Wertz sent a gasp through the Polo Grounds crowd when he belted a long drive to center field – sure extra bases and a Cleveland lead. But Giants center fielder Willie Mays, with his back to the infield, made an amazing over-the-shoulder catch near the 460-foot sign, wheeled and made a leaping throw back to the infield. Marvin Grissom relieved Liddle and completed the inning without incident.

The crowd still was talking about that play in the 10th inning when Rhodes was called on to pinch-hit with two runners on base. On Lemon's first pitch, Rhodes hit a high fly ball down the right-field line that settled, barely, into the short bleachers for a three-run homer that ended one of the most dramatic games in World Series history.

1959 Dodgers Sweep Playoff

Gil Hodges raced home from second base with two out in the 12th inning on a wild throw by Milwaukee shortstop Felix Mantilla, giving the Dodgers a sweep of their best-of-three playoff series with the Braves and bringing Los Angeles its first National League pennant.

The Dodger victory at Memorial Coliseum was set up by a three-run game-tying rally in the ninth inning after Milwaukee righthander Lew Burdette had carried a 5–2 lead into the final frame. The Dodgers loaded the bases in their tying rally on singles by Wally Moon, Duke Snider and Hodges. Two runs scored on Norm Larker's single and another on Carl Furillo's sacrifice fly.

The winner came after the first two batters had been retired in the 12th. Bob Rush walked Hodges, Joe Pignatano singled and Furillo hit a high bouncer behind second base. Mantilla gloved and made an off-balance throw that bounced past first baseman Frank Torre.

The Braves, who had dropped a 3–2 series-opening loss at Milwaukee after the teams had tied for the N.L. lead with 86–68 records, led all the way in the second game until the ninth.

SEPTEMBER

30

1916 GIANTS' STREAK ENDS AT 26

Red Smith and Sherry Magee keyed a five-run seventh-inning explosion with back-to-back home runs and the Boston Braves went on to record an 8–3 victory in the second game of a doubleheader, snapping the New York Giants' incredible 26-game winning streak.

The longest streak in baseball history had reached its zenith in the opener of the twin bill at New York's Polo Grounds when Rube Benton shut out the Braves, 4–0, continuing the Giants' long run of near-perfect baseball. The teams entered the seventh inning of the nightcap tied 2–2, but the Braves disappointed 38,000 New York fans with their sudden onslaught.

The streak started September 7 with a win over Brooklyn and the Giants ran up six victories over St. Louis, five over Pittsburgh, four each over Philadelphia and Cincinnati and three over Chicago and Boston. Their run, which lifted them from last place to fourth in the National League standings, was interrupted by a 1–1 September 18 tie with Pittsburgh.

The longest previous major league winning streak was 21 games, set back in 1880 by the old National League's Chicago Cubs.

1927 RUTH THE SHOWMAN HITS 60TH HOMER

Babe Ruth, adding yet another entry to his ever-growing aura of immortality, bashed his 60th home run of the season off Washington lefthander Tom Zachary and broke his own major league record of 59 set six years earlier.

Babe Ruth *(left) blasted 60 homers for the 1927 New York Yankees and teammate* **Lou Gehrig** *(right) drove in 175 runs.*

In typical Ruth fashion, he did it with panache and flair during New York's 4–2 victory at Yankee Stadium. Batting in the eighth inning with a man on base in a 2–2 game, Ruth belted a 1–1 Zachary pitch into the right-field bleachers. The crowd roared, Ruth strutted around the bases and teammates pounded their bats against the wooden floor of the dugout, making a thundering noise.

When the bleacher crowd greeted him with another ovation upon his return to right field in the top of the ninth, he playfully marched around the outfield, bringing another roar from the stands.

The Bambino had hit home runs No. 58 and 59 the day before to tie the record he set in 1921, his second New York campaign.

1945 GREENBERG BLASTS BROWNS

Detroit slugger Hank Greenberg, who had returned to baseball three months earlier after a four-year hitch in the military, belted a grand slam home run through the dark and misty St. Louis sky to give the Tigers a dramatic American League pennant-clinching 6–3 victory over the Browns.

Greenberg's ninth-inning blast off St. Louis righthander Nelson Potter brought the Tigers back from a 3–2 deficit in the first game of a scheduled final-day doubleheader at Sportsman's Park. With the Tigers' pennant secure, the second game was called off, giving Detroit a final 1½-game cushion over Washington.

The Senators, who had concluded their season, needed a St. Louis sweep to force a playoff. And the Browns lifted their hopes by carrying their slim lead into the ninth inning.

But pinch-hitter Hub Walker led off with a single and Skeeter Webb was safe on a fielder's choice. After the runners were sacrificed to second and third, Doc Cramer was walked intentionally, loading the bases. Greenberg blasted the pennant-winner just inside the left-field foul pole.

Hank Greenberg's *slam clinched a pennant for the Tigers.*

A STAR IS BORN

1926: Robin Roberts, a Hall of Fame righthander who recorded 286 victories in a 19-year major league career.

★ ★ ★

1932: Johnny Podres, the lefthander who pitched the seventh-game clincher in Brooklyn's first and only World Series championship (1955).

MILESTONES IN SPORTS

1913

Francis Ouimet pulled off a shocker when he beat British stars Harry Vardon and Ted Ray in a playoff, becoming the first amateur ever to win the U.S. Open golf tournament.

1934

Dizzy Dean beat the Cincinnati Reds, 9–0, for his 30th victory of the season – and the N.L. pennant-clincher for the St. Louis Cardinals.

1951

Jackie Robinson's 14th-inning home run gave Brooklyn a 9–8 final-day victory over Philadelphia and forced a tie with the New York Giants for the N.L. pennant.

1962

The bumbling, stumbling expansion New York Mets lost their major league-record 120th game – 5–1 to the Chicago Cubs.

1972–1992

Two milestones: Pittsburgh's Roberto Clemente and Kansas City's George Brett joined baseball's 3,000-hit club – 20 years apart.

1984

Perfecto: California's Mike Witt retired all 27 Texas Rangers he faced in a 1–0 season-ending victory at Arlington Stadium.

1984

The Los Angeles Rams set an NFL record when they scored three safeties in a 33–12 victory over the New York Giants.

1988

Toronto's Dave Stieb, one out away from a no-hitter for the second time in six days, was denied again when Baltimore's Jim Traber blooped a single to right field. Stieb won his one-hitter, 4–0.

OCTOBER 1

1975 Ali Is Still Champ

A subdued and businesslike Muhammad Ali, forsaking his "float like a butterfly, sting like a bee" style, retained his heavyweight boxing championship when a battered and bruised Joe Frazier failed to answer the bell for the 15th round of the "Thrilla in Manila."

Ali, who had split his previous two fights with Frazier, chose to stand and slug it out with the former champion, refraining from his usual clowning. He dominated the early rounds, but the ever-relentless Frazier fought back and took control before tiring.

That's when the 33-year-old Ali really came on. From the 12th through the 14th rounds, he punished the 31-year-old challenger and Frazier, his right eye swollen shut and obviously exhausted, was held back when the bell rang for the final round.

A STAR IS BORN

1945: Rod Carew, a seven-time American League batting champion who finished his 19-year career in 1985 with a .328 average and 3,053 hits.

★ ★ ★

1953: Grete Waitz, the Norwegian distance runner who won the New York City Marathon nine times.

★ ★ ★

1963: Mark McGwire, a current major league first baseman.

★ ★ ★

DEATH OF A LEGEND

1975: Larry MacPhail (baseball).

★ ★ ★

1984: Walter Alston (baseball).

★ ★ ★

1984: Billy Goodman (baseball).

★ ★ ★

1961 Maris Gets 61st Homer

New York Yankee right fielder Roger Maris accomplished what no player in the long history of baseball had been able to do when he drove a fourth-inning pitch from Boston righthander Tracy Stallard into the right-field stands at Yankee Stadium for his 61st home run of the season.

The blow came on the final day of the regular campaign and allowed Maris to pass the immortal Babe Ruth on the one-season home run charts. Ruth's record of 60 home runs had stood since 1927 and a June ruling by Commissioner Ford Frick guaranteed that it will stand a while longer as the official mark for a 154-game schedule. Maris hit his 59th home run in the Yankees' 154th game and his record-breaking 61st came in game No. 162.

No matter how it is cataloged in the record book, Maris' home run broke new ground. And it came in dramatic fashion, giving the Yankees and Bill Stafford a 1–0 victory over the Red Sox before 23,154 delirious fans.

Maris hit a 2–0 pitch on his second trip to the plate after flying out in the opening inning. As soon as he made contact, a loud roar engulfed the stadium and Maris momentarily stood transfixed before beginning his triumphant trot around the bases.

New York Yankee **Roger Maris** *watches the flight of record-breaking home run No. 61 in a regular season-ending game against Baltimore.*

1932 Dramatic Ruth Calls Homer

A dramatic, in-your-face home run by Babe Ruth broke a 4–4 tie in the fifth inning and sent the New York Yankees on their way to a 7–5 victory and a commanding 3–0 lead over the Chicago Cubs in the World Series.

Ruth, exhibiting his ever-present flair for the dramatic, stepped to the plate to face Charlie Root with the game tied and a full house at Wrigley Field screaming and taunting with every pitch. There were hard feelings between the teams and emotions were high.

Ruth, who had homered off Root in the first inning, looked at two balls and two strikes as the intensity rose to fever pitch. Then, suddenly, the Yankees' Bambino made a sweeping gesture toward the center-field stands, as if to say that's where he intended to deposit Root's next offering.

Whether that's what Ruth meant, nobody knows for sure – he would not say. But he hit the next pitch over the center-field fence and then trotted triumphantly around the bases.

MILESTONES IN SPORTS

1903

Pittsburgh 7, Boston 3 in the first World Series game ever played.

1944

The St. Louis Browns, long the doormat of the American League, ended 43 years of frustration by defeating the New York Yankees, 5–2, on the final day of the season and capturing their first-ever pennant.

1950

Dick Sisler hit a dramatic three-run homer in the 10th inning of the season finale to give the Philadelphia Phillies a 4–1 victory over second-place Brooklyn and their first N.L. pennant in 35 years.

1967

The Boston Red Sox continued their "Impossible Dream" and capped one of the greatest pennant races in history when they defeated Minnesota, 5–3, on the final day of the season and clinched their first A.L. flag since 1946.

1977

Soccer great Pele drew 75,646 fans to the New Jersey Meadowlands for his farewell game. He played half of the exhibition game with each of his two former teams—the New York Cosmos and Santos of Brazil.

1988

Florence Griffith-Joyner, alias FloJo, completed her Olympic dash to glory by running the third leg for the victorious U.S. women's 400-meter relay team and winning a third gold medal.

OCTOBER 2

A STAR IS BORN

1932: Maury Wills, the six-time National League stolen base champion who swiped a then-record 104 for the Los Angeles Dodgers in 1962.

★ ★ ★

1946: Bob Robertson, an 11-year major league first baseman best remembered for his three-homer N.L. Championship Series game for Pittsburgh in 1971.

★ ★ ★

1962: Mark Rypien, a current National Football League quarterback.

1978 DENT BURNS RED SOX

Light-hitting Bucky Dent lifted a seventh-inning fly ball over the inviting left-field wall at Boston's Fenway Park for a three-run homer and propelled the New York Yankees to a tension-filled 5–4 victory over the Red Sox in a one-game playoff that decided the American League East Division championship.

The victory capped the Yankees' amazing comeback from a 14-game July deficit and earned them a chance to play Kansas City in the A.L. Championship Series. The playoff became necessary when Boston won its final regular-season game and the Yankees lost to Cleveland.

The Red Sox broke to a 2–0 lead against 24-game winner Ron Guidry on Carl Yastrzemski's second-inning home run and Jim Rice's sixth-inning RBI single. The Yankees could manage only two hits through six innings off Boston starter Mike Torrez.

But Chris Chambliss and Roy White singled in the seventh and Dent, a .243 hitter, lifted a fly ball that got a boost from the wind and settled onto the screen atop Fenway's Green Monster. The Yankees added another seventh-inning run and Reggie Jackson's eighth-inning homer increased the lead to 5–2.

The Red Sox rallied for two eighth-inning runs and had two runners on base in the ninth, but relief ace Goose Gossage came in and retired Rice and Yastrzemski to end the A.L.'s first title playoff since 1948.

MILESTONES • IN SPORTS •

1916

Philadelphia great Grover Cleveland Alexander stopped the Boston Braves, 2–0, for his major league-record 16th shutout of the season.

1921

New York slugger Babe Ruth capped an amazing season by blasting home run No. 59 off Boston's Curt Fullerton in a 7–6 Yankee victory.

1938

Bullet Bob Feller, Cleveland's 19-year-old flamethrower, struck out a major league-record 18 Detroit hitters during a 4–1 loss to the Tigers.

1950

Chicago quarterback Jim Hardy fired six touchdown passes, five to Bob Shaw, as the Cardinals routed the Baltimore Colts, 55–13.

1970

Thirty-one persons, including 14 players from the Wichita State football team and Coach Ben Wilson, died when a plane transporting them to a game in Logan, Utah, crashed in the Colorado Rockies near Denver.

1980

WBC heavyweight champion Larry Holmes dominated comeback-minded Muhammad Ali and recorded a technical knockout over the former champ when he couldn't answer the bell for the 11th round of a bout in Las Vegas.

1983

The Green Bay Packers scored 35 second-quarter points and 49 in the first half of a 55–14 rout of the Tampa Bay Buccaneers.

1908 INDIAN PITCHER PERFECT

Cleveland's Addie Joss joined select company when he retired all 27 Chicago White Sox batters he faced and became the second pitcher in modern baseball history to throw a perfect game.

Joss, who won for the 24th time this season, is the first pitcher to accomplish the feat since Boston's Cy Young overpowered Philadelphia in a 1904 contest. The righthander needed to be perfect in the game at Cleveland because Chicago 40-game winner Ed Walsh allowed only four hits and one run while striking out 15.

Joss was not so dominant, striking out three, but he was in total control in lowering his earned-run average to a sparkling 1.16. The Indians scored the only run when Joe Birmingham singled in the third inning.

St. Louis Cardinals ace **Bob Gibson** *(45) is congratulated by teammates after his dominating World Series Game 1 performance against the Detroit Tigers.*

1968 GIBSON FANS 17 TIGERS

Bob Gibson, the hard-throwing St. Louis righthander who posted a National League-record 1.12 earned-run average during the regular season, put on one of the most dazzling World Series displays ever witnessed when he struck out a record 17 Detroit Tigers in a 4–0 Game 1 victory at Busch Stadium.

Gibson allowed five hits and outpitched Detroit 31-game winner Denny McLain in a heralded matchup that proved to be one-sided. It was apparent early that it was going to be as Gibson struck out seven of the first nine batters he faced and the Cardinals staked him to a 3–0 lead in the fourth inning.

The Tigers never came close. As Gibson piled up strikeout after strikeout, it became apparent they were overmatched. Gibson closed the game in a blaze of glory. He fanned Al Kaline to open the ninth and got Norm Cash for his 16th strikeout, surpassing Sandy Koufax's Series record of 15. Willie Horton became victim No. 17 on a called third strike.

MILESTONES
• IN SPORTS •

1920

A long-standing record: St. Louis Browns first baseman George Sisler got his 257th hit of the season.

1946

The St. Louis Cardinals became National League champions when they defeated the Brooklyn Dodgers, 8–4, and completed their two-game sweep of baseball's first pennant playoff.

1962

The San Francisco Giants rallied for four ninth-inning runs and a 6–4 victory over the Los Angeles Dodgers in the decisive third game of an N.L. pennant playoff.

1971

Pittsburgh first baseman Bob Robertson exploded for a postseason record-tying three home runs and led the Pirates to a 9–4 Game 2 victory over San Francisco in the N.L. Championship Series.

1973

The new World Football League was formed to compete against the powerful NFL.

1982

Robin Yount hit two home runs and Milwaukee rolled to a 10–2 final-day victory over Baltimore that staved off a late collapse and gave the Brewers their first-ever A.L. East Division title.

1987

Los Angeles Dodgers pitcher Orel Hershiser ended San Diego catcher Benito Santiago's rookie-record hitting streak at 34 games.

1990

George Brett went 1 for 1 in Kansas City's season finale and finished with a .329 average, becoming the first player to win batting titles in three different decades.

OCTOBER

3

1951

THOMSON'S MIRACLE

Bobby Thomson's electrifying three-run homer capped a four-run ninth-inning rally that gave the never-say-die New York Giants a 5–4 victory over Brooklyn in the rubber match of a three-game playoff to decide the National League pennant.

The victory at New York's Polo Grounds concluded the most exciting pennant race in history and the N.L.'s second pennant playoff – the first to go three games. The Giants had appeared hopelessly buried at 13½ games behind the front-running Dodgers on August 12 , but they rebounded to win 37 of their final 44 to force a tie. After splitting the first two games of the playoff, they appeared hopelessly buried in the finale, facing a 4–1 ninth-inning deficit against 20-game winner Don Newcombe.

But Alvin Dark and Don Mueller opened the frame with singles and Monte Irvin fouled out. Whitey Lockman followed with a double that made the score 4–2 and sent Dodger Manager Chuck Dressen to his bullpen for reliever Ralph Branca.

The righthander's third pitch to Thomson was drilled toward the left-field seats. As the capacity crowd sat in stunned silence, the ball disappeared into the stands. When the fans finally grasped what had transpired, pandemonium broke loose as Thomson danced wildly around the bases.

Bobby Thomson, *the man who hit the fabled 'Shot Heard 'round the World'*

Brooklyn Game 4 hero **Cookie Lavagetto** *(center) with Dodger run-scorers* **Al Gionfriddo** *(left) and* **Eddie Miksis.**

1947

COOKIE BURNS BEVENS

In a bizarre twist to a strange game, New York's Bill Bevens surrendered a two-out, two-run ninth-inning double to Brooklyn pinch-hitter Cookie Lavagetto – a hit that ruined his bid for a first-ever World Series no-hitter and cost the Yankees a victory.

The dramatic turn of events at Brooklyn's Ebbets Field gave the Dodgers an unlikely 3–2 victory and a 2–2 tie in the fall classic. Their good fortune was a product of both Lavagetto's clutch blow and Bevens' wildness, which cost him a fifth-inning run (two walks and a groundout) and put the tying and lead runners on base in the ninth.

With Bevens clinging to his no-hitter and a 2–1 advantage entering the final frame, the righthander retired Bruce Edwards on a fly ball. But Carl Furillo walked, the ninth base on balls surrendered by Bevens, Spider Jorgensen fouled out and pinch-hitter Pete Reiser drew a free pass.

That brought up Lavagetto, batting for Eddie Stanky. On Bevens' second pitch, the righthanded hitter swung late and hit a drive to the opposite field. The ball bounced off the right-field wall as both runners scampered home, spoiling Bevens' date with destiny.

A STAR IS BORN

1931: Glenn Hall, a hockey Hall of Fame goaltender and an 11-time NHL All-Star during his 18 professional seasons.

★ ★ ★

1940: Jean Ratelle, a hockey Hall of Fame center who scored 491 goals and 1,267 points over a 22-year NHL career.

★ ★ ★

1951: Dave Winfield, a current major league outfielder and designated hitter.

★ ★ ★

1954: Dennis Eckersley, a current major league pitcher.

★ ★ ★

DEATH OF A LEGEND

1986: Vince DiMaggio (baseball).

★ ★ ★

1989

SHELL MAKES HISTORY

Art Shell, the 15-year Raiders offensive tackle and recent inductee into the Pro Football Hall of Fame, became the first modern-era black coach in the National Football League when he was selected by Los Angeles Owner Al Davis to replace Mike Shanahan.

Shell, a Raiders assistant, took over the coaching reins after the team struggled to a 13 start. He became the first NFL black head since the league's formative years, when running back Fritz Pollard served three years as player-coach for the Hammond (Ind.) Pros. Since Pollard, no black had advanced beyond the job of offensive or defensive coordinator.

Ironically, Shell broke football's color barrier on the same date that Frank Robinson was named baseball's first black manager (for Cleveland) in 1974.

OCTOBER

4

A STAR IS BORN

1934: Sam Huff, a football Hall of Fame linebacker with the Chicago Bears and Washington Redskins from 1956–69.

★ ★ ★

1963: A.C. Green, a current National Basketball Association forward.

★ ★ ★

DEATH OF A LEGEND

1981: Fred Lindstrom (baseball).

★ ★ ★

1955

DODGERS END FRUSTRATION

Johnny Podres ended more than a half century of frustration for Brooklyn baseball fans when he pitched an eight-hit shutout and, with a major defensive assist from left fielder Sandy Amoros, gave the Dodgers their long-awaited first World Series championship.

Game 7 winner **Johnny Podres** *leads the locker room cheer for Brooklyn's first World Series victory.*

The 2–0 Game 7 victory at Yankee Stadium snapped the Dodgers' World Series losing streak at seven. Pennant winners in 1916, 1920, 1941, 1947, 1949, 1952 and 1953, they had lost on each occasion, the last five to the hated Yankees. And for a few brief moments in the finale, it didn't look like 1955 would be any different.

The key play occurred in the sixth inning with the Dodgers holding a 2–0 advantage. After Billy Martin drew a leadoff walk and Gil McDougald bunted safely, Yogi Berra slashed a drive down the left-field line that appeared headed for extra bases. But Amoros, who had just entered the game, raced to the foul line, extended his arm and made a spectacular catch. His quick throw to the infield allowed the Dodgers to complete a double play.

The amazing catch stunned the Yankees and gave new life to Podres, who shut down the New Yorkers the rest of the way without incident.

MILESTONES • IN SPORTS •

1906

The powerful Chicago Cubs won their 116th game and completed the season with an unprecedented .763 winning percentage.

1963

Speedy Scot, with Ralph Baldwin in sulky, recorded an easy straight-set victory in the Kentucky Futurity and became the second standardbred in history to win the Triple Crown of trotting.

1964

Kansas City's Bobby Hunt tied an AFL record when he intercepted four passes in the Chiefs' 28–7 victory over Houston.

1970

Major league umpires, seeking higher compensation for postseason work, ended their unprecedented one-day strike against baseball and returned for the second games of the A.L. and N.L. championship series.

1980

Oklahoma 82, Colorado 42: the highest-scoring game in major college football history.

1986

New York Yankee relief ace Dave Righetti saved both ends of a doubleheader and brought his major league-record total to 46.

1987

The NFL average attendance dropped from 59,824 one week to 16,947 the next as the league used replacement players while the regulars were on strike.

1948

INDIANS WIN A.L. PLAYOFF

Two home runs by player-Manager Lou Boudreau and a three-run shot by Ken Keltner provided all the scoring Gene Bearden needed as he pitched the Cleveland Indians to an 8–3 victory over the Boston Red Sox in the first pennant playoff in American League history.

The one-game, winner-take-all battle, played before a subdued capacity crowd at Fenway Park, was decided in Cleveland's four-run fourth inning, when Keltner's big blow chased Boston starter Denny Galehouse. Bearden went on to record his 20th victory, shutting the Red Sox down on five hits and giving the Indians their second A.L. pennant and first since 1920.

Cleveland playoff heroes: (left to right) pitcher **Gene Bearden, Lou Boudreau** *and* **Ken Keltner.**

Boudreau, whose team had suffered a tough final-day loss to Detroit that threw the A.L. race into a tie, got things rolling with a first-inning home run off Galehouse. He got the Indians started in their big fourth with the first of his two singles and he hit his second home run in the fifth off Ellis Kinder.

Boston had earned its one-game shot at the Indians with a 10-5 final-day victory over the New York Yankees.

1987

TIGERS CATCH JAYS

Larry Herndon hit a home run off Jimmy Key and Detroit lefthander Frank Tanana put the finishing touches on one of the great collapses in baseball history when he shut out Toronto, 1–0, on the final day of the season and helped the Tigers clinch the American League East Division title.

The loss was the seventh straight for the stunned Blue Jays and their third in a row to the Tigers in a season-closing series. Toronto had won its 96th game on September 26 and owned a 3 1/2- game lead with seven to play.

The Blue Jays saw that lead dwindle to one when they dropped a 13-inning decision to Detroit and then lost three straight to Milwaukee. The Tigers won the first two games of the season-closing series at Tiger Stadium and suddenly owned a one-game lead entering the finale.

Tanana fired a six-hitter in the clincher.

1985 Robinson Gets 324th

Eddie Robinson, the man who pushed Grambling State into national prominence, became the winningest college football coach in history when his Tigers posted a 27–7 victory over Prairie View A&M at the Cotton Bowl in Dallas.

Robinson, the king of black college football, edged past former Alabama coaching great Paul (Bear) Bryant when he posted his 324th career victory in a game that drew 36,652 fans and more than 500 journalists. Bryant had retired after the 1982 season with 323 career wins.

Robinson's record-setter came in his 45th year as a coach and amid much hoopla. The Grambling sideline, knowing victory was well in hand, was one big celebration through most of the final quarter. When the game ended, Robinson was mobbed by his players as friends, well-wishers and photographers swarmed around like bees.

1947 Catch Ruins Yanks

The Brooklyn Dodgers, who averted a Game 4 World Series loss when pinch-hitter Cookie Lavagetto stroked a two-out, two-run ninth-inning double that ruined Bill Bevens' no-hit bid, pulled another rabbit out of their caps in an 8–6 victory over New York in Game 6 at Yankee Stadium.

The Dodgers, down 3–2 in the fall classic, jumped to a 4–0 lead in the must-win game, fell behind 5–4 and then regained the advantage with a four-run sixth-inning rally capped by Pee Wee Reese's two-run single. Would the Dodgers' 8–5 lead hold up? The Yankees quickly put two runners on base in their half of the inning and Joe DiMaggio stepped to the plate with a chance to answer that question.

He didn't waste any time, blasting a Joe Hatten pitch toward the left-field bullpen. But just as it appeared the ball would disappear for a three-run homer, Dodgers left fielder Al Gionfriddo, inserted into the game as a defensive replacement between innings, raced over and made a twisting catch near the 415-foot sign, pulling the ball back to safety.

The Yankees threatened one more time in the ninth, but Hugh Casey came on to close out the victory.

Brooklyn Manager **Burt Shotton** *hugs little* **Al Gionfriddo**, *the Dodgers' savior in Game 6 of the 1947 World Series.*

October 5

A Star Is Born

1824: Henry Chadwick, a Hall of Famer known as the "Father of Baseball" because of his contributions as a sportswriter and innovator.

★ ★ ★

1889: Jim Bagby Sr., a righthanded pitcher who won 31 games for the World Series-champion Cleveland Indians in 1920.

★ ★ ★

1965: Mario Lemieux, a current National Hockey League center.

★ ★ ★

1965: Patrick Roy, a current National Hockey League goaltender.

★ ★ ★

1967: Rex Chapman, a current National Basketball Association guard.

★ ★ ★

Death of a Legend

1954: Oscar Charleston (baseball).

★ ★ ★

1969: Walter Hagen (golf).

★ ★ ★

1979: Ken Strong (football).

★ ★ ★

Milestones in Sports

1928

Little Leo Diegel defeated Al Espinosa, 6 and 5, to win the PGA Championship at Five Farms Club in Baltimore. The tournament had been won by Walter Hagen four straight times.

1942

Rookie pitcher Johnny Beazley handcuffed New York, 4–2, and the St. Louis Cardinals completed their stunning five-game World Series victory over the powerful Yankees.

1953

Billy Martin's record-tying 12th World Series hit, a run-scoring single in the bottom of the ninth inning, capped the New York Yankees' six-game fall classic victory over the Brooklyn Dodgers.

1967

Boston righthander Jim Lonborg allowed one hit and one walk in one of the most dominating performances in World Series history—a 5–0 Game 2 victory over the St. Louis Cardinals.

1986

Los Angeles running back Eric Dickerson capped his 207-yard, two-touchdown day with a 42-yard TD run that gave the Rams a 26–20 overtime victory over Tampa Bay. It was the longest overtime TD run in history.

1990

NFL Commissioner Paul Tagliabue fined Cincinnati Coach Sam Wyche $30,000 for refusing to allow a female reporter into his team's locker room.

1941 Owen's Passed Ball

The New York Yankees, apparent Game 4 World Series losers to Brooklyn when Tommy Henrich fanned on a third-strike delivery from Hugh Casey, got new life when Dodger catcher Mickey Owen let the ball get away and turned it into a four-run rally that produced a 7–4 victory.

"Only in Brooklyn" was the wailing cry heard from 33,813 shocked fans at Ebbets Field after their Dodgers had let a sure victory turn into a 3–1 fall classic deficit. Leading 4–3 with two out in the ninth on a sweltering afternoon, "victory" is what it appeared to be when Henrich missed one of Casey's sharp-breaking curves and so did Owen, allowing the ball to bounce back to the screen.

Given another chance with Henrich now on first, the Bronx Bombers struck fast. Joe DiMaggio followed with a single and Charlie Keller doubled home both Henrich and DiMaggio. After Bill Dickey drew a walk, Joe Gordon doubled home two more runs.

Reliever Johnny Murphy closed out the victory in one of the most fantastic turnarounds ever witnessed.

OCTOBER

6

1993 JORDAN RETIRES, SHOCKS WORLD

In a stunning announcement that shifted the balance of power in the National Basketball Association, Chicago Bulls star Michael Jordan retired, saying the monotony of his routine had eclipsed the gratification of the rewards.

In a news conference attended by NBA Commissioner David Stern and televised live around the world, Jordan said he had accomplished everything he possibly could in basketball and had nothing more to prove. He will be giving up the final three years of a contract that pays $3.9 million per season, but analysts estimate his marketing endeavors net him $28 million annually.

Jordan leaves on the heels of Chicago's third straight NBA championship and he takes with him seven consecutive scoring titles. He has been generally acclaimed as the greatest player in the history of the professional game and his incredible exploits have been heralded world-wide.

The high-flying guard is coming off a personally tumultuous year in which his father was killed in an apparent roadside robbery and he had to defend himself from gambling charges. He said those problems had nothing to do with his decision to leave the sport he has dominated since 1984.

1963 L.A. PULLS OFF SWEEP

The opportunistic Los Angeles Dodgers scratched out a pair of runs on two hits and Sandy Koufax made them stand up for a 2–1 victory at Dodger Stadium, completing a shocking four-game World Series sweep of the New York Yankees.

Koufax allowed six hits and struck out eight in his second complete-game effort of the fall classic. He had outdueled Yankee ace Whitey Ford in a 5–2 first-game victory and beat Ford again in the clincher.

Ford surrendered only two hits, but one was a mammoth fifth-inning home run by Frank Howard. After the Yankees had tied on Mickey Mantle's seventh-inning blast, the Dodgers got the game-winner in the bottom of the frame without a hit.

Jim Gilliam opened the inning by hitting a chopper that Yankee third baseman Clete Boyer fielded. His throw was on target, but first baseman Joe Pepitone lost the ball amid the white-shirted crowd and Gilliam streaked all the way to third. He scored on Willie Davis' sacrifice fly.

Los Angeles' two-game Series winner **Sandy Koufax** *(right) poses with the enemy, New York Yankee slugger* **Bill Skowron.**

MILESTONES IN SPORTS

1926

Babe Ruth added to his long line of slugging records when he blasted three home runs in Game 4 of the World Series at St. Louis' Sportsman's Park – a 10–5 Yankee victory over the Cardinals.

1955

Scott Frost, with Joe O'Brien in sulky, captured the Kentucky Futurity and harness racing's first Triple Crown. Scott Frost already had won the Hambletonian and Yonkers Trot.

1969

Baltimore completed its three-game A.L. sweep of Minnesota and the Amazin' Mets completed their N.L. sweep of Atlanta in baseball's first League Championship Series, setting up a showdown in the World Series.

1978

Kansas City third baseman George Brett blasted three solo home runs off New York ace Catfish Hunter in Game 3 of the A.L. Championship Series, but the Yankees still posted a 6–5 victory.

1985

San Francisco quarterback Joe Montana threw an NFL-record 57 passes, piling up 429 yards and five touchdowns in the 49ers' 38–17 pounding of Atlanta.

1985

Phil Niekro, the Yankees' 46-year-old knuckleballer, became the oldest pitcher to throw a shutout when he earned his 300th career victory in a season-closing 8–0 decision over Toronto.

1986

San Diego's Charlie Joiner became the NFL's all-time leader in receiving yardage and Seattle's Steve Largent moved into fourth place on the all-time list during the Seahawks' 33–7 victory over the Chargers.

1991

Pitching on the final day of the regular season, New York Mets righthander David Cone tied an N.L. record with 19 strikeouts in a 7–0 victory over Philadelphia.

1980 HOWE SWEET IT IS

Art Howe stroked a two-run homer and drove in four runs to support the six-hit pitching of Joe Niekro and give the Houston Astros a 7–1 victory over Los Angeles in a one-game playoff to decide the National League West Division championship.

The victory allowed the Astros to avoid becoming the goats in one of the great collapses of baseball history. Needing only one victory to clinch the franchise's first-ever N.L. West title, Houston arrived in Los Angeles for a season-closing series and proceeded to lose three straight one-run decisions, all decided by Dodger home runs. That left the teams tied with 92–70 records and forced a playoff that would be contested at Dodger Stadium.

The sagging Astros needed a lift, and they got it from Howe. Houston jumped to a 2–0 lead in the first inning off Dave Goltz, thanks to two Dodger errors, and added two more runs in the third on Howe's homer. His two-run single capped a three-run fourth-inning and Niekro, seeking his 20th victory, coasted home.

A STAR IS BORN

1905: Helen Wills-Moody, one of the great women tennis players of all time. She won eight Wimbledon singles championships and seven U.S. titles.

★ ★ ★

1960: Albert Lewis, a current National Football League defensive back.

★ ★ ★

1965: Ruben Sierra, a current major league outfielder.

1904

The New York Highlanders defeated Boston, 3–2, giving Happy Jack Chesbro his 41st victory of the season.

1916

Georgia Tech 222, Cumberland College 0: the granddaddy of football blowouts.

1935

Goose Goslin singled home Mickey Cochrane with the winning run in the bottom of the ninth inning, giving the Detroit Tigers a 4–3 Game 6 victory over Chicago and their first-ever World Series.

1945

Green Bay's 41-point first-quarter explosion buried the Detroit Lions and the Packers cruised to a 57–21 victory.

1977

With two out and nobody on base, the Los Angeles Dodgers stunned Philadelphia with a three-run ninth-inning rally that produced a 6–5 victory in Game 3 of the N.L. Championship Series.

1984

Major league umpires agreed to let Commissioner Peter Ueberroth arbitrate their dispute over postseason pay and returned from a one-week strike to work the final game of the N.L. Championship Series.

A STAR IS BORN

1905: Chuck Klein, a Hall of Fame outfielder who won an N.L. Triple Crown for Philadelphia in 1933 and finished his 17-year career with a .320 average.

★ ★ ★

DEATH OF A LEGEND

1925: Christy Mathewson (baseball).

★ ★ ★

1991: Leo Durocher (baseball).

1984

Payton Runs Past Legendary Brown

Chicago's Walter Payton, ending his long pursuit of Jim Brown's ghost, ran six yards with a third-quarter pitch from quarterback Jim McMahon and became the greatest career rusher in National Football League history.

Chicago's **Walter Payton**, *the NFL's all-time leading rusher.*

The historic run came in a 20–7 victory over New Orleans at Chicago and moved him past former Cleveland great Brown, who compiled 12,312 yards in an outstanding career that lasted from 1957 through 1965. Payton, competing in his 10th NFL campaign, finished the day with 154 yards and a career total of 12,400.

The game was stopped after the record run so officials could present him the ball. The 100-yard game was also Payton's record-setting 59th, breaking a tie with Brown.

1952

Martin Saves Yankees

Billy Martin sprinted in from his second base position and made a shoetop catch of a bases-loaded popup that saved a 4–2 New York lead and propelled the Yankees to a Game 7 World Series victory over Brooklyn.

The Yankees were on the verge of letting their fourth straight Series championship slip away when the alert Martin performed his rescue act. Trying to protect a two-run lead in the deciding seventh game, Yankee reliever Vic Raschi walked Carl Furillo, got pinch-hitter Rocky Nelson on a popup, surrendered a single to Billy Cox and walked Pee Wee Reese, loading the bases. New York Manager Casey Stengel called Bob Kuzava from the bullpen.

Kuzava got the dangerous Duke Snider on a popup for the second out and then induced Jackie Robinson to hit a popup near the mound, a sure rally-killer. But Kuzava stood transfixed, waiting for first baseman Joe Collins to make the play and Collins circled desperately, looking for a ball he couldn't see. As all three runners sprinted around the bases, Martin sized up the situation and sprinted in. He made the shoetop catch and Kuzava retired the Dodgers in the final two innings.

Mickey Mantle *(left) and* **Gene Woodling** *(right) blasted Game 7 home runs and* **Bob Kuzava** *turned in a sterling relief job as the Yankees finished off the Dodgers in the World Series.*

1984

Padres Catch Cubs

Tony Gwynn broke a 3–3 seventh-inning tie with a two-run double and the San Diego Padres went on to record a 6–3 victory over Chicago in a tense fifth game of the National League Championship Series.

The victory, San Diego's record-setting third straight after losing the first two games of the best-of-five playoff, gave the Padres their first-ever World Series berth. The loss was a bitter pill for the Cubs, who appeared to be on their way to ending a 39-year fall classic famine.

Even after blowing their 2–0 NLCS advantage, the Cubs opened a 3–0 lead in Game 5 on Leon Durham's two-run first-inning homer and Jody Davis' second-inning solo shot. They appeared to be in great shape with Rick Sutcliffe on the mound looking for his 16th consecutive victory.

But the Padres scored twice against the talented righthander in the sixth and broke open the game in the fateful seventh. The tying run scored when Durham let Tim Flannery's grounder go through his legs and the go-ahead runs came home when Gwynn's smash bounced wildly over second baseman Ryne Sandberg's shoulder. Gwynn scored on a single by Steve Garvey.

Relief ace Goose Gossage came in to close out the stunning victory.

OCTOBER

8

1908 CUBS HANDLE GIANTS

Chicago manufactured four third-inning runs off Christy Mathewson and Mordecai (Three Finger) Brown made them stand up for a 4–2 victory over the New York Giants in the wild and raucous culmination to the greatest pennant race in baseball history.

The game was a replay of the September 23 contest at New York's Polo Grounds that was declared a tie because of a baserunning blunder by New York first baseman Fred Merkle, costing the Giants an apparent victory. The replay became necessary when both teams ended the season with 98–55 records.

As 26,000-plus screaming fans jammed into the Polo Grounds and thousands more watched from Coogan's bluff and the elevated railroad tracks that overlooked the park, the Giants jumped to a 1–0 first-inning lead on Mike Donlin's RBI single. But Brown was called into the game in relief of starter Jack Pfiester and quickly shut down the New York offense.

The Cubs got started in the third when Joe Tinker tripled and scored on a single by Johnny Kling. A walk to Johnny Evers and doubles by Frank Schulte and Frank Chance produced three more runs.

Brown allowed only one run the rest of the way, putting the finishing touch on the Cubs' third consecutive National League pennant.

1956 LARSEN HAS PERFECT DAY

Don Larsen, a journeyman righthander who couldn't get through the second inning of his first start against Brooklyn, achieved the ultimate in pitching excellence three days later when he threw the first no-hitter and perfect game in World Series history.

The 27-year-old, using a new no-windup delivery, retired all 27 Dodgers he faced in his 2–0 Game 5 victory before 64,519 stunned fans at Yankee Stadium. He outdueled 39-year-old Brooklyn starter Sal Maglie, who matched him pitch for pitch through 11 batters before Mickey Mantle slammed a fourth-inning delivery into the right-field stands.

From that point on, all attention was focused on the amazing Larsen, who continued his unfailing three-up, three-down success and entered the ninth inning with six strikeouts and a 2–0 lead.

He quickly retired Carl Furillo on a fly ball and Roy Campanella on a grounder. Dale Mitchell, a career .312 hitter, stepped to the plate to bat for Maglie. As a nation of fans sat on the edge of their seats, Larsen worked the count to 1–2 before firing his 97th pitch – a called third strike.

Brooklyn Dodgers Owner **Walter O'Malley** *gives a tip of the hat to New York Yankee* **Don Larsen** *after his World Series Game 5 perfect game.*

MILESTONES IN SPORTS

1927

The New York Yankees, called by many the greatest team ever assembled, wrapped up their second World Series championship with a 4–3 victory over Pittsburgh, completing a four-game sweep.

1933

Boston Redskins star Cliff Battles became the NFL's first 200-yard rusher when he gained 215 in a 21–20 victory over the New York Giants.

1961

Green Bay's Paul Hornung exploded for 33 points in a 45–7 victory over Baltimore, scoring on four touchdowns, six extra points and a field goal.

1961

New York lefty Whitey Ford extended his record World Series scoreless-innings streak to 32 when he pitched five shutout innings in Game 4 against Cincinnati before leaving with an ankle injury.

1966

Wyoming's Jerry DePoyster set an NCAA record when he kicked three field goals of more than 50 yards in a 40–7 victory over Utah. DePoyster's kicks were 54, 54 and 52 yards.

1973

The New York Mets beat the Cincinnati Reds, 9–2, in the Game 3 main event of the N.L. Championship Series. Mets shortstop Bud Harrelson and the Reds' Pete Rose fought to a draw in the celebrated secondary event.

A STAR IS BORN

1909: Bill Hewitt, a football Hall of Fame end for the Chicago Bears and Philadelphia Eagles in the 1930s and '40s.

★ ★ ★

1917: Billy Conn, the world light heavyweight champion from 1939–41 best remembered for his near-miss upset of heavyweight champion Joe Louis.

★ ★ ★

1955: Bill Elliott, an race car driver who won the Daytona 500 two times and captured the NASCAR national championship in 1988.

★ ★ ★

1965: Matt Biondi, the American swimmer who won five gold medals, a silver and a bronze at the 1988 Seoul Summer Olympic Games.

1988 COLUMBIA ENDS LOSING STREAK

Solomon Johnson ran two yards for the go-ahead touchdown with 5:13 remaining and Columbia University fans held their breath as a last-second Princeton field goal attempt fell short, ensuring the Lions' 16–13 victory and ending the longest losing streak in major college football history.

The Lions had not won in 44 games over five years when they squared off at Lawrence A. Wein Stadium against Princeton as 21-point underdogs. But a cold rain helped keep the teams on even terms and the Lions got a big 182-yard rushing effort from Greg Abbruzzese.

Even so, they trailed 13–9 with time running out in the fourth quarter when they put together the winning drive. When the last-second field goal attempt fell short, ecstatic fans stormed the field and tore down both goal posts.

The victory was the Lions' first since beating Yale in 1983 and their first non-losing game since a tie against Dartmouth three weeks later.

1934 CARDINALS PERSEVERE

The St. Louis Cardinals blasted six Detroit pitchers for 17 hits and withstood a garbage-throwing tirade by frustrated Tiger fans en route to an 11–0 Game 7 conclusion to a hard-fought World Series.

Commissioner **Kenesaw Mountain Landis** *(in hat) confers with managers, players and umpires after the wild garbage-throwing melee that halted Game 7 of the World Series.*

The mood of the Detroit faithful, festive at the beginning of the afternoon, turned ugly when St. Louis left fielder Joe Medwick slid hard into Tiger third baseman Marv Owen on a sixth-inning triple. After Medwick scored to increase the Cardinal lead to 9–0, he returned to leftfield for a shower of bottles, fruit, vegetables and any other debris the fans could find to throw.

With the situation quickly getting out of control, Commissioner Kenesaw Mountain Landis, watching from his box seat, interceded and ordered Medwick removed from the game. The move had a calming effect and Dizzy Dean completed his six-hit shutout, capping the Cardinals' rise from a 3–2 World Series deficit.

The game actually was decided in a seven-run third inning that was keyed by player-Manager Frank Frisch's three-run double.

A STAR IS BORN

1889: Rube Marquard, a Hall of Fame pitcher who won 201 games in an 18-year major league career in the first quarter of the century.

★ ★ ★

1898: Joe Sewell, a Hall of Fame infielder in the 1920s and '30s who batted .312 over his 14-year major league career.

★ ★ ★

1903: Walter O'Malley, the long-time owner of the Dodgers who moved the team from Brooklyn to Los Angeles after the 1957 season.

★ ★ ★

1958: Mike Singletary, one of the National Football League's best inside linebackers over his 12-year career with the Chicago Bears.

★ ★ ★

1970: Kenny Anderson, a current National Basketball Association guard.

DEATH OF A LEGEND

1950: George Hainsworth (hockey).

1958 YANKEE RALLY SHOCKS BRAVES

Yankee Game 7 heroes: (left to right) **Bill Skowron, Bob Turley** *and* **Elston Howard.**

Moose Skowron's three-run eighth-inning homer broke open a tight game and the New York Yankees went on to defeat Milwaukee, 6–2, becoming the second team in baseball history to recover from a 3–1 deficit and win a World Series.

Skowron's blow capped a four-run explosion that snapped a 2–2 tie and made a winner of Bob Turley, who was brilliant in 6$^{2}/_{3}$ innings of relief for Don Larsen. Turley, who had worked in Games 5 and 6, escaped from a bases-loaded jam in the third inning and went on to yield two hits and one run – a game-tying Del Crandall homer – the rest of the way.

The decisive rally started with two out when Yogi Berra doubled and was singled home by Elston Howard. Andy Carey followed with another single and Skowron connected off Braves' starter Lew Burdette.

The victory was sweet revenge for the Yankees, who had dropped a tough seven-game Series to the Braves last year and then fell behind, three games to one, in this fall classic. The New Yorkers secured their record 18th World Series crown with consecutive 7–0, 4–3 and 6–2 victories.

1966 ORIOLE PITCHING ZIPS DODGERS

Baltimore lefthander Dave McNally punctuated one of the most dominating team pitching performances in history when he fired a four-hit, 1–0 shutout at the Los Angeles Dodgers and concluded the Orioles' shocking sweep of the defending champions.

The Game 4 victory at Baltimore's Memorial Stadium was decided on a fourth-inning home run by American League Triple Crown winner Frank Robinson off Don Drysdale. But the Series victory was decided by an Orioles staff that compiled a 0.50 earned-run average and gave the pitching-rich Dodgers a taste of their own medicine.

Little did anyone suspect that when the Dodgers scored a third-inning run on a bases-loaded walk in Game 1, that would be their last of the series. Moe Drabowsky, in relief of McNally, shut them down the rest of the way in that 5–2 opener, Jim Palmer pitched a four-hit 6–0 shutout in Game 2 and Wally Bunker allowed six hits in a 1–0 Game 3 win.

OCTOBER 9

MILESTONES IN SPORTS

1910

Cleveland's Nap Lajoie got eight hits in a final-day doubleheader against St. Louis, apparently passing Ty Cobb for the A.L batting title. Seven were bunt singles, leading to an investigation by A.L. President Ban Johnson.

1916

Boston lefty Babe Ruth bested Brooklyn's Sherry Smith in a memorable World Series Game 2 pitching duel, allowing six hits in a 14-inning 2–1 victory.

1919

Cincinnati 10, Chicago 5: The "Black Sox" go down to defeat in Game 8 of the World Series.

1928

Babe Ruth's second three-home run World Series barrage in three years gave the New York Yankees a 7–3 victory over St. Louis and their second straight fall classic sweep.

1964

Ayres, with John Simpson in sulky, became the third trotter to win a Triple Crown when he captured the Kentucky Futurity.

1977

The New York Yankees scored three ninth-inning runs in Game 5 of the A.L. Championship Series, securing a 5–3 victory over Kansas City and their second straight pennant.

1983

Buffalo quarterback Joe Ferguson completed 38 of 55 passes for 419 yards and five touchdowns in a 38–35 NFL overtime victory over Miami.

OCTOBER

10

1968 TIGERS RALLY, BEAT GIBSON

Mickey Lolich's five-hit pitching and a misjudged fly ball were too much for Bob Gibson to overcome as Detroit completed its record-tying comeback from a three games to one deficit and defeated the St. Louis Cardinals, 4–1, in Game 7 of the World Series.

The victory was the record-tying third of the fall classic for the paunchy Tiger lefty, who emerged as the Series pitching star over more likely candidates Gibson and Denny McLain, a 31-game winner for the Tigers during the regular season. Gibson had been phenomenal in two earlier Series victories and entered Game 7 with a record seven straight Series wins.

To no one's surprise, the final game remained scoreless through six well-pitched innings. But with two out in the seventh, lightning struck when Norm Cash and Willie Horton singled and Jim Northrup lifted a deep fly to center.

Curt Flood, an outstanding defensive outfielder, broke in on the ball, realized his mistake and backtracked. Too late. The ball bounced off the wall, two runs scored and a Bill Freehan double made it 3–0. The teams traded ninth-inning runs and the Tigers were World Series champions.

1924 SENATORS CAPTURE FIRST WORLD SERIES

The Washington Senators, long the doormat of the American League, captured their first World Series championship when a harmless-looking ground ball inexplicably hopped over the head of New York third baseman Fred Lindstrom in the 12th inning of Game 7 at Griffith Stadium.

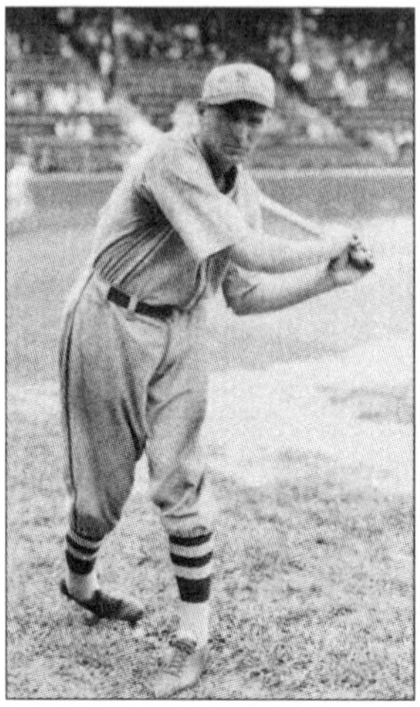

Fred Lindstrom *was victimized by two bad-hop grounders.*

To say that Lady Luck was on Washington's side is an understatement. The Giants were seemingly in control of the Series finale, holding a 3–1 lead with one out in the eighth inning. But the Senators loaded the bases with two out and player-Manager Bucky Harris hit a ground ball to third.

As Lindstrom prepared to make a routine play, the ball hopped wildly over his head and two runs scored, tying the game. Aging Walter Johnson was called from the Washington bullpen and the once-dominant righthander responded with four shutout innings.

Washington got three big breaks during its winning rally. Muddy Ruel, given new life when Giants catcher Hank Gowdy stumbled and dropped his foul popup, doubled and Johnson reached when shortstop Travis Jackson booted his grounder. That's when Earl McNeely's routine shot, just like Harris' in the eighth, hopped over Lindstrom's head, allowing Ruel to score the Series-deciding run.

1920 INDIANS GO ON A BINGE

Cleveland players Elmer Smith, Jim Bagby and Bill Wambsganss all took giant steps into the baseball record book as the Indians defeated Brooklyn, 8–1, in one of the most memorable World Series contests ever played.

With the fall classic deadlocked at two games apiece, the Indians struck quickly against Dodger starter Burleigh Grimes. Charlie Jamieson and Wambsganss singled and Tris Speaker bunted for a hit, loading the bases in the bottom of the first inning. Smith stepped to the plate and promptly belted the first grand slam home run in World Series history.

Cleveland's **Bill Wambsganss** *tags out Brooklyn's* **Otto Miller**, *completing the first unassisted triple play in World Series history.*

The score remained 4–0 until the fourth, when Bagby, a 31-game winner during the regular season, stepped to the plate with two runners aboard. He, too, connected – for the first Series homer by a pitcher.

But the capper came in the Brooklyn fifth when Pete Kilduff singled, moved to second on Otto Miller's hit and broke for third when Clarence Mitchell smashed a drive toward right-center field. Second baseman Wambsganss picked it off, stepped on second to force Kilduff and wheeled around to tag Miller. The first Series triple play also was unassisted.

MILESTONES IN SPORTS

1926

Aging Grover Cleveland Alexander rescued St. Louis in Game 7 of the World Series when he struck out Yankee slugger Tony Lazzeri with the bases loaded in the seventh inning – a game eventually won by the Cardinals, 3–2.

1957

The Milwaukee Braves captured their first World Series championship when Lew Burdette recorded his record-tying third fall classic victory – a 5–0 shutout of the New York Yankees in Game 7.

1961

The New York Mets and Houston Colt .45s filled their rosters during the N.L.'s first-ever expansion draft.

1980

George Brett's upper-deck Yankee Stadium blast off New York's Goose Gossage gave the Kansas City Royals a 4–2 victory and three-game A.L. Championship Series sweep of the Yankees.

1981

Southern California running back Marcus Allen rushed for 211 yards in a 13–10 loss to Arizona – his fifth straight 200-yard effort.

1987

San Francisco's Jeffrey Leonard homered in his fourth straight N.L. Championship Series game against St. Louis, helping the Giants to a 4–2 victory and a 2–2 Series tie.

A STAR IS BORN

1905: Wally Berger, a major league outfielder who set a rookie home run record (38) in 1930.

★ ★ ★

1946: Gene Tenace, a 15-year major leaguer remembered for his record-tying four-home run World Series in 1972 for the Oakland Athletics.

1991 Chip Beck Shoots 59, Ties Record

Veteran tour player Chip Beck, lifting his game to a plateau that only one man had previously reached, shot the second 59 in the history of PGA tournament play during the third round of the Las Vegas Invitational at the Sunrise Golf Club.

The 35-year-old Beck, who has been playing on the tour for 13 years, joined Al Geiberger as the only golfers to achieve a sub-60 score in a PGA-sponsored event. Geiberger shot his 59 in the 1977 Memphis Classic and it remained unmatched for 14 years.

But then along came Beck, who recorded 13 birdies and five pars while claiming a share of the third-round lead with Bruce Lietzke. Beck's milestone round came over a 6,914-yard Sunrise course, Geiberger's over the 7,193-yard Colonial Country Club course in Memphis.

Geiberger's round consisted of 11 birdies, an eagle and six pars.

1980 Phillies Win Wild Battle

Philadelphia's Pete Rose bowled over Houston catcher Bruce Bochy and scored the winning run in the 10th inning, helping the Phillies overcome the Houston Astros, 5–3, in one of the wildest and most controversial National League Championship Series games ever played.

Most of the Game 4 controversy took place in the fourth inning after Phillies Bake McBride and Manny Trillo had led off with singles. The next batter, Garry Maddox, hit a soft line drive toward the mound and Houston pitcher Vern Ruhle fielded the ball, throwing to first base for an apparent double play. Philadelphia players streamed out of the dugout, insisting Ruhle had trapped the ball and, during the confusion, Astros first baseman Art Howe went over and stepped on second, claiming a triple play.

The debate carried on for 20 minutes with umpire Doug Harvey finally ruling the play a catch and granting the double play. He said time had been called before the triple play was recorded. The Phillies failed to score in the inning.

The Phillies did score three runs in the eighth, however, to gain a 3–2 lead and the Astros tied it in the ninth on a Terry Puhl single. The Phillies won in the 10th when Rose scored on Greg Luzinski's double and Trillo doubled home Luzinski.

1972 Reds Triumph On Wild Pitch

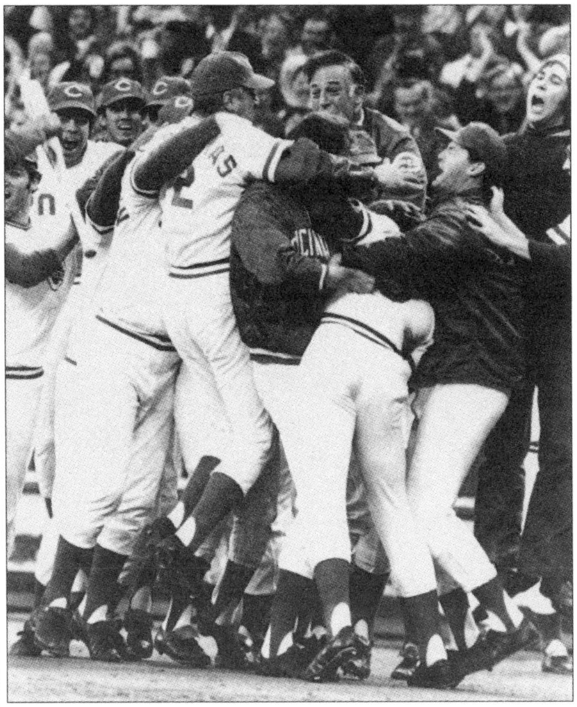

It's celebration time for the Cincinnati Reds after winning the N.L. Championship Series on a Pittsburgh wild pitch.

Pinch-runner George Foster raced home on a ninth-inning wild pitch by Pittsburgh reliever Bob Moose, giving the Cincinnati Reds a narrow 4–3 victory in the decisive fifth game of the National League Championship Series at Riverfront Stadium.

The Pirates were clinging to a slim 3–2 advantage when the ninth inning opened, but Cincinnati catcher Johnny Bench, the National League's regular-season home run champion, took care of that with a shot over the right-field fence off Pirates reliever Dave Giusti.

Tony Perez and Denis Menke followed with singles and Giusti was replaced by Moose. Cesar Geronimo's deep fly to right sent Foster, running for Perez, to third and Moose got a second out on an infield pop. But with Hal McRae pinch-hitting for pitcher Clay Carroll, Moose's pitch bounced in front of the plate and skipped past catcher Manny Sanguillen as Foster raced home to a wild victory celebration near the Reds' dugout.

So ended the first National League playoff series to go the five-game distance.

A Star Is Born

1897: George Preston Marshall, a pro football Hall of Famer who founded the Washington Redskins.

★ ★ ★

1906: Dutch Clark, a pro football Hall of Fame quarterback for the Portsmouth Spartans and Detroit Lions in the 1930s.

★ ★ ★

1939: Maria Bueno, an outstanding Brazilian tennis player who won four U.S. singles championships and three Wimbledon titles.

★ ★ ★

1961: Steve Young, a current National Football League quarterback.

★ ★ ★

1965: Chris Spielman, a current National Football League linebacker.

Death of a Legend

1959: Bert Bell (football).

October 11

Milestones in Sports

1911

Detroit's Ty Cobb and the Chicago Cubs' Frank (Wildfire) Schulte were named recipients of the first Chalmers MVP awards.

1913

Philadelphia lefthander Eddie Plank's two-hitter defeated Christy Mathewson and the New York Giants, 3–1, in the decisive fifth game of the World Series.

1943

New York's Spud Chandler pitched a 10-hit shutout and the Yankees closed out the St. Louis Cardinals, 2–0, in the fifth and deciding game of the World Series.

1971

The United States captured its fourth straight Davis Cup championship with a slim 3–2 victory over Romania.

1981

Los Angeles' LeRoy Irvin became the fourth player in pro football history to return two punts for touchdowns in the same game, running 75 and 84 yards during the Rams' 37–35 victory over the Atlanta Falcons.

OCTOBER

12

A STAR IS BORN

1906: Joe Cronin, a Hall of Fame infielder and .301 hitter in 20 major league seasons, a manager, a front-office executive for the Red Sox and president of the American League.

★ ★ ★

1906: Rick Ferrell, a Hall of Fame catcher who batted .281 over 18 major league seasons.

★ ★ ★

1936: Tony Kubek, a New York Yankee shortstop who went on to greater fame as a baseball broadcaster.

★ ★ ★

DEATH OF A LEGEND

1969: Sonja Henie (figure skating).

★ ★ ★

1986: Norm Cash (baseball).

★ ★ ★

1986 SOX RALLY NIPS ANGELS

Boston center fielder Dave Henderson drilled a dramatic two-run ninth-inning homer to keep the Red Sox's pennant hopes alive and then hit an 11th-inning sacrifice fly to give them a 7–6 victory over California in Game 5 of the American League Championship Series at Anaheim Stadium.

Boston savior **Dave Henderson** *smiles broadly as he is greeted at the plate by* **Bill Buckner** *(6) and* **Dave Stapleton** *after his dramatic game-tying home run.*

With the Red Sox, down three games to one, on the brink of elimination and the Angels within one strike of their first-ever A.L. pennant, Henderson fouled off two pitches and then shocked 64,223 celebrating Angels fans when he drilled a 2-2 Donnie Moore offering into the left-field seats, giving the Red Sox a 6–5 lead.

But the Angels weren't ready to die, either. They fought back to tie in the bottom of the ninth on Rob Wilfong's RBI single and loaded the bases with one out, only to let Boston reliever Steve Crawford off the hook with two harmless fly ball outs. The score remained tied until the 11th, when Henderson delivered his bases-loaded sacrifice fly.

Henderson, ironically, had appeared to be destined for goat horns after accidentally knocking Bobby Grich's sixth-inning drive over the center-field fence while trying to make a catch, giving the Angels a lead they held until the fateful ninth.

1992 MONK CATCHES STEVE LARGENT

Washington wide receiver Art Monk caught three straight fourth-period passes from quarterback Mark Rypien and moved past former Seattle great Steve Largent as the all-time top receiver in National Football League history.

Monk's record-setting 10-yard sideline catch came in the closing minutes of the Redskins' 34–3 Monday night victory over the Denver Broncos. It was the t hird straight pass thrown his way and career catch No. 820 – one more than Largent managed in an outstanding career that ended after the 1989 campaign.

Monk, a 13-year veteran, has totaled 11,211 yards, 13.7 per catch, and 60 touch-downs. He has caught at least one pass in137 consecutive games, which ranks third on the career list behind Largent (177) and Ozzie Newsome (150).

Monk finished his historic game with seven catches for 69 yards. Ironically, Monk caught five passes for 69 yards on December 23, 1989, against Seattle – in Largent's final professional game.

1929 A'S POST 10-RUN INNING

Jimmie Dykes' two-run double capped Philadelphia's incredible 10-run seventh-inning comeback and the Athletics held on for a 10–8 victory over Chicago in Game 4 of the World Series at Shibe Park.

The A's sudden offensive explosion wiped out an 8–0 Cubs advantage and turned a potential 2–2 Series tie into a 3–1 advantage. It appeared the A's were hopelessly buried as they entered the seventh inning down by eight runs and facing a pitcher, Charlie Root, who had allowed only three hits.

Al Simmons, the American League's top RBI man, ended the shutout with a long home run to open the inning. Consecutive singles by Jimmie Foxx, Bing Miller, Dykes and Joe Boley added two more runs and, after pinch-hitter George Burns had popped out, Max Bishop stroked another RBI single.

Mule Haas, facing reliever Art Nehf, followed with a line drive to center that Hack Wilson lost in the sun. Haas circled the bases with a three-run inside-the-park homer, making the score 8–7.

After Mickey Cochrane walked, Simmons and Foxx singled, Miller was hit by a pitch and Dykes delivered his winning blow.

Suddenly down 10–8, the shocked Cubs went meekly the rest of the way.

MILESTONES IN SPORTS

1948

The New York Yankees, third-place finishers last season under Bucky Harris, pulled a shocker when they named Casey Stengel as their new manager.

1963

No. 2-ranked Texas overpowered top-ranked Oklahoma, 28–7, in a much-publicized college football confrontation at the Cotton Bowl in Dallas.

1967

St. Louis righthander Bob Gibson ruined Boston's "Impossible Dream" when he pitched a three-hitter and beat the Red Sox, 7–2, in Game 7 of the World Series.

1976

New York's Don Murdoch tied an NHL rookie record by scoring five goals in a 10–4 Rangers rout of Minnesota.

1982

Milwaukee's Paul Molitor banged out a World Series-record five hits, teammate Robin Yount added four and Mike Caldwell pitched a three-hitter to lead the Brewers to a 10–0 Game 1 victory over St. Louis.

1986

Chicago's Walter Payton became the first NFL player to go over 20,000 all-purpose yards when he rushed for 76 and caught passes for 30 more in a 20–7 victory over Houston.

1987

The Minnesota Twins defeated Detroit, 9–5, in Game 5 of the A.L. Championship Series, winning their first pennant in 22 years.

MILESTONES
· IN SPORTS ·

1921

Art Nehf pitched a four-hitter and the Giants beat the Yankees, 1–0, in the Game 8 conclusion to the first all-New York World Series.

1947

All-Stars 4, Maple Leafs 3 in the first NHL All-Star Game at Toronto.

1963

Mickey Wright captured her fourth LPGA Championship in six years when she beat Mary Lena Faulk, Mary Mills and Louise Suggs by two strokes at Las Vegas.

1971

Roberto Clemente collected three hits as the Pirates treated their home fans to a 4–3 victory over Baltimore in the first World Series night game ever played.

1985

New York Giants quarterback Phil Simms completed 40 of his NFL record-tying 62 pass attempts for 513 yards in a 35–30 loss to Cincinnati.

1960

Maz Pulls Yankee Plug

Pittsburgh second baseman Bill Mazeroski pulled the plug on the vaunted New York Yankee machine with a ninth-inning Game 7 home run that brought a dramatic conclusion to one of the most exciting World Series ever played.

Pittsburgh's **Bill Mazeroski** *dances around the bases after his World Series-ending home run against the Yankees.*

Mazeroski, leading off the final inning with the score tied 9–9, hit Ralph Terry's second pitch over the left-field fence at Forbes Field and then danced jubilantly around the bases. The home run brought down the curtain on a Series in which the resourceful Pirates had been outhit, 91–60, and outscored, 55–27.

The Pirates broke on top with two runs in the first off Bob Turley and two more in the second off Bill Stafford. But the powerful Yankees fought back on a Moose Skowron homer in the fifth and routed starter Vern Law in a four-run sixth that was capped by Yogi Berra's three-run blast.

When the Yankees added two runs in the top of the eighth, things looked bleak for the Pirates. But the Bucs quickly struck back with five runs of their own in the bottom of the inning – three on a shocking home run by backup catcher Hal Smith.

Down by two, the Yanks fought back again, tying the score in the top of the ninth and setting the stage for Mazeroski. It took him only one memorable swing.

OCTOBER

13

A STAR IS BORN

1876: Rube Waddell, a Hall of Fame pitcher who won 191 games in the first decade of the 1900s.

★ ★ ★

1931: Eddie Mathews, a Hall of Fame third baseman who blasted 512 home runs over his 17-year major league career.

★ ★ ★

1957: Reggie Theus, a 13-year National Basketball Association guard who scored 19,015 career points.

★ ★ ★

1962: Jerry Rice, a current National Football League wide receiver.

★ ★ ★

1967: Javier Sotomayor, the Cuban who became the world's first 8-foot high jumper in 1989.

DEATH OF A LEGEND

1974: Sam Rice (baseball).

★ ★ ★

1984: George Kelly (baseball).

1903

First World Series

Bill Dinneen pitched a four-hit shutout and outdueled a tired Deacon Phillippe as the Boston Red Sox completed their shocking eight-game victory over Pittsburgh in a 3–0 finale to baseball's first world championship series.

Phillippe was tired because he had worked 36 tough innings going into the eighth game, with three victories and a loss to show for his efforts. Dinneen had pitched 26 himself, but he was getting plenty of help from teammate Cy Young. That two-against-one pitching matchup was primarily responsible for the Red Sox's ability to upset the heavily-favored Pirates.

Holding a 4–3 advantage in the best-of-nine postseason playoff, the upstart American League champs broke through against the Pirates' workhorse in the fourth inning on Hobe Ferris' two-run single. With Dinneen continuing to mow down the Pirates, the Red Sox added a sixth-inning run on another Ferris single. That's all the righthander needed to give the Red Sox their fourth straight Series triumph and to notch his third win of the Series.

1914

Braves Finish Miracle Sweep

In a World Series conclusion that was just as astonishing as their run to the National League pennant, the Miracle Braves of Boston swept past the heavily-favored Philadelphia Athletics and claimed baseball's highest prize.

"Swept" as in four straight. The 3–1 finale at Braves Field was a fitting conclusion to one of the great upset stories of the century.

The Braves, who had made a miraculous run from last place in mid-July to a $10^1/_2$-game victory margin in the N.L. pennant race, handled the Athletics with ease. The A's, winners of three of the last four World Series, simply could not solve a pitching staff that featured Dick Rudolph, Bill James and Lefty Tyler.

Rudolph, who had pitched a 7–1 first-game victory, was just as good in the finale, allowing seven hits and walking one while outdueling Bob Shawkey. Rudolph got all the runs he needed on Johnny Evers' two-run fifth-inning single.

Pitcher **Bill James,** *a key figure for the Miracle Braves.*

OCTOBER

14

1905 SERIES ENDS IN SHUTOUT

New York Giants righthander Christy Mathewson brought the World Series to its fifth-game conclusion the same way he had opened it – with a shutout. His 2–0 whitewashing of the Philadelphia Athletics was the perfect ending for a Series in which the losing team never was able to score a run.

Mathewson won the opener 3–0, the A's Chief Bender answered with a 3–0 Game 2 shutout, Mathewson pitched a 9–0 third-game victory and teammate Joe McGinnity was a 1–0 winner in Game 4. Mathewson pitched a six-hitter in the finale and outdueled Bender, who allowed just five hits himself.

Mathewson finished the fall classic with three shutouts in six days, permitting just 14 hits while striking out 18 and walking one.

Christy Mathewson *threw nothing but zeroes at the Athletics in the World Series.*

1976 YANKS END FRUSTRATION

A towering ninth-inning home run by first baseman Chris Chambliss off Kansas City relief ace Mark Littell brought a dramatic conclusion to Game 5 of the American League Championship Series and ended 12 years of New York Yankee frustration.

New York Yankee first baseman **Chris Chambliss.**

The first Yankee pennant since 1964 became official when Chambliss' drive disappeared over the right-center field fence, giving the Yankees a 7–6 victory over the Royals and triggering one of the wildest mob scenes ever witnessed.

Joyous fans rushed out of the stands and mobbed Chambliss, who was trying to circle the bases. Second base had been removed before he could get there and he never could reach third or home. When the celebration finally concluded, more than $100,000 in damage had been done to Yankee Stadium.

Both teams scored early in the must-win contest, but the favored Yankees carried a 6–3 lead into the eighth inning. The Royals refused to die, however, and tied the score on a dramatic three-run homer by George Brett.

Chambliss, the leadoff batter in the bottom of the ninth, hit Littell's first pitch and put the Yankees in their 29th World Series.

A STAR IS BORN

1896: Oscar Charleston, a Negro League star and Hall of Famer who is considered one of the great center fielders of all time.

★ ★ ★

1910: John Wooden, a basketball Hall of Famer as both a coach and a player. He directed UCLA to 10 national championships, including seven straight from 1967–73.

★ ★ ★

1946: Al Oliver, an 18-year major leaguer who compiled a .303 career average before retiring in 1985.

★ ★ ★

1947: Charlie Joiner, an 18-year NFL receiver who caught 750 passes for 12,146 yards.

★ ★ ★

DEATH OF A LEGEND

1969: Arnie Herber (football).

★ ★ ★

1988: Vic Raschi (baseball).

1992 CABRERA'S HIT LIFTS BRAVES

Francisco Cabrera, a backup catcher who had three hits during the regular season, lined a two-out bases-loaded single to left field, driving in two runs and giving the Atlanta Braves a stunning 3–2 National League Championship Series-clinching victory over the Pittsburgh Pirates.

Cabrera, batting in the ninth inning of the tension-filled Game 7 at Atlanta's Fulton County Stadium, hit a 2–1 pitch from Pirates reliever Stan Belinda through the infield. Left fielder Barry Bonds charged the ball and made a strong throw to the plate, but Atlanta runner Sid Bream eluded catcher Mike LaValliere's tag. That gave the Braves their second straight pennant and sent the Pirates down to NLCS defeat for the third year in a row.

The loss was especially bitter for seventh-game starter Doug Drabek, who had carried a 2–0 lead into the decisive ninth. But Terry Pendleton led off with a double and sure-handed second baseman Jose Lind made an error on a ground ball. When Drabek walked Bream to load the bases, Belinda was called into the game.

Pendleton scored on Ron Gant's sacrifice fly. Belinda walked Damon Berryhill and retired Brian Hunter on an infield pop, setting the stage for Cabrera.

MILESTONES IN SPORTS

1906

The Chicago White Sox, baseball's "Hitless Wonders," completed their shocking World Series upset of the powerful Chicago Cubs (116-game winners) with an 8–3 victory at South Side Park.

1916

Englishman Jim Barnes sank a four-foot putt on the 36th hole and defeated Jock Hutchison, 1-up, in the inaugural PGA Championship at the Siwanoy Country Club in New York.

1951

Detroit's Jack Christiansen returned two punts for touchdowns, but the Los Angeles Rams overcame his heroics and beat the Lions, 27–21.

1968

Jim Hines of the United States ran the 100-meter dash in a world-record 9.95 seconds while capturing the gold medal in the Summer Olympic Games at Mexico City.

1972

Gene Tenace became the first player in history to hit home runs in his first two World Series at-bats as he led the Oakland Athletics to a 3–2 Game 1 victory over Cincinnati.

1984

Kirk Gibson's two home runs and five RBIs carried the Detroit Tigers to an 8–5 World Series-clinching Game 5 victory over San Diego.

1991

The New York Rangers' Mike Gartner scored his 500th career goal.

1992

The Toronto Blue Jays powered their way to a 9–2 victory over Oakland in Game 6 of the A.L. Championship Series, giving Canada its first baseball pennant.

1946 SLAUGHTER'S MAD DASH

Enos Slaughter's mad dash around the bases caught the Boston defense sleeping and gave the St. Louis Cardinals the winning run in their 4–3 seventh-game World Series victory over the Red Sox at Sportsman's Park.

A happy group of St Louis Cardinals celebrate their World Series victory over the Red Sox.

The play was set up when Slaughter led off the eighth inning of a 2–2 game with a single. He had to hold when Whitey Kurowski popped out while attempting to sacrifice and Del Rice flied out, but Harry Walker lined a shot into left-center field and Slaughter set sail.

Boston center fielder Leon Culberson cut the ball off quickly, wheeled and threw to shortstop Johnny Pesky. Everyone in the park, including Pesky, expected a first-and-third situation, but Slaughter had other ideas. He hit the third-base bag and kept right on going. Pesky, surprised by the bold move, hesitated before making a throw that pulled catcher Roy Partee up the line as Slaughter slid home safely.

Boston threatened in the ninth, but Harry Brecheen retired two batters with runners on first and third to secure the championship.

1988 GIBSON HOMER SHOCKS A'S

Kirk Gibson, limping badly and wincing with every painful swing, blasted a 3–2 Dennis Eckersley pitch over the right-field fence with two out in the ninth inning to give Los Angeles a 5–4 victory over Oakland in an unbelievable conclusion to Game 1 of the World Series.

The fantastic finish looked like something straight out of a Hollywood script. The Athletics, on the strength of Jose Canseco's second-inning grand slam, carried a 4–3 lead into the ninth and turned the game over to Eckersley, baseball's best reliever.

Eckersley quickly retired the first two batters and then issued a rare walk to pinch-hitter Mike Davis. The ailing Gibson was called up to pinch-hit for pitcher Alejandro Pena.

Gibson, who had injured his leg before the Series, was in obvious pain as he stepped to the plate. He couldn't put pressure on his bad leg and his swings were almost one-handed. When the count reached 2–2, Davis stole second. On a 3–2 offering, the grimacing Gibson put everything he had into one last swing – and connected. He hobbled around the bases as the Dodger Stadium crowd and a national television audience watched in disbelief.

It was the first time a World Series game had been decided on a come-from-behind home run in the final inning.

A STAR IS BORN

1858: John L. Sullivan, last of the bare-knuckle heavyweight boxing champions who reigned from 1882–92.

★ ★ ★

1909: Mel Harder, a 20-year major league pitcher who won 223 games for the Cleveland Indians.

★ ★ ★

1945: Jim Palmer, a Hall of Fame pitcher and 268-game winner in 19 seasons with the Baltimore Orioles.

★ ★ ★

1970: Mike Peplowski, a current National Basketball Association center.

★ ★ ★

DEATH OF A LEGEND

1963: Horton Smith (golf).

★ ★ ★

1985: Max Zaslofsky (basketball).

★ ★ ★

1989 GRETZKY PASSES POINT RECORD

Wayne Gretzky scored a game-tying goal with 53 seconds remaining in regulation to pass former great Gordie Howe as the National Hockey League's all-time top point-scorer. Then, for good measure, the Great One scored again in overtime to give the Los Angeles Kings a 5–4 victory over Edmonton.

Fittingly, Gretzky's coronation took place at Edmonton's Northlands Coliseum – the arena where he played for nine seasons and led the Oilers to four Stanley Cup championships. He was traded to Los Angeles last year and completed his record run in a Kings uniform before the Oilers fans he had thrilled for so long with his mind-boggling exploits.

Needing two points to tie Howe's record of 1,850, Gretzky assisted on an early goal to pull within one. But with time running out and the Kings trailing 4–3, it appeared the record would have to wait for another day.

Not so. The crowd erupted when Gretzky dramatically swept a backhander past Edmonton goaltender Bill Ranford in the final minute to tie the score. After the game had been stopped for a brief ceremony, Gretzky capped his big night with the overtime winner.

Howe needed 26 seasons to compile his record point total, most of them with Detroit. The amazing Gretzky passed his mark in season No. 10.

OCTOBER 15

MILESTONES IN SPORTS

1923
The beginning of a dynasty: The New York Yankees clinched their first World Series championship with a 6–4 victory over the New York Giants.

1925
The Pittsburgh Pirates became the first team to recover from a 3–1 World Series deficit when they defeated Washington, 9–7, in Game 7.

1972
Chicago's Stan Mikita joined the NHL's 1,000-point club when he assisted on a goal in a 3–1 loss to St. Louis.

1977
Arkansas kicker Steve Little tied the 2-week-old NCAA record of Texas' Russell Erxleben when he booted a 67-yard field goal in a college football game against Texas.

1986
The New York Mets scored three runs in the ninth inning and three in the 16th to claim the N.L. pennant with a 7-6 victory over Houston. It was the longest postseason game ever played.

1987
The NFL Players Association ordered its members to end their 24-day in-season strike and return to their teams, even though agreement had not been reached on a new contract.

1988
Oklahoma rushed for an NCAA-record 768 yards in a 70–24 college football rout of Kansas State.

OCTOBER

16

A STAR IS BORN

1883: Will Harridge, a Hall of Fame baseball executive who served as American League president for 27 years (1931–58).

★ ★ ★

1900: Goose Goslin, a Hall of Fame outfielder who compiled a .316 career average over 18 major league seasons.

★ ★ ★

1940: Dave DeBusschere, a basketball Hall of Fame forward who scored 14,053 points over a 12-year NBA career in the 1960s and '70s, and a former major league pitcher.

★ ★ ★

1941: Tim McCarver, a catcher who compiled a .271 average over 21 major league seasons and went on to a second career as a baseball broadcaster.

★ ★ ★

1969: Juan Gonzalez, a current major league outfielder.

★ ★ ★

1962 GIANTS, McCOVEY FALL INCHES SHORT

New York second baseman Bobby Richardson snared a vicious line drive off the bat of San Francisco slugger Willie McCovey, bringing a pulsating end to another Yankee World Series victory and leaving the Giants a few inches short.

With the Yankees holding a precarious 1–0 lead and starter Ralph Terry working on a two-hitter in the game at Candlestick Park, the Giants finally got their offense untracked in the ninth. Pinch-hitter Matty Alou led off with a bunt single and Terry recorded two outs. But Willie Mays doubled to right, putting the tying and winning runs in scoring position.

Up stepped the 6-foot-4, 225-pound McCovey, swinging his bat like a toothpick and anxious to give the Giants their first championship since 1954. Terry was anxious to atone for his 1960 World Series-ending pitch that Pittsburgh's Bill Mazeroski hit for a home run.

On a 1–1 count, the left-handed slugger hit a line smash that appeared to be headed for right field. But Richardson took one step to his left, threw up his glove and the ball nestled in. The Yankees were champions for the second straight year – by inches.

New York Yankee pitcher **Ralph Terry** *gets a victory ride after stopping San Francisco in Game 7 of the World Series.*

1968 USOC BANS PROTESTORS

Tommie Smith used an incredible burst of speed to shoot past his competitors and set a world record in the 200-meter final in the Mexico City Olympic Games, but the sensation he caused in winning that race was nothing compared to the furor that would arise after the awards ceremony.

Smith, who became the first 200-meter sprinter to break 20 seconds (19.83), and John Carlos, the bronze medal winner, used their moment in the Olympic sun to deliver a message to the American public – and Olympic officials quickly delivered another kind of message to the athletes.

The two American sprinters stepped onto the dais barefooted with prominently displayed civil rights buttons. When the national anthem was played and the American flag raised, both bowed their heads deeply and raised a black-gloved fist in a black-power salute.

They later explained that the clenched fist symbolized black strength and unity and the bare feet were a reminder of black poverty in the U.S. The bowed heads were to express their belief that the words of freedom in the national anthem applied only to white-skinned Americans.

The protest outraged International Olympic Committee officials, who ordered the United States Olympic Committee to discipline the athletes. Under threat of having the entire U.S. contingent banished from the Games, the USOC suspended Smith and Carlos and banned them for life from Olympic competition.

1985 CLARK BLASTS DODGERS

St. Louis first baseman Jack Clark drove a Tom Niedenfuer fastball into the left-field seats with two on and two out in the ninth inning, shocking a packed Dodger Stadium house and giving the Cardinals a National League Championship Series-clinching 7–5 victory over Los Angeles.

Clark's dramatic Game 6 home run came after the Dodgers had taken a 5–4 lead in the bottom of the eighth on Mike Marshall's solo homer. The Dodgers, in fact, had led most of the afternoon, scoring single runs in the first two innings and two in the fifth – the second on Bill Madlock's third Series home run. The Cardinals scored three in the seventh.

Willie McGee singled to open the fateful ninth for St. Louis and Ozzie Smith walked. Both advanced when Tom Herr bounced to first for the second out. That brought up Clark, who delivered his game-winning homer.

MILESTONES • IN SPORTS •

1910

A.L. President Ban Johnson officially declared Detroit's Ty Cobb league batting champion in the wake of Nap Lajoie's suspicious eight-hit final-day doubleheader performance against the St. Louis Browns.

1912

A dropped fly ball by New York center fielder Fred Snodgrass opened the door for two 10th-inning Boston runs and a 3–2 World Series-deciding victory over the Giants.

1964

Don Schollander became the first swimmer to win four golds in one Olympic Games when he anchored the American 4 X 200-meter freestyle relay team to victory at Tokyo.

1969

The Amazin' New York Mets completed their run to glory with a 5–3 Game 5 World Series victory over Baltimore.

1971

Toronto's Norm Ullman assisted on a goal and picked up his 1,000th career point in a 5–3 loss to the New York Rangers.

1976

Texas A&M kicker Tony Franklin connected on 64- and 65-yard field goals – in the same game, a 24–0 victory over Baylor.

1989 Series Shuts Down After Earthquake

It was the most unforgettable World Series game never played. At 5:04 p.m., with 60,000-plus fans jammed into San Francisco's Candlestick Park and feverishly awaiting the introduction of the Oakland Athletics and Giants players before Game 3, a not-so-funny thing happened. The ballpark began to shake, the press box waved precariously and all electric power shut down. The Bay Area had been hit by an earthquake.

Amazingly, everybody assembled for this fall classic event remained calm and even festive. But that mood changed quickly when radio and television began reporting massive destruction and loss of lives, the result of a tremor that measured 7.1 on the Richter scale.

The scene at San Francisco's Candlestick Park after a major earthquake forced postponement of World Series Game 3.

Baseball Commissioner Fay Vincent acted quickly by postponing the game and ordering Candlestick Park officials to get the fans out of the stadium in an orderly fashion before it turned dark. His quick action proved to be wise.

A crowd that a few hours earlier had been so excited about a baseball game vacated Candlestick Park quickly to face the somber realities of death and devastation.

1979 Pirate 'Family' Rules

Willie Stargell, *the father figure in Pittsburgh's 'Family.'*

Willie Stargell, affectionately known as "Pops" by his Pittsburgh teammates, blasted a two-run sixth-inning homer and Pirate relievers Grant Jackson and Kent Tekulve made it stand up in a 4–1 seventh-game World Series victory over Baltimore.

The victory at Baltimore's Memorial Stadium climaxed a valiant comeback from a three games to one Series deficit for the team that billed itself as the "Family." In becoming the fourth team in history to accomplish that feat, the Pirates relied on some lusty hitting and a pitching staff that permitted just two Oriole runs over the last 28 innings of the Series.

The Orioles broke on top in the Game 7 finale when second baseman Rich Dauer muscled up and hit a third-inning homer. But Pittsburgh starter Jim Bibby, with $4^{1}/_{3}$ innings of hitless relief from Jackson and Tekulve, shut down the Orioles the rest of the way while the Pirate bats were getting untracked.

After Bill Robinson singled in the sixth inning, Stargell blasted a Scott McGregor pitch for a 2–1 lead. The Pirates added a pair of ninth-inning runs and Tekulve closed the door on the Bucs' first World Series championship since 1971.

October 17

Milestones in Sports

1948

The Green Bay Packers intercepted seven Bob Waterfield passes and cruised to a 16–0 victory over the Los Angeles Rams.

1960

New National League franchises were officially awarded to interests in New York and Houston.

1971

Steve Blass pitched a four-hitter and the Pittsburgh Pirates squeezed out a 2–1 victory over Baltimore in the deciding seventh game of the World Series.

1974

Joe Rudi's seventh-inning Game 5 home run off Los Angeles relief ace Mike Marshall gave the Oakland Athletics a 3–2 victory over the Dodgers and their third straight World Series championship.

1987

Minnesota 10, St. Louis 1 in the first World Series game played under a roof – the Hubert H. Humphrey Metrodome.

1989

The Calgary Flames scored a record-tying two shorthanded goals in 4 seconds and three goals in 27 seconds of the third period en route to an 8–8 tie with Quebec.

A Star Is Born

1907: Paul Derringer, a righthanded pitcher who won 223 major league games over 15 seasons in the 1930s and '40s.

★ ★ ★

1946: Bob Seagren, an outstanding American pole vaulter who won the gold medal in the 1968 Summer Olympics at Mexico City and broke the world outdoor record in the event five times.

★ ★ ★

1966: Danny Ferry, a current National Basketball Association forward.

★ ★ ★

Death of a Legend

1972: Turk Broda (hockey).

★ ★ ★

1977: Cal Hubbard (football, baseball).

1954 Burk Throws 7 Touchdowns

Philadelphia quarterback Adrian Burk, putting on one of the most dazzling passing displays in National Football League history, fired a record-tying seven touchdown passes in a 49–21 victory over the winless Redskins at Washington.

Burk tied the record set in 1943 by Chicago quarterback Sid Luckman, who threw for seven touchdowns in a game against the New York Giants. Burk's record-matching throw, to Pete Pihos, came with 10 seconds left to play.

Pihos caught three touchdown passes, Bobby Walston caught three and Tony Ledbetter pulled in one. The 26-year-old former Baylor star completed 19 of 27 passes for 229 yards and he also starred with his foot.

Burk, who doubles as a punter, pinned the Redskins at their 2, 3 and 9-yard line with punts, making it easy on the unbeaten Eagles' defense. The highlight of the game for Washington was Dale Atkeson's 99-yard kickoff return midway through the second quarter.

OCTOBER

18

MILESTONES IN SPORTS

1950

Connie Mack, the 87-year-old founder and patriarch of the Philadelphia Athletics, ended his 50-year active career and named Jimmie Dykes as the team's new manager.

1953

Willie Thrower, credited with being the first black quarterback in NFL history, made his one and only appearance with the Chicago Bears, completing three passes in eight attempts for 27 yards against San Francisco.

1953

The Los Angeles Rams' Woodley Lewis totaled 120 yards in punt returns and 174 in kickoff returns during a 31–19 victory over Detroit.

1960

The New York Yankees stunned the baseball world when they released 70-year-old Manager Casey Stengel, five days after the Bronx Bombers' World Series loss to Pittsburgh.

1967

The American League granted Athletics Owner Charles O. Finley permission to move his team to Oakland and awarded expansion franchises to Kansas City and Seattle.

1968

American sprinter Lee Evans knocked an incredible seven-tenths of a second off the world record in the 400-meter run, clocking 43.8 in his gold medal-winning performance at the Mexico City Olympic Games.

1968 BEAMON'S RECORD LEAP

American long jumper Bob Beamon, flapping his arms like a bird trying to gain height, soared an incredible 29 feet, 2 1/2 inches and shattered the world record for the event by almost 2 feet.

Beamon's amazing performance came on his opening jump during competition in the Summer Olympic Games at Mexico City. The 22-year-old New Yorker sped down the runway, got tremendous height off the board and cut through the thin mountain air like a knife before landing in uncharted territory. Nobody had ever topped 28 feet, much less 29.

The crowd of 45,000 at Olympic Stadium sat in disbelief as the numbers 8.90 (meters) were placed on the scoreboard. Then came a mighty roar as the 6-foot-3 Beamon jumped up and down wildly in front of the stands. The previous world best for the event was 27–4 3/4.

American **Bob Beamon** *soars into the record book.*

1977 JACKSON KILLS DODGERS WITH POWERFUL BAT

Reggie Jackson, putting on the greatest power display in postseason history, blasted three home runs on three swings and powered the New York Yankees to a World Series-clinching 8–4 victory over Los Angeles.

Jackson's barrage was a fitting conclusion to the Yankees' first championship since 1962. It also was sweet vindication after a turmoil-filled regular season in which he fought with Manager Billy Martin and other Yankee players.

Jackson actually started his long-ball barrage two days earlier, when he connected in the eighth inning of a 10–4 New York loss at Los Angeles. And he continued it in the Game 6 finale when, in his first official at-bat in the fourth inning, he hit Burt Hooton' s first pitch into the right-field stands at Yankee Stadium. The two-run shot gave the Yankees a 4–3 lead.

Jackson batted again in the fifth with a man on and hit Elias Sosa's first pitch into the right-field seats. He stepped up again leading off the eighth and rocketed a Charlie Hough offering into the center-field bleachers. Four official at-bats, four homers – an unprecedented feat. His five homers for the Series also were a record.

The beneficiary of Jackson's power show was pitcher Mike Torrez, who won his second Series game.

1924 THE HORSEMEN AND A GHOST

A Ghost galloped in Illinois and the Four Horsemen rode at New York's Polo Grounds. Two legends were born on the same day. The Four Horsemen were Notre Dame quarterback Harry Stuhldreher and running backs Elmer Layden, Don Miller and Jim Crowley. They were so proficient in leading the undefeated Irish to a 13–7 victory over Army that sportswriter Grantland Rice was moved to write:

"Outlined against a blue-grey October sky, the Four Horsemen rode again. In dramatic lore, they are known as Famine, Pestilence, Destruction and Death. These are only aliases. Their real names are Stuhldreher, Miller, Crowley and Layden....."

Miller ran for 148 yards, Crowley 102 and Layden 60 with a touchdown. But those numbers do not compare to those compiled on the same day by Red Grange, Illinois' Galloping Ghost. Helping to dedicate new Memorial Stadium against a tough Michigan team, Grange put on a memorable performance.

He returned the opening kickoff 95 yards for a touchdown and recorded TD runs of 67, 56 and 44 yards in the first 12 minutes as the Illini rolled to a 27–0 halftime lead. Grange added a 13-yard touchdown run in the third quarter and threw a 20-yard TD pass in the fourth. He accounted for 402 total yards in the Illini's 39–14 victory – 212 yards rushing on 15 carries, 126 yards on three kickoff returns and 64 yards on six pass completions in eight attempts.

Grange capped his big afternoon by intercepting a Michigan pass. The defeat ended the Wolverines' 20-game unbeaten streak.

Illinois' Galloping Ghost, **Red Grange**, *working his magic against Michigan.*

A STAR IS BORN

1933: Forrest Gregg, a football Hall of Fame tackle who went on to coach Cleveland, Cincinnati and Green Bay of the NFL.

★ ★ ★

1939: Mike Ditka, a football Hall of Fame tight end who went on to coach the NFL's Chicago Bears for 11 seasons.

★ ★ ★

1942: Willie Horton, a slugging outfielder who belted 325 home runs over 18 major league seasons in the 1960s and '70s.

★ ★ ★

1956: Martina Navratilova, an outstanding women's tennis player who has won nine Wimbledon singles titles, four U.S. Opens, three Australian Opens and two French Opens.

★ ★ ★

1958: Thomas Hearns, an outstanding boxer who has held championships in five different weight classifications.

October 19

1981 Monday Homer Shocks Expos

A two-out, ninth-inning home run by Rick Monday ruined the prospect of baseball's first Canadian pennant and gave the Los Angeles Dodgers a 2–1 National League Championship Series-clinching victory over the Montreal Expos.

Playing on a windy, 40-degree afternoon at Montreal, Game 5 developed into a pitcher's duel between the Dodgers' Fernando Valenzuela and the Expos' Ray Burris. The Expos scored a first-inning run but were shut down the rest of the way. The Dodgers broke through in the fifth when Monday singled and eventually scored on Valenzuela's ground ball.

And that's the way it stayed until the fateful ninth, when Montreal ace Steve Rogers was called in to replace Burris and quickly retired the first two batters. That brought it down to Rogers, who had permitted just two runs in his last 42 innings, against Monday, who was 1 for 5 with four strikeouts entering the final game. Rogers had shut down the Dodgers, 4-1, in a one-sided Game 3 victory.

But the Dodger outfielder won the battle when he drilled a Rogers pitch over the center-field fence, shocking the 36,491 revved-up fans at Olympic Stadium and giving Los Angeles the lead. Valenzuela, with one-out relief from Bob Welch, secured the pennant in the bottom of the inning.

The victory advanced the Dodgers to a World Series date with the New York Yankees and left the Expos and their fans wondering "what if?".

1968 Toomey Is 'Greatest'

Bill Toomey, a 29-year-old California English teacher, walked away from the Summer Games at Mexico City as the "world's greatest athlete" after setting an Olympic record in winning the prestigious decathlon.

Toomey compiled 8,193 points in the grueling two-day event, 192 more than American Rafer Johnson managed in his record-setting performance of 1960 but 126 below the world mark held by West German Kurt Bendlin. Toomey excelled in the running events and turned in an exceptional 45.6-second time in the 400 meters that gave him 1,021 points.

His weakness was the field events and he needed a pressure pole vault to keep him in medal contention. After missing on his first two vaults, Toomey faced the prospect of not getting any points in the event. But he made it over 13–9$^{1}/_{2}$ on his final try and remained in the lead.

Toomey held a 56-point advantage over second-place Bendlin going into the final event – the 1,500-meter run. He needed a time of 4:35.1 to set a world record, but crossed the finish at 4:57.1.

A Star Is Born

1876: Mordecai (Three Finger) Brown, a Hall of Fame pitcher who won 208 games over a 12-year career. He is best remembered for his great duels against Christy Mathewson.

★ ★ ★

1961: Tim Belcher, a current major league pitcher.

★ ★ ★

1962: Evander Holyfield, a boxer who once held the heavyweight championship.

★ ★ ★

1965: Brad Daugherty, a current National Basketball Association center.

★ ★ ★

Death of a Legend

1954 : Hugh Duffy (baseball).

★ ★ ★

1990: Lew Worsham (golf).

★ ★ ★

Milestones in Sports

1936

The University of Minnesota was the No. 1-ranked team when the Associated Press released its first college football poll.

1985

Rob Houghtlin's 29-yard field goal with time running out gave No. 1-ranked Iowa a 12–10 victory over No. 2-ranked Michigan in a Big Ten showdown at Iowa's Kinnick Stadium.

1985

Brigham Young quarterback Robbie Bosco passed for 585 yards in a 45–23 college football victory over New Mexico.

1985

Nebraska kicker Dale Klein tied an NCAA record when he booted seven field goals during a 28–20 victory over Missouri.

1986

Kansas City's Lloyd Burruss returned two interceptions for touchdowns and picked off another pass for good measure in the Chiefs' 42–41 victory over San Diego.

1989

Another 1,000-point man: Quebec's Peter Stastny scored a goal in a 5–3 victory over Chicago.

Montreal's **Maurice (Rocket) Richard** *(right), hockey's first 500-goal scorer.*

1957 Richard Gets 500th

Montreal's Maurice (Rocket) Richard, already the highest-scoring player in National Hockey League history, blazed new territory when he slapped a 20-foot shot past Chicago goalie Glenn Hall for career goal No. 500.

The milestone shot came at 15:32 of the opening period and sent the Canadiens on their way to a 3–1 victory. When the ankle-high drive settled into the net, 14,405 fans at the Montreal Forum began a long, loud ovation as the Rocket raised his arms in triumph and leaped into the arms of teammate Jean Beliveau.

Linesman George Hayes retrieved the puck for Richard, who returned it to the bench for safekeeping. Richard, beginning his 16th professional season, is the oldest player in the NHL at age 36.

Richard also assisted on a Doug Harvey goal and Beliveau added a third-period clincher.

OCTOBER 20

A STAR IS BORN

1931: Mickey Mantle, a Hall of Fame center fielder who blasted 536 home runs in an outstanding 18-year career with the New York Yankees. He also earned three MVP citations and an A.L. Triple Crown.

★ ★ ★

1932: Roosevelt Brown, a football Hall of Fame tackle for the New York Giants from 1953–66.

★ ★ ★

1938: Juan Marichal, a Hall of Fame pitcher who won 243 games over a 16-year major league career.

★ ★ ★

1953: Keith Hernandez, an outstanding defensive first baseman who batted .298 over a 16-year major league career.

★ ★ ★

DEATH OF A LEGEND

1906: Buck Ewing (baseball).

★ ★ ★

1953: Harry Cameron (hockey).

★ ★ ★

1988 HERSHISER, DODGERS ZIP PAST A'S

Los Angeles righthander Orel Hershiser put a fitting cap on his highlight-filled season when he stopped the Oakland Athletics on four singles and pitched the Dodgers to a 5–2 World Series-clinching victory at the Oakland Coliseum.

Hershiser's Game 5 performance was not his best of the year, but it was more than enough to complete one of the biggest upsets in Series history. The undermanned Dodgers, playing without regular-season MVP Kirk Gibson and pitcher Fernando Valenzuela because of injuries, nevertheless made short work of the powerful A's – and with surprising ease.

Hershiser's final-game performance was not a surprise. He had closed the regular season with a record-breaking 59 consecutive scoreless innings and he had pitched the Dodgers' N.L. Championship Series clincher against the New York Mets – a shutout, naturally. He also had stopped the A's, 6–0, on a second-game Series three-hitter.

He got all the offensive support he needed in the finale from two unlikely sources. Mickey Hatcher, who had hit one regular-season home run, muscled up for his second of the Series – a two-run shot in the first. Then Mike Davis, looking for his first Series hit, blasted a two-run shot in the fourth.

MILESTONES IN SPORTS

1963

Oakland Raiders running back Clem Daniels rushed for 200 yards and a pair of touchdowns in a 49–26 American Football League victory over the New York Jets.

1964

Johnny Keane, who directed the St. Louis Cardinals to a seventh-game World Series victory over New York five days earlier, stunned the baseball world when he signed a contract to manage the Yankees in 1965.

1979

John Tate captured the vacant WBC heavyweight championship when he scored a unanimous 15-round decision over Gerrie Coetzee in Pretoria, South Africa.

1984

Washington State running back Rueben Mayes rushed for 216 yards and scored five touchdowns as the Cougars overcame a 28–7 halftime deficit to Stanford and recorded a 49–42 victory.

1990 REDS FINISH SWEEP

Jose Rijo pitched brilliantly after surviving a first-inning jam and his Cincinnati teammates squeezed out a pair of eighth-inning runs that allowed the Reds to complete their shocking four-game World Series sweep of the powerful and heavily-favored Athletics at Oakland.

Rijo was touched for a double by Willie McGee and a run-scoring single by Carney Lansford in the opening frame, but the Reds righthander was untouchable from that point on. He allowed three walks – and that's it. He mowed down the A's inning after inning and received two-out ninth-inning relief from Randy Myers in securing the 2–1 victory, his second win of the Series.

Oakland's Dave Stewart wasn't bad himself, making that single run stand up until the eighth. The Reds loaded the bases with nobody out in that inning and scored on a ground ball by Glenn Braggs and a sacrifice fly by Hal Morris.

Jose Rijo *was a key performer in Cincinnati's shocking World Series sweep of the Oakland A's.*

1982 GAME 7 COMEBACK POWERS CARDINALS

Milwaukee catcher **Ted Simmons** *watches the flight of his Game 2 World Series home run against St. Louis.*

Keith Hernandez delivered a clutch two-run sixth-inning single to tie the game and George Hendrick singled home the go-ahead run, sending the St. Louis Cardinals on their way to a 6–3 World Series-clinching victory over Milwaukee.

The Game 7 triumph at Busch Stadium was secured by the strong right arm of Cardinals relief ace Bruce Sutter, who worked two hitless innings in relief of starter Joaquin Andujar. Sutter was given a little extra cushion when Darrell Porter and Steve Braun singled home eighth-inning insurance runs.

The Brewers, playing in their first World Series, carried a 3–1 lead into the sixth, one run coming on Ben Oglivie' s fifth-inning home run and two more coming in the sixth on a Cardinal error and Cecil Cooper's sacrifice fly.

But St. Louis went to work in its half of the sixth when Ozzie Smith hit a one-out single, Lonnie Smith doubled and pinch-hitter Gene Tenace walked, loading the bases. Hernandez, batting against lefty Bob McClure in relief of starter Pete Vuckovich, drove a single to right, scoring the Smiths. Hendrick followed with another single and the Cardinals had the lead.

OCTOBER 21

1989 HOUSTON BLITZES SMU

Houston, putting its quick-striking offensive machine into high gear, rolled to a 95–21 victory over Southern Methodist in a performance that shattered numerous NCAA individual and team records.

The Cougars became the first college football team to gain 1,000 yards in a single game, rolling up 1,021 and breaking the former NCAA mark of 883 set by Nebraska in 1982. They did most of their damage through the air and the principal culprit was quarterback Andre Ware.

Ware completed 25 of 41 passes for 517 yards and six touchdowns – in the first half. He sat out most of the second and watched backup David Klingler fire four more TD passes. Ware set the NCAA record for passing yardage in a half, for TD passes in a quarter (5) and for passing yards in a quarter (340).

SMU is playing its first season of football after two years off because of NCAA sanctions.

1975 FISK SAVES RED SOX

A dramatic, 12th-inning home run by Boston catcher Carlton Fisk brought down the curtain on a memorable World Series Game 6 and forced a seventh-game showdown between the Red Sox and Cincinnati Reds.

Fisk, leading off the inning in the wee hours of the morning, connected with a pitch from Pat Darcy and hit a towering drive down the left-field line at Fenway Park. The only question was fair or foul and that was answered when the ball bounced off the foul pole and Fisk jubilantly danced around the bases. The Red Sox had a 7–6 victory and baseball fans had a special memory.

The game was intense and exciting from the start. Boston jumped to a 3–0 lead on Fred Lynn's first-inning home run, but the Reds scored the next six runs, two coming on a Ken Griffey triple and two more on a George Foster double.

Trailing 6–3 in the bottom of the eighth, Bernie Carbo made history when he hit his second pinch-hit homer of the Series, tying a 16-year-old record. The clutch three-run blow also tied the game.

The Red Sox threatened to win in the bottom of the ninth when they loaded the bases with nobody out, but reliever Will McEnaney escaped the jam. Boston dodged a bullet in the 11th when right fielder Dwight Evans made a spectacular catch, robbing Joe Morgan of a home run. The Reds got two men on in the top of the 12th but again failed to cash in, setting the stage for Fisk.

Three important cogs in Cincinnati's high-powered Big Red Machine: (left to right) **George Foster, Joe Morgan** *and* **Ken Griffey.**

MILESTONES IN SPORTS

1973

Los Angeles Rams star Fred Dryer became the first player to record two safeties in one game – a 24–7 triumph over the Green Bay Packers.

1973

Reggie Jackson and Bert Campaneris belted two-run homers and Oakland captured its second straight World Series with a 5–2 Game 7 win over the New York Mets.

1976

The Philadelphia 76ers gave a reported $3 million to the New York Nets for star forward Julius Erving.

1980

The Philadelphia Phillies posted a 4–1 Game 6 victory over Kansas City and captured the first World Series championship in the long history of the franchise.

1984

Cleveland kicker Steve Cox booted the second-longest field goal in NFL history (60 yards), but the Browns lost to Cincinnati, 12-9.

A STAR IS BORN

1928: Whitey Ford, the stylish Hall of Fame lefthander who won 236 games over 16 major league seasons for the New York Yankees.

★ ★ ★

1928: Vern Mikkelsen, an NBA star of the 1950s who scored 10,063 points over 10 seasons with the Minneapolis Lakers.

★ ★ ★

1959: George Bell, a former major league outfielder.

★ ★ ★

1976 BIG RED MACHINE ROLLS OVER OUTMANNED YANKEES

Johnny Bench drilled a pair of homers and drove in five runs as Cincinnati's Big Red Machine steamrolled its way to a 7–2 victory over the New York Yankees and a quick-and-easy World Series sweep.

Enhancing its reputation as one of the greatest teams ever assembled, Cincinnati concluded a season that featured 102 regular-season victories, a three-game sweep of Philadelphia in the National League Championship Series and the four-game blitz of the Yankees.

Even more telling was the Reds' two-year totals of 210 victories, a 6–0 Championship Series record and two World Series titles. They became the first repeat N.L. winners since the 1921 and '22 New York Giants and they spoiled the Yankees' first World Series appearance since 1964.

Bench did most of the Game 4 damage, blasting a two-run homer in a three-run fourth inning and a three-run shot in a four-run ninth.

OCTOBER

22

A STAR IS BORN

1907: Jimmie Foxx, a Hall of Fame catcher-infielder who blasted 534 home runs and batted .325 over his 20-year major league career.

★ ★ ★

1923: Pete Pihos, a football Hall of Fame end for the Philadelphia Eagles from 1947–55.

★ ★ ★

1925: Slater Martin, a basketball Hall of Fame guard who enjoyed championship success with Minneapolis and St. Louis in the 1950s .

★ ★ ★

1963: Brian Boitano, a two-time world champion figure skater and a gold medalist for the U.S. in the 1988 Winter Olympic Games at Calgary.

DEATH OF A LEGEND

1917: Bob Fitzsimmons (boxing).

★ ★ ★

1927: Ross Youngs (baseball).

★ ★ ★

1990: Frank Sinkwich (football).

1972

Tenace Has Blast As A's Win Series

Oakland catcher Gene Tenace concluded his memorable first World Series with a bang, driving in two runs and lifting the Athletics to a 3–2 seventh-game victory over Cincinnati.

Gene Tenace *came off Oakland's bench to play World Series long ball with Cincinnati.*

The fall classic championship was the Athletics' first in Oakland and first since 1930, when they played in Philadelphia. Tenace had a lot to do with the victory, delivering a memorable performance that ranks among the best ever.

The Oakland regular-season backup, who had hit only five home runs during the regular season, made history by connecting in his first two World Series at-bats, keying a 3–2 Game 1 victory for the A's.

In the finale, he singled in a first-inning run and doubled home a run in the sixth, when the A's built a 3–1 lead. The Mets could never catch up as they faced 21-game winner Catfish Hunter, 19-game winner Ken Holtzman and bullpen ace Rollie Fingers in relief of starting pitcher Blue Moon Odom.

Tenace finished the Series with a .348 batting average, a record-tying four home runs and nine RBIs.

MILESTONES
• IN SPORTS •

1927

Ten-year New York Giants star Ross Youngs, a career .322 hitter and future Hall of Famer, died of Bright's disease.

1933

Primo Carnera successfully defended his heavyweight boxing championship with a 15-round unanimous decision over Paulino Uzcudun in a bout at Rome.

1950

An NFL blowout: The Los Angeles Rams defeated the Baltimore Colts, 70-27.

1961

Erich Barnes of the New York Giants tied an NFL record when he returned a Dallas interception 102 yards for a touchdown in a 17–16 loss to the Cowboys.

1988

Nebraska set an NCAA record when it defeated Kansas State, 48–3, and recorded its 27th straight winning football season.

1975

Reds Survive Game 7 Scare

Joe Morgan looped a soft ninth-inning single into center field to drive home Ken Griffey and the powerful Cincinnati Reds, extended to the limit by the upstart Boston Red Sox, posted a World Series-clinching 4–3 victory in a seventh-game thriller at Fenway Park .

In what will be remembered as one of the classic World Series ever contested, the seventh game fittingly went down to the final inning and a two-out hit. Morgan's game-winner was set up when Griffey walked to open the inning and advanced to third on a sacrifice and groundout. Pete Rose walked, setting up the Reds' second baseman for hero honors.

The Reds, who had dropped a heart-breaking Game 6 thriller when Carlton Fisk banged a 12th-inning homer off the left-field foul pole, found themselves trailing early when the Red Sox scored three times in the third off Don Gullett. But with relievers Jack Billingham, Clay Carroll and Will McEnaney checking the Red Sox the rest of the way, Cincinnati clawed its way back.

Tony Perez made it 3–2 with a two-run sixth-inning homer and the Reds tied in the seventh on a Rose single. After Morgan's game-winner, McEnaney retired the Red Sox 1–2–3 in the bottom of the ninth to secure the championship..

1975

WFL Calls It Quits

The 10-team World Football League, unable to compete against the more affluent National Football League without television or season-ticket support, threw in the towel before the 12th week of games in its second campaign.

The decision to go out of business was primarily a case of not wanting to throw good money after bad. In its short lifespan, the league walked a fiscal tightrope and reportedly lost more than $30 million. A number of franchises failed to meet payrolls, shifted to other cities or went bankrupt.

The biggest problems were the league's inability to land a major television contract and sagging attendance, which had declined to an average of 13,331 over the last five weeks. The 6–4 vote to disband left 380 players without jobs.

The league played its full 20-game summer schedule last year with the Birmingham Americans beating the Florida Blazers in the inaugural World Bowl championship game.

October 23

1993 Late Blast Stuns Phils

Toronto left fielder Joe Carter connected for a dramatic three-run, ninth-inning home run off Philadelphia reliever Mitch Williams, giving the Blue Jays an 8–6 victory and their second consecutive World Series championship.

Carter's gargantuan blast over the left-field fence at Toronto's SkyDome ended a see-saw Game 6 battle in which the Phillies had overcome a four-run deficit. Trailing 5–1 entering the seventh, Philadelphia rallied for five runs, three coming on Lenny Dykstra's fourth Series home run.

After Larry Andersen had pitched out of a bases-loaded jam in the eighth inning, Williams took over in the ninth and walked leadoff batter Rickey Henderson. Williams, known as Wild Thing because of his penchant for walking batters and pitching behind in the count, retired Devon White but surrendered a single to Paul Molitor, his 12th Series hit.

That brought up Carter, who missed badly on a 2–1 slider before belting Williams' next pitch and dancing euphorically around the bases. It was the first time a team trailing in the last inning of the final game had won a World Series with a home run.

The Blue Jays, who had become the first non-American-based World Series champions the year before, also became baseball's first Series repeat champs since the New York Yankees in 1977–78.

1971 Sooners Win in a Rush

If it wasn't the most dominating offensive display in history, it was close. The powerful Oklahoma Sooners unleashed their devastating wishbone attack on Kansas State, rushing for an NCAA single-game record 711 yards, scoring on 11 of 12 possessions and pounding out a 75–28 victory at Manhattan, Kan.

It wasn't pretty. The Sooners controlled the clock and ran from their triple-option wishbone at will, scoring the first 10 times they touched the ball. They put together drives of 67, 80, 59, 80, 49 and 71 yards in a mechanical first half that produced a 41–14 lead.

The devastation continued after intermission and the No. 2-ranked Sooners were not stopped until their reserves fumbled the ball away with 1:35 remaining in the game.

The big gun in the offensive explosion was Greg Pruitt, who romped for a Big Eight Conference-record 294 yards on 17 carries and scored three touchdowns. Reserve halfback Roy Bell scored four times and Oklahoma quarterback Jack Mildren twice.

Bill Butler scored all four touchdowns for Kansas State, which actually held a 7–0 lead early in the contest.

A STAR IS BORN

1906: Gertrude Ederle, the first woman to swim the English Channel and a winner of three swimming gold medals in the 1924 Paris Olympic Games.

★ ★ ★

1931: Jim Bunning, a 17-year major league pitcher who won 224 games and pitched a 1964 perfect game.

★ ★ ★

1940: Pele, generally considered the greatest soccer player in history. He played on three Brazilian World Cup champions and spent the end of his career playing in the U.S. for the New York Cosmos.

★ ★ ★

1962: Doug Flutie, the 1984 Heisman Trophy-winning quarterback from Boston College who later played in the USFL, NFL and CFL.

★ ★ ★

MILESTONES IN SPORTS

1910

Jack Coombs earned his record-tying third victory as the Philadelphia Athletics wrapped up their five-game World Series triumph over the Chicago Cubs with a 7–1 win.

1949

Detroit's Don Doll picked off four Chicago passes to key a 24–7 victory over the Cardinals.

1960

An NFL first: Detroit's Jim Martin kicked two 50-plus-yard field goals in the Lions' 30–17 victory over Baltimore.

1979

New York Yankee Manager Billy Martin made off-field headlines again when he split the lip of a Minnesota marshmallow salesman in a Bloomington, Minn., barroom fight.

1982

Northwestern University freshman Sandy Schwab completed 45 of 71 passes, an NCAA-record-tying 17 for 208 yards to Jon Harvey, in a 49–14 loss to Michigan.

Philadelphia pitcher **Jack Coombs** *was a three-time winner in a quick-and-easy five-game World Series.*

1945 Dodgers Break Barrier

Kansas City Monarchs shortstop **Jackie Robinson** *before signing with Brooklyn.*

Brooklyn President Branch Rickey, daring to go where every other baseball executive has feared to tread, made history when he announced that 26-year-old Negro League star Jackie Roosevelt Robinson had been signed to play for the Dodgers' Montreal Class AAA affiliate.

Robinson thus becomes the first black player in Organized Baseball since 1884, when Moses Fleetwood Walker competed in the young National League. The former four-sport UCLA star and Kansas City Monarchs shortstop was hand-picked by Rickey to break baseball's color barrie.

Robinson, a former second lieutenant in the U.S. Army, was best known at UCLA for his prowess as a football running back. He signed his historic pact in Montreal, in the presence of Royals officials and Branch Rickey Jr., son of the Dodgers president.

OCTOBER 24

MILESTONES IN SPORTS

1943

The Green Bay Packers intercepted nine Detroit passes, seven off quarterback Frank Sinkwich, in a 27–6 victory over the Lions.

1948

Chicago's Bill Blackburn returned two interceptions for touchdowns in a wild 35-point third quarter that lifted the Cardinals to a 49–27 victory over the Boston Yanks.

1970

Christos Papanicolaou, a Greek who perfected his technique while attending college in the United States, became the first pole vaulter ever to clear 18 feet when he soared 18–0$^{1}/_{4}$ at an Athens-Belgrade meet.

1977

Boy Wonder Steve Cauthen became the first jockey to pass $5 million in purse winnings in one year.

Steve Cauthen, *racing's first $5-million man.*

1992 JAYS WIN FOR CANADA

Dave Winfield, the 41-year-old inspiration of the Toronto Blue Jays, drove in two runs with an 11th-inning double and the Jays held on for a 4-3 Game 6 victory at Atlanta that gave Canada its first-ever World Series championship.

Winfield's two-out ground ball double just inside the third-base bag scored Devon White, who had been hit by a Charlie Leibrandt pitch, and Roberto Alomar, who had singled. Then the Blue Jays had to survive a desperation Braves rally in the bottom of the inning .

Atlanta got one run back on Brian Hunter's RBI grounder and just missed tying the game when Otis Nixon, bunting with a runner on third, was thrown out by pitcher Mike Timlin on a bang-bang play at first base to end the game.

Nixon had kept the Braves away from elimination in the ninth inning when he slapped a two-out base hit to left field, scoring Jeff Blauser and knotting the score at 2–2. The Braves scored their first run in the third on a Terry Pendleton sacrifice fly.

Toronto scored its early runs on a first-inning error and Candy Maldonado's fourth-inning home run off Steve Avery.

The Toronto **Blue Jays** *celebrate Canada's first World Series championship.*

1987 HRBEK SLAMS CARDS

The Minnesota Twins, trailing the St. Louis Cardinals 5–2 and on the verge of elimination in Game 6 of the World Series, exploded for eight runs in the fifth and sixth innings and recorded an 11–5 victory that set up a seventh-game showdown.

As was their custom during the regular season, the Twins muscled up during their winning rally and turned the Metrodome into a crescendo of noise and confusion. First Don Baylor belted a game-tying two-run homer off John Tudor. Then first baseman Kent Hrbek took center stage.

With the hanky-waving Minnesota fans now into the game, the Twins loaded the bases in the sixth off Bob Forsch. Cardinals Manager Whitey Herzog brought lefty Ken Dayley in to face the lefthanded-hitting Hrbek, who promptly smashed his first pitch over the center-field fence.

Hrbek danced around the bases with an upraised fist as the crowd roared. The Twins added an eighth-inning run and the celebration really began.

1981 ARIZONA STATE WINS SLUGFEST

In the greatest offensive slugfest ever staged, Arizona State overpowered Stanford, 62–36, and the teams combined to break five NCAA college football records and 11 Pacific-10 marks.

The Sun Devils rolled up 743 total yards and the Cardinal 693, an NCAA-record combined total of 1,436, and the combined passing yardage for the two teams was 1,092 yards, another NCAA mark.

The top gun in this offensive explosion was Arizona State quarterback Mike Pagel, who passed for 466 yards and a Pac-10-record seven touchdowns. His primary target was split end Bernard Henry, who caught nine of this throws for 160 yards.

Stanford quarterbacks John Elway (270) and Steve Cottrell (311) combined for a conference team record of 581 passing yards. Elway completed 10 of 17 for 270 yards and three TDs before leaving in the second quarter with a concussion. Darrin Nelson caught nine passes for 237 yards – and he rushed for 84 more.

Pagel threw two touchdown passes to Henry, Eric Redenius and Ron Wetzel and one to Jerome Weatherspoon.

A STAR IS BORN

1926: Y.A. Tittle, a pro football Hall of Fame quarterback who passed for 28,339 yards in a 17-year career.

★ ★ ★

1962: Jay Novacek, a current National Football League tight end.

★ ★ ★

DEATH OF A LEGEND

1972: Jackie Robinson (baseball).

★ ★ ★

MILESTONES IN SPORTS

1947

Columbia University, recovering from a 20–7 halftime deficit, defeated powerful Army, 21–20, and ended the Cadets' 32-game college football unbeaten streak.

1979

The San Diego Chargers lost to the Oakland Raiders, 45–22, but Dan Fouts (303 yards) became the first NFL quarterback to pass for 300 yards in four consecutive games.

1980

WBA heavyweight champion Mike Weaver knocked out Gerrie Coetzee in the 13th round of a title bout in Sun City, Bophuthatswana.

1981

Back-to-back seventh-inning home runs by Steve Yeager and Pedro Guerrero gave the Los Angeles Dodgers a 2–1 victory over the New York Yankees and a 3–2 edge in the World Series.

1987

The Minnesota Twins closed out their first World Series championship with a 4–2 Game 7 victory over St. Louis behind the pitching of Frank Viola and Jeff Reardon.

1986 METS WIN A SHOCKER

Mookie Wilson's routine ground ball bounced through the legs of Boston first baseman Bill Buckner as Ray Knight raced home with the winning run, giving the New York Mets a 6–5 victory in a wild and crazy conclusion to Game 6 of the World Series.

The 10-inning victory at Shea Stadium deadlocked the fall classic at three games apiece and brought the Mets back from what looked like certain death. The Red Sox had taken a 6–3 lead in the top of the 10th on Dave Henderson's home run and an RBI single by Marty Barrett, setting up the Mets' amazing deathbed comeback.

Red Sox reliever Calvin Schiraldi opened the inning by retiring Wally Backman and Keith Hernandez on fly balls. Two out, nobody on base. But Gary Carter kept the Mets' faint hopes alive with a single and Kevin Mitchell followed with another base hit.

Schiraldi got a two-strike count on Knight, who looped a single to center, scoring Carter and sending Mitchell to third. That brought up Wilson to face reliever Bob Stanley in an epic battle. It lasted for 10 pulsating pitches and Wilson fouled off four two-strike deliveries. Stanley's seventh pitch was wild, allowing Mitchell to score the tying run. His 10th pitch produced the ground ball that Buckner booted.

Dejected Boston **Red Sox** *players contemplate one that got away.*

OCTOBER 25

A STAR IS BORN

1923: Bobby Thomson, a .270 career hitter over 15 major league seasons who is best remembered for the pennant-winning home run he hit for the New York Giants in their 1951 playoff victory over Brooklyn.

★ ★ ★

1940: Bob Knight, the controversial Indiana coach who has directed the Hoosiers to three NCAA basketball championships.

★ ★ ★

1948: Dave Cowens, a basketball Hall of Fame center who scored 13,516 points over 11 NBA seasons, 10 with the Boston Celtics.

★ ★ ★

1948: Dan Issel, a former star forward who scored 27,482 career points over 15 ABA and NBA seasons.

★ ★ ★

1966: Wendel Clark, a current National Hockey League left winger.

★ ★ ★

DEATH OF A LEGEND

1981: Pete Reiser (baseball).

★ ★ ★

1991: Bill Bevens (baseball).

1964 WRONG WAY DASH

Minnesota defeated San Francisco, 27-22, in a National Football League game at Kezar Stadium, but the final score was pushed out of the spotlight by Vikings defensive end Jim Marshall's unintentional dash to football infamy.

The Vikings held a 10-point fourth-quarter lead when Marshall scooped up a 49er fumble and lumbered 60 yards untouched to the end zone – his own. Marshall described what happened next:

"I thought they (the frantic Viking coaches and players) were cheering me on. About the 5-yard line I looked around and things just didn't seem right. Fran (Minnesota quarterback Tarkenton) was yelling at me from the sidelines and pointing in the opposite direction. I couldn't think of anything else to do, so I threw him the ball."

Marshall "threw" the ball out of the end zone and the 49ers were awarded a safety, which didn't affect the final outcome of the game. It did, however, put him in the company of California defender Roy Riegels, who made a similar misplay in the 1929 Rose Bowl game. Riegels' infamous wrong-way run cost the Golden Bears a one-point loss to Georgia Tech.

1990 HOLYFIELD DECKS DOUGLAS

The short but sweet heavyweight title reign of James (Buster) Douglas came to a crashing halt when the champion took a powerful right to the jaw from challenger Evander Holyfield in the third round of a fight at Las Vegas.

As Douglas tumbled to the canvas, rolled onto his back and took the count that ended his eight-month dream, Holyfield stood stoically in his corner, ready to accept the passing of the championship baton.

The 30-year-old Douglas, who had pulled a shocking upset in February with a 10th-round knockout of then-champion Mike Tyson, was making his first defense of the title he probably never expected to own. The loss dropped his record to 30–5–1 while the up-and-coming Holyfield won his 25th straight fight.

OCTOBER

26

MILESTONES
IN SPORTS

1960

The American League, trying to jump ahead of the National League in the expansion race, okayed the shift of the Washington Senators to Minneapolis and awarded franchises to Washington and Los Angeles, to begin play in 1961.

1980

The St. Louis Cardinals sacked Baltimore quarterback Bert Jones 12 times in a 17–10 National Football League victory over the Colts.

1980

Houston bulldozer Earl Campbell rushed for 202 yards and a pair of touchdowns in a one-sided 23–3 victory over Cincinnati.

1982

Steve Carlton, Philadelphia's 37-year-old lefthander, captured the N.L. Cy Young Award for an unprecedented fourth time.

1989

Paul Tagliabue, the National Football League's seventh elected commissioner, officially began his tenure as Pete Rozelle's replacement.

1990

A milestone: Los Angeles' Wayne Gretzky became the National Hockey League's first 2,000-point man when he assisted on a goal in a 6–2 loss to the Winnipeg Jets.

1985 LATE ROYALS RALLY SHUFFLES THE CARDS

The Kansas City Royals, on the verge of elimination in Game 6 of the World Series, pulled a rabbit out of their caps and escaped with a controversy-filled 2–1 victory over the cross-state St. Louis Cardinals.

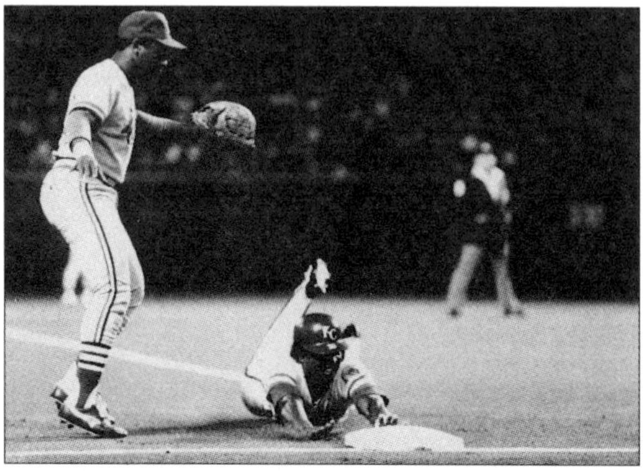

St. Louis third baseman **Terry Pendleton** *watches Kansas City's* **Frank White** *slide safely during the all-Missouri Series.*

The Redbirds, holding a three games to one Series advantage and a 1–0 lead entering the ninth inning of the sixth contest at Royals Stadium, stumbled badly when an umpire's decision went against them. The controversy surrounded a ground ball hit by pinch-hitter Jorge Orta to open the inning. First baseman Jack Clark fielded the ball and tossed to pitcher Todd Worrell covering first, apparently in time.

"Safe," said umpire Don Denkinger, and the Cardinals protested vehemently. When play continued, Steve Balboni lifted a foul popup that Clark inexplicably failed to catch. Given new life, Balboni grounded a single into left field.

After Jim Sundberg's sacrifice attempt had resulted in a force at third, both runners advanced on a one-out passed ball by catcher Darrell Porter. Hal McRae was walked intentionally to fill the bases and pinch-hitter Dane Iorg, a former Cardinal, drove a single to right field, scoring two teammates and giving the Royals an improbable victory.

The Cardinals had scored their only run on a looping two-out eighth-inning single by pinch-hitter Brian Harper off Royals starter Charlie Leibrandt.

1970 ALI'S HAPPY RETURN

The tough, $3^{1}/_{2}$-year boxing exile of Muhammad Ali came to a quick end when the former heavyweight champion scored a third-round technical knockout of Jerry Quarry in a non-title bout at Atlanta.

Ali, who was stripped of his title and sent into exile because of his refusal to be inducted into the armed services on religious grounds, dominated the nine-minute bout and remained unbeaten.

Ali came out dancing and jabbing and was simply too much for the slow-moving Quarry. Fighting a younger opponent for the first time, the 28-year-old Ali opened a big gash over the 25-year-old Quarry's left eye in the third round.

After examining the cut between rounds, Quarry's trainer threw in the towel.

A STAR IS BORN

1899: Judy Johnson, a Hall of Fame third baseman in the old Negro Leagues and a long-time major league scout.

★ ★ ★

1906: Primo Carnera, the huge Italian heavyweight who held the world championship for a year in the early 1930s.

★ ★ ★

1911: Sid Gillman, a former NFL end who went on to a pro football Hall of Fame coaching career.

★ ★ ★

1921: Joe Fulks, a basketball Hall of Fame forward who starred during the NBA's formative years.

★ ★ ★

1949: Steve Rogers, a righthanded pitcher who won 158 games over 13 years with the Montreal Expos.

★ ★ ★

DEATH OF A LEGEND

1931: Charles Comiskey (baseball).

★ ★ ★

1929 SECRET WEAPON ALBIE BOOTH DESTROYS ARMY

There was no reason to expect that once-beaten Yale could stay in the game against powerful and unbeaten Army, and the Cadets quickly confirmed that suspicion when they raced to a 13–0 first-quarter lead in a college football game at the Yale Bowl.

But Elis Coach Mal Stevens was just teasing the mighty Cadets. He unveiled his secret weapon in the second quarter and shot down Army's hopes for an undefeated season and national championship.

The secret weapon was Albie Booth – a fleet-footed, 5-foot-6, 140-pound sophomore quarterback who proved to be much more than the huge, slow-footed Cadets could handle.

Little Albie carried on almost every play of a second-quarter scoring drive that he capped with a short run. Then his 35-yard journey to the end zone in the third quarter and extra-point kick gave Yale a 14–13 lead.

But Booth saved the best for last. Fielding an Army punt on his own 35-yard line, he electrified the 80,000 crowd with a 65-yard return for Yale's final touchdown, which he capped with another extra-point kick. Albie Booth had scored every point in Yale's shocking 21–13 upset.

MILESTONES IN SPORTS

1967

New Mexico tight end Emilio Vallez caught an NCAA record-tying 17 passes for 257 yards in the Lobos' 75–12 loss to Texas-El Paso.

1973

Alabama rushed for an NCAA-record 748 yards, with a record four players topping the 100-yard barrier. The Crimson Tide defeated Virginia Tech, 77–6.

1984

Iowa quarterback Chuck Long set an NCAA record with 22 straight completions in a 24–20 victory over Indiana.

1984

Wichita State kicker Sergio Lopez-Chavero kicked field goals of 54, 54 and 51 yards in a 23–6 victory over Drake.

1985

Kansas City righthander Bret Saberhagen fired a five-hitter and the Royals wrapped up their first World Series championship with an 11–0 seventh-game victory over St. Louis.

1991

New Orleans kicker Morten Andersen kicked a 60-yard field goal in a 20–17 loss to Chicago, matching the second longest in NFL history.

Washington State record-setter **Rueben Mayes.**

1991 TWINS HOLD OFF BRAVES

Gene Larkin's pinch-hit single over a drawn-in outfield scored Dan Gladden from third base in the 10th inning and gave the Minnesota Twins a pulsating 1–0 victory over Atlanta in Game 7 of the "worst-to-first" World Series.

In a tense and exciting conclusion to a Series full of memorable moments and outstanding performances, Minnesota starter Jack Morris traded pitches – and zeroes – with Atlanta's John Smoltz. Smoltz left after 7 1/3 scoreless innings, Morris worked all 10.

Both teams had chances, but the game remained scoreless as Atlanta mounted its best threat in the eighth. After Lonnie Smith led off with a single, Terry Pendleton drove a Morris pitch off the left-center-field wall at Minnesota's Metrodome. Smith, unable to find the ball, hesitated between first and second and failed to score on Pendleton's double.

Smith was stranded at third when Morris got an infield out and Sid Bream hit into an inning-ending double play. The Twins secured their second Series championship in five years when Gladden doubled to lead off the 10th, moved to third on a sacrifice and danced home on Larkin's hit. The run ended the battle of teams that had risen from last-place division finishes in 1970 to pennants.

The **Minnesota Twins** *had plenty to celebrate after beating Atlanta in one of the most exciting World Series ever played.*

OCTOBER 27

A STAR IS BORN

1922: Ralph Kiner, a Hall of Fame slugger and seven-time N.L. home run champion during a 10-year career that produced 369 homers.

★ ★ ★

1930: Bill George, a football Hall of Fame linebacker over a 15-year NFL career with the Chicago Bears and Los Angeles Rams (1952–66).

★ ★ ★

1964: Mary T. Meagher, a winner of three swimming gold medals at the 1984 Los Angeles Olympic Games and a world record-holder in the 100-meter butterfly.

★ ★ ★

DEATH OF A LEGEND

1955: Clark Griffith (baseball).

★ ★ ★

1984: Larry Foust (basketball).

1984 MAYES RUSHES FOR RECORD

Washington State running back Rueben Mayes exploded for 357 yards and three touchdowns, breaking one of college football's most cherished records and leading the Cougars to a 50–41 victory over Oregon in a titanic offensive struggle at Eugene, Ore.

Mayes topped the single-game rushing record set by Georgia Tech back Eddie Lee Ivery six years earlier – by a single yard. He started slowly with 41 first-quarter yards but picked up steam with a 156-yard second period. He ran for 73 yards in the third quarter and finished with 87, breaking the record with 1:12 remaining on a four-yard run.

Mayes, who scored on runs of 2, 69 and 12 yards, carried 39 times and averaged 9.2 yards per attempt. He had run for 216 yards and five touchdowns in the previous week's 49–42 victory over Stanford.

The Cougars compiled 663 total yards, the Ducks 478. Mayes also entered the record books for most yardage in consecutive games. He had run for 216 yards against Stanford, giving him a two-game total of 573.

1986 METS CLOSE OUT BOSTON

Keith Hernandez drove in three runs and Sid Fernandez and Jesse Orosco turned in clutch relief performances as the New York Mets, miracle comeback winners in Game 6, claimed an 8–5 seventh-game decision over Boston and their second-ever World Series championship.

Hernandez stroked a two-run bases-loaded single in a three-run sixth-inning rally that brought the Mets back from a 3–0 deficit and he contributed a sacrifice fly in their three-run seventh. Fernandez kept the Mets in the game with 2 1/3 shutout innings when the Red Sox threatened to run away early and Orosco protected the New York lead with shutout pitching in the eighth and ninth.

Ray Knight contributed a solo seventh-inning home run to the Mets cause and Darryl Strawberry hit a solo shot in the eighth after the Red Sox had pulled to within 6–5.

Boston had gained its early advantage on back-to-back third-inning home runs by Dwight Evans and Rich Gedman and a run-scoring single by Wade Boggs. Evans doubled home two runs in the eighth.

OCTOBER

28

A STAR IS BORN

1937: Lenny Wilkens, a Hall of Fame guard who scored 17,772 career points and a current NBA coach.

★ ★ ★

1949: Bruce Jenner, a 1976 U.S. Olympic gold medalist in the decathlon at Montreal.

1981 DODGERS BLITZ YANKS

Pedro Guerrero drove in five runs to key a 9–2 victory over New York as the Los Angeles Dodgers completed their four-straight blitz of the Yankees after losing the first two games of the World Series.

Duplicating the victory pattern the Yankees had used against them in winning the 1978 fall classic, the Dodgers won the third, fourth and fifth games to take a 3–2 advantage and then entered the fifth inning of Game 6 locked in a 1–1 tie. Not for long.

With George Frazier on the mound after starter Tommy John had surprisingly been removed for a pinch-hitter, the Dodgers struck quickly. Ron Cey snapped the tie with a single and Guerrero made it 4–1 with a two-run triple.

Guerrero contributed a two-run single in the sixth and added a solo home run in the eighth as Burt Hooton and Steve Howe combined on a Series-clinching seven-hitter.

Frazier suffered his third loss of the Series, tying the record for futility set by Lefty Williams of the 1919 Black Sox.

1962 TITTLE GOES ON TD TEAR

New York quarterback Y.A. Tittle, playing catch with his receivers like the Washington players weren't even there, fired a National Football League record-tying seven touchdown passes to lead the Giants to a 49–34 victory over the Redskins at Yankee Stadium.

New York quarterback **Y.A. Tittle** *blistered Washington for seven touchdown passes in one game.*

Tittle matched the one-game record set first in 1943 by Chicago's Sid Luckman and equaled by Philadelphia's Adrian Burk in 1954 and Houston's George Blanda last year. He completed 27 of 39 throws for 505 yards and enjoyed one stretch of 12 consecutive completions.

He needed his record-tying performance to stave off a Redskin team that had not lost in six weeks and to offset the four-touchdown pass performance of second-year Washington quarterback Norm Snead.

The 35-year-old Tittle connected on three TD tosses to Joe Walton, two to Joe Morrison and one each to Del Shofner and Frank Gifford. Shofner was his favorite target, catching 11 passes for a club-record 269 yards. Gifford caught Tittle's sixth and longest touchdown strike of the day – a 63-yarder.

MILESTONES IN SPORTS

1973

Gail Goodrich scored 49 points and Elmore Smith set an NBA record with 17 blocked shots as the Los Angeles Lakers posted a 111–98 victory over Portland.

1973

Eddie Maple rode Secretariat to victory in the Canadian International Championship Stakes at Woodbine Race Course, ending the 1973 Triple Crown winner's fabled career.

1978

Northwestern Louisiana's Joe Delaney rushed for 299 yards and four touchdowns in a 28–18 victory over Nicholls State.

1989

Tony Alford broke a Western Athletic Conference record when he rushed for 310 yards and three touchdowns in Colorado State' s 50–10 victory over Utah.

Los Angeles Lakers sharpshooter **Gail Goodrich.**

1989 QUAKE SERIES ENDS

The Oakland Athletics mercifully brought down the curtain on baseball's first Bay Area World Series with a 9–6 victory over the San Francisco Giants – 11 days after a major earthquake had forced postponement of Game 3 while spreading death and destruction throughout Northern California.

The A's formula for success was simple – score early and often. They jumped to an 8–0 advantage after 5 1/2 innings and held on to complete their four-game sweep – a victory that was lost in the shadow of the tragedy that surrounded it.

For more than a week, Commissioner Fay Vincent and other officials had debated whether to finish the fall classic or cancel it in deference to the earthquake's victims. After more than a week, it finally was decided to play and the A's picked up right where they had left off, posting a 13–7 victory.

Rickey Henderson got them off to a good start with a Game 4-opening home run and pitcher Mike Moore doubled home two in a three-run second. A three-run fifth all but sealed victory.

MILESTONES
• IN SPORTS •

1971

George Foreman, strengthening his bid for a heavyweight title shot, made Brazilian Luis Pires his 32nd straight professional victim with a fourth-round technical knockout at New York's Madison Square Garden.

1973

Buffalo's O.J. Simpson became the first player in NFL history to pass the 1,000-yard rushing barrier in seven games when he carried a record 39 times for 157 yards in a 23–14 victory over Kansas City.

1977

Texas kicker Russell Erxleben booted a 60-yard field goal in the Longhorns' 26–0 victory over Texas Tech – his NCAA-record third 60-yard field goal of the season.

1983

Gill Fenerty exploded for a 337-yard, six-touchdown performance as his Holy Cross team crushed Columbia, 77–28.

1988

Iowa's Chuck Hartlieb completed 44 of 60 passes for 558 yards and three touchdowns, but the Hawkeyes still dropped a 45–34 Big Ten battle to Indiana.

1921 TINY CENTRE STUNS POWERFUL HARVARD

Quarterback Bo McMillin broke through right tackle on a keeper, cut left and ran 32 yards down the sideline for a third-quarter touchdown, giving little Centre College a stunning 6–0 victory over powerful Harvard.

The Praying Colonels, considered a patsy for a Harvard team that had built a 35-game unbeaten streak dating back to 1916, had other ideas when they squared off against the Crimson at Harvard Stadium in Cambridge, Mass. The teams had met in 1920 and Centre played Harvard to a 14–14 halftime tie before collapsing in the second half of a 31–14 Crimson victory.

But this time the Colonels refused to wilt, putting on a valiant defensive display. It was 0–0 at the half and still scoreless when McMillin broke free. Rebuffing every Harvard offensive thrust, the Colonels held on to post one of the most unbelievable upsets in the history of football.

And Harvard's hopes for another perfect season were dead.

Centre College quarterback **Bo McMillin** *breaks free on his 32-yard game-deciding touchdown run against previously unbeaten Harvard.*

OCTOBER 29

1987 HEARNS REGAINS TITLE

Thomas (Hit Man) Hearns, forced into a brawling style because of the wild rushes of his opponent, knocked out Argentine Juan Roldan at 2:01 of the fourth round and became the first boxer to win titles in four different weight categories.

Hearns' Las Vegas victory gave him the vacant World Boxing Council middleweight title. But he did not get it without a battle. Roldan threw style and technique out the window and continuously charged Hearns, throwing round-house and unconventional punches.

To say Roldan was relentless is an understatement. At the opening bell, he charged Hearns like a mad bull and forced him into evasive maneuvers. He flailed away and Hearns rocked him with a big right midway through the round, sending him to the canvas. He got up, took the mandatory eight count and charged right back at Hearns. As the first round was ending, Hearns put Roldan down again.

Not at all discouraged, Roldan resumed his pursuit in the second round. Again he went down, this time from a left hook. And still he came. Hearns finally ended the fight in the fourth round with two savage rights.

Hearns previously had held the welterweight, super welterweight and light heavyweight championships.

A STAR IS BORN

1953: Denis Potvin, a hockey Hall of Famer who set career records for goals, assists and points by a defenseman over his 15 NHL s easons.

★ ★ ★

1959: Mike Gartner, a current NHL right winger and a member of the league's 500-goal club.

★ ★ ★

DEATH OF A LEGEND

1965: Bill McKechnie (baseball).

★ ★ ★

1979 MAYS HANDED BASEBALL BAN

Hall of Famer Willie Mays, the No. 2 all-time leading home run hitter and one of the most popular players ever to put on a baseball uniform, sadly severed all ties to the sport when he accepted a job with a new Atlantic City casino-hotel.

Mays had been given an ultimatum by Commissioner Bowie Kuhn: choose between the $100,000-per-year casino job or his $50,000 job with the New York Mets. But, he warned, Mays would not be allowed to maintain ties with baseball if he chose the offer from Bally Manufacturing Company, owner of the multimillion-dollar Park Place Hotel.

"I'm not into gambling," said an obviously unhappy Mays. "The company is into gambling, not me. I don't gamble that much. That shouldn't stop me from making a living. I think anybody regrets it when his name is dragged through something like this."

Mays, who hit 660 home runs and compiled a .302 average in 22 seasons with the Giants and the Mets, will become the special assistant to the president – primarily a community relations job.

OCTOBER

30

MILESTONES IN SPORTS

1943

It took Toronto's Gus Bodnar only 15 seconds to score his first goal in his NHL debut—a 5–2 victory over the New York Rangers.

1954

Rochester defeated Boston, 98–95, as the NBA unveiled its 24-second shot clock.

1955

New York's Jim Patton returned a punt and a kickoff for touchdowns in the Giants' 35–7 victory over Washington.

1971

Michigan State's Eric Allen claimed college football's coveted single-game rushing record when he rolled up 350 yards in the Spartans' 43–10 victory over Purdue.

1975

A milestone: Boston's John Bucyk notched his 500th NHL goal in a 3–2 victory over St. Louis.

Boston's **John Bucyk,** *another 500-goal man.*

1974 Ali 'Ropes' Foreman

He bobbed, he weaved, he dodged and he ducked. Muhammad Ali, evidently trying to show that big George Foreman could not hurt him, did all those things as the heavyweight champion flailed away.

Ali's "rope-a-dope" strategy paid dividends in the eighth round. After spending the first seven laying against the ropes and taking everything Foreman had to offer without fighting back, Ali knocked out his arm-weary opponent and reclaimed the heavyweight crown that had been stripped from him more than seven years earlier.

Ali, 32 years old and still making wild predictions, had said before the title bout in Kinshasa, Zaire, that Foreman would fall from exhaustion by the end of the 10th round. He wasn't far off.

The champion, who had won his three previous title fights in a combined 11:35, took Ali's bait but never could deliver the big blow—or even hurt the challenger. When an exhausted Foreman stumbled in the eighth round, Ali stepped up with a left-right combination that sent him to the canvas.

It was all over and Ali had won the heavyweight championship for a second time, matching Floyd Patterson's record. Foreman was making his third defense of the title he won in January 1973 from Joe Frazier.

A STAR IS BORN

1898: Bill Terry, a Hall of Fame first baseman in the 1920s and '30s who batted .341 over 14 major league seasons.

★ ★ ★

1927: Joe Adcock, a slugging first baseman who blasted 336 home runs over 17 major league seasons in the 1950s and '60s.

★ ★ ★

1936: Jim Perry, a 215-game winner over 17 major league seasons in the 1960s and '70s.

★ ★ ★

1962: Danny Tartabull, a current major league outfielder.

★ ★ ★

DEATH OF A LEGEND

1954: Wilbur Shaw (auto racing).

1971 Cornell Star Marinaro Sets Rushing Record

Cornell record-setter **Ed Marinaro.**

Cornell running back Ed Marinaro became major college football's all-time leading rusher when he carried for 272 yards in a victory over Columbia and passed former Oklahoma star Steve Owens' career mark of 3,867 yards.

Marinaro entered the contest at Cornell's Schoellkopf Field needing seven yards to pass Owens. He ran six yards on his first carry of the day and broke the record on his second—a three-yard dive. He went on to hurdle the magic 4,000-yard barrier, raising his career total to 4,132.

The big senior tailback also scored a pair of touchdowns in leading the undefeated Big Red to a 24–21 victory. The win kept Cornell tied with Dartmouth for the Ivy League lead.

Marinaro is the first major college player to surpass 4,000 yards in a three-year career. Eight small-college runners have run farther, but all did it as four-year varsity players. He also became the first college player to post nine 200-yard games in a career.

His fourth 200-yard performance of the season tied a record set by former Southern Cal star O.J. Simpson in 1968.

1966 Unitas Passes Tittle

Baltimore quarterback Johnny Unitas overtook Y.A. Tittle as the greatest passing quarterback of all time and celebrated his achievement by leading the Colts to a 17–3 National Football League victory over the Los Angeles Rams.

Unitas disappointed the 57,898 Los Angeles fans by picking apart the Rams with a 13-of-22, 252-yard performance that included a pair of touchdown passes to John Mackey. But he also gave them a lasting memory when he hooked up on a 31-yard third-quarter pass with Raymond Berry, lifting his career yardage total past Tittle's NFL mark of 28,339.

Mackey was a big factor in Unitas' milestone performance. He caught an 89-yard touchdown pass in the opening period and grabbed a 17-yarder in the second.

Unitas finished the day with 28,375 career passing yards.

MILESTONES
· IN SPORTS ·

1948

Washington's Slingin' Sammy Baugh threw for 446 yards and four touchdowns and teammate Dan Sandifer returned two of his four interceptions for TDs as the Redskins pounded the Boston Yanks, 59–21.

1978

New York Yankee lefthander Ron Guidry capped his 25–3 campaign with the A.L. Cy Young Award.

1981

Purdue's Scott Campbell passed for 516 yards, but Ohio State was too much for his Boilermakers in a 45–33 Buckeye victory.

1981

Florida State's Greg Allen ran for a freshman-record 322 yards in a 56–31 victory over Western Carolina.

1987

Chris Antley became the first jockey to win nine races in a single day, riding four winners at Aqueduct and then crossing the Hudson River to ride five more at the Meadowlands.

1959

LSU Nips Ole Miss On Cannon Blast

The Tigers of Louisiana State University, their backs planted squarely against the wall as they tried to defend their national championship and protect their No. 1 ranking, simply reached into their offensive arsenal and pulled out a Cannon. A Billy Cannon.

Their predicament was simple. No. 3-ranked Mississippi was in Baton Rouge and the determined Rebels had every intention of snapping LSU's 18-game winning streak and leaving town with a 7–0 record. And sure enough, Ole Miss carried a 3–0 lead into the fourth quarter of the intense defensive struggle, courtesy of a 22-yard field goal by Ed Khayat that was set up by Cannon's first-quarter fumble.

LSU's **Billy Cannon** *breaks through Mississippi's defense on his game-deciding 89-yard punt return.*

But Cannon was not about to let a game of this magnitude end on that note. So the All-America running back stepped into the spotlight and decked the Rebels' national championship hopes with one explosive fourth-quarter gallop.

Fielding a bouncing Jake Gibbs punt at his own 11-yard line with 10 minutes left to play, Cannon hit the first wave of tacklers and absorbed several hits, somehow remaining on his feet. Suddenly he broke free and it was off to the races—89 yards and the winning touchdown. Final: LSU 7, Mississippi 3.

OCTOBER

31

A STAR IS BORN

1900: Cal Hubbard, the only member of both the baseball and pro football Hall of Fames. He was a baseball umpire and an NFL tackle.

★ ★ ★

1902: Wilbur Shaw, an outstanding automobile racer who won the Indianapolis 500 three times in four years (1937, '39 and '40).

★ ★ ★

1914: Jersey Joe Walcott, a former world heavyweight boxing champion (1951).

★ ★ ★

1947: Frank Shorter, the U.S. distance runner who won the marathon gold medal in the 1976 Montreal Olympic Games.

★ ★ ★

1963: Fred McGriff, a current major league first baseman.

★ ★ ★

DEATH OF A LEGEND

1983: George Halas (football).

1987

Deal Of the Decade

In an extraordinary three-team trade that one National Football League official called "the deal of the decade," three-time rushing champion Eric Dickerson was sent by the Los Angeles Rams to the Indianapolis Colts.

To get the 27-year-old superstar, the Colts had to put together a huge package of draft picks and players. They started their maneuvering by sending the rights to linebacker Cornelius Bennett, the unsigned second pick of the 1987 college draft, to the Buffalo Bills for their 1988 and '89 first-round draft picks, a 1988 second-round pick and fourth-year running back Greg Bell.

The Colts added their own No. 1 and No. 2 selections in 1988, a second-rounder from '89 and running back Owen Gill to the package and sent it to the Rams for Dickerson. The Bills get Bennett, the Colts get Dickerson and the Rams get six first and second-round draft picks and two veterans.

The Rams were willing to part with the record-setting Dickerson because of his demands to renegotiate his contract.

1950

NBA Breaks Color Barrier

Arnie Risen scored 20 points to lead the Rochester Royals to a season-opening 78–70 home victory over Washington, but the real significance of this game was the appearance of Capitols forward Earl Lloyd, the first black to play in a National Basketball Association game.

Lloyd's historic debut beat the debut of another black, Boston's Chuck Cooper, by one day. Lloyd, a 6-foot-6, 220-pound forward who carried a reputation as a defensive specialist, scored six points, grabbed 10 rebounds and handed out five assists in a solid first effort.

Cooper played the next night in the Celtics' 107–84 loss to Fort Wayne, scoring nine points and grabbing two rebounds. Cooper was the first black to be drafted by an NBA team—on the second round out of Duquesne. Lloyd was an eighth-round selection out of West Virginia State.

Cooper also holds the distinction of being the first black to sign an NBA contract.

Boston's **Chuck Cooper**, *the NBA's second black player.*

NOVEMBER

1

A STAR IS BORN

1931: Vic Power, a slick-fielding first baseman who compiled a .284 batting average from 1954-65.

★ ★ ★

1932: Al Arbour, the former NHL coach who directed the New York Islanders to four straight Stanley Cup championships (1980–83) en route to more than 700 career victories.

★ ★ ★

1936: Gary Player, the South African golf great who won nine major championships and each of the Big Four titles at least once.

★ ★ ★

1960: Fernando Valenzuela, a current major league pitcher.

★ ★ ★

1938

SEABISCUIT PULLS UPSET

Seabiscuit, widely expected to fall under the winning spell of 1937 Triple Crown winner War Admiral, shot from the starting gate and held off all advances from the champion colt en route to a stunning three-length victory in a match race at Baltimore's Pimlico track.

A crowd of 40,000 witnessed the demise of War Admiral, which went off at 1–4 and figured to be a sure bet. But Seabiscuit and jockey George Woolf had other ideas, which became apparent as soon as the starting gate clanked open.

Woolf lashed his 5-year-old California colt to the front and moved him quickly to the rail. He slowed up on the first turn, giving Seabiscuit a breather and forcing Charlie Kurtsinger to pull up War Admiral. Recognizing the dilemma, Kurtsinger quickly moved War Admiral to the outside and pulled even on the backstretch, setting the stage for an exciting finish.

The horses were neck and neck around the final turn, but War Admiral, having exhausted himself catching up, ran out of gas. Seabiscuit pulled away on the stretch and finished with a track-record 1:56 3/5 over the 1 3/16-mile course.

1913

DORAIS, IRISH PASS TEST IN SHOCKING VICTORY OVER ARMY

Notre Dame quarterback Gus Dorais, giving new meaning to the forward pass, stunned powerful Army with a never-before-witnessed aerial display that produced a 35–13 Fighting Irish victory at West Point, N.Y.

In the first notable intersectional game in Notre Dame history, Dorais unleashed a wide-open attack that resulted in 13-of-17 passing for 243 yards and a touchdown. That TD was a 25-yard first-quarter bomb to Knute Rockne for Notre Dame's first score.

Whereas most teams had used the forward pass (legalized in 1906) only in end-of-the-game desperation or on plays designed to deliver the ball to a receiver at a predetermined spot, Dorais hit his pass catchers in full flight and balanced his attack with solid running from his backs. Most of his completions were on short routes that set up two touchdown runs apiece by Ray Eichenlaub and Joe Pliska.

The passing strategy was the brainchild of Coach Jesse Harper, who was hungry to bring his team national attention.

Gus Dorais, *who went on to NFL fame as coach of the Detroit Lions (above), helped usher in the passing era as a quarterback at Notre Dame.*

1959

MONTREAL STAR PLANTE INTRODUCES GOALIE MASK

Montreal's **Jacques Plante,** *pre-goalie mask.*

Montreal goaltender Jacques Plante, having taken a shot to the face 20 minutes earlier, stepped back into the nets with a new look – an innovative hockey mask that helped ease his nerves for the remainder of the Canadiens' 3–1 victory over the New York Rangers in a game at Madison Square Garden.

It was the first time Plante had worn the mask during a regular National Hockey League game, but he had been using it for some time during practices. He had designed it with the help of a Montreal businessman, but Coach Toe Blake would not let him use it in regular play, thinking it limited his vision and made him susceptible to 95-mph slap shots.

Blake's attitude changed, however, when Plante was nailed by a first-period shot and retired to the dressing room for stitches. Without a backup goalie, Blake told Plante he could use the mask if he returned to the ice. Plante told his coach he would not go back without it – either for that game or ever again.

Before the mask, Plante had taken several hundred stitches in his face while suffering four broken noses, two cracked cheek bones and a fractured skull.

MILESTONES
• IN SPORTS •

1966

A National Football League franchise was awarded to New Orleans interests on All Saints Day.

1971

The new 10-team World Hockey Association announced its franchise lineup and committed to begin play in October 1972.

1982

National League owners blocked the re-election of Commissioner Bowie Kuhn and ended his sometimes-stormy 14-year reign over baseball.

1985 TULSA RUNS WILD

The Tulsa Hurricane piled up 554 rushing yards and 637 yards of total offense in rolling to a 42–26 victory over Wichita State at Cessna Stadium. But the real story of this game was the combined effort of quarterback Steve Gage and running back Gordon Brown.

Both rushed for more than 200 yards in the Hurricane's option attack, becoming the first teammates ever to top that barrier in the same game. Gage, who also completed five passes for 83 yards, ran for 206 yards on 26 carries and scored a pair of touchdowns. Brown carried 23 times for 214 yards and scored once.

Tulsa had a slim 14–13 halftime lead and a 21–19 third-quarter advantage, but the Hurricane broke loose in a 21-point final quarter. Gage scored both of his TDs in that period and Tulsa scored on drives of 72, 67 and 81 yards.

A STAR IS BORN

1903: Travis Jackson, a Hall of Fame shortstop who played in the 1930s and '40s for the New York Giants.

★ ★ ★

1914: Johnny Vander Meer, a 15-year major league pitcher best remembered for his back-to-back no-hitter feat of 1938.

★ ★ ★

1928: Leon Hart, the big end from Notre Dame who won the Heisman Trophy in 1949.

★ ★ ★

1934: Ken Rosewall, the Australian tennis star who captured four Australian, two French and two U.S. championships from 1953–72.

★ ★ ★

1958: Willie McGee, a current major league outfielder.

★ ★ ★

1960: Said Aouita, a current Moroccan record-setting distance runner.

★ ★ ★

DEATH OF A LEGEND

1973: Earle (Greasy) Neale (football).

★ ★ ★

1992 NO MAGIC FOR LAKERS

Los Angeles Lakers star Magic Johnson, who had announced his return to professional basketball five weeks earlier despite his status as HIV-positive, changed his mind and retired again because of the health concerns being expressed by other players who would have to compete against him.

The 33-year-old Johnson made his announcement four days before the start of the National Basketball Association season. He had played in five of the Lakers' eight preseason games, averaging 10.4 points and 12 assists.

But recent comments by other NBA stars, the most vocal by Utah's Karl Malone, seemed to catch Johnson by surprise. Many players expressed concern about facing Johnson in a competitive situation where scrapes and cuts are common hazards of the trade.

"This is not based on his doctor's advice," said Dr. Michael Mellman, who said Magic is fit to play. Johnson had retired originally in November 1991 when he first tested positive for HIV, the virus that causes AIDS. But he came back to play for the U.S. "Dream Team" in the Olympic Games at Barcelona and then decided to revive his NBA career. He had been assured that the risk factor to other athletes was "infinitesimally small."

MILESTONES · IN SPORTS ·

1958

An NFL-record crowd of 90,833 turned out at the Los Angeles Coliseum to watch the Rams defeat the Chicago Bears, 41–35.

1972

Steve Carlton, whose 27 victories accounted for almost half of the last-place Philadelphia Phillies' total, was voted the N.L. Cy Young Award.

1974

Honoring a request from baseball home run king Hank Aaron, the Atlanta Braves traded him to Milwaukee, the city where he started his career in 1974 and where he hit 398 of his 733 career homers.

1976

San Diego lefthander Randy Jones, a 22-game loser just two years earlier, captured the N.L. Cy Young Award after his 22-victory campaign for the Padres.

Philadelphia ace **Steve Carlton** *accepts his Cy Young Award from N.L. President Warren Giles.*

NOVEMBER 2

1990 NBA TEAMS SET A FAST PACE

New Denver Coach Paul Westhead unveiled his run-run-run offense to Nuggets fans at McNichols Arena and the result was predictable – a 162–158 Golden State victory that set a National Basketball Association record for combined points in a regulation game.

Using the same up-and-down, limited-defense, fast-shooting style that had allowed his Loyola-Marymount college basketball teams to set numerous NCAA scoring records, Westhead unleashed his exciting strategy in the NBA season-opener for both teams. The Warriors didn't seem to mind, building a record-setting 87–83 halftime advantage and then holding off the Nuggets in the late going.

The 320 combined points surpassed the previous record of 318 set in 1984, when the Nuggets beat San Antonio, 163–155. The 170 halftime points topped the 166 scored by Syracuse and San Francisco in a 1963 contest.

Chris Mullin led the way for Golden State with 38 points while Tim Hardaway added 32 points and 18 assists. Orlando Woolridge scored 37 points and Walter Davis added 33 for the Nuggets.

NOVEMBER

3

MILESTONES IN SPORTS

1929

The NFL's Providence team made history when it played host to the Cardinals – in the first-ever pro football game under the lights.

1968

Jim Turner kicked six field goals and his New York Jets teammates added a touchdown in a 25–21 NFL victory over the Buffalo Bills.

1973

Big Texas running back Roosevelt Leaks pounded his way to 342 yards on 37 carries and the Longhorns pounded Southern Methodist University, 42–14.

1973

Purdue freshman Mike Northington tied a Big Ten record when he scored five touchdowns in the Boilermakers' 48–23 victory over Iowa.

1973

A milestone: Chicago's Stan Mikita became the National Hockey League's sixth 1,000-point scorer when he assisted on the Blackhawks' only goal in a 3–1 loss to St. Louis.

1989

The Soviet invasion: Golden State's Sarunas Marciulionis and Atlanta's Alexander Volkov became the first Russians to play in the National Basketball Association.

1952 Kentucky Cancels Schedule

The University of Kentucky, the NCAA Tournament champion in three of the last five years and one of the most dominant basketball programs in the country, canceled its 21-game 1952–53 schedule as the result of an NCAA investigation that uncovered numerous rule violations.

The drastic action came after the NCAA announced that it would recommend next January that Kentucky be put on probation for all sports in 1952–53 because of infractions that occurred from 1947–50. Bradley, another basketball power, also was censured, but the Braves will just have to sit out the 1953 NCAA Tournament.

The NCAA said that Kentucky athletes had received pay and some were illegally certified as eligible for NCAA participation with the knowledge of Adolph Rupp and his assistant coaches. Several Wildcats had been implicated earlier in the 1951 "fix" scandals, but no mention of that was made in the NCAA's report.

Kentucky and Bradley officials said they would comply with the NCAA punishment, although Rupp said he thought the decision was harsh.

1990 Houston Wins Wild Shootout

Houston quarterback **David Klingler** *passed for 563 yards and seven touchdowns in a wild shootout at the Astrodome.*

In a wild shootout at the Astrodome, Houston's David Klingler and Texas Christian University's Matt Vogler put on the greatest aerial display in football history. The Cougars emerged from the game battered and bruised, but their 56–35 victory kept a national-best 12-game winning streak intact.

This was no place for the weak of heart. Vogler, making his second collegiate start at quarterback, completed 44 of 79 passes for an NCAA-record 690 yards. Five of those throws were for touchdowns to different receivers, all of whom topped 100 yards for the afternoon.

Klingler wasn't too shabby, either. He completed 36 of 53 throws for 563 yards and seven touchdowns – his second straight seven-TD performance. Marcus Grant caught three of those TD throws for 103 yards.

The teams combined for NCAA records in total offense (1,563 yards) and passing yards (1,253). None of the 12 scoring drives consumed more than 1:39 of playing time. Houston totaled 827 yards and averaged 9.5 yards per play.

Vogler's 100-yard receivers and TD catchers were Cedric Jackson, Kelly Blackwell, Stephen Shipley, Kyle McPherson and Richard Woodley.

1973 Catch 22: An NCAA Record

Brigham Young quarterback Gary Sheide passed for 408 yards and six touchdowns in a 56–21 romp past New Mexico, but his biggest accomplishment was reflected in the numbers posted by teammate Jay Miller.

Miller, a wide receiver, caught an NCAA single-game record 22 passes, three of which went for touchdowns. He broke the 6-year-old mark of 20 set by Tulsa's Rick Eber in 1967. Twenty of his catches came on throws by Sheide and the record-breaker and his 22nd reception were on four-yard throws by backup quarterback Randy Litchfield.

Sheide connected with Miller on TD passes of 33, 17 and 6 yards and threw scoring passes of 13, 2 and 7 yards to Wayne Bower. He finished his big afternoon with 32 completions in 50 attempts with one interception.

Miller caught three passes for 61 yards in the first quarter, six for 74 in the second, four for 54 in the third and nine for 74 in the fourth. He totaled 263 yards overall.

A STAR IS BORN

1908: Bronko Nagurski, an outstanding fullback-defensive tackle for the Chicago Bears from 1930–43 and a charter member of the pro football Hall of Fame.

★ ★ ★

1918: Bob Feller, a Hall of Fame righthander for the Cleveland Indians and a 266-game winner over 18 seasons.

★ ★ ★

1936: Roy Emerson, the 1960s Australian tennis great who recorded more grand slam tournament victories (12) than any other male player.

★ ★ ★

1949: Larry Holmes, the former heavyweight boxing champion (1978–85) who finished his career with a 54–4 record.

★ ★ ★

MILESTONES
· IN SPORTS ·

1934

Detroit pounded Pittsburgh, 40–7, in an NFL game, but the Steelers took consolation as the first team to score against the Lions after six shutout victories.

1960

Philadelphia's Wilt Chamberlain scored 44 points in a 136–121 victory over Detroit, but he also set an NBA record by missing all 10 of his free throw attempts.

1971

Los Angeles Lakers great Elgin Baylor announced his retirement, nine games into his 14th NBA season. Baylor finished his outstanding career with 23,149 points – an average of 27.4 per game.

1984

The NFL's Seattle Seahawks returned four interceptions for touchdowns, all 58 yards or longer, and blasted the Kansas City Chiefs, 45–0.

1976 FREE-AGENT ERA BEGINS

The Montreal Expos, the team that compiled baseball's worst record last season, ushered in a new era of free agency when they selected Baltimore slugger Reggie Jackson with the first pick in the game's first re-entry draft.

Third baseman **Sal Bando** *was one of the many Oakland Athletics players who drew a lot of attention in baseball's first re-entry draft.*

The proceedings at New York's Plaza Hotel were the aftermath of the historic Basic Agreement hammered out last July by Players' Association director Marvin Miller and the club owners. The agreement contained the parameters for a draft of players who have played out their contract options and are "free" to sign agreements with other major league teams.

Almost "free". Under terms of the draft to determine negotiating rights to 26 available players, teams were allowed to select as many as they wished – until a player was picked for the 12th time. Players not selected or picked only once became free to bargain with any team and those clubs losing players were allowed to retain negotiating rights.

Among the high-profile stars drawing the most attention were Jackson, Sal Bando, Don Baylor, Dave Campbell, Rollie Fingers, Wayne Garland, Bobby Grich, Don Gullett, Joe Rudi and Gene Tenace.

NOVEMBER

4

A STAR IS BORN

1911: Joe (Ducky) Medwick, the Hall of Fame outfielder who batted .324 over a 17-year major league career in the National League (1932–48).

★ ★ ★

1930: Dick Groat, a former National League batting champion who batted .286 over a 14-year career in the 1950s and '60s.

★ ★ ★

DEATH OF A LEGEND

1950: Grover Cleveland Alexander (baseball).

★ ★ ★

1955: Cy Young (baseball).

★ ★ ★

1942 GORDON WINS MVP

In a shocking slap to the face of Boston slugger Ted Williams, New York Yankee second baseman Joe Gordon was named the American League Most Valuable Player in a vote by the Baseball Writers Association of America.

It was the second consecutive year that the unpopular Williams had lost a close vote that many thought should have gone his way. Last season the Splendid Splinter batted .406 and led the A.L. with 37 home runs, but lost the MVP voting to New York's Joe DiMaggio .

But that was understandable because DiMaggio was coming off a season in which he hit in a major league-record 56 straight games and led in runs batted in with 125. Gordon's numbers paled in comparison.

Williams won the A.L. Triple Crown, batting .356 with 36 homers and 137 RBIs. The Boston left fielder also led the A.L. in slugging average (.648), runs scored (141), walks (145) and total bases (338). Gordon batted .322, hit 18 homers and drove in 103 runs – but he played for a pennant winner.

Williams likely was hurt by the running feud he carries on with the writers who handle the voting.

New York second baseman **Joe Gordon,** *pictured with Yankee Owner* **Jacob Ruppert** *in 1939, edged Ted Williams for the 1942 American League MVP award.*

1989 SUNDAY SILENCE GETS REVENGE

Sunday Silence, gaining sweet revenge against the colt that cost him horse racing's Triple Crown earlier in the year, edged Easy Goer by a neck and captured the $3 million Breeder's Cup Classic at Florida's Gulfstream Park.

The 3-year-old son of Halo won for the third time in four career meetings with Easy Goer and established himself as the clear-cut Horse of the Year favorite. Sunday Silence had edged Easy Goer in both the Kentucky Derby and Preakness Stakes, but suffered an eight-length loss to his arch-rival in the Triple Crown-deciding Belmont Stakes.

Easy Goer, based on that Belmont victory, went off as the 1–2 betting choice at Gulfstream. But jockey Pat Day let him fall behind by 11 lengths at the half mile and the colt needed everything he could muster to catch up at the 6-furlong mark. Sunday Silence, ridden for the first time by Chris McCarron, pulled away again and held off a late challenge.

Sunday Silence ran the $1^1/4$-mile course in $2:00^1/5$ to capture the rich first prize.

NOVEMBER

5

1977 NCAA Denies Pass Record

Grambling State quarterback Doug Williams became the most prolific passer in college football history when he threw for 378 yards in a 65–0 victory over Langston, but the strong-armed youngster was denied a place in the NCAA record books because of a technicality beyond his control.

Williams was simply caught in the middle. He had thrown for 5,121 yards in his first three seasons when Grambling competed as a Division I-AA team. But the Tigers moved up to Division I-A status in the off-season before Williams' senior campaign, negating any shot he had at breaking the career passing record.

The 7,551 career passing yards Williams had attained after the Langston game were two more than the major college record John Reaves managed as Florida's quarterback from 1969–71. But only 2,430 were compiled as a Division I-A passer, securing Reaves' continued status as the NCAA career record-holder.

Williams was nearly un-stoppable in Grambling's lopsided victory over outmanned Langston, completing 23 of 30 pass attempts and throwing for five touchdowns.

1927 Hagen Wins 4th Consecutive PGA

Veteran Walter Hagen, down by three after the first hole of the afternoon round, recovered his composure and roared back to claim a 1-up victory over young Joe Turnesa and his record fourth straight PGA Championship.

The 1927 season was enjoyable for **Walter Hagen.** *After serving as captain of the triumphant U.S. Ryder Cup team (above), he earned his fourth consecutive PGA Championship victory.*

The outlook was bleak for Hagen as Turnesa took a 2-up advantage into the afternoon round at the Cedar Crest Country Club in Dallas and then promptly won the first hole, putting the defending champion in serious trouble. But Hagen, his resolve facing a severe test, fought back like a caged tiger.

He won the second and third holes, lost the fourth and then pulled back within one with a birdie putt on seven. Hagen finally caught the youngster with another birdie on 12 and took the lead on 14, when he carded a par four and Turnesa slipped to a double bogey .

The last four holes were halved, with Hagen missing a three-foot birdie putt on 15 and Turnesa missing golden opportunities to tie with short putts on 16 and 18. But Hagen held and the PGA title was his for the fourth time since 1923, when he lost in a dramatic playoff to Gene Sarazen.

Hagen's consecutive PGA finals victories were fashioned against four different opponents: Jim Barnes, William Mehlhorn, Leo Diegel and Turnesa.

1982 Cavs' Streak Reaches 24

Otis Birdsong scored 27 points and Darwin Cook added 19 to pace the New Jersey Nets to a 99–91 victory that extended the Cleveland Cavaliers' National Basketball Association-record losing streak to 24 games.

The loss was Cleveland's fifth in as many games this season after finishing the 1981–82 campaign 0–19. The streak is three games worse than the former record of 21 held by Detroit, which lost 14 games to end the 1979–80 season and its first seven in 1980–81. Philadelphia set the one-season record with 20 straight losses in 1973.

The Cavs fought hard to end their misery, but a late rally fell a little short. Cleveland pulled to within 93–89 on Geoff Huston's basket with 48 seconds remaining, but Cook made two free throws and Foots Walker made four more to insure New Jersey's third victory in five games.

A STAR IS BORN

1891: Earl (Greasy) Neale, a football Hall of Fame coach for the Philadelphia Eagles from 1941–50.

★ ★ ★

1952: Bill Walton, a basketball Hall of Fame center who helped UCLA set an NCAA record with 88 straight victories and later played on two NBA championship teams.

★ ★ ★

DEATH OF A LEGEND

1970: Charlie Root (baseball).

★ ★ ★

MILESTONES • IN SPORTS •

1961

St Louis' Bill Stacy returned two Dallas interceptions for touchdowns and the Cardinals defeated the Cowboys, 13-17, in an NFL game.

1966

Brigham Young quarterback Virgil Carter passed for 513 yards and ran for 86 more to set an NCAA record for total yards by one player during a 53–33 victory over Texas Western.

1977

Brigham Young sophomore quarterback Marc Wilson set an NCAA single-game passing record when he threw for 571 yards in the Cougars' 38–24 victory over Utah.

1976

The Seattle Mariners selected Kansas City outfielder Ruppert Jones and the Toronto Blue Jays nabbed Baltimore shortstop Bob Bailor as the first picks in the expansion draft to stock the new A.L. teams.

1978

A coaching milestone: Oakland's John Madden earned his 100th NFL victory when the Raiders downed the Kansas City Chiefs, 20–10.

1976 Campbell Opens Up Free-Agency Vault

Reliever Bill Campbell, who jumped into the big-money spotlight with a career year for the Minnesota Twins last season, signed a four-year, $1 million contract with the Boston Red Sox, perhaps opening the vault door for other members of baseball's first crop of free agents.

Reliever **Bill Campbell** *made history when he signed a free-agent contract with the Boston Red Sox.*

Campbell signed his contract 48 hours after team owners had gathered in New York to participate in an historic re-entry draft. During those proceedings, the owners obtained negotiating rights from the list of 26 players who had played out their option and were considered free agents under terms of the new Basic Agreement that eliminated the antiquated reserve system.

The 6-foot-3 Campbell, selected on the first round by Boston and St. Louis, also was picked by 11 other teams. But he opted for the Red Sox, who gave him a lucrative contract that ranks among the biggest in baseball history. The numbers will be noted by other free agents like Reggie Jackson, Bobby Grich and Rollie Fingers.

A STAR IS BORN

1861: James Naismith, the man who is credited with inventing basketball in 1891 and the namesake for the basketball Hall of Fame.

★ ★ ★

1887: Walter Johnson, the Hall of Fame righthander who won 416 games in 21 seasons (1907-27) for the Washington Senators.

★ ★ ★

1953: John Candelaria, a current major league pitcher.

★ ★ ★

DEATH OF A LEGEND

1922: Morgan Bulkeley (baseball).

★ ★ ★

1931: Jack Chesbro (baseball).

★ ★ ★

1979: Chick Evans (golf).

★ ★ ★

1974 Dodger Earns Honor

Los Angeles Dodgers righthander Mike Marshall put the cap on the greatest iron man pitching performance in decades when he became the first relief pitcher ever to capture a prestigious Cy Young Award.

Although the strong-minded and controversial Marshall is not a popular figure among the nation's sportswriters, nobody would deny that the rubber-armed veteran earned the honor. He appeared in a major league-record 106 games and pitched a relief-record 208 innings, a remarkable ledger of endurance never before rivaled.

The 31-year-old Marshall, who easily outpolled Dodger teammate Andy Messersmith, held the previous records of 92 games and 179 innings, both set in 1973. He also appeared in a record 14 straight games in late June and early July and set another mark with 83 games finished. He completed the season with 15 victories and 21 saves.

Marshall was awarded 17 of the 24 first-place votes for 96 points – 30 more than Messersmith, who compiled a 20–6 record in a starting role.

Los Angeles iron man **Mike Marshall** *is congratulated by catcher* **Joe Ferguson** *after one of his 21 saves.*

MILESTONES IN SPORTS

1966

Philadelphia's Timmy Brown returned a pair of Dallas kickoffs 93 and 90 yards for first- and second-quarter touchdowns as the Eagles edged the Cowboys, 24–23.

1971

Lydell Mitchell set a Penn State career rushing record when he bolted for 209 yards and scored five touchdowns in the Nittany Lions' 63–27 victory over Maryland.

1973

Triple Crown winner Secretariat said an official goodbye to the horse racing wars when he was paraded in full silks by jockey Ron Turcotte before 32,990 boisterous fans at Aqueduct race course in New York.

1981

Prohibitive favorite Larry Holmes survived a seventh-round knockdown and retained his WBC heavyweight crown with an 11th-round technical knockout of Renaldo Snipes at Pittsburgh.

1982

Mississippi quarterback Kent Austin set a major college record for completion percentage when he connected on 18 of 19 attempts for 269 yards and two touchdowns in a 45–14 victory over Tulane.

1993 Holyfield Beats Bowe

Evander Holyfield, ignoring a 20-minute delay caused by a parachutist crashing into the ring, scored an exciting majority decision over Riddick Bowe and reclaimed the heavyweight championship he had lost to Bowe almost a year earlier.

Holyfield became the third man to win the heavyweight crown at least twice, joining Muhammad Ali and Floyd Patterson in that distinction. He did most of his damage in the middle rounds, Bowe dominating early and at the finish.

Holyfield, choosing to mix clever boxing with his usual toe-to-toe style, rocked the bigger champion in the fifth and 10th rounds. In the fifth, he sent Bowe reeling with three shots to the head but couldn't finish him off. In the 10th, he shocked the champion with a four-punch combination.

The fight was punctuated by a bizarre seventh-round incident in which a man on a propeller-driven parachute crashed into the Caesars Palace (Las Vegas) outdoor ring, hitting the ropes and tumbling into the crowd. He was beaten up by several fans and removed, handcuffed, on a stretcher. During the confusion, Bowe's pregnant wife, Judy, fainted and also was taken away on a stretcher.

The loss was the first in 35 decisions for the 246-pound Bowe. Holyfield, a 217-pounder, is 30–1.

NOVEMBER

7

A STAR IS BORN

1936: Al Attles, the basketball Hall of Famer who scored 6,328 points as an NBA player in the 1960s and won 557 games as an NBA coach in the 1970s.

★ ★ ★

1938: Jim Kaat, a 25-year major league lefthander in a career that spanned four decades and produced 283 victories.

★ ★ ★

1944: Joe Niekro, a 22-year major league pitcher who won 221 games.

★ ★ ★

DEATH OF A LEGEND

1978: Gene Tunney (boxing).

1991 HIV Virus Forces Magic's Retirement

Earvin (Magic) Johnson, whose contagious smile and mesmerizing talent helped lead the National Basketball Association into an era of great prosperity, brought a nation to its knees when he announced he was ending his 12-year career because he had tested positive for HIV, the virus that causes AIDS.

Johnson's shocking disclosure at the Los Angeles Forum brought a massive outpouring of emotion from friends, fans and other observers throughout the country. It came as the result of routine tests and Johnson emphasized that he does not have AIDS at this time, only the virus that leads to it.

The 32-year-old Johnson, who said that his wife had tested negative, added that he hoped his decision to make it public would increase national awareness of the dreaded disease. And sure enough, clinics and hospitals around the nation reported an immediate upsurge in AIDS testing.

The Lakers will be losing one of the greatest stars in the history of the NBA. After leading Michigan State to an NCAA championship as a sophomore, Magic led the Lakers to five NBA titles in 12 seasons, including the first back-to-back titles by any team in 19 years.

But that's only part of his phenomenal story. Johnson, considered one of the great playmakers of all time, finished with an NBA career-record 8,932 assists. He also finished with career averages of 19.7 points, 7.3 rebounds and 11.4 assists. Magic earned three Most Valuable Player citations.

MILESTONES IN SPORTS

1943

Playing in the rain and mud at Detroit, the Lions and New York Giants battled to a 0–0 tie – the last scoreless deadlock in NFL history.

1964

The Braves, who had moved from Boston to Milwaukee in 1953, received permission from the National League to transfer to Atlanta after the 1965 campaign.

1970

Argentine Carlos Monzon recorded a 12th-round knockout of Italy's Nino Benvenuti and claimed the world middleweight championship in a stunning upset at Rome, Italy.

1972

Cincinnati catcher Johnny Bench, coming off a 45-home run season, was named National League Most Valuable Player for the second time in three years.

1976

Minnesota's Sammy White caught a 37-yard touchdown strike from quarterback Fran Tarkenton with 53 seconds remaining, bringing his receiving yardage total to 210 and giving the Vikings a 31–23 victory over the Detroit Lions.

1968 Berenson Has 6-Goal Game

Red Berenson, who had not scored a goal in more than a week and had managed just three all season, connected six times in a one-game explosion against the Flyers that helped St. Louis to an 8–0 National Hockey League victory at the Philadelphia Spectrum.

St. Louis Blues center **Red Berenson** *(7).*

The six goals, all off Flyers goalie Doug Favell, fell one short of the single-game record set by Quebec's Joe Malone in 1920. It was the first six-goal effort in 24 years and only the sixth overall. Detroit's Syd Howe was the last to accomplish the feat in 1944 and the other four six-goal games were recorded in the 1920 and '21 seasons, when the NHL was still an infant league.

It did not appear early that this game would produce anything out of the ordinary. Berenson scored in the first period to break his slump, but was otherwise held in check. Not so in the second period, when the center blazed four shots past Favell.

He added another in the third and closed with a third-period assist on a Camille Henry goal.

1925 Tiny Kick Keys Upset

A first-quarter Tiny Lewis field goal and a five-day rainstorm that turned Chicago's Soldier Field into a treacherous sea of mud proved to be a deadly combination for the powerful Michigan Wolverines, who watched their hopes for a national championship slowly wash away.

Lewis gave heavy-underdog Northwestern all the points it needed for a 3–2 upset that rocked the college football world. Michigan had entered the game undefeated and had outscored its five opponents, 180–0.

But luck was more of a factor than talent on this unpleasant day. Both teams spent the rainy afternoon sliding, fumbling and punting – trying not to make a crucial mistake and hoping the other team would.

Michigan's came in the opening quarter when Lewis converted a Benny Friedman fumble into his 18-yard field goal. The Wildcat defense held Michigan to 35 total yards and did not allow a first down. The Wolverines' only points came on a final-quarter intentional safety.

1970 Dempsey's 63-Yarder

In a National Football League comeback that fell just short of miraculous, New Orleans recorded a 19–17 victory over the Detroit Lions at Tulane Stadium.

Record-setting New Orleans kicker **Tom Dempsey.**

"Miraculous" might be an understatement. When Detroit kicker Errol Mann booted an 18-yard field goal that gave the Lions a 17–16 lead with 11 seconds remaining, the Saints appeared to be in a hopeless situation. But. . .

On the first play from scrimmage after Mann's field goal, Al Dodd caught a 17-yard pass from New Orleans quarterback Billy Kilmer, giving the Saints a first down at their own 45. Two seconds remained. Time, perhaps, for one "Hail Mary" end zone throw? But no. The optimistic Saints sent in their field goal unit.

With everybody in the stadium expecting a fake, kicker Tom Dempsey actually booted the ball. It sailed high and straight, but did it have the distance – 63 yards, seven yards longer than the previous best National Football League field goal? Dempsey, who was born with half a right foot and had to wear a special shoe approved by the league, couldn't tell.

"I saw the referee's hands go up and heard everybody start yelling and I knew it was good," he said later. It was Dempsey's fourth field goal of the game.

1952 Richard Sets Record

Montreal's Maurice Richard, living up to his well-earned nickname, fired a rocket past Chicago goaltender Al Rollins and surpassed Nels Stewart as the greatest regular-season goal scorer in National Hockey League history.

Richard's 325th goal came on a low drive into the corner of the net during the second period of the Canadiens' 6–4 victory at the Montreal Forum. The record-setter came off a pass from Butch Bouchard, Richard's teammate for his entire 11-year career.

The crowd of 14,562 got a double treat in the second period. First Elmer Lach scored his 200th career goal, then Richard connected. Dick Gamble scored twice and Floyd Curry and Paul Meger once each to account for Montreal's other goals.

Richard had scored his record-tying goal October 29 and then went scoreless for three games. He also holds NHL records for career playoff goals and most goals in a season.

November 8

Milestones in Sports

1942

Cleveland quarterback Parker Hall threw an NFL-record seven interceptions and the Green Bay Packers put them to good use in a 30–12 victory over the Rams.

1954

American League owners approved the sale of the Philadelphia Athletics franchise to Arnold Johnson and the transfer of the team to Kansas City.

1959

Minneapolis Lakers forward Elgin Baylor exploded for an NBA-record 64 points in a game against Boston.

1958

Ohio State defensive tackle Jim Marshall returned an interception for one touchdown and a blocked punt for another as the Buckeyes fought Purdue to a 14–14 tie.

1966

Baltimore's Frank Robinson, the American League Triple Crown winner, became the first player to win MVP honors in both leagues.

1981

The Miami Dolphins squeezed out a 30–27 overtime victory over New England, giving Coach Don Shula his 200th NFL career win.

1986

Tulsa's Steve Gage became the first NCAA quarterback to run and pass for more than 200 yards (212 and 209) in a 34–27 victory over New Mexico.

A Star Is Born

1896: Bucky Harris, a Hall of Fame infielder known as the "Boy Wonder" when he was player-manager for Washington in the 1920s. He went on to win 2,160 games as a major league manager.

★ ★ ★

1942: Angel Cordero Jr., an outstanding jockey who won three Kentucky Derbys and more than 6,000 career races.

★ ★ ★

Death of a Legend

1977: Bucky Harris (baseball).

★ ★ ★

1980 Wilson Lights Up Sky

Illinois quarterback Dave Wilson lit up the skies of Columbus, O., with an unprecedented aerial display, but Ohio State surived his blitz and recorded a 49–42 victory that kept it tied for the Big Ten Conference lead.

Wilson, who is competing under a court order preventing the conference from barring him on academic grounds, was nearly unstoppable in a record-shattering performance that rallied the Illini from a 35–7 deficit. He set an NCAA record with 621 passing yards and tied NCAA marks for pass attempts (69), completions (43) and total plays (76). The previous best yardage total (571) had been compiled by Brigham Young's Marc Wilson in 1977.

Wilson also fired six touchdown passes, two to Gregg Dentino. Lost in the shadow of his performance was the 284-yard, four-touchdown effort of Ohio State's Art Schlichter. The Buckeye quarterback completed 11 straight passes in the first half when Ohio State (8–1) built its big lead.

Dave Wilson *passed for a record 621 yards, but Illinois still lost to Ohio State.*

NOVEMBER

9

A STAR IS BORN

1935: Bob Gibson, a Hall of Fame righthander who won 251 games over 17 seasons with the St. Louis Cardinals.

★★★

1942: Tom Weiskopf, a British Open winner in 1973 and the longest hitter on the PGA Tour in the 1960s and '70s.

★★★

1958: Ted Higuera, a current major league pitcher.

★★★

1962: John Battle, a current National Basketball Association guard.

★★★

1963: Anthony Bowie, a current National Basketball Association guard.

★★★

1946

0-0: Army Ties Irish

In what had been billed as the greatest offensive battle in the history of college football, No. 1-ranked Army and No. 2-ranked Notre Dame crossed up the experts by playing to a 0–0 tie before a packed house at Yankee Stadium.

The result caught everybody by surprise. Army, riding a 25-game winning streak, entered the contest 7–0, having outscored its opposition 208–55. Notre Dame was 5–0, having rolled up a 177–18 advantage over its opponents. Both teams had firepower and a lot was at stake.

Notre Dame targeted talented Army running backs Glenn Davis and Doc Blanchard for its defensive thrust and held the stars to 80 yards on 35 carries. The Cadets went after Irish quarterback Johnny Lujack, holding him to six pass completions and nine yards on the ground. Notre Dame managed 225 yards of total offense, Army 195.

Notre Dame did put together a second-quarter 85-yard march that was stopped at the Army 3 and Lujack made a saving tackle on Blanchard when he broke clear in the third quarter.

The unexpected result meant that the coveted top ranking would have to be decided by the pollsters, not the teams on the field.

Army's 1-2 running punch of **Doc Blanchard** *(left) and* **Glenn Davis** *was silenced by Notre Dame.*

MILESTONES
· IN SPORTS ·

1953

The U.S. Supreme Court, reaffirming its earlier position, ruled 7–2 that baseball is a sport, not a business, and therefore is not subject to the nation's antitrust laws.

1957

Montreal's Claude Provost set an NHL record for fastest goal at the beginning of a period when he scored at 4 seconds of the second stanza in a 4–2 Canadiens' victory over Boston.

1972

Boston's John Bucyk joined the NHL's 1,000-point club when he scored a goal in an 8–3 victory over Detroit.

1984

Larry Holmes retained his IBF heavyweight championship when he scored a 12th-round technical knockout of Bonecrusher Smith in a bout at Las Vegas.

1988

Laffit Pincay rode two winners at California's Hollywood Park and joined Bill Shoemaker as the only jockeys with 7,000 career triumphs.

1982

Eye Problem KOs Leonard

Sugar Ray Leonard, the former light welterweight Olympic boxing champion and a winner of 32 professional fights over an impressive 5½-year career, announced his retirement because of an eye injury that his doctor said could prove troublesome in future bouts.

Leonard announced his decision during an ostentatious ceremony at the Baltimore Civic Center. A crowd of 10,000, including Muhammad Ali and other celebrities, gave him a wild sendoff as he said goodbye while standing in the ring where he fought his first professional bout in 1977.

The boxing world is losing one of its most popular performers. Leonard's flamboyant style and lightning-quick reflexes have mesmerized fight fans and opponents alike. He has held both the welterweight and junior middleweight championships, losing the welterweight crown once to Roberto Duran and winning it back in a rematch. That was his only career loss.

In his last fight, Leonard suffered a partially detached retina that required surgery. Ophthalmologist Ronald Michels had given his 26-year-old patient the go-ahead to fight again, but strongly advised against it.

1989

Bucks Win in 5 Overtimes

Tony Brown's three-point bomb started Milwaukee on a nine-point run in the fifth overtime and the Bucks held on to record a 155–154 victory over Seattle in the longest National Basketball Association game since the 1954 adoption of the 24-second clock.

Milwaukee's run started with Brown's three-pointer and ended with a Jeff Grayer layup, but the SuperSonics fought back with an 8–0 run of their own that almost forced a sixth overtime. That would have matched the 1951 record set by the Indianapolis Olympians and Rochester Royals – a pre-shot clock game that the Olympians won, 75–73.

Regulation ended in a 103–103 tie when Milwaukee's Fred Roberts hit a late free throw and the ensuing overtimes ended at 110–110, 120–120, 127–127 and 138–138. Seattle's Dale Ellis forced two extra sessions with final-second jumpers.

Ellis scored 53 points, 20 of them in the extra periods. Ricky Pierce scored 36 for the Bucks.

Seattle hit 52 of 117 shots from the field and 46 of 60 free throws. The Bucks were 56 of 111 and 39 of 49.

1928 Irish Win For Gipper

In a classic battle that may well have been decided in the Notre Dame locker room at halftime, the Fighting Irish handed powerful Army its first loss of the season – a 12–6 shocker at New York's Yankee Stadium.

Notre Dame's inspirational **George Gipp** *in 1920.*

The inspiration for Notre Dame's emotional victory came from Coach Knute Rockne's halftime speech. With his 4–2 Irish team locked in a scoreless battle with the 6–0 Cadets, Rockne told his troops about a deathbed plea delivered eight years earlier by Irish star George Gipp, who had just led Notre Dame to its second straight unbeaten season.

"When the breaks are beating the boys, tell them to go in there and win just one for the Gipper," Gipp told his tearful coach. Rockne never forgot. He just waited for the right time and told his 1928 team, "this is the day and you are the team." Fired up, Notre Dame played a strong second half, overcoming a 6–0 Army lead and scoring the winning touchdown on John Niemiec's fourth-quarter pass to Johnny O'Brien.

Army returned the ensuing kickoff 55 yards and drove inside the Notre Dame 5-yard line, but the game ended with the Cadets on the 1 and out of timeouts.

1990 Suns Bomb Denver

In a National Basketball Association contest that gave new meaning to the term "run and gun," the Phoenix Suns posted a 173–143 victory over Denver that set several offensive records.

Beating the Nuggets at their own full-court-pressure, instant-offense game, the Suns looked like they were running a layup drill as they hit 17 of their first 19 shots and roared to an unprecedented 107-point first half – 17 more than the previous record of 90, set the previous week by the Nuggets. Phoenix also set first-half records with 43 field goals and 33 assists and broke loose for a record 57 second-quarter points – 22 by rookie Cedric Ceballos.

There was even talk of the NBA's first 200-point game for a while, but the Suns' frantic pace slowed in the second half and they could do no better than match the NBA regulation-game point record set by the 1959 Boston Celtics.

The game also was a milestone for Phoenix Coach Cotton Fitzsimmons, who recorded his 700th career victory.

November 10

Milestones in Sports

1945

No. 1 Army 48, No. 2 Notre Dame 0 in a much-publicized "Game of the Century" that fell considerably short of expectations.

1978

WBC heavyweight champion Larry Holmes knocked out Alfredo Evangelista in the seventh round of a title fight at Las Vegas.

1984

Wyoming's Kevin Lowe (302) and South Dakota State's Ricky Wegher (231) combined for a major college-record 533 rushing yards in a game won by the Cowboys, 45–29.

1984

Wild Again, a 31–1 longshot, held off Slew o' Gold and Gate Dancer to capture the $3 million Breeder's Cup Classic in the inaugural Breeder's Cup series at Hollywood Park.

1985

Miami quarterback Dan Marino completed his eighth pass to Mark Duper, a 50-yard touchdown bomb with 41 seconds remaining, to give the Dolphins a 21–17 victory over the New York Jets. Duper's catches totaled 217 yards.

A Star Is Born

1896: Jimmie Dykes, an outstanding player, coach and manager in a baseball career that spanned nearly 50 years (1917–64).

★ ★ ★

1919: Clyde (Bulldog) Turner, a pro football Hall of Fame center-linebacker from 1940-52 and later coach of the New York Titans.

★ ★ ★

1934: Norm Cash, a former American League batting champion (1961) who belted 377 home runs in a 17-year major league career.

★ ★ ★

1963: Mike Powell, the current long jumper who broke Bob Beamon's 23-year-old record in 1991 with a leap of 29-4½.

★ ★ ★

1963 Howe Scores 545th Goal

Detroit star Gordie Howe whipped a shorthanded shot past Montreal goaltender Charlie Hodge and officially dethroned former Canadiens' marksman Maurice (Rocket) Richard as the greatest regular-season goal-scorer in National Hockey League history.

Howe's 545th career goal came at 15:06 of the second period after teammates Bruce MacGregor and Alex Faulkner had given Detroit a 2–0 lead. Red Wings goalie Terry Sawchuk took care of the rest, making 39 saves while treating Detroit fans to a 3–0 victory – his NHL record-tying 94th career shutout.

But Sawchuk took a backseat to Howe, who now owns the "grand slam" of hockey. Besides ranking as the top all-time goal-scorer, Howe holds NHL career records for points (1,221), assists (676) and games played (1,132). He also has won a record six Hart Trophies as the player adjudged most valuable to his team.

Both Howe and Richard set their records in 18 seasons. Sawchuk matched the career shutout mark of former Montreal goalie George Hainsworth.

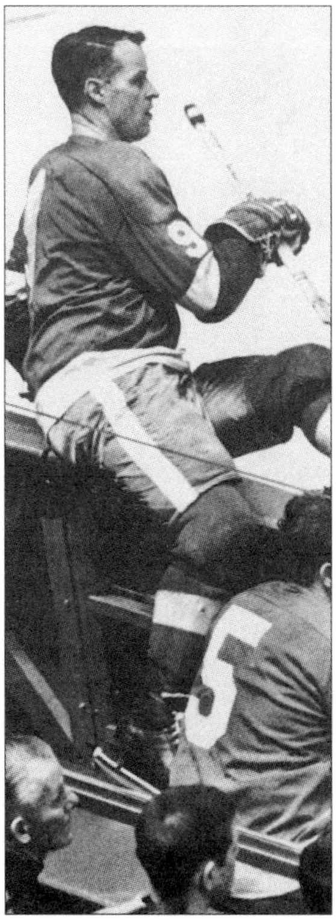

Detroit star **Gordie Howe.**

NOVEMBER

11

A STAR IS BORN

1891: Rabbit Maranville, a Hall of Fame shortstop who compiled 2,605 hits over 23 major league seasons from 1912–35.

★ ★ ★

1899: Pie Traynor, a Hall of Fame third baseman who collected 2,416 hits over 17 seasons with Pittsburgh in the 1920s and '30s.

★ ★ ★

1912: Hal Trosky, a slugging first baseman who produced six straight 100-RBI seasons for Cleveland in the 1930s.

★ ★ ★

1951: Fuzzy Zoeller, a current PGA Tour golfer who owns major-tournament victories in the Masters and U.S. Open

★ ★ ★

1978 Georgia Tech's Ivery Sets Rushing Record

Georgia Tech record-setter **Eddie Lee Ivery.**

Georgia Tech running back Eddie Lee Ivery braved wind and snow and all the defense the Air Force could muster to keep his appointed rounds – an NCAA-record 356-yard rushing performance during the Yellow Jackets' 42–21 victory at Colorado Springs.

It was not the kind of day that invites record-setting performances. The temperature was 22 degrees at kickoff, a 16-mile per hour wind was whipping up anything that wasn't tied down and light snow was falling. Ivery gave no hint of great things to come when he gained 11 yards on his first four carries.

But then he picked up steam and rendered the Air Force helpless. He gained 345 yards on his final 22 carries and finished the day averaging 13.7 yards per attempt. Boosting that average were touchdown jaunts of 73, 80 and 57 yards.

The one negative in his performance was a fumble – at the end of his record-setting 21-yard run. Ivery broke the 7-year-old mark of Michigan State's Eric Allen, who ran for 350 yards in a 1971 contest against Purdue.

MILESTONES • IN SPORTS •

1972

Michigan State pulled off a stunning upset for retiring Coach Duffy Daugherty when it handed powerful Ohio State its first loss of the season, a 19–12 setback at East Lansing, Mich.

1972

Utah State quarterback Tony Adams set an NCAA single-game passing record when he threw for 561 yards in a 44–16 victory over arch-rival Utah.

1979

Denver's Rick Upchurch returned three punts for 30 yards in a 45–10 victory over New England, lifting his career punt return total to 2,209 yards and becoming the NFL's all-time leader.

1981

The Minnesota North Stars broke loose for eight second-period goals and overpowered Winnipeg, 15–2.

1987

Boston fireballer Roger Clemens, who finished 20–9 with a 2.97 ERA, became only the fourth pitcher in baseball history to win consecutive Cy Young Awards.

1911 Thorpe Kicks Stun Harvard

Jim Thorpe, *the all-everything football star for Carlisle Industrial School.*

Jim Thorpe, whose status was questionable going into what figured to be a mismatch at Harvard Stadium, kicked four field goals and led his underdog Carlisle Industrial School team to a shocking 18–15 victory over the Crimson.

Thorpe, who spent most of the pregame limping around on a heavily bandaged right leg, was everywhere once the action started. He carried the ball, he recklessly threw his body around on defense and he did whatever was necessary to slow down once-beaten Harvard.

The 25,000 disappointed Crimson fans saw firsthand why he is considered one of the world's greatest pure athletes.

Harvard held a 9–6 halftime lead, but Carlisle took control in the third period. Thorpe carried the ball into position for Possum Powell to score on a short TD run and then added a pair of field goals. His fourth three-pointer of the contest came in the final quarter from 48 yards out and provided the winning points.

That kick became important later in the game when Harvard's Robert Storer picked up a blocked punt and sprinted into the end zone.

The defeat was the second in a row for Harvard, which lost to Princeton the previous week.

1990 Thomas Gets 7 Sacks

Kansas City linebacker Derrick Thomas set a National Football League record by sacking Seattle quarterback Dave Krieg seven times, but the only thing anybody talked about was the one that slipped away.

That happened in the final seconds of the game at Kansas City's Arrowhead Stadium with the Chiefs holding a 16–10 lead. Krieg took the snap, dropped back and was hit by Thomas, apparently a sack victim for the eighth time.

But somehow Krieg wriggled free and launched a 25-yard pass into the end zone. Seahawk Paul Skansi outleaped a swarm of Kansas City defenders and, with Norm Johnson's extra-point kick, Seattle had a shocking 17–16 victory.

"I thought I had him," said a stunned Thomas. "He just stumbled back, caught his balance and threw the pass." Thomas, who broke the 1983 record of six sacks by San Francisco's Fred Dean, lifted his nine-week total to 15. His third of the day forced a Krieg fumble that teammate Dan Saleaumua recovered in the end zone.

1979 Eagles Kick Dallas

The Philadelphia Eagles, riding the momentum supplied by Tony Franklin's monster field goal, built a 24–7 lead and held off a furious Dallas rally to hand the Cowboys a 31–21 defeat at Irving, Tex.

Franklin provided the game's big blow with seconds remaining in the opening half when he booted a 59-yard field goal, the second longest in National Football League history. The kick was only four yards shorter than the 63-yard record-setter by New Orleans' Tom Dempsey in 1970.

And it capped a 10-point spurt by the Eagles that put them in position to win their first game ever at Texas Stadium. Philadelphia had taken a 14–7 lead 46 seconds earlier when backup quarterback John Walton, replacing injured Ron Jaworski, fired a 29-yard touchdown pass to Charlie Smith. After a Randy Logan interception, Franklin delivered his bomb.

Even when the Eagles increased their lead to 17 points on Jaworski's third-quarter TD pass to Harold Carmichael, victory was far from assured. Dallas quarterback Roger Staubach threw a pair of touchdown passes in the final six minutes to pull the Cowboys within three, but Wilbert Montgomery streaked 37 yards for an insurance TD with 1:01 remaining.

Montgomery finished the game with 126 yards and topped the 1,000 barrier for the second straight year. He became the first Eagles runner to reach the plateau in consecutive seasons.

1920 Baseball Selects 1st Commissioner

Stern-faced **Kenesaw Mountain Landis** *took the reins in 1920.*

Embarking on what they termed a new era for baseball, the 16 major league owners, meeting for three hours at a Chicago hotel, selected United States District Court Judge Kenesaw Mountain Landis as the first commissioner of the game, replacing the three-man National Commission that had ruled since 1903.

Landis was given dictatorial powers over the owners and players with a mandate to clean up the National Pastime and make it more appealing to the fans. Triggering the owners' drastic decision was the rumors of scandal surrounding Chicago White Sox players "fixing" the 1919 World Series.

The owners, seeing that Landis was unwilling to give up his position on the bench, decided on a proposal whereby he could continue his jurist duties while serving as the game's first commissioner. It took Landis only a few minutes to say yes to the idea.

The Judge will have final say over all disputes and other matters pertaining to baseball.

A Star Is Born

1893: Carl Mays, a 208-game major league winner best remembered for throwing the pitch that killed Cleveland shortstop Ray Chapman.

★ ★ ★

1912: Tuffy Leemans, a pro football Hall of Fame fullback for the New York Giants from 1936–43.

★ ★ ★

1944: Ken Houston, a football Hall of Fame defensive back for the Houston Oilers and Washington Redskins from 1967–80.

★ ★ ★

1961: Nadia Comaneci, the Rumanian gymnast who won three gold medals, two silver and one bronze at the 1976 Montreal Olympic Games. She was the first gymnast to score a perfect 10 during competition.

Death of a Legend

1993: Bill Dickey (baseball)

1985 Flyers Goalie Lindbergh Dies In Car Crash

Philadelphia Flyers goaltender Pelle Lindbergh, the 1984 Vezina Trophy winner and one of the top young netminders in the National Hockey League, died at a New Jersey hospital, two days after a fiery automobile crash had left him brain dead.

Doctors, with permission from Lindbergh's family, took him off life support and performed a five-hour operation to remove his organs for transplant. That surgery climaxed an emotional two-day roller-coaster for friends, family and hockey fans throughout North America.

Lindbergh suffered severe brain damage, spinal cord injuries and broken bones when his Porsche skidded into a concrete wall in Somerdale, N.J. He was rushed to the hospital where he was put on life support, with no hope of recovery. Two passengers in the car were listed in stable condition.

The talented 26-year-old Swede compiled a 40–17–7 record last year while leading the Flyers to the Stanley Cup finals, where they lost to Edmonton. He posted three shutouts and a 12–6 record in the playoffs.

November 12

Milestones in Sports

1892

William (Pudge) Heffelfinger became the first known professional football player in the United States when he accepted a $500 payment to play for the Pittsburgh-based Allegheny Athletic Association team.

1931

The largest crowd (13,542) ever to witness a sports event in Toronto turned out for the dedication of new Maple Leaf Gardens, but the Chicago Blackhawks spoiled the occasion by handing the Leafs a hard-fought 2-1 defeat.

1964

Fred Hutchinson lost his long battle with cancer when he died at age 45 in Bradenton, Fla. – less than a month after resigning as manager of the Cincinnati Reds.

1967

Green Bay's Travis Williams tied an NFL record when he returned a pair of kickoffs for touchdowns in the Packers' 55–7 victory over the overmatched Cleveland Browns. The Packers scored 35 points in the opening quarter.

1972

Miami's Don Shula became the first NFL coach to reach the 100-victory plateau within 10 seasons when the Dolphins overpowered New England 52–0. Seventy-one of those victories were compiled in Shula's seven-year stint as coach of the Baltimore Colts.

NOVEMBER

13

1967 PACERS DROP BOMB

It appeared the Dallas Chaparrals had secured an American Basketball Association victory over Eastern Division leader Indiana when John Beasley hit a short jump shot with one second left for a 118–116 lead. But appearances can be deceiving.

The desperate Pacers inbounded the ball at their own baseline to Jerry Harkness and the reserve forward turned quickly and heaved the ball goalward as the final buzzer sounded. Swish! The 92-foot three-point shot (by ABA rules) gave the Pacers a most unlikely 119–118 victory and a 12–3 record.

The basket was just Harkness' second of the game and he finished with seven points. The bomb, Indiana's first three-pointer of the contest, negated 30-point performances by Dallas' Bob Verga and Cliff Hagan and left the stunned Chaparrals players shaking their heads in amazement.

The end line-to-end line shot was the longest ever made in a professional basketball game.

A STAR IS BORN

1951: Gilbert Perreault, a hockey Hall of Fame center who scored 512 goals and 1,326 points in 17 NHL seasons with Buffalo.

★ ★ ★

1963: Vinny Testaverde, a current NFL quarterback.

1992 BOWE BEATS HOLYFIELD

Riddick Bowe, answering critics who had questioned his fortitude and desire, scored an impressive 12-round unanimous decision over Evander Holyfield and claimed the undisputed heavyweight championship of the world.

Unleashing a steady barrage of powerful punches in the title bout at Las Vegas, Bowe staggered the smaller champion several times and sent him to the canvas with a left-right combination in the 11th round. Holyfield was up quickly and took the mandatory eight count, but he simply held on the rest of the way.

The 25-year-old Bowe's firepower was too much for the 30-year-old champion. He dominated the fight from the start and the only things that kept Holyfield on his feet were pride and determination. That was especially true in a classic 10th round in which Bowe staggered his opponent with a vicious assault that failed to produce a knockdown.

But in the end, Holyfield was simply overmatched. The victory was Bowe's 32nd in as many fights. Holyfield, who had won the championship two years ago, suffered his first loss in 29 bouts.

1964 PETTIT REACHES 20,000-POINT CAREER MARK

The St. Louis Hawks could not win the game, but star forward Bob Pettit won the personal war when he became the first player in National Basketball Association history to score 20,000 career points.

Pettit's milestone basket came in the second quarter of the Hawks' 123–106 loss to the Cincinnati Royals at Cincinnati. When Pettit hit his short jumper, the contest was stopped and he was presented with the game ball.

The 31-year-old Pettit went on to score 29 points in the game, giving him a night-ending total of 20,022. He accomplished the feat in his 11th NBA season while carrying a career average of just over 26 points.

The Royals' victory was their second in a three-day span over the Hawks.

Jerry Lucas keyed the charge with a 30-point effort and Jack Twyman added 25. Oscar Robertson, who was back in the lineup for the first time after suffering a debilitating eye injury, scored 22 points for the Royals.

MILESTONES IN SPORTS

1949

The Chicago Cardinals set an NFL scoring record when they waltzed past the outmanned New York Bulldogs, 65–20.

1966

Rookie Garo Yepremian kicked six field goals, four in the second period, as the Detroit Lions defeated Minnesota, 32–31.

1966

It was the Don Meredith show as the Dallas quarterback passed for 406 yards and a pair of touchdowns in a 31–30 victory over Washington.

1971

Colorado running back Charlie Davis set a sophomore rushing record when he exploded for 342 yards in a victory over Oklahoma State.

1971

Penn State halfback Lydell Mitchell scored four touchdowns in a 35–3 victory over North Carolina State and set a major college record with 25 TDs in a single season.

1979

A baseball first: St. Louis' Keith Hernandez and Pittsburgh's Willie Stargell were named co-National League MVPs.

1985

Lynette Woodard made history when she became the first woman to compete for the world-renowned Harlem Globetrotters.

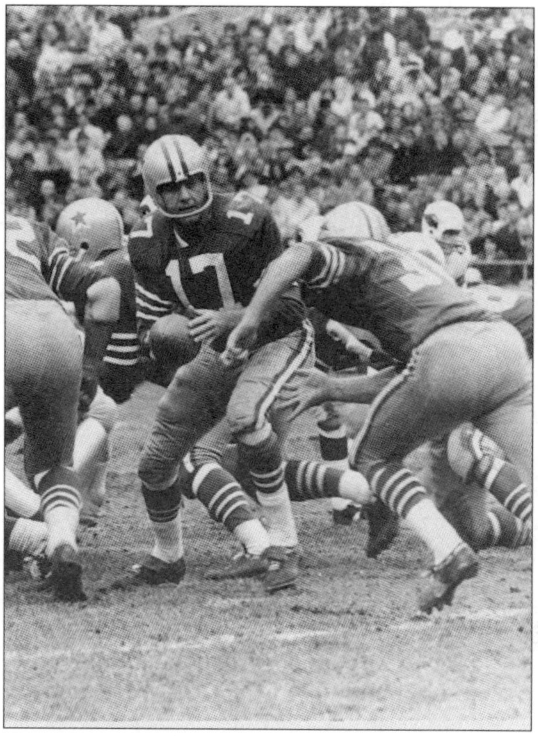

Dallas Cowboys quarterback **Don Meredith** *(17) was unstoppable against Washington.*

MILESTONES
IN SPORTS

1943

Washington quarterback Sammy Baugh staged a one-man show, firing four touchdown passes and intercepting four Frank Sinkwich throws in a 42–20 victory over Detroit.

1964

An NBA first: Baltimore teammates Gus Johnson (41) and Walt Bellamy (40) reached the 40-point barrier in the same game – a 127–115 victory over the Los Angeles Lakers.

1964

Detroit's Gordie Howe scored on a breakaway at the Montreal Forum and became the most prolific scorer in National Hockey League history, topping the career mark of 626 goals (regular season and playoffs) by former Canadien Rocket Richard.

1965

Gary Cuozzo, subbing for the injured Johnny Unitas, fired five touchdown passes and led the Baltimore Colts to a 41–21 NFL victory over Minnesota in Minneapolis.

The classic form of Washington quarterback **Sammy Baugh.**

NOVEMBER 14

A STAR IS BORN

1929: Jimmy Piersall, the ever-controversial outfielder who batted .272 over a 17-year American League career in the 1950s and '60s.

★ ★ ★

1955: Jack Sikma, the high-scoring forward-center who finished his 14-year NBA career with 17,287 points.

★ ★ ★

1960: Aaron Broten, a current National Hockey League left winger.

★ ★ ★

DEATH OF A LEGEND

1929: Joe McGinnity (baseball).

★ ★ ★

1970 Marshall Players Die in Plane Crash

Seventy-five persons, including the Marshall University football team and coaching staff, were killed when the charter plane carrying them from North Carolina to Huntington, W. Va., crashed and burned near the Tri-State Airport in the Appalachian Mountains.

The tragedy, the worst ever involving an athletic team, occurred at 7:40 p.m. in a light fog and rain after a 40-minute flight from Kinston, N.C. The Thundering Herd had played an afternoon game against East Carolina.

Included among the dead were 37 players, Marshall's entire coaching staff, a West Virginia legislator and members of the Big Green Boosters Club. Also included was the flight crew of four and a baggage handler.

The DC-9 twin-jet was owned by Southern Airways out of Atlanta. It had been in communication with the airport just before the crash and there was no indication anything was wrong.

It was the nation's third airliner crash of the year and the second involving a college football team. Thirty-one persons, including 14 Wichita State players and Coach Ben Wilson, died when their chartered plane crashed October 2 in the Rocky Mountains near Denver.

1993 Shula Catches The Papa Bear

The Miami Dolphins, overcoming adversity after losing second-string quarterback Scott Mitchell to a shoulder injury, held on for a 19–17 victory over Philadelphia and handed Don Shula his National Football League-record 325th coaching victory.

The Dolphins, playing more than half the game with third-string quarterback Doug Pederson, rallied from a 14–13 deficit on two second-half Pete Stoyanovich field goals and let their swarming defense take care of the rest.

Stoyanovich's 46-yarder in the final period proved to be the winner as the 63-year-old Shula stretched his career coaching record to 325–153–6 over 31 seasons. The previous record-holder, Chicago's George (Papa Bear) Halas, compiled a 324–151–31 mark over 40 campaigns.

The Dolphins scored on an eight-yardpass from Mitchell to Terry Kirby and Mark Higgs' one-yard run. Philadelphia got a pair of scoring passes from veteran Ken O'Brien, who took the Eagles to the Miami 23 in the closing minutes before a fumble cut the rally short.

1943 Luckman Fires 7 TD Passes

Chicago quarterback Sid Luckman, venturing into uncharted territory, fired seven touchdown passes and threw for 453 yards while leading the Bears to a 56–7 victory over the New York Giants at the Polo Grounds.

Luckman either established or helped establish six National Football League records with his unprecedented passing explosion. The seven TD passes broke the record of six set earlier this year by Sammy Baugh and his 453 yards bettered the one-game record of 333 held by Cecil Isbell.

The Bears gained a single-game record 702 total yards and a record 508 through the air, thanks to a late 55-yard pass thrown by backup quarterback Bob Snyder.

The carnage was witnessed by 56,681 fans who saw Luckman connect on two scoring passes to Jim Benton and Hampton Pool and one each to Connie Berry, George Wilson and Harry Clark. He completed 23 of the 30 passes he attempted and the Bears scored 14 points in each quarter.

The victory raised Chicago's record to 7–0–1.

Sid Luckman *(right) with Bears Coach* **George Halas.**

NOVEMBER

15

A STAR IS BORN

1928: Gus Bell, a major league outfielder who batted .281 and hit 206 home runs over a 15-year career in the 1950s and '60s.

★ ★ ★

1950: Mac Wilkins, the discus thrower who won an Olympic gold medal at Montreal in 1976 and a silver medal eight years later at Los Angeles.

★ ★ ★

DEATH OF A LEGEND

1983: Charley Grimm (baseball).

★ ★ ★

1985: Riggs Stephenson (baseball).

★ ★ ★

1960 Baylor Scores 71 In Record Binge

Elgin Baylor, *the Los Angeles Lakers' top gun.*

The 10,132 fans who ventured to Madison Square Garden for a National Basketball Association doubleheader got plenty for their money – a thrilling one-point overtime battle in the first game and a record-setting scoring outburst in the second.

The fans still were talking about the Detroit Pistons' 115–114 first-game victory over Boston when smooth Los Angeles Lakers forward Elgin Baylor went to work in the nightcap. The former Seattle University star made the New York Knicks look helpless while scoring an NBA-record 71 points in a 123–108 Lakers victory.

The 6-foot-5 Baylor, using every move and trick in his vast repertoire, connected on 28 field goals and 15 free throws, including a 15-of-20 effort from the field in his 34-point first half. He scored 37 more points after intermission to top his own previous NBA record of 64.

He scored his record-breaking basket with 1:35 remaining and then added three more before leaving to a standing ovation.

1969 Knicks Start Season 17-1

Willis Reed scored 27 points, grabbed 11 rebounds and keyed a New York explosion that carried the Knicks to a 113–98 victory over Boston and lifted their record to 17–1.

The victory at New York's Madison Square Garden before 19,500 jubilant fans set a record for the best start in the 24-year history of the National Basketball Association. It topped the 16–1 start accomplished by the 1966–67 St. Louis Hawks and came at the expense of the defending NBA-champion Celtics, who are playing this season without the great Bill Russell.

It looked like an entirely different Boston team. With 7-foot Henry Finkel now stationed in the middle, Reed dominated play. A 14–2 first-quarter spurt gave the Knicks a 34–20 lead and they increased their margin to 25 by the midway point of the final quarter, never letting the Celtics back in the game.

Reed connected on 11 of his 19 shots from the floor and 5 of 8 from the free throw line. He received ample support from Walt Frazier, who scored 21 points, and Dave DeBusschere, who had 18.

1969 Shaw Throws 9 TD Passes

San Diego State quarterback Dennis Shaw fired a major college NCAA-record nine touchdown passes, a record-setting six to Tim Delaney, and the Aztecs remained unbeaten with a 70–21 victory over New Mexico State at San Diego.

Shaw completed 26 of 42 passes for 441 yards and did most of his damage in a 49-point Aztec first half. Four of his first-half throws went for touchdowns to Delaney (2, 22, 34 and 31 yards) and three more went to Tom Reynolds (14, 33 and 7 yards).

After a scoreless third quarter in which Shaw fired three interceptions, he came back to throw 30 and 9-yard TD strikes to Delaney in the final period. Brian Sipe, Shaw's backup, accounted for the other Aztec touchdown with a 28-yard fourth-quarter throw to Eugene Carter.

The previous major college single-game record was seven touchdown passes, set by Tulsa's Jerry Rhome in 1964. Providing the perfect cap for this record-setting game was New Mexico State quarterback Rhett Putman, who threw three touchdown passes of his own to account for all of the Aggies' scoring.

MILESTONES • IN SPORTS •

1901

James Jeffries successfully defended his heavyweight championship when he scored a sixth-round technical knockout of Gus Ruhlin at San Francisco.

1964

Babe Parilli fired five touchdown passes and Gino Cappelletti totaled 24 points as the Boston Patriots ended Buffalo's nine-game unbeaten streak with a 36–28 AFL victory at Buffalo.

1952

An NBA-record 13 players fouled out of an overtime game between Syracuse and Baltimore. The Nationals lost eight, the Bullets five.

1973

Bobby Orr scored three goals and handed out four assists to lead the Boston Bruins to a 10–2 NHL thumping of the New York Rangers.

1975

Pittsburgh's Tony Dorsett rambled through the Notre Dame defense for 303 yards and the Panthers scored a 34–20 victory over the Fighting Irish.

Boston Patriots quarterback **Babe Parilli.**

1957

Notre Dame Ends Oklahoma Streak

Dick Lynch ran three yards for a fourth-quarter touchdown on a fourth-and-goal play, giving Notre Dame a gigantic 7–0 upset victory that ended Oklahoma's four-year major college-record 47-game winning streak.

Lynch scored the game-winner with 3:50 remaining in the contest at Norman, Okla. The winning 80-yard drive was keyed by quarterback Bob Williams' 10-yard pass to Dick Royer and an eight-yard burst by Lynch.

The Sooners, who had not lost since a 1953 game against Notre Dame, bunched at the line on the game-winning play, anticipating a handoff to fullback Nick Pietrosante. But Williams faked to him, rolled out and pitched to Lynch.

The defeat ended an amazing run in which the Sooners won their last nine games of 1953 and then went undefeated in 1954, '55 and '56, winning three straight national championships. They were 7–0 this season and rated as prohibitive 18-point favorites against Notre Dame.

But the Fighting Irish, coming off consecutive losses to Navy and Michigan State after opening 4–0, had other ideas. They managed 17 first downs to nine for Oklahoma, outgained them in rushing yards, 169–98, and outpassed them, 79–47.

Notre Dame's **Dick Lynch** *streaks for the touchdown that ended Oklahoma's record streak.*

1968

Michigan Back Johnson Sets Rushing Mark

Michigan running back Ron Johnson broke loose for five touchdowns and a major college rushing-record 347 yards as the fourth-ranked Wolverines prepped for a Big Ten Conference showdown against Ohio State by blasting Wisconsin, 34–9.

Johnson, running on a rain-slick field, set the tone for his adventurous afternoon when he took a handoff on Michigan's second play from scrimmage and ran 35 yards for a touchdown. But the Badgers refused to be intimidated and actually owned a 9–7 advantage when the teams broke for intermission.

Johnson quickly took care of that. He ran 67 yards for a touchdown 25 seconds into the third quarter, ran one yard for another score after a Tom Curtis interception and bolted 60 yards later in the period to give the Wolverines a commanding 27–9 lead.

He iced his big day with a 49-yard TD dash 20 seconds into the fourth quarter—on his final carry. Johnson's 347 yards broke the NCAA record of 340 set six weeks earlier by Mercury Morris of West Texas State.

1982

57-Day NFL Strike Ends

The longest strike in sports history came to a merciful end when the National Football League players and owners reached agreement on a five-year contract that opens the door for the season to resume in four days.

The 57-day strike, the first-ever interruption of the regular-season schedule, cost the league $240 million in gate and television revenues and forced cancellation of 112 games. Only a part of those games will be made up under a revised schedule that calls for regular-season play to end January 2, a week later than originally planned.

Under the new format, each team will play nine regular-season contests, including the two that were played before the strike began September 21. Six extra teams will earn playoff berths, bringing the postseason total to 16.

The strike was seven days longer than the work-stoppage that crippled baseball last year. But it was worthwhile to the players, who received $1.3 billion in salaries and benefits.

A Star Is Born

1946: Jo Jo White, an outstanding NBA guard who scored 14,399 points and handed out 4,095 assists over 12 seasons.

★★★

1950: Harvey Martin, a hard-rushing defensive end for the Dallas Cowboys from 1973–83.

★★★

1964: Dwight Gooden, a current major league pitcher.

★★★

November 16

Milestones in Sports

1957

Boston center Bill Russell set an NBA record when he pulled down 49 rebounds during a Celtics' victory over the Philadelphia Warriors.

1962

Wilt Chamberlain exploded for 73 points, 45 in the first half, in a Philadelphia victory over New York. It was only the fourth-highest career point total by the amazing 7-footer.

1973

Dave Cowens scored 14 points in the final quarter as Boston pulled away from Milwaukee for a 105–90 NBA victory, ending the Bucks' 13-game winning streak.

1980

Tampa Bay quarterback Doug Williams completed 30 of 55 passes for 486 yards and four touchdowns, but the Bucs still dropped a 38–30 decision to Minnesota.

1991

The No. 2-ranked Miami Hurricanes squeaked out a 17–16 victory over No. 1 Florida State when a last-second 34-yard Seminole field goal attempt barely missed wide right.

NOVEMBER 17

A STAR IS BORN

1930: Bob Mathias, the American who captured decathlon gold medals in consecutive Olympic Games (1948 and '52).

★ ★ ★

1944: Tom Seaver, a Hall of Fame righthander who won 311 games and three Cy Young Awards in a 20-year career that ended in 1986.

★ ★ ★

1945: Elvin Hayes, a basketball Hall of Fame forward who scored 27,313 points over a 16-year career.

DEATH OF A LEGEND

1987: Paul Derringer (baseball).

1956 JIM BROWN SCORES 43

The great Jim Brown brought his regular-season collegiate career to an unforgettable conclusion when he set a major college scoring record of 43 points during Syracuse's 61–7 victory over Colgate at Archbold Stadium.

Brown rushed for 197 yards on 22 carries, but it was his scoring outburst that drew national attention. He scored six touchdowns and added seven conversion kicks to top the single-game record of 42 points set by Mississippi's Arnold (Showboat) Boykin in 1951.

Brown scored all 27 of Syracuse's first-half points on touchdown runs of 1, 15, 50 and 8 yards and three conversions. He scored on 19 and 1-yard bursts in the second half and added four more kicks that brought his point total to 43. But he didn't hog all the attention.

Quarterback Chuck Zimmerman sneaked over the goal line in the third quarter for the first Orangeman touchdown not scored by Brown. Ferd Kuczala and Dan Ciervo added third and fourth-quarter touchdown runs.

Jim Brown, *Syracuse's 43-point scorer.*

1968 HEIDI WINS NFL MATCHUP

Daryle Lamonica fired a 43-yard touchdown pass to Charlie Smith with 42 seconds remaining and Preston Ridlehuber recovered a fumble on the ensuing kickoff for another touchdown, giving the Oakland Raiders an exciting 43–32 victory over the New York Jets in a nationally-televised contest at Oakland.

Nationally televised, that is, except for the final 61 seconds – when Oakland wrapped up its American Football League victory. In what forever will be remembered as the "Heidi Game," NBC-TV pulled the plug on its football coverage precisely at 7 p.m. Eastern time so it could show its regularly-scheduled program (Heidi) in its entirety.

The reaction from football fans around the country caught NBC by surprise. Irate callers flooded its switchboard and the complaints grew more vociferous as scoring updates were flashed across the bottom of the screen. The switchboard became so overloaded it blew a fuse and NBC, stung by the reaction, promised to avoid such future plug-pulling.

The game featured the two glamour teams of the AFL. Defending champion Oakland got four TD passes from Lamonica and the Jets got a touchdown run and TD pass from colorful quarterback Joe Namath. Oakland started its winning drive precisely at the point the game was pulled off the air.

1991 LIONS' UTLEY IS PARALYZED

Detroit Lions offensive guard Mike Utley suffered a paralyzing injury when he landed on his head while handling a routine pass-blocking assignment during the Lions' 21–10 National Football League victory over the Los Angeles Rams.

Utley remained paralyzed but in stable condition at a Detroit hospital after 2 1/2 hours of surgery for a neck injury that occurred when his head hit the artificial surface of the Pontiac Silverdome field. He was blocking the Rams' David Rocker, who jumped to try and deflect an Erik Kramer pass. Rocker landed on Utley, who fell forward and suffered his neck-snapping injury.

The 6-foot-6, 290-pounder fractured his sixth cervical vertebrae. He underwent surgery to decompress some tissue and fragments that were pressing against the spinal cord. Doctors said the operation went as smoothly as could be expected, but refused to predict whether the paralysis would be permanent.

"It was a very severe injury to his spinal cord," said Dr. Phillip Mayer, who performed the operation. When asked if the injury would put an end to Utley's professional career, Mayer responded, "In all probability, yes."

Utley is a third-year professional out of Washington State University.

MILESTONES IN SPORTS

1926

The Blackhawks made their first game at old Chicago Coliseum a memorable one, defeating the Toronto St. Pats, 4–1.

1965

Major league owners tabbed retired Air Force lieutenant general William D. Eckert to succeed Ford Frick as baseball's fourth commissioner.

1971

Muhammad Ali knocked down Buster Mathis four times en route to a unanimous 12-round decision in a non-title bout at Houston's Astrodome.

1971

Oakland lefthander Vida Blue became the youngest player to win an MVP citation and only the fifth to capture both the Cy Young and MVP in the same season.

1983

Three former or current Kansas City Royals – Willie Wilson, Willie Aikens and Jerry Martin – became the first active players ever to be sent to prison for drug violations when a federal judge handed them a three-month sentence for attempting to purchase cocaine.

The old and the new: Former Commissioner **Ford Frick** *(left) introduces his replacement,* **William D. Eckert.**

NOVEMBER 18

A STAR IS BORN

1885: Phog Allen, a college basketball coach who compiled 746 victories over a 37-year career (1920–56), most of which was spent at Kansas.

★ ★ ★

1925: Gene Mauch, a former major league manager who compiled 1,902 victories from 1960–87.

★ ★ ★

1926: Roy Sievers, a 17-year major league outfielder who batted .267 and belted 318 home runs in the 1950s and '60s.

★ ★ ★

1956: Tony Franklin, a former kicker who booted the second longest field goal (59 yards) in NFL history.

★ ★ ★

1956: Warren Moon, a current National Football League quarterback.

★ ★ ★

DEATH OF A LEGEND

1980: Conn Smythe (hockey).

1967 O.J.'s Run Nips UCLA

Southern Cal halfback **O.J.Simpson** *and Coach* **John McKay.**

O.J. Simpson pulled off a breathtaking 64-yard run and third-ranked Southern California pulled off an exciting upset with a 21–20 victory over No. 1-ranked UCLA at the Los Angeles Coliseum.

The winning point was scored on Rikki Aldridge's extra-point kick with 10:38 remaining after Simpson exploded around left end and cut back to the middle, outrunning a host of UCLA defenders to the end zone.

That fourth-quarter jaunt came a few minutes after UCLA quarterback Gary Beban had thrown a 20-yard touchdown pass to Dave Nuttall. But Bruins' kicker Zenon Andrusyshyn shanked the extra-point kick, a miss that would prove costly.

The victory gave the 9–1 Trojans the Pacific 10 Conference's automatic Rose Bowl bid and put them back in contention for a national championship. Simpson finished the day with 177 rushing yards, 13 coming on a second-period touchdown run. Southern Cal also scored a first-half TD when Pat Cashman returned a Beban interception 55 yards.

1940 Cornell Gives Up Victory

Cornell University officials, reacting to a report by referee Red Friesell that he had mistakenly allowed the Big Red an extra play in their 7–3 victory over Dartmouth, relinquished all claim to the win in an unprecedented act of sportsmanship that snapped their unbeaten streak at 18 games.

The controversial play occurred in the final seconds of a game at Hanover, N.H. Trailing 3–0 to an underdog Dartmouth team, Cornell drove to the Big Green 6-yard line and ran three plays to the 1. Friesell penalized Cornell for an illegal substitution and Walt Scholl threw incomplete into the end zone, apparently ending Cornell's hopes.

But Friesell had lost count of the downs and the Big Red ran one more play – a six-yard pass from Scholl to Bill Murphy for a touchdown. Cornell had escaped Dartmouth's upset bid – or so it seemed.

When Friesell submitted a report to the Eastern Intercollegiate Football Association admitting his mistake, Cornell Coach Carl Snavely reviewed film and told Athletic Director James Lynah and President Ezra Day that the fifth down had indeed occurred.

Day sent a telegram to Dartmouth Athletic Director William T. McCarter relinquishing claim to the victory. End of controversy.

1966 Sandy Koufax Retires at 30

Los Angeles Dodger lefthander Sandy Koufax capped his latest National League season of domination with the shocking announcement that he is ending his 12-year major league career.

Koufax's unexpected retirement came on the heels of a 27–9 season in which he fashioned a 1.73 earned-run average and struck out 317 batters. He was awarded his third Cy Young Award, his second straight, and was a key figure in the Dodgers' run to the N.L. pennant and their four-game sweep of Baltimore in the World Series.

The reason? Koufax said he fears causing permanent damage to his arthritic left elbow, which has become increasingly painful over the last three seasons. Koufax, who is forfeiting his $125,000 yearly salary, requested that the Dodgers put him on the voluntarily retired list.

The fireballing lefty has been phenomenal in the last half decade. Since 1961, he has compiled 129 victories and earned a major league-record five straight ERA titles. He is 97–27 over the last four years and he has thrown no-hitters in each of the last four seasons, including a perfect game last year against the Chicago Cubs. His ERA in eight World Series games is an incredible 0.95.

Koufax is leaving at the still-tender age of 30.

MILESTONES • IN SPORTS •

1945

Green Bay star Don Hutson, the NFL's career leader in touchdown receptions, caught his 99th and last TD pass from Irv Comp in a game against the Boston Yanks.

1949

Jackie Robinson, who broke the color barrier for the Brooklyn Dodgers in 1947, capped his .342 season by becoming baseball's first black MVP.

1970

Joe Frazier successfully defended his heavyweight title with a second-round knockout of Bob Foster at Detroit.

1974

Denver quarterback Charley Johnson passed for 445 yards and two touchdowns, but the Broncos dropped a 42-34 decision to the Kansas City Chiefs.

1978

Vanderbilt's Frank Mordica rushed for 321 yards and scored five touchdowns as the Commodores posted a 41–27 victory over the Air Force.

1980

Kansas City's George Brett, who flirted all season with the magical .400 batting average before settling for a final .390, was named A.L. MVP.

1984

Buffalo rookie Greg Bell ran for 206 yards, including an 85-yard touchdown burst, as the Bills broke their 11-game losing streak with a 14-3 victory over Dallas.

NOVEMBER

19

1961 BLANDA THROWS 7 TDs

Houston quarterback George Blanda shredded New York's defense for an American Football League-record seven touchdown passes and tied the one-game professional mark for scoring tosses shared by two former National Football League stars.

Blanda, who matched the feats of Chicago Bears quarterback Sid Luckman (1943) and the New York Giants' Adrian Burk (1954) while leading the Oilers to a 49–13 pasting of the Titans in a game at Houston, added another dimension to his record-tying effort. He also kicked all seven of Houston's point-after conversions.

Blanda broke his own AFL record of four touchdown passes, set last year in the circuit's inaugural season. Three went to 1959 Heisman Trophy winner Billy Cannon, three to Bill Groman and one to Charley Hennigan. The scoring tosses covered 28, 6, 78, 66, 6, 46 and 11 yards.

Blanda completed 20 of 32 passes for 418 yards. Luckman, unlike Blanda, threw his touchdown passes to five different receivers and finished with 433 passing yards in a 56-7 victory over the Giants. Burk needed three receivers and threw for only 242 yards in a 49-21 win over Washington.

1966 PARSEGHIAN SETTLES FOR 10–10 TIE

Notre Dame Coach **Ara Parseghian** *received plenty of criticism for playing it safe against Michigan State.*

Winning wasn't everything, at least not to Notre Dame Coach Ara Parseghian when his No. 1 Fighting Irish met No. 2-ranked Michigan State at Spartan Stadium in one of the most ballyhooed battles of unbeatens ever staged.

Parseghian, content to protect his team's top ranking and believing the pollsters would see things his way, sat on the ball over the final minute and a half of a 10–10 tie rather than try for the victory.

Parseghian's decision created a storm of controversy. Fans from all over the country as well as Michigan State players criticized the controversial decision and one of the two major polls obviously agreed, dropping the Fighting Irish to No. 2 behind the Spartans.

Parseghian, however, seemed to be relieved with the result. The Irish trailed most of the game, finally tying the score on Joe Azzaro's 28-yard field goal early in the final period. Michigan State had jumped ahead 10–0 in the second quarter on Regis Cavender's four-yard run and Dick Kenney's 47-yard field goal.

Notre Dame's hopes were further dimmed by the loss of quarterback Terry Hanratty, who separated his shoulder in the opening quarter. But Coley O'Brien replaced Hanratty and fired a 34-yard touchdown pass to Bob Gladieux that kept the Irish in the game.

The controversy centered around Notre Dame's final possession, which started at the Irish 30 with 1:24 left to play. The Irish ran the ball three times and O'Brien sneaked for a first down on fourth and one. After O'Brien was dropped for a seven-yard loss, he ran one more time as the clock expired.

Azzaro missed a potential game-winning 41-yard field goal on Notre Dame's previous possession.

1978 GIANTS FUMBLE VICTORY

In a shocking reversal to a game that appeared to be over, Philadelphia defender Herm Edwards picked up a New York Giants fumble with 20 seconds remaining and ran 26 yards for a touchdown that gave the Eagles a 17–12 victory at Giants Stadium.

The shock factor was increased by the realization that all the Giants had to do was fall on the ball. No handoff. No chance for a misplay. Just take the snap, put a knee down and head for the locker room.

That's what Giants quarterback Joe Pisarcik and most of his teammates had in mind. But the New York coaches inexplicably called for a handoff to fullback Larry Csonka and the Giants experienced their worst nightmare.

Pisarcik never got control of the snap and the ball bounced onto the artificial turf and right into the arms of Edwards. He was off to the races.

"That's the most horrifying ending to a ball game I've ever seen," said Giants Coach John McVay. It was even more horrifying when you consider that the Eagles had no timeouts remaining.

A STAR IS BORN

1921: Roy Campanella, a Hall of Fame catcher whose Dodger career was cut short by a paralyzing automobile accident in 1958.

★ ★ ★

1947: Bob Boone, the 19-year major leaguer who caught a record 2,225 games from 1972–90.

★ ★ ★

DEATH OF A LEGEND

1976: Wayne Millner (football).

MILESTONES • IN SPORTS •

1961

Cleveland's Jim Brown ran for an NFL-record 242 yards and four touchdowns as the Browns posted an easy 45–24 victory over the Philadelphia Eagles.

1983

Edmonton's Jari Kurri scored five goals and Wayne Gretzky added three goals and five assists as the Oilers overpowered New Jersey, 13–4.

Edmonton's five-goal scorer **Jari Kurri.**

1983

Los Angeles Lakers center Kareem Abdul-Jabbar joined Wilt Chamberlain as the only players to score 30,000 career points.

1989

The United States soccer team qualified for its first World Cup since 1950, beating Trinidad and Tobago, 1–0, at Port-of-Spain.

1989

Steffi Graf beat Martina Navratilova, 6–4, 7–5, 2–6, 6–2, in the final of the Virginia Slims Championship at New York, finishing the year with an 85–2 singles record.

1982 Cal Beats The Band

If it wasn't the most spectacular finish to a college football game, it certainly was the most unusual. Stanford had taken a 20–19 lead over California on a 35-yard Mark Harmon field goal with four seconds remaining in the traditional "Big Game" at Berkeley, Calif., and disappointed fans already were filing out of Memorial Stadium when. . .

Harmon squibbed his kickoff downfield and California's Kevin Moen fielded the ball at the Golden Bears' 43-yard line. After running 10 yards and with the Stanford pursuit closing in, Moen fired an overhand lateral pass toward Richard Rodgers on the left sideline. After a short gain, Rodgers also lateraled, to Dwight Garner at the Stanford 44.

Garner, in the clutches of the Cardinal defense, was falling to the ground when he tossed another lateral – back to Rodgers at the 48. Rodgers headed down the middle of the field and again lateraled, this time to Mariet Ford. Ford advanced from the Stanford 46 to the 25 when he, too, approached trouble. Running at full speed without much choice, he creatively tossed the ball blindly over his right shoulder, hoping somebody would be in the right spot at the right time.

Voila! Moen, the man who originated the play, grabbed the ball and headed for the end zone. The Stanford band had already advanced into the area, thinking the game was over. The band members unwittingly provided a corridor of interference for Moen, who burst into the end zone, knocked over a trombone player and scored.

Five laterals, a touchdown and a miraculous victory. Cal 25, Stanford 20. The game's conclusion was not without controversy. Stanford claimed Garner should have been pronounced down and the game pronounced over before he got off his lateral. Other complaints centered around illegal laterals and the band being prematurely on the field. But all was overlooked in the confusion and the play went into the books as a 57-yard kickoff return by Moen – with, of course, a little help from his friends.

A STAR IS BORN

1866: Kenesaw Mountain Landis, the former federal judge who served as baseball's first commissioner from 1920–44.

★ ★ ★

1869: Clark Griffith, a Hall of Fame pitcher, one of the founding fathers of the American League in 1901 and a long-time president of the Washington Senators.

★ ★ ★

1929: Don January, the 1967 winner of the PGA Championship and a consistent winner on the PGA Tour for many years.

DEATH OF A LEGEND

1982: Bob Short (baseball).

1977 Payton Sets Rushing Mark

Walter Payton, *Chicago's 275-yard rusher.*

MILESTONES IN SPORTS

1934

Toronto's Busher Jackson scored an NHL-record four third-period goals and the Maple Leafs recorded a 5–2 victory over the St. Louis Eagles.

1960

Four interceptions by St. Louis' Jerry Norton keyed the Cardinals' 26-14 victory over Washington.

1982

Dwight Muhammad Qawi, formerly Dwight Braxton, retained his world light heavyweight title with an 11th-round technical knockout of Eddie Davis at Atlantic City.

1983

The Atlanta Falcons recorded a stunning 28–24 NFL victory over San Francisco when Steve Bartkowski's 47-yard desperation pass was deflected at the goal line to Billy Johnson, who scored as time expired.

1990

Boston ace Roger Clemens was suspended for the first five games of the 1991 season and fined $10,000 for his heated exchange with the umpires in Game 4 of the A.L. Championship Series.

November 20

Walter Payton, weak from influenza and suffering from hot and cold flashes, inflicted a different kind of suffering on the Minnesota Vikings when he ran for a National Football League-record 275 yards and sparked the Chicago Bears to a 10–7 victory.

The 23-year-old Payton, staging his revival act during a game at Chicago's Soldier Field, topped the 273-yard record Buffalo's O. J. Simpson set last season. The third-year professional carried the ball 40 times and raised his season yardage to 1,404, leaving him 600 yards short of Simpson's one-season rushing record with four games remaining to play.

The 204-pounder scored the Bears' only TD on a one-yard run in the second quarter. He ran for 144 first-half yards on 26 carries and pulled within five of Simpson's record with a 58-yard fourth-quarter dash.

Payton picked up three yards on his next carry and followed with a four-yarder that gave him the record. The victory pulled the Bears to within a game of the Vikings in the NFC Central Division.

Simpson's 273-yard effort came in a 27-14 loss to the Detroit Lions. He gained his yards on 11 fewer carries than Payton needed and scored touchdowns on runs of 48 and 12 yards.

Simpson also owns the third-best single-game total, achieved in a 1973 Buffalo victory over New England. Simpson rushed for 250 yards in that contest, carrying the ball 29 times and scoring a pair of touchdowns.

NOVEMBER

21

MILESTONES
· IN SPORTS ·

1971

The New York Rangers matched an NHL record when they exploded for eight third-period goals en route to a 12–1 victory over California.

1981

Brigham Young quarterback Jim McMahon shredded the Utah defense for 552 yards in the Cougars' 56–28 victory.

1982

It was business as usual as the National Football League resumed action after the players had ended their record 57-day strike.

1987

Brown scored a touchdown with 47 seconds remaining and recorded a 19–16 victory over Columbia – the Lions' NCAA-record 41st consecutive loss.

1987

Southwestern Louisiana quarterback Brian Mitchell showed his versatility when he rushed for 271 yards and four touchdowns and passed for another 205 yards in a 35–28 victory over Colorado State.

QB **Brian Mitchell,** *Southwestern Louisiana's Mr. Versatility.*

1981 ALLEN ENDS RAMPAGE

Southern Cal record-setter **Marcus Allen.**

Southern California tailback Marcus Allen ended his record-setting season in a blaze of glory when he scored on a five-yard touchdown run with 2:14 remaining to give the Trojans a 21–20 victory over arch-rival UCLA at the Los Angeles Coliseum.

Allen's game-deciding dash capped a 219-yard effort that brought his record one-season rushing total to 2,342 and ended UCLA's Rose Bowl and national championship hopes. Allen, college football's first 2,000-yard rusher, finished the year with a 5.81-yard per carry average and 23 touchdowns. He also finished with an unprecedented eight 200-yard games while either tying or setting 12 NCAA records.

His second TD run against the Bruins capped Southern Cal's recovery from a 21–12 final-quarter deficit. Frank Jordan cut the margin to six points with his third field goal and a Troy West interception with 4:53 remaining set up Allen's game-winner.

The victory was not secured, however, until Trojan George Achica blocked Norm Johnson's 46-yard field goal attempt as time expired.

1931 TROJAN RALLY SHOCKS IRISH

A 33-yard field goal by Johnny Baker capped a fourth-quarter rally by Southern California and gave the Trojans a dramatic 16–14 victory over Notre Dame, dropping the curtain on the Fighting Irish's 26-game unbeaten streak.

Notre Dame, which had not lost since the final game of the 1928 season, appeared to be in full control of its destiny. With 52,000 fans cheering them on at 1-year-old Notre Dame Stadium, the 6–0–1 Fighting Irish capped a 55-yard second-quarter drive with a short Steve Banas touchdown run and Marchy Schwartz scored from three yards out in the third period, extending the advantage to 14–0.

There was not much hope for a Southern Cal victory when the Trojans began their shocking comeback that featured two long drives and a pair of Gaius Shaver touchdown runs. The Trojans appeared to be out of miracles, however, when Notre Dame tackle Joe Kurth broke through and blocked Baker's game-tying extra-point attempt with about 4 minutes left to play.

But Notre Dame's relief was short-lived. Southern Cal got the ball back for one last thrust and Shaver hit passes of 50 yards to Raymond Sparling and 23 yards to Robert Hall – the Trojans' first completions of the day – and Baker took care of the rest.

1987 KNIGHT DOES IT AGAIN

Bob Knight, never at a loss for controversy, added another international incident to his growing resume when he threw a temper tantrum and pulled his Indiana basketball team off the floor during an exhibition game against the touring Soviet Nationals.

Knight, who hit a Puerto Rican policeman in a celebrated 1979 incident when he was coaching the United States team in the Pan American Games, performed his disappearing act during a contest at Indiana's Assembly Hall.

With his team trailing the Russians, 66–43, in the second half, Knight got into a heated discussion with one of the referees. The argument turned nasty and the Indiana coach was whistled for his third technical foul of the game – bringing an automatic ejection.

Knight left the court all right, but not without his team. He pulled the Hoosiers off the floor and led them into the locker room. The Soviets were awarded a forfeit victory.

A STAR IS BORN

1905: Fred Lindstrom, a Hall of Fame infielder who batted .311 over a 13-year major league career in the 1920s and '30s.

★ ★ ★

1916: Sid Luckman, a football Hall of Fame quarterback for the Chicago Bears (1939-50) and the first National Football League player to throw seven touchdown passes in one game.

★ ★ ★

1920: Stan (The Man) Musial, a Hall of Fame outfielder-first baseman and one of the outstanding hitters of all time. He finished his 22-year St. Louis career with 3,630 hits, 475 home runs, seven National League batting championships and a career average of .331.

★ ★ ★

1932: Jim Ringo, a football Hall of Fame center for Green Bay and Philadelphia from 1953–67.

★ ★ ★

1944: Earl Monroe, a basketball Hall of Fame guard who scored 17,454 points over a 13-year NBA career.

★ ★ ★

1966: Troy Aikman, a current National Football League quarterback.

★ ★ ★

DEATH OF A LEGEND

1958: Mel Ott (baseball).

★ ★ ★

1959: Max Baer (boxing).

★ ★ ★

1970: Newsy Lalonde (hockey).

★ ★ ★

1988: Carl Hubbell (baseball).

★ ★ ★

MILESTONES · IN SPORTS ·

1945

Cleveland receiver Jim Benton caught 10 passes for an NFL-record 303 yards and scored a touchdown as the Rams posted a 28–21 victory over the Lions at Detroit.

1951

Detroit's Jack Christiansen, who 5 1/2 weeks earlier became the first player to return two punts for touchdowns in one game, did it again when he burned Green Bay for 72- and 89-yard scores in a 52–35 victory at Detroit.

1959

The new AFL held its first college draft with teams making such first-round choices as Gerhard Schwedes, Don Meredith, Billy Cannon and Monty Stickles.

1974

The new NFL sudden-death overtime rule was put to a test for the first time by the Denver Broncos and Pittsburgh Steelers – and the result was a 35–35 tie.

1981

Quarterback Warren Moon scored a pair of second-half touchdowns and directed a late Edmonton drive to the winning field goal as the Eskimos defeated Ottawa, 26–23, and captured their fourth straight Grey Cup title.

1981

San Diego tight end Kellen Winslow tied an NFL record when he hauled in five touchdown passes in the Chargers' 55–21 victory over Oakland.

1986

Edmonton's Wayne Gretzky, playing in his 575th NHL game, scored his 500th career goal into an empty net as the Oilers beat Vancouver, 5–2.

NOVEMBER 22

1950 19-18: AN NBA LOW

Larry Foust's basket with six seconds remaining, only the eighth field goal of the game, gave the Fort Wayne Pistons a 19–18 victory over Minneapolis in the lowest-scoring contest in National Basketball Association history.

For those fans looking for excitement, Minneapolis was not the place to be on this night. The Pistons took an 8–7 first-quarter lead, fell behind 13–11 at halftime and then turned on the defensive juice, holding the Lakers to five second-half points.

That's quite an accomplishment, considering Minneapolis had big George Mikan at center. Mikan scored a game-high 15 points, but he could not stop the slow-down tactics of the Pistons.

The 37 total points were one below the modern NBA record and the eight field goals were five below the previous mark. Fort Wayne' s victory ended Minneapolis' home winning streak at 29 and was its first on the road this season.

The Pistons' high scorer was John Oldham with five points, one more than teammate Paul Armstrong. Minneapolis attempted 18 shots, Fort Wayne 13.

1965 CLAY KEEPS TITLE

Cassius Clay, much like a cat taunts and plays with a mouse before moving in for the kill, humiliated former heavyweight champion Floyd Patterson through 12 painful rounds before recording a technical knockout in a title bout at the Las Vegas Convention Center.

The younger, faster and quicker Clay toyed with the only two-time champion in heavyweight boxing history while retaining his crown before 7,402 disgruntled and restless fans. It appeared Clay could have put away his 30-year-old opponent at any time, but he danced around the ring, taunting, jabbing, screaming and delivering major blows to Patterson's sagging dignity.

Patterson appeared helpless against the 23-year-old champion, although he never stopped trying. Clay simply had too many tools and he was content to mock and carry Patterson for as long as the referee permitted.

That was most of 12 rounds. The referee finally stepped in and ended the one-sided proceedings as the fans cheered their approval.

Patterson won the heavyweight title in 1956, lost it to Ingemar Johansson in 1959 and regained it the next year in a rematch. His bid to win it for an unprecedented third time well could have been the final fight of his career.

1986 YOUNG TYSON POUNDS BERBICK, CLAIMS HIS HEAVYWEIGHT CROWN

Promoter **Don King** *gives a big lift to new heavyweight champion* **Mike Tyson.**

Mike Tyson, a powerful young slugger from Catskill, N.Y., became the youngest champion in heavyweight boxing history when he dropped Trevor Berbick at 2:35 of the second round in a World Boxing Council title bout at Las Vegas.

Tyson showed his awesome power by knocking Berbick to the canvas twice in a second round that bordered on the comical. The first knockdown was courtesy of a left hook delivered at the end of a flurry early in the round. Berbick jumped to his feet quickly and signaled that he was okay.

But he spent the rest of the round clinching and holding on – until Tyson caught him with a left hook to the temple that sent him reeling. Berbick tried heroically to get back to his feet, stumbling twice to the canvas and reeling around the ring before finally rising at the count of nine. The referee took one look at the dazed champion and threw his arms around his shoulders, signaling the end of the fight.

Tyson achieved his championship at the tender age of 20 years and five months. The previous youngest champion was Floyd Patterson, who was 21 years and 11 months when he knocked out Archie Moore in 1956 and claimed Rocky Marciano's vacated title. Tyson is 28–0 as a professional with 26 knockouts.

Berbick was making his first defense of the crown he wrested from Pinklon Thomas in March.

A STAR IS BORN

1926: Lew Burdette, a righthanded workhorse pitcher who compiled 203 victories over an 18-year major league career.

★ ★ ★

1943: Billie Jean King, one of the all-time great women tennis players and the moving force behind formation of the women's professional tour in the 1970s.

★ ★ ★

1943: Yvan Cournoyer, a hockey Hall of Fame right winger who scored 428 goals and played on 10 Stanley Cup winners over a 15-year career with Montreal.

★ ★ ★

1950: Greg Luzinski, a major league outfielder who hit 307 home runs over a 15-year career.

★ ★ ★

1967: Boris Becker, a West German tennis star who has won three Wimbledon titles and one U.S. and Australian championship.

NOVEMBER

23

MILESTONES
IN SPORTS

1947

Washington's Slingin' Sammy Baugh connected on six touchdown passes and the Redskins routed the Chicago Cardinals, 45–21.

1957

Dick Christy capped his 29-point afternoon by kicking a 36-yard field goal as time expired, giving North Carolina State a 29–26 victory over South Carolina. Christy also ran for four touchdowns and kicked two extra points in the game that decided the Atlantic Coast Conference championship for the Wolfpack.

1958

Cleveland's Bobby Mitchell returned a punt and a kickoff for touchdowns and the Browns recorded a 28–14 victory over the Philadelphia Eagles.

1968

Houston scored seven fourth-quarter touchdowns and 76 second-half points en route to a 100–7 victory over outmanned Tulsa in a game that fittingly was played at the Astrodome.

1975

Minnesota quarterback Fran Tarkenton set a National Football League career record when he completed his 2,840th pass during the Vikings' 28–13 victory over San Diego.

1984 FLUTIE'S MIRACLE TAMES HURRICANES

Gerard Phelan, answering more than a few prayers and punctuating a Doug Flutie miracle, caught a 48-yard "Hail Mary" pass from his diminutive quarterback on the final play of the game and gave the Eagles a stunning 47–45 nationally televised victory over Miami at the Orange Bowl.

Phelan's 11th catch of the day was a fitting conclusion to one of the greatest quarterback duels ever staged. Boston College's Flutie completed 34 of 46 passes for 472 yards and three touchdowns. Miami's Bernie Kosar hit on 25 of 38 attempts for 447 yards and a pair of TDs.

The Hurricanes appeared to have the game safely tucked away when Melvin Bratton scored his fourth touchdown of the game on a one-yard run with 28 seconds remaining, giving Miami a 41–38 advantage. Not so.

Flutie quickly whisked the Eagles downfield. The winning play started at the Miami 48-yard line, but Flutie's throw actually covered 64 yards in the air. Phelan simply outfought the defenders for the ball.

Boston College miracle worker **Doug Flutie.**

1968 HARVARD RALLY CATCHES YALE

Capping one of the most unbelievable comebacks in college football history, Pete Varney caught a two-point conversion pass from quarterback Frank Champi with no time left on the clock and gave Harvard a 29–29 tie with arch-rival Yale in "The Game" at Harvard Stadium.

Unbelievable because Harvard trailed the Elis, 29–13, with less than a minute remaining. Both teams sported unblemished records and the Ivy League championship appeared to belong to Yale. But. . .

Champi, who had replaced starter George Lalich late in the first half, fired a 15-yard touchdown pass to Bruce Freeman, cutting the deficit to 10 with 42 seconds left. Gus Crim pulled the Crimson to within striking distance when he bulled his way into the end zone for a two-point conversion – after a Yale penalty had given Harvard a second chance.

Things suddenly got interesting when Harvard's Bill Kelly recovered the ensuing onside kick at the Yale 49. Champi ran 14 yards, Yale committed a face-mask penalty and Crim ran 14 more yards, putting Harvard on the 8. With 4 seconds remaining, Champi took the snap and fired a TD pass to Vic Gatto.

Amazingly, it was 29–27. When Varney caught his conversion pass, Harvard had a tie that looked much more like a victory to those who were there.

A STAR IS BORN

1934: Lew Hoad, an Australian tennis champion who won consecutive Wimbledon titles in 1956 and '57.

★ ★ ★

1940: Luis Tiant, a major league pitcher who won 229 games in a career that ended in 1982.

★ ★ ★

1956: Shane Gould, a record-setting Australian swimmer who won five medals at the 1972 Munich Olympic Games.

★ ★ ★

DEATH OF A LEGEND

1948: Hack Wilson (baseball).

★ ★ ★

1991 SANDS RUNS WILD

Tony Sands, a 5-foot-6 scatback who had enjoyed only moderate success in his four seasons at Kansas, ended his college football career in spectacular fashion when he exploded for an NCAA-record 396 yards in the Jayhawks' 53–29 season-closing victory over Missouri.

It took the diminutive Sands a record 58 carries to top the mark of 386 yards set earlier this season by San Diego State's Marshall Faulk. He gained 240 of his yards in a big second half and broke Faulk's record in the final minute of the game.

Sands, who also scored four touchdowns, had to work for his record. He averaged 6.8 yards per carry and his long gainer was 38 yards. He finished his senior campaign with 1,442 yards and the Jayhawks completed their first winning season since 1981 with a 6-5 record.

Record-setting Kansas running back **Tony Sands.**

MILESTONES · IN SPORTS ·

1949

An NBA record: The Syracuse Nationals defeated the Anderson Packers, 125–123, in five overtimes.

1967

Minnesotan Jerry Hansen was clocked at 194.8 miles per hour in his Lola-Chevy, a record for the Daytona International Speedway. Hansen was qualifying for the American Road Race of Champions.

1977

Miami quarterback Bob Griese fired six touchdown passes and the Dolphins destroyed St. Louis, 55–14, in a Thanksgiving Day matchup.

1985

Ned Armour, a former track star who had never played college football, caught two touchdown bombs and British Columbia rolled to a 37–24 Grey Cup victory over Hamilton at Montreal.

1957

ROOKIE BROWN SETS NFL RUSHING MARK

NOVEMBER 24

Cleveland rookie Jim Brown exploded for a National Football League-record 237 yards and spiced his big day with four touchdowns as the Browns retained their Eastern Conference lead with a 45–31 victory over the Los Angeles Rams.

The Browns, playing before 65,407 fans at Cleveland, had to rally from a 28–17 third-quarter deficit. The comeback was orchestrated by backup quarterback Milt Plum, who took over when starter Tom O'Connell suffered a second-quarter injury.

Plum's best weapon was the 220-pound Brown, who added 14 yards onto the NFL single-game rushing record set last year by Los Angeles' Tom Wilson. Brown also raised his league-leading rushing total to 769 yards and lifted his season touchdown total to nine.

The former Syracuse star's most spectacular touchdown came in the second period on a play that should have resulted in a turnover. He took a hand-off from Plum, fumbled as he was hit at the line of scrimmage, took two steps and caught the ball again and raced 69 yards for the TD. He later added touchdown runs of 1, 1 and 4 yards.

Rookie **Jim Brown,** *the Cleveland Browns' record-setting running back.*

1960

WILT GRABS 55 REBOUNDS

Philadelphia's Wilt Chamberlain took a big step forward in his continuing personal battle with Boston center Bill Russell when he grabbed 55 rebounds in a game against the Celtics, breaking Russell's previous National Basketball Association record by four.

Chamberlain scored 34 points to go along with his record rebound performance, but Russell got the last laugh when the Celtics walked away with a 132–129 victory in the game at Philadelphia.

Russell scored only 18 points, but he helped key a 37-point fourth-quarter Boston spurt that secured the victory.

Chamberlain wiped out the record of 51 rebounds Russell set in a game last February against Syracuse. Russell also grabbed 49 rebounds in a 1957 contest – the third highest total in history.

The trio of Tom Heinsohn, Sam Jones and Bob Cousy provided most of the offense for the Celtics. Heinsohn scored 26 points, Jones 25 and Cousy 23.

1988

ANTI-DRUG IDEA GETS APPROVAL

Sports ministers and officials from more than 100 countries embraced an anti-drug charter and recommended that the International Olympic Committee create an itinerant panel to test athletes around the world on short notice.

While there was no insurance such a charter could be enforced, it did provide a statement of support for the IOC's effort to combat performance-enhancing drug use by athletes. The anti-drug charter was approved by acclamation by Olympic representatives meeting in Moscow.

The basic guidelines for testing and sanctions were drawn up five months ago by representatives of 28 countries at a conference in Canada. The traveling panel, an extension of those guidelines, would conduct short-notice testing of athletes during training and become a permanent arm of the IOC Medical Commission.

The big question was how many of the 167 countries represented by the IOC would participate in the plan.

A STAR IS BORN

1938: Oscar Robertson, a basketball Hall of Fame guard who scored 26,710 points over an outstanding 14-year NBA career that ended in 1974.

★ ★ ★

1940: Paul Tagliabue, National Football League commissioner.

★ ★ ★

1943: Dave Bing, a basketball Hall of Fame guard who scored 18,327 points over a 12-year NBA career in the 1960s and '70s.

★ ★ ★

1948: Rudy Tomjanovich, a former NBA forward and current coach of the Houston Rockets.

★ ★ ★

DEATH OF A LEGEND

1990: Fred Shero (hockey).

NOVEMBER

25

MILESTONES IN SPORTS

1925

Red Grange, playing his first professional game for the Chicago Bears, was held to 36 rushing yards in a scoreless tie with the Chicago Cardinals.

1934

The Lions, playing their first season in Detroit, suffered their first-ever defeat, 3–0, at the hands of the Green Bay Packers. The Lions had won their first 10 games.

1948

Philadelphia's Howie Dallmar tied his own NBA record for futility when he missed all 15 of his field goal attempts in a game against Washington.

1976

O.J. Simpson rushed into the NFL record book when he ran for 273 yards and two touchdowns in Buffalo's 27–14 loss to the Detroit Lions.

1981

Milwaukee righthander Rollie Fingers became the first relief pitcher ever to win the A.L. Most Valuable Player award, edging Oakland's Rickey Henderson in a close vote.

1985

Clemson's Grayson Marshall set an NCAA record when he handed out 20 assists during the Tigers' 83–57 victory over Maryland-Eastern Shore.

1989

Seventh-ranked Miami overpowered No. 1 Notre Dame, 27–10, at the Orange Bowl, ending the Fighting Irish's 23-game winning streak.

1971

TURKEY DAY SHOWDOWN

Nebraska running back Jeff Kinney romped for 174 yards and scored four touchdowns to lead top-ranked Nebraska to a 35–31 victory over No. 2-ranked Oklahoma in a Thanksgiving Day shootout billed as the "Game of the Century."

The battle at Norman, Okla., lived up to all expectations – and beyond. Nebraska, 10–0 and riding a 29-game unbeaten streak, had entered the game averaging 38.9 points and holding opponents to 6.4. The 9–0 Sooners were an offensive machine, averaging 45 points – while giving up 16.2. But if the Cornhuskers appeared to have a defensive edge, you never would have known once the game started.

Neither team seemed capable of stopping the other. Oklahoma piled up 467 yards and scored in every quarter. The game see-sawed back and forth, Oklahoma holding a 17–14 halftime advantage and a 31–28 lead midway through the final quarter. Two of the Sooners' touchdowns came on Jack Mildren runs and two more on surprising Mildren-to-Jon Harrison passes – surprising because the Sooners operated out of a wishbone and seldom threw the ball.

It all came down to a dramatic 74-yard Nebraska drive engineered by quarterback Jerry Tagge. The key play was provided by Johnny Rodgers, who earlier had scored a touchdown on an electrifying 72-yard punt return. Rodgers made a diving third-down catch to keep the drive alive and Kinney provided the capper – a two-yard run with 1:38 remaining.

A STAR IS BORN

1902: Eddie Shore, a hockey Hall of Famer generally considered the greatest defenseman of all time. He spent all but half a season of his 14-year career with the Boston Bruins.

★ ★ ★

1914: Joe DiMaggio, a Hall of Fame outfielder for the New York Yankees for 13 seasons. The .325 career hitter is considered by some the best all-around player in baseball history.

★ ★ ★

1933: Lenny Moore, a football Hall of Fame halfback for the Baltimore Colts from 1956–67.

★ ★ ★

1963: Bernie Kosar, a current National Football League quarterback.

DEATH OF A LEGEND

1944: Kenesaw Mountain Landis (baseball).

1950

MICHIGAN TOPS OHIO STATE IN SNOW BOWL

Tony Momsen blocked a Vic Janowicz punt and recovered it in the end zone for a second-quarter touchdown that gave underdog Michigan a 9–3 victory over Ohio State in a driving snowstorm at Ohio Stadium.

The Wolverines' surprising victory, coupled with Northwestern's 14–7 upset of Illinois, gave them an unlikely Big Ten Conference championship and Rose Bowl berth. Michigan (5–3–1) accomplished that feat without making a first down or completing a pass while rushing for just 27 yards.

The snow was so bad the players could not be seen from the press box. Strong winds complicated the situation and temperatures hovered near 10 degrees. The teams spent the afternoon punting – Michigan kicking 24 times and Ohio State 21.

The Buckeyes struck first on a 27-yard Janowicz field goal after blocking a quick-kick attempt in the first quarter. Michigan got its first points moments later when Allen Wahl blocked a Janowicz punt out of the end zone for a safety. The winning points came just 47 seconds before halftime when Momsen broke in on Janowicz, blocked another punt and fell on it in the end zone.

The Buckeyes managed only three first downs and 41 total yards. The snow was so thick that brooms were used to clear it away for first-down measurements.

1980

LEONARD GETS HIS REVENGE

With the plea of "No mas, no mas," Roberto Duran threw in the towel in his rematch with Sugar Ray Leonard and surrendered the WBC welterweight title he had won from him six months earlier.

New welterweight champion **Sugar Ray Leonard** *celebrates after* **Roberto Duran's** *'No mas' surrender in New Orleans.*

In a startling conclusion to a title bout at the New Orleans Superdome, the 29-year-old Panamanian champion stepped away from Leonard during eighth-round action, turned to the referee and made his plea, which is Spanish for "no more." Duran claimed later that he was suffering stomach cramps that were growing progressively worse.

The 24-year-old Leonard had controlled the fight from the outset and was ahead on all cards. The style, shuffle and quickness that had been missing when he suffered his only career loss to Duran in Montreal were back and Leonard was dishing out a lot of punishment. Most observers concluded that Duran simply lost heart.

MILESTONES · IN SPORTS ·

1961

St. Louis' Jerry Norton became the first NFL player to intercept four passes in a game twice, running two back for touchdowns. But the Cardinals still dropped a 30–27 decision to the Pittsburgh Steelers.

1963

Navy quarterback Roger Staubach was named winner of the Heisman Trophy.

1968

Another Heisman: Southern California running back O.J. Simpson captured college football's top honor.

1975

Boston center fielder Fred Lynn made baseball history when he earned the American League MVP – the first time a rookie had been so honored.

1982

It took WBA heavyweight champion Larry Holmes 15 rounds, but he retained his title with a unanimous decision over Tex Cobb at Houston.

1988

No. 1-ranked Notre Dame defeated No. 2 Southern California, 27–10, and finished its college football regular season 11–0.

Roger Staubach, *Navy's Heisman Trophy winner, was a man of many awards in the 1963 postseason.*

1991 BADGER BOB DIES AT 60

Bob Johnson, the upbeat, inspirational coach who led the Pittsburgh Penguins to last year's Stanley Cup championship, died of brain cancer, three months after a life-threatening tumor had been diagnosed. He was 60.

The August announcement of Johnson's affliction caught everybody by surprise and shocked the professional hockey world. He was coming off his greatest career triumph and had given Pittsburgh its first-ever championship. Before Johnson introduced his energetic, enthusiastic and positive-thinking approach, the Penguins had failed to even reach the playoffs in seven of the previous eight seasons.

That type of success was not unusual for the man known as Badger Bob. He had coached the University of Wisconsin to three NCAA championships and he helped build the Calgary Flames into a National Hockey League power. He was only the second American coach to lead a team to the Stanley Cup championship.

Johnson had been confined to his Colorado Springs home since an August operation to remove a brain tumor. Doctors had decided to treat a second tumor with radiation. A Penguins spokesman said Johnson had been in a coma for about a week.

Pittsburgh Penguins Coach **Bob Johnson** *in 1990.*

1976 PANTHER STAR DORSETT ENDS FINAL SEASON IN A BIG RUSH

Just call it the Tony Dorsett show. Never mind that No. 1-ranked Pittsburgh concluded an 11–0 regular season and boosted its national championship hopes with a 24–7 victory over arch-rival Penn State, the game at Pittsburgh's Three Rivers Stadium clearly was a showcase for the Panthers' record-setting senior.

Running through a good Nittany Lions defense like it wasn't even there, Dorsett finished his regular-season career with an impressive 224-yard, two-touchdown effort that solidified his status as the greatest career rusher and scorer in college football history. His performance against the Nittany Lions was both artistic and intimidating.

After Penn State jumped to a 7–0 first-quarter lead, Dorsett tied the game with a six-yard second-quarter dash. But the speedy 22-year-old was just getting started. He shredded the Penn State defense for 173 second-half yards and provided the winning touchdown on a 40-yard third-quarter run.

When all of the numbers were added up, Dorsett owned NCAA individual records for career rushing yards (6,082), career scoring (356 points) and 1,000-yard seasons (4). He tied career marks for touchdowns (59) and 100-yard games (33).

1989 RAMS' FLIPPER CATCHES ON

With his team trailing New Orleans 17–13 and less than 3 minutes remaining, Willie (Flipper) Anderson decided to take matters into his own hands – literally. The result was an amazing comeback victory for the Los Angeles Rams and a National Football League receiving record for Anderson.

First Anderson caught a 46-yard pass from quarterback Jim Everett to set up Buford McGee's five-yard touchdown run that cut the Saints' lead to 17–10. Then, after the Rams had regained possession, Anderson caught a game-tying 15-yard TD pass with 1:02 remaining . The Rams claimed their 20–17 victory 6:38 into overtime when Mike Lansford kicked a 31-yard field goal – set up by Anderson's 14 and 26-yard receptions.

Anderson finished the afternoon with 15 catches for a record 336 yards, far outdistancing the previous mark of 309 set by Kansas City's Stephone Paige in 1985. His outstanding effort kept the 8–4 Rams in title contention in the NFC West Division race.

NOVEMBER 26

A STAR IS BORN

1892: Joe Guyon, a football Hall of Fame halfback during the formative years of the National Football League.

★ ★ ★

1910: Lefty Gomez, a Hall of Fame pitcher who won 189 games and compiled a 6–0 World Series record in the 1930s and '40s for the New York Yankees.

★ ★ ★

1942: Jan Stenerud, a football Hall of Fame kicker who scored an NFL career-record 1,699 points and booted 373 field goals in a 19-year career that ended in 1985.

★ ★ ★

1959: Mike Moore, a current major league pitcher.

★ ★ ★

DEATH OF A LEGEND

1991: Bob Johnson (hockey).

NOVEMBER

27

MILESTONES IN SPORTS

1947

A close call: A.L. Triple Crown winner Ted Williams lost the Most Valuable Player vote by one point to New York Yankee Joe DiMaggio.

1949

Philadelphia's Steve Van Buren became the NFL's second 200-yard rusher and first in 16 years when he romped for 205 yards in a 34–17 victory over the Pittsburgh Steelers.

1960

Detroit's Gordie Howe opened his own NHL club when he assisted on a goal for his unprecedented 1,000th point in the Red Wings' 2–0 victory over Toronto.

1960

The Denver Broncos, trailing Buffalo 38–7, rallied for a 38–38 tie in a record-setting AFL game.

1980

Instant victory: The Chicago Bears recorded a 23–17 Thanksgiving Day victory over Detroit when Dave Williams returned the overtime kickoff 95 yards for a touchdown.

1926 Tiny Carnegie Tech Stuns Notre Dame

Carnegie Tech, a little team with a big heart, delivered a swift kick to the pride and national championship hopes of powerful Notre Dame when it pulled off a stunning 19–0 upset of the Fighting Irish before 45,000 fans at Pittsburgh's Forbes Field.

Playing under the direction of assistant coach Tommy Mills while Knute Rockne was in Chicago watching the Army-Navy game, the unbeaten Irish ran into a buzzsaw. They were outhustled and outplayed, both offensively and defensively.

While Notre Dame Coach **Knute Rockne** *(in suit) was in Chicago on a scouting mission, his powerful Irish team was banished by underdog Carnegie Tech.*

Tech took surprising control of the contest in the second quarter when Bill Donohoe scored on a 13-yard run and Cy Letzelter tallied on a four-yarder. Tech increased its lead on two third-quarter Howard Harpster field goals and then turned matters over to a hard-nosed defense that allowed Notre Dame only one serious scoring threat – in the closing minutes of the game.

Tech finished its big afternoon with 11 first downs, five more than Notre Dame. Tech's second touchdown was set up by a blocked punt and two Fighting Irish passes were intercepted.

There was much speculation after the game about Rockne's absence. If the coach was so overconfident that he took off on a scouting mission, what message did that relay to his players? Carnegie Tech answered that question with its stunning upset.

1954 Eskimos Pull Upset

Jackie Parker's electrifying 85-yard touchdown run with a wild lateral capped a shocking fourth-quarter Edmonton rally that gave the Eskimos a major 26–25 upset victory over Montreal in the Grey Cup final at Toronto's Varsity Stadium.

Parker scooped up a wild pitch by Montreal's Chuck Hunsinger and ran for the winning score after quarterback Bernie Faloney had directed the Eskimos on a 103-yard drive, wiping out a 25–14 deficit. The Alouettes appeared to be in control of the game when they stretched their 18–14 halftime lead in the third quarter.

Montreal had entered the Canadian Football League's championship game as a prohibitive favorite. Many, in fact, considered the Alouettes the most powerful team ever developed in Canada. Edmonton's victory was the first for a team from the Western portion of the country since 1948.

1966 72-41: Bombs Away

A.D. Whitfield scored three touchdowns and Brig Owens and Charley Taylor added two apiece as the Washington Redskins ran over, around and through the New York Giants for a record-setting 72–41 National Football League victory before 50,439 fans at Washington.

The contest set records for combined points (113) and points by one team in a regular-season game. The Chicago Bears had scored 73 in a 1940 NFL championship game romp over the Redskins. The game ended, strangely, with Washington's Charlie Gogolak kicking a 29-yard field goal – because "he needed the practice." That was the only three-pointer in a game filled with big plays.

Taylor scored his touchdowns on passes of 32 and 74 yards from quarterback Sonny Jurgensen. Owens scored on a 62-yard run with a fumble recovery and a 62-yard interception return – his third pickoff of the game. Whitfield scored on a 63-yard run, Bobby Mitchell ran 45 yards for a score and Rickie Harris returned a punt 52 yards for a fourth-quarter TD.

Washington scored 13 first-quarter points, 21 in the second period, 14 in the third and 24 in the fourth. The Giants also did some offensive damage, actually outgaining the Redskins in total yards, 389–341. But quarterbacks Tom Kennedy and Gary Wood were intercepted five times.

A STAR IS BORN

1903: Johnny Blood McNally, a halfback during the NFL's formative years and a charter member of the pro football Hall of Fame.

★ ★ ★

1958: Mike Scioscia, a current major league catcher.

★ ★ ★

1960: Ken O'Brien, a current National Football League quarterback.

★ ★ ★

1961: Randy Milligan, a current major league first baseman.

★ ★ ★

DEATH OF A LEGEND

1971: Joe Guyon (football).

★ ★ ★

1987: Babe Herman (baseball).

★ ★ ★

1964 Trojan Rally Shocks Irish

It took only 30 minutes to unravel what Notre Dame had spent an entire season building. A halftime away from their 10th straight victory and a likely national championship, the Fighting Irish were stunned when Southern Cal rallied from a 17-point deficit for a 20-17 victory.

The Trojan comeback before 83,840 delighted fans at the Los Angeles Coliseum put a damper on what had been a near-perfect season for the Fighting Irish and new Coach Ara Parseghian. Southern Cal's comeback began when Mike Garrett ran one yard for a touchdown after the Trojans had moved 66 yards with the second-half kickoff.

When Notre Dame failed to respond on its next two possessions, Southern Cal pulled within 17–14 on Craig Fertig's 23-yard fourth-quarter TD pass to Fred Hill. Fertig's 15-yard strike to Rod Sherman moments later completed the startling turnaround.

Heisman Trophy-winning quarterback John Huarte completed 18 of 29 passes for 272 yards and a touchdown for Notre Dame.

Milestones in Sports

1906

Heavyweight champion Tommy Burns barely retained his title when he fought to a 20-round draw with Jack O'Brien in a bout at Los Angeles.

1925

Montreal goalie Georges Vezina collapsed in the net during an NHL game and later was diagnosed with tuberculosis – the disease that took his life four months later.

1938

Promising Chicago White Sox pitcher Monty Stratton saw his career come to a premature end when his right leg was amputated at the knee after a hunting accident in Greenville, Tex.

1956

Brooklyn righthander Don Newcombe, coming off a 27–7 season for the N.L. pennant-winning Dodgers, was named winner of baseball's first Cy Young Award as the game's top pitcher.

1969

The New York Knicks set an NBA record when they defeated the Cincinnati Royals, 106–105, for their 18th straight victory.

1982

The Edmonton Eskimos captured their record fifth consecutive Grey Cup championship with a 32–16 victory over the Toronto Argonauts.

1982

The United States defeated France, 4–1, and captured its second straight Davis Cup title and fourth in five years.

1981 Bear Gets Record Win

Legendary Alabama Coach Paul (Bear) Bryant added another feather to his houndstooth cap when he directed the Crimson Tide to a season-ending 28–17 victory over arch-rival Auburn – the record-setting 315th of his career.

Bryant's milestone victory moved him past Amos Alonzo Stagg on the all-time college football coaching list. Stagg's 314 victories were compiled over 57 seasons at Springfield (Mass.) College, Chicago and Pacific. The 68-year-old Bryant needed 37 years at Maryland, Kentucky, Texas A&M and Alabama.

The record-setter came in Alabama's final game of the season, a contest in which the favored Crimson Tide stumbled its way through three quarters. The 78,170 fans who had packed into Legion Field at Birmingham, Ala. were apprehensive when the upstart Tigers carried a 17–14 lead into the final period.

But Bryant's fate was in capable hands. A 38-yard touchdown pass from Walter Lewis to Jesse Bendross and a 15-yard TD run by Linnie Patrick gave Alabama its ninth victory and kept everybody from having to wait till next year.

November 28

Alabama football Coach **Paul (Bear) Bryant.**

1929 Cardinal Star Scores 40

Chicago Cardinals scoring machine **Ernie Nevers.**

Chicago running back Ernie Nevers, setting a National Football League standard that may never be broken, scored all of the Cardinals' points in a 40–6 victory over the cross-city rival Chicago Bears.

The former Stanford star almost single-handedly gave the Cardinals the Chicago city championship for the first time since 1927, running for six touchdowns and kicking four extra points. Nevers scored on runs of 20, 4, 6, 1, 1 and 10 yards.

But Nevers wasn't Chicago's only weapon. The Cardinal defense kept the Bears bottled up all afternoon, allowing only one big play . The Bears scored in the third quarter when Walt Horn connected with Garland Grange on a 50-yard touchdown pass.

A Star Is Born

1942: Paul Warfield, a football Hall of Fame wide receiver from 1964–77.

★ ★ ★

1965: Matt Williams, a current major league third baseman.

★ ★ ★

Death of a Legend

1939: James Naismith (basketball).

★ ★ ★

1977: Bob Meusel (baseball).

★ ★ ★

1985: Johnny (Blood) McNally (football).

NOVEMBER

29

A STAR IS BORN

1923: Minnie Minoso, a five-decade major leaguer who batted .298 over a 17-year career. He made brief appearances in 1976 and 1980 as promotional stunts.

★ ★ ★

1959: Neal Broten, a current National Hockey League center.

★ ★ ★

1960: Howard Johnson, a current major league infielder-outfielder.

★ ★ ★

1968: Pedro Martinez, a current major league pitcher.

★ ★ ★

1968: Dee Brown, a current National Basketball Association guard.

★ ★ ★

1976 YANKS SIGN REGGIE JAX

Reggie Jackson *started swinging for the Yankees in 1976.*

The New York Yankees, anxious to build on the American League pennant they captured last season, dipped into the new free-agent pot and pulled out its biggest prize – former Oakland and Baltimore slugger Reggie Jackson.

The Yankees lured Jackson to the Big Apple with a five-year contract worth $2.9 million. The brash, outspoken Jackson, who hit 27 homers and drove in 91 runs last season for the Orioles, was introduced to the New York media in what looked more like a coronation than an unveiling.

Presiding over the gala affair was Yankee Owner George Steinbrenner while veteran stars Thurman Munson and Roy White were on hand to present Jackson with his new uniform.

That uniform came at the expense of the Montreal Expos, who made a more lucrative offer to the 6-foot, 200-pounder, and the Philadelphia Phillies and Los Angeles Dodgers, teams Jackson had favored in his early negotiations. Those teams were pursuing a player who has hit 281 home runs in nine full major league seasons.

Jackson is the second free-agent to sign since baseball's first re-entry draft November 4.

MILESTONES IN SPORTS

1924

Bill Boucher scored three goals and the Canadiens dedicated the new Montreal Forum with a 7–1 NHL victory over Toronto.

1934

With CBS Radio doing its first-ever national broadcast of an NFL game, the Chicago Bears defeated the Detroit Lions, 19–16, on Thanksgiving Day.

1987

The New Orleans Saints stopped Pittsburgh, 20–16, and clinched the first winning season in the franchise's 20-year history.

1987

Jerry Kauric's 49-yard field goal with 1:10 remaining gave the Edmonton Eskimos a 38–36 victory over Toronto in the Grey Cup championship game at Vancouver.

1989

The Oklahoma Sooners set an NCAA record when they exploded for 97 first-half points en route to a 173–101 victory over U.S. International.

1969 KNICKS' STREAK SNAPPED AT 18

Jimmy Walker and Eddie Miles combined for 51 points and the struggling Detroit Pistons brought an end to the longest winning streak in National Basketball Association history with a 110–98 victory over the New York Knicks at Madison Square Garden.

The Knicks' record 18-game run, which started October 23 with a victory over the same Pistons, was snapped by a team with a 7–13 record. The New Yorkers, who are 23–2 after their 36-day success cruise, had set the record the previous night with an emotional come-back victory over the Cincinnati Royals.

But the Knicks appeared tired and listless against the Pistons. They managed to stay even through three quarters, but their normal defensive intensity was just not there. After gaining an 84–84 tie early in the final period, Miles gave Detroit the lead with a jump shot and the Pistons pulled steadily away.

Walt Frazier scored 24 points for the Knicks, who lost for the first time in the month of November. The Pistons outshot the Knicks from the floor, 49.4 percent to 40.7.

1992 JETS' LINEMAN IS PARALYZED

New York Jets defensive end Dennis Byrd suffered a paralyzing injury when he collided with teammate Scott Mesereau while trying to tackle Kansas City quarterback Dave Krieg during a National Football League game at Giants Stadium.

Byrd suffered a non-displaced fracture of the C–5 vertebra in his neck when he drove his head into the sternum of Mesereau, a Jets defensive tackle, during third-quarter action of the Chiefs' 23–7 victory. Krieg, standing in the pocket as Byrd and Mesereau charged toward him from opposite sides, stepped up to avoid contact and the two players hit each other, Byrd suffering his neck injury and Mesereau getting the wind knocked out of him.

Byrd's lower body was paralyzed, but there was some sensation in his feet and toes. Doctors attending the 26-year-old at Lenox Hill Hospital remained optimistic, but would not speculate about a recovery. Byrd will undergo a four-hour operation to stabilize the neck and stop the swelling. He also could face respiratory problems because the muscles between his ribs are paralyzed.

New York Jets defensive end **Dennis Byrd** *(90) before his paralyzing accident.*

1974 TROJANS BOMB IRISH IN COMEBACK BLITZ

High-stepping **Anthony Davis** *was the key to Southern Cal's stunning victory over Notre Dame.*

It looked like a typical day at the office. Notre Dame, 9–1 and the best defensive team in the country, owned a 24–0 lead over 8–1–1 Southern California with 1 minute left in the first half. Ho hum!

A packed house at the Los Angeles Coliseum was consoled when Anthony Davis caught a seven-yard touchdown pass from Pat Haden, sending the Irish into halftime with a 24–7 lead. And there was excitement when Davis took the second-half kick-off and raced 100 yards for another TD.

Suddenly playing with renewed vigor – and hope – the Trojans continued their assault. Davis scored again, from six yards out, and again, from four. Southern Cal had an amazing 27–24 lead. But the Trojans weren't through – not by a long shot.

Haden fired a pair of third-quarter TD passes to J.K. McKay and a fourth-quarter strike to Shelton Diggs. Charles Phillips got into the scoring column with a 58-yard interception return.

When all the numbers were added up, Southern Cal had a 55–24 victory and the Fighting Irish had red faces. The Trojans, unbelievably, had scored 49 second-half points and 55 in 17 minutes of action.

And the assault came against a Notre Dame defense that had entered the game ranked No. 1 nationally and had allowed only nine touchdowns in its previous 10 games.

A STAR IS BORN

1931: Bill Walsh, the former NFL coach who led the San Francisco 49ers to three Super Bowl titles in the 1980s.

★ ★ ★

1962: Bo Jackson, the 1985 Heisman Trophy winner who went on to fame and fortune as a two-sport (baseball and football) professional star.

★ ★ ★

1956 PATTERSON CLAIMS TITLE

Young Floyd Patterson, a 2–1 underdog to his 20-year veteran opponent, claimed the vacant world heavyweight boxing championship with a fifth-round technical knockout of Archie Moore in a title bout at Chicago.

Patterson, who at the tender age of 21 became the youngest heavyweight champion in history, exploded into the national spotlight when he dropped the reigning light heavyweight champ two times in the fifth round before the referee stepped in and halted the fight.

The knockdown blow was a left hook that seemed to come out of nowhere. Moore, who claims to be 39, struggled to his feet by the count of nine but Patterson sprang at him with both hands and quickly dropped him again. Somehow Moore regained his feet, but the referee wisely ended the onslaught.

Two of the three judges had Patterson ahead through four rounds, another had the fighters even. But it was apparent from the beginning that it was just a matter of time before Patterson's superior quickness would spell doom for Moore.

Patterson succeeds former heavyweight champion Rocky Marciano, who retired undefeated last year.

1979 LEONARD WINS WILD SLUGFEST

Sugar Ray Leonard, showing that his Olympic boxing success was no fluke, scored an exciting 15th-round technical knockout of previously undefeated Wilfred Benitez and claimed the world welterweight boxing championship.

The evenly matched and punishing bout at Las Vegas came to an end six seconds before the final bell when referee Carlos Padilla stepped between the fighters. The groggy Benitez had just climbed off the canvas, courtesy of a Leonard left hook.

The decision ended one of the most entertaining fights in years. Although Leonard was ahead on all cards, both boxers dished out their share of punishment.

Leonard used his superior quickness to score frequently against the Puerto Rican champion. Benitez fired away with overhand rights to the head of his 23-year-old challenger. The only early knockdown was recorded by Leonard in the third round – with another left hook.

The victory was Leonard's 26th straight since turning professional while Benitez lost for the first time in 39 professional bouts.

"We threw punches that would have rocked a volcano," Leonard said after the victory.

NOVEMBER 30

MILESTONES IN SPORTS

1941

The Chicago Bears used a 49-point second-half explosion to defeat the Philadelphia Eagles, 49-13, in an NFL game.

1986

Heavy underdog Hamilton pulled off a Grey Cup shocker when it defeated Edmonton, 39–15, in the CFL championship game at Vancouver.

1987

Two-sport star Bo Jackson rushed for 221 yards and the NFL's Los Angeles Raiders rushed past Seattle, 37–14.

1989

Jockey Kent Desormeaux set a one-year record when he rode his 547th winner during a meet at Laurel (Md.) Race Course.

1990

Boston's Larry Bird became the 15th 20,000-point scorer in NBA history during a game against the Washington Bullets.

1991

Minnesota's Bobby Smith assisted on a goal during the North Stars' 4–3 victory over Toronto, becoming the 32nd member of the NHL's 1,000-point club.

1991

Guy Forget defeated American Pete Sampras in a four-set match that clinched France's first Davis Cup victory in 59 years and set off a nationwide celebration.

DECEMBER

1

MILESTONES IN SPORTS

1924

The newly-formed Boston Bruins dropped the first NHL puck on American soil when they scored a 2–1 victory over the Montreal Maroons at Boston Arena.

1936

Yale end Larry Kelley was named second winner of college football's prestigious Heisman Trophy.

1959

LSU halfback Billy Cannon was the runaway choice for college football's 25th Heisman Trophy.

1973

Jack Nicklaus became golf's first Two Million Dollar Man when he recorded a one-stroke victory over Mason Rudolph in the Walt Disney World Classic.

1984

A Golden Anniversary: Boston College quarterback Doug Flutie won the Heisman Trophy.

1984

Greg Page captured the WBA heavyweight championship when he knocked out Gerrie Coetzee in the eighth round of a bout at Sun City, Bophuthatswana.

1990

The Davis Cup returned to the United States for the first time since 1982 when the doubles team of Rick Leach and Jim Pugh recorded a four-set victory over Australians Pat Cash and John Fitzgerald for an insurmountable 3-0 American lead.

1945 ARMY GUNS DOWN NAVY

The unstoppable forces of Doc Blanchard and Glenn Davis combined for five touchdowns and Army closed the door on its second straight college football national championship with a 32–13 thumping of arch-rival Navy at Philadelphia's Municipal Stadium.

U.S. President **Harry Truman** *(center) showed his neutrality by moving to the Navy side of the field after watching the first half from the Army side.*

Army's Mr. Inside and Mr. Outside put on an impressive show for the 100,000 spectators that included President Harry Truman, top officers from both branches of the military and members of the President's cabinet in the first peacetime meeting between the schools since 1941 – a week before the Japanese attack on Pearl Harbor.

The bulldozing Blanchard scored on first-period runs of 1 and 17 yards as Army built a 20–0 lead and he added a 46–yard interception return for a touchdown just 48 seconds into the second half. The elusive Davis scored on a first-quarter 48-yard run and a final-period dash of 27 yards.

Army, completing consecutive undefeated seasons for the first time in its storied history, had all the points it needed after the first quarter. Seldom attempting a pass and working against Navy's eight-man line, Coach Red Blaik's Cadets managed only five first downs after their early explosion.

Navy scored on a 61-yard pass from quarterback Bruce Smith to Clyde Scott just before halftime and on Joe Bartos' 26-yard run in the fourth quarter.

A STAR IS BORN

1902: Red Badgro, a football Hall of Fame end whose National Football League career spanned from 1927–36 with three New York teams.

★ ★ ★

1911: Walter Alston, a baseball Hall of Fame manager who directed the Brooklyn and Los Angeles Dodgers to 2,040 regular-season victories and four World Series championships in 23 seasons.

★ ★ ★

1939: Lee Trevino, an outstanding golfer who won the U.S. Open, British Open and PGA Championship two times each.

★ ★ ★

1948: George Foster, a former major leaguer who hit 348 home runs and batted .274 over an 18-year career that ended in 1986.

DEATH OF A LEGEND

1975: Nellie Fox (baseball).

★ ★ ★

1987: Punch Imlach (hockey).

1951 BOYKAN SCORES 7 TDs

It was a day for showboating in Starkville, Miss., and Mississippi halfback A.L. (Showboat) Boykin certainly did that. Boykin set a major college record and humbled arch-rival Mississippi State in the process when he scored seven touchdowns in the Rebels' lopsided 49–7 victory over the Bulldogs.

Boykin scored on runs of 85, 21, 14, 12, 14, 1 and 5 yards in his 42-point effort. He finished the day with 187 yards on 14 carries, an average of 13.4 yards per rush.

Ole Miss quarterback Jimmy Lear, not letting Boykin hog all the fun, contributed seven conversion-kick points to round out the scoring for the 6–3–1 Rebels.

1954 17 IN HUGE TRADE

The Baltimore Orioles and New York Yankees put their official stamp on the biggest trade in baseball history – a 17-player deal that changed the face of both teams and sent shivers through baseball's hot stove league.

Bringing new meaning to the term "restructuring," the O's and Yankees performed the transaction in two stages. On November 18, nine players were exchanged with the Yankees getting pitchers Bob Turley and Don Larsen and shortstop Billy Hunter for pitchers Harry Byrd and Jim McDonald, catchers Hal Smith and Gus Triandos, shortstop Willie Miranda and outfielder Gene Woodling.

The deal was concluded after the major league draft with eight more players changing organizations. This time the Yankees got the numbers advantage, picking up pitcher Mike Blyzka, outfielders Jim Fridley and Ted Del Guercio, first baseman Dick Kryhoski and catcher Darrell Johnson for pitcher Bill Miller and infielders Kal Segrist and Don Leppert.

Pitcher **Bob Turley** *changed from a Baltimore to New York uniform as part of a whopping 17-player trade.*

1950 NAVY SHOCKS NO. 2 ARMY

Underdog Navy, inspired by a pair of second-quarter touchdowns and a defense that refused to give an inch, snapped No. 2-ranked Army's 28-game unbeaten streak with a shocking 14–2 triumph before 101,000 fans at Philadelphia's Municipal Stadium.

With President Harry Truman watching from the Navy side of the field, the gang-tackling Midshipmen smothered the vaunted Army running game and picked off five passes en route to their first triumph over the Cadets since 1943. A seven-yard touchdown run by quarterback Bob Zastrow and his 30-yard TD pass to Jim Baldinger provided all the scoring Navy needed.

Army managed just one first down and three rushing yards in the first half and could not get its offense rolling until the final quarter. But in that wild period, the Cadets moved to Navy's 21, 15, 6 and 3-yard lines, only to have passes intercepted or fumble the ball away on each occasion.

Three interceptions of Bob Blaik passes came in the final 15 minutes, both teams lost the ball twice on fumbles and Army blocked a Navy kick. But all the Cadets could manage was a third-quarter safety.

It was the first time Army had failed to score a touchdown since 1947. The Cadets, three touchdown favorites, were trying to close out their third consecutive undefeated season and sixth in their last seven.

Oklahoma currently is ranked No. 1.

1972 A.D. BREAKS IRISH WITH 6-TD BURST

Sophomore tailback Anthony Davis broke Notre Dame's back with two long kickoff returns and scored four more touchdowns on short runs as Southern Cal laid claim to college football's national championship with a 45–23 victory over the Fighting Irish at the Los Angeles Memorial Coliseum.

Davis, a 5-foot-9, 185-pound speedster, scored on runs of 1, 5, 4 and 8 yards, but most of the damage came on his long returns. He brought back the opening kickoff 97 yards to spark the Trojans' 19-point first quarter and then returned a third-quarter kickoff 96 yards after Notre Dame had pulled to within two points at 25-23.

Davis' six-touchdown explosion and Southern Cal's 11th straight victory (the Trojans are unbeaten in 16 contests) was witnessed by 75,243 fans and a national television audience. Southern Cal is the nation's only undefeated major college team.

Davis, who ran for 99 yards on 22 carries, passed the 1,000-yard mark and brought his 1972 touchdown total to 18. Tom Clements threw three TD passes for Notre Dame.

1975 ARCHIE'S SECOND HEISMAN

Ohio State mini-mite Archie Griffin, who finished his outstanding college football career with a major-college record of 5,176 rushing yards, made history when he became the first player to win the coveted Heisman Trophy two times.

The talented 5-foot-8, 184-pound halfback, who last season became the fifth junior to win the award, easily outdistanced his competitors in voting by 888 sportswriters and broadcasters throughout the nation. Griffin totaled 1,800 points to 730 for California running back Chuck Muncie and 708 for Southern Cal's Ricky Bell. Griffin and Ohio State Coach Woody Hayes flew to New York's Downtown Athletic Club for the announcement.

Griffin, who also set a major-college record with 31 consecutive 100-yard rushing games, is the 38th running back to win the award inaugurated in 1935 and the fourth Ohio State player.

Ohio State's **Archie Griffin**, *the first two-time Heisman winner.*

A STAR IS BORN

1940: Willie Brown, a football Hall of Fame defensive back over a 16-year career that ended in 1978 with the Oakland Raiders.

★ ★ ★

1963: Ron Sutter, a current National Hockey League center.

★ ★ ★

1973: Monica Seles, the Yugoslavian tennis star and former No. 1-ranked women's player whose career was put on hold when she was attacked and stabbed by a fan while playing in a 1993 tournament.

★ ★ ★

DECEMBER 2

MILESTONES IN SPORTS

1905

The University of Chicago snapped Michigan's incredible five-year unbeaten streak at 56 games with an emotional 2–0 victory over the Wolverines at Chicago.

1907

Tommy Burns defended his heavyweight championship for a fifth time with a 10th-round knockout of Gunner Moir at London.

1944

No. 1-ranked Army overpowered No. 2 Navy, 23–7, in a battle of college football titans at Baltimore's Municipal Stadium.

1959

The American Football League became a reality when the circuit's eight teams selected 425 players in its first college draft.

1962

A Grey Cup marathon ended with Winnipeg beating Hamilton, 28–27, for the Canadian Football League championship. The game at Toronto became a two-day affair when play was suspended because of a dense fog.

1969

The NHL continued its expansion with the addition of Vancouver and Buffalo teams that will begin play in 1970–71.

1989

Houston's Andre Ware became the first black quarterback to win a Heisman Trophy.

DECEMBER

3

1982 HEARNS BEATS BENITEZ

Thomas (Hit Man) Hearns, deviating from his normal slug-it-out style, jabbed his way to a majority decision over Wilfred Benitez and captured the World Boxing Council super-welterweight championship on a majority decision at the New Orleans Superdome.

Hearns, a former World Boxing Association welterweight champion, circled, jabbed and hooked the champion, but refused to mix it up in the center of the ring. The strategy was effective as Hearns scored one knockdown and earned lopsided decisions from two of the three judges.

Hearns, who raised his record to 36–1, simply outboxed Benitez, a well-respected counterpuncher who has lost only twice in 46 fights. Only in the 10th round did the opponents stand toe to toe and that lasted only about a minute before Hearns began circling again.

By the fifth round, Hearns was in control and he delivered a right hand that staggered Benitez, who stayed up by balancing his gloves on the canvas. It was scored a knockdown. Benitez was given credit for a ninth-round knockdown, but replays showed that Hearns simply stumbled on his own.

Hearns said later that he injured his right hand midway through the fight and used it sparingly thereafter.

1956 WILT HAS BIG DEBUT

Wilt Chamberlain, the 7-foot Philadelphian who could change the face of college basketball, made a sensational debut for the University of Kansas when he poured in a school-record 52 points in the Jayhawks' 87–69 season-opening victory over Northwestern before 15,000 enthusiastic fans at Lawrence, Kan.

Chamberlain scored all of the Jayhawks' points as they raced to a quick 11–2 lead. With most of his baskets coming on dunk shots, the slender giant totaled 25 points in the first half, 27 in the second. He played all but 31 seconds of his varsity debut.

Wilt Chamberlain *soared to a 52-point effort in his Kansas college debut.*

Chamberlain, who carried a 42-point scoring average his senior season for Philadelphia's Overbrook High School and once scored 74 in a prep contest, broke the Kansas record of 44 points in a game shared by Clyde Lovellette and B.H. Born.

Kansas and Coach Dick Harp were the winners in the major recruiting battle for Chamberlain's services two years ago. Wilt the Stilt was pursued by well over 100 major colleges and universities.

1950 LIONS' BOX HAS BIG DAY

Detroit's Cloyce Box fell two yards short of setting a National Football League single-game record for receiving yardage, but his four-touchdown, 302-yard pass-catching effort was good enough to lead the Lions to an impressive 45–21 victory over the Colts in a game at Baltimore's Memorial Stadium.

Box caught three TD passes from quarterback Bobby Layne and another from Fred Enke. He finished the day with 12 receptions for 302 yards, one short of the 303-yard NFL record Cleveland's Jim Benton set in 1945. Benton caught 10 passes and scored just one TD.

Box and halfback Doak Walker accounted for all of Detroit's points. Walker scored two touchdowns, kicked a 42-yard field goal and converted on all six TD conversion attempts. Layne completed 16 of 27 passes for 341 yards.

MILESTONES • IN SPORTS •

1946

Army halfback Glenn Davis, following in the footsteps of teammate Doc Blanchard the year before, won the 12th Heisman Trophy.

1943

Notre Dame's Angelo Bertelli became the second quarterback to win a Heisman Trophy.

1950

Los Angeles' Tom Fears enjoyed the biggest pass-catching day in NFL history when he pulled in 18 for 189 yards and two touchdowns in the Rams' 51–14 victory over Green Bay.

1966

Lew Alcindor, making his varsity debut for UCLA, scored a school-record 56 points as the Bruins rolled to a 105–90 victory over Southern Cal.

1972

New York's Bobby Howfield celebrated his 36th birthday by kicking six field goals, the final from 42 yards with two seconds remaining, as the Jets edged New Orleans, 18–17, at Shea Stadium.

1979

Another Southern Cal halfback captured the Heisman Trophy: Charles White.

1993

The Atlanta Hawks routed Houston, 133–111, ending the Rockets' NBA record-tying streak of season-opening victories at 15.

A STAR IS BORN

1923: Tom Fears, a football Hall of Fame end who caught 400 passes for 5,397 yards over nine seasons (1948–56) with the Los Angeles Rams.

★ ★ ★

1937: Bobby Allison, a current stock car racer who won the Daytona 500 three times and captured the NASCAR national championship in 1983.

★ ★ ★

1951: Rick Mears, a four-time winner of the Indianapolis 500 and a three-time CART national champion.

★ ★ ★

1965: Katarina Witt, a four-time world champion figure skater from East Germany who captured Olympic gold medals in 1984 and '88.

Tom Fears, *the record-setting pass-catcher of the Los Angeles Rams.*

MILESTONES • IN SPORTS •

1945

Army fullback Doc Blanchard pulled off a college football coup when he became the first junior to win a Heisman Trophy.

1956

Notre Dame's Paul Hornung edged Tennessee's Johnny Majors in the Heisman Trophy voting, becoming the first player from a losing team to win the award.

1961

Floyd Patterson defended his heavyweight crown with a fourth-round knockout of Tom McNeeley in Toronto.

1961

The Washington Redskins broke an NFL color barrier when they made Syracuse running back Ernie Davis the first black No. 1 draft pick in league history.

1982

Another junior Heisman winner: Georgia's Herschel Walker edged Stanford's John Elway and SMU's Eric Dickerson.

1988 SANDERS COMPLETES RECORD RUN

Oklahoma State running back Barry Sanders, announced as the Heisman Trophy winner just hours earlier, closed out his regular season with a record-setting binge that sparked the Cowboys to a 45–42 victory over Texas Tech in Tokyo.

Sanders, the eighth junior to win the coveted Heisman, closed his campaign with a 257-yard, four-touchdown effort that set and extended single-season NCAA records. His final total of 2,553 yards surpassed Marcus Allen's one-season rushing record (2,342 yards in 1981) and he finished with 39 touchdowns, 10 more than any player in history.

Sanders scored the Cowboys' first two TDs, one on a 56-yard dash, and their last two. In between came a pair of touchdown passes from Mike Gundy to Hart Lee Dykes. The first of those TD passes gave Oklahoma State (9–2) a 24–21 lead and the Cowboys never trailed again.

The Cowboys of the Big Eight Conference will play Western Athletic Conference champion Wyoming in the Holiday Bowl. Texas Tech finished its season at 5–6.

A STAR IS BORN

1930: Harvey Kuenn, a former A.L. batting champion for Detroit who batted .303 over a 15-year career that ended in 1966.

★★★

1931: Alex Delvecchio, a hockey Hall of Fame iron man center who scored 456 goals while missing just 43 games in 22 seasons (1950–74) with Detroit.

★★★

1955: Dave Taylor, a current National Hockey League right winger.

★★★

1957: Lee Smith, a current major league relief pitcher.

★★★

1963: Sergei Bubka, the outstanding Ukrainian pole vaulter who was the first to clear 20 feet, both indoor and out (1991).

★★★

DEATH OF A LEGEND

1944: Roger Bresnahan (baseball).

★★★

1952: James Norris Sr. (hockey).

★★★

1988: Wally Berger (baseball).

DECEMBER 4

1971 MAJORS KEYS VOLS' UPSET

An opportunistic Tennessee defense forced six turnovers and Bobby Majors broke Penn State's back with 195 yards in kick returns as the Volunteers ended the Nittany Lions' 15-game winning streak with a 31–11 upset at Knoxville's Neyland Stadium.

The loss, spoiling Penn State's perfect record and killing the Nittany Lions' hopes for a national championship, came in the final regular-season game for both teams. Cornerback Conrad Graham returned a first-quarter Penn State fumble 76 yards for a touchdown and linebacker Jackie Walker returned an interception 43 yards for another score, but Majors still grabbed the spotlight.

The All-America safety had two kickoff returns of more than 50 yards and brought back a Penn State punt 44 yards for a second-quarter score. He helped the 9–2 Volunteers win the battle of field position and the Tennessee defense took care of the rest, holding the nation's most prolific scoring offense to a second-quarter field goal and a fourth-quarter Lydell Mitchell touchdown.

The Cotton Bowl-bound Nittany Lions had not lost since mid-season last year. The one consolation for Penn State was Mitchell's one-season NCAA-record 29th touchdown.

1960 HORNUNG BREAKS SCORING RECORD

Green Bay halfback Paul Hornung accounted for 23 points and set a one-season National Football League scoring record while lifting the Packers to a 41–13 victory over the Chicago Bears at Wrigley Field.

Hornung brought his season point total to 152 by scoring two touchdowns, kicking two field goals and converting five extra-point kicks. He eclipsed the record of 138 points set by former Packer receiver Don Hutson in 1942.

Hornung gave Green Bay a second-quarter lead with a 21-yard field goal and Willie Davis added to it by blocking a Chicago punt and recovering the ball in the end zone for a touchdown. Hornung booted a 41-yard field goal before halftime and caught a 17-yard Bart Starr TD pass early in the third period – his first touchdown reception of the year.

Hornung added a fourth-quarter touchdown on a 10-yard run and closed his day with 68 yards on 14 carries. Teammate Jim Taylor rushed for 140 yards and Starr completed 17 of 23 passes for 227 yards and two touchdowns.

The Packers' victory, witnessed by 48,410 fans, was their first at Wrigley Field since 1952.

Green Bay golden boy **Paul Hornung.**

DECEMBER

5

MILESTONES
· IN SPORTS ·

1924

Hamilton's Red Green scored five goals in the Tigers' 10–3 National Hockey League victory over the Maple Leafs at Toronto.

1947

Joe Louis pulled off a tough 15-round split decision over Jersey Joe Walcott and retained his heavyweight title in a bout at New York's Madison Square Garden.

1950

Ezzard Charles made his fifth heavyweight title defense a successful one with an 11th-round knockout of Nick Barone at Cincinnati.

1974

The Birmingham Americans captured the first World Football League championship when they defeated the Florida Blazers, 22–21, in the World Bowl game at Birmingham, Ala.

1981

An easy choice: Southern California running back Marcus Allen, the most prolific one-season rusher in NCAA history (2,342 yards), walked away with a Heisman Trophy.

1992

Former Pittsburgh slugger Barry Bonds signed the richest contract in baseball history, a six-year, $43 million free-agent deal with the San Francisco Giants.

1969

TEXAS WINS SHOWDOWN

Jim Bertelsen ran two yards for the game-tying touchdown and kicker Happy Feller added the extra point that gave No. 1-ranked Texas a thrilling 15-14 victory over No. 2 Arkansas in a Southwest Conference showdown at Fayetteville, Ark.

The triumph, the 19th straight for the Longhorns, did not come easily. Arkansas, riding a 15-game winning streak of its own, had built a 14–0 lead on first and third-quarter touchdowns while shutting down a Longhorn Wishbone attack that had averaged 44 points per game. The Razorbacks entered the final period apparently headed for an impressive victory.

But that's when Texas quarterback James Street went to work. On the first play of the quarter, Street broke free on a 42-yard touchdown dash and then ran for a two-point conversion. After Danny Lester killed an Arkansas drive at the Texas 8-yard line with an interception, Street struck again – like lightning.

On a daring fourth-and-three play, Street shocked the run-focused Razorbacks with a 44-yard bomb to Randy Peschel, who finally was tackled at the Arkansas 13. Two plays later, Bertelsen scored.

Arkansas mounted a final drive, but Tom Campbell sealed the verdict for Texas with an interception. Bill Burnett scored Arkansas' first touchdown on a one-yard run and Chuck Dicus caught a 29-yard TD pass from Bill Montgomery in the third period.

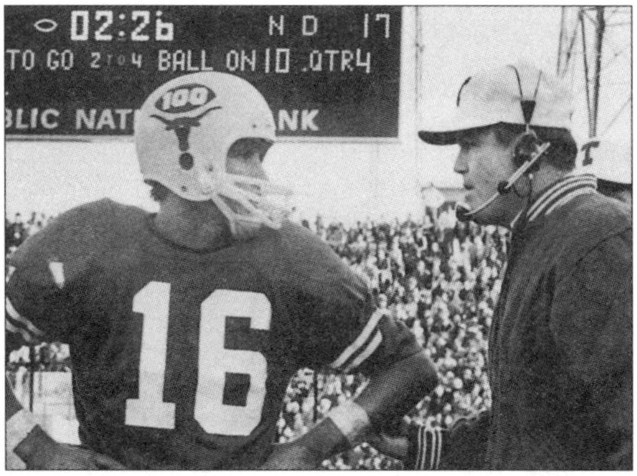

Texas Coach **Darrell Royal** *(right) and quarterback* **James Street.**

1978

ROSE JOINS PHILLIES

The Pete Rose promotional tour shut down its short-term operation with the announcement that the hustling 16-year Cincinnati veteran had signed a four-year, $3.2 million free-agent contract with the Philadelphia Phillies.

Rose, a recent entry into baseball's 3,000-hit club and a vital cog in Cincinnati's mid-1970s Big Red Machine, told a packed news conference at baseball's winter meetings in Orlando, Fla., that he had opted for the Phillies over such high bidders as Atlanta, Pittsburgh, the New York Mets and Kansas City.

Rose, who becomes the highest paid player in baseball, had taken an innovative approach to his free agency by jetting around the country and inviting selected teams to make offers. That bidding had reached as high as $1 million per year, but the three-time National League batting champion reportedly accepted a lower offer from the Phillies – a team that dropped out and then re-entered the bidding.

Pete Rose *displays his new Philadelphia uniform, apparently to the delight of Phillies reliever* **Tug McGraw.**

A STAR IS BORN

1947: Jim Plunkett, the former Stanford Heisman Trophy winner (1970) who led the Oakland-Los Angeles Raiders to Super Bowl victories in 1981 and '84.

★ ★ ★

1957: Art Monk, a current National Football League wide receiver.

★ ★ ★

DEATH OF A LEGEND

1951: Shoeless Joe Jackson (baseball).

★ ★ ★

1971

ELLISON BREAKS RUSHING RECORD

Los Angeles running back Willie Ellison rushed into the National Football League record books with a 247-yard blitz that paced the Rams to a 45–28 victory over New Orleans before 73,610 fans at the Memorial Coliseum.

Ellison compiled his record on 26 carries and eclipsed the AFL-NFL mark of 243 yards set by Buffalo's Cookie Gilchrist in a 1963 American Football League game. Gilchrist needed 36 carries.

Ellison got the Rams off to a fast start with an 80-yard touchdown romp in the first two minutes and passed Gilchrist with a four -yard run in the final minute. He broke Tom Wilson's 15-year-old Rams record of 223 yards early in the fourth quarter.

With Ellison running wild and quarterback Roman Gabriel firing three touchdown passes, the Rams rolled to their easy victory. Travis Williams contributed a 105-yard kickoff return to the carnage as Los Angeles built a 35–7 halftime advantage.

MILESTONES IN SPORTS

1939

Iowa halfback Nile Kinnick edged Michigan halfback Tom Harmon in a close Heisman vote.

1973

Sandy Hawley, unhurt after falling from his mount in the fourth race, came back to claim his record-setting 485th victory of the season when he rode Night Train Lane in the ninth at Laurel Race Course.

1980

Thomas Hearns, making the first defense of his WBA championship, scored a sixth-round knockout of challenger Luis Primera at Detroit.

1986

Miami quarterback Vinny Testaverde recorded the most lopsided victory in the 52-year history of the Heisman Trophy voting, outdistancing Temple's Paul Palmer by a whopping 1,541 points.

1992

American Jim Courier held off Switzerland's Jakob Hlasek, 6–3, 3–6, 6–3, 6–4, to give the United States a 3–1 victory and its 30th Davis Cup title.

1961 DAVIS WINS HEISMAN

Ernie Davis, the talented running back who eclipsed most of Jim Brown's rushing and scoring records at Syracuse University, became the 27th athlete and first black to receive a Heisman Trophy when he was honored during ceremonies at New York's Downtown Athletic Club.

Davis, who rushed for 2,386 yards and scored 220 points in a three-year career that produced two All-America citations, outdistanced another black, Ohio State fullback Bob Ferguson, in voting by 1,091 sportswriters and broadcasters from around the nation.

The 6-foot-2, 210-pound halfback rushed for 686 yards on 98 carries as a sophomore, 877 on 112 carries as a junior and 823 on 150 carries this season as a senior. With Davis leading the charge in 1959, the Orangemen captured a national championship.

His 35 touchdowns were 10 more than Brown managed from 1954–56 and his 220 points broke Brown's career mark of 187. Brown rushed for 2,091 career yards.

DECEMBER 6

A STAR IS BORN

1896: George Trafton, a football Hall of Fame center who made his name in the NFL's formative years with the Chicago Staleys and Bears.

★ ★ ★

1899: Jocko Conlan, a baseball Hall of Fame umpire in the National League from 1941–64.

★ ★ ★

1921: Otto Graham, the Hall of Fame quarterback who ran and passed the Cleveland Browns to seven AAFC and NFL championships in 10 seasons (1946–55).

★ ★ ★

1925: Andy Robustelli, a Hall of Fame defensive end who missed only one game in 14 seasons with the Los Angeles Rams and New York Giants (1951–64).

★ ★ ★

1967: Kevin Appier, a current major league pitcher.

DEATH OF A LEGEND

1942: Amos Rusie (baseball).

★ ★ ★

1955: Honus Wagner (baseball).

★ ★ ★

1985: Burleigh Grimes (baseball).

★ ★ ★

1970 ANOTHER RAIDER MIRACLE

Warren Wells caught a deflected 33-yard desperation pass from Daryle Lamonica in the end zone and 43-year-old George Blanda kicked the extra point with one second remaining, giving the Oakland Raiders a near-miraculous 14–13 victory over the Jets in a National Football League thriller at New York.

The Raiders, tied with Kansas City atop the AFC West Division, appeared to be in a hopeless situation when they received a punt with 30 seconds left and started the winning drive from their own 30 – without any timeouts.

Lamonica immediately went deep for Wells and Jets defender Earlie Thomas helped his cause with pass interference.

Oakland heroes **Daryle Lamonica** *(right) and* **George Blanda.**

Now positioned at the New York 33, the Raiders misfired on two passes before Lamonica fired his game-winner.

Wells was sandwiched by Thomas and W.K. Hicks and the Jets collided while going for the ball, Thomas tipping it forward. Wells pulled it in and Blanda kicked the point.

It was the fourth time Blanda had either won or tied a game with a kick in the final 16 seconds.

1984 SUKOVA SHOCKS MARTINA

Helena Sukova, a 19-year-old Czech looking for her first major title, handed Martina Navratilova a shocking 1–6, 6–3, 7–5 setback in the semifinals of the Australian Open, ending her record winning streak at 74 matches and ruining her dream of a tennis grand slam.

Navratilova had not lost since January and was looking for the 100th title of her career. She also was looking for the final link of a one-season grand slam after earlier victories in the French, Wimbledon and U.S. championships.

Sukova was the master on this day. Playing before an enthusiastic crowd in Melbourne, Australia, Sukova appeared easy pickings for her 28-year-old opponent when she went down quietly in a quick-and-easy first set.

But Sukova, using a strong serve and precision passing, suddenly took control. She claimed the second set and jumped to a 3–0 lead in the third before Navratilova could fight back. Martina evened the count at 4–4, but Sukova broke in the 11th game and stubbornly kept up the pressure as Navratilova saved five match points before finally falling.

DECEMBER

7

1977 HOWE SWEET IT IS AGAIN

Gordie Howe, the 49-year-old patriarch of professional hockey, blazed a new trail when he notched his 1,000th career goal, ending a 10-game scoring slump and sparking the New England Whalers to a 6–3 World Hockey Association victory over the Birmingham Bulls.

The historic goal was greeted by an uncertain silence as more than 10,000 spectators in the non-hockey stronghold of Birmingham, Ala., tried to digest exactly what had happened. But when Howe's Whaler teammates flooded the ice for congratulations, the crowd gave him a long standing ovation. The goal was scored from three feet, 1:36 into the first period.

It was the 147th of Howe's WHA career after 26 National Hockey League campaigns that produced 786 regular-season goals and 67 in the playoffs for the Detroit Red Wings. Howe spent three seasons with the WHA's Houston Aeros playing with sons Mark and Marty before moving to the Whalers this season. He had been sitting on 999 goals for almost a month.

"Thank God it's over," said a relieved Howe, who added that the milestone chase had turned into a major distraction for both him and his media-hounded teammates. Howe had been playing with an injured wrist.

1968 68 POINTS: MURPHY SETS NCAA MARK

Calvin Murphy, Niagara's rapid-fire scoring machine, set an NCAA one-game record against Division I competition when he exploded for 68 points in a 118-110 Purple Eagles' victory over Syracuse at the Niagara Falls, N.Y., Student Center.

Murphy, the nation's second-leading scorer last season, connected on 24 field goals and 20 free throws to break the single-game record of 66 points scored by Washington & Lee's Jay Handlan against Furman in 1951. The talented junior guard scored 34 points in each half.

Murphy, whose previous high game was 57 points last season against Villa Madonna, trails only Furman's Frank Selvy (100 points), Villanova's Paul Arizin (85) and Temple's Bill Mlkvy (73) on the all-time single-game charts. But they all performed their scoring feats against non-Division I teams.

1980 AROUSED 49ERS PLAY CATCHUP

San Francisco comebackers **Ray Wersching** *and quarterback/holder* **Joe Montana** *(16).*

Down 35–7 at halftime and testing the patience of 37,949 normally faithful fans at Candlestick Park, the San Francisco 49ers rallied behind the passing of Joe Montana to tie the game in regulation and then won in overtime, 38–35, on Ray Wersching's 36-yard field goal.

The comeback, the biggest in National Football League history, was completed with 1:55 remaining in regulation when Lenvil Elliott ran seven yards for a touchdown and a 35–35 tie. San Francisco's overtime drive for the winning field goal was aided by a roughing penalty.

It was a tale of two halves. New Orleans owned the first, with Archie Manning throwing three touchdown passes. The Saints vaulted to a 21–0 lead, surrendered a 57-yard TD punt return to San Francisco's Freddie Solomon and then added 14 more points for their 28-point lead. They outgained the 49ers, 324–21, before intermission.

But Montana led his team to a pair of touchdowns in both the third and fourth quarters. He hit Dwight Clark on a 71-yard TD bomb and threw 14 yards to Solomon.

A STAR IS BORN

1925: Max Zaslofsky, a former NBA scoring champion (1948) and a 10-year star during the league's formative years.

★ ★ ★

1947: Johnny Bench, a Hall of Fame catcher over 17 major league seasons and the cornerstone of Cincinnati's Big Red Machine of the mid-1970s.

★ ★ ★

1956: Larry Bird, a nine-time All-NBA first-team performer and three-time MVP who led the Boston Celtics to three championships in the 1980s.

★ ★ ★

DEATH OF A LEGEND

1962: Bobo Newsom (baseball).

MILESTONES • IN SPORTS •

1929

Leo Diegel, who ended Walter Hagen's four-year run of PGA Championship victories the previous year, won his second straight PGA title with a 6 and 4 triumph over Johnny Farrell at Los Angeles.

1949

Notre Dame end Leon Hart, who never played in a losing college football game, became the second lineman to win a Heisman Trophy.

1973

Los Angeles guard Jerry West set an NBA record with 10 steals in a game at Seattle, but the SuperSonics got the last laugh with a 115–111 victory over the Lakers.

1985

Auburn running back Bo Jackson edged Iowa quarterback Chuck Long by a record-low 45 points in voting for the Heisman Trophy.

1990

And then there were 24: The NHL added expansion franchises in Ottawa and Tampa, Fla.

1990

Shawn Bradley, Brigham Young's 7-foot-6 freshman center, tied an NCAA record when he blocked 14 shots in the Cougars' 90–86 victory over Eastern Kentucky.

1949 Heisman Trophy winner **Leon Hart.**

1940 VENGEFUL BEARS RIP 'SKINS, 73-0

The Chicago Bears, still fuming over disparaging remarks by Washington Owner George Preston Marshall and several of his players after a 7–3 loss three weeks earlier, exploded for a record 11 touchdowns and buried the Redskins, 73–0, in the National Football League championship game at Washington's Griffith Stadium.

The most lopsided professional game of all-time was decided on the game's second play when Chicago's Bill Osmanski broke free for a 68-yard scoring run. The Bears added two more first-quarter TDs, one in the second quarter, four in the third and three in the fourth. Ten different players scored with only Harry Clark crossing the goal line twice.

Chicago's **George McAfee** *gets tripped up after a short gain against the Redskins in the NFL championship game.*

The victory was sweet revenge for the Monsters of the Midway, who had complained about the officiating after the Redskins' earlier victory. That prompted Marshall to state, "The Bears are crybabies. When the going gets tough, the Bears quit."

That's all the motivation Bears Owner and Coach George Halas needed to work his team into a frenzy. Chicago intercepted eight Washington passes, three of which were returned for touchdowns, and scored on runs of 68, 1, 42, 23, 44, 2 and 1 yards. Quarterback Sid Luckman, running the new T-formation to precision, also threw a 30-yard scoring pass to Ken Kavanaugh.

MILESTONES IN SPORTS

1948

High-scoring SMU junior Doak Walker became the second underclassman to win the coveted Heisman Trophy.

1966

Roger Maris, the man who broke Babe Ruth's one-season home run record in 1961, was traded by the New York Yankees to St. Louis for third baseman Charlie Smith.

1977

Atlanta Braves Owner Ted Turner, suspended last December for "tampering" with prospective free agents, was reinstated by Commissioner Bowie Kuhn.

1978

Roberto Duran, out of contenders for the lightweight championship he had defended 12 times, scored an eighth-round knockout over Monroe Brooks in his first bout as a welterweight.

1987

An NHL oddity: Philadelphia goalie Ron Hextall scored into an empty net as the Flyers defeated Boston, 5–2.

DECEMBER 8

1961 WILT'S SCORING RECORD

The incomparable Wilt Chamberlain exploded for a National Basketball Association-record 78 points, but his Warriors lost a 151–147 triple-overtime heart-breaker to the Los Angeles Lakers before 4,022 fans in the second game of an NBA doubleheader at the Philadelphia Convention Center.

Chamberlain single-handedly kept the Warriors in the contest, which also included a 63-point effort by the Lakers' Elgin Baylor. He connected on 31 of 62 field-goal attempts and 16 of 31 free throws while grabbing 43 rebounds. He had 53 points in regulation.

The 78-point outburst broke the NBA record of 71 set last season by Baylor. The slick Laker forward performed that feat in regulation, a record that will stand for now. In this game, Baylor connected on 23 field goals and 17 shots from the foul line.

The game was tied at 109 at the end of regulation, at 121 after one overtime and at 133 after two. Paul Arizin was Philadelphia's second-leading scorer with 19 points. Jerry West backed up Baylor with 32.

In the doubleheader opener, the Detroit Pistons recorded a 133-107 victory over the Chicago Packers. The high scorer in that game was Chicago's Walt Bellamy with 23 points.

1963 COOKIE CRUMBLES JETS WITH 243-YARD EFFORT

Cookie Gilchrist, Buffalo's 251-pound battering-ram fullback, rumbled for a single-game record 243 yards and scored five touchdowns as the Bills overwhelmed the New York Jets, 45–14, in an American Football League game witnessed by 20,222 enthusiastic fans at Buffalo's War Memorial Stadium.

The Gilchrist show started early with a four-yard touchdown run and ended late with a six-yarder. In between, the 28-year-old bruiser ran 1, 1 and 19 yards for touchdowns in a one-sided contest the Bills led at halftime, 24–7.

Gilchrist, who led the AFL with 1,096 yards last season, reached his record 243-yard total on 36 carries and made life easy for quarterback Daryle Lamonica, who made his first professional start. Lamonica completed 10 of the 16 passes he attempted for 115 yards and a touchdown.

The previous-best AFL or NFL single-game rushing effort was 237 yards, accomplished twice by Cleveland's Jim Brown (1957 and '61). The five touchdown runs also tied a single-game record for the 3-year-old AFL.

A STAR IS BORN

1958: George Rogers, the former Heisman Trophy-winning running back (1980) from South Carolina who went on to a short NFL career.

★★★

1967: Jeff George, a current National Football League quarterback.

★★★

DEATH OF A LEGEND

1958: Tris Speaker (baseball).

★★★

1985: Bill Wambsganss (baseball).

★★★

DECEMBER

9

1934 GIANTS SNEAK PAST STUMBLING BEARS

The New York Giants, turning in desperation to basketball-style sneakers to give them much-needed traction on an icy field, scored 27 points in the final 10 minutes and captured their first National Football League championship with a 30–13 victory over the heavily-favored Chicago Bears.

The game at New York's Polo Grounds was a slip-and-slide affair with the undefeated, untied Bears holding a 10–3 halftime advantage. That's when Giants Coach Steve Owen dispatched clubhouse attendant Abe Cohen in search of shoes that he hoped would give his players better footing on a treacherous field.

Cohen returned with bags full of sneakers – and just in time. The Bears owned a 13–3 lead on a Bronko Nagurski touchdown run and two Jack Manders field goals and just 10 minutes remained. But that would be enough.

Suddenly able to cut and turn, the Giants blitzed a team that had defeated them twice in the regular season. Quarterback Eddie Danowski hit Ike Frankian with a 28-yard touchdown pass, halfback Ken Strong ran 42 and 11 yards for TDs and Danowski capped the scoring with a nine-yard run.

Final: 30–13. The Bears had outscored their previous opponents, 286–86.

New York Coach **Steve Owen** *got his team in step and the Giants went on to overwhelm the Bears.*

MILESTONES • IN SPORTS •

1949

The National Football League brought its membership to 13 with the addition of All-America Football Conference franchises Cleveland, Baltimore and San Francisco, ending the AAFC's four-year run as an independent circuit.

1967

After spending 16 hours in a Detroit hospital for a kidney ailment, 40-year-old Gordie Howe returned to the ice and scored a goal and assist in the Red Wings' 3–2 victory over the New York Rangers.

1973

St. Louis placekicker Jim Bakken, who set an NFL record by kicking seven field goals in a 1967 game against Pittsburgh, booted six more in a 32–10 victory over the Falcons at Atlanta.

1976

Rookie New York Coach Lou Holtz shocked the football world when he walked away from his five-year contract with the Jets, saying he wanted to return to college coaching.

1989

The NHL's board of governors voted to expand the league from 21 to 28 teams by the year 2000, with franchise entry fees set at $50 million.

A STAR IS BORN

1931: Cliff Hagan, a basketball Hall of Fame forward who scored 14,870 points over 10 NBA seasons with the St. Louis Hawks and three ABA campaigns in Dallas.

★ ★ ★

1932: Bill Hartack, an outstanding jockey who won the Kentucky Derby five times and the Preakness Stakes three times in the 1950s and '60s.

★ ★ ★

1938: Deacon Jones, a Hall of Fame defensive end and one of the NFL's most feared pass rushers. He was part of the Los Angeles' Rams' Fearsome Foursome front line in the 1970s.

★ ★ ★

1942: Dick Butkus, a Hall of Fame middle linebacker and one of the NFL's most intimidating players during a nine-year career with the Chicago Bears.

★ ★ ★

1953: World B. Free, a fast-shooting guard who scored 17,955 points over a 13-year NBA career that ended in 1988.

DEATH OF A LEGEND

1965: Branch Rickey (baseball).

1977 TOMJANOVICH SERIOUSLY HURT IN NBA FIGHT

In what Houston Coach Tom Nissalke termed "the most malicious thing I've ever seen in basketball," Rockets forward Rudy Tomjanovich took a roundhouse punch from burly Los Angeles forward Kermit Washington that fractured his jaw, broke his nose and resulted in a serious concussion.

Tomjanovich, who was hospitalized in intensive care, was belted in the third period of Houston's 116–105 National Basketball Association victory over the Lakers at the Los Angeles Forum. The unfortunate Tomjanovich was actually just an innocent bystander when a fight broke out between the solid 6-foot-8 Washington and 7-foot Houston center Keven Kunnert.

Kunnert was knocked to the hardwood floor and Tomjanovich rushed over to act as peacemaker. But Washington heard him coming, whirled around and delivered a haymaker punch that knocked Tomjanovich off his feet. The 6-foot-8 Houston star fell backward and hit his head on the floor. The next thing he knew he was lying in a Los Angeles hospital bed. Tomjanovich is the Rockets' captain and the NBA's 15th leading scorer.

Washington could face serious NBA penalties and disciplinary action from Commissioner Larry O'Brien. The NBA has been reeling from a recent upsurge in fighting.

1955 'SWEET' SUGAR CLAIMS TITLE

Sugar Ray Robinson, reclaiming the championship mantel he had discarded three years earlier, captured the middleweight crown for a record third time when he recorded a quick-and-easy knockout of Carl (Bobo) Olson in the second round of a bout at Chicago.

Robinson, appearing sharp and confident, caught Olson with a big right to the jaw at 2:51 of the second round. The 27-year-old Olson, a two-time loser to Robinson before his retirement, fell to the canvas and failed to get up by the mandatory 10 count.

It was no contest as Robinson rekindled memories of the boxer once rated as the "best ever pound for pound." Robinson first gained the middleweight crown in 1951 when he beat Jake LaMotta and then regained it later in the year when he beat Randy Turpin after losing to the Englishman on points.

The 35-year-old Robinson, also a former welterweight champion, gave up the crown for a show business career in 1952. But the call of the ring was too strong and he resumed boxing in January, after a $2^1/_2$-year layoff.

December 10

MILESTONES IN SPORTS

1965

Emile Griffith, defending his world welterweight title for an 11th time, scored a unanimous 15-round decision over Manny Gonzalez at New York.

1968

Heavyweight champion Joe Frazier needed 15 rounds to defend his crown with a unanimous decision over Oscar Bonavena at Philadelphia.

1971

The New York Mets gave up on fireballing righthander Nolan Ryan, trading the 24-year-old along with three prospects to California for six-time All-Star shortstop Jim Fregosi.

1971

Kareem Abdul-Jabbar scored a career-high 55 points as the Milwaukee Bucks raised their record to 25–4 with a 120–104 victory over Boston at Milwaukee.

1975

Bill Veeck, the maverick owner who once sent a midget to bat for the St. Louis Browns, was readmitted to baseball when A.L. owners voted to allow him to purchase the Chicago White Sox from John Allyn for $9.75 million.

1982

Michael Dokes claimed the WBA heavyweight championship with a first-round technical knockout of Mike Weaver at Las Vegas.

1992

The NHL expanded to 26 teams with the addition of California and Florida franchises.

1989 Largent Gets Record

Seattle quarterback Dave Krieg's one-yard touchdown pass to Curt Warner with 3:51 remaining gave the Seahawks a 24–17 National Football League victory over Cincinnati , but an earlier scoring pass drew more attention.

Record-setting Seattle receiver **Steve Largent.**

That came just before halftime when Krieg, looking for a secondary receiver after a pattern had broken down, found veteran Steve Largent open in the back of the end zone. The 10-yard touchdown reception was the record-setting 100th of Largent's NFL career, moving him past former Green Bay great Don Hutson on the all-time list.

The catch also enabled the 35-year-old Largent to become the NFL's first 13,000-yard receiver.

A STAR IS BORN

1959: Mark Aguirre, a current National Basketball Association forward.

★ ★ ★

DEATH OF A LEGEND

1946: Walter Johnson (baseball).

★ ★ ★

1977: Adolph Rupp (basketball).

1977 Jockey Tops $6 Million

Little Steve Cauthen, horse racing's 17-year-old wonder, became the first jockey to earn purses totaling $6 million in one year when he rode Little Happiness to victory in a six-furlong sprint at Aqueduct.

The sixth-race victory, worth $15,000, pushed the 96-pound wonder past the magic mark with $7,540 to spare. The Kentucky farmboy had entered the meet needing $14,760 for the milestone and he picked up $7,300 with a first-race victory and a fourth-race second-place finish.

Little Happiness, a 3-year-old filly, was Cauthen's 475th winner of the year. The victory drew boisterous shouts from the fans, handshakes from fellow jockeys and a trophy from the New York Racing Association.

Cauthen had reached the previously uncharted territory of $5 million in October. He rode the first half of the year as a 16-year-old apprentice with a weight allowance, but the victories just kept right on coming when he made the switch to journeyman status.

Racing's Six Million Dollar Man has recorded one six-winner day, four five-winner days and 13 four-winner days.

1965 Robinson Ends Boxing Career

Sugar Ray Robinson, boxing's most popular champion in an era when the sport was king, ended his 25-year career in a gaudy but heartwarming retirement ceremony at New York's Madison Square Garden.

Robinson, who posted a 174–19–6 record over 25 years, was honored by a packed house and a number of celebrities who gathered ring side. The 44-year-old, who entered the ring for a last time dressed in his familiar trunks and robe, was greeted by a deafening ovation and four of the five former champions he had dethroned for the middleweight crown in an eight-year span.

On hand, also decked out in fighting garb, were Randy Turpin, who Robinson defeated in 1951, Carl (Bobo) Olson (1955), Gene Fullmer (1957) and Carmen Basilio (1958). Missing was Jake LaMotta, the champion Robinson had defeated in 1951 when he claimed the title for a first time. Robinson also held the welterweight title from 1946–51.

After speeches from various dignitaries, Robinson took the microphone for a brief farewell. Then it was all over and the "best fighter pound for pound boxing had ever seen" departed as Joel McCrea serenaded him with "Auld Lang Syne."

Sugar Ray Robinson, *pictured with manager George Gainford in 1939, was a talented 17-year-old when he began his long career.*

DECEMBER

11

MILESTONES · IN SPORTS ·

1949

In the battle of Chicago, Bears quarterback Johnny Lujack broke Sammy Baugh's one-game pass yardage record (446) when he threw for 468 yards and six touchdowns in a 52–21 victory over the Cardinals.

1950

Major league owners ousted Commissioner A.B. (Happy) Chandler, voting 9–7 against renewing his contract for another term.

1960

The Los Angeles Rams brought an end to the four-year, 47-game touchdown-throwing streak of Baltimore quarterback Johnny Unitas with a 10–3 victory over the Colts at the Memorial Coliseum.

1972

New York's Don Maynard caught seven passes and passed Raymond Berry on the all-time NFL career receptions list with 631, but the Jets dropped a 24–16 decision to the Oakland Raiders.

1977

Philadelphia's Tom Bladon set an NHL record for defensemen when he scored eight points (four goals, four assists) in the Flyers' 11–1 victory over Cleveland at Philadelphia.

1983

John Henry became the first racehorse to pass the $4 million barrier when he captured the Hollywood (Fla.) Turf Cup with Chris McCarron in saddle.

1949

Browns Complete Four-Year Sweep

The Cleveland Browns, one of the most dominant teams in the history of professional football, brought down the curtain on the All-America Football Conference with a 21–7 victory over San Francisco in the league's fourth and final championship game.

Dub Jones, *part of Cleveland's unstoppable AAFC offensive arsenal.*

The Browns, who compiled a 52–4–3 record over four seasons and won all four title games, ignored the mud and rainy conditions at Cleveland's Municipal Stadium in dispatching the 49ers. They scored touchdowns in the first, third and fourth periods and let their rock-solid defense take care of the rest.

Edgar Jones got Cleveland on the board with a two-yard run and Marion Motley added to the lead with a 63-yard burst off tackle in the third period. When San Francisco cut the lead in half on Frankie Albert's 23-yard pass to Paul Salata early in the fourth quarter, Browns chief engineer Otto Graham drove his team to the clinching touchdown on 10 plays.

The four-yard TD run by Dub Jones with six minutes remaining closed the door on the maverick circuit. The Browns, 49ers and Colts will begin play next season in the National Football League under a merger agreement.

1969

Toomey Sets Record

Olympic champion Bill Toomey, finally realizing his dream after nine previous misses, put together a strong second-day performance that lifted him to a world-record total of 8,417 points during decathlon competition in the Southern Pacific Amateur Athletic Union meet at UCLA.

Toomey made his 10th run at West German Kurt Bondlin's 2-year-old world record a successful one. He entered the final day of competition needing 3,872 points and came away with 3,969, including a career-best 14–0¼ pole vault.

Toomey also ran the 110-meter hurdles in 14.3 seconds, threw the discus 152–6, hurled the javelin 215–8 and ran the 1,500 meters in 4:39.4. Highlights of his first day of competition included a career-best shot put of 47–2¼, a 10.3 in the 100 meters and a 25–5½ long jump.

Fresno State's John Warkentin finished a distant second with 7,440 points.

A STAR IS BORN

1924: Felix (Doc) Blanchard, a three-time All-America running back for Army and the 1945 Heisman Trophy winner. He was Army's Mr. Inside and teammate Glenn Davis was Mr. Outside.

★ ★ ★

DEATH OF A LEGEND

1959: Jim Bottomley (baseball).

★ ★ ★

1977

Winless Bucs Break Jinx

Mike Washington, Richard Wood and Greg Johnson scored touchdowns on interceptions and Tampa Bay exploded out of its two-year funk with a 33–14 victory at New Orleans – the first triumph in Buccaneers history after 26 consecutive losses.

The victory touched off a wild celebration that started in the final minute of the game with Bucs players chanting, "It's disgraceful, it's disgraceful" at the Saints. That was a reference to a pregame comment by New Orleans quarterback Archie Manning that it would be "disgraceful" to lose to the Bucs.

"Whatever Archie Manning said, I agree with him," said Bucs Coach John McKay. "He said it would be a disgrace to lose, and it is."

The Bucs, who had never scored on an interception in their two seasons, got a 45-yard return by Washington in the third quarter and a 10-yarder by Wood in the fourth. Johnson caught a deflected Manning pass in the end zone to put icing on the cake. The 33 points were a team record.

Tampa Bay picked off six passes and recorded five sacks.

A STAR IS BORN

1912: Henry Armstrong, an outstanding boxer who held the featherweight, lightweight and welterweight titles simultaneously in 1938.

★ ★ ★

1932: Bob Pettit, a basketball Hall of Fame forward for 11 NBA seasons in the 1950s and '60s. He was the first player to score 20,000 career points.

★ ★ ★

1946: Emerson Fittipaldi, a Brazilian auto racer who won two Formula One championships and an Indianapolis 500 (1989).

★ ★ ★

1962: Tracy Austin, a two-time U.S. Open champion and the youngest player to win the prestigious event. .

DEATH OF A LEGEND

1977: Frank Boucher (hockey).

1965 SAYERS TIES TD RECORD

Chicago rookie Gale Sayers exploded for a National Football League record-tying six touchdowns and the Bears rolled to a lopsided 61–20 victory over San Francisco, avenging a 52–24 season-opening loss to the 49ers.

Sayers set the stage for the Wrigley Field crowd when he caught an 80-yard scoring bomb from quarterback Rudy Bukich in the opening quarter and then added touchdown runs of 21 and 7 yards in the second period. After bringing his TD total to five with third-quarter runs of 50 and 1 yards, the former Kansas star capped his big day with a scintillating 85-yard punt return.

Sayers, who picked up 113 yards on nine carries, brought his season touchdown total to 21, breaking the NFL record of 20 set by Baltimore's Lenny Moore last year. The six-touchdown game matched the 1929 effort of the Chicago Cardinals' Ernie Nevers against the Bears and a 1951 outburst by Cleveland's Dub Jones against Chicago.

Chicago running back **Gale Sayers.**

DECEMBER 12

MILESTONES IN SPORTS

1965

In a wild shootout at Baltimore, Paul Hornung scored five touchdowns and the Green Bay Packers powered their way to a 42–27 NFL victory over the Colts.

1971

The Los Angeles Lakers set an NBA record when they won their 21st consecutive game, a 104–95 decision over the Atlanta Hawks. Milwaukee had won 20 straight the previous year.

1971

Chicago great Bobby Hull became the NHL's fifth 1,000-point scorer when he assisted on a goal during the Blackhawks' 5–3 victory over Minnesota at Chicago.

1977

Los Angeles forward Kermit Washington, who sent Houston's Rudy Tomjanovich to the hospital with a roundhouse punch during a December 9 game, was fined $10,000 and suspended at least 60 days by NBA Commissioner Larry O'Brien.

1986

James (Bonecrusher) Smith captured the WBA heavyweight championship with a first-round technical knockout over Tim Witherspoon at New York.

1987

With Mookie Blaylock recording an NCAA single-game record with 13 steals, Oklahoma set a team record with 34 en route to a 152–84 victory over Centenary.

1937 'SKINS, BAUGH TAME BEARS

Washington rookie Sammy Baugh, adding a new dimension to the run-dominated game with his rifle arm, broke a fourth-quarter tie with a 35-yard touchdown pass to Ed Justice and the Redskins held on to record a 28–21 victory over Chicago in the National Football League championship game at Wrigley Field.

Baugh completed 17 of 35 passes for 335 yards and three touchdowns against the bigger Bears, two of the TD strikes coming in the final period to wipe out a 21–14 Chicago advantage. The Bears had built their lead on a 10-yard Jack Manders run and a pair of Bernie Masterson TD passes – 37 yards to Manders and three to Ed Manske.

But Baugh, a Texas Christian University product, fired 40 yards to Wayne Millner for a third-quarter touchdown and tied the game with an exciting 78-yard strike to Millner after almost getting sacked in the final period. Baugh's game-winner to Justice was set up by a fake punt.

The Redskins' victory was a perfect conclusion to their first season in Washington.

Washington rookie 'slinger' **Sammy Baugh.**

1981 ALI RETIRES AFTER LOSING TO BERBICK

Muhammad Ali, conceding that "Father Time caught up with me" after losing a unanimous 10-round decision to Trevor Berbick, ended a colorful, controversial and successful boxing career that had started 20 years earlier when he fought under the name Cassius Clay.

The 39-year-old Ali, who won the heavyweight championship three times in a career that got a jump start with a gold-medal victory in the 1960 Olympic Games at Rome, called it quits for the third time after being pounded by the 27-year-old Berbick in a bout at Nassau on the Bahamas. "I could feel his youth," Ali said. "I'm finished. I've got to face the facts. For the first time, I could feel that I'm 40 years old."

Ali, who claimed his first heavyweight title with a knockout of Sonny Liston in 1964, finished with a 56–5 record, including career-ending losses to heavyweight champion Larry Holmes and Berbick. Holmes scored a technical knockout over Ali last October when he ended a two-year retirement. Ali's other losses were to Joe Frazier, Ken Norton and Leon Spinks, fighters he also defeated at least once in his storied career.

Ali said he would have retired even if the decision had gone the other way. "I didn't have the ability to make certain attacks. I didn't have any excuses. I'm finished."

DECEMBER

13

1983 GRETZKY SCORING STREAK HITS 31

Edmonton gunner Wayne Gretzky broke his own National Hockey League record when he scored in his 31st consecutive game, but The Great One was upstaged by the New York Islanders and center Butch Goring during a contest at the Nassau Coliseum.

With Goring notching four goals and Mike Bossy adding two, the Islanders produced a one-sided 8–5 victory for the 15,850 New Yorkers who braved a snowstorm to see this battle of top NHL teams. The crowd got its money's worth early when Bossy scored twice in a three-minute span of the first period and Goring added his first as the Islanders raced to a 5–1 lead and never looked back.

With Goring scoring twice in the second stanza, the lead increased to 7–2. He closed out his big night at 17:15 of the final period.

Gretzky's assist on a Willy Lindstrom goal broke his own record 30-game scoring streak and he added his 300th NHL goal in the closing minutes. But it was too little, too late as the Islanders recorded their ninth straight victory over the NHL's top point team – all three meetings last year during the regular season, four consecutive in the Stanley Cup finals and both meetings so far this year.

A STAR IS BORN

1913: Archie Moore, the world light-heavyweight champion from 1952–60 in a boxing career that produced a 199–26–8 record.

★ ★ ★

1924: Larry Doby, the man who broke the A.L. color barrier in 1947 with Cleveland. He was a .283 hitter over 13 major league seasons (1947–59).

★ ★ ★

1938: Gus Johnson, an outstanding NBA guard for 10 seasons in the 1960s and '70s, nine of them with the Baltimore Bullets.

★ ★ ★

1943: Ferguson Jenkins, a righthanded pitcher who recorded 284 victories in a 19-year career that ended in 1983.

★ ★ ★

1960: Richard Dent, a current National Football League defensive end.

★ ★ ★

1961: Gary Zimmerman, a current National Football League offensive tackle.

★ ★ ★

1969: Sergei Fedorov, a current National Hockey League center.

★ ★ ★

DEATH OF A LEGEND

1990: Alice Marble (tennis).

★ ★ ★

1977 EVANSVILLE TEAM DIES IN CRASH

A chartered DC-3 carrying the University of Evansville's basketball team among its 29 passengers crashed into a hill in rain and dense fog near Dress Regional Airport, killing everybody aboard.

The plane, en route to Nashville, Tenn., where the team was scheduled to catch a bus for Murfreesboro for a game at Middle Tennessee State, apparently experienced engine trouble and tried to turn back shortly after takeoff. The crash site, about a mile and a half from the airport, was littered with letter jackets and gym bags, many bearing the logo of the Evansville Aces.

Four people were alive when help reached the crash site, but they all died later. Rescuers were unable to check inside the wreckage because of the fires. Among the dead were 14 players, Coach Bob Watson and school-associated personnel ranging from team managers to alumni. The freshman-dominated team, playing its first season in Division I, had won one of its first four games under a new coaching staff. Evansville Athletic Director Jim Byers said classes were being canceled and a memorial service was being planned.

The airplane tragedy was the first involving a sports team since 1970, when members of the Marshall and Wichita State football squads were killed in crashes six weeks apart.

MILESTONES IN SPORTS

1975

Carlos Monzon retained his WBA middleweight championship with a fifth-round knockout of Tunesian Gratien Tonna in Paris.

1976

The Pacific-8 Conference, looking to become the Pacific-10, extended invitations for Western Athletic Conference powers Arizona and Arizona State to join.

1978

An NBA rarity: Boston's Dave Cowens fouled out as a player and later was ejected as a coach from the Celtics' 112–105 loss to Houston.

1980

San Diego quarterback Dan Fouts passed for 339 yards in a 21–14 victory over Seattle and set two NFL records: most passing yards in a season (4,407) and most 300-yard games in a season (7).

1980

Niatross, with Clint Galbraith in sulky, easily defeated a field of five in an invitation race at Greenwood Raceway and became harness racing's first $2 million career winner.

1983 DETROIT DEFEATS DENVER IN 186-184 SLUGFEST

A layup and two free throws by Isiah Thomas gave Detroit a six-point lead and the Pistons held on for a frantic 186–184 triple-overtime victory over Denver in the highest-scoring game in National Basketball Association history.

The game at Denver's McNichols Sports Arena produced several records, including a combined total of 370 points that surpassed the previous mark of 337 (San Antonio-Milwaukee in 1982). The teams also combined for a record 144 field goals, Detroit set a team mark with 74 field goals and both Detroit and Denver topped the previous league high for points by a single team.

Thomas was the main man for Detroit with 47 points, while John Long added 41 and Kelly Tripucka 35. Denver's Kiki Vandeweghe led all scorers with 51 and Alex English contributed 47.

The game was tied at 145 at the end of regulation, at 159 after the first overtime and at 171 after the second.

Thomas hit a key 3-point shot in the first overtime and Tripucka scored all 12 of Detroit's points in the second extra session.

Detroit guard **Isiah Thomas** *soared for 47 points in the highest-scoring NBA game ever played.*

1984 Dickerson Rushes In

Los Angeles running back Eric Dickerson finished his record-breaking season with a 98-yard effort, but the San Francisco 49ers spoiled the occasion by handing the Rams a 19–16 loss at Candlestick Park.

Dickerson, who sat out most of the fourth quarter, finished with a one-season National Football League-record 2,105 yards, 102 more than Buffalo's O.J. Simpson gained in 1973. Dickerson had broken Simpson's record (2,003 yards) last week when he rambled for 215 yards in a game against Houston.

But it took Dickerson 15 games to catch Simpson, who played only 14 in his record-setting campaign. The National Football League has since gone to a 16-week season. Dickerson completed his 14th game with 1,792 yards on 326 carries.

The victory was San Francisco's regular-season-record 15th and ninth in a row. Quarterback Joe Montana led the way with a pair of early touchdown passes that built a 14–3 lead. Dickerson gained all but three of his yards in the first half.

A STAR IS BORN

1922: Charley Trippi, a Hall of Fame halfback and quarterback who rushed for 3,506 yards in nine NFL seasons with the Chicago Cardinals (1947–55).

★ ★ ★

1939: Ernie Davis, the 1961 Heisman Trophy-winning running back from Syracuse who died of leukemia before he could play in the NFL.

★ ★ ★

1946: Stan Smith, a former tennis star who won the 1971 U.S. Open and 1972 Wimbledon singles championships.

★ ★ ★

DEATH OF A LEGEND

1920: George Gipp (football).

★ ★ ★

1980: Elston Howard (baseball).

★ ★ ★

1985: Roger Maris (baseball).

★ ★ ★

1960 New Teams Draft Players

New York Yankee pitchers **Eli Grba** *(left) and* **Bobby Shantz**, *the first players selected in baseball's first expansion draft.*

In an unprecedented draft that signaled a new era of baseball growth and expansion, the two new members of the American League stocked their rosters and began planning strategy for their inaugural seasons.

The Washington Senators and Los Angeles Angels, the newcomers to a baseball fraternity that had remained 16 strong for more than a half century, selected 28 players apiece from the pool of 120 submitted by the eight holdover clubs. The Senators and Angels paid $75,000 per player – a total of $2.1 million.

They also were given the option of drafting up to eight minor league players at $25,000 apiece. The Angels picked three, the Senators two.

Angels General Manager Fred Haney opened the proceedings at A.L. President Joe Cronin's office by selecting 26-year-old New York Yankee pitcher Eli Grba. Senators G.M. Ed Doherty opted for Yankee left-hander Bobby Shantz. The selections continued alternately, with both teams looking for a good mix of veterans and youngsters.

1988 Miami Wins First Game

A 17-foot jump shot by Los Angeles Clippers forward Ken Norman bounced off the rim with two seconds remaining and the expansion Miami Heat held on for an 89–88 victory – their first as a member of the National Basketball Association after 17 losses.

When Norman's shot bounced away, the entire Miami team raced to center court at the Los Angeles Sports Arena to celebrate the history-making moment. The 17-game losing streak was an NBA record to open a season, but it fell three games short of Philadelphia's 1972–73 record for one-season ineptitude and seven games short of Cleveland's two-season (1981-83) losing run.

Miami's scoring was evenly spread among Pat Cummings (15 points), Grant Long (15), Billy Thompson (15) and Jon Sundvold (14). The Heat built a 12-point second-half lead (72-60), but had to fight off a frantic Clippers rally.

Los Angeles gradually narrowed its deficit and finally scored six consecutive points to pull within 85–84 with 2:23 remaining. Cummings stretched the lead with a jumper, but Danny Manning answered for the Clippers. Rory Sparrow and Manning matched jump shots to set up the tense conclusion.

Ironically, the Clippers also were the victims for the first NBA victory by the expansion Charlotte Hornets. The Heat's victory just took a little longer and was a little more dramatic.

DECEMBER 14

MILESTONES • IN SPORTS •

1920

Jack Dempsey toyed with Bill Brennan before knocking him out in the 12th round and retaining his heavyweight championship at New York's Madison Square Garden.

1965

Kansas City fullback Mack Lee Hill, 25, died after going into convulsions following an operation to repair a ruptured knee ligament. Hill had suffered the injury two days earlier against Buffalo.

1982

Los Angeles sniper Marcel Dionne joined hockey's exclusive 500-goal club when he connected during a 7–2 Kings loss at Washington.

1985

UCLA needed a record eight overtimes to post a 1–0 victory over American University and claim the NCAA soccer championship.

1986

Miami quarterback Dan Marino, topping the 400-yard passing plateau for an NFL-record seventh time, fired a 20-yard overtime strike to Mark Duper and the Dolphins claimed a 37–31 NFL victory over the Los Angeles Rams.

1991

Michigan wide receiver Desmond Howard was a runaway Heisman winner, outdistancing Florida State quarterback Casey Weldon by 1,574 points.

DECEMBER 15

1973 WALTON GANG PREVAILS

UCLA's Walton Gang, playing without its leader for more than 21 minutes, shook off adversity and overpowered North Carolina State, 84–66, in a much-ballyhooed battle of unbeaten basketball powers at the St. Louis Arena.

With 6-foot-11 Bill Walton chained to the bench for 21:07 after picking up his fourth foul midway through the first half, the Bruins' NCAA-record 79-game winning streak appeared to be in jeopardy. The Wolfpack, featuring 7-4 center Tom Burleson and high-flying forward David Thompson, had entered the nationally televised contest with a two-season 29-game winning streak and was primed to dethrone a champion.

But the Waltonless Bruins, winners of seven straight NCAA Tournament crowns, refused to wilt. With Keith Wilkes and Dave Meyers carrying the load, UCLA stayed close until Walton returned with 9:53 remaining.

Walton scored the first basket of a nine-point run that broke a 54–54 tie and opened a lead. Wilkes, who held Thompson to 17 points while scoring 27, contributed four to the winning run. Walton scored 11 points and grabbed 10 rebounds in 18:53 of play.

N.C.-State, coming off an undefeated 1972–73 season, sat out last year's NCAA Tournament while on probation for recruiting violations.

A STAR IS BORN

1940: Nick Buoniconti, a former Miami linebacker (1969–76) who played for the Dolphins' 1973 and '74 Super Bowl champions.

★ ★ ★

DEATH OF A LEGEND

1953: Ed Barrow (baseball).

★ ★ ★

1968: Jess Willard (boxing).

★ ★ ★

MILESTONES • IN SPORTS •

1955

Minneapolis defeated Syracuse, 135–133, in a three-overtime thriller that set an NBA record for most combined points in a game.

1970

Australian lefthander Rod Laver passed a tennis milestone when he became the first to top $200,000 in one-year winnings.

1963

Cleveland's Jim Brown ran for 125 yards on 28 carries in the Browns' 27–20 victory at Washington, pushing his NFL one-season record to 1,863 yards.

1973

Tennessee 11, Temple 6: the lowest-scoring college basketball game since 1938.

1973

Canadian Sandy Hawley rode Charlie Jr. to victory in the third race at Laurel Race Course, becoming the first jockey to record 500 wins in one year.

1980

Dave Winfield became the highest-paid player in team sports history when the New York Yankees signed him to a 10-year free-agent contract worth an estimated $16 million.

1974 A's CATFISH TO TEST FREE-AGENT WATERS

Oakland righthander Jim (Catfish) Hunter, the reigning Cy Young winner and American League earned-run average champion, became the most prominent unrestricted free agent in baseball history when arbitrator Peter Seitz ruled in his favor while hearing a dispute with Athletics Owner Charles O. Finley.

The 28-year-old Hunter, now free to sell his services to any of the 24 major league teams, could become the highest-paid performer in the game. He will not come cheap after a 25–12 1974 campaign and a five-year stretch that has produced 106 victories.

With Hunter leading the way, the A's have captured three straight World Series.

The Hunter-Finley dispute stemmed from a contract issue regarding deferred payments. Hunter contended Finley did not honor the agreement and therefore voided the contract. Finley said there was no contract violation, just disagreement over interpretation.

While certainly interesting, the case does not have long-term implications for other players or the reserve clause in general.

1946 BEARS CLAW GIANTS

A 19-yard touchdown run by Chicago quarterback Sid Luckman broke a fourth-quarter tie and the Bears went on to capture their fifth National Football League championship with a 24–14 victory over the New York Giants in a scandal-marred contest at the Polo Grounds.

The title game opened with a cloud of suspicion swirling around Giants quarterback Frank Filchock. Reports had circulated that Filchock and fullback Merle Hapes had been offered bribes by professional gamblers. Hapes, admitting the charge, was suspended but Filchock, denying the accusations, was allowed to play.

Filchock fought through the adversity and fired a pair of touchdown passes – 38 yards to Frank Liebel and five to Steve Filipowicz – as the Giants surprisingly held the powerful Bears to a 14–14 tie through three quarters.

But Chicago broke the game open in the fourth when Luckman faked a handoff on an apparent sweep left and bolted down the right sideline for the winning score.

New York Giants Coach **Steve Owen** *(right) with quarterback* **Frank Filchock**, *the focus of a pre-title game scandal.*

MILESTONES
• IN SPORTS •

1929

The Blackhawks christened new Chicago Stadium with a 3–1 NHL victory over the Pittsburgh Pirates.

1930

Golf grand slam winner Bobby Jones was honored as the first recipient of the Amateur Athletic Union's prestigious Sullivan Award.

1940

Heavyweight champion Joe Louis dashed the hopes of challenger Al McCoy with a sixth-round technical knockout in a title match at Boston.

1972

The Miami Dolphins posted a 16–0 victory over Baltimore, completing the first unbeaten and untied 14-game regular season in NFL history.

1974

Green Bay Coach Dan Devine became head of Notre Dame's football program, replacing Ara Parseghian.

1979

Minnesota defensive end Jim Marshall played in his NFL-record 282nd consecutive regular-season game before ending his outstanding 20-year career.

1973

2,003: Simpson's Rushing Odyssey

Buffalo's O.J. Simpson, ending his pursuit of Jim Brown's rushing record in style, rambled for 200 yards in a 34–14 victory over the New York Jets at Shea Stadium and raised his season total to an incredible 2,003.

Buffalo record-setter **O.J. Simpson** *at work.*

Simpson, needing just 61 yards to surpass Brown's National Football League one-season rushing record of 1,863, passed that mark when he ran for six yards just 10:34 into the game. After a brief celebration, Simpson set his sights on the magic 2,000-yard plateau, a barrier once beyond the comprehension of most football fans.

The Bills, having built a big lead over the hapless Jets, spent the second half trying to get Simpson his yardage. The former Southern Cal star brought his total to 2,003 when he ran seven yards with 6:28 remaining. He went to the sideline, where he stayed the rest of the game.

Simpson's 2,003 yards were achieved on 332 carries. He enjoyed a record 11 100-yard games and reached 200 three times, including 250 and 219-yard efforts in games against New England.

1945

Rams Win on Safety

A wind-blown pass that struck the goalpost and bounced back into the end zone gave the Cleveland Rams a first-quarter safety and the ultimate winning margin in their 15–14 National Football League championship game victory over the Washington Redskins at Cleveland.

Playing in a sub-zero temperature with gusty winds that made the afternoon miserable, the Rams and Redskins waged a spirited battle. The safety occurred when Washington quarterback Sammy Baugh, backed up against his own end zone, tried to throw deep and watched his wobbly pass blow into the upright, breaking a scoreless tie.

The Redskins bounced back when Frank Filchock, replacing Baugh, threw a 38-yard touchdown pass to Steve Bagarus in the second quarter, but Cleveland reclaimed a 9–7 advantage on Bob Waterfield's 37-yard strike to Jim Benton moments later.

The safety loomed big in the third quarter when Waterfield connected on a 53-yard TD pass to Jim Gillette and the Rams missed the extra point. Filchock's eight-yard touchdown pass to Bob Seymour closed out the scoring.

Washington kicker Joe Aguirre missed field goal attempts of 46 and 31 yards in the fourth quarter.

Washington's 'Mr. Typical Fan,' and the goalpost struck by **Sammy Baugh's** *pass.*

DECEMBER

16

A STAR IS BORN

1962: William (The Refrigerator) Perry, a current National Football League defensive tackle.

★ ★ ★

DEATH OF A LEGEND

1940: Billy Hamilton (baseball).

★ ★ ★

1980

Jets Taste Futility

Shorthanded goals by Bob Bourne and Anders Kallur in a four-goal New York first period sent the second-year Winnipeg Jets on their way to a National Hockey League-record 30th consecutive game without a victory—a 6–2 loss to the Islanders at Nassau Coliseum.

The Islanders made quick work of the young Jets by jumping to a 4–0 advantage in an eight-minute span of the opening stanza. Kallur struck first at 13:23, beating goalie Pierre Hamel. Bourne scored shorthanded at 16:09, Kallur beat Hamel in a shorthanded situation moments later and Denis Potvin added a power-play goal.

The Jets, who have not won since mid-October, got goals from Danny Geoffrion and Tim Trimper, but they were too little too late. The powerful Islanders were in control all the way.

The previous NHL mark for futility belonged to the 1975–76 Kansas City Scouts, who went 27 games without a victory.

DECEMBER

17

A STAR IS BORN

1939: Peter Snell, the New Zealander who captured both the 800-meter and 1,500-meter gold medals at the 1964 Tokyo Summer Olympic Games.

★ ★ ★

1957: Bob Ojeda, a current major league pitcher.

★ ★ ★

MILESTONES IN SPORTS

1972

O.J. Simpson gained 101 yards in Buffalo's 24–17 victory over Washington and captured the NFL rushing title with 1,261 yards, 45 more than the Redskins' Larry Brown.

1974

Chris McCarron, a 19-year-old apprentice jockey, set a one-year victory record when he made Ohmylove his 516th winner in a seven-furlong test at Laurel Race Course.

1983

Angel Cordero rode Chieftain's Command to victory in the Firenze Handicap at Aqueduct Park, equaling Bill Shoemaker's one-season record for stakes winners with 46.

1984

Miami quarterback Dan Marino fired four touchdown passes, extending his one-season NFL-record total to 48, as the Dolphins posted a regular season-closing 28–21 victory over Dallas at the Orange Bowl.

1991

The rout of the century: Cleveland defeated Miami, 148–80, in the most lopsided NBA game in history.

1933

HUNGRY BEARS WIN FIRST TITLE GAME

Chicago end Billy Karr caught a lateral from Bill Hewitt and raced 19 yards for the winning score as the Bears posted a 23–21 victory over the New York Giants in the National Football League's first championship game.

Chicago's helmetless **Bill Hewitt** *laterals to* **Billy Karr** *on the winning touchdown play in the NFL's first official championship game.*

Karr's touchdown capped a see-saw battle that pitted Eastern Division winner New York (11–3) against the Western Division-champion Bears (10–2–1) at Chicago's Wrigley Field. Before 1933, the NFL had consisted of one division and the title had been decided by regular-season play.

George Halas' Bears broke on top with a pair of Jack Manders field goals, but the Giants answered with a 29-yard Harry Newman-to-Red Badgro touchdown pass. After Manders had kicked a 15-yard field goal in the third quarter, New York scored again for a 14–9 lead.

Karr scored the first of his two TDs on an eight-yard pass from Bronko Nagurski to reclaim the lead for Chicago in the third quarter, but Newman hit Ken Strong for eight yards to put the Giants back on top in the fourth.

The Bears' game-winner came with less than a minute remaining. Nagurski took a hand-off and fired a 13-yard pass to Hewitt, who lateraled to Karr in full stride near the sideline.

1944

FRITSCH RUINS GIANT DREAM

Fullback Ted Fritsch ran for one touchdown and caught a 26-yard pass for another and the Green Bay Packers made the second-quarter scores stand up for a 14–7 victory over the New York Giants in the National Football League championship game at the Polo Grounds.

Played before 46,016 fans, the game featured teams that had managed eight regular-season victories despite war-depleted rosters. The Giants had reached the title game behind a defense that had allowed just 75 points in 10 games.

But the Packers struck twice in the second quarter and that was all they needed. Fritsch's first touchdown came on a one-yard fourth-down run and the second came on a pass from quarterback Irv Comp, who used the aging Don Hutson as a decoy.

Hutson lined up on the left side, slanted across the field and began waving his arms near the right sideline. Comp faked a throw to him, whirled and hit Fritsch all alone in the flat. Fritsch ran untouched into the end zone.

1956

FIRED-UP ILLINI END DONS' RUN

George BonSalle scored 19 points and a fired-up Illinois team handed San Francisco an embarrassing 62–33 thrashing at Champaign, Ill – the Dons' first defeat after an NCAA-record 60 straight victories.

San Francisco's streak, which had started in December 1954 and encompassed two NCAA Tournament championships, came to a thudding halt as the Fighting Illini outplayed the Dons in every facet of the game.

The 4–0 Illini raced to an 8–0 lead and did not allow San Francisco to score from the field in the first three minutes. Using a tough man-to-man defense, Illinois built a 31–15 halftime lead and increased the margin to as much as 32 after intermission.

"I don't know if we could have beaten Illinois even if we had played our best," said San Francisco Coach Phil Woolpert, who had directed the Dons to a 5–0 record without graduated stars Bill Russell and K.C. Jones. "Illinois was really fired up."

A STAR IS BORN

1886: Ty Cobb, a Hall of Fame outfielder who compiled a .367 average and 4,191 hits over 24 seasons. He is considered by some the greatest player in baseball history.

★ ★ ★

DEATH OF A LEGEND

1960: Art Nehf (baseball).

★ ★ ★

1971: Bobby Jones (golf).

★ ★ ★

1974: Harry Hooper (baseball).

★ ★ ★

DECEMBER 18

1932 BEARS GO INDOORS, CAPTURE NFL TITLE

Red Grange caught a one-yard fourth-quarter scoring pass from Bronko Nagurski and the Chicago Bears added a safety for a 9–0 victory over the Portsmouth Spartans in a playoff game that decided the National Football League championship.

The one-game playoff, necessitated when both teams finished their regular seasons with six victories, was played indoors. Scheduled for Wrigley Field, the contest was switched to Chicago Stadium because of snow and extreme cold.

Because of an improvised dirt-covered field that was 80 yards long and flanked on both sides by walls, special ground rules were set up to keep the ball in the middle of the field and to cover any strange situations that might arise. None did as the teams played three scoreless quarters.

The Bears finally broke through in the fourth after gaining a first down at the Portsmouth 7-yard line. Nagurski ran six yards on first down and then was stopped on two more tries. He took a fourth-down handoff, retreated the necessary five yards into the Bears backfield and lofted a game-deciding pass to Grange. A bad end zone snap gave Chicago a late safety.

1949 EAGLES SLOSH PAST RAMS

The Philadelphia connection of quarterback **Tommy Thompson** *(left) and tight end* **Pete Pihos** *was too much for the Los Angeles Rams in the NFL title game.*

With Los Angeles' high-powered passing attack grounded by a driving rain and muddy field, the Philadelphia Eagles splashed their way to a 14–0 victory over the Rams and claimed their second straight National Football League championship in the first title game played on the West Coast.

The Eagles, a burly, run-oriented team that relied on defense to keep the score close, thrived under the adverse conditions they faced at the Memorial Coliseum. With NFL rushing champion Steve Van Buren gaining 196 yards on 31 carries (both title-game records), Philadelphia controlled the ball and kept it out of the hands of Los Angeles quarterbacks Bob Waterfield and Norm Van Brocklin.

The Rams, who had scored 360 points in 12 league games, never could get going on the wet field. They managed just seven first downs, none by rushing, and gained 98 yards in the air. One of their punts was blocked by Eagles rookie Leo Skladany, who returned it two yards for a touchdown.

Philadelphia's first TD had come on a 31-yard second-quarter pass from Tommy Thompson to Pete Pihos. Van Buren took care of the rest.

MILESTONES IN SPORTS

1930

The illustrious reign of Adolph Rupp as Kentucky basketball coach opened with a 67–19 victory over Georgetown (Ky.) at Lexington.

1964

Cincinnati's Oscar Robertson scored a career-high 56 points, including 18 in the final quarter, as the Royals posted a 111–107 NBA victory over the Los Angeles Lakers.

1967

Joe Frazier, reinforcing his status as No. 1 heavyweight contender, scored a third-round technical knockout over Marion Conner at Boston Garden and raised his professional record to 19–0.

1977

Chicago's Walter Payton, who needed 199 yards to overtake O.J. Simpson's one-season rushing record, was held to 47 by the New York Giants and finished with 1,852, the third-best total in NFL history.

1977

The Tampa Bay Bucs, who had ended their NFL-record 26-game losing streak a week earlier, made it two in a row with a regular season-ending 17–7 victory over St. Louis at Tampa Stadium.

1983 GRETZKY ZIPS TO 100

Edmonton center Wayne Gretzky added yet another feather to his crowded cap when he scored two goals and a pair of assists during a 7–5 victory at Winnipeg, giving him 100 points after just 34 games this season.

In setting a National Hockey League record for fastest 100 points, Gretzky also extended his record consecutive-games point-scoring streak to 34. He got three of his points in the opening period when he assisted on Mark Messier and Ken Linseman goals and scored himself, helping the Oilers to a 4–1 lead.

He scored his second goal – and 100th point – early in the second stanza and Paul Coffey added a goal that stretched Edmonton's lead to 6–1. The goals were Nos. 36 and 37 for Gretzky and the assists were Nos. 62 and 63.

The Oilers lifted their NHL-best record to 24–7–3 for 51 points, 20 more than second-place Vancouver in the Smythe Division.

DECEMBER

19

MILESTONES

• IN SPORTS •

1913

Heavyweight champion Jack Johnson retained his title after fighting to a 10-round draw against Jim Johnson in Paris.

1917

Five teams officially began play under the banner of the National Hockey League.

1917

Montreal players Joe Malone of the Canadiens and Harry Hyland of the Wanderers became the NHL's first five-goal scorers in games against Ottawa and Toronto on the same day.

1965

Jim Brown scored his record 126th – and last – NFL touchdown and won his eighth rushing title (1,544 yards) as Cleveland closed its regular season with a 27–24 victory at St. Louis.

1971

Houston safety Ken Houston set a career and one-season record for touchdown interceptions when he performed the feat on consecutive John Hadl passes in the Oilers' 49–33 victory over San Diego.

1976

A single-engine plane that buzzed Baltimore's Memorial Stadium in the closing moments of Pittsburgh's 40–14 AFC playoff victory over the Colts crashed in the almost-empty upper deck 15 minutes after the game, injuring the pilot and three other people.

1948

Browns Go Undefeated In AAFC

Bruising fullback Marion Motley rambled for three touchdowns and Edgar Jones added two more as the Cleveland Browns continued their three-year domination of the All-America Football Conference with a 49–7 championship game rout of Buffalo and completed professional football's first undefeated, untied season.

Bruising fullback **Marion Motley** *(76) was too much for* **Buffalo** *in the AAFC championship game.*

The Bills were no match for the mighty Browns on a frigid, snowy afternoon at Cleveland Stadium. Suffocating the Bills with a defense that allowed just 167 total yards while forcing eight turnovers that led directly to six touchdowns, Cleveland took a 14–0 halftime lead on Jones' three-yard run and George Young's 18-yard return of a fumble recovery.

The Browns really turned on the offensive juice after intermission. The 232-pound Motley scored on touchdown runs of 29, 31 and five yards, Jones caught a nine-yard scoring pass from Otto Graham and Lou Saban returned one of five Buffalo interceptions 39 yards. The Browns finished with 336 total yards.

Cleveland's 15–0 season included three victories over Buffalo by a combined 122–34 score. Three National Football League teams had gone through seasons with only ties marring their record and the Chicago Bears twice had made it through perfect regular seasons, only to suffer defeat in the NFL championship game.

1984

Gretzky Reaches 1,000

Edmonton scoring machine Wayne Gretzky became the youngest player to notch 1,000 National Hockey League points when he assisted on a first-period goal during the Oilers' 7–3 victory over the Los Angeles Kings.

Gretzky blasted a shot off the post on a breakaway 1:41 into the game, but the puck bounced to teammate Mike Krushelnyski, who banged it home. The assist gave the amazing 23-year-old 1,000 points in 424 games covering less than six seasons – almost 300 games and four seasons faster than Montreal's Guy Lafleur reached the plateau.

Gretzky went on to score two goals and add three more assists in the game, raising his totals to 390 goals (28th on the career list) and 615 assists (20th). Career scoring leader Gordie Howe retired with 1,850 points over 22 campaigns.

A STAR IS BORN

1894: Ford Frick, a former N.L. president and baseball commissioner (1934–51) best remembered for putting the asterisk next to Roger Maris' home run record in 1961.

★ ★ ★

1924: Doug Harvey, a Hall of Fame defenseman for six Montreal Stanley Cup winners in a 19-year NHL career that ended in 1969.

★ ★ ★

1926: Bobby Layne, a Hall of Fame quarterback who passed for 26,768 yards over 15 NFL seasons (1948–62) with four teams.

★ ★ ★

1934: Al Kaline, a Hall of Fame outfielder over 22 seasons with the Detroit Tigers and the youngest man ever to win a batting title (.340 in 1955).

★ ★ ★

1957: Kevin McHale, a former National Basketball Association forward.

★ ★ ★

1961: Reggie White, a current National Football League defensive end.

★ ★ ★

1948

Eagles Numb Cardinals

Steve Van Buren rumbled five yards through the snow and a near-frozen Chicago defensive line to score the only touchdown of the game and give the Philadelphia Eagles their first National Football League championship – a 7–0 decision over the Cardinals at Shibe Park.

Playing in a Philadelphia blizzard that limited vision, made footing treacherous and numbed fingers and toes, neither team was able to mount much of an offensive thrust. Other than a first-quarter 68-yard Tommy Thompson-to-Jack Ferrante bomb that was called back because of an offsides penalty, there was nothing even resembling a scoring drive until the Eagles broke through in the fourth quarter.

That breakthrough was set up by a Chicago mistake. When a Ray Mallouf handoff squirted free and Philadelphia's Bucko Kilroy recovered at the Cardinal 17, the Eagles were in business. Three plays later, Van Buren, the NFL's leading rusher for two years, carried five yards for a touchdown.

MILESTONES
• IN SPORTS •

1966

The NBA awarded a new franchise to Seattle interests, bringing its membership to 11 with another team to be added before the 1967–68 season.

1973

Another 1,000-point man: Montreal's Henri Richard reached the milestone with an assist during a 2–2 tie at Buffalo.

1980

The New York Jets defeated the Dolphins, 24–17, at Miami in an NFL game televised nationally by NBC Sports – without announcers or commentators.

1981

In a record-setting start, Winnipeg's Doug Smail scored five seconds into an NHL game against St. Louis. The Jets won the matchup at Winnipeg, 5–4.

1983

Montreal glamour boy Guy Lafleur notched his 500th career goal in a 6–0 victory at New Jersey.

1979

FLYERS MATCH NHL UNBEATEN RECORD

Behn Wilson capped a desperation Philadelphia surge with a third-period power-play goal that allowed the Flyers to earn a 1–1 tie with Pittsburgh and extend their National Hockey League record-tying unbeaten streak to 28 games.

Behn Wilson's *goal kept Philadelphia's unbeaten streak intact.*

With 17,077 fans at the Philadelphia Spectrum loudly cheering them on, the Flyers came out for a supercharged final period that saw them outshoot the Penguins, 16–6. But, like the two periods before, they couldn't get the puck past goaltender Greg Millen and the frustration mounted.

Swarming all over the Penguins, the Flyers finally connected when Dennis Vervegaert found Wilson alone at the side of the net and the defenseman shot it home with 4:08 remaining, sending the crowd into delirium. The tie allowed the Flyers to match the 28-game unbeaten streak put together by the 1977–78 Montreal Canadiens.

The Penguins had taken their 1–0 lead on a first-period power-play goal by Ron Stackhouse and then turned matters over to Millen. The hot goalie extended his scoreless-period streak to five before giving up Wilson's tying goal. The 22-year-old Millen was undefeated in eight games entering the contest after sitting out seven weeks with a hamstring injury.

After the final buzzer, red and black balloons cascaded out of the stands and pre-printed cards floated down like confetti, bearing a special message: "28. You were there."

DECEMBER

20

A STAR IS BORN

1881: Branch Rickey, a 59-year executive best remembered for hiring Jackie Robinson to break baseball's color barrier in 1947.

★ ★ ★

1900: Gabby Hartnett, the Chicago Cubs' Hall of Fame catcher who batted .297 over a 20-year career that ended in 1941.

★ ★ ★

1928: Jack Christiansen, a Hall of Fame defensive back and punt returner for the Detroit Lions from 1951–58.

★ ★ ★

1942: Bob Hayes, the former 100-yard dash world record-holder, 100-meter Olympic gold medalist and All-Pro football player for the Dallas Cowboys.

★ ★ ★

DEATH OF A LEGEND

1972: Gabby Hartnett (baseball).

1981

TRACY CATCHES NAVRATILOVA

Tracy Austin, down a set and 0–2 in the second to Martina Navratilova, roared back for a convincing 2–6, 6–4, 6–2 victory in the Toyota Series final at East Rutherford, N.J., and staked her claim as the No. 1 woman player in the world.

The 19-year-old Californian, who defeated Navratilova earlier in the year for the U.S. Open championship, scored victories on successive days against Chris Evert-Lloyd and Navratilova in the season-ending tournament. That brought her 1981 records against Evert- Lloyd to 2–1 and Navratilova to 4–2.

"I think I should be No. 1," Austin said, even though she missed almost five months of the season because of injury. Her comeback against Navratilova backed up that belief.

After getting blitzed in the opening set and falling behind in the second, Austin started attacking from all over the court. She broke Navratilova in the third game, broke her again for a 5–4 lead and then steadily pulled away.

1987

RICE BREAKS TD RECORDS

San Francisco wide receiver Jerry Rice broke a scoreless second-quarter tie with an end-around touchdown run and then caught two scoring passes in a 28-point second half as the 49ers scored a 35–7 victory over Atlanta in a record-setting National Football League battle at Candlestick Park.

Most of the record setting was handled by Rice, the speedy touchdown-catching machine who increased his season record total to 21. Rice, who has scored at least three touchdowns in five consecutive games, set another NFL record by catching at least one TD pass in his 12th consecutive contest.

Rice's touchdown catches came on 20- and one-yard strikes from quarterback Steve Young, who directed an offense that amassed 461 yards. While the second half was one-sided, it was not without its dramatic moments.

Atlanta's Sylvester Stamps and San Francisco's Joe Cribbs added to the Rice excitement when they tied an NFL record by returning consecutive kickoffs for touchdowns. Stamps traveled 97 yards after Rice's 20-yard TD reception and Cribbs answered for the 49ers with a 92-yard return.

San Francisco's record-setting **Jerry Rice.**

DECEMBER

21

A STAR IS BORN

1892: Walter Hagen, an outstanding early-century golfer who captured two U.S. Opens, five PGA Championships and four British Opens.

★ ★ ★

1911: Josh Gibson, a Hall of Fame catcher who was known as the Babe Ruth of the Negro Leagues.

★ ★ ★

1926: Joe Paterno, the college football coach who has guided Penn State to two national championships while earning four Coach of the Year citations.

★ ★ ★

1948: Dave Kingman, a major league slugger who belted 442 home runs in a 16-year career that ended in 1986.

★ ★ ★

1954: Chris Evert, the women's tennis great who won 18 major titles and earned five No. 1 world rankings in a career that ended in 1989.

★ ★ ★

1959: Florence Griffith-Joyner, a three-gold medal winner in the 1988 Olympic Games and former world record-holder in the 100- and 200-meter dashes.

★ ★ ★

1960: Andy Van Slyke, a current major league outfielder.

1984 HURT BOSCO SPARKS BYU

Robbie Bosco, hampered by a first-quarter knee and ankle injury that severely limited his mobility, fired a 13-yard touchdown pass to tight end Kelly Smith with 1:23 remaining to give Brigham Young a come-from-behind 24–17 victory over Michigan and a claim to college football's national championship.

Bosco, the national leader in total offense, had led the undefeated and No. 1-ranked Cougars to the tying touchdown moments earlier – a seven-yard pass to Glen Kozlowski. Bosco, who was intercepted three times and fumbled twice, was playing in pain after being injured on a late first-quarter hit by Michigan's Mike Hammerstein. The big tackle was slapped with a personal foul.

But that was little consolation to BYU fans, who saw Bosco go to the sideline and their championship aspirations suffer a severe blow. And sure enough, after the Cougars had eked out a 10–7 halftime lead, Michigan took a 17–10 advantage on a 10-yard scoring pass from Chris Zurbrugg to Bob Perryman and a 32-yard field goal by Bob Bergeron.

Bosco's heroics (343 yards passing, two TDs) put BYU in position to claim its first-ever national title, although critics pointed to the Cougars' soft schedule. Every other major-college team has at least one loss.

1974 STABLER SLUGS MIAMI

Oakland quarterback Ken Stabler fired four touchdown passes, the final with 26 seconds remaining to Clarence Davis, giving the Raiders a 28–26 American Football Conference playoff victory over Miami and ending the Dolphins' two-year reign as Super Bowl champions.

Stabler's desperation eight-yard scoring pass into a crowded end zone capped an eight-play 68-yard drive and was thrown with Miami defensive end Vern Den Herder hanging onto his ankles. Stabler, who threw for 293 yards, completed six passes on the winning drive.

The game was a seesaw battle that opened with Miami's Nat Moore returning the kickoff 89 yards for a touchdown. Of the game's 60 minutes, the Dolphins were either ahead or tied for 55:58 with Oakland leading twice – at 14–10 and 21–19. The Raiders' second lead was the result of a 72-yard Stabler strike to Cliff Branch.

But Miami didn't take long to regain the advantage on Benny Malone's 29-yard run.

Oakland Raiders quarterback **Ken Stabler.**

MILESTONES IN SPORTS

1926

In a shocking baseball trade, the St. Louis Cardinals sent five-time N.L. batting champion and three-time .400 hitter Rogers Hornsby to the New York Giants for infielder Frank Frisch and pitcher Jimmy Ring.

1941

Bears 37, Giants 9: An NFL championship game rout at Chicago.

1975

The Buffalo Sabres capped a 14–2 victory over Washington with an NHL record-tying eight-goal explosion in the third period.

1975

George Blanda closed out his 26th professional season by kicking four extra points and becoming football's first 2,000-point scorer as his Raiders posted a 28–20 victory over Kansas City at Oakland.

1989

Ohio University's Dave Jamerson gave new meaning to the words "hot shooting" when he scored an NCAA-record 14 three-point field goals and 60 points in a 110–80 victory over Charleston.

SPORTS THE NEW YORK TIMES, WEDNESDAY, DECEMBER 22, 1926.

Hornsby Trade Arouses St. Louis; Landis Not to Interfere

ST. LOUIS AROUSED OVER HORNSBY DEAL

RANGERS CONQUER PIRATE SIX, 1 TO 0

MISS WILLS LOSES MATCH TO TILDEN

N. Y. A. C. PRESENTS YACHTING TROPHIES

ST. PAUL'S DOWNS TIGER FRESHMEN, 1-0

The headline in the **New York Times** *delivers the shocking news of* **Rogers Hornsby's** *trade to the Giants.*

1981 A LONG, LONG STORY

Doug Schloemer's 15-foot jumper with one second remaining gave Cincinnati a 75–73 victory over Bradley and ended the longest Division I basketball game in NCAA history – a seven-overtime thriller at Peoria, Ill.

Schloemer's basket provided the only points of the final extra session and just the 13th and 14th for the Bearcats after regulation. Both teams used stalling tactics throughout the overtimes and only once did either lead by more than two points after regulation.

That was in the fifth overtime, when Bradley went ahead by four. But Cincinnati's Mike Williams made a pair of free throws and Kevin Geffney's 10-foot shot tied the game again.

The 3-hour, 15-minute marathon broke the record of six overtimes set by Niagara and Siena in 1953 and matched by Minnesota and Purdue two years later.

MILESTONES IN SPORTS

1894

The United States Golf Association, which would become the governing body of golf, was founded.

1924

Toronto's Babe Dye joined the growing list of five-goal scorers when he helped the St. Patricks to a 10–2 victory at Boston.

1971

The Los Angeles Lakers defeated Baltimore, 127–120, and extended their incredible winning streak to 27 games, breaking the major league sports team mark of 26 set by baseball's 1916 New York Giants.

1974

A 500-goal man: Boston's Phil Esposito gave home fans something extra to cheer in the Bruins' 5–4 victory over Detroit.

1974

Bobby Orr, a 26-year-old Boston defenseman, joined teammate Phil Esposito in the spotlight when he scored a goal and assist against the Red Wings and became the youngest NHL player to amass 800 career points.

1990

A 1,000-point man: Pittsburgh defenseman Paul Coffey reached the milestone with an assist in a 4–3 victory over the New York Islanders .

1915 BASEBALL GETS PEACE

American and National league officials, tiring of the costly two-year battle against the maverick Federal League, broke down and signed a peace treaty that grants immunity to all players who competed in the outlaw circuit.

Feeling the pinch of player raids that had diluted the quality of its product, baseball agreed to pay $600,000 for distribution to eight Federal League teams and to allow two Federal League owners – Charles Weeghman of the Chicago Whales and Phil Ball of the St. Louis franchise – to purchase existing Major League teams. The Federal League accepted the settlement and shut down operations.

Weeghman was granted permission to purchase the National League's Cubs and Ball was given the okay to buy the A.L.'s Browns. While no provisions were adopted for distribution of players, anyone who competed in the Federal League became eligible to play in the major leagues. That, of course, includes several big-name stars who had jumped to the rebel circuit.

Only the Federal League's Baltimore franchise refused to accept the terms, filing a suit against baseball under the Sherman Antitrust Act.

DECEMBER 22

A STAR IS BORN

1862: Connie Mack, the former catcher, manager and team owner of the Philadelphia Athletics in a baseball career that spanned almost seven decades.

★ ★ ★

1938: Matty Alou, an outfielder who batted .307 over a 15-year career that ended in 1974.

★ ★ ★

1944: Steve Carlton, a hard-throwing lefthander who won 329 games and a record four Cy Young Awards over a 24-year career that ended in 1988. He ranks second on the all-time strikeout list with 4,136.

★ ★ ★

1948: Steve Garvey, a .294 hitter over 19 seasons (1969–87) and the N.L. record-holder for consecutive games played (1,207).

1969 PISTOL SHOOTS DOWN BEAVERS

Pistol Pete Maravich, Louisiana State's unstoppable scoring machine, fired in 46 points, including an NCAA-record 30 on free throws, as the once-beaten Tigers defeated Oregon State, 76–68, in a fight-marred contest at Corvallis, Ore.

Maravich was on fire from the free-throw line, hitting 30 of 31 attempts, but he was only 8 for 23 from the field. He also was on fire around the referees, who charged him with three of LSU's seven technical fouls. Pete's father, LSU Coach Press Maravich, was charged with two technicals.

The tone for the game was set in the first half when LSU's Al Sanders slugged it out with Oregon State's Vince Fritz as players from both teams rushed onto the court. It took officials five minutes to clear the floor and Sanders was ejected.

The Beavers took a 14-point lead early in the second half, but Maravich hit a pair of free throws and LSU exploded for nine consecutive field goals to take control. Maravich's 46 points were a Gill Coliseum record.

Oregon State got 32 points from Gary Freeman in his first game of the season.

1946 GRAHAM SPARKS BROWNS

Rookie quarterback Otto Graham fired a 16-yard touchdown pass to Dante Lavelli with less than five minutes remaining and the Cleveland Browns held off the New York Yankees, 14–9, capping the All-America Football Conference's first season with a championship game victory at Cleveland Stadium.

The touchdown finished off a 76-yard drive highlighted by a 24-yard Graham-to-Edgar Jones pass. Graham, who completed 16 of 27 throws for 213 yards, capped his big afternoon by insuring victory with a late interception.

Cleveland wide receiver **Dante Lavelli, Otto Graham's** *favorite target in the AAFC championship game.*

The Browns dominated the game statistically, but the Yankees almost pulled out a victory. Cleveland rolled up 315 total yards to New York's 146, but the Yankee defense held at key moments and their offense did just enough to throw a scare into the stronger Browns.

After Cleveland forged a 7–3 halftime lead on Marion Motley's one-yard second-quarter plunge, the Yankees drove 80 yards and took the lead on Speck Sanders' two-yard third-quarter run. The New Yorkers made the advantage stand up until the fourth quarter.

DECEMBER 23

1962 EXTRA, EXTRA! TEXANS WIN

Tommy Brooker connected on a 25-yard field goal 2:54 into the second overtime, giving the Dallas Texans a 20–17 victory over the Houston Oilers in the American Football League's third championship game – the longest contest in professional history.

Brooker's sudden-death kick brought an end to the 77-minute, 54-second battle that dethroned the AFL's two-time defending champion. Neither team had scored since Charlie Tolar's one-yard burst brought Houston even with 5:38 remaining in regulation.

Tolar's TD completed the Oilers' comeback from a 17–0 halftime deficit built on a pair of Abner Haynes touchdowns – a 28-yard reception from Len Dawson and a two-yard run – and Brooker's 16-yard field goal. Quarterback George Blanda brought the Oilers back with a third-quarter 15-yard scoring pass to Willard Dewveall and a 31-yard fourth-quarter field goal.

Blanda completed 23 of 46 passes for 261 yards, but the Texans picked off five – including one in the second overtime. That was swiped by defensive lineman Bill Hull, who killed an Oilers' drive and returned the ball 23 yards to set up the Texans' winning drive.

1972 IMMACULATE RECEPTION

Pittsburgh rookie Franco Harris grabbed a deflected fourth-down pass and streaked 60 yards for the winning touchdown in a near-miraculous conclusion to an American Football Conference divisional playoff game between the Steelers and Oakland Raiders at Three Rivers Stadium.

Harris' touchdown, with five seconds remaining, wiped out a 7–6 Oakland lead and gave the Steelers a 13–7 triumph and their first berth in an AFC championship game. The situation appeared hopeless with the Steelers facing a fourth-and-10 at their own 40-yard line and 22 seconds remaining on the clock.

But quarterback Terry Bradshaw faded back and fired a pass toward Frenchy Fuqua. Raiders defensive back Jack Tatum got to it first and fisted the ball backward, apparently insuring an Oakland victory. But Harris, the right man in the right spot, picked the ball off, fended off an attempted tackle by Jimmy Warren and scored on the "Immaculate Reception."

The Raiders had taken their lead less than a minute earlier when quarterback Ken Stabler capped an 80-yard drive with a 30-yard run and George Blanda added the extra point. Pittsburgh had led to that point on 18- and 29-yard Roy Gerela field goals.

1975 BASEBALL GETS FREE-AGENCY

Los Angeles Gold Glovers **Andy Messersmith** *(left) and* **Steve Garvey,** *just a few weeks before Messersmith was pronounced a free agent by a labor arbitrator.*

In a monumental ruling that threatens baseball's long-controversial "reserve system," labor arbitrator Peter Seitz ruled that pitchers Andy Messersmith and Dave McNally no longer were bound to their contracts and were free to sell their services to the highest bidder.

Seitz's landmark decision tears a gaping hole in a system that binds a player contractually to a team until he either is traded or retires. The reserve clause had been attacked two times in courts over the last half century, but had withstood both challenges.

Not this time. Messersmith, a 39-game winner over the last two seasons with the Los Angeles Dodgers, pitched his 1975 "option year" without a contract and claimed he should be a free agent. McNally, a four-time 20-game winner with Baltimore, became more of a symbolic figure when he retired halfway through his first Montreal season.

Seitz suggested that a solution on free agency be worked out through the collective bargaining process. Ironically, the basic agreement expires December 31.

A STAR IS BORN

1935: Paul Hornung, a Heisman Trophy winner (1956) and a three-time point-scoring champion in the NFL for Green Bay. The Hall of Fame back holds the all-time mark of 176 points in one season (1960).

★ ★ ★

1942: Jerry Koosman, a lefthanded pitcher who won 222 games in a 19-year career that ended in 1985.

★ ★ ★

1947: Bill Rodgers, a champion distance runner who won the Boston and New York City marathons four times each from 1975–80.

★ ★ ★

1962: Jerry Reynolds, a current National Basketball Association guard/forward.

★ ★ ★

1963: Jim Harbaugh, a current National Football League quarterback.

★ ★ ★

MILESTONES IN SPORTS

1933

Montreal great Howie Morenz became the NHL's all-time top goal scorer when he connected for No. 251 in the Canadiens' 3–0 victory over Detroit.

Los Angeles Rams quarterback **Norm Van Brocklin.**

1951

A 73-yard, fourth-quarter touchdown strike from Norm Van Brocklin to Tom Fears lifted the Los Angeles Rams to a 24–17 NFL championship game victory over the Cleveland Browns.

1978

The New York Islanders' Bryan Trottier put on a one-man show with five goals and three assists in a 9–4 victory over the rival New York Rangers.

1979

Atlanta's Garry Unger, nursing a shoulder injury, saw his NHL-record consecutive-games streak of 914 end when the Flames defeated St. Louis, 7–3.

1980

The Winnipeg Jets ended their NHL-record winless streak at 30 games when they defeated the Colorado Rockies, 5–4, in a game at Winnipeg.

1982 NAIA School Upsets Virginia

Chaminade University, a tiny NAIA school that did not even have a basketball team seven years earlier, pulled off one of the biggest upsets in college history when it shocked No. 1-ranked Virginia, 77–72, in Honolulu, Hawaii.

The Cavaliers, 8–0 and featuring 7-foot-4 All-America Ralph Sampson, stopped in Hawaii on their way back from a tournament in Japan. They had scored easy victories over the Silverswords the last two seasons and this year's encounter figured to be another major mismatch.

But Chaminade had other ideas and made that clear by racing to a 7–0 lead. Virginia fought back, but the Silverswords entered the halftime break tied 43–43.

Virginia appeared to take control in the second half, jumping to a seven-point lead. But this time Chaminade fought back and claimed a shocking 70–68 advantage with 1:37 remaining. Three free throws by Mark Wells and two more by Jim Durham in the final seconds sealed the victory for Cinderella.

Just as shocking as the upset was the play of sophomore center Tony Randolph, who gave away eight inches to the towering Sampson but outscored him, 19–12.

A STAR IS BORN

1921: Bill Dudley, a Hall of Fame do-everything back who spent nine seasons in the NFL between 1942 and '53.

★★★

1950 Browns Rule NFL In Rookie Season

Lou Groza's 16-yard field goal with 28 seconds remaining lifted Cleveland to an exciting 30–28 victory over the Los Angeles Rams and gave the Browns their first National Football League championship – in their rookie NFL season.

Paul Brown *gets a victory ride from jubilant Cleveland players after the NFL-rookie Browns had dispatched Los Angeles in the league championship game.*

The winning points, set up by quarterback Otto Graham with a 58-yard drive, provided sweet vindication for the team that had ruled the now-defunct All-America Football Conference for the last four years. When the Browns entered the NFL with Baltimore and San Francisco, everybody predicted they would be lucky to post a winning record in the "big time."

After a 10–2 regular season and a victory over New York in a playoff game, Cleveland claimed the last big piece of its championship puzzle. But not without a struggle. The Rams scored on their first play from scrimmage – an 82-yard TD bomb from Bob Waterfield to Glenn Davis – and set the tone for what would become a knockdown, drag-out offensive battle. It took the Browns only three minutes to tie on a 32-yard Graham-to-Dub Jones touchdown pass.

Dickie Hoerner gave the Rams another lead on a three-yard run, but Graham answered with touchdown tosses of 35 and 39 yards to Dante Lavelli. Hoerner scored again on a one-yard run and a fumble-recovery TD gave the Rams a comfortable 28-20 lead entering the fourth quarter.

It was a situation made for Graham. First he engineered a 65-yard drive that he capped with a 14-yard TD strike to Rex Baumgardner. Then he started the winning drive from the Cleveland 32, running for 19 yards on the first play. Three pass completions put the ball on the Rams' 11 and a one-yard run set up Groza's winning kick.

The Browns were champions of the league that was supposed to bring them to their knees.

MILESTONES IN SPORTS

1967

Lew Alcindor scored 21 points and UCLA matched college basketball's second-longest winning streak with a 114–63 victory over Notre Dame, the Bruins' 39th triumph in a row.

1974

Bart Starr, the man who quarterbacked the Green Bay Packers through one of the most glorious runs in NFL history in the 1960s, was named coach of the sagging team.

1977

Ken Stabler's 10-yard TD pass to Dave Casper 58 seconds into a second overtime gave Oakland a 37–31 first-round NFL playoff victory over Baltimore in the third-longest professional football game ever played.

1961 Oilers Repeat As AFL Champs

George Blanda fired a 35-yard touchdown pass to Billy Cannon and kicked a 46-yard field goal as the Houston Oilers defeated San Diego, 10–3, and claimed their second American Football League championship in as many tries.

The Oilers, who scored a professional-record 513 points during a 10–3–1 regular season, were anything but offensive against the Chargers at San Diego. The Oilers managed 160 passing yards and 96 on the ground while throwing six interceptions and losing a fumble.

But the Chargers were just as bad. The Oilers defense held San Diego to 79 rushing yards, intercepted four passes and recovered two fumbles. Houston carried a tenuous 3–0 lead into the final period, thanks to Blanda's 46-yard second-quarter field goal.

The game-breaker came on a third-down play from the San Diego 35 when Blanda, under pressure, spotted Cannon at the 17 and lofted a pass his way. The former Heisman Trophy winner outleaped defenders, sidestepped a tackler and ran into the end zone.

The Chargers avoided a shutout in the fourth quarter when Jack Kemp directed a drive that ended with a 12-yard field goal by George Blair.

DECEMBER

25

A STAR IS BORN

1927: Nellie Fox, a little second baseman who played 19 seasons (1947–65) and compiled a .288 career average.

★ ★ ★

1945: Ken Stabler, an outstanding NFL quarterback who passed for 27,938 yards over a 15-year career in the 1970s and '80s.

★ ★ ★

1946: Larry Csonka, a bulldozing fullback who carried the load for Miami's 1973 and '74 Super Bowl championship teams and an 8,000-yard career rusher.

★ ★ ★

1957: Rickey Henderson, a current major league outfielder.

★ ★ ★

DEATH OF A LEGEND

1989: Billy Martin (baseball).

★ ★ ★

1971 MIAMI WINS MARATHON

Garo Yepremian delivered a 37-yard field goal 7:40 into the second overtime period, giving the Miami Dolphins a 27–24 American Conference divisional playoff victory over Kansas City in the longest game in National Football League history.

Underdog Miami lost the battle against Kansas City's **Ed Podolak**, *but won its war against the Chiefs.*

The 82-minute, 40-second Christmas Day battle at Kansas City's Municipal Stadium was a series of missed opportunities for the Chiefs, who had appeared in two of the first four Super Bowls.

They led, 24–17, when Miami's Bob Griese hit Marv Fleming with a seven-yard game-tying touchdown with 1:36 remaining in regulation. And when Ed Podolak ran the ensuing kickoff back 78 yards, normally reliable kicker Jan Stenerud missed a 31-yard field goal attempt that could have won the game. A 42-yard Stenerud kick in the first overtime period was blocked.

The Dolphins, a first-time playoff contestant, scored TDs on one-yard runs by Larry Csonka and Jim Kiick. Podolak was a one-man wrecking crew for the Chiefs. The running back rushed for 85 yards, caught eight passes for 110 more and returned three kickoffs for 153 yards. He scored touchdowns on a seven-yard pass from quarterback Len Dawson and a three-yard run.

But it wasn't enough to ensure victory.

1984 NAIA GIANT KILLER STRIKES AGAIN

Chaminade, the little Hawaiian school that could, pulled off its fourth major upset of a Division I basketball power in three years and captured the Western Airlines Chaminade Classic in Honolulu.

The Silverswords' latest victim was 9–0 Southern Methodist, a talented team ranked fourth and sixth in the latest wire-service polls. Chaminade's 71–70 victory over the Mustangs in the final followed an equally shocking semifinal win over Louisville.

Chaminade, which has an enrollment of 1,070 students, first captured national headlines in 1982 when it upset No. 1-ranked Virginia featuring 7-foot-4 All-America Ralph Sampson.
The Silverswords followed that shocker last year with a victory over Louisville. The Silverswords now are 11–4 and ranked eighth among NAIA schools.

SMU appeared to be in business when Jon Koncak hit a basket with 12 seconds remaining for a 70–69 lead and then blocked a Chaminade shot with three seconds remaining. But the Silverswords got the ball back with less than a second to play and Keith Whitney sent shockwaves through the arena when he sank a 20-foot fadeaway jumper off the inbounds pass as the final horn sounded.

Whitney led Chaminade with 21 points. Koncak led SMU with 24.

MILESTONES IN SPORTS

1956

A record for frustration: Fort Wayne's Corky Devlin tied a mark shared by two other NBA players when he missed all 15 field-goal attempts in a game against the Minneapolis Lakers at Rochester, N.Y.

1984

New York's Bernard King exploded for 60 points, but the Knicks still dropped a 120–114 decision to the New Jersey Nets.

1989 BILLY MARTIN DIES IN CRASH

Billy Martin, the fiery, hot-tempered motivator who managed the New York Yankees a record five times, died in a tragic automobile accident near his home in Binghamton, N.Y. He was 61.

Martin was a passenger in a pickup truck driven by long-time friend William Reedy of Detroit. The truck skidded off an icy road, slid 300 feet down an embankment and came to a stop at the foot of Martin's driveway.

Martin was rushed to the hospital, but efforts to revive him proved futile. Reedy, who sustained a broken hip and rib injuries, was charged with driving while intoxicated.

The ever-controversial Martin, who was serving as a special Yankee advisor, had ended his fifth and last Yankee managerial stint in June 1988. He had maintained an on-again, off-again relationship with New York Owner George Steinbrenner, an equally volatile personality who fired Martin four times and hired or re-hired him five.

Billy Martin *as manager of the New York Yankees in 1985.*

Martin managed the Yankees to a World Series victory in 1977 and an A.L. pennant in 1976.

1955 OTTO SAYS FAREWELL TO THE NFL

Cleveland quarterback **Otto Graham** *(right) shares a locker-room laugh with his father after guiding the Browns to victory in his final professional game.*

Otto Graham, bidding a stylish farewell to professional football after a glorious 10-year run, scored two touchdowns and threw for two more as the Cleveland Browns overwhelmed the Rams, 38–14, in the National Football League championship game at the Los Angeles Memorial Coliseum.

Graham, lured back to the Browns for one final season after retiring the previous year, was never more masterful. After the Browns had built a 10–7 lead on Lou Groza's 26-yard field goal and a 65-yard interception return by Don Paul, the venerable quarterback took over.

He fired a 50-yard scoring strike to Dante Lavelli in the second period, scored on runs of one and 15 yards in the third and closed out his big effort with a 35-yard pass to Ray Renfro in the final quarter. He finished with 14 completions for 202 yards.

He also finished with an amazing record. Graham directed the Browns to All-America Football Conference championships in each of the league's four years and three NFL titles after the AAFC closed down. His other three teams lost in NFL championship games.

1960 DEAN RUINS PACKERS

Philadelphia rookie Ted Dean returned a Green Bay kickoff 58 yards to set up the game-winning touchdown and then ran the final five yards for the score as the Eagles handed the Packers a tough 17–13 National Football League championship game loss at Philadelphia.

Dean's heroics became necessary when Green Bay quarterback Bart Starr fired a seven-yard touchdown pass to Max McGee 1:53 into the final period for a 13–10 Packers lead. Dean returned the ensuing kickoff to the Green Bay 39 and Eagles quarterback Norm Van Brocklin directed a penalty-aided drive for the winning score.

The Packers, making their first title-game appearance since 1944, scored first on a pair of Paul Hornung field goals. But Van Brocklin's 35-yard touchdown pass to Tommy McDonald and a Bobby Walston field goal gave the Eagles a 10–6 halftime advantage. After a scoreless third period, Starr connected with McGee.

The game ended with Green Bay threatening at the Eagles' 9-yard line.

A STAR IS BORN

1924: Glenn Davis, Army's "Mr. Outside" who earned All-America honors three times and won the 1946 Heisman Trophy.

★ ★ ★

1935: Norm Ullman, a hockey Hall of Fame center who scored 1,229 NHL points before extending his career with two seasons (1975–77) in the WHA.

★ ★ ★

1947: Carlton Fisk, a 24-year major league catcher who blasted more than 400 home runs before retiring in 1993.

★ ★ ★

1954: Ozzie Smith, a current major league shortstop.

DEATH OF A LEGEND

1989: Doug Harvey (hockey).

★ ★ ★

1908 BOXING'S FIRST BLACK CHAMP

Jack Johnson, brutalizing Tommy Burns for 14 rounds and flashing his best I-told-you-so smile all the way, sent shock waves rippling through white America when he became the first black heavyweight champion of the world.

The fight in Sydney, Australia, was nothing more than an exhibition for the big slugger from Galveston, Tex. He floored Burns with a right in the opening round and then carried the champion the rest of the way until Sydney police jumped in the ring to stop the fight.

When it was over, Burns was a bloody mess, Johnson clean and refreshed. "I figured Burns had something coming to him," said Johnson, who had endured racial slurs throughout the week leading up to the fight. "I certainly wished to give him his $35,000 worth."

That was a reference to the agreement that Burns would get $35,000 for the bout, Johnson $5,000. But Johnson was not about to quibble because he had pursued the champion halfway around the world seeking the match. Burns had finally relented, going against the unwritten boxing taboo on fighting blacks. Burns had held the crown since 1905.

DECEMBER 26

MILESTONES IN SPORTS

1925

West 6, East 0 in the first East-West Shrine Game, an annual college football all-star classic to benefit crippled children.

1943

Sid Luckman threw five touchdown passes and the Chicago Bears rolled to a 41–21 NFL championship game victory over Washington at Wrigley Field.

1946

After a six-year halt of competition because of World War II, the United States swept to a 5–0 victory over defending champion Australia in the Davis Cup final.

1954

Cleveland quarterback Otto Graham ran for three touchdowns and passed for three more as the Browns broke Detroit's two-year hold on the NFL championship with a convincing 56–10 victory over the Lions at Cleveland.

1965

Pete Gogolak kicked three field goals and Buffalo's top-ranked defense took care of the rest as the Bills posted a 23–0 victory over San Diego in the AFL championship game.

1982

Chicago back Walter Payton became professional football's fourth 10,000-yard rusher when he gained 104 in the Bears' 34–26 victory over the Los Angeles Rams.

DECEMBER

27

A STAR IS BORN

1943: Roy White, a .271 hitter in a 15-year career (1965–79) with the New York Yankees.

★ ★ ★

1959: Andre Tippett, a current National Football League linebacker.

★ ★ ★

MILESTONES
IN SPORTS

1967

UCLA stretched its winning streak to 40, the second longest in NCAA history, with a 95–55 victory over Minnesota at Los Angeles.

1974

Ohio State record-setter Archie Griffin became the fifth junior to win a Heisman Trophy.

1981

Edmonton's Wayne Gretzky scored his 100th point of the season – in the Oilers' 38th game.

1989

Kentucky set an NCAA record with 21 three-point field goals, but North Carolina still powered its way to a 121–110 victory over the Wildcats at Louisville.

1991

Golden State's Tim Hardaway set an NBA record when he missed all 17 of his field-goal attempts in a game at Minneapolis, but Chris Mullin scored 36 points and the Warriors still posted a 106–102 victory.

1959 COLTS TRIP GIANTS AGAIN

The Baltimore Colts, using 24-point fourth-quarter burst to wipe out a 9–7 deficit, rolled to their second consecutive National Football League championship with a 31–16 victory over the New York Giants at Baltimore.

The Colts had been frustrated all afternoon by a stingy Giants defense that limited their powerful running game to 73 yards and leading rusher Alan Ameche to 30. But lightning struck in the final 15 minutes.

First quarterback Johnny Unitas scored on a four-yard run, giving Baltimore the lead. Then Unitas fired a 12-yard touchdown pass to Willie Richardson after an Andy Nelson interception. Johnny Sample picked off a New York pass and returned it 42 yards for a TD, increasing the Colts' lead to 28–9, and another Sample interception set up a 32-yard Steve Myhra field goal.

The Giants, who had built their lead on three Pat Summerall field goals, finally reached the end zone with 32 seconds remaining on a 32-yard pass from quarterback Charley Conerly to Bob Schnelker.

The Colts had scored an early TD on Unitas' 59-yard bomb to Lenny Moore.

1953 LAYNE, LIONS CROWN BROWNS

Bobby Layne fired a 33-yard touchdown pass to Jim Doran with 2:08 remaining and Doak Walker's conversion gave the Detroit Lions a 17–16 victory over Cleveland and their second straight National Football League championship.

Layne's scoring pass wiped out a 16–10 Browns advantage and threw 54,577 fans at Detroit's Briggs Stadium into an uproar. The Lions had defeated the powerful Browns, 17–7, in the 1952 title game.

Cleveland had built its lead on three Lou Groza field goals and a nine-yard third-quarter run by Chick Jagade. The Browns were forced to stick to the ground all afternoon because of a mysterious slump by quarterback Otto Graham, who managed to complete just two of 15 passes for a measly 20 yards.

The Lions scored their first touchdown on Walker's one-yard dive after a first-quarter Graham fumble and Walker added a 23-yard second-quarter field goal. Layne took Detroit 80 yards for the go-ahead touchdown.

The victory was sealed in the closing minute when rookie Carl Karilivacz intercepted Graham's desperation pass.

Strong-armed Detroit quarterback **Bobby Layne.**

Cleveland quarterback **Frank Ryan.**

1964 BROWNS REGAIN WINNING FORM

Gary Collins caught three second-half touchdown strikes from quarterback Frank Ryan and the underdog Cleveland Browns posted a 27–0 victory over Baltimore in a National Football League championship game witnessed by 79,544 ecstatic fans at Cleveland's Municipal Stadium.

After the teams played to a first-half scoreless tie, 40-year-old Lou Groza broke the ice with a 43-yard third-quarter field goal. Then lightning struck in the form of a 46-yard run by Jim Brown that set up Ryan's 18-yard TD pass to Collins and a 42-yard Ryan-to-Collins bomb that really broke the game open. Another Groza field goal and Collins' 51-yard touchdown reception closed out Cleveland's unexpected scoring burst.

Collins finished with five receptions for 130 yards and Ryan outpassed Colts veteran Johnny Unitas, 206–89. Cleveland also held a 142–92-yard advantage on the ground. Every one of Collins' five receptions was either for a touchdown or a first down. Ryan connected on 11 of his 18 throws, most of them deep patterns. The Browns had entered the game with a reputation as a running team.

1958 COLTS TRIP GIANTS IN NFL CLASSIC

DECEMBER 28

Alan Ameche, Baltimore's bulldozer fullback, slammed across the goal line 8:15 into the National Football League's first overtime and the Colts captured their first championship with a 23–17 victory over the New York Giants in what has been hailed as the greatest football game of all time.

Baltimore's **Alan Ameche** *bulls through the Giants' defense for the winning touchdown in the so-called greatest football game ever played.*

Played before a national television audience and a crowd of 64,185 at New York's Yankee Stadium, the game attracted the kind of attention that previously had been reserved for pennant and championship-deciding baseball games. The nail-biting intensity of a fast-paced final quarter and overtime period were pluses for the attention-starved NFL.

The Giants struck first on a 36-yard Pat Summerall field goal, but the rest of the half belonged to quarterback Johnny Unitas and the Colts. After Ameche's two-yard touchdown run gave Baltimore its first lead in the second quarter, Unitas connected on a 15-yard scoring toss to Raymond Berry for a 14–3 halftime advantage.

The Giants got back into the game with a third-quarter defensive stand that kept Baltimore from pulling away and a key play on their next possession. Quarterback Charley Conerly connected deep with Kyle Rote, who fumbled on the Colts' 25-yard line, but Alex Webster picked up the ball and ran to the 1. Mel Triplett's plunge and a later 15-yard Conerly TD pass to Frank Gifford gave the Giants a 17–14 lead.

The Colts responded with a desperate 73-yard drive to the tying field goal. Three passes from Unitas to Berry netted 62 of the yards and Steve Myhra's 20-yard kick knotted the score with seven seconds remaining in regulation.

After holding the Giants on their first possession of the league's first-ever sudden-death overtime period, the Colts made it look easy. Combining Unitas passes and Ameche runs, Baltimore quickly moved to a first down at the New York 1. Ameche bulled over for the winner.

A STAR IS BORN

1900: Ted Lyons, a Hall of Fame pitcher who won 260 games for the Chicago White Sox over a 21-year career that ended in 1946.

★ ★ ★

1920: Steve Van Buren, a bruising Hall of Fame fullback who led the NFL in rushing four times during an eight-year career (1944–51) with the Eagles.

★ ★ ★

1929: Terry Sawchuk, a hockey Hall of Fame goaltender (1949–70) who set the career record for shutouts with 103.

★ ★ ★

1960: Ray Bourque, a current National Hockey League defenseman.

★ ★ ★

DEATH OF A LEGEND

1983: Jimmy Demaret (golf).

★ ★ ★

1975 STAUBACH SAYS A 'HAIL MARY'

Dallas quarterback Roger Staubach, 50 yards from the end zone and reduced to a prayer in a National Conference divisional playoff game at Minnesota, got the answer he wanted when Drew Pearson hauled in his "Hail Mary" pass with 24 seconds remaining to give the Cowboys a 17–14 victory over the Vikings.

"I guess it was a 'Hail Mary' pass," Staubach said later. "You throw it up and hope he catches it." That's exactly what happened. The long, looping throw came up short and Pearson fought through defenders to make the catch and then rolled into the end zone. The play completed an 85-yard drive, which was kept alive by an earlier 25-yard Staubach-to-Pearson pass on a fourth-and-16 play. Vikings Coach Bud Grant screamed for a call of offensive pass interference, to no avail.

Minnesota had seemingly taken control of the game when Brent McClanahan ran one yard for a touchdown to cap a 70-yard drive with 5:24 remaining, giving the Vikings a 13–10 advantage. Dallas had scored earlier on Doug Dennison's four-yard run and Toni Fritsch's 24-yard field goal.

MILESTONES IN SPORTS

1944

The Maurice (Rocket) Richard scoring touch was on display in a five-goal, three-assist effort that sparked Montreal to a 9–1 victory over Detroit.

1947

The Chicago Cardinals, with Elmer Angsman and Charley Trippi scoring two touchdowns apiece, shocked Philadelphia, 28–21, in the NFL championship game.

1952

Doak Walker ran 67 yards for a third-quarter touchdown and the Detroit Lions pulled away from the Browns for a 17–7 NFL championship game victory at Cleveland.

1966

Australia claimed its third straight Davis Cup victory when Roy Emerson overpowered India's Ramanathan Krishman in straight sets for an insurmountable 3–1 Aussie lead.

1968

Arthur Ashe keyed a 4–1 American tennis victory over Australia that returned the Davis Cup to the United States for the first time since 1963.

DECEMBER

29

1963 U.S. Regains Prize

Chuck McKinley, facing a must-win situation after teammate Dennis Ralston had lost earlier in the day to Roy Emerson, recorded a grueling four-set triumph over big John Newcombe and returned the Davis Cup to the United States after a four-year absence.

McKinley, who earlier had combined with Ralston for a doubles victory, dropped a tough first set and then fought back for a 10–12 , 6–2, 9–7, 6–2 victory in the match at Adelaide, Australia. McKinley negated the 19-year-old's booming serve with a strong ground game that gave the U.S. a final 3–2 advantage.

The turning point came in the third set with McKinley trailing, 2–4, and trying to break service. Leading 40–30 in the game, McKinley was handcuffed by a monster second serve that was not called by the linesman. Newcombe pleaded with the linesman, who stuck to his call. The umpire eventually ruled it out for a double fault and the unnerved Newcombe never recovered.

McKinley could have lost his poise after the grueling opening set. The American staved off four match points, only to lose, but the adversity seemed to inspire him.

Emerson had crushed Ralston earlier in the day, 6–2, 6–3, 3–6, 6–2. The Australians had won the coveted trophy four straight years.

1963 Bears Intercept Title-Bound Giants

Quarterback Billy Wade ran for a pair of Chicago touchdowns and the Bears, aided by a knee injury that severely hampered the mobility of New York quarterback Y.A. Tittle, recorded a 14–10 victory over the Giants in the National Football League championship game at bitterly cold Wrigley Field.

Wade's first score, a two-yard run, completed a short Chicago drive set up by Larry Morris' 61-yard interception return to the Giants' 5. His second, a one-yard third-quarter run, closed the scoring after Don Chandler's 13-yard field goal had given New York a 10–7 advantage.

Chicago defensive end **Ed O'Bradovich** *fights off tacklers after intercepting a championship game pass by New York quarterback Y.A. Tittle.*

Tittle, who had thrown for 3,145 yards and 36 touchdowns during the Giants' 11–3 regular season, wrenched his knee in the second quarter after firing a 14-yard scoring strike to Frank Gifford. Tittle finished the afternoon with five interceptions, the final one on a desperation heave into the Chicago end zone with 10 seconds remaining.

Richie Petitbon picked off the throw that sealed the Bears' victory.

1957 Rote Sparks Lions

Tobin Rote, starting in place of injured quarterback Bobby Layne, ran for one touchdown and passed for four more as the underdog Detroit Lions powered their way to a shocking 59–14 National Football League championship game victory over Cleveland before 55,263 delirious fans at Briggs Stadium.

After Jim Martin had opened the scoring with a 31-yard field goal, Rote ran one yard for a touchdown and Gene Gedman followed suit in a surprising 17-point first-quarter explosion. The Browns' Jimmy Brown ran 29 yards to cut the lead to 10, but the Lions turned up the pressure.

On a fake second-quarter field goal, Rote stood up and fired a 26-yard scoring pass to Steve Junker to extend the lead. Terry Barr's 19-yard interception return for a touchdown gave the Lions a commanding 31–7 halftime lead.

Rote connected on second-half touchdown passes to Jim Doran (78 yards), Junker (23) and Dave Middleton (32). Backup quarterback Jerry Reichow closed the scoring with a 16-yard toss to Howard (Hopalong) Cassady.

The title victory capped a season that had started with the resignation of Coach Buddy Parker, who didn't believe the Lions could be competitive.

Detroit Lions quarterback **Tobin Rote.**

MILESTONES · IN SPORTS ·

1961

A typical Wilt Chamberlain day: 60 points in a 123–118 Philadelphia victory over the Los Angeles Lakers.

1966

Bob Seagren broke his own world indoor pole vault record when he soared 17–1 during competition in the Knights of Columbus Games at Saskatoon, Saskatchewan.

1977

Female baseball writer Melissa Ludtke of Sports Illustrated filed suit against major league baseball, the New York Yankees and various New York City officials because she was denied access to the locker room to interview players during the World Series.

1984

The Wayne Gretzky watch: Edmonton's Great One scored his 100th point in the Oilers' 35th game of the season.

1992

John Daly, the Cinderella winner of the 1991 PGA Championship, withdrew from the pro tour to enter an alcohol rehabilitation facility.

A STAR IS BORN

1881: Jess Willard, the huge heavyweight boxer who unseated champion Jack Johnson in 1915 and lost the crown to Jack Dempsey four years later.

★ ★ ★

1936: Ray Nitschke, a Hall of Fame middle linebacker and defensive anchor for Green Bay teams that won five NFL titles and two Super Bowls from 1958–72.

★ ★ ★

1946: Laffit Pincay Jr., a jockey who rode one Kentucky Derby and three Belmont winners and ranks second only to Bill Shoemaker in career victories.

★ ★ ★

1978 Ohio State Fires Hayes

Woody Hayes, the crusty, growling football coach who directed Ohio State to 205 victories and two national championships over 28 seasons, was fired the day after he punched a Clemson player near the end of his team's 17–15 loss in the Gator Bowl classic.

The news was delivered by Athletic Director Hugh Hindman at a press conference in Jacksonville, Fla. Hindman said he had asked Hayes to resign, but the coach refused. After conferring with Ohio State President Harold Enarson, he told Hayes of the decision.

There was some speculation Buckeye officials had been looking for an excuse to fire the 65-year-old Hayes. If so, he certainly provided them with a good one. The controversy started with 1:58 remaining in the Gator Bowl when Clemson linebacker Charlie Bauman intercepted an Ohio State pass and was knocked out of bounds at the Ohio State sideline.

Suddenly, Hayes went wild and started swinging at Bauman. No explanation was given, although one report said the youngster taunted him by waving the ball in his face. Ohio State player Ken Fritz tried to intervene and was punched in the face by his irate coach, who stormed from the field with a police escort after the game.

ABC, which televised the game nationally, showed only a brief replay from a bad angle. But next-day television replays confirmed that Hayes indeed had thrown a punch at Bauman. When news reached Columbus, O., after the firing, reaction ranged from indignation to praise.

It was not the first controversy that had swirled around Hayes. He had been on school and Big Ten probation several times for various on-field tirades, the latest last season when he reportedly hit a television cameraman. He was not a favorite among league referees and officials.

Hayes, who started at Ohio State in 1951, compiled a 205–61–10 record with the Buckeyes and a 238–72–10 overall mark that included stints as coach of Denison and Miami of Ohio. His Buckeye teams won national championships in 1954 and '68 and he was named college football's top coach in 1957 and '75.

Long-time Ohio State Coach **Woody Hayes.**

A STAR IS BORN

1883: Lester Patrick, a pre-NHL hockey star who went on to earn Hall of Fame credentials as a coach and executive.

★ ★ ★

1935: Sandy Koufax, a Hall of Fame lefthander who won three Cy Young Awards and five straight ERA titles for the Los Angeles Dodgers in the 1960s.

★ ★ ★

1961: Ben Johnson, the Canadian sprinter who set several 100-meter world records that later were revoked because of drug use. He was stripped of his 1988 Olympic gold medal.

DEATH OF A LEGEND

1967: Charlie Conacher (hockey).

★ ★ ★

1970: Sonny Liston (boxing).

1978 WHA Merges Into NHL

Bringing down a costly curtain on the World Hockey Association, the rival National Hockey League agreed to absorb four WHA franchises and let them compete next season in the NHL as expansion teams.

The Edmonton Oilers, New England Whalers, Quebec Nordiques and Winnipeg Jets will become official members of the NHL – but not without a price. Each franchise will pay a $6 million entry fee and most of their players will be made available to the existing 17 NHL teams. The four newcomers will be allowed to protect two skaters and two goaltenders from their current rosters before restocking through an expansion draft. That concession was especially important to the Oilers, who now will be able to protect young superstar Wayne Gretzky.

The NHL decided to handle the move as expansion to avoid problems with the players' union. Two of the former WHA franchises, Birmingham and Cincinnati, will receive an unspecified reimbursement for their agreement to dissolve.

The sudden NHL expansion forced the league to do some division shuffling. The Whalers will compete next season in the Norris Division, the Nordiques in the Adams, the Jets and Oilers in the Smythe. Current National Hockey League member Washington will move from the Norris to the Patrick.

December 30

MILESTONES · IN SPORTS ·

1936

Stanford and one-hand set shot artist Hank Luisetti snapped Long Island University's 43-game winning streak with a 45–31 upset at New York's Madison Square Garden.

1956

Alex Webster ran for a pair of touchdowns as the New York Giants rolled to a 27-point halftime lead en route to a 47–7 victory over Chicago in the NFL championship game at Yankee Stadium.

1962

Jerry Kramer kicked three field goals and Jim Taylor ran seven yards for a touchdown as the Green Bay Packers won their second straight NFL championship with a 16–7 victory over the New York Giants.

1963

Venerable Gordie Howe scored his unprecedented 600th career goal midway through the opening period of Detroit's 2–1 victory over the Boston Bruins.

1981

Edmonton's Wayne Gretzky scored into an empty net to cap a five-goal explosion that lifted his season total to 50 in 39 games. The Oilers beat Philadelphia, 7–5.

1990

Orlando guard Scott Skiles broke a 13-year-old NBA record when he handed out 30 assists in the Magic's 155–116 victory over Denver.

DECEMBER

31

1974 Yankees Land Catfish

The New York Yankees, throwing out an estimated $3.75 million contract offer as bait, landed 28-year-old righthander Catfish Hunter, the most prized free-agent catch in American sports history.

Hunter, who posted a 25–12 record last season and 106 victories over the last five with the Oakland A's, signed a five-year contract with the Yankees on New Year's Eve, ending an unprecedented bidding war that drew numerous team officials to the law offices of Cherry, Cherry and Flythe in Ahoskie, N.C., near Hunter's hometown.

The reigning A.L. Cy Young winner and earned-run average champion, who had led the A's to three straight World Series titles, was declared an unrestricted free agent on December 15 when arbitrator Peter Seitz upheld his claim that Oakland Owner Charles O. Finley had breached his contract.

A STAR IS BORN

1928: Hugh McElhenny, a Hall of Fame running back who rushed for 5,281 yards in a 13-year NFL career that ended in 1964.

★ ★ ★

1961: Rick Aguilera, a current major league relief pitcher.

★ ★ ★

DEATH OF A LEGEND

1990: George Allen (football).

★ ★ ★

1972 Clemente Dies at 38

Four-time National League batting champion Roberto Clemente, leading the Puerto Rican effort to help Nicaraguan earthquake victims, died when a cargo plane loaded with relief supplies crashed into the ocean shortly after takeoff from San Juan International Airport.

The talented Pittsburgh outfielder, a .317 career hitter, a former N.L. Most Valuable Player (1966) and a recent inductee into baseball's elite 3,000-hit club, was one of five people aboard the DC-7 that went down about a mile from the airport. Clemente was flying to Nicaragua because he wanted to make sure the supplies would get to those who needed them most.

The 38-year-old Clemente, the most popular sports figure in his native Puerto Rico, is a certain Hall of Famer. The 12-time All-Star got his 3,000th – and final – hit on September 30 when he doubled off New York's Jon Matlack. The strong-armed right fielder led the Pirates to World Series victories in 1960 and '71.

Dallas masked man **Dick Daniels** *(left) reaches for Green Bay's* **Willie Wood** *on a fourth-quarter punt return during the 'Ice Bowl' championship game.*

1967 Packers Ice the Cowboys

Green Bay quarterback Bart Starr, out of timeouts and facing a do-or-die situation at the Dallas 2-foot line, dived into the end zone with 13 seconds remaining and gave the Packers a 21–17 victory over Dallas and their third straight National Football League championship.

Starr's winning dive capped a 12-play, 68-yard drive on the frozen turf of Green Bay's Lambeau Field. Facing a game-time temperature of minus-13 degrees and a stiff wind that made it seem even colder, the teams waged a titanic "Ice Bowl" battle that would decide the participant in Super Bowl II.

The Packers, looking for their fifth NFL title in seven years, appeared better suited for the conditions when they jumped to a 14–0 lead on Starr touchdown passes of eight and 43 yards to Boyd Dowler. But the Cowboys fought back on George Andrie's seven-yard return of a Green Bay fumble, Danny Villanueva's 21-yard field goal and a 50-yard TD pass to Lance Rentzel.

Trailing 17–14 with 4:50 remaining, Starr directed the dramatic final drive that featured 12 and nine-yard completions to Donny Anderson and a 19-yarder to Chuck Mercein. Anderson ran two yards to the one and then carried twice for about a foot, setting up Starr's TD dive.

MILESTONES • IN SPORTS •

1935

A 20–20 basketball tie? Courtesy of an official scorer's error, Notre Dame and Northwestern recorded an NCAA first.

1958

Alex Olmedo produced one of the major upsets in Davis Cup final history when he beat Australian champ Ashley Cooper in four sets and gave the United States an insurmountable 3–1 lead.

1961

Paul Hornung, on leave from the Army, scored 19 points and the Green Bay Packers destroyed the New York Giants, 37–0, in the NFL championship game at Green Bay's City Stadium.

1973

In a classic battle of unbeatens, Notre Dame turned back the Crimson Tide of Alabama, 24–23, in a Sugar Bowl shootout that decided college football's national championship.

1975

Alabama 13, Penn State 6 in college football's first indoor Sugar Bowl, played at the New Orleans Superdome.

1988

Pittsburgh center Mario Lemieux became the first NHL player to score eight points in a game twice in one season. His five-goal, three-assist effort sparked the Penguins' 8–6 victory over New Jersey.

1989

In a blinding fog that seriously obscured game action for 65,534 fans at Solider Field and a national television audience, the Chicago Bears groped their way to a 20–12 NFC divisional playoff victory over the Philadelphia Eagles.

INDEX

A

B

C

D

E

F

G

I

J

K

L

M

N

S

T

U